THE CAKRASAMVARA TANTRA
(The Discourse of Śrī Heruka)

The *Treasury of the Buddhist Sciences* series is copublished by the American Institute of Buddhist Studies and Wisdom Publications in association with the Columbia University Center for Buddhist Studies and Tibet House US.

The American Institute of Buddhist Studies (AIBS) established the *Treasury of the Buddhist Sciences* series to provide authoritative translations, studies, and editions of the texts of the Tibetan Tengyur (*bstan 'gyur*) and its associated literature. The Tibetan Tengyur is a vast collection of over 4,000 classical Indian Buddhist scientific treatises (*śāstra*) written in Sanskrit by over 700 authors from the first millennium CE, now preserved mainly in systematic 7th–12th century Tibetan translation. Its topics span all of India's "outer" arts and sciences, including linguistics, medicine, astronomy, socio-political theory, ethics, art, and so on, as well as all of her "inner" arts and sciences such as philosophy, psychology ("mind science"), meditation, and yoga.

THE DALAI LAMA

Message

The foremost scholars of the holy land of India were based for many centuries at Nālandā Monastic University. Their deep and vast study and practice explored the creative potential of the human mind with the aim of eliminating suffering and making life truly joyful and worthwhile. They composed numerous excellent and meaningful texts. I regularly recollect the kindness of these immaculate scholars and aspire to follow them with unflinching faith. At the present time, when there is great emphasis on scientific and technological progress, it is extremely important that those of us who follow the Buddha should rely on a sound understanding of his teaching, for which the great works of the renowned Nālandā scholars provide an indispensable basis.

In their outward conduct the great scholars of Nālandā observed ethical discipline that followed the Pāli tradition, in their internal practice they emphasized the awakening mind of *bodhichitta*, enlightened altruism, and in secret they practised tantra. The Buddhist culture that flourished in Tibet can rightly be seen to derive from the pure tradition of Nālandā, which comprises the most complete presentation of the Buddhist teachings. As for me personally, I consider myself a practitioner of the Nālandā tradition of wisdom. Masters of Nālandā such as Nāgārjuna, Āryadeva, Āryāsaṅga, Dharmakīrti, Candrakīrti, and Śāntideva wrote the scriptures that we Tibetan Buddhists study and practice. They are all my gurus. When I read their books and reflect upon their names, I feel a connection with them.

The works of these Nālandā masters are presently preserved in the collection of their writings that in Tibetan translation we call the Tengyur (*bstan 'gyur*). It took teams of Indian masters and great Tibetan translators over four centuries to accomplish the historic task of translating them into Tibetan. Most of these books were later lost in their Sanskrit originals, and relatively few were translated into Chinese. Therefore, the Tengyur is truly one of Tibet's most precious treasures, a mine of understanding that we have preserved in Tibet for the benefit of the whole world.

Keeping all this in mind I am very happy to encourage a long-term project of the American Institute of Buddhist Studies, originally established by the late Venerable Mongolian Geshe Wangyal and now at the Columbia University Center for Buddhist Studies, and Tibet House US, in collaboration with Wisdom Publications, to translate the Tengyur into English and other modern languages, and to publish the many works in a collection called *The Treasury of the Buddhist Sciences*. When I recently visited Columbia University, I joked that it would take those currently working at the Institute at least three "reincarnations" to complete the task; it surely will require the intelligent and creative efforts of generations of translators from every tradition of Tibetan Buddhism, in the spirit of the scholars of Nālandā, although we may hope that using computers may help complete the work more quickly. As it grows, the *Treasury* series will serve as an invaluable reference library of the Buddhist Sciences and Arts. This collection of literature has been of immeasurable benefit to us Tibetans over the centuries, so we are very happy to share it with all the people of the world. As someone who has been personally inspired by the works it contains, I firmly believe that the methods for cultivating wisdom and compassion originally developed in India and described in these books preserved in Tibetan translation will be of great benefit to many scholars, philosophers, and scientists, as well as ordinary people.

I wish the American Institute of Buddhist Studies at the Columbia Center for Buddhist Studies, Tibet House US, and Wisdom Publications every success and pray that this ambitious and far-reaching project to create *The Treasury of the Buddhist Sciences* will be accomplished according to plan. I also request others, who may be interested, to extend whatever assistance they can, financial or otherwise, to help ensure the success of this historic project.

May 15, 2007

TREASURY OF THE BUDDHIST SCIENCES

The Cakrasamvara Tantra

(The Discourse of Śrī Heruka)

Śrīherukābhidhāna

A Study and Annotated Translation
by David B. Gray

Edited by Thomas F. Yarnall

TREASURY OF THE BUDDHIST SCIENCES SERIES
TENGYUR TRANSLATION INITIATIVE

COPUBLISHED BY
THE AMERICAN INSTITUTE OF BUDDHIST STUDIES AND WISDOM PUBLICATIONS
IN ASSOCIATION WITH THE COLUMBIA UNIVERSITY CENTER FOR BUDDHIST STUDIES
AND TIBET HOUSE US

Wisdom

Treasury of the Buddhist Sciences series
Tengyur Translation Initiative
A refereed series published by:

American Institute of Buddhist Studies
Columbia University
80 Claremont Avenue, Room 303
New York, NY 10027
www.aibs.columbia.edu

Wisdom Publications
199 Elm Street
Somerville, MA 02144 USA
www.wisdompubs.org

In association with Columbia University's Center for Buddhist Studies and Tibet House US.
Distributed by Wisdom Publications.

Library of Congress Cataloging-in-Publication Data for the previous edition is as follows:

Tripiṭaka. Sūtrapiṭaka. Tantra. Cakrasamvaratantra English.
The Cakrasamvara Tantra : the discourse of Śrī Heruka (Śrīherukābhidhāna) / a study and annotated translation by David B. Gray ; editing and design by Thomas F. Yarnall.
p. cm. — (Treasury of the Buddhist sciences)
"Co-published with Columbia University's Center for Buddhist Studies and Tibet House US."
Includes bibliographical references and index.
ISBN 978-0-9753734-6-0 (alk. paper)
1. Tripiṭaka. Sūtrapiṭaka. Tantra. Cakrasamvaratantra—Commentaries. I. Gray, David B., 1969– II. Yarnall, Thomas, F. III. Title.

BQ2180.C3522Z52 2007
294.3'85--dc22

2007060677

ISBN 978-1-949163-02-5 (hardcover) 978-1-949163-03-2 (ebook)

22 21 20 19 3 4 5

Cover design by Gopa&Ted2. Set in Diacritical Adobe Garamond 11/14.

Printed on acid-free paper and meets the guidelines for permanence and durability of the Production Guidelines for Book Longevity of the Council on Library Resources.

♲ This book was produced with environmental mindfulness. For more information, please visit wisdompubs.org/wisdom-environment.

Printed in the United States of America.

Contents

Series Editor's Preface xi
Author's Preface xvii

PART ONE: INTRODUCTION

1. Introduction to the Cakrasamvara Tantra
   The Cakrasamvara and the Yoginī Tantras 3
   Dating the Text 11
   Cakrasamvara Literature 15
2. Traditional History of the Cakrasamvara Tantra
   Mythic Root Texts 28
   The Origin of Heruka 35
3. Contents and Contexts
   The Triple Wheel Maṇḍala 54
   Ḍākinīs, Yoginīs, and Women 77
   Consecration and the Sexual Yogas 103
   Mantras and Magic 131
4. Texts and Translation
   Texts Employed 137
   Translation Methodology 145
   Technical Notes 151

PART TWO: TRANSLATION

1. The Descent of the Maṇḍala 155
2. The Procedure of Wheel Worship 164
3. The Procedure of Consecration and Fee [Payment] 171
4. The Procedure Called 'The Nonduality of the Heroes and Yoginīs' 178
5. The Procedure of Selecting the Letters of the Root Mantra 181
6. The Procedure of Selecting the Hero's Six Armor [Mantras] 186
7. The Procedure of Selecting the Mantra 188
8. The Procedure of Selecting the Reversed Yoginī Mantras 194
9. The Procedure of the Ritual Actions of the Root Mantra 196
10. The Achievement of the Triple Body and the Procedure of the Ritual Actions of the Essence Mantra 202
11. The Procedure of Characterizing the Seven-lived One 206

12. The Procedure of the Ritual Actions of the Quintessence 209
13. The Procedure of the Applications of the Armor Mantra..... 214
14. The Procedure of the Donkey Form Yoga for Becoming Śrī Heruka 217
15. The Procedure of the Syllabic Signs 222
16. The Procedure of Examining the Characteristics of the Seven Yoginīs 226
17. The Procedure of the Signs, Gestures, and Perambulant Forms of All Yoginīs.............................. 232
18. The True Procedure of the Colors, Characteristics, and Signs of All Yoginīs................................ 236
19. The Procedure of Pointing Out the Gestures of the Yoginīs... 239
20. The Procedure of the Symbolic Hand Gestures of the Yoginīs . 243
21. The Procedure of the Characteristics of the Visual Body Gestures 246
22. The Procedure of the Characteristics of the Distinctive Limb Gestures 248
23. The Procedure of the Characteristics of the Ḍākinīs' Signs and Insignia.................................. 250
24. The Procedure of the Symbolic Speech of the Four Classes ... 256
25. The Procedure of Completely Hiding the Root Mantra 263
26. The Procedures of Inspecting the Disciple and the Vows..... 265
27. The Procedures of the Conduct, Observances, Worship, and Sacrificial Cakes............................ 271
28. The Procedures of the Inner Fire Sacrifice and Class Oneness.. 282
29. The Procedures of the Messenger's Defining Marks and the State of Empowerment 289
30. The Procedure of Mantra Selection Bound in the Muraja Drum 292
31. The Procedure of the Rites of Eating, Fire Sacrifice and the Sacrificial Cakes, and the Hand Signs................ 297
32. The Procedures of the Animal Sacrificial Victims, the Means of Achieving the Zombie, and the Creation Stage 300
33. The Reverential Procedure of Secret Worship 305
34. The Procedure of Summoning via the Fire Sacrifice of the Nondual Messenger 308
35. The Procedure of the Nondual Ritual Action and the Method of Cheating Black Death......................... 312

36. The Procedure of Summoning the Reality Worship 317
37. The Procedure of Inner Mastery 320
38. The Procedure of the Yoginīs' Place and the Heroes' Secret Abode 322
39. The Procedure of Vision and Loud Laughter 325
40. The Procedures of Subjugating the Five Social Classes and Mahāmudrā 327
41. The Procedure of Laying Down the Maṇḍala of the Twenty-four Syllables 329
42. The Procedure of the Laughter Mantra and the Magic of the Yoginīs' Forms 338
43. The Procedure of Accomplishing the Ritual Actions of the Quintessence [Mantra] 343
44. The Procedure of the Six Yoginīs' Ritual Actions with the Seven Syllable [Mantra] 350
45. The Six Yoginī Ritual Actions and the Summoning of the Power of Speech 353
46. The Procedure of Ritual Actions with the Five ha Syllables . . . 358
47. The Procedure of All Ritual Actions of the Sarvabuddhaḍākinī Mantra 360
48. The Procedure of the Maṇḍala of the Hidden Abode of All Heroes and Ḍākinīs 364
49. The Procedure of Transforming the Victim Who Is Born Seven Times 367
50. The Procedure of the Domination Fire Sacrifice and the Teaching of the Stages in Relation to the Seats, etc. 370
51. Creation Stage Esoteric Instruction 376

Glossaries 385
Conspectus Siglorum 405
Bibliography 409
Index 437

Series Editor's Preface

The Indo-Tibetan Buddhist tantric tradition is one of the most profound and vast products of Indian and Tibetan civilizations. Though some have been inclined to read the literature of this tradition as being the perverse product of a community of delusional and sociopathic yogins, they still acknowledge that it provides a remarkable wealth of data on the contents of the human individual subconscious and collective unconscious—a rich mine of insight for depth-psychological researchers. More seriously, it seems much more likely (and more realistic) that this literature represents the normally esoteric codification of the manuals for and results of extraordinary psychic explorations on the part of sophisticated, determined, and courageous Indian and Tibetan philosopher-adventurers, which is how yogin and yoginī adepts (*siddha*) might properly be described. These individuals were practitioners of Mahāyāna Buddhism, immersed in the evolutionary world of the bodhisattva who lives in a time-stream of millions of lifetimes, aiming to evolve—through the meritorious activities of generosity, morality, and tolerance, and through the psychic and sustained intellectual development of contemplative skill and wisdom-insight—toward the evolutionary summit of buddhahood.

They define buddhahood as the total and eternal freedom from suffering—attained through the perfection of the understanding of the self and the universe and the processes of life and death—conjoined with the perfection of the compassion that enables a buddha-being to assist others in their own evolutionary progress with maximal effectiveness. They progress within the Mahāyāna way from the exoteric practice of the transcendences (*pāramitā*) to the esoteric practices of the Tantras in order to accelerate such evolutionary development, compressing into a single lifetime or a few lifetimes biological and psychological transformations that would normally take lifetimes of positive efforts during thousands or millions of deaths and rebirths.

The tantric communities of India in the latter half of the first Common Era millennium (and perhaps even earlier) were something like "Institutes of Advanced Studies" in relation to the great Buddhist monastic "Universities." They were research centers for highly cultivated, successfully graduated experts in various branches of inner science (*adhyātmavidyā*), some of whom were still monastics and could move back and forth from university (*vidyālaya*) to "site" (*pīṭha*), and many of whom had resigned vows of poverty, celibacy, and so forth, and were living in the classical Indian *saṁnyāsin* or *sādhu* style. I call them the "psychonauts" of the tradition, in parallel with our "astronauts," the materialist scientist-adventurers whom we admire for their courageous explorations of the "outer space" which we consider the matrix of material reality. Inverse astronauts, the psychonauts voyaged deep into "inner space," encountering and conquering angels and demons in the depths of their subconscious minds.

These tantric communities seemed to have understood full well the real dangers of falling prey to the forces lurking in such psychic depths—hence the secrecy and warnings of the dangers of the Tantras. As a skillful response to such dangers, the mandala universes of the tantric *imaginaire*—such as that of Chakrasamvara, located on the summit of Mount Meru in the Buddhist cosmos, and associated with Mt. Kailash on earth—are realms wherein such explorations can be conducted safely. Just as astronauts have to wear elaborate metal and plastic space suits to venture into the moonscape or the pressureless reaches of outer space, so the holographically visualized life-forms (*iṣṭhadevatā*, or "chosen deities") such as Chakrasamvara are embodiments and identities that the adepts can inhabit in order to penetrate areas where otherwise their normal embodiments and identities would be destroyed. These inner scientist adepts claim to have developed such extreme stability of contemplative attention and imagination that they can persist in the continuum of awareness from waking into lucid dream state, and that in the latter they can consciously manifest their body as that of a systematically imagined divine buddha-form, acting in the dream with the identity of being a perfect buddha-deity of the Chakrasamvara mandala palace community. They further claim that they can build on that ability and do the same thing in contemplatively induced out-of-body experience, manifested when the ordinary, coarse body has been stabilized in cataleptic trance, in simulation of near-death and post-death, between-state (*antarābhava*, *bar do*) experiences. They thus contend that they can traverse death and rebirth in these subtle, dream-like planes numerous times in a single lifetime, and that they can thereby radically accelerate their evolutionary progress toward what they define as the buddha condition.

Our understanding of these ideas and practices is complicated by the fact that these psychonauts lived in societies in various Indian nations and in Tibet wherein there were numerous other spiritual practitioners who were not Mahāyāna Buddhists, but tribal shamans, local sorcerers, and religious worshippers of Mahavira, Shiva, Vishnu, and Shakti in India, and later in

Tibet of the buddha-deities of the Bön practitioners, possibly derived from Zoroastrian deities. Among these, the Shaivite adepts seem to have been the most closely associated with the Chakrasamvara community, since the world of this Tantra seems intimately interactive with the forms of the esoteric Shaivite world. This is all the more interesting, since Shiva himself seems almost a yogin or adept god—"God" as a yogin—with the creation and destruction of the world being the practice of a divine yogin.

The Buddhist myth of Chakrasamvara seems to take aim at the destructive aspect of Shiva—the "world-destroyer" Rudra aspect for which he is well known—seeking to overwhelm its forms and transmute its energies into the bodhisattva enterprise. The most terrible symbol of this is the depiction of the buddha-deity Chakrasamvara standing with his two feet planted on deity forms, his right foot on the back of the neck of Rudra, and his left on the breasts of his consort, Kālarātri. Hindu scholars in the past have understandably found this insulting; and it certainly would be an aggressive affront if these forms were intended for public display. However, they were of course not so intended. Rather, these are esoteric imaginary forms; they are intended as aids (counter-archetypes) to enable one to overwhelm the archetypes of familiar cosmic deities—of whom one is in awe or is deeply afraid—in one's own deep psyche as one rises to the challenge of directly confronting naked reality, without depending on God or Goddess to know everything and to take care of everyone but assuming those responsibilities oneself out of the abundantly messianic drive of the bodhisattva. This powerful symbol thus represents oneself maturing into union with the divine enlightened identity, not depending on any enlightened or divine being outside oneself. This is similar to the shocking Ch'an Buddhist expression, "If you meet a buddha on the road, kill him!" Nobody is getting killed here, and no Rudra is being insulted in the Tantra; it is simply a matter of the practitioner overcoming within herself or himself any vestige of the childish imaginings that the goal state of divine enlightenment is anything outside of one's own self, or belongs to anyone other than oneself.

The present study, critical edition, and annotated translation of the major scripture of the Mother Tantra division of the Unexcelled Yoga Tantras represents a remarkable achievement on the part of Dr. Gray. It would have been exceptional at the hand of a senior scholar with decades of experience, and so is all the more admirable as the work of a young scholar in the early part of his career, though it has taken him about a decade to bring it up to this outstanding level. Immersing ourselves in this scripture, as we did in the process of editing Dr. Gray's amazing work, is an exhilarating and somewhat daunting process. There is even a tinge of dread, as its enlightened author prudently intended it to be kept esoteric, not to be widely available to an unprepared public, in order of course to avoid the types of dangers outlined above. Because of the tremendous importance of this major source of the Mother Tantra division of Unexcelled Yoga, Dr. Yarnall and myself honored the extraordinary work of David Gray by making strenuous efforts to make sure every detail was clarified, every potentially misunderstandable point was meticulously presented. In this way we have endeavored to follow the example set by His Holiness the Dalai Lama who in forewords to several books on Buddhist Tantra (some including descriptions and representations of rather fierce ritual images) has expressed his wise counsel to the effect that, 'Well, traditionally (and probably still now) it would be better not to publish this at all; but if it is going to be published inevitably anyway, it is important to explain it clearly and authoritatively so as to avoid damaging misunderstandings.'

Sigmund Freud, in discovering and expounding the subconscious with its *id*, full of polymorphously perverse *eros* and murderous *thanatos*, unbridled lust and aggression, is not urging us to go out and commit incest, rape, and murder. Yet many people still today do think of Freud as perverse, or at least a bit unsavory, as they themselves live in denial that such impulses exist in the civilized human mind, and of course especially in themselves. Educated persons with any knowledge of psychoanalytic theory and practice, of course, are quite clear on the greatness of Freud et al.'s discoveries and contributions. The modern reception of the Buddhist and Hindu Tantras has been similarly mixed, thought of as "obscene" (Snellgrove), "vulgar" (de la Vallée Poussin), "atrocious," "transgressive," and so forth. Of course, we must accept the possibility that they all may be right—we indeed may be encountering here a perverse, demonic cult, sanitized by centuries of pious rationalization. But we must likewise accept the possibility (as I certainly believe) that we are encountering some of the results of an extraordinary inner science, which explored the unconscious of the individual to learn how to transform its energies from negative to positive. Whichever the case, for the moment the present work stands as a major milestone in our progress toward understanding and more fully appreciating this complex, ancient tradition.

We are very pleased and proud to publish this magnificent work today, and so to provide another key resource that makes possible the beginnings of the solid study of this recondite and important tradition. Though the Tantra itself is a part of the Kangyur, not the Tengyur, its translation is fully interconnected with numerous commentaries from the Tengyur, and so it fits perfectly into our *Treasury*. Therefore, I congratulate David Gray, intrepid translator and meticulous scholar, for this wonderful accomplishment, I thank Dr. Yarnall for his great effort and painstaking care in designing and editing such a complex text, and we invite modern explorers of the Buddhist Tantras to encounter, for the first time, a clear picture of the root textual source of the cult of Chakrasamvara, the "Superbliss Wheel" Buddha.

Robert A. F. Thurman
Jey Tsong Khapa Professor of Indo-Tibetan Buddhist Studies, Columbia University
Director, Columbia Center for Buddhist Studies
President, American Institute of Buddhist Studies
President, Tibet House US

February 18, 2007
New Year's Day, Fire Pig Year

Copublishers' Preface to the 2019 Printing

Since the AIBS first printed this book in 2007 Dr. Gray has published three related books, one containing the Sanskrit and Tibetan editions for the *Cakrasamvara Tantra* (Gray 2012, AIBS), and two volumes containing Tsong Khapa's commentary on this tantra (Gray 2017, AIBS; and Gray 2019, AIBS and Wisdom Publications). For this new 2019 printing, now copublished by AIBS and Wisdom, we have fixed minor typos and have reformatted the book to include many of the new aesthetic elements from our new copublished series. However, since all three of Dr. Gray's more recent books (2012, 2017, 2019) refer to pages from the first 2007 printing of this tantra, we have minimized and implemented all changes in such a way as to maintain the original pagination in this new 2019 printing.

Author's Preface

This book is a study and translation of the *Cakrasamvara Tantra*, a Buddhist ritual text composed in India during the eighth century by an unknown author or group of authors. It is a work of central importance to the development of tantric Buddhism in India, and it remains an important scripture in many tantric Buddhist communities. Its study and practice is maintained by the Nevārī Buddhist community in the Kathmandu valley, as well as by many Tibetan Buddhists, not only in Tibet itself but in other regions influenced by Tibetan Buddhism, including Mongolia, Russia, China, and elsewhere, as Tibetan lamas have been living and teaching in diaspora.

The first part of this work consists of a study of the Tantra and its historical significance. While not exhaustive, it does explore a number of important issues, including the dating and provenance of the text and its commentarial tradition. I highlight evidence indicating that the *Cakrasamvara Tantra* developed in a non-monastic setting, and was composed via the active appropriation of elements of both text and practice belonging to non-Buddhist groups, most notably the Kāpālikas, an extreme and quasi-heretical Śaiva group focusing on transgressive practices.

Since appropriation invariably entails transformation, I also explore the strategies taken by Buddhists to transform the *Cakrasamvara Tantra* into a bona fide Buddhist text. These strategies included both active erasure of Śaiva elements and the addition and overlay of standard Buddhist terms and concepts. They also include the development of a mythic discourse that explains this appropriation in a manner that privileges the Buddhist perspective, and reduced the Śaiva other to a subordinate position. Buddhists also advocated internalized meditative practices that bracketed and neutralized the transgressive exercises that are actually prescribed by the text.

These changes apparently took place as the text and its concomitant tradition of ritual and meditative practice were incorporated into the curricula of several monastic Buddhist communities in Northeastern India, most notably at Vikramaśīla in what is now West Bengal, where a number of the text's commentators thrived. This process was underway by the ninth century, and continued unabated until these institutions were destroyed during the thirteenth and fourteenth centuries. Fortunately, by this time the Cakrasamvara tradition, in both its textual and praxical manifestations, was already transmitted to and established in Nepal and Tibet. Its transmission is ongoing, largely due to the work of Tibetan lamas and their disciples around the world.

The second section of this book is an annotated translation of the *Cakrasamvara Tantra.* It is based on my own edition of the incomplete Sanskrit manuscripts, the Tibetan translations, and extensive consultation of the Sanskrit and Tibetan commentaries. My edition of the Sanskrit and Tibetan texts was published in Gray 2012. The *Cakrasamvara Tantra* is a difficult and obscure text, so its translation necessitated frequent and sometimes lengthy annotations. Many of these consist of discussion and analysis of the disparate sources, which often disagree on the reading of a given section of the text. Many also consist of my translations from the commentaries, often accompanied by the Sanskrit when I am working from manuscripts or hard-to-obtain Indian editions. I generally do not provide the Tibetan when quoting from the texts in the Kangyur and the Tengyur; unless otherwise noted, I work mainly from the now widely available *sde-dge* edition of the Tibetan canon.

* * *

This study could not have been written without the assistance that has been provided by many individuals and institutions. My initial research into the *Cakrasamvara Tantra* began when I was a graduate student at Columbia University, studying under Robert Thurman, Ryuichi Abé, Gary Tubb, and Matthew Kapstein. I had the good fortune of being able to spend a year studying in India and Nepal with the financial and logistical support of Columbia University and the American Institute of Indian Studies. While there, I was fortunate to receive the hospitality of the Central Institute of Higher Tibetan Studies in Sarnath, the Office of H.H. The Dalai Lama Tenzin Gyatso, and the Library of Tibetan Works and Archives in Dharamsala. Much of my work at this time was largely conducted under the guidance of Geshe Yeshe Thapkay of the Central Institute of Higher Tibetan Studies, Geshe Yama Tseden and Geshe Tenzin Dargyay at Namgyal Monastery in Dharamsala, and Lelung Rinpoche, both in the United States and Dharamsala. I would also like to thank the Oriental Institute in Vadodara, the Kesar Library in Kathmandu, and the Institute for Advanced Studies of World Religions in Carmel, NY for so graciously allowing me to study manuscripts in their collections, and for providing me with microfilm and microfiche copies, as well as photocopies, of those that were essential for my work.

Work on this volume began during my tenure as a Woodrow Wilson postdoctoral fellow at Rice University. This would not have been possible without the support of the Woodrow Wilson Foundation, and, at Rice University, the Center for the Study of Cultures, the School of Humanities, and the Department of Religious Studies. I would like to particularly thank Werner Kelber, Sandra Gilbert, William Parsons, Anne Klein, and Jeffrey Kripal for their support and encouragement during this period. The work was completed at Santa Clara University, with the support of the College of Arts and Sciences and the Religious Studies Department. I would like to thank Catherine Bell, Paul Crowley, and David Pinault for their support during this period. I would also like to thank Iain Sinclair, who kindly provided me with detailed criticisms resulting from his careful reading of my dissertation, and Nobumi Iyanaga, who also provided me with helpful feedback on topics related to this work. I would particularly like to acknowledge the detailed feedback and criticism provided by the editor of this series, Robert Thurman. The editor of this volume, Thomas Yarnall, likewise provided indispensable and meticulous editorial support and critical advice. This volume would not have been possible without their assistance. Any and all faults, however, are solely my own responsibility.

Last but not least, I would like to thank my wife, Diana Iong, whose support and assistance has been indispensable from this project's inception eight years ago until its completion now. I would also like to thank our parents, Harry B. Gray III, Patricia Hope Allen-Hunt, Raymond L. Hunt, David Kam Hon Iong, and Silvia Sau Wan Lee Iong, without whom this work would not have been possible.

Dedicated to the Memory of

David Kam Hon Iong, 容 錦 漢 (1934–2000)

and

Harry B. Gray III (1938–2003)

Part One

Introduction

1. Introduction to the Cakrasamvara Tantra

1.1 The Cakrasamvara and the Yoginī Tantras

The texts and practices associated with the *Cakrasamvara Tantra* collectively constitute one of the most important contemporary traditions of esoteric or tantric Buddhism, still practiced in distinct lineage traditions by Nevārī Buddhists in Nepal as well as by Tibetan Buddhists of three of the four major schools, namely the Sa-skya, bKa'-brgyud, and dGe-lugs. It was also evidently quite popular in India, at least in Northern India during the late tenth through late thirteenth centuries when the second transmission of Buddhism to Tibet took place, as is attested by the hundreds of texts associated with the Cakrasamvara tradition that were translated into Tibetan during this time. It was extensively disseminated in India, as there is evidence of its spread as far south as Śrī Laṅka.[1] The *Cakrasaṁvara Tantra* was translated at least twice into Tibetan, and through the medium of Tibetan it has also been translated into Mongolian and Chinese.[2] There are also surviving copies of Cakrasamvara related texts in pre-modern Uighur[3] and Chinese translation.[4] Nevertheless, it remains a tradition that is still largely

[1] A Śrīlaṅkan history, the *Nikāya-saṅgraha* or *Sāsanāvatāra-caritaya*, composed around 1400 CE by Devarakṣita, alias Dharmakīrti of Gaḍalādeṇiya (Chandra 1984, 106), lists thirty-four tantric texts studied by the *Abhayagirivāsins*. These include not only the *Cakrasamvara Tantra* but also the "Herukādbhuta Tantra," which Chandra identifies with the *Herukābhyudaya Tantra* (HA). There is also a text listed as the "Sarvabuddha Tantra," which is likely the *Sarvabuddhasamayoga* (JS). See Chandra 1984, 108–110, and also Mudiyanse 1967, 17.

[2] There is a Mongolian translation of the entire Tibetan canon, including the Cakrasamvara related literature. There is a modern Chinese translation of the *Cakrasamvara Tantra* produced by Chinese practitioners of Tibetan Buddhism, made from the standard (Mardo) revised Tibetan translation. It is entitled 勝樂略續. There is no definitive evidence that a Chinese translation was made during the pre-modern period.

[3] See Kara and Zieme 1976 for an edition and German translation of an incomplete Uighur Cakrasamvara maṇḍala meditation text, one which was evidently translated from a Tibetan work of the Sa-skya school.

[4] Beckwith has published the contents of a Yuan dynasty collection of tantric Buddhist texts attributed to 'Phags-pa (1235–1280), a Sa-skya lama who was the nephew of Sa-skya Paṇḍita and teacher of Kublai Khan. This collection consists of what appear to be Chinese translations of Tibetan Buddhist works, and it is entitled "The Secret Collection of the Quintessential Path of the Mahāyāna." (大乘要道密集). The second text in this collection is entitled: 依吉祥上樂輪方便智慧雙運道玄義卷. Beckwith does not translate

unknown outside of the Asian cultural worlds where it has been practiced, as very few of its texts have been edited and translated into Western languages.[5]

The text most usually known as the *Cakrasamvara Tantra* (CS)[6] has several different names. At the conclusion of the surviving Sanskrit manuscripts, the text refers to itself as the "Great King of Yoginī Tantras called the Śrī Cakrasamvara" (*śrīcakrasamvara-nāma-mahāyoginī-tantra-rāja*). The term *Cakrasamvara* literally means the "Binding of the Wheels," and it is usually taken as referring to the Tantra's maṇḍala, which is called the "triple wheel" (*tricakra*), due to the maṇḍala's three wheels which are believed to pervade the cosmos, which in the traditional Indian perspective was also seen as threefold.[7] The later tradition also relates it to the inner anatomy of the subtle body, which the maṇḍala is also thought to pervade. The subtle body, too, was thought to consist of "wheels" or energy centers oriented along the vertical axis of the central channel (*avadhūtī*).

The Tantra, however, refers to itself by another name at the end of every chapter, and this name is the *Śrīherukābhidhāna*, "Discourse of Śrī Heruka," Śrī Heruka or Heruka being the name of the maṇḍala's central deity. The text itself is relatively short, consisting of approximately seven

---

this title (1984, 12), but it might be translated as "The Volume on the Hidden Meaning of the Way of Uniting Wisdom and Art according to the *Śrī Cakrasamvara*." That is, I take 上樂 as a translation of *samvara* following the Tibetan *bde-mchog*, while 輪 commonly translates *cakra*. The only peculiarity is their inversion here. This collection has been preserved in Taiwan, where it has been published three times between 1962 and 1981.

[5] The text entitled *Śrī-Cakraśaṁvara-Tantra*, published by Sir John Woodruff under the alias "Arthur Avalon" as vol. 7 of his "Tantrik Texts" series, is *not* a translation of the Tantra itself, but rather a series of Cakrasamvara ritual texts, translated from the Tibetan by Kazi Dawa-Samdup (1919). With regard to the explanatory tantras and commentaries, see my note on these subjects in the respective sections below. Elizabeth English (2002) has translated an important *sādhana* or meditative practice text centering around the goddess Vajravārāhī, the central goddess of the *Cakrasamvara Tantra*, who is also the central figure in her own cult.

[6] I will abbreviate this name as CS throughout the notes for this text. See the *Conspectus Siglorum* for identification of the *sigla* used in the notes to this text.

[7] For a discussion of an alternate understanding of *samvara* or *śamvara* as "supreme bliss," see section 2.2 below.

hundred stanzas.[8] It is a rather cryptic text, largely lacking the narrative structure that its name suggests it will have—for this reason, the text is also widely known as the *Laghusamvara*, or "*Samvara* Light," due to the belief that it is a condensed version of a much larger source text.

The full title in the colophon, "Great King of Yoginī Tantras called the *Śrī-Cakrasamvara*," draws explicit attention to the class of "Yoginī Tantras" in which tantras such as the *Cakrasamvara* and the *Hevajra* were classified by the Indian commentarial tradition. The *Cakrasamvara Tantra* also, in several places, draws attention to a rival class which it calls the "Yoga Tantras," which, in contradistinction to later Tibetan systems of tantric classification, includes tantras such as the *Guhyasamāja*.[9] The *Yoginī Tantras* correspond to what later Tibetan commentators termed the "Mother Tantras" (*ma rgyud*), while tantras such as the *Guhyasamāja* were classified as "Father Tantras" (*pha rgyud*), both of which were placed in the ultimate class known as the "Unexcelled Yoga Tantras" (*rnal 'byor bla med kyi rgyud*).[10]

The Yoginī Tantras were well-known for their focus on sexual yogas, and according to some commentators, this is the reason for their superiority. The *Vajrapañjara*, an explanatory tantra for the *Hevajra*, which is one of the most important Yoginī Tantras along with the *Cakrasamvara*, describes the tantra classes as follows:

> The method of the perfection of wisdom is called "yoginī,"
> who is served for the sake of union with the great consort

---

[8] This is the number traditionally given for its length in the commentarial literature. It is roughly accurate, but at this point an exact count is not possible as all surviving mss. are incomplete, and the commentaries and Tibetan translations do not agree, as there are many verse fragments and entire verses that are attested in one source but not another. This seems to indicate that the CS was never finalized, but remained an unstable text with numerous variant mss. throughout its history.

[9] The CS mentions the "Yoga Tantras" in chapters twenty-six and thirty-three.

[10] For a traditional account of this classification schema see Snellgrove 1988. Note that the labels "Mother Tantra" and "Father Tantra" appear to have been developed by Tibetan scholars and do not seem to be attested in the surviving Sanskrit sources. The latter term *rnal 'byor bla med kyi rgyud* is often presented as a Sanskrit term, namely *anuttarayoga-tantra*. Tibetan versions of Sanskrit texts such as the *Vajrapañjara* and its commentary do provide evidence for terms such as *anuttarayoga* (see passage translated immediately below). See Gibson 1997 for a discussion of Tibetan contributions in the area of tantric Buddhist textual taxonomy.

> (*mahāmudrā*). The *Vajrapañjara* of the yoginī is called the "Yoginī Tantra." The art of all perfections is attained through meditative states (*dhyāna*) alone. The *Hevajra maṇḍala*, the *Sarvabuddha[samayoga]*, the *Guhyagarbha*, the *Vajrāmṛta*, the *Cakrasamvara*, and the *[Vajra-]pañjara*[11] are famed as the six Yoginī Tantras. The Yoga Tantras were taught for the sake of disciplining men. Yoginī Tantras were taught in order to assemble women. *Action Tantras* [were taught] for the inferior, and the *Practice* [*Tantras*][12] for everyone else. Superior Yoga (*rnal 'byor mchog*) is taught for superior beings, and Unexcelled Yoga (*rnal 'byor gong med*) for those who surpass [them].[13]

Devakulamahāmati comments on this passage as follows:

> *Action Tantras* involve the external visualization of the deity as food, and so forth, and the earnest practice of purification, silence, and so forth. *Action yoga* involves visualization [of the deity] external to oneself. Yoga is the visualization of the experiential unity (*ekarasa*) of oneself and the wisdom [hero] who arises from one's own wheel. Superior Yoga is engaging in the great secret of supreme joy which arises from the embrace with one's consort (*vidyā*). Unexcelled Yoga (*rnal 'byor bla med*) involves dependence upon the supreme bliss that arises from the union of the vajra of one's deity with the lotus.[14]

He depicts the two highest tantric classes as entailing sexual union with a consort. This is a matter which bears further investigation, as one would not

[11] The six tantras listed here appear to be: 1. *Hevajra Tantra* (HV), Tōh. 417; 2. *Sarvabuddha-samayoga-ḍākinījālasamvara* (JS), Tōh. 366; 3. *Guhyagarbha*, presumably the *Śrīguhyagarbha-tattvaviniścaya*, Tōh. 832; 4. *Vajrāmṛta*, Tōh. 435; 5. *Cakrasamvara* (CS), Tōh. 368; 6. *Vajra-pañjara*, Tōh. 419.

[12] Literally "that which is not *kriyā*" (*bya min*, *akriyā*), a term that designates the *caryātantra* class. See Gyurme and Kapstein 1991, 2:19 n. 256.

[13] *Vajrapañjara*, 54b.

[14] Devakulamahāmati, *ḍākinīvajrajāla-tantrarāja-tattvapauṣṭikapañjika-nāma*, 90b–91a.

expect that normative Buddhist organizations, centered as they are upon the institution of celibate monasticism, would give rise to spiritual disciplines that would require a violation of the vow of celibacy.

The term *yoginī* in the name *Yoginī Tantra* points to the unusual social context in which these texts arose. It appears almost certain that the Yoginī Tantras, with their focus on sexual practices, the transgressive consumption of "polluting" substances such as bodily effluvia, female deities such as yoginīs and ḍākinīs, and fierce male deities, such as the Heruka deities—who are closely modeled on Śaiva deities such as Mahākāla and Bhairava, and bear the accoutrements of charnel ground dwelling yogins—did not solely derive from a mainstream monastic Buddhist context. Instead, they seem to have developed among and/or been influenced by liminal groups of renunciant yogins and yoginīs, who collectively constituted what might be called the "siddha movement." This movement has been outlined in great detail by Ronald Davidson in his 2002 book. Of particular interest here is the strong influence of the Śaiva groups, including the Kāpālikas, on the development of the Buddhist Yoginī Tantras, a topic on which Alexis Sanderson has written an influential series of essays.

The Buddhist Yoginī Tantras, like the Hindu tantric traditions to which they are closely related, appear to have originated in a distinct subculture[15] which could be termed "the cult of the charnel ground,"[16] consisting of antinomian yogins, yoginīs, and various renunciants who chose a deliberately transgressive lifestyle, drawing their garb and, in part, sustenance from the liminal space of the charnel ground that was the privileged

---

[15] Dick Hebdige defined the term "subculture" as "cultures of conspicuous consumption"; he elaborates that "it is through the distinctive rituals of consumption, through style, that the subculture at once reveals its 'secret' identity and communicates its forbidden meanings. It is basically the way in which commodities are used in a subculture which mark the subculture off from more orthodox cultural formations." (1979, 103) The charnel ground cult did indeed have its distinctive style, characterized by ornamentation derived from the charnel grounds (skulls, bones, ash, etc.), as well as "distinctive rituals of consumption," such as the extraction and consumption of power substances from human corpses. Hebdige's definition is also cited by Hugh Urban, who relies upon his and Bourdieu's work in explicating the development of a distinct identity by the Kartābhajās in colonial Bengal. See Urban 2001a, 60 ff., and especially 241 n. 5.

[16] I have adapted Tsuda's term "cult of the cemetery," as "cemetery" is not an appropriate translation for *śmaśāna*. This expression was first employed by Shinichi Tsuda in his 1978 essay; see also Tsuda 1990.

locus for their meditative and ritual activities. The Śaiva Kāpālikas constituted the best-known group in this subculture, as attested by the numerous references to them in Sanskrit literature.[17] The Kāpālikas have been characterized as having been engaged in a pursuit of power, one that often involved the transgression of social mores and rules of purity.[18] This power-centered ideology and its concomitant advocacy of transgressive, heteropraxic conduct is a central feature of the Yoginī Tantras as well, and it is valorized in the *Cakrasamvara Tantra* as the yoginī's heteropraxy or "conduct of the left" (*vāmācāra*).

Alexis Sanderson has argued convincingly that Śaiva-Kāpālika sources made an important impact on the Buddhist Yoginī Tantras, and has likewise claimed that Buddhist Yoginī Tantras are intertextually dependent upon them. While many of his claims have yet to be substantiated,[19] he identifies

---

[17] To conclude that the Śaiva Kāpālikas were the dominant subculture based on the predominance of references to them in *extant* Sanskrit literature presumes that this literature is roughly representative of that actually composed in medieval India. This literature is exhaustively documented in David Lorenzen's (1971, 1989) works.

[18] See Sanderson 1985, 190–216.

[19] He argues in one article that "Chapters 15 to 17 of the Buddhist Laghusaṁvara (Herukābhidhāna), which teaches a secret jargon of monosyllables (*ekākṣaracchoma*) (15), and the characteristics by means of which the Buddhist adepts may recognize females as belonging to one or the other of seven Yoginī-families (16) and seven Ḍākinī-families (17) equals the *samayācāracestā vidhāna* chapter of the Yoginīsaṁcāra section of the Jayadrathayāmala. Chapter 19 of the Laghusaṁvara, on the characteristics of the Yoginīs known as Lāmas, equals chapter 29 of the Siddhayogeśvarīmata." (1994, 94–95) Obviously, a detailed study of the textual passages in question would be necessary to demonstrate exactly what "equals" means here, and it may not even be possible to establish conclusively that one text borrowed from the other, excluding other possibilities that, say, both drew from a third source. Sanderson has also published a lengthier study (2001), in which he has compared in greater detail several instances of intertextuality between the CS and Śaiva texts. In this article, entitled "History through Textual Criticism in the Study of Śaivism, the Pañcarātra and the Buddhist Yoginītantras," Sanderson argues that the Śaiva versions of the textual passages are the sources for the Buddhist versions, due to the fact that the Śaiva texts provide the clearest readings, while the Buddhist versions of the text are often ungrammatical. However, as Davidson has noted, Sanderson's assumption that the clearest reading is the earliest one violates the longstanding rule in textual criticism of *difficilior lectio*, which holds that the more challenging reading is often the earliest, given the tendencies of later editors and copyist to "correct" difficult readings. (2002b, 386 n. 105) Sanderson has not, in fact, demonstrated that the more grammatical Śaiva texts are earlier; their grammaticality itself does not demonstrate this. While Sanderson is certainly correct that the Buddhist Yoginītantras were significantly influenced by Śaiva Kāpālika practices (and, very likely, texts as

at least one point where Buddhist Yoginī Tantras, including the *Cakrasamvara Tantra*, appear to have borrowed from a non-Buddhist source.[20]

The non-normative nature of the Yoginī Tantras is indicated by their textual structure. These texts generally jettisoned the textual conventions of earlier esoteric Buddhist scriptures such as the *Sarvatathāgata-tattvasaṁgraha Sūtra*, which followed the textual model of the earlier Mahāyāna sūtras, and often assumed instead the discursive style found in Śaiva scriptures, with the texts presenting themselves as records of conversations between a god and goddess.[21] More specifically, the *Cakrasamvara Tantra* and its early commentaries exhibit traces of Śaiva influence, traces which inspired different commentarial responses.[22] These involve the appearance of names of Śaiva deities, namely Mahābhairava, Rudra, and Mahākāla/Mahākālī. One case, in chapter two, was eradicated in later editions of the text.[23] The earliest com-

well), the undoubtedly complex relationships that exist between Śaiva and Buddhist tantric textual traditions will only be determined conclusively once all of the surviving texts have been critically edited and published.

[20] This concerns the textual passage in the CS and other Yoginī Tantras listing the 24 site pilgrimage circuit, which will be discussed in section 3.1 below.

[21] Texts which assume this model include, for example, the *Caṇḍamahāroṣaṇa Tantra* (Tōh. 431, partially edited in George 1974), and the *Vajravārāhī-abhibhava Tantrarāja* (Tōh. 378).

[22] I have identified five cases, in chs. 2, 19, 41, 42, and 50. All of these are discussed in the notes to the respective chapters, and some are also discussed below.

[23] This eradication occurs in CS ch. 2 v. 17, where the principal goddess, Vajravārāhī, is described as "facing the deity Śrī Heruka" (*śrīherukadevābhimukhāṁ*). However, Jayabhadra's commentary reads here "facing Mahābhairava" (*mahābhairavābhimukham*), a reading confirmed by the parallel passage in the *Abhidhānottara Tantra* (AU). It seems likely that sometime following the composition of Jayabhadra's commentary the text was revised in order to efface an embarrassingly obvious reference to a Hindu deity. The second chapter also contains a second possible example of such transformation. In v. 14, Śrī Heruka is described as "the terror of Mahābhairava" (*mahābhairavabhīṣaṇam*). The parallel passage in the AU mss., however, informs the reader that he "has the form of Mahābhairava" (H 147a.3, I 599b.6, J 238.5–6: *mahābhairavarūpiṇam*). One should note that both readings make sense in light of the myth of Heruka's subjugation of Bhairava. I suspect that the AU's reading is the original reading here. Unfortunately, Jayabhadra does not comment on this text, but I suspect that the AU's reading is older, in part because it is confirmed by the statement in ch. 32 that Heruka has "Bhairava's form" (*bhairavākāraṁ*). Interestingly, Bhavabhaṭṭa provides a third reading that completely removes all reference to Mahābhairava, namely "the terror of the Mahāraurava [hell]" (Pandey 2002, 32: *mahārauravabhīṣaṇam*). This reading makes less sense, and may represent a partially successful attempt to emend the text.

mentator, Jayabhadra,[24] generally accepts these traces but explains them in a Buddhist fashion, arguing that Mahābhairava, mentioned in chapter two as Vajravārāhī's consort, is actually a buddha (*bhagavān*). Likewise, when chapter sixteen describes a clan of yoginīs as companions of a Śaiva deity, "the hero Rudra," Jayabhadra explains that they were born in Śrī Heruka's clan.[25] However, one of his successors at Vikramaśīla, Bhavabhaṭṭa, emended the text in these places to more orthodox Buddhist readings.[26]

Now it is important to note that most if not all of these deities, while likely originating in Hindu circles, have Buddhist analogues. For example, there is a Buddhist Mahākāla, as well as a Buddhist version of Bhairava, Vajrabhairava. What is of particular interest is not so much the presense of these names in the text, but the consternation that these names caused among the early commentators. In particular, the attempts to erase or thoroughly transform these names in the text indicates that at least some Buddhists, such as Bhavabhaṭṭa, were uncomfortable with the presence of Śaiva names in the text. Such emendations were undoubtedly the work of Buddhists working in monastic contexts, who were likely troubled by these instances of slippage, in which the names of major Śaiva deities appear in the place of Buddhist deities.[27]

---

[24] See sections 1.2 and 1.3 below for discussions of the dating of the CS, its commentaries, and its commentators.

[25] He likewise claims, in the context of ch. 42, that the "Mahākālī" mentioned in the text is Vajravārāhī. See the notes to these chapters in the translation below.

[26] Bhavabhaṭṭa quite consistently effaces these references and replaces them with more neutral names. In some cases, such as the case in ch. 2, he was apparently successful, with surviving CS mss. exhibiting his emendation. In other cases, such as those in chs. 16, 41, and 42, he apparently was not. Ch. 50 presents an exception to this pattern. In a section where the CS Sanskrit text is missing, only Bhavabhaṭṭa preserves the reading which attests Śaiva influence, namely "The Mahākāla mantrin should repeat [mantra]" (*mahākālo japen mantrī*). In place of *mahākāla*, the Tibetan translations attest the word "always," *rtag tu* (PM 245a, SL 142b).

[27] The categories of "Hindu" and "Buddhist" deities are, of course, problematic, since both traditions borrowed from one another quite extensively. There was significant appropriation of elements of Śaiva iconography by Buddhists, as Phyllis Granoff (1979) has pointed out. But there was also significant appropriation by Hindus from Buddhist tantric sources, as Bühnemann (1999 and 2000) has shown. While deities such as Mahākāla and Bhairava were adopted into the tantric Buddhist pantheons, they clearly originated as Hindu deities, and their presence in the *Cakrasamvara Tantra* evidently caused discomfort to Buddhist commentators such as Bhavabhaṭṭa.

In the case of the Yoginī Tantras such as the *Cakrasamvara Tantra*, it appears that the ninth century was crucial with regard to their acceptance within Buddhist monastic institutions, and was the period when such altertions were made.[28] It is unclear why texts such as the *Cakrasamvara* were apparently only slightly rather than significantly emended. Perhaps this was due to their prestige. If widespread belief in the efficacy of the text's rituals and meditations was the primary factor leading to their inclusion within Buddhist monastic curricula, this very same prestige may have seriously limited the possibility for emending the text. This limitation, however, was not a problem, for creative hermeneutics could achieve what actual alteration could not. This was the province of the commentators, whose work was essential in establishing the *Cakrasamvara Tantra* as a Buddhist text.

1.2 Dating the Text

It is not currently possible to date the *Cakrasamvara Tantra* precisely. Its *terminus ante quem* is clearly the late tenth century, when it was first translated into Tibetan by Rin-chen bZang-po with the assistance of Padmākaravarman.[29] However, the long and rich commentarial tradition points to a much earlier composition of the text; the earliest commentary, that written by Laṅka Jayabhadra,[30] was probably composed during the early- to mid-ninth century. According to Tāranātha, he was the third tantric preceptor at

[28] Not only is the ninth century the period when we see clear development of sophisticated tantric Buddhist exegetical systems, but it is also the period when there is clear evidence of the spread in South India of tantric Buddhism as a self-conscious movement. For example, a Śrī Laṅkan history, the *Nikāya-saṁgraha*, reports that during "the reign of Sena I (846–866), vājiriya-vāda was introduced to the Vīrāṅkura monastery by a monk of the *Vajraparvata-nikāya* of India, and the king accepted these doctrines." (Chandra 1984, 108, citing Mudiyanse 1967, 8) Of course, the so-called "Vajrayāna" originated in earlier textual production during the seventh and eighth century, giving rise to earlier transmissions to China and Tibet. But it may have taken longer for esoteric Buddhism to emerge as a self-consciously distinct movement in India, and the late eighth or ninth century seems the most likely period for this to have occurred. It is interesting as well that this Śrī Laṅkan text gives recognizable but distinct designations for this movement, i.e., *vājiriya-vāda* and *Vajraparvata-nikāya*.

[29] According to Tucci, Rin-chen bZang-po studied in India from 975–988 CE (1988, 3–4); it would have been during this period that they produced their translation.

[30] His name and his origin in Śrī Lanka is confirmed by the colophon of the Sanskrit ms. of his commentary. (D 61b.2)

Vikramaśīla,[31] which was founded by King Dharmapāla (c. 775–812) at the end of the eighth century.[32] Since the first two preceptors, Buddhajñānapāda and Dīpaṁkarabhadra, served during Dharmapāla's reign,[33] Jayabhadra likely was active as a scholar during the early- to mid-portion of the ninth century.

The *Cakrasamvara Tantra*'s *terminus post quem* is the early eighth century. This is provided by the fact the *Cakrasamvara Tantra*, in its third, twenty-seventh, and thirtieth chapters, mentions by name several other tantras, including the *Sarvatathāgata-tattvasaṁgraha Sūtra*, *Guhyasamāja Tantra*, *Vajrabhairava Tantra*, *Śrī Paramādya*, and the *Samvara*, which here refers to the *Samayoga* or *Sarvabuddhasamayoga-ḍākinījālasamvara* (JS).[34] The *Cakrasamvara Tantra*, in its final form, must postdate these texts. While their exact dates are unknown, there is no firm evidence that any of these texts, aside from the *Sarvatathāgata-tattvasaṁgraha Sūtra*, existed prior to the eighth century.[35] On the other hand, all of these texts (except for the *Vajrabhairava*) are listed by Amoghavajra in his *Index of the Vajraśekhara Sūtra Yoga in Eighteen Sections*,[36] which shows that they existed in some

---

[31] See Chimpa and Chattopadhyaya 1970, 18, 325–29. I consider evidence such as this to be an important source for the construction of the history of tantric Buddhism. While it is of course possible that Tāranātha's list is erroneous (and it is evidently the case that his historical works do contain some errors, one of which will be noted below), I see no reason to *assume* from the outset that it is erroneous, unless additional evidence proves it to be. In fact, as Templeman has argued, there is good reason to believe that his works maintain greater fidelity to earlier Indian sources than did many later Tibetan historical works; moreover he also critically evaluated the Indian and Tibetan materials at his disposal (see Templeman 1981). In this case, there is good reason to provisionally accept it as evidence, as elements of Tāranātha's account are confirmed by other sources of information (as will be noted below). There are further reasons to believe that Jayabhadra's is the earliest extant Cakrasamvara commentary, as will be discussed in section 1.3 below.

[32] See Willemen 1983, 21.

[33] See Davidson 2002b, 311, and Chimpa and Chattopadhyaya 1970, 325.

[34] See the notes to chs. 3, 27, and 30 of the translation below for the canonical citations of these texts.

[35] The dating of the *Tattvasaṁgraha* has been the subject of considerable study in Japan. Regarding this see, for example, Matsunaga 1977 and 1980.

[36] 金剛頂經瑜伽十八會指歸 (T. 869). For a detailed, annotated English translation of this important text, see Geibel 1995.

form when he composed this work following his return to China from South Asia in 746 CE.[37] They may date, as has been conjectured, to the early eighth century, but it is certainly possible that some of these texts may date to the late seventh century.[38]

While there is no evidence suggesting that the *Cakrasamvara Tantra* was composed prior to Amoghavajra's return to China, there is evidence suggesting that the text was composed soon afterward, by the mid- to late eighth century. Ronald Davidson has previously noted that there are citations "from the *Laghusaṁvaratantra* (*bDe mchog gi rgyud*, Tōh. 368)" in Vilāsavajra's *Ārya-Nāmasaṁgītiṭīkā-mantrārthāvalokinī-nāma.*[39] Since Vilāsavajra was active in the mid- to late-eighth century,[40] this would be a startling discovery, as it would firmly date the text, in some version at least, to this period.

It turns out, however, that most of the passages in this text that are identified as quotes from the *Samvaratantra* (*bde mchog gi rgyud*) derive not from the *Cakrasamvara/Laghusamvara* but are quotations from the *Samayoga.*[41] In Indian Buddhist texts the appellations *samvara* or *samvaratantra* are typically a shorthand designation for the latter text. This was the case not

---

[37] See Chou 1945, 292, which consists of a biography of Amoghavajra.

[38] The *Guhyasamāja*, *Samayoga*, and *Śrī Paramādya* are all listed in Amoghavajra's index, and are also attested in the rNying-ma "Eighteen Tantras of the Māyājāla Class," as Eastman has pointed out in his (1981) seminar paper. Matsunaga has conjectured that "the first half of the 8th century was the formative period of the *Guhyasamāja-tantra* while the text in its present form was completed in the latter half of the 8th century." (1978, xxvi) He very well may be correct, but it is also possible that the *Guhyasamāja* as well as these other texts may have been composed as early as the late seventh century.

[39] See Davidson 1981, 7–8.

[40] Vilāsavajra was one of the preceptors of Buddhajñānapāda, who served at the newly founded Vikramaśīla under King Dharmapāla. See Davidson 1981, 6 and 2002b, 311.

[41] The following passages in Vilāsavajra's AN correspond to passages in the JS: (1) AN 29b: *'di nyid dpal bde mchog gi rgyud las gsungs pa ste / nam mkha' kun gyi skabs na dpal // rdo rje sems dpa' de bzhin gshegs /*; JS 152a: */ nam mkha' kun gyi skabs na dpal // rdo rje sems dpa' de bzhin gshegs //* (2) AN 67b: */ de nyid las gsungs pa'ng bde ba ni saṁ zhes pa la sogs pa'o /*; JS 151a: */ shaṁ zhes bya ba bde bar bshad /* (3) AN 102a: */ de ltar yang dpal bde mchog gi rgyud las gsungs pa / kun tu kun nas thams cad du // bdag nyid rtag tu rnam pa kun // sangs rgyas la sogs brtan gyo kun // kun gyi dngos por bdag gyur to /*; JS 151b: */ kun tu kun nas thams cad ni // bdag nyid rtag tu rnam pa kun // sangs rgyas la sogs brtan gyo kun // kun gyi dngos por bdag gyur to /.*

only in Vilāsavajra's commentary, but in others as well.[42] Generally, when Indian commentators refer to the *Cakrasamvara* they use the name *Laghu-samvara* or *Cakrasamvara*. However, it turns out that there is one instance in his commentary where Vilāsavajra does quote the *Cakrasamvara Tantra*, from its second chapter.[43] He also makes a reference to its forty-eighth chapter.[44] While it is not possible to date the *Cakrasamvara Tantra* earlier than the tenth century on the basis of the extant manuscripts and translations alone, Vilāsavajra's commentary suggests that the text was compiled in some form by the late eighth century. The Cakrasamvara is thus traceable to the latter end of an epoch of Indian history, namely the seventh and eighth centuries, which a preponderance of data suggests was a crucial era in the development of tantric Buddhism. Concerning this epoch, Naudou has suggested: "Let us recognize that the arguments invoked in order to justify that chronology are not all of equal value; certain can assuredly be proven false, but, from whichever angle one approaches the problem, all lead us to the end of the 7th and to the 8th century."[45]

---

[42] For example, Indrabhūti, in his *Jñānasiddhi*, quotes a passage that he identifies as "stated in the *Samvara Tantra*" (Samdhong and Dwivedi 1988, 144: *samvaratantre nigaditam*), which is equivalent to the text at JS 152a and 153a. In addition, Nāgabodhi, in his *Samājasādhanavyavasthāna*, quotes the *Samvara* (at QT 9.3–4), which corresponds to text at JS 153a.

[43] The quote occurs as follows at AN 67a: */ glang chen ko rlon gos su gyon // zhes pa ni dpal 'khor lo bde mchog gi rgyud las te /*. This corresponds to the following text in CS ch. 2: *hasticarmaviruddhaṁ ca*, which in Mardo's translation reads: *glang po'i pags pa rnam par bgos* (PM 214b).

[44] The reference occurs as follows at AN 66b: *// keng rus mche ba gtsigs pa po // ha la ha la gdong brgya pa // zhes pa ni / de la keng rus ni dpal bde mchog 'khor lo'i rgyud las so /*. He begins by quoting the last half of verse 67 from the *Mañjuśrī-nāmasaṁgīti*, which occurs as follows in Davidson's edition: *daṁṣṭrākarālakaṅkālo halāhalaśatānanaḥ* (1981, 54). He continues, writing "As for that, *skeleton* [occurs] in the *Cakrasamvara Tantra*." This may be a reference to CS ch. 48, which occurs as follows: *vikaṭadaṁṣṭriṇām eva ca kaṁkālamahākaṁkāla*; PM 244a: */ de bzhin mche ba rnam gtsigs dang // keng rus keng rus chen po dang /*.

[45] Naudou (1980, 79) comes to this conclusion via a review of the various attempts to date the tantras, and has argued that a great deal of evidence, none of which is absolutely firm in and of itself, points to the seventh and eighth centuries as the period of greatest activity in the development of the tantras. Regarding the numerous problems evident in past attempts to date the tantras, see Wedemeyer 2001.

1.3 Cakrasamvara Literature

The *Cakrasamvara Tantra* is a very cryptic text. While this is due in part to its relative brevity, and in part to the somewhat simplified and prosaic form of Sanskrit in which it is written (a form which was increasingly common from the early medieval period onward),[46] it is largely the text's contents and their treatment that account for its obscurity. Like most tantras, it is primarily a ritual text, dedicating most of its fifty-one chapters to the description of rites such as the production of the maṇḍala, the consecration ceremonies performed within it, as well as various other ritual actions such as *homa* fire sacrifices, enchantment with mantras, and so forth. Moreover, like many tantras, and perhaps more than most, it fails to give sufficient information for the performance of these rituals.[47] It also often obscures crucial elements, particularly the mantras, which the text typically presents in reverse order, or which it codes via an elaborate scheme in which both the vowels and consonants are coded by number.[48]

The text was thus written so as to require commentary. This was no doubt due to the imperative of secrecy, which the text itself repeatedly demands of its adepts. Only initiated adepts were to receive the Root Tantra (*mūlatantra*), and they would have required oral instructions from their gurus in order to understand it. It probably did not take long, however, for Buddhists to begin composing literature to expand upon and explain the root texts. Indeed, the earliest surviving commentary (Jayabhadra's) was probably composed within fifty years of the Root Tantra itself.

There are three general genres of Cakrasamvara commentarial literature: the "explanatory tantras" (*vyākhyātantra*); commentaries on the root text; and ritual literature, such as *sādhanas*, *maṇḍalavidhis*, *abhiṣekavidhis*, and so forth, which describe in detail meditative and ritual practices. Among these, the greatest uncertainty surrounds the explanatory tantras. Generally, these are independent but closely related tantras that were later

[46] For a more thorough description of the Sanskrit preserved in the surviving mss., see section 4.1 below.

[47] This is a common issue in the history of esoteric Buddhism. A famous example of this involves Kūkai's decision to travel to China after acquiring a copy of the Chinese translation of the *Mahāvairocana-sūtra* and failing to understand its ritual components. Regarding this, see Abé 1999, 108–111.

[48] Regarding the mantra coding in the CS, see section 3.4 below.

subsumed within the tradition surrounding the *Cakrasamvara Tantra*. The decision of what is and is not an explanatory tantra seems to have been somewhat arbitrary, given the great diversity of texts so classified. Perhaps to address this taxonomic confusion, the Tibetan exegete Bu-ston composed a list of seven types of explanatory tantras, as follows:

> With regard to [those texts] taken to be explanatory tantras, it is claimed that they fall into seven types: 1) those which clarify that which is unclear; 2) those which complete the incomplete; 3) those of different methodology; 4) those which summarize the meaning [of a text]; 5) those which correspond to a portion [of a text]; 6) those which give rise to definitive understanding; and 7) those which discern the word and meaning [of the text]. (DS 47–48)

This is not, properly speaking, a list of different types of explanatory tantras, but rather a list of their functions. As such, it may be useful as the basis of a polythetic taxonomy of this genre of literature, with all examples being expected to contain some, but not necessarily all, of these functions.[49]

Such functional diversity also undoubtedly facilitated the *ex post facto* classification of bodies of related texts, with one selected as the "Root Tantra" and the others relegated to the role of its explanatory tantras. This is apparently what took place in the Cakrasamvara tradition. Bu-ston listed nine tantras as explanatory tantras of the Cakrasamvara. These are, to use the common short-hand names: the *Abhidhānottara* (AU);[50] *Vajraḍāka* (VD); *Ḍākārṇava* (DM);[51] *Herukābhyudaya* (HA); *Yoginīsaṁcāra* (YS);[52] *Samvarodaya* (SU);[53] *Caturyoginīsampuṭa* (Tōh. 376); *Vārāhī-abhisambodhi* (Tōh. 377); and the *Sampuṭa* (SP).[54] All but the last of these texts are classi-

---

[49] Regarding polythetic classificatory schemas and their relevance in the study of religion, see Smith 1982, 1–18.

[50] The *Abhidhānottara* is partially edited and translated in Kalff 1979.

[51] The Apabhraṁśa version of the *Ḍākārṇava* is edited in Chaudhuri 1935.

[52] The Sanskrit and Tibetan versions of the *Yoginīsaṁcāra* are edited in Pandey 1998.

[53] The *Samvarodaya* is partially edited and translated in Tsuda 1974.

[54] The first *kalpa* of the *Sampuṭa* is edited and translated in Elder 1978, and edited only in Skorupski 1996.

fied by Bu-ston as "uncommon" (*thun mong ma yin pa*) explanatory tantras, meaning that they belong solely to the Cakrasamvara tradition. The *Sampuṭa*, on the other hand, is a "common" (*thun mong ba*) explanatory tantra, meaning that it is shared by more than one tradition, in this case the Cakrasamvara and Hevajra traditions.[55]

A period of approximately five hundred years separates the composition of the *Cakrasamvara Tantra* and the exegetical activities of the Tibetan scholar Bu-ston (1290–1364 CE),[56] and there is no doubt that the identification of the Cakrasamvara explanatory tantras evolved slowly. The early Cakrasamvara commentaries, composed during the ninth and early tenth centuries, make no mention of this issue. The earliest reference to Cakrasamvara explanatory tantras occurs in commentaries dating to the late tenth or eleventh centuries. Durjayacandra apparently refers to six explanatory tantras in his commentary, although his text is ambiguous.[57] Meanwhile, Atīśa Dīpaṁkaraśrījñāna, in a text likely composed during the early- to mid-eleventh century,[58] mentions three explanatory tantras.[59]

---

[55] Bu-ston provides a useful resume of the contents of these nine texts in his RP, describing each text at the following locations: AU 396–407; VD 407–11; DM 411–18; HA 418–20; YS 420–21; SU 421–23; *Caturyoginīsampuṭa*, 423; *Vārāhyabisambodhi*, 423–24; SP 424–29.

[56] Regarding the life of Bu-ston see Ruegg 1966.

[57] Durjayacandra's commentary reads "the *Ḍāka*, the *Udaya*, the *Saṁcāra*, the *Abhidhānottara Tantra*, the *Sampuṭa Tantra*, and 'the four' should be understood to be explanatory tantras." (RG 246b: */ mkha 'gro 'byung ba kun spyod dang // de bzhin mtshan mchog bla ma'i rgyud // kha sbyor rgyud dang bzhi po ni // bshad pa'i rgyud du shes par bya /*) The *Ḍāka/ mkha 'gro* could refer either to the *Vajraḍāka* or the *Ḍākārṇava*, while the *Udaya/'byung ba* could refer to any or all of the following three texts: the *Samvarodaya*, the *Herukābhyudaya*, and possibly the *Vajravārāhyabhibhava-Tantrarāja* (Tōh. 378). The Tibetan *bzhi po* could be a reference to the *Caturyoginīsampuṭa*. I read *mtshan mchog* as an irregular translation of *Abhidhānottara*. Tsong Khapa discusses this quote at KS 3b–4a, which I comment upon in my translation of this work (Gray 2017, 34).

[58] Atīśa lived from 982–1054 CE, and journeyed to Tibet in 1040 CE. See Chattopadhyaya 1967, 66, 311, 364.

[59] In his *Abhisamayavibhaṅga*—a commentary on Lūipa's *sādhana* entitled the *Śrībhagavad-abhisamaya*—Atīśa states: "I will explain gathering together the essential points from the *Abhidhāna[-uttara]* (*nges brjod*), the *[Heruka-]Abhyudaya* (*mngon 'byung*), and the *Ḍāka* (*mkha' 'gro*). Here the object of explanation is the process of the path of definitive meaning, which is the topic of the Yoginī Tantras, including the *Khasama Mahātantra* and the four explanatory tantras that elucidate it." (AV 186a) Again, it is not clear if by *mkha' 'gro* Atīśa is referring to the *Vajraḍāka* or the *Ḍākārṇava*.

Most of these texts appear to be independent works, and internally contain no indication that they are subsidary to the *Cakrasamvara Tantra*, although many make reference to a vast ur-text known as the *Abhidhāna* or *Khasama Tantra*. Some, such as the *Abhidhānottara* and *Yoginīsaṁcāra*, do indeed "complete the incomplete," filling in crucial details that are missing in the "Root Tantra" itself.[60] Some of these texts, such as the *Abhidhānottara*, *Vajraḍāka*, and *Ḍākārṇava*, are also much larger than the *Cakrasamvara Tantra*.

It seems likely that these texts were identified later (by the late tenth century) as Cakrasamvara explanatory tantras. The rationale for doing so was probably just that they were seen to be closely related texts. I suspect that the Cakrasamvara was privileged simply because it had by that time become the most popular text of this body of closely related literature. This is indicated by the Tibetan canon, which contains over a dozen translations of Indian commentaries on the *Cakrasamvara Tantra*, and many more Cakrasamvara ritual texts. The texts identified as its explanatory tantras generally have only one commentary each, with far fewer corresponding ritual texts. While it is possible that the Tibetans themselves, wittingly or unwittingly, engaged in selective translation, I find this unlikely, and suspect rather that their translation choices reflect, approximately if not precisely, the intellectual currents in North Indian Buddhist communities.[61]

---

[60] For example, with regard to the maṇḍala, the Cakrasamvara lists only the names of the deities in the three wheels, as well as their corresponding pilgrimage places. It omits, however, the correlations to body parts and constituents, which is crucial for the "body maṇḍala" practice. This information is provided, however, in the *Abhidhānottara* and *Yoginīsaṁcāra*, as will be discussed in section 3.1 below.

[61] This point is impossible to prove as we have no independent means of confirming the contents of the libraries of the great Northern Indian monastic centers, all of which were destroyed within a few centuries of the recommencement of the transmission of Buddhism to Tibet. While Tibetan sources typically present the translators as faithful transmitters of Indian Buddhism, it is possible (if not likely) that Tibetan preferences played some role in their selection of texts to translate. It is also possible that socio-political factors impacted this transmission process. One might wonder, for example: to what extent did the Indian Buddhist reception of Tibetan pilgrim-translators affect the range of possibilities open to them in their study of Buddhist texts? Certainly Tibetan hagiographies portray Tibetan students such as Marpa the Translator studying with figures such as Nāropa, Śāntibhadra, Maitrīpa, and Jñānaḍākinī who—though influential—were nevertheless institutionally marginal. See Trungpa 1982, 9–33. These figures were "institutionally marginal" insofar as their tantric teaching activities occurred on the margins of (if not entirely outside of) the major

That said, there is evidence suggesting that the identification of the *Cakrasamvara Tantra* as the Root Tantra of the tradition was somewhat arbitrary. Some early commentators, such as Bhavabhaṭṭa, express the notion that the "light" version of the *Cakrasamvara Tantra* derives from a much larger root text.[62] This seems to be closely related to the distinction between a "root tantra" and an "appendix" (*uttaratantra*),[63] which may be a precursor to the concept of the explanatory tantra. The colophon of the *Cakrasamvara Tantra* refers to itself as follows: "It is the king and master of all teachings, the great hero Śrī Heruka, and the appendix of an appendix (*uttarottaraṁ*), and it appears in the *Discourse of Śrī Heruka* as the end of the one hundred thousand [stanza] Great King of Tantras." For the Indian Buddhist who wrote this colophon, the existing *Cakrasamvara Tantra* is merely an "appendix of an appendix," deriving ultimately from a much larger text that is also called the *Discourse of Śrī Heruka* (*Śrīherukābhidhāna*). Bhavabhaṭṭa comments here that "The word **and**[64] shows that it is an **appendix of an appendix** that summarizes the import of another tantra."[65] This problematizes the Tibetan conclusion that the *Cakrasamvara Tantra* is a root tantra.[66] It also points to the *Abhidhānottara Tantra*, which

monastic centers. For example, Nāropa's hagiography indicates that he began his tantric teaching career only after he had left Nālandā, while Śāntibhadra is portrayed as never having studied or taught in such institutions. While it is possible that Tibetans were drawn to them on account of their charisma, it is also possible that they were excluded from the formal study of the tantras at the established monastic centers, as Yi-jing evidently was centuries earlier at Nālandā. See my discussion of this in section 3.2 below.

62 See section 2.1 below for a discussion of this issue. The commentaries of Bhavabhaṭṭa and other Indian commentaries are discussed below in the present section.

63 An appendix (*uttaratantra*) is an auxiliary text, added to a tantra, which is believed to in some way complete that tantra's meaning.

64 When translating commentarial passages, I place in bold the terms that are being commented upon, in order to clarify the relationship between source text and commentary. Here Bhavabhaṭṭa is commenting upon the title given in the colophon of the CS mss.

65 Pandey 2002, 596: *cakārāt tantrāntarārthasamuccāyakam uttarottaraṁ vyākhyātam.*

66 This is a problem on which Tibetan commentators such as Bu-ston and Tsong Khapa spent a good deal of time. For a survey of this issue, see Tsuda 1974, 27–45, as well as my translation of Tsong Khapa's commentary (Gray 2017). Note, however, that Tsuda errs in assuming that the term *Samvara* in older Indian literature refers to the CS or *Cakrasamvara* (1974, 37). See my discussion of this issue in section 1.2 above.

seems to have been considered the appendix to this larger *Abhidhāna* text. The *Abhidhānottara* is clearly one of the oldest of the explanatory tantras, as it preserves Śaiva readings dating to the ninth century, some of which were emended in the root tantra itself. But although the *Abhidhānottara* in several cases preserves older readings, it is clearly not older than the *Cakrasamvara Tantra*, as it mentions this text by name.[67] Its preservation of older readings is likely a result of the fact that it was apparently a less popular text, as indicated by the dearth of commentaries upon it. On the other hand, many of the explanatory tantras, such as the *Samvarodaya*, *Vajraḍāka*, and *Ḍākārṇava*, appear to have been composed later than the oldest strata of texts, which certainly includes the *Cakrasamvara* and *Abhidhānottara Tantras*. This is because the former texts, unlike the latter texts composed during the eighth century, contain technical Buddhist terminology relating to the perfecting stage (*niṣpannakrama*), indicating that they were likely composed no sooner than the ninth century, as I will discuss in section 3.1 below.

Shinichi Tsuda has suggested that the identification of the *Samvarodaya Tantra* as a Cakrasamvara explanatory tantra is also problematic.[68] Tsuda's doubt was also apparently shared by the Nevārī Buddhist community, which emphasizes the Cakrasamvara tradition. The Nevārīs, however, did not evidently value highly the *Cakrasamvara Tantra* text itself, of which they preserved only one incomplete manuscript, and two late copies made from it. The Nevārīs placed far greater emphasis on the *Samvarodaya*, of which approximately a dozen manuscripts survive.[69] At least one of these manuscripts,[70] copied in 1702, refers to itself as the *Herukābhidhāna-mahātantrarāja*, which implies that, for one copyist at least, the *Samvarodaya Tantra* eclipsed the *Cakrasamvara Tantra*, usurping the name by which that latter was known in the Nevārī manuscript tradition.

While the exact history of the *Cakrasamvara* and its related tantras remains unclear, the history of the Cakrasamvara commentarial tradition is

---

[67] Where the CS text at ch. 27 v. 20 reads *samvare* in a list of texts, the AU mss. read *cakrasamvare* (H 140a.1, I 596b.2, J 226.5). As a result, the final form of the AU must postdate the composition of the CS.

[68] See Tsuda 1974, 27–45.

[69] See Tsuda 1974, 1–4.

[70] This is the ms. of which a facsilime (microfiche no. MBB II-89) is preserved in the collection at the Institute for Advanced Studies of World Religions (Carmel, NY).

far more clear. A date for the composition of the *Cakrasamvara Tantra* in the mid- to late-eighth century is supported by the general trajectory of the commentarial tradition, which appears to have begun during the ninth century, by which point the *Cakrasamvara Tantra* must have become incorporated into the curricula of Northern Indian Buddhist monasteries, most notably at Vikramaśīla in Northeastern India. This suggests, albeit weakly, that the text may have been composed in Northeastern India, a hypothesis that also seems to be confirmed by botanical evidence as well.[71]

Moreover, the authors of five of the eleven extant commentaries that treat the entire Root Tantra were associated with Vikramaśīla monastery. The earliest Cakrasamvara commentary is that composed by Laṅka Jayabhadra, who was likely active during the early to mid-ninth century. His commentary, which survives in two Sanskrit manuscripts as well as in Tibetan translation,[72] is very important as it gives us an early view into the process of the adaptation of the *Cakrasamvara Tantra* to the Buddhist monastic context. This process, as argued above, was characterized by the elision of non-Buddhist elements (such as the names of Śaiva deities) and their replacement with Buddhist substitutes. Its relatively early date is also attested by the significant number of later commentators who depend upon it.

This adaptive process was already well underway by the time of Bhavabhaṭṭa.[73] He was the fifth tantric preceptor at Vikramaśīla, succeeding

[71] I refer the reader to Stephen Hodge's (1994) study "Considerations on the Dating and Geographic Origins of the *Mahāvairocanābhisaṁbodhi-sūtra.*" Therein Hodge argues, partly on the basis of botanical evidence, that this text was likely composed somewhere in the sub-Himalayan track of India and Nepal. While I have not undertaken as detailed a study as Hodge with regard to the *Cakrasamvara Tantra*, a preliminary survey seems to suggest that the *Cakrasamvara Tantra* was also likely composed in this region. The various rituals described in the Tantra require a significant number of plant products. Many of these, such as camphor and sandalwood, were widely available throughout India given their use in incense. However, a number of rituals require the use of flowers, which are not easily transported and must, presumably, be used fresh. Two of the flowers most commonly called for in the *Cakrasamvara Tantra—karavīra* (*Nerium indicum*) and *campaka* (*Michelia champaca*)—are native to the Northeastern region, and may indicate that the ritual portions of the text, at least, were composed in this area. See Hodge 1994, 72–74, 80–83.

[72] See the *Conspectus Siglorum* below for a complete list of the commentarial sources used in my annotated translation.

[73] Bhavabhaṭṭa's name is recorded in the colophons of Tibetan translations of his texts as "Bhavabhadra" (e.g., Tōh. 1403, fol. 256a; Tōh. 1415, fol. 208b). The Sanskrit mss. of his

Jayabhadra's successor, Śrīdhara, and was thus likely active during the late ninth century. He may be the Mahāsiddha Bhadrapāda, who according to tradition was a disciple of Kāṇha. As Kāṇha was a contemporary of King Devapāla (c. 812–850 CE),[74] this also seems to point to a late ninth century date for Bhavabhaṭṭa. His commentary is clearly dependent upon Jayabhadra's, reproducing large portions of it. It is, however, much larger and more comprehensive, and it also contradicts Jayabhadra at numerous points, often providing more normative Buddhist readings where Jayabhadra gives the older, Śaiva readings. Bhavabhaṭṭa also often attests multiple readings, indicating that there were at least three distinct versions of the *Cakrasamvara Tantra* circulating by this time.

Bhavabhaṭṭa was succeeded at Vikramaśīla by another Cakrasamvara commentator, Bhavyakīrti, who was probably active during the early tenth-century. His commentary is shorter and less ambitious than his predecessor's, following Jayabhadra's commentary more closely, and thus appearing to represent a more conservative commentarial tradition, one which did not accept all of Bhavabhaṭṭa's emendations and interpretative innovations. His commentary is preserved in Tibetan translation only.

The next Cakrasamvara commentator based at Vikramaśīla was Durjayacandra, the eighth preceptor at Vikramaśīla, who was active during the late tenth century when Rin-chen bZang-po met with him there.[75] His commentary was particularly important for the Sa-skya school in Tibet, as that school's founder, the Tibetan exegete Sachen Kun-dga' sNying-po, relied heavily upon it.

Finally, Tathāgatarakṣita, the tenth preceptor at Vikramaśīla, also composed a commentary. He is undoubtedly the same Tathāgatarakṣita who composed the *Yoginīsaṁcāra-nibandha* (Tōh. 1422), which he translated with Rin-chen-grags during the late eleventh century.[76] He also helped Dharma blo-gros translate *Candrakumāra's *Herukābhyudaya* commentary

---

Cakrasamvara commentary, however, give the correct reading, Bhavabhaṭṭa. See Pandey 2002, 597.

[74] See Snellgrove 1959, 1:14.

[75] See Tucci 1988, 35.

[76] Rin-chen-grags (1040–1112 CE, r. 1102–1110), also known as Ba-ri Lo-tsva-ba, succeeded dKon-mchog rgyal-po to the Sa-skya throne.

(Tōh. 1421), which according to that text's colophon was translated at Vikramaśīla, confirming the tradition reported by Tāranātha.[77]

There are also six complete commentaries written by five authors who were apparently not associated with Vikramaśīla. Among these, the oldest is that written by Kambala, and it rivals in importance Jayabhadra's commentary. According to legend, Kambala was from Oḍḍiyāna in the Northwest,[78] and was strongly associated with the dissemination of the Yoginī Tantras. He has been dated by Dowman to the mid- to late-ninth century, although there is a tradition in Tibetan Buddhist historiography that places him earlier, in the eighth century.[79] On the other hand, there is still another Tibetan tradition which sees him as a guru of the Mahāsiddha Tilopa,[80] who was active during the latter half of the tenth century (if we accept Wylie's dating of his disciple Nāropa as 956–1040 CE).[81] But there is an alternate tradition that holds that Kambala was not Tilopa's guru, but rather his guru's guru, which would bring him back to the late ninth century.[82]

In any event, Kambala's commentary is relatively early and important, since, with Jayabhadra's, it is one of the two commentaries on which many later writers rely. Indeed, several commentaries depend significantly on Kambala's work. Devagupta's commentary is basically an expansion of Kambala's. Indrabhūti's commentary likewise relies upon it, and is clearly a later work, as it relies upon the four joys system of exegesis which was borrowed from the *Hevajra* tradition, and which is not found in the earliest

---

77 See Candrakumāra, 120a.

78 In the Swat valley of modern Pakistan, as Kuwayama (1991) has demonstrated.

79 See Dowman 1985, 184–185. One account of the Cakrasamvara lineage passing through Vajravārāhī places Kambala quite early, as a master of king Indrabhūti. This points to the Kambala who visited Indrabhūti with Vilāsavajra, and who thus may have lived during the late eight century. If so, this was not likely the same Kambala who composed the Cakrasamvara commentary. Regarding this, see Dowman 1985, 184–185.

80 See Torricelli and Naga 1995, 69 n. 32.

81 Wylie 1982, 691; see also Newman 1998, 347 n. 10.

82 See Cuevas 2003, 228 n. 53. This tradition, reported in bKa'-brgyud sources, holds Kambala to be the teacher of Lalitavajra (Rol-pa'i rDo-rje), who in turn was one of Tilopa's gurus.

commentaries.[83] According to Tāranātha, Indrabhūti was a disciple of Kambala, which might date him to the tenth century.[84]

There are two commentaries attributed to Vīravajra. While little is known concerning this author, they are clearly relatively late works, dating to the eleventh century.[85] They are very sophisticated works, and represent a high point of Indian tantric Buddhist scholarship. His commentaries are also among the most thorough. He relies both upon Jayabhadra and Kambala, as well as Bhavabhaṭṭa and Durjayacandra, and he is also quite erudite, quoting from a number of other sources, including Yogācāra texts and a number of other tantras.

Lastly, there is the *Śrītattvaviśadā-nāma-śrīsamvaravṛtti*, attributed to the author *Śāśvatavajra (rTag-pa'i rDo-rje), about whom very little is known. He appears to have been active relatively late.[86] His commentary, while erudite, is quite different from the others, and somewhat difficult to use due to its lack of chapter divisions. I have, however, referred to it in several instances.

---

[83] Bhavabhaṭṭa's commentary appears to be the earliest CS commentary to employ the four joys terminology, suggesting that it became popularized by the late ninth to early tenth centuries.

[84] See Templeman 1983, 34–35. Clearly, Kambala lived no later than the tenth century, as one of his texts, the *Navaślokī*, was translated into Chinese (T. 1516) during the early eleventh century by Dharmapāla, who likely brought the text with him upon departing India in the late tenth century. Regarding this translation and Dharmapāla, see Tucci 1956, 211–215, and JAN Yün-hua 1966, 39–41.

[85] The name *Vīravajra (dPa'-bo rDo-rje) appears as a very early figure in several lineage lists as a disciple of the master 'Gro-ba bdugs-bying, culminating in the figure of Kambala (Roerich 1949, 362, 552), but this could not possibly be the same Vīravajra who commented on the CS, as he relies significantly on Kambala's work. In his PD commentary, he refers to the commentaries of Bhavabhaṭṭa and Durjayacandra, which dates his work on this text to no earlier than the late tenth century, when the latter was active (See PD 394a). His commentary on the *Sampuṭa Tantra* (*Sarvatantranidānamahāguhya-Śrīsampuṭa-nāma-tantrarājaṭīkā-ratnamāla-nāma*, Tōh. 1199) was translated during the late eleventh century by Rin-chen-grags (1040–1112 CE), so he clearly lived no later than this time.

[86] His two works related to the CS (his TV commentary and also his *śrīcakrasamvara-ṣeka-kriyākrama*, Tōh. 1470) were both translated during the fourteenth century by Bu-ston (1290–1364 CE). According to the colophon of his commentary (TV 352a), he was the principal disciple of dGa'-byed bDag-po, a figure I have not been able to identify.

In the course of translating the *Cakrasamvara Tantra* I have turned to all eleven of the Indian commentaries that treat the entire scripture,[87] as well as to several of the Tibetan commentaries, namely those by Sachen Kun-dga' sNying-po (1092–1158), Bu-ston Rin-chen-grub (1290–1364), and Tsong Khapa bLo-bzang Grags-pa (1357–1419). Among these, Sachen's is relatively independent, although it relies particularly strongly on Durjayacandra's commentary. Sachen follows the translation of Mal-gyo Lotsāwa, to which I have not referred except via his quotations. Bu-ston takes into account multiple translations and also a large number of the Indian commentaries. Tsong Khapa also takes them into account, and is aware of the works of Sachen and Bu-ston. He relies particularly heavily on Bu-ston's commentary, which he often quotes at length.[88]

I often translate portions of these commentaries in the notes to my translation of the *Cakrasamvara Tantra*, especially at points where the root scripture is obscure and the commentaries help clarify the meaning. Indeed, there are numerous passages where the commentaries were essential aids to my own understanding of the text. While I have tried as much as possible to take into consideration a large number of these commentaries throughout my translation, I have tended to privilege the earlier commentaries for which there are also surviving Sanskrit manuscripts, namely those by Jayabhadra and Bhavabhaṭṭa. In addition, I have also found Kambala's and Vīravajra's commentaries to be particularly helpful, especially in the ritual portions of the text, as they are often the only commentaries which explain

---

[87] There are two additional commentaries that I did not employ in this translation. One is the *Laghutantraṭīkā* attributed to Vajrapāṇi, available both in Tibetan translation (Tōh. 1402) and also a Sanskrit ed. (Cicuzza 2001). It is one of the three "Bodhisattva commentaries" celebrated by the later Tibetan tradition. Like the other Bodhisattva commentaries, it is heavily influenced by the *Kālacakra Tantra* and its exegetical tradition, and thus cannot possibly date earlier than the late tenth century. On the dating of the *Kālacakra Tantra*, see Orofino (1994b, 15–16), who argues for its composition between 967 and 1026 CE; Newman (1998, 342–43) argues for a later date, between 1025 and 1040 CE. While it is a fascinating and important text, it comments on only the first ten and a half verses of the first chapter of the CS, which significantly reduced its utility for this present work. Lastly, Sumatikīrti's brief "commentary" (Tōh. 1411) is simply a synopsis of the text. It is quoted in its entirety by Tsong Khapa in his commentary, and I treat it at length in my translation of that work (Gray 2017).

[88] See my translation of Tsong Khapa's commentary (Gray 2017) for a detailed discussion of the sources employed by him.

these challenging portions of the text. I also translate comments that are of unusual interest, even when the Root Tantra is relatively clear.

One problem with this methodology is that while it may assist the reader in understanding the Tantra, it does violence to the texture of the commentaries themselves, some of which are interesting works in their own right. Take, for example, Vīravajra's comments on the opening verse of the Tantra:

> Moreover, as soon as one has praised and made supplications with the speech of the heroes and heroines, having prostrated without rising and worshipped with the fivefold ambrosia, **and now** is stated. Now, as it is desirable that the topic of the Tantra be shown at the beginning, it says: **I will explain the secret**. The referent of **secret** is twofold: the creation stage and the perfecting stage. There are two secrets of the creation stage: 1) visualizing the solitary hero, and 2) visualizing the maṇḍala's wheels. Why are they secret? It is because they concern, as the *Śrī Paramādya* states, the entry of the gnosis hero into the heart. As the *Vajraśekhara* states, "in this very secret vehicle, total entry achieves the victors' state."[89] As for the perfecting stage, it is secret because it is endowed with the four seals (*mudrā*) and the four arts (*upāya*). Why is it secret? It is because bliss and emptiness are not realized without practicing it, that is, by Brahmā, Viṣṇu, Mahādeva, the disciples (*śrāvaka*), or the solitary buddhas (*pratyekabuddha*).[90] Thus it says in this text, **the happiness of the divine and human states** do **not amount to one sixteenth** of Vajradhara's.[91] Also, the *Sampuṭa* states: "it is

[89] While I have surveyed these very long texts (presumably Tōh. 487 or 488, and Tōh. 480), I have not been able to identify the locations of these quotes.

[90] This appears to be a paraphrase of a passage in the first chapter of the first *kalpa* of the *Sampuṭa Tantra*: "It is secret because it is not the experiential scope of Viṣṇu, Śiva, Brahmā, the disciples, or the solitary buddhas." (Skorupski 1996, 217: *hariharahiraṇyagarbhaśrāvakapratyekabuddhānām agocaratvād rahasyaṁ*)

[91] This is a variant of CS ch. 1 v. 15. See my translation and notes below.

secret because it is the experiential scope (*gocara*) of all buddhas and bodhisattvas."[92]

I will explain shows the purpose of the text. It was previously attained by the heroes and heroines, and now is realized by the yogins. What is the text like? As it says, **concisely, not extensively**, it is not extensive, being condensed from the one hundred thousand stanza [text] which is itself condensed from the [text of] one hundred thousand chapters. Thus it is an **appendix of an appendix**. If we clearly state that which it will discourse upon, it is **union with Śrī Heruka**. His defining mark is the self-nature of the three bodies, and with regard to the cause of that, the method of the creation and perfecting [stages], **Heruka** signifies the buddhas and bodhisattvas. **Union** indicates wisdom; it is the actual woman, the wisdom of emptiness of the twelfth [bodhisattva] stage. The cause of that, the wisdom of the creation and perfecting [stages], is signified by the lady (*yoṣid, btsun mo*). With regard to wisdom and art, there is the perfecting stage wisdom and art that perfects the solitary hero and the maṇḍala's wheels, and there is the perfecting stage wisdom and art of the *karmamudrā, dharmamudrā, samayamudrā* and *mahāmudrā*. The defining characteristics of these will be explained later. Now **union** (*saṁyoga*) is unification (*samāyoga*). There is unification by directly giving rise to the realization of bliss which is devoid of the eighty instinctual natures,[93] and by giving rise to the consciousness which

---

[92] The text in *Sampuṭa* (ch. 1 section 1) omits *bodhisattva*, reading simply *rahasyaṁ buddhagocaraṁ* (Skorupski 1996, 219).

[93] The "eighty natures" (*aśītiprakṛti*) in the *Guhyasamāja* system are mental states which serve as obscurations to the realization of the three clear lights, and are divided into 33 feminine, 40 masculine, and 7 neuter forms. For a complete list see Wayman 1977, 185–88. Here Vīravajra glosses these eighty natures as "instinctual" (*rnam par rtog pa'i*). Normally I would translate this as "conceptual," but here I translate it as "instinctual" since the eighty natures designate unconscious instinctual patterns. Many thanks to Dr. Robert Thurman for pointing this out.

> accords with its object through direct vision of the *mahāmudrā*, which is the emptiness of the sphere of reality (*dharmadhātu*). Here this is not the total union with the emptiness of *dharmadhātu* that is the gnosis of the eleventh [bodhisattva] stage.
>
> What is the [Tantra's] purpose? It is the **means of achieving all desired aims**. The yogins' desired aims are the worldly powers that are the good qualities of the desire realm, the common powers that are the meditative states (*dhyāna*) and the formless [realm] concentrations, and the supreme achievement, the gnosis of the buddhas and bodhisattvas. (PD 354b–355b)

Vīravajra employs here the "purpose and relevance" (*dgos-'brel*) method of tantric exegesis which became the standard hermeneutical device employed by commentators on the Yoginī Tantras.[94] And while portions of this might be usefully extracted for footnotes, doing so violates the texture of the commentary itself. While this is unavoidable in a work of this sort, the study and translation of the commentaries themselves remains a desideratum.

2. Traditional History of the Cakrasamvara Tantra

2.1 Mythic Root Texts

Diachronic study of the commentaries is helpful in ascertaining the history of the tradition. However, this is *not* the traditional history as understood by the commentators themselves. Like all Mahāyāna Buddhist scriptural productions, the *Cakrasamvara Tantra* is believed to be a revealed scripture, representing the authentic speech of a buddha. Unlike most other Buddhist scriptures, however, this tantra is not located in the teaching activity of the historical Buddha Śākyamuni. This is marked textually by the unconventional opening of the Tantra, which does not begin with the standard opening background verse (*nidāna*) that graces virtually all other Buddhist scriptures. Asserting the claim that the text is the authentic

[94] This method is admirably described by Broido 1983b.

speech of the Buddha (*buddhavacana*),[95] the standard *nidāna* verse always begins: "Thus I have I heard: at one time…" (*evaṁ mayā śrutam ekasmin samaye…*). This is typically followed by a statement that the Blessed Lord was staying in such-and-such a place in the company of a group of monks, nuns, laypersons, bodhisattvas, and so forth.

In the Nikāya scriptures the speaker is Śākyamuni, teaching in settings recognizably within the area of Northeastern India that was the scope of his peregrinations. Mahāyāna Buddhist scriptures reference an expanded cosmology including multiple buddhas and buddhalands, expanding the potential range of teachers and teachings. Some of the early Buddhist tantras, such as the *Sarvatathāgata-tattvasaṁgraha Sūtra*, contain elaborate opening scenarios which feature buddhas such as Vairocana in supramundane settings such as Akaniṣṭha, the highest heaven of the form realm (*rūpa-dhātu*).[96] Other tantric texts contain opening scenarios that must have seemed shocking to more conservative Buddhist communities. Such was the case with the *nidāna* verse of the *Guhyasamāja*, famous for its strong erotic savor: "Thus have I heard: at one time the Blessed Lord was residing in the vulvae of the adamantine ladies, the essence of the body, speech and mind of all tathāgatas."[97] This verse or its variants occur in a number of other tantras, which no doubt reflects its popularity in tantric Buddhist circles.[98]

In contrast to this established convention, the *Cakrasamvara Tantra* and other texts, such as the *Samayoga*, jettison the *nidāna* verse entirely, beginning instead with the laconic "and now" (*atha*). The presence of this

---

[95] Regarding the concept of *buddhavacana* and its transformation in Mahāyāna scholastic literature, see Lopez 1995 and McMahan 1998.

[96] For the Sanskrit text of the *Tattvasaṁgraha nidāna*, see Yamada 1981, 3–4; for a translation, see Gray 2001, 383–4.

[97] Matsunaga 1978, 4: *evaṁ mayā śrutam ekasmin samaye bhagavān sarvatathāgata-kāyavāk-cittahṛdaya-vajrayoṣidbhageṣu vijahāra /.*

[98] It likewise occurs in the *Hevajra Tantra* and its related literature; see Snellgrove 1959, 2:2. A variant occurs in the *Caṇḍamahāroṣaṇa* as follows: "Thus have I heard: at one time the Blessed Lord Vajrasattva was residing in the vulva of Vajradhātvīśvarī, the essence of the body, speech, and mind of all tathāgatas, with many hosts of adamantine yogins and yoginīs." (George 1974, 18: *evaṁ mayā śrutam ekasmin samaye bhagavān vajrasattvaḥ sarvatathāgata-kāyavākcittahṛdaya-vajradhātvīśvarībhage vijahāra / anekaiś ca vajrayogiyoginīgaṇaiḥ*). This verse is also interesting in that it changes the unusual locative plural *bhageṣu* to the locative singular *bhage*.

and the corresponding absence of the standard opening verse inspired considerable controversy, which the commentator Bhavyakīrti summarizes as follows:

> Now, some hold that this [*Cakrasamvara* text] was selected from the *One Hundred Thousand Stanza Root Tantra*, and that since that Root Tantra states, "Thus have I heard," and so forth, there is no statement of it in this appendix (*uttaratantra*). Additionally, some claim that it is because the Lord is in the non-located nirvāṇa, which is why [the text] says "always abides in the the universal nature." Furthermore, it is held that it shows that in the unteachable teaching the teacher and what is to be taught are one, and hence it is said that the [text itself, which is] the body of mantra, is the Buddha Lord. Others assert that it teaches the Mahāyāna in the same manner as the *Mañjuśrī-nāma-saṁgīti*, and so forth, which also lack "Thus have I heard." I, Bhavyakīrti, hold that since the primal buddhas know no cessation, this teaching formulation has a beginningless continuum, existing even before Śākyamuni, as has been well stated by tens of millions of buddhas and heroes. This means that when the *Prajñāpāramitā*, and so forth, wane due to the power of time, the burning eon, and so forth, the Lord Śākyamuni teaches them again. The *Śrī Cakrasamvara* is not like that, for it exists without interruption in inexpressible buddhalands, and it is experienced through meditative states, and so forth, by the heroes and heroines such as Īśvarī. This is the significance of text such as "and then" (*atha*). (SM 2b–3a)

The first theory that Bhavyakīrti mentions, that this text begins with *atha* because it was derived from a much longer tantra, appears to be generally accepted. As this hypothetical source text no longer exists, its exact nature was also a source of controversy. Generally, it was believed to be a massive text of one hundred thousand stanzas, called either the "Discourse" (*abhidhāna*) or "Sky-like" (*khasama*). Thus, like many other tantric traditions, this tradition claims that its relatively brief text originates in a lost original of one hundred thousand stanzas. That number was presumably chosen in response to the standard set by the *Prajñāpāramitā Sūtra* of that length, which appears to be the only Buddhist text to have actually reached that length. As this claim was made many times by many different traditions, there seems to have occurred a progressive inflation, with some commentators upping the ante and claiming an even larger length for this mythic text. The *Ḍākārṇava*, a Cakrasamvara explanatory tantra, thus tripled the size of the mythic root text: "In the *Laghusamvara*, which is derived from the three hundred thousand verse *Abhidhāna*, the chapters are linked to reality in accordance with the letters, from *A* until letter *Kṣ*." (DM 242b–243a) Similarly, the *Herukābhyudaya* claims that there are two source texts: "The Essence Tantra was taught abridged from one hundred and three hundred thousand [stanza texts]."[99] (HA 7a) The commentator Vīravajra further upped the ante, positing a massive text of one hundred thousand chapters. He does so in the context of commenting upon the text of the first chapter, "more lofty than the lofty" (*uttarād api cottaraṁ*), which he reads nominally, as a statement that this tantra is an appendix derived from another appendix: "Why is 'the appendix also [derived] from an appendix?' There is the Root Tantra of one hundred thousand chapters, and subsequent to it is the hundred thousand stanza *Khasama*, and the fifty one chaptered [text] is the subsequent appendix." (PD 355b) This theory does not make much sense, however, as it is hard to see how a short text of seven hundred stanzas could contribute much as an appendix to the far vaster texts from which it supposedly derives.

Even if one accepts the hypothesis that the Tantra derived from a much larger source text, many commentators felt that it was necessary to "read" into the extremely concise first chapter the background information that a *nidāna* usually provides. The *Cakrasamvara Tantra* and related tantras contain a verse which came to be identified as their *nidāna* verse, despite the fact that it does not conform to the venerable Buddhist model. It reads: "The hero made of all ḍākinīs, Vajrasattva, supreme bliss, always abides in the universal nature, the secret that is supreme and delightful."[100]

---

[99] The commentator *Candrakumāra (*zla-ba gzhon-nu*) writes in his *Śrīherukābhyudaya-mahāyoginī-tantrarāja-katipayākṣarapañjikā* that "The 'one hundred thousand' is the one hundred thousand [versed] *Abhidhāna*. And there is also an extensive *Abhidhāna* of three hundred thousand verses." / *'bum phrag ni mngon par brjod pa'i 'bum pa'o // rgyas par mngon par brjod pa 'bum phrag gsum yang ngo* / (105a).

[100] This occurs in CS ch. 1 as follows: *rahasye parame ramye sarvātmani sadā sthitaḥ // sarva-ḍākinīmayaḥ sattvo vajrasattvaḥ paraṁ sukhaṁ*. It undoubtedly derives from the variant found

According to the *Vajraḍāka* explanatory tantra, this text esoterically codes the standard *nidāna* verse.[101]

Advocates of the *Cakrasamvara Tantra* claim that this "*nidāna*" embodies an esoteric knowledge that is timeless. This represents an alternative legitimation strategy that permits the rejection of historically based lineage claims. Insofar as they appear in the world, they appear simply as a recurrent revelation from a timeless source, one that is hence continually accessible to those who possess the esoteric knowledge. This is the claim made by Bhavyakīrti; and it was also the claim of his predecessor at Vikramaśīla, Bhavabhaṭṭa, who argued that it was taught by the Dharmakāya Buddha Mahāvajradhara, as follows:

> The teacher is Mahāvajradhara in his form of four faces, and so forth. He also exists directly as an emanation. This Tantra exists by being taught from time beginningless. Whenever sentient beings lack merit it wanes, and through their merit it thrives [again]. The teacher and the one who is taught, and so forth, are illusory, and the deeds of the tathāgatas are inconceivable. Here the solicitor was the Blessed Lady Vajravārāhī, and the compiler Vajrapāṇi. It was taught in order to restore it for all.[102]

---

in the older *Sarvabuddhasamayoga*: "the hero made of all buddhas, Vajrasattva, Supreme Bliss, always abides in the universal nature, the secret that is supreme and delightful." (JS 151b: */ sems dpa' sangs rgyas kun gyi dngos // rdo rje sems dpa' bde ba'i mchog / gsang ba mchog gi dgyes pa na // thams cad bdag nyid rtag tu bzhugs /*)

[101] The *Vajraḍāka*'s commentary here is quite complex, as it connects both the text of the "Yoginī Tantra *nidāna*" and the text of another line in CS ch. 1, "existing in the beginning, middle, and end" (*ādimadhyāntasaṁsthitaṁ*) to the beginning of the standard *nidāna* (*evam mayā śrutaṁ ekasmin samaye*), as follows: "As for **existing in the beginning, middle, and end**, the **beginning** is the **secret,** the awareness of the previous source of 'thus.' The **end** is that which is **delightful**, which depends on that which is 'heard.' The **middle** is **supreme**; 'by me' is very holy. **Existing** is the **universal nature**, and it is 'at one time'." (VD 90a)

[102] Pandey 2002, 2 (emended by my reading of the text at F 2b.5–3a.1): *caturmukhādirūpo mahāvajradharo deśakaḥ / sa ca sākṣād eva nirmāṇāvasthitaḥ / tantraṁ cedam anādikāla-deśyatvenāvasthitaṁ / sattvānām apuṇyaṇ kadācin nirodhati / kadācit puṇyāt pratitiṣṭhati / tac ca deśyadeśakādi māyopam idaṁ tathāgatānāṁ caritam acintyam / itaś ca bhagavatī vajravārāhy adhyeṣikā / vajrapāṇiḥ saṁgātā / sāmānyena pratyarpitaṁ śāsanatvāt tasya /.*

Bhavabhaṭṭa thus denies that this teaching originated in an historical teaching encounter, asserting instead that it is primordial and eternal, appearing in the world when the collective karma of sentient beings is appropriate. Moreover, Bhavabhaṭṭa claims that the *Cakrasaṃvara Tantra* was taught in its short form due to the compassion of numerous awakened beings, who teach it for the sake of those who, understandably, lack the patience to tackle the long version(s) of the scripture:

> Furthermore, the Tantra is accomplished setting forth its entire import through the teacher of four faces, and so forth, the teaching, and those who are to be taught. It is taught by the sugatas, but they do not give rise to it in the manner of cause and effect, happiness or unhappiness, lust or hatred, the well-done or poorly done, and so forth. Here [it says this Tantra is] "well-spoken by tens of millions of buddhas and also tens of millions of heroes."[103] Elsewhere [it says]: "that which was stated by the past buddhas will be stated by the future ones, and that which the present complete buddhas state again and again is extolled in this *Māyājāla Mahātantra*."[104] Regarding their utterance, which is here the teaching, the *Śrī Cakrasaṃvara* appears as a result of the Buddha's teaching—at unlimited times—the same words, and so forth, from the perspective of both meaning and text. Desiring thus to teach this, the Blessed Lord said "And now," and so forth. The Blessed Lord, drawing from the one hundred thousand [stanza] Root Tantra, teaches for the sake of devotees of the *Śrī Cakrasaṃvara* who desire brevity. Due to Vajravārāhī's solicitation, there was this reply by the Blessed Lord, "And now," and so forth.[105]

[103] This passage occurs in CS ch. 48 as: *subhāṣitaṃ buddhakotīṇāṃ vīrāṇāṃ koṭīṇām eva ca*. Note that Bhavabhaṭṭa reads here *koṭim* rather than *koṭīṇām*.

[104] This is a quote from the *Mañjuśrīnāmasaṃgīti* (v. 12–13 in Davidson's edition). See Davidson 1981, 20, 50.

[105] Pandey 2002, 2–3 (emended by my reading of the text at F 3a.1–6): *athavā caturmukhādideśakadeśyadeśanādisakalārthābhidhāyi tantraṃ siddhaṃ sugatā deśayanti na tu*

Of course, the notion that a great text of one hundred thousand or more stanzas was reduced to a short text of a mere seven hundred might seem troubling to some, given the fact that its import could hardly be retained in such a short text. Bhavabhaṭṭa assures the reader that this is not the case and that it remains true to the original, despite the fact that over ninety-nine percent of it was stripped away. He also reads into the text additional details, providing a narrative framework for a text that is virtually stripped of narrative elements:

> The relevance of "I will explain the secret" is that the Root Tantra is completed. The *Śrī Cakrasamvara Tantra*, then, cannot produce additional material. This is because it fulfills the import of that. It differs only in being a condensed text. Indeed, [the statement] that "due to that cause of my being solicited by Vajravārāhī, **I will explain the secret**" is relevant [here.] The solicitation is [implied] by the statement, "**Listen to what is taught in the Tantra.**" It would truly not be felicitous for there to be a Dharma teaching for which there is no solicitation. This is because this would incur disrespect for the teaching that is foremost. Is it necessary that the Goddess is the solicitor? It is reported that in the Root Tantra that there is a solicitor who is an attendant in the lineage of the gurus. Therefore, here too it is understood that there is an attendant. According to some the Blessed Lord is the solicitor and the Blessed Lady is the teacher. [This is possible because] the intention of the tathāgatas is inconceivable.[106]

---

kurvanti yathā kāryakāraṇādi sukhaduḥkhādi rāgadveṣādi sukṛtaduṣkṛtādi ca / uktaṁ ceha / subhāṣitaṁ buddhakoṭīnāṁ vīrāṇāṁ koṭim eva ca iti / anyatra yātīte bhāṣitā buddhair bhāṣiṣyante hy anāgatāḥ / pratyutpannāś ca saṁbuddhā yā bhāṣante punaḥ punaḥ / māyājāle mahātantre yā cāsmin sampragīyata iti / bhāṣaṇaś ceha deśanaiva arthato granthataś ca samānapadādi buddhair anavadhikālaṁ deśyamānaṁ śrīcakrasamvaratantram avatarati / tad evaṁ deśayitukāmo bhagavān āha athāta ityādi / bhagavān śrīcakrasamvarādhimuktānāṁ arthāya lakṣaparimāṇān mūlatantrāt tad ākṛṣya deśayate hi saṁkṣeparucaya iti / vajravārāhyā 'dhyeṣitasya bhagavataḥ prativacanam etad athāta ityādi /.

106 Pandey 2002, 3 (emended by my reading of the text at F 3b.1–5): *mūlatantram evākarīkṛtya rahasyam vakṣya iti sambandāḥ / tataḥ hi nārthāntarīkartum śrīcakrasamvaratantraṁ śakyam / atraiva tadarthaparisamāpteḥ / bhedas tu granthasaṁkṣepamātreṇa / athavā yato*

Issues such as the identities of the teacher, solicitor, and so forth, may seem minor, particularly in the case of a text for which its advocates claim a timeless existence. However, these issues were important for Buddhists such as Bhavabhaṭṭa as they grounded the text in "history" as richly imagined by the tradition, providing the basis for the production of lineages. Indeed, at least two such lineages for the *Cakrasamvara Tantra* emerged, rooted in two revelations of the text by awakened beings in the world.[107] Since one of these awakened beings was the Tantra's primary goddess, Vajravārāhī, it was necessary to claim for her at least the status of the text's solicitor or even perhaps the text's teacher. This latter claim reverses the expected gender roles, and while Bhavabhaṭṭa apparently does not favor it, he was not willing to dismiss it as impossible, given the importance of Vajravārāhī in this Yoginī Tantra tradition.

2.2 The Origin of Heruka

While the central deity of the *Cakrasamvara Tantra*—known as Heruka, Śrī Heruka, and also Samvara and Śamvara—appears in the world of Buddhist literature in noticeable form in the eighth century, it is possible to construct a genealogy for him that goes back considerably further in Indian history.

The name Samvara, which is also attested as Śamvara and Śambara, has the most ancient lineage. This term does not appear as a proper name in the *Cakrasamvara Tantra* itself. The noun *samvara* is derived from the verb *saṁ-√vṛ*, meaning to "bind," "enclose," or "conceal." A common meaning of *samvara* is "vow." It occurs several times in the *Cakrasamvara Tantra* in this sense, including in the title for chapter twenty-six. A secondary meaning is a "sanctuary," derived from its sense of concealment. This occurs once, at the beginning of chapter fifteen. It occurs numerous times in compound, usually in the well-known compound *ḍākinījālasamvara*, which I

---

vajravārāhy adhyeṣito 'ham ataḥ kāraṇād rahasyaṁ vakṣya iti yojyam / tantre nigaditaṁ śṛṇv iti vacanād adhyeṣaṇām eva / anadhyeṣitasya na hi dharmadeśanā śreyasī / unnatyai dharmadeśanāyā evāgauravasambhavāt / adhyeṣikā devīti ko niyama iti cet / guruparamparāto hi śrūyate mūlatantre sevādhyeṣiketi / tata ihāpi seveti gamyate / bhagavān adhyeṣako bhagavatī deśaketi kecit / acintyarūpo hi tathāgatānām abhiprāyaḥ /.

[107] According to gZhon-nu dPal, there were two distinct lineages of transmission of the *Cakrasamvara Tantra*: 1) from Cakrasamvara to Vajravārāhī to the Mahāsiddha Lūipa, and 2) from Vajradhara to Vajrapāṇi to the Mahāsiddha Saraha. See Roerich 1976, 380–397.

translate as the "the binding of the ḍākinīs' network." This is a very important concept in this text; the compound is given great prominence, occurring twice in the first chapter, where it is equated with "union with Śrī Heruka" (*śrīherukasasaṁyoga*), as well as with Vajrasattva, the "hero made of all ḍākinīs." It is likewise equated with the "unification of all heroes" (*sarvavīrasamāyoga*) at the end of chapter thirty-one. This compound is clearly derived from the *Sarvabuddhasamayoga-ḍākinījālasamvara Tantra*, in which the concept of the *ḍākinījālasamvara* is equated with the "union of all Buddhas."

As Claudio Cicuzza has pointed out, the term *samvara* in this context clearly implies the sense of "union."[108] The spiritual implications of this term are quite significant, as is nicely illustrated by the following passage in the *Samvarodaya Tantra*:

> The union (*samvaraṁ*) of all Buddhas resides in the syllable *evaṁ*. Physical, verbal, and mental action is the ultimate union of all forms (*sarvākāraikasamvaraṁ*). Union (*samvaraṁ*) is supreme bliss, awakening which cannot be spoken or shown. It is the secret of all buddhas, the assembly that is the supreme union (*samvaraṁ varaṁ*).[109]

While "union" is a sound translation of *samvara* in this context, I prefer translating it literally as "binding" in the context of the compound in which it almost always occurs in this text, *ḍākinījālasamvara*, since this translation seems more congruous with the metaphor of the "net." This translation also reflects the root meaning of the Tibetan term used to translate *samvara* in this compound, *sdom pa*. The "ḍākinīs' network" here refers to the Cakrasamvara maṇḍala, which is dominated by the "three wheels" of the ḍākinīs and their consorts. Its "binding" is the process of union or mystical identification in which the adept engages via creative visualization, thereby achieving "union with Śrī Heruka." This term thus refers to the "body maṇḍala" practice in which the adept visualizes the three wheels of the maṇḍala within his/her own body. That is, he or she experiences his or her body as the sacred space of the maṇḍala, constituted as a

---

108 See Cicuzza 2001, 16.

109 My translation of SU 3.17c–19b, from the text ed. by Tsuda (1974, 79); cf. the translation by Cicuzza (2001, 16) and Tsuda (1974, 246–47).

"net" or network of the ḍākinīs and their consorts. Success in this practice is thought to yield profound results, including the achievement of the "adamantine body" (*vajradeha*) which prevents untimely death, as well as the gnosis that results from the achievement of union with Śrī Heruka.

As the *Samvarodaya* suggests, this term refers not only to praxis, but also to the promised result of this practice, "supreme bliss," which is awakening. This sense of *samvara* is attested by its interpretive Tibetan translation as "Supreme Bliss" (*bde mchog*). While *vara* does mean "supreme," the derivation of "bliss" from *saṁ* is based upon an old Indian Buddhist interpretive etymology, which Bhavabhaṭṭa describes as follows: "Since bliss is signified by joining together, *saṁ* is bliss, as it is said: 'bliss is called *saṁ*.' Moreover, this is also the worldly palatal syllable *śaṁ*."[110] This explanation is based upon the fact that in Sanskrit the prefix *saṁ-*, like the Latin prefix *con-*, suggests conjunction, union, togetherness, and so forth.

Bhavabhaṭṭa also acknowledges the alternate spelling of the term as *śamvara* or *śambara*. This name appears to have a venerable history. It is attested in the first chapter of the *Sarvabuddhasamayoga*, which reads: "*śaṁ* is said to be bliss; it is the great bliss of all buddhas. Since this bliss is supreme, he is Śamvara, the one who employs all illusions." (JS 151a)

The name Śamvara or Śambara brings to mind the figure of Dāsa Śambara of the *Ṛg Veda*, the enemy of Indra.[111] Asko Parpola has argued that "buffalo-shaped" deities are remnants of a pre-Āryan buffalo cult, and are *asuras* who are the enemies of the gods, whose classical descendents

---

[110] Pandey 2002, 6: *saṁskārasya sukhavācakatvāt saṁ sukhaṁ 'sukhaṁ sam iti cākhyātam' iti vacanāt / yo 'yaṁ laukikaḥ śaṁśabdaḥ sa tālavya eva.* While Bhavabhaṭṭa does not give much credence to the theory that it is the palatal syllable *śaṁ* that designates bliss, this theory may have derived from the vedic indeclinable term *śaṁ*, which means "auspiciously, fortunately, happily," and so forth (Monier-Williams 2002, 1054 col.2).

[111] According to Macdonell, Śamvara is mentioned about twenty times in the *Ṛg Veda*, such as in the following cases: "Indra shook the summit of heaven when he cut down Śambara (1.54.4). He found Śambara dwelling in the mountains (2.2.11) and struck down from the mountain (1.130.7; 6.26.5). He struck down from the great mountain the Dāsa Śambara, the son of Kulitara (4.30.14). He struck down from the height Śambara, who thought himself a little god (7.18.20)." (1898, 161) Several other verses depict him as dwelling in the forts of the Dāsas, which Indra cast down. For a study of these materials, see Parpola 1988.

include the Buffalo Demons Mahiṣāsura, Śumbha, and Niśumbha,[112] who are also thought to derive from non-Āryan sources.[113] Parpola includes the Cakrasamvara deity Śamvara/Heruka in this class.[114] He stresses that the power of "illusion" (*māyā*) is typically attributed to the *asuras*, and that this power primarily manifests as the ability to assume multiple shapes, as do demons Mahiṣāsura, and so forth, in their combat with the Goddess.[115] As noted above, the *Samayoga* attributes to Śamvara the ability to "employ all illusions." And while he is typically depicted in human form, he also has a "donkey form," introduced in chapter fourteen. Furthermore, by mastering his mantra, the adept is promised the power to "assume many thousands of forms."[116]

A link, albeit tenuous, between the vedic and tantric materials is provided by the *Arthaśāstra*, which contains the following spell to render a victim unconscious:

> I bow down to Bali the son of Virocana, to Śamvara of a hundred illusions, and to Bhaṇḍīrapāka, Nāraka, Nikumbha and also Khumba. I bow down to Devala and to Nārada; I bow down to Sāvarṇi Gālava. By imploring them great sleep has been produced for you.[117]

---

[112] The names Śumbha and Niśumbha appear in the Trailokyavijaya mantra coded in CS ch. 30, although they also appear in mantras of many other tantras such as the *Sarvatathāgatatattvasaṁgraha*. See Snellgrove 1987, 137–44, 153.

[113] The theory that the Śumbha-Niśumbha myth in the *Devī-Māhātmya* is derived from non-Āryan mythic traditions was earlier argued by Coburn (1984 and 1991). Parpola goes on to suggest that the name Heruka derives from the Tamil term *eṛu* or its cognates, which means "bull, male of any animal remarkable for its strength, male buffalo." (1992, 298)

[114] See Parpola 1992, 298. While no buffalo-headed form of Samvara/Śamvara is attested in any Cakrasamvara textual source of which I am aware, there is a deity known as "Mahiṣa Samvara," deriving from the Śrī Vajrabhairava cycle, who is worshipped within the vihāra *āgaṁs* of Patan and Kathmandu. See Decleer 1998, 296. For an image of this deity, see Huntington and Bangdel 2003, 284.

[115] See Parpola 1992, 297.

[116] See my translation of CS ch. 9 below.

[117] *Arthaśāstra* 14.3.19–20: *baliṁ vairocanaṁ vande śatamāyaṁ ca śamvaraṁ / bhaṇḍīrapākaṁ nārakaṁ nikumbhaṁ khumbam eva ca // devalaṁ nāradaṁ vande vande sāvarṇigālavam / eteṣām anuyogena kṛtaṁ te svāpanaṁ mahat //*, ed. in Kangle 1986, 1.274.

Like Davidson,[118] I do not mean to imply that worship of Śamvara/Heruka continued unbroken from vedic times onward.[119] Yet this passage, probably composed by the early centuries CE,[120] points to a continuation of the *asura* cult into the classical period, from which Buddhists apparently drew inspiration as they developed new cults of deities who were viewed as manifesting hostility to the classical Hindu deities such as Śiva and Viṣṇu, just as the *asura* were the perpetual foes of the older vedic deities such as Indra.

The link may have been suggested to the Buddhists by the Hindus, who during the first half of the first millennium of the Common Era wrote numerous polemical attacks on Buddhism and other "heretical" religions such as Jainism. These include the legends in the *Purāṇas* which resorted to the older vedic myth of the unending battle between the gods and *asuras* to account for the origins of heresy. Many of these, such as the myth of the destruction of the Triple City (*tripurāntaka*), describe the heresies as tricks devised by the gods to deceive the militarily superior *asuras*, who could only be defeated if they took up the practice of heresy.[121] The origin myths of the tantric Buddhist deities, one of which will be discussed at length below, were likely composed in reaction to such hostile discourse. Buddhist versions reproduce Hindu polemical discourse in describing a hostile encounter between Buddhist and Hindu deities, but, naturally, resolve it with the victory of the former over the latter.

The figure of Heruka appears to have a somewhat less venerable history than that of Śambara. As Davidson has pointed out, the earliest refer-

---

[118] See Davidson 2002b, 214. I am indebted to Ronald Davidson, whose excellent book brought to my attention this passage, as well as the important passages in the *Subāhuparipṛcchā Tantra*, discussed below.

[119] Other scholars, however, may wish to imply this. I refer to Thomas McEvilley, who in his fascinating but highly speculative article, "An Archaeology of Yoga," argues that tantric sexual yoga developed in the proto-historical Indus Valley civilization. He also argues this in a more recent (2002) article, which is far less detailed but more broadly comparative.

[120] There is considerable uncertainty concerning the dating of the *Arthaśāstra*. Tradition, of course, attributes it to the early Mauryan period, and it does appear quite likely that the *Arthaśāstra* as it now stands contains material that may date to this era. There is evidence of later interpolations, suggesting, as Scharfe has argued, that the text was compiled during the first or second centuries CE. See Scharfe 1993, 293.

[121] For detailed studies of these legends see O'Flaherty 1971, 1976, and 1983.

ence to Heruka appears to be in the *Subāhuparipṛcchā Tantra,*[122] where "Heruka" is not the fierce cosmic savior that he is in the later tantric origin myths, but rather appears to be classified among demonic beings: "At night gods, titans (*asura*), goblins (*piśāca, sha za,* 食 肉), and *heruka*s (*khrag 'thung ba,* 食 血) wander unresisted in the world, harming beings and wandering on."[123] Here the *heruka*s are characterized as ferocious and demonic creatures, whose terrible nature is indicated in both the Tibetan and Chinese interpretative translations, which label them as "blood drinkers."[124]

Soon afterward, Heruka appears in the *Samayoga*[125] in recognizable form, that of a fierce charnel ground deity, the guise assumed by the Buddha Vajradhara in his effort to subdue evil doers.[126] This text presents an origin myth that portrays Heruka's appearance as presaged by a period of chaos and evil in the world. At some point in the distant past:[127]

---

122 This text was probably composed in India during the seventh century. It was translated by Śubhakarasiṁha in 726 CE, and presumably brought with him when he arrived in Chang-an in 716 CE. See Abé 1999, 151, and Davidson 2002b, 213.

123 This translates the Tibetan version of the text (*Subāhuparipṛcchā,* 188b). The Chinese translation adds *nāga*s to the list, and groups together the *piśāca* and *heruka* as "classes of evil demons who drink blood and eat flesh." (T.895.18.720a10: 及 食 血 肉 諸 惡 鬼 類)

124 *khrag 'thung ba* is in fact the standard Tibetan translation of Heruka, although the name is quite often transliterated instead. This translation is likely based upon an Indian interpretive etymology, given the fact that Śubhakarasiṁha independently translated the term in the same way into Chinese.

125 As noted above, the *Samayoga* was likely composed sometime during the late seventh or early eighth centuries.

126 This is according to the Heruka creation myth that will be discussed below. Interestingly, the *Samayoga* commentarial tradition also equates Vajradhara and Heruka. In JS *kalpa* nine, the nine dramatic sentiments are listed and equated with deities. Compassion (*karūṇa*) is associated with Vajradhara (JS 178b). Surativajra, however, associates compassion with Heruka (426a). Indranāla provides another variant of the conversion myth, writing: "Vajradhara manifested in the body of Heruka in order to discipline Indra, the chief of the gods, with compassion." (368a) This is fascinating, as it portrays Heruka, like the Śambara of vedic lore, as the enemy of Indra. Later versions of the myth replace Indra with more contemporary Śaiva deities.

127 According to the commentator Surativajra (400a), the story takes place in the *kṛtayuga* during the time of Kāśyapa Buddha, while Indranāla (296a) sees it as occurring six eons ago during the lifetime of the Buddha Vīracandra.

> At that time all beings were extremely violent and perverse. Due to extremely vicious violence, [beings] fell down wailing. Dying, those beings were reborn as extremely perverse ones due to their habitual tendencies. Their minds blessed by Māra, they were extremely perverse ones, [such as spirits who cause] fever, poison, and goitre,[128] and ḍākinīs,[129] *yakṣas*, astral spirits (*graha*),[130] devils,[131] and obstacle demons.[132] They devastated the triple world, devouring even spiritual practitioners. Even gods, and so forth, were killed. The teachings were also destroyed. Then the gods, together with Indra, came before Brahmā. And Brahmā and the gods with Indra proceeded to take refuge in Viṣṇu. And Brahmā, Viṣṇu, and the gods came before Mahādeva. Then Brahmā, Viṣṇu, and Mahādeva[133] took refuge in Vajrin. (JS 157a–b)

According to the commentator Indranāla, "Vajrin" refers to Buddha Mahāvajradhara,[134] who assembles all buddhas with the gesture (*mudrā*) of the "vajra snap" in order to secure their help in suppressing the vicious ones. The *Samayoga* continues:

---

[128] The Tibetan translation here is *dbyig dug nad*, presumably translating *gaṇḍamāla*, namely goiter, or perhaps any other disease causing inflammation and abscess in glandular tissues.

[129] The Tibetan translation here reads *phra men ma*, an obscure term that is also used to translate *ḍākinī* in ch. 8 of the *Laṅkāvatāra Sūtra*. (Compare the Tibetan at fols. 155b and 157b with the Sanskrit in Vaidya 1963, at p. 102 line 26, and p. 105 v. 15.) No doubt the meat-eating demonic variety of ḍākinī is intended here.

[130] The *gdon* or *graha* are evil spirits believed to cause mental and physical illness.

[131] *bdud* or *māra*, presumably here a generic class of evil spirits, not Death himself.

[132] *rnam par log 'dren*, presumably a translation of *vināyaka*. In his commentary, Indranāla lists these different classes of spirits, and then comments: "The hosts of great vicious ones, such as devils, obstacles, and so forth, quickly arose and pervaded all of the worlds." (296b–297a)

[133] The text here reads *dbang chen*, Mahendra, which I read as Mahādeva to conform to the pattern set by the text. Surativajra's commentary (402a) confirms this reading.

[134] Indranāla 297a.

> Just through the "vajra snap" the buddhas together with Vajradhara spread everywhere throughout all of the worlds and cosmic realms like sesame seeds. As the extremely perverse and violent would not be benefited through peaceful [means], all of the tathāgatas manifested the ferocity that is the reality of wisdom and art. If the triple world is burned by them, fervent, in fierce forms, what need is there to speak of the three cosmic realms being scorched by all fervent buddhas? (JS 157b)

This is followed by a fascinating but rather ambiguous passage describing the birth of Heruka, evidently through the generation of yogic heat via controlled breathing:

> Now, the mind is firmly focused on the tip of the nose. Through the heat of a long nasal breath,[135] he arises through union with a consort by means of the Victor. That very Blessed Lord emerges as a yogin, an Adamantine Fierce one. Greatly Glorious Vajraheruka is very terrifying, blazing with ash; his visage blazes blue for beings, and his maṇḍala of light blazes red. He is as fierce as the end-time of great destruction. Greatly blazing, his voice blazes, like a charnel ground fire. He has a crown of skulls, fierce like the end-time of great destruction. Possessing the methods such as ferocity, he is as terrifying as a charnel ground, with various faces, and eyebrows arched in anger. With his blazing gaze and dance, he incinerates the triple world, along with Rudra,[136] Mahādeva, Viṣṇu,[137] the Sun, the

---

[135] Surativajra comments here that "**the mind is firmly focused on the tip of the nose** means that the mind is focused in the secret space (*mkha' gsang du*) of the divine couple of Śrī Heruka, the nonduality of wisdom and art, appearing as the syllable *hūṁ*, into the drop of which dissolve the buddhas of the ten directions. The **breath** of the nose of the secret vajra is lengthened and heated through the thirty-two syllables. From this he arises via birth from the womb of the consort Gaurī, and so forth, of Heruka's maṇḍala." (402a)

[136] *gu lang*, which, according to the *Tibetan-Sanskrit Dictionary*, has been used to translate the names Śiva and Rudra (Negi 1993–2002, 2:487).

[137] *nye dbang* (*upendra*), a name of Viṣṇu.

> Moon, Yama, and Brahmā, reducing them to ash. They are all brought by the sounding of his vajra, vajra skull-staff, and bell, and become ash, and are restored again. The shadows that are the evil spirits could not endure the sun of his blazing. The devils, and so forth, all were born again, and this king, who is able to consume the blood of the vicious ones, sported with them in the charnel ground. They were all joined with the vajra, and with the blazing ḍākinī maṇḍala he cleansed the cosmos of the extremely vicious and violent beings, establishing them in the awakening of the buddhas in purified buddhalands. Through all of his unexcelled behavioral modes,[138] such as adamantine lust and ferocity, the cosmos and its beings who are infinite [like] the realm of space were purified. (JS 157b–158a)

This text does not vilify the Hindu deities, despite the fact that they are gratuitously roasted in Heruka's process of cosmic house cleansing. They are rather portrayed as victims of the cosmic disorder, and as progressively seeking refuge in the hierarchy of cosmic beings, which naturally culminates in the ultimate refuge, the Buddha Mahāvajradhara. The cosmic disorder is the result of an apparently inevitable process of *karmic* conditioning, although the traditional Buddhist villain, Māra, apparently stirs up trouble by "blessing" the evil-doers.

The version of the story that would eventually predominate, however, is far more polemical, and clearly portrays Śaiva deities—Rudra and/or Bhairava—as the culprits of the cosmic disorder. This change was perhaps unavoidable, as the deity Heruka is clearly modeled on the figure of Śiva in his destructive manifestation, closely approximating the iconography of the deity Bhairava. This change was likely influenced by the general proliferation of religious polemical literature during the mid-first millennium of the Common Era. In particular, this transformation may have been triggered by the famous account of Vajrapāṇi's subjugation and conversion of Mahādeva in the *Sarvatathāgata-tattvasaṁgraha Sūtra*.[139]

---

[138] *rtog pa*, presumably in translation of *kalpa*, *kalpanā*, and so forth.

[139] This important myth has been studied at length by Snellgrove (1987, 134–141) and Davidson (1991). See also Nobumi Iyanaga 1985 for an important study of this and other

Several well known Tibetan versions of Heruka's origin myth have received critical attention.[140] This myth, in its full form, likely post-dates the Tantra itself, which contains only tantalizing hints of the myth's cosmic show-down resulting in Heruka and Vajravārāhī's subjugation of Bhairava and Kālarātri. The most prominent is that which occurs in chapter fifty-one, as follows:

> On a stalk on the summit of the mountain are a universal lotus and the vowels and consonants. [There] he treads upon Gaurī's Lord, his body embraced by the Adamantine Bell. Contemplate the supreme state, the Great King Śrī Heruka, endowed with half of twenty-four and with hosts of heroes and yoginīs.

This relatively sparse description of the central deities and their subdued Hindu foes is greatly developed in the commentarial literature. For example, Abhayākaragupta describes the Cakrasamvara maṇḍala as follows:

> In the Samvara maṇḍala there is a variegated lotus atop Mount Sumeru within an adamantine tent (*vajrapañjara*).[141] Placed on it is a double vajra, which sits as the base of a court in the middle of which is the Blessed Lord. He stands in the archer (*ālīḍha*) stance[142] on Bhairava and

accounts of the subjugation of Hindu deities. See also my translation below of Indrabhūti's version of the Heruka origin myth, which summarizes the STS myth.

[140] See Davidson 1991 for a study and partial translation of Grags-pa rGyal-mtshan's *The Origination of Heruka* (*dpal he ru ka'i byung tshul*). The account given by Bu-ston's *Illumination of the General Meaning of the Laghusamvara Tantra* (*bde mchog nyung ngu rgyud kyi spyi rnam don gsal*) is studied and partially translated in Gray 2001, 487–89, and 2003, 52.

[141] The term *pañjara* is usually translated as "cage" (see Apte 1965, 580.1); however, I translate it as "tent" following the Tibetan translation, *gur*. In the tantric context, the protective net of vajras is not understood to trap the inhabitants within it (in the manner of a cage), but rather to protect them from baleful outside elements (in the manner of a tent).

[142] The stance taken in archery by a left-handed person, with the right leg extended and the left leg contracted, bent slightly at the knee. There has been some confusion with regard to the *ālīḍha* and *pratyālīḍha* concerning which leg is extended. Newman (1990, 124–25 n. 4) cites the *Nāṭyaśāstra* (10.70c–71b) and the Tibetan *Mahāvyutpatti* (#4266, 4267) in support of the interpretation of *ālīḍha* as a stance with the right leg extended and the left contracted. See also Harle 1971.

> Kālarātri who lie on a solar disk atop the pericarp of the lotus. He is black and has four faces which are, beginning with the front [and continuing around counter-clockwise], black, green, red, and yellow, each of which has three eyes. He has a tiger skin and has twelve arms. Two arms holding a vajra and a vajra-bell embrace Vajravārāhī. Two of his hands hold up over his back a white elephant hide dripping with blood. His other [right hands hold] a *ḍamaru* drum, an axe, a flaying knife (*kartri*), and a trident. His remaining left [hands hold] a khatvanga staff marked with a vajra, a skull-bowl filled with blood, a vajra noose, and the head of Brahmā. A garland of fifty moist human heads hangs about his neck. He has the six insignia,[143] and a sacred thread made of human sinew.[144] He has a row of five skulls above his forehead, and a crest of black dreadlocks topped by a left-oriented crescent moon and a double vajra. He is endowed with a fierce meditative state (*vikṛtadhyāna*) and bears his fangs. He brings together in one the nine dramatic sentiments (*navarasa*).[145]

Until recently, there did not appear to be any surviving Indic accounts of the Heruka origin myth, aside from a paucity of references of the sort seen in the text above. Davidson surmises that this is likely due to the late development of the myth in India, which he suggests may have been composed by the Indians involved in the transmission of the related traditions to Tibet.[146] There is, however, at least one Indian version of the myth that rivals, if not exceeds, the complexity of the Tibetan versions of the tale, and is likely their source. It occurs in Indrabhūti's commentary (c. tenth

[143] These are the six insignia of a Kāpālika yogin: a necklace, crest jewel, earring, choker, the sacred thread, and ash. See my discussion of these below.

[144] Reading the variant *naharu*, which means sinew according to Sanderson (1994, 98 n. 4).

[145] My translation of Abhayākaragupta's *Niṣpannayogāvalī* (from the Sanskrit in Bhattacharyya 1949, 23). See also Sanderson 1994, 91.

[146] See Davidson 1991, 219.

century)[147] on the *Cakrasamvara*.[148] Given the importance of this account, I translate it here in full:

> Regarding the instruction concerning the great secret of the distinctive fruit in this chapter, "next" (*atha*) [indicates the line] in the first chapter, "**Existing in the beginning, middle, and end, difficult to obtain in the triple world**." As for the meaning of this, the **beginning** [indicates] the emergence of the enlightened activity of the reality body in the gnostic communal enjoyment body from the sphere of reality, which was from the beginning connected to the body of reality itself. The **middle** is the emergence of the communal enjoyment body as Vajradhara's mansion atop Mt. Sumeru. The **end** is the body which manifests from the measureless magic of maṇḍala emanation, the inseparable [pair] Heruka and Vajrayoginī, who abide having created the true maṇḍala in Jambudvīpa, for the sake of taming the worldly deities of the Desire Realm. **I will explain the triple body** which is supreme and unexcelled together with the background (*nidāna*) in order that there will be no doubt that the secret will be attained through simply knowing the process of meditating on the path **in accordance with union**.
>
> To summarize, in the beginning—in accordance with the previous origination of the wheel of wisdom—the Buddha created the palace of the sphere of reality in the expanse of pure wisdom. From the inseparable sphere of the reality body and wisdom inseparable, there was the glorious communal enjoyment body, Mahāvajradhara, in Akaniṣṭha, the realm of great happiness. There dwell changelessly,

147 See above (p. 24) for a discussion of Indrabhūti's likely dates.

148 Davidson (1991, 233 n. 46) notes that Indrabhūti is one of the Indian sources for the myth, citing IC 4a–b. At the point of Davidson's citation, however, Indrabhūti only refers to the myth, a fact which probably contributed to Davidson's conclusion. Indrabhūti's fuller account, translated below, occurs in the context of his commentary on CS ch. 10, a fact that is not insignificant, as we shall see.

through the method of inseparability, measureless great bodhisattvas of the ninth stage, goddesses who are bodhisattvas, and tathāgatas. The lustful ones who are to be disciplined, and their principal teacher, Mahādeva, came to the palace atop Mt. Sumeru, and all of these evil ones were disciplined. The Tathāgata Mahāvajradhara himself, and the Reverend Vajrapāṇi who is inseparable from him, disciplined them as described in the *Śrī Tattvasaṁgraha.*[149]

Vajrapāṇi asked Vajradhara, "Blessed Lord, How should I proceed with the criminal sentient beings such as Mahādeva, and so forth, who have not been peacefully trained by all Tathāgatas?" Then the Blessed Lord Vairocana, through the blessing of all tathāgatas, settled into the concentration called the "Wisdom Vajra of the Great Art of All Tathāgatas." As soon as he was equipoised, the atoms of all of the spheres of all the tathāgatas burst forth, and they assembled on the peak of Mt. Sumeru as a palace made of vajras and precious jewels. It was perceived in the same way by all of the tathāgatas, and resided in the curl of hair (*śrīvatsa*) at the heart of the Blessed Lord Vairocana. As soon as he uttered [the syllable] *hūṁ*, luminous light from the heart of Vajrapāṇi pervaded all of the three realms. The great god Mahādeva, and so forth, surrounded by a great host of [beings] who dwelt everywhere, in all of the realms, far-flung clouds and oceans of the world,[150] were summoned by the iron goad of the *samaya* of all tathāgatas, and gathered there. All the lords of the three worlds such as Mahādeva completely surrounded the palace [on Mt. Sumeru], aghast with their jaws dropping, muttering anxious words, and seeking refuge in Vajrapāṇi. The god known as Mahādeva fell to the ground unconscious.

149 The following is a summary of the text of the *Tattvasaṁgraha*, corresponding to the Tibetan translation at 49a–53b, and the Sanskrit at Yamada 1981, 157–169.

150 This line, *'jig rten gyi khams rab 'byams sprin rgya mtsho thams cad na* (IC 50a), indicates that Mahādeva summoned all sorts of beings, including the terrestrial, celestial, and aquatic.

There Vajrapāṇi called out to all of the gods, saying, "Listen to my command! If you all want to live, then take refuge in Buddha, Dharma, and Saṁgha!"

Then they replied, "We go for refuge in the Buddha, Dharma, and Saṁgha, together with the *mudrā* host." Being pacified, those sentient beings who did not endeavor to turn away from evil were blessed by being annihilated.

Then the Blessed Lord said to the Great Bodhisattva Vajrapāṇi, "Great Bodhisattva, if we do not reanimate this Maheśvara or Mahādeva, there will be no point in his striving to listen with a diminished life-force. But if we revive him, even he could become a good person!"

Thinking "So be it!" Vajrapāṇi spoke the essence mantra for reviving the dead, which is: *Oṁ vajrāyur jñāna bhāṁ*. As Śrī Vajrapāṇi uttered these adamantine words, the essence mantra blazed upon the soles of his feet. In order to purify them, he pressed Mahādeva with his left foot, and the goddess Umādevī with his right. Then Mahādeva, through being touched by the sole of Vajrapāṇi's foot, experienced the bliss of the many concentrations (*samādhi*), *dhāraṇīs*, and doors of liberation of all the tathāgatas. Offering up his body at the feet of Vajrapāṇi, Mahādeva passed beyond numerous world systems, as many as there are grains of sand in thirty-two Gaṅgā rivers, or as there are atoms in a world system, and he became a buddha known as Soundless Lord of Ashes (*Bhasmeśvaranirghoṣa*) in the world system called Ash Parasol (*Bhasmacchatrā*). On account of this the body of Mahādeva exclaimed: "Ah! The wisdom of awakening of all the buddhas is indeed unexcelled! I have been established in nirvāṇa through being pressed with the mantric words!"

Then that buddha created a manifestation which entered into the body of Mahādeva, who then said, "Ah! What a wonder is the secret wisdom and bliss of all buddhas, on account of which this corpse has returned to the world of the living!" Then the body of Mahādeva was revived and blessed, for the sake of all the beings of this world, and so that all the criminals would be disciplined. He was established as the crown prince in Jambudvīpa.

After Vajrapāṇi pressed down the head of Mahādeva, he had a crescent moon on the left side of his dreadlocks. All of the tathāgatas gave him a trident to bear, and bestowed the adamantine name consecration, [calling him] "Excellent Adamantine Spell" (*Vajravidyottama*). Then Vajravidyottama Bodhisattva, circling with his blazing vajra trident like a whirling firebrand, worshipped them with an offering of dance and said, "Ah! Buddhahood is attained through contact with the supreme foot due to the unexcelled spirit of awakening of all buddhas!"

In the Paranirmitavaśavartin [heaven] he disciplined criminals as the Fierce One Trailokyavijaya; the obstacle demons (*vināyaka*)[151] were disciplied in the Nirmāṇarati [heaven] by the Fierce One Vajrajvālānalārka,[152] in Tuṣita by Vajragarbha, in the Yāma [heaven] by the Fierce One Vajrahūṁkāra, and on the peak of Sumeru by Vajrapāṇi. Then Mahāvajradhara established himself as the manifestation body Śrī Heruka, who is inseparable from the Four Bodies [of a buddha]. Vairocana [offered him his] palace which is the maṇḍala with perfected wheels. Amitābha [offered him]

---

[151] This term, used in the plural here, does not appear to refer to Gaṇeśa in particular, but to a generic class of spirits.

[152] The deity Vajrajvālānalārka appears in the Dharmadhātuvagīśvara Maṇḍala, in which he is described as follows by Abhayākara in his *Niṣpannayogāvālī*: "In the southeast is Vajrajvālānalārka, who is black and who has four faces endowed with the erotic, heroic, disgusting, and compassionate sentiments, which are dark blue, yellow, white, and red. He has eight arms, the right ones of which hold a vajra, sword, an arrow, and a discus, the left of which hold a bell, a noose, a bow, and a banner attached to a khatvanga staff. He stands in the archer's pose (*ālīḍha*), stepping upon Viṣṇu and his wife." *agnau vajrajvālānalārkaḥ kṛṣṇaḥ śṛṅgāravīrabibhatsakaruṇarasānvitacaturmukhaḥ atha caitāni nīlapītasitaraktāni aṣṭabhujo 'sau savyair vajrāsiśaracakrabhṛd vāmair ghaṇṭāṁ pāśaṁ cāpaṁ khaṭvāṅgāsaktapatākaṁ ca bibharti sapatnīkaṁ viṣṇum ālīḍhenākramya sthitaḥ* / (Bhattacharyya 1949, 59–60)

the vase of nectar in a brimming skull bowl. Amoghasiddhi worshipped him with the gods [who consecrate] the sense media and the blessing goddesses. Through the complete gnosis of mantra that is a glorious treasure, Akṣobhya consecrated him with his vajra, [giving him] unexcelled authority as Lord of the Clan. Vajrasattva taught him the supreme bliss of the play of passion in the form of the fierce Samvara who completely embodies the nine dramatic sentiments. He emanated from his body the host of fierce ones [who were to subdue] the lord who led astray the triple world....[153] Since these twenty-four fierce ones proceeded to pervade the sky, the earth's surface, and the underworld, the Supreme Lord of the maṇḍala together with the door and quarter guardians [exist] internally, externally, and in all times. There was a previous origination of this gnosis in the *kṛtayuga* of the first eon. In the *tretā*, *dvāpara*, and final *kali yuga*s, Bhairava and Kālarātri dwelt in Magadha, at the center of the lotus of Jambudvīpa, due to the supreme sovereignty of *karma*. As a result, there were the eight Bhairavas in the *pīlavas*, *upapīlavas*,[154] and charnel grounds. The four gods together with their goddesses [came] from the sky to the places they call the seats (*pīṭha*). The celestial musicians (*gandharva*), without feminine accompaniment, [came from] the sky to the places called [subsidiary] seats (*upapīṭha*).[155] On earth the two *yakṣa*s with their wives seized the places known as fields (*kṣetra*), and the subsidiary fields (*upakṣetra*) were seized by *yakṣa*s who dwelled there with their wives in the manner of lords of wealth. The demons (*rākṣasa*) and demonesses (*rākṣasī*) seized the *chandoha* and enjoyed themselves in

---

[153] I am omitting here a list of the twenty-four mantras of the twenty-four fierce ones. See IC 51b.

[154] These categories of pilgrimage place occur in the *Hevajra Tantra* but not in the *Cakrasamvara Tantra*. See Snellgrove 1959, 1:69–70. The remaining categories of pilgrimage place are listed in CS ch. 50 below.

[155] The text here omits the *upa-* (*nye-*) prefix.

> mountain ravines. At the *upachandoha* the attendants of the demons together with their mates engaged in perversions. In the meeting-places (*melāpaka*) the serpent-deity lord couples united. In the subsidiary meeting-places (*upa-melāpaka*) the two serpent-deity servants, the husbands together with their wives, wandered and played. In the charnel grounds (*śmaśāna*) the serpents (*uraga*) endeavored to obstruct reason. The two servants of the serpents, together with their wives, operated in the subsidiary charnel grounds (*upaśmaśāna*) from the underworld.
>
> Having taken control of the three realms, they overpowered the world. In these twenty-four places they [behaved like] worldly ones, acting out their lust and hatred. Wherever they were, Īśvara-Bhairava and Umā engaged in love-play, along with their retinue.
>
> The Blessed Lord Heruka, together with Vajrayoginī, voiced resounding, fierce, terrible laughter, a miracle for the purpose of disciplining the evil ones, through the wisdom and enlightened activity of the deity host of the maṇḍala's wheels. The earth greatly trembled and the realms of the world quaked. Through engagement, control, enjoyment, and dissolution, the names of those disciplined were attached to the heroes and yoginīs who disciplined them. (IC 49b–52a)

This myth serves several purposes. It provides an account for the appearance in the world of the deity Heruka as well as the teaching attributed to him, including the *Discourse of Śrī Heruka* (*Cakrasamvara Tantra*). It narrates the appearance of the maṇḍala, which is structured around the three wheels inhabited by twenty-four deity couples, corresponding to the twenty-four pilgrimage places. It also accounts for the fact that Heruka and his retinue appear with the accoutrements and even the names of Śaiva deities. This myth, via projective inversion, attributed to the Hindus the very heretical qualities for which the Cakrasamvara tradition was suspect in Buddhist circles.[156]

Heruka himself appropriates the appearance of the Hindu deity Bhairava, a fact acknowledged in the Tantra itself, wherein he is described as having "Bhairava's form" (*bhairavākāraṁ*).[157] A master of illusions, he, along with his entourage, is described by his Buddhist advocates as taking on the appearance of Bhairava and his host, as a compassionate strategy (*upāya*) for the conversion of their followers. According to Indrabhūti, this process had four stages: "engagement, control, enjoyment, and dissolution." Engagement and control evidently refer to the actual subjugation of the deities. According to Grags-pa rGyal-mtshan, "enjoyment" entailed taking on the forms and behavior of the subdued deities to be subdued. He wrote that Heruka and his host

> enjoyed both their food and their ornaments. Since they enjoyed their food, flesh, and blood in the tantric feast (*gaṇacakra*) they are called the "Glorious Host of Blood Drinking Deities." Moreover, they stole their ornaments, which is the reason why Heruka and his retinue took as their ornaments the six insignia (*ṣaṇmudrā*), the human head necklace, the tiger hide undergarment, and so forth.[158]

Bu-ston adds that they also forcibly stole the girls of the subdued gods, and enjoyed with them the "four joys" (*caturānanda*), i.e., the sexual yogas.[159]

With regard to their "dissolution," this is basically a form of what has been termed "compassionate killing."[160] Grags-pa rGyal-mtshan wrote that Heruka and his host "dissolved the consciousnesses of Mahādeva's annihilated deity host into clear light. The Buddha predicted that in the future

---

156 Regarding the subject of "projective inversion," see Dundes 1991. The apparent heresy of the Cakrasamvara tradition will be discussed in sections 3.2 and 3.4 below.

157 See ch. 32 below. As noted above, the AU variant of CS ch. 2 also describes him as having the form of Mahābhairava (*mahābhairavarūpiṇaṁ*).

158 Grags-pa rGyal-mtshan, *dpal he ru ka'i byung tshul*, 299.4.

159 See DS 63.

160 See Cantwell 1997 for a discussion of this from the perspective of the rNying-ma tradition.

[Mahādeva would become] the 'Tathāgata Lord of Ashes'."[161] Finally, their "control" over these deities is symbolized by their use of their bodies as seats.[162]

This myth represents the adoption of non-Buddhist elements while at the same time representing the subordination of these elements within a Buddhist cosmic hierarchy, graphically represented by the placement of the Śaiva deities under the feet of their Buddhist vanquisher. The myth provides an elaborate fourfold scheme for this process of the appropriation and subordination of a non-Buddhist tradition. It is clearly a reaction to Hindu myths such as the myth of the destruction of the Triple City (*tripurāntaka*), of which Buddhists were aware.[163] The Cakrasamvara commentator Bhavyakīrti made an elaborate apologetic defense of the violence implicit in this text, arguing that "being endowed with great compassion, and having realized the reality of selflessness, one will not fall even if one practices the ten non-virtues for the sake of beings." (SM 29b) He further defended it by referring to examples from Hindu mythology, including the *tripurāntaka* myth: "Rudra destroyed the Triple City, and the army of Viṣṇu demolished eighteen massive armies"[164] (SM 30a); and descriptions such as: "the sage (*ṛṣi*), whose mind was burned with the fire of wrath, incinerated like wood the king's army with the fire of malediction." (SM 30a) However, he claimed that unlike the wise and compassionate Buddhists who commit acts of violence, "these heretics, because they kill, give rise to the suffering of the hells, and so forth" (SM 30a), thus propounding an ethical double standard with regard to the employment of violence by religious figures. It should be of no surprise that this contentious myth of the tradition's origin attracted negative attention. In fact, this Buddhist myth of

---

161 Grags-pa rGyal-mtshan, *dpal he ru ka'i byung tshul*, 299.4–330.1.

162 Grags-pa rGyal-mtshan, *dpal he ru ka'i byung tshul*, 300.1. He refers here to the prediction made in the *Sarvatathāgata Tattvasaṁgraha Sūtra*, which Indrabhūti does not mention, giving only his future name and world system. See Snellgrove 1987, 138, and Yamada 1981, 169.

163 Concerning the myth of the Triple City, see O'Flaherty 1976, 180–204.

164 The text here reads *a kṣo hi*, a transliteration of *akṣauhiṇī*, referring to an army consisting of 21,870 elephants, 21,870 chariots, 65,610 horses, and 109,350 foot soldiers (Monier-Williams 2002, 4.1).

Heruka inspired a Śaiva counter-myth, which was based upon the Hindu model of the *tripurāntaka* narrative.[165]

3. Contents and Contexts

3.1 The Triple Wheel Maṇḍala

It is not an accident that Indrabhūti recounts Heruka's origin myth in the context of the *Cakrasamvara Tantra*'s tenth chapter. For this chapter introduces the concept of the three levels of embodiment of a buddha, and Indrabhūti sees the manifestation in the world of Śrī Heruka and his maṇḍala as a process of emanation. This is a process which proceeds from the inconceivable and non-localizable reality body to the communal enjoyment body manifestation of Vajradhara and his palace atop the axial peak Mount Sumeru, and which culminates in the manifestation of the Cakrasamvara maṇḍala—of Heruka with his consort and retinue—embedded in the landscape of Jambudvīpa, the Indian subcontinent.

According to the first verse of this chapter, "nondual union with Śrī Heruka" is essential for the realization of the triple body (*trikāya*),[166] which is equivalent to the gnosis of a buddha (*buddhajñāna*), the knowledge of reality that is the product of a buddha's awakening experience. According to commentators such as Bhavabhaṭṭa, this is because the nature of Śrī Heruka is the nature of the triple body which is the universe;[167] in other words, to

[165] The thirteenth century Kaśmīri author Jayadratha recorded this Śaiva counter-myth in his *Haracaritacintāmaṇi*. This myth involves the typical *tripurāntaka* scenario. The gods are being oppressed by demons who are invincible due to their devotion to Śiva. Bṛhaspati thus devises the heresy of the Buddhist tantras, replete with their images of Buddhist deities trampling Hindu deities, which causes the demons to lose their faith in Śiva. This, of course, gives Śiva the opportunity to destroy them. See Sanderson 1994, 93–94.

[166] The CS follows the classical Yogācāra theory of the three bodies of a buddha, making no mention of Haribhadra's four bodies theory. This may be because it was composed prior to Haribhadra's composition of his *Abhisamayālaṁkāra* commentaries. Regarding the triple body theory and Haribhadra's revision of it, see Makransky 1997. Haribhadra was a student of Śāntarakṣita and a contemporary of Kamalaśīla, and thus flourished during the late eighth and/or early ninth centuries; see Ruegg 1989b, 153. This, however, does not constitute proof for the dating of the Tantra, as the commentators such as Bhavabhaṭṭa, who definitely postdate Haribhadra, also ignore his theory. This may be because they were more inclined toward the classical Yogācāra perspective.

[167] See Bhavabhaṭṭa's comments on the first four verses of ch. 10 in the translation below.

realize Śrī Heruka is to realize the nature of the universe which is one's own nature.

This union is to be achieved via meditation on the Cakrasamvara maṇḍala. The Cakrasamvara maṇḍala focuses upon a central deity couple, Śrī Heruka and Vajravārāhī. They are surrounded by the four "essence yoginīs," Ḍākinī, Lāmā, Khaṇḍarohā, and Rūpiṇī. Together these six deities constitute the central "gnosis wheel" (*jñānacakra*) of the maṇḍala. They are surrounded by three concentric wheels—the blue colored mind wheel (*cittacakra*), the red colored speech wheel (*vākcakra*), and the white colored body wheel (*kāyacakra*)—each of which consists of eight deity couples.[168] The periphery of the maṇḍala is protected by eight fierce goddesses positioned in the cardinal directions and quarters.[169] This constitutes the maṇḍala palace. It is, in turn, surrounded by the "eight great charnel grounds," which clearly mark the tradition as a pre-eminent product of the charnel ground culture of the siddha movement. Like other tantric traditions, the most basic form of meditation practice for this tradition is the creation stage (*utpattikrama*) practice in which one visualizes oneself as the deity Heruka, surrounded by his retinue, in the maṇḍala palace atop the pinnacle of Mt. Sumeru, stacked atop the elemental disks that support the cosmos. The description of the Cakrasamvara maṇḍala occupies a significant portion of the text.[170] However, the Root Tantra itself does not provide sufficient information for the visualization of the maṇḍala; this information is rather found in the tradition's *sādhana* texts, which provide detailed meditation instructions.[171]

---

168 See Table One below for a list of these deities and their correlations.

169 These are the four theriomorphic gatekeeper goddesses, Kākāsyā (Crow Face), Ulūkāsyā (Owl Face), Śvānāsyā (Dog Face), and Śūkarāsyā (Pig Face). In the quarters are positioned Yamadāhī, Yamadūtī, Yamadaṁṣṭriṇī, and Yamamathanī.

170 CS ch. 2 describes its construction, and ch. 3 the rite of consecration performed within it. Ch. 4 lists the 24 ḍākinīs of three wheels, and ch. 48 the 24 heroes. Ch. 41 lists the twenty-four pilgrimage places to which they are linked. The latter portion of ch. 50 describes the classes of pilgrimage place, and ch. 51 provides a brief account of the maṇḍala's setting.

171 Regarding the tantric Buddhist creation stage, see Yarnall 2003 and Cozort 1986 for a discussion from the dGe-lugs perspective; Harding 1996 for a study from the rNying-ma perspective; Dawa-Samdup (1919, 73–140) for a translation of a Cakrasamvara *sādhana* describing the maṇḍala visualization practice; and English 2002 for a detailed study, edition, and translation of an important Vajravārāhī *sādhana*.

This union is further deepened by meditation on what the tradition terms the "body maṇḍala" (*kāyamaṇḍala*), in which the maṇḍala is mapped onto the practitioner's body, which is transformed into a "network of ḍākinīs" (*ḍākinījāla*). Here the maṇḍala serves as what Tambiah has termed an "indexical symbol," capable of shifting between multiple levels of referentiality.[172] The tradition presupposes that the maṇḍala, along with the deities who inhabit it, pervades the cosmos at its various levels, including the microcosmic level of the body. As the Tantra states in chapter forty-eight concerning the male and female deities who inhabit the maṇḍala:

> The entire world is completely pervaded by the twenty-four heroes. The heroes' ḍākinīs, the yoginīs Pracaṇḍā, and so forth, should be seen as positioned in the wheels. He who is adept in all rites and who desires power should always, well-equipoised, visualize himself as consisting of the three wheels. By means of what was previously taught and the established method, worship the binding of the ḍākinīs' network, which is indeed the great wheel which is the abode of all powers, and which was well-spoken by tens of millions of buddhas and also tens of millions of heroes.

Accordingly, the Cakrasamvara adept, who is shown the maṇḍala in the context of his or her consecration, is to engage in an intensive practice of meditation which involves visualizing the maṇḍala—which is thought to pervade the triple world of ancient Indian cosmology—within his or her body. The practitioner's body is linked to the larger cosmos via the three wheels of the maṇḍala, which are correlated to the triple world cosmology—to the heavens, earth, and underworlds, respectively—and also to the three bodies of a buddha, namely to the reality body (*dharmakāya*), the communal enjoyment body (*saṁbhogakāya*), and the manifestation body (*nirmāṇakāya*), respectively.

---

[172] Tambiah wrote, in his essay "A Performative Approach to Ritual," that indexical symbols "have a duplex structure, because they combine two roles: they are symbols which are associated with the represented object by a conventional semantic rule, and they are simultaneously also indexes in existential pragmatic relation with the objects they represent." (1985, 156)

Each wheel is the abode of eight deity couples, for a total of twenty-four. These are correlated to twenty-four sacred sites scattered around the Indian subcontinent and the surrounding mountainous areas. Moreover, each of the twenty-four goddesses is correlated to a body part. In this regard the wheels are arranged hierarchically along the body's vertical axis, with the mind wheel more or less occupying the head and uppermost parts of the torso, the speech wheel corresponding to the upper torso and vocal organs, and the body wheel corresponding to the lower torso, legs, and feet. A detailed list of the wheels, their deities, and correlations is provided in Table One below.

Table One: The Three Wheels of the Cakrasamvara maṇḍala*

Mind Wheel

	Sacred Place	**Seed (*bīja*)**	**Goddess**	**Body Part**	**Consort**	**Bodily Constituent**
E	Pullīramalaya	puṃ	Pracaṇḍā	head	Khaṇḍakapāla	teeth & nails
S	Jālandhara	jāṃ	Caṇḍākṣī	crown	Mahākaṇkāla	head & body hair
W	Oḍiyāna	oṃ	Prabhāvatī	right ear	Kaṅkāla	skin & filth
N	Arbuda	aṃ	Mahānāsā	back of neck	Vikaṭadaṃṣṭrī	flesh
NE	Godāvarī	goṃ	Vīramatī	left ear	Surāvairī	tendons
NW	Rāmeśvarī	rāṃ	Kharvarī	between the eyebrows	Amitābha	bones
SW	Devīkoṭa	deṃ	Laṅkeśvarī	eyes	Vajraprabha	kidneys**
SE	Mālava	māṃ	Drumacchāyā	shoulders	Vajradeha	heart

* The CS itself lists the sacred places in ch. 41, the female deities in ch. 4, and the male deities in ch. 48, but does not provide the additional correlations. Some of this is found in the commentaries on these chapters, such as the commentary on ch. 4 by Kambala and Devagupta. Here I relied on the explanatory tantras, particularly: the *pīṭhāyoginī* ch. of the AU, translated and edited in Kalff 1979; chs. 4 and 13 of the YS (edited in Pandey 1998); and ch. 7 of the SU (edited and translated in Tsuda 1974). I have also consulted the Tibetan translation of Lūipa's BA, and Atīśa's AV commentary on this. See also the edition and annotated translation of Umāpatideva's *śrīvajravārāhīsādhana* in English 2002.

** The AU (J 109.2) and YS (13.7, Pandey 1998, 38) both read here *bukke*, "in the heart," which is redundant since the next element on the list is *hṛdaya*. The Tibetan translation of both is *mkhal ma*, "kidney." Kalff argues that *bukke* is a corruption of *vṛkka*, "kidney." I believe that he is correct, and that the readings *bukke/bukka* resulted from an incorrect Sanskritization from the Pāli *vakkaṃ* (see Table Two below).

[Table One (Cont'd)]

Speech Wheel

	Sacred Place	Seed (*bīja*)	Goddess	Body Part	Consort	Bodily Constituent
E	Kāmarūpa	kāṃ	Airāvatī	armpits	Aṅkuraka	eyes*
S	Oḍra	oṃ	Mahābhairavā	breasts	Vajrajaṭila	bile
W	Triśakuni	triṃ	Vāyuvegā	navel	Mahāvīra	lungs
N	Kośala	koṃ	Surābhakṣī	tip of the nose	Vajrahūṃkāra	large intestine
NE	Kaliṅga	kaṃ	Śyāmādevī	mouth	Subhadra	small intestine
NW	Lampāka	laṃ	Subhadrā	throat	Vajrabhadra	stomach
SW	Kāñcī	kāṃ	Hayakarṇī	heart	Mahābhairava	feces
SE	Himālaya	hiṃ	Khagānanā	perineum**	Virūpākṣa	part of the hair

* The AU here reads *akṣiṇī* (Kalff 1979, 319); the SU gives the alternate reading *cakṣur* (7.8, Tsuda 1974, 94). The YS gives the corrupt reading *kakṣayor*, corrected in the Tibetan translation to *mig gnyis* (4.3, Pandey 1998, 39, 228). While these are relatively consistent, this is nonetheless an anomalous reading that does not fit the remainder of the list. It is one of only two points where the Sanskrit does not correspond to the Pāli of the *Mahāsatipaṭṭhāna Sutta*, which reads here *yakanaṃ*, "liver." I wonder if here as well the Sanskrit resulted from a misreading of a Pāli text. Perhaps the Tibetan translation of *mchin pa* ("liver") for *bukka* in the SU (7.7, Tsuda 1974, 94, 183) reflects a misplaced recognition that the liver should be in this list.

** The Sanskrit here reads *meḍhrake* in the *Yoginīsaṃcāra* (Pandey 1998, 121); *meḍhre* in the *Abhidhānottara* (J 110.1); and *meḍhrasthāne* in the *Samvarodaya* (7.11, Tsuda 1974, 94). The term *meḍhra* usually means penis, but so too does *liṅga*, correlated to Pretapuri below. Unlike *liṅga*, this term is less common, and appears to have been a source of confusion for the Tibetan translators. It is translated in the Tibetan version of the *Yoginīsaṃcāra* as the "root of the penis" (Pandey 1998, 310: *mtshan rtsar*). Kalff (1979, 159) follows the Tibetan here in making his translation, and he also notes several other variants in Tibetan texts, including the reading "anus" in the AU translation (*bzhang sgo*) and "rectum" (*rgyu zhabs*) in the translation of Śūraṅgavajra's commentary. The translation of Dārika's *sādhana* reads "bladder" (200b). Lūipa's *Śrībhagavad-abhisamaya* gives the vague reading "genital region" (AV 190b: *'doms*).

(cont'd)

[Table One (Cont'd)]

Body Wheel

	Sacred Place	Seed (*bīja*)	Goddess	Body Part	Consort	Bodily Constituent
E	Pretapuri	preṃ	Cakravegā	penis	Mahābala	phlegm
S	Gṛhadevatā	gṛṃ	Khaṇḍarohā	anus	Ratnavajra	pus
W	Saurāṣṭra	sauṃ	Śauṇḍinī	thighs	Hayagrīva	blood
N	Suvarṇadvīpa	suṃ	Cakravarmiṇī	calves	Ākāśagarbha	sweat
NE	Nagara	naṃ	Suvīrā	toes*	Heruka	fat
NW	Sindhu	siṃ	Mahābalā	dorsal feet**	Padmanarteśvara	tears
SW	Maru	maṃ	Cakravartinī	big toes	Vairocana	saliva
SE	Kulutā	kuṃ	Mahāvīryā	knees	Vajrasattva	snot

English translates *meḍhra* as "penis" and *liṅge* "sexual organ" (2002, 275; see also p. 511 n. 577). While we cannot do better on the basis of the Sanskrit alone, I would be inclined to translate *liṅga* as penis, as this is its usual referent in Cakrasamvara literature, and I would translate *meḍhra* with a more vague reading, such as "sexual organ" or "pubic region," following the Tibetan *'doms*. Given the variance in the Tibetan translations, I am inclined to tentatively identify this spot as the perineum, which could be considered the "root of the penis" in men, located as it is between the sexual organ and anus.

* The AU (Kalff 1979, 286) and YS (13.7, Pandey 1998, 122) both read here *aṅgulīṣu*, which could refer either to the toes or fingers, excluding the big toe and thumb. The SU, however, reads *pādāṅgulau*, which confirms that it is a toe or the toes that is being referred to here. Other texts, such as the BA, read *sor mo rnams* (190b), which could include both fingers and toes. I translate this as "toe" because it fits the pattern of the body wheel, which otherwise correlates only with body parts on the legs or in the genital region.

** Literally *pādapṛṣṭhayoḥ*, the "back side" or dorsal surface of the two feet.

In "body maṇḍala" practice, the meditator imagines the deity couples in their divine abodes, which are, on the macrocosmic level, the sacred spaces of South Asia, and, on the microcosmic level, the parts on the surface of one's body listed in the fourth column of Table One above. In the meditation, the practitioner visualizes the deities in these places while intoning the corresponding seed syllable, a process known as the placement of the seed syllables (*bījanyāsa*).[173] The purpose of this is to strengthen one's sense of identity with the cosmos that is the maṇḍala, and with the divinities who reside within it, particularly with Heruka, who, the Tantra tells us, pervades the universe.[174]

One of the purposes of this identification is to effect the creative re-imagination of one's body, which is to be seen no longer as filthy and incomplete, but as the perfect, divine abode of the deities. It is thus noteworthy that this tradition borrowed from an earlier Buddhist meditation tradition that sought to establish the very conviction that the body is in fact foul and impermanent. This borrowing concerns the list of body constituents correlating to the twenty-four male deities in Table One above. This list is a bit peculiar, as it lacks the organization along the vertical axis of the prior list, consisting mainly of internal and external organs as well as bodily effluvia. This list is almost identical to an earlier list given in a text of the Pāli canon, the *Scripture on the Foundations of Mindfulness* (*Mahāsatipaṭṭhāna Sutta*), a pivotal early Buddhist meditation text that is still highly valued in the Theravāda tradition.[175] In this text, the list is given for the purpose of the common meditation technique of analyzing the body into its constituent parts. The text takes a quite dispassionate tone, and if anything exhibits the revulsion toward the body which was quite common in early

[173] For more information on this practice, see the *sādhanas* that are available in translation (e.g., Kawa Samdup 1919, esp. 114–119). See also Elizabeth English's 2002 study and translation of a closely related *sādhana*, and Kelsang Gyatso 1997, which is a guidebook written for contemporary English-speaking practitioners.

[174] Most notably in a passage in CS ch. 50 (quoted and discussed below).

[175] For a translation of this text, see Walshe 1995, 335–350. For a discussion of the associated meditation practices, see King 1992, 67–69. Buddhaghoṣa also comments in detail on the thirty-two elements in the *sutta*'s list, highlighting in particular the foulness of these elements. See *Visuddhimagga* 8.81–138, translated in Ñāṇamoli 1976, 268–283.

Buddhist discourse. The lists, as they occur in the *Yoginīsaṁcāra Tantra* and the *Mahāsatipaṭṭhāna Sutta*, are compared in Table Two below.[176]

It is quite remarkable that the Cakrasamvara tradition takes this very same list, which admittedly contains some quite unpleasant elements, and correlates them to the male deities. The aim here is to completely re-envision one's body as the pure abode of the maṇḍala deities, an abode which is in fact co-extensive with the universe. This visualization is extended even to the conventionally most foul and objectionable of body parts and bodily substances, perhaps to challenge the meditator to overcome his deeply ingrained conditioning concerning the body. No doubt for this reason, the second mantra that the adept is to recite at the conclusion of this meditation is as follows: *oṁ vajraśuddhāḥ sarvadharmā vajraśuddho 'haṁ*, "Oṁ All things are vajra-purified, and vajra-purified am I."

[176] There are remarkable parallels between these two lists, as Kalff (1979, 197) has noted. The *Mahāsatipaṭṭhāna Sutta* (MSP) list is somewhat longer, containing several items omitted from the YS and other CS texts. However, they are listed in almost identical order, the only exception being "bile," *pitte/pittaṁ*, which is the second in the Speech Wheel list in the CS literature, but which occurs further down in the MSP, just before *semhaṁ*, "phlegm." The CS literature also has at least one element that does not occur in the MSP, and that is the anomalous *sīmanta*, "hairline" or "part of the hair." The terms *akṣiṇī/cakṣur/kakṣayor*, "both eyes," also does not occur in the MSP, unless it is a faulty Sanskritization from the Pāli *yakanaṁ*, "liver," which is in fact the corresponding item in the MSP list. There are also some other minor differences. Where the MSP reads "skin" (*taco*), the YS reads "skin and filth." Filth (*mala*), being a common attribute of the skin, is probably a later addition. Likewise, where the YS reads "bones" (*asthiṣu*), the MSP reads "bones and bone-marrow" (*aṭṭhī aṭṭhimiñjā*).

Table Two: Bodily Constituents in the *Cakrasamvara* literature and the Pāli Canon

Yoginī Saṁcāra[177]	*Mahāsatipaṭṭhāna Sutta*[178]
nakhadantayoḥ	nakhā dantā
keśaromayoḥ	keśā lomā
tvaṅmalayoḥ	taco
māṁse	maṁsaṁ
naharuṣu	nahārū
asthiṣu	aṭṭhī aṭṭhimiñjā
bukkaṁ	vakkaṁ
hṛdayaṁ	hadayaṁ
akṣiṇī[179]	yakanaṁ
pitte	pittaṁ
phupphuse	papphāsaṁ
antre	antaṁ
guṇavartau	antaguṇaṁ
udare	udariyaṁ
purīṣe	karīsaṁ
sīmante	- - -
śleṣma[ni]	semhaṁ
pūye	pubbo
lohite	lohitaṁ
prasvede	sedo
meda[si]	medo
aśruṣu	assu
kheṭe	khelo
siṅghāṇake	siṅghāṇikā

[177] Source: *Yoginīsaṁcāra* 4.2–4, ed. in Pandey 1998, 38–40. Note that most of the items in this list are cited in the locative case because the text is referencing the bodily locations where the twenty-four male deities are to be visualized.

[178] Source: Rhys-Davids and Carpenter 1982, 293.

[179] As noted above, the YS reads *kakṣayor* here; *akṣiṇī* is the reading preserved in the AU.

As Sferra points out, in tantric Buddhist texts such as this the term "purification" (*viśuddhi*)

> deals with the crucial theme of the essential nature of things, not merely as aiming at theoretical definitions, but also as a starting point of the practice that leads to awakening. In this second context we see the term "purification" is used in two different ways. One the one hand it indicates pureness, Buddha's nature itself, the ever shining and pure condition that is always present in all things. This pureness represents one of the foundations on which the practice and doctrine of the Buddhist Tantras is based and which can be exemplified by the formulas *viśuddhis tathatā* and *tathatātmikā śuddhiḥ*. On the other hand, the term indicates "purification" and therefore a process or a means: *yayā sarvabhāvā nirdoṣā bhavanti sā viśuddhiḥ*. (1999, 85–86)

The purpose of this practice is to recondition one's conception and image of one's body, a reconditioning that is effected via the metaphor and practice of the maṇḍala. This is possible due to the flexibility of the maṇḍala as an indexical symbol, as it permits cross-referentiality between the bodies of individual practitioners, the cosmos, and the social world, in turn effecting the production of distinct subjectivities and the inextricably related, hierarchically organized social spaces. That is, the maṇḍala, as enacted in ritual and meditative practice, mediates between the microcosm of the practitioner's body, the macrocosm of the cosmos, and the intermediary world of India's sacred sites. As David Gellner has suggested:

> Such practices as these make clear that the maṇḍala model applies equally to the universe as a whole, to the country (*deśa*) Nepal, to each city, to each temple and shrine, and, Tantrically, to the worshipper's own body. The realization of one's own identity with these larger designs is the attainment of salvation. (1992, 191)

For the tradition itself, the various meditative and ritual techniques focusing upon the maṇḍala have tremendous soteriological value. A wide array of practices—ranging from "outer" practices such as pilgrimage to "inner" meditative techniques—are deployed to encourage creative identification of the body with the larger universe as an essential means of reshaping one's identity for the purpose of achieving awakening.[180]

The Cakrasamvara maṇḍala and the practices surrounding it also have political implications that should not be ignored. An interesting feature of the maṇḍala, as noted above, is its correlation of the twenty-four deity couples with twenty-four sites scattered across South Asia.[181] From the Buddhist standpoint, this list is notable for its *absence* of any of the well-known Buddhist pilgrimage sites. This may be an indication that this list ultimately derives from a non-Buddhist source. Alexis Sanderson has argued that the passage in the *Cakrasamvara Tantra* that lists these twenty-four sacred sites derives from Śaiva scriptural sources.[182] The issue of textual dependence aside, the myth of Heruka's origin can be profitably read as an indirect acknowledgment of the tradition's debt to non-Buddhist or marginally Buddhist groups such as the Kāpālikas.

In addition to composing the myth of the origin of the Cakrasamvara maṇḍala, its adherents also sought to re-encode the maṇḍala to bolster its identification as Buddhist. One tried and true method for re-encoding was to correlate suspect entities with classical Buddhist categories.[183] Chapter

---

[180] I explore in greater depth the implications of the "body maṇḍala" and related practices with respect to identity construction in my article, "Mandala of the Self: Embodiment, Practice, and Identity Construction in the Cakrasamvara Tradition" (2006).

[181] This correlation is justified via the myth of Heruka's subjugation of Bhairava and his host, as detailed above. These twenty-four sites are also correlated with ten classes of pilgrimage site, as is detailed below in Table Three. This list and its correlations also occur in several other Yoginī Tantras. See, for example, Snellgrove 1959, 1:69–70.

[182] Sanderson argues that the passage in question (in CS ch. 41) derives from a "Kāpālika scripture," the *Tantrasadbhāva*. He claims that the Buddhist list presents a garbled version of the latter's list (which correlates deity classes with sacred sites), mistakenly listing *gṛhadevatā* ("household deity") as a place name (1994, 94–95). Sanderson is likely correct about this, but see also Davidson's criticisms of this claim. Davidson notes that the list is not particularly associated with Śaiva/Kāpālika sites either, and argues that the textual history of these texts is not sufficiently well-known to demonstrate clear affiliation. Davidson suggests that both may derive from an earlier source, which might be either Kāpālika or Buddhist (2002b, 206–211). Whatever the ultimate origin of this list, it is clear that the list is analomous in a Buddhist context, and that the list as it occurs in Yoginī Tantras such as the *Cakrasamvara* is defective insofar as it presents *gṛhadevatā* as a place name.

[183] For example, texts in the Cakrasamvara tradition, such as the YS ch. 2, and Lūipa's BA *sādhana*, correlate the 37 goddesses of the Cakrasamvara maṇḍala with the 37 Elements

fifty of the *Cakrasamvara Tantra* correlates the ten types of pilgrimage places with the ten bodhisattva stages (*bhūmi*), providing them with a normative Mahāyāna Buddhist association, as illustrated below in Table Three. Doing so links this text and its external practices of pilgrimage and internal meditation practices with the rich Mahāyāna Buddhist tradition of viewing progress along the spiritual path as a pilgrimage.

Leading to Awakening (*bodhipakṣikadharma*) of the classical Abhidharma. Regarding this, see Wayman 1973, 3–11.

Table Three: Cakrasamvara Pilgrimage Sites and the Bodhisattva Stages

	Type of Sacred Site	**Pilgrimage Site**	**Bodhisattva Stage**
1.	Seat (*pīṭha*)	Pullīramalaya, Jālandhara, Oḍḍiyāna, Arbuda	Joyous (*pramuditā*)
2.	Subsidiary Seat (*upapīṭha*)	Godāvarī, Rāmeśvarī, Devīkoṭa, Mālava	Immaculate (*vimalā*)
3.	Field (*kṣetra*)	Kāmarūpa, Oḍra	Illuminating (*prabhākarī*)
4.	Subsidiary Field (*upakṣetra*)	Triśakuni, Kośala	Effulgent (*arciṣmatī*)
5.	Chandoha	Kaliṅga, Lampāka	Facing (*abhimukhī*)[184]
6.	Upachandoha	Kāñcī, Himālaya	Very-difficult-to-conquer (*sudurjayā*)
7.	Meeting Places (*melāpaka*)	Pretapuri, Gṛhadevatā	Far Reaching (*dūraṅgamā*)
8.	Subsidiary Meeting Places (*upamelāpaka*)	Saurāṣṭra, Suvarṇadvīpa	Immovable (*acalā*)
9.	Charnel Grounds (*śmaśāna*)	Nagara, Sindhu	Accomplished (*sādhumatī*)
10.	Subsidiary Charnel Grounds (*upaśmaśāna*)	Maru, Kulutā	Cloud of Truth (*dharmameghā*)

Such correlating evidently was not sufficient to fully assuage Buddhist discomfort. After providing this correlation, the text concludes with the following passage:

[184] The Tantra here reverses the typical order of *sudurjayā* and *abhimukhī*, which are usually the fifth and sixth stages, respectively.

> This teaching of Śrī Heruka concerns the inner stages. With respect to the ten perfections and stages there is the barbaric language (*mlecchabhāṣaṁ*)[185] of the yoginīs. The hero's body, by nature mobile and immobile, is in heaven, the underworld, and in the mortal worlds. The teaching regarding Pullīramalaya, and so forth, is that they are positioned both outside and inside.

The text suggests that the Buddhist assumption of non-Buddhist terminology and practice (such as a non-Buddhist pilgrimage circuit), is an example of the "barbaric language" of the yoginīs which is found throughout the text. This language is not "foreign" from the perspective of the Indian cultural world; it is "foreign" or "barbaric" only from the normative Buddhist perspective. Such appropriation is justified by the myths of conversion, and also here via the claim for the omnipresence of Śrī Heruka. That is, since "the hero's body, by nature mobile and immobile, is in heaven, the underworld, and in the mortal worlds," therefore it pervades all pilgrimage sites, Buddhist and non-Buddhist alike. The text, however, backs away from this claim to totalizing all-inclusiveness, limiting the "teaching of Śrī Heruka" to "the inner grounds," which probably reflects the likely political reality that Buddhists did not have control over many or any of the sites listed in chapter forty-one. This may represent a case where the attempted conversion of Indian sacred spaces by Buddhists was less than successful.[186]

Buddhists thus tended to de-emphasize the literal, "outer" interpretation of the maṇḍala as a map of external pilgrimage places, and emphasized instead an inner interpretation which involved the re-mapping of the maṇḍala onto the body.[187] This was effected ritually through meditative practices such as Lūipa's "body maṇḍala." This re-mapping was reinforced in

---

185 In the Tibetan translation *mlecchabhāṣaṁ* is not translated literally, but figuratively as "symbolic speech" (PM 245b, SL 142b: *brda yi skad*).

186 Tibetan biographies of siddhas such as Kṛṣṇācārya portray them as engaged in struggles with aggressive Śaiva ḍākinīs for control of these sacred sites. Regarding this phenomenon, see Templeman 1999.

187 This is a venerable pattern; Yi-xing and Śubhakarasiṁha, in their commentary on the *Mahāvairocana-abhisambodhi Sūtra*, likewise sought to purge the Buddhist practice of *homa* (fire sacrifice) of its "heretical" associations by emphasizing the "inner" visualized practice, without which the "outer" ritual practice is useless. See Strickmann 1983, 444.

Buddhist discourse through the development of taxonomies of disciples that categorized practitioners in accordance with the degree of sophistication of their praxis. In one such taxonomy, the Indian Buddhist scholar-saint Abhayākaragupta posited five classes of practitioners, whose status was determined by the nature of their practice. Regarding these, he wrote:

> There are five types of disciples, distinguished as the lesser, the middling, the lesser amongst the great, the middling amongst the great, and the greatest of the great. In terms of the lesser, the outer regions such as the "seats" (*pīṭha*), and so forth, are taught. This is stated in the *Vimalaprabhā*. Here the seats, and so forth, such as Jālandhara are taught so that the childish might wander the land; this is not applicable to everyone. This is because the Vajrayoginīs who are born among the brahmin, warrior (*kṣatriya*), commoner (*vaiśya*), and servant (*śūdra*) classes, and among the outcastes, live also in the cities, and they also exist in lands such as Tibet and China. This is not taught in the concise tantras, but it does say in the extensive tantras that the seats (*pīṭha*), and so forth, are in all countries and in all cities. In terms of the middling, the seats, and so forth, of the goddesses of the maṇḍala are arranged as the foundation of the maṇḍala palace.
>
> In terms of the lesser amongst the great, the seats, and so forth, are taught to be the head, and so forth, in the body, by the process wherein the pilgrimage circuit of the childish is completely transformed by the syllables *puṁ*, and so forth. The channels that run between them are also referred to as the goddesses. In terms of the middling amongst the great, by means of the perfecting stage there is placement with respect to the Vajradevīs, who are esteemed as the seats, and so forth, that are in the head, and so forth, which exist thus in the body, and as the natural actuality of the channels which run between them, without the [use of] seed syllables, and so forth. The greatest of the great who abide in the perfecting stage create the *bodhicitta* of inseparable emptiness and compassion as mastery of all of the wheels of the maṇḍala—which are the reality of the stages

> (*bhūmi*) and the perfections (*pāramitā*)—by means of the seats, and so forth, which are the natural actuality of the eyes, and so forth, in the body. In terms of the above, there are statements such as "great gnosis abides in one's own body, free of all thought."[188]

Passages such as this one from Abhayākara's text served two general Buddhist political interests. The first was to de-emphasize a non-Buddhist pilgrimage circuit, which was to be replaced by a "superior" internal meditative praxis. Abhayākara's taxonomy privileges the subtle perfecting stage practices, while downplaying external practices such as pilgrimage. This passage also exhibits a transformation with respect to the status of women, whose participation in the rituals of the early tradition was requisite, but who are eliminated in the "great" modes of practice, via the reduction of the female to abstract presences in the (presumed male) body of the adept.[189]

The second political interest served involved Abhayākara's acknowledgment and open approval of the transmission of the tradition to other cultural contexts. The mention of Tibet and China is surely not accidental, as these were major destinations for its transmission, of which erudite Indian Buddhists such as Abhayākaragupta were certainly aware. Abhayākara thus legitimates the re-mapping of the sacred sites of the tradition to the landscape of Tibet and China, which re-mapping was ongoing as he was writing in the eleventh century, and with which he was involved.[190]

External pilgrimage was not a problem provided that Buddhists were in control of the sites in question. This sort of interpretive flexibility was an essential factor in the transformations the tradition had to undergo as it crossed boundaries. These included the boundary between the liminal renunciant groups and the mainstream monastic Buddhist communities in South

---

[188] Abhayākaragupta, *Śrīsampuṭa-tantrarājaṭīkāmnāyamañjarī-nāma*, 152a–b. The quotation at the end of this passage is from HV 1.1.12: *dehasthaṁ ca mahājñānaṁ sarvasaṁkalpavarjitaṁ* (Snellgrove 1959, 2:2).

[189] The implications of this will be explored in sections 3.2 and 3.3 below.

[190] Abhayākaragupta has been dated to the late eleventh and early twelfth century. According the Tibetan historical tradition, Abhayākara was an instructor of the Tibetan rMa Lotsawa, who studied in India and Nepal at this time. See Roerich 1949, 219. See also Sperling 1994, 808 n. 5, and also Singh 1968, 179–198.

Asia, as well as the cultural and geographic boundaries the tradition crossed as it was transmitted across Asia.[191]

Abhayākaragupta exemplifies an interpretive trend in the Cakrasamvara and related traditions, a trend which involved increasing emphasis on the internalized yogic anatomy highlighted in the perfecting stage practices. It is important to note that there is no overt reference to these practices in the *Cakrasamvara Tantra* itself. It appears that categories of the creation stage (*utpattikrama*) and perfecting stage (*niṣpannakrama*) were products of the interdependent processes of tantric composition and commentarial systematization that occurred in Indian Buddhist monastic settings from the late eighth century onward, and, in particular, in the Ārya school of Guhyasamāja exegesis that produced the *Piṇḍīkṛtasādhana* and the *Pañcakrama*.[192] Cakrasamvara commentators writing from the ninth century onward typically portrayed the perfecting stage as the "ultimate import" of the text, a necessary strategy as the Root Text itself does not mention the perfecting stage in any direct or literal fashion. Fortunately, these commentators had at their disposal a long tradition of sophisticated interpretative strategies that permitted the creative discovery or uncovering of the hidden import of the text.[193]

---

[191] For a discussion of the mapping of the Cakrasamvara maṇḍala over the Kathmandu valley, see Gellner 1992, 190–92. There have been numerous studies regarding the remapping of the Cakrasamvara maṇḍala across the landscape of the Tibetan cultural world, ranging from Karzha in the far Southwest (Stutchbury 1999), the Himalayas (Macdonald 1990), Tsari in the Southeast (Huber 1999a), and Amdo in the Northeast (Buffetrille 1999). See also Huber 1990 for a discussion of the controversy this remapping triggered in Tibet.

[192] It is clear that the categories *utpattikrama* and *niṣpannakrama* were developed by the late eighth to early ninth century as these terms appear in the root *Hevajra Tantra*. These categories also appear and are systematically developed in the Ārya tradition of Guhyasamāja exegesis, which arguably originated around this same time (while Mimaki and Tomabechi have argued that these Ārya texts were most likely composed during the ninth or tenth centuries [1994, ix], Wedemeyer notes [2001, 254–256] that Mimaki elsewhere has acknowledged that texts attributed to one of the pivotal Ārya tradition writers, Āryadeva, are datable to the late eighth century). Davidson has argued for the ninth century as the period when tantric commentarial systematization occurred (2002a, 56 ff.), which matches well my provisional dating for the development of the Cakrasamvara commentarial tradition. However, it appears that here the Cakrasamvara tradition itself was somewhat derivative, largely relying on developments occurring in the context of the Guhyasamāja and Hevajra traditions.

[193] These interpretive strategies fall under the rubric of what has been called "Buddhist hermeneutics." Regarding this, see the volume *Buddhist Hermeneutics*, edited by Donald Lopez (1988). See especially the articles by Broido, Kapstein, and Thurman, as well as Lopez's introduction. See also Broido 1982, 1983a, 1983b.

While the sophisticated commentarial apparatus that would characterize later tantric scholarship may not have been developed until after the *Cakrasamvara Tantra* was composed, it is clear that many of these practices themselves had been developed by the mid- to late eighth century. The "creation stage" techniques of visualizing both individual deities and their maṇḍala environments were already a well-developed feature of tantric practice by the eighth century, and had evolved from far older Buddhist visualization techniques.[194]

By the late seventh century Indian Buddhists were also composing tantric texts such as the *Mahāvairocana-abhisambodhi Tantra* that advocated "signless" meditations which were apparently seen as alternatives or augments to the visualization exercises. Buddhaguhya's *Piṇḍārtha* commentary on this text, which was likely composed in the late eighth century, provides an interesting explanation of one such technique. In it he first describes the generation of a visualized image of the deity via a four-branched recitation practice.[195] This is followed by a description of the "concentration (*samādhi*) without perceptual forms," which presupposes mastery of the previous visualization techniques. He explains:

> First you should actualize all the four branches of recitation for a while as before, and then analyze the manifestation of the created (*parikalpita*) colour, shape, and so on, of your tutelary deity who is identical to yourself, breaking them down into atoms. Or it is also acceptable to do this by way of the reasoning that is unborn and unarising from the very beginning, or similarly by way of the technique of

[194] Of particular note are the visualization techniques described by Buddhaghoṣa (active during the fifth century in Śrī Laṅka) in his *Visuddhimagga* (VM). In addition to the well-known visualization techniques employing disks (*kasiṇa*) made of earth or other substances (VM chs. 4–5, translation in Ñāṇamoli 1976, 1:122–184), individuals can be employed as objects of concentration, as is described in the section on the meditation on loving kindness (VM 9.1–76, translation in Ñāṇamoli 1976, 1:321–340). Regarding the importance of vision and visualization techniques in both early and Mahāyāna Buddhism, see also Kloetzli 1983, Gethin 1997, and McMahan 2002.

[195] This is the generation of a visualized image of Mahāvairocana from the seed syllables *a*, *ā*, *aṁ*, and *aḥ*, succinctly described in the previous section of his commentary. Buddhaguhya associates this visualized image with the *saṁbhogakāya* and *nirmāṇakāya* levels of embodiment. See Hodge 2003, 520–521.

> drawing-in the vital energy (*prāṇa*) through the yoga of turning your mind inside, or by way of not focusing on its appearance [as colour and shape]. In accordance with that realization, you should then actualize the mind which is just self-aware, free from the body image of your tutelary deity and without appearance [as subject and object], and mentally recite your *vidyā* mantra as appropriate. (Hodge 2003, 522)

Buddhaguhya lists four possible techniques for further "perfecting" the visualized image of the "creation stage," a perfection that implies its dissolution. Although he does not use the terminology of the later tradition, it does seem reasonable to see this as an early attempt at systematizing what must have been a diverse array of advanced meditative techniques, some of which would eventually be included under the rubric of the "perfecting stage."

Two of the techniques described by Buddhaguhya support David Germano's argument that the perfecting stage covers two distinct rubrics, which are

> an earlier body of practice focused on the absence of images and a later system of techniques focused on the human body as a directly sensed reality. The first aspect indicates formless types of contemplation directly on the ultimate nature of one's mind utterly devoid of any fabricated or spontaneous visual images. Often discussed as the dissolution of visual images back into the visionary, one could explain them as a felt experience of being grounded in the body, guided by the felt gravity of the body's presence without any cathexis to external images. They can also be understood in part as attempts to formally incorporate the non-esoteric styles of meditation on emptiness (that were increasingly normative in orthodox monastic environments) into Tantric practice and ideology. (Germano 1994, 220)

In addition to this aspect, which may correlate to Buddhaguhya's "unborn reasoning," Germano also describes a second aspect, which likewise appears comparable to Buddhaguhya's "technique of drawing-in the vital energy (*prāṇa*) through the yoga of turning your mind inside." Germano continues, writing:

> The second rubric of perfection phase contemplation signifies *internal* meditations on a subtle or imaginal body-image through visualizing its triune elements known as "the channels, winds, and nuclei" (*rtsa rlung thig le*). This is in contrast to focusing on *external* visualizations of deities in front of oneself, or as one's self, or even internal visualizations of constellations of such deities as a "body maṇḍala." These types of perfection phase meditations are innovative and distinctive in the history of Buddhist Tantra in that they introduce overtly sexual symbolism as the basis for contemplation through reliance on non-anthropomorphic representations of a subtle body. Correspondingly they mark a move towards *felt* tactile sensations (especially sexual bliss and the sensation of warmth) rather than exclusive reliance on our capacity for vision. In this way it marks a movement toward embodiment and processes internal to our body, with sexuality involving intensely tactile felt presences in contrast to vision, the coolest and most metaphysical of our senses. (Germano 1994, 221)

The *Cakrasamvara Tantra* does not explicitly address the subtle body, with its channels, winds, drops, and energy centers (*cakras*), or the meditations involving these. These are, however, important topics for the commentators. Several of the explanatory tantras do address the topic of the perfecting stage. The *Samvarodaya Tantra* and *Ḍākārṇava Tantra*s, for example, explicitly discuss the structure of the subtle body.[196] This likely indicates that these texts were in fact composed after the *Cakrasamvara Tantra* itself. Interestingly, the portions of the *Samvarodaya Tantra* that discuss the perfecting stage exhibit several instances of intertextuality with texts of the Āryā tradition of Guhyasamāja exegesis, such as the *Pañca-*

[196] The SU does this in chs. 3 and 5–7; see Tsuda 1974, 243–247, 251–263. Ch. 5 of the DA likewise provides a detailed accounting of four *cakras* and 120 channels. See DA 153b–155a.

krama.[197] This probably indicates that this text (or at least these portions of it) was not completed until after the Āryā texts were composed.[198]

Other explanatory tantras such as the *Vajraḍāka* express criticism of the "contrived" (*bcos ma*) meditations and rituals of the "lower" tantras, and uphold an alternative, namely the "natural" (*rnal ma* or *sahaja*) state of natural repose in the body that is the product of perfecting stage practice. The *Vajraḍāka Tantra* explains:

> In order to realize the natural union, you must practice the contrived meditations and contrived [mantra] repetitions. And once you have realized the natural union through the outer, contrived disciplines, you no longer need to bother with the contrivances. For example, having obtained a boat, you cross to the other side of the river, and once you have crossed you abandon it; it is just so with the contrivances. Those who clear away the outer actions produced by the contriving mind, such as the maṇḍala, and so forth, are praised as being of foremost worth, since all successes abide in them. Those who follow the literal treatises in which the actuality of the Victor is unknown, such as those written by the sages (*ṛṣi*), and those who follow the tantras mentally yet engage in worldly, contrived actions, are begging for misery with much exertion. Therefore, those who engage in the procedures of ritual actions (*kriyāvidhi*) such as the maṇḍala, and so forth, are unliberated, outer men who produce only afflictions. Being unrealized they will not awaken, insofar as they have misconceptions. Yet if they thoroughly understand purification, those things that they desire will naturally arise.

---

[197] Tsuda identifies an instance of intertextuality with the *Pañcakrama* at SU 6.11–12 (1974, 260 n. 1, 2) and also with the *Caturdevīparipṛcchā* at SU 2.28–29 (1974, 243 n. 1). SU ch. 3 is also correlated by Tsong Khapa to the five stages of the *Pañcakrama*. See Tsuda's notes to this chapter (1974, 243–246).

[198] Of course, the dependence might be the other way, with the authors of the *Pañcakrama*, and so forth, relying on the SU, but I find this possibility far less likely, given the great influence which the Āryā tradition had on tantric Buddhist scholars across the spectrum of traditions.

> The nature of cause and effect does not exist ultimately; yet due to the luminosity that is the nature of things, it is also not [mere] emptiness. The repose (*vihāra*) of the diverse aspects of all distinct natures is like a jewel in the ocean, which has the mode of being without beginning or end. The mundane are always involved with conventional practices; the supramundane go against that. Existence and non-existence are not known to be intrinsic. Those who are thoroughly realized through this method are not liberated lacking perfection. If you rely on the natural path, you will be liberated no matter what you do. *Saṁsāra* and *nirvāṇa*, the actuality of misery and bliss, which augment, respectively, error and virtue, all abide naturally. (VD 124b–125a)

The term *sahaja* here is probably employed as it was by Buddhajñānapāda in his *Dvikramatattvabhāvanā-mukhāgama* (Tōh. 1853), designating "the outcome of both the developing and perfecting practices, but not as a member of a schema of joy or ecstasy."[199] This text also is unlikely to have been composed prior to the ninth century.

One common element in both the *Cakrasamvara Tantra* and the perfecting stage practices is the emphasis placed on sexuality as an essential element of the spiritual path. This notion was a radical one, directly at odds with the practice of celibacy that Buddhists had emphasized for over a millennium. The *Cakrasamvara Tantra*, in its third chapter and also elsewhere, advocates the deployment of sexuality in its second and third consecrations. These were later understood as conferring upon the adept the authority to practice the perfecting stage sexual yogas. However, as I will argue below, there is no overt evidence in the *Cakrasamvara Tantra* itself for any of these sexual yogas. Rather, the purpose of these consecrations appears to have been the production of sexual fluids that were deemed to be powerful and empowering substances in their own right. The nature of these practices and their relation to the sexual yogas, and well as the concomitant issue of the status of women in this tradition, are the subjects of the next two sections below.

---

[199] Davidson 2002a, 60. See Davidson's discussion of Buddhajñānapāda's use of this term.

3.2 Ḍākinīs, Yoginīs, and Women

One of the central enigmas of the Yoginī Tantras concerns the figures of the yoginīs or ḍākinīs,[200] and their relation to the sexual practices described in these texts. The ḍākinīs, who are particularly emphasized in the *Samayoga* and *Cakrasamvara Tantras*, were initially viewed as a class of nefarious quasi-human or non-human beings, similar to the dreaded flesh-eating *rākṣasa/rākṣasī* demons. Such is their portrayal in the *Laṅkāvatāra Sūtra*, a Mahāyāna scripture composed in India during the fourth century, although mention of the ḍākinīs was likely added to this text no earlier than the sixth century.[201] This text threatens carnivores with the following fate:

> The [carnivore] is born again and again as one who is ill-smelling, contemptuous, and insane among the families of the caṇḍāla, the pukkasa, and among the ḍomba.[202] From the womb of a ḍākinī he will be born into a carnivorous family, and then into the womb of a rākṣasī and a cat; he belongs to the lowest class of men.[203]

---

200 These figures are used interchangeably in the CS and related texts such as the AU. In fact, in the parallel passages between the CS and the AU, one text often reads one of these terms, while the other text reads the other. Generally, the CS uses the term *ḍākinī* more often than the AU or any other of the Yoginī Tantras that I have studied.

201 Regarding the dating of the *Laṅkāvatāra*, its *terminus ante quo* is 443 CE when it was first translated into Chinese. There is evidence, however, pointing to its existence in India many decades earlier during the fourth century. See Sutton 1991, 13–19. Note, however, that the term *ḍākinī* does not appear in Bodhiruci's sixth century Chinese translation of this passage, or in a similar passage that precedes it. In both cases, the term *rākṣasī* (羅 殺 女) stands in the place of *ḍākinī* (T.16.671.564b18–19, 563a24–25). However, the terms *ḍāka* and *ḍākinī* (T.16.671.565a6: 荼 伽 荼 伽 女) occur in the following chapter, which presents a *dhāraṇī* for protection from possession by evil spirits, including the ḍākinīs. This may indicate the growth of belief in ḍākinīs as terrifying spirits beginning in the sixth century. I am grateful to Nobumi Iyanaga for bringing Bodhiruci's translation to my attention.

202 The caṇḍāla and ḍomba are well-known outcaste groups; the term *pukkasa* is a Prakrit term probably derived from *pulkasa*, which evidently designates another outcaste group, "a despised mixed-tribe" (Monier-Williams 2002, 638.2).

203 *Laṅkāvatāra Sūtra*, 8.14–15: *durgandhiḥ kutsanīyaś ca unmattaś cāpi jāyate / caṇḍāla-pukkasakule ḍombeṣu ca punaḥ punaḥ // ḍākinījātiyonyāś ca māṁsāde jāyate kule / rākṣasī-mārjārayonau ca jāyate 'sau naro 'dhamaḥ //* (Vaidya 1963, 105); cf. Suzuki 1932, 221.

Around the same time that the ḍākinīs appear in the *Laṅkāvatāra*, Dharmakīrti brings to our attention the existence of Ḍākinī Tantras, which are evidently notorious for advocating observances (*vrata*) involving perverse or transgressive practices. This discussion occurs in Dharmakīrti's *Svavṛtti* on his *Pramāṇavārttika*, which was likely composed by the late sixth or early seventh century,[204] in the context of a passage addressing the issue of whether or not "success" (*siddhi*) in magical procedures involving mantras is dependent upon adherence to ethical norms (*dharma*).[205] His answer was:

> No, for it is evident that there are observances in the Ḍākinī and Bhaginī Tantras, and so forth, which are incompatible with ethical norms and are replete with violence, theft, sexual intercourse, perverse actions, and so forth, and through which there is distinctive success.[206]

Dharmakīrti clearly identifies them as non-Buddhist teachings, as follows:

> Violence, sexual union, the doctrine of the Self, and so forth, are explained as being the causes of bad and good results in mantra ritual texts that are Buddhist and non-Buddhist, [respectively]. How could both be true if one is designated as being incompatible [with ethical norms]? Since there is no verdict on this matter as a ritual text of antithetical import accords with the other [perspective], there is no certainty [with regard to this issue].[207]

---

[204] Toshihiko Kimura (1999) has argued persuasively that Dharmakīrti lived c. 550–620 CE, contra several other attempts to date him either somewhat earlier or somewhat later.

[205] I interpret *dharma* here in its normative rather than descriptive sense, as described by Richard Gombrich (1996, 34–37). For a similar normative use of the term, see the *Agañña Sutta*, *Dīgha Nikāya* 27.7–8, translated in Walshe 1995, 408–409.

[206] *na / dharmaviruddhānām api krauryasteyamaithunahīnakarmādibahulānāṁ vratānāṁ ḍākinībhaginītantrādiṣu darśanāt / taiś ca siddhiviśeṣāt /* (Gnoli 1960, 163; translation mine). See also the translations in Davidson 1981, 8, and Sanderson 2001, 11–12 n. 10.

[207] This passage occurs as follows in Dharmakīrti's root text in the context of the above passage: *tathā hi bauddhetarayor mantrakalpayor hiṁsāmaithunātmadarśanādayo 'nabhyudaya-hetavo 'nyathā varṇyante / tat katham ekatra viruddhābhidhāyi dvayaṁ satyaṁ syāt / tatrārthāntarakalpane tad anyatrāpi tulyam ity arthānirṇayāt kvacid apratipattiḥ /* (Gnoli 1960, 123; translation mine).

Alexis Sanderson has argued convincingly that the Ḍākinī and Bhaginī Tantras were Śaiva texts,[208] and while there may be no connection between these and the later Buddhist Yoginī Tantras, which were also notorious for their apparent advocacy of transgressive violence and sexuality, the similarity is striking, and points toward the "ritual eclecticism" that was common in early medieval India.[209]

During the sixth and seventh centuries in India when Dharmakīrti was writing, Mahāyāna Buddhists were certainly engaged in the production of ritual texts and practices involving the use of mantras, maṇḍalas, and so forth. Indeed, for centuries they had been increasingly practicing ritual and meditative techniques, many of which would retrospectively be included under rubrics such as *vajrayāna, mantrayāna*, and so forth. The slow increase of ritual and meditative texts translated into Chinese during the mid-first millennium has been well-documented,[210] and Buddhist authors writing during the seventh century, such as Śāntideva and Bhāvaviveka, demonstrate an increasing familiarity with and acceptance of the accoutrements of esoteric Buddhism, such as the magical use of mantras.[211] There is even evidence that ritual practices involving maṇḍalas were performed at Nālandā during the seventh century, although evidently there was some secrecy surrounding these performances.[212] As Matthew Kapstein has argued:

---

[208] See Sanderson 2001, 12 n. 10.

[209] See Phyllis Granoff's fascinating (2000) essay for a discussion of this phenomenon.

[210] See, for example, Chou 1945, and Matsunaga 1977, 1978, and 1980.

[211] Regarding the esoteric Buddhist elements in the works of these authors, see Davidson 1999, and Kapstein 2001, 233–255.

[212] Yi-jing (義净), a Chinese pilgrim who studied at Nālandā during the latter half of the seventh century, reported in his *Records of Eminent Monks of the Great Tang who Sought the Dharma in the Western Regions* (大唐西域求法高僧傳) that "When I, Yi-jing, was at Nālandā, I repeatedly tried to enter the maṇḍala, but my hopes were in vain as I was unable to produce sufficient merit, which shattered my aspiration to propagate these extraordinary teachings." (T. 2066.51.7a.11–12) The term I translate here as *maṇḍala* is 壇場, *tan-chang*. The character *tan* typically means altar, but can designate a maṇḍala in tantric texts (see Soothill and Hodous 1937, 446). The term *tan-chang* here clearly means maṇḍala, as the term *chang* implies an expanse of space that would be occupied by a maṇḍala, but not by the typical altar.

> [T]he practice of "incantation and ritual," directed to both ultimate and mundane ends, had become normal Mahāyāna practice, and not merely popular cult shunned by the learned clergy, prior to the sixth century, and probably as early as the third. Over the course of the centuries the volume of ritual lore incorporated into the Mahāyāna in this fashion increased without any but general doctrinal restriction.... It was only after this corpus had grown sufficiently massive to take on a life of its own however, that conditions came to favor the emergence of the mantranaya and later Vajrayāna as distinct ways of Buddhist practice.... [T]his development occurred within a century or two following Bhāvaviveka's day, and perhaps had begun already during his lifetime. Once it took place, it became possible to attempt an *ex post facto* classification of the whole mass of mantric lore that had accumulated during the preceding centuries. Thus, the so-called "outer tantras" had been part and parcel of Mahāyāna practice long before anyone ever conceived of them as a class apart. (2001, 245)

While much of esoteric Buddhist ritual appears to have derived from the appropriation of non-Buddhist rituals, it is important to note that this appropriation involved a complex and creative process which took place over many centuries.[213] Indeed, Buddhists appropriated and thoroughly transformed the vedic fire sacrifice (*homa*), but this appropriation appears to have taken place quite early in Buddhist history, leading to an extended period of transformation culminating in the tantric Buddhist version of this rite.[214] Buddhists, however, were aware of the popularity of non-Buddhist

---

[213] I use the term "appropriation" as defined by Tony Stewart and Carl Ernst, as a process "wherein the borrowed item is transformed through the process of incorporation, thus fundamentally altering both the appropriated and the appropriator." (2003, 587)

[214] Giovanni Verardi has argued for the early Buddhist appropriation of the *homa* rite in his (1994) monograph. For more information concerning the Buddhist *homa* rite, see Payne 1991, as well as the various essays in Staal 1983, vol. 2.

versions of the *homa* rite, and wrote apologetic defenses arguing for the superiority of their version of it.[215]

The Yoginī Tantras seem to represent a later instance of Buddhist appropriation of non-Buddhist practices, one which was underway no later than the eighth century. They are characterized by the transgressive practices which Dharmakīrti labeled *hīnakarma*, which were associated with non-Buddhist groups such as the Kāpālika, as well as, increasingly, some members of the Buddhist communities. These were likely accepted only by relatively few Buddhists at this time, and resisted by some. Xuan-zang's biographer, Hui Li, reports that when King Harṣa Śīlāditya was travelling in Orissa he was reproached for his support of Nālandā by "Hīnayāna" monks, who argued that "The Monastery of Nālanda and its 'sky-flower' doctrine is not different from the Kāpālika sect." (Beal 1911, 159) This may represent resistance to the growing popularity of esoteric Buddhism in major monastic centers such as Nālandā.

The Buddhist adaptation of Kāpālika-type practices remained controversial for several centuries. During the eighth century, when Tibetans were beginning their project of receiving, translating, and assimilating Buddhist texts and practices, some Tibetans had serious misgivings concerning the tantras that contained transgressive elements, which culminated in an attempt at censorship during the imperial period, circa the late eighth century.[216] According to the Tibetan scholar and historian Bu-ston:

> Tibet's king and high-ranking ministers observed that dishonest sentient beings of the future would not understand the profound intentional import [of the texts], and would apprehend the symbols literally. Without even the slightest unification of art and wisdom, they would be educated in the mantras without being bound to even a

---

[215] See Strickmann's summary of Yi-xing and Śubhakarasiṁha's defense of the Buddhist *homa* rite (1983, 425–426).

[216] The translation activity during the Tibetan imperial period occurred over a period of about two hundred years, from the mid-seventh to mid-ninth centuries. Karmay has concluded: "Already towards the end of the 8th century A.D. there was the question of whether the Tantras, especially the anuttarayoga-tantras, were to be practiced literally. Finally, it was decided that such Tantras should be translated into Tibetan only when royal permission was given." (1980a, 151)

> single commitment concerning [what behaviors are] to be avoided or cultivated. These practitioners of the immodest, deviant, semblant tantras of the heretics would denigrate the Teachings of the Buddha and engage in a method of destroying both self and other. Hence it was decided through royal proclamation that there was to be no translation of the Mahāyoga Tantras except when permission is granted.[217]

Apparently, during the imperial period the Tibetan kings were particularly concerned with the rites of black magic (*abhicāra*)—including rites to destroy the king—that are included in many of the tantras, and which occur prominently in the Unexcelled Yoga Tantras such as the *Cakrasamvara*.[218]

Controversy concerning these texts continued in India well beyond the eighth century. Ānandagarbha, writing during the ninth century,[219] makes the more general statement that the *Guhyasamāja* as a whole was taught for the purpose of converting a certain type of non-Buddhist religious practitioner. He wrote that the *Guhyasamāja* was taught in order to bring into the Buddhist fold[220] those

---

217 Bu-ston, *rgyud sde spyi'i rnam par gzhag pa*, 127.

218 While we do not know which tantras were actually censured during the imperial period, we do know that some were selectively translated, with transgressive passages excluded. The absence of passages describing the fierce *abhicārahoma* rite in the early dynastic translation of the *Sarvadurgatipariśodhana Tantra* (SDP) was evidently due to censorship. Van der Kuijp reports that "Grags-pa rgyal-mtshan refers to some earlier exegetes who opined that these two passages were lacking in the SDP because earlier kings and ministers had prohibited their translation out of fear of antagonistic tantric practitioners. He, however, is of the view that they were indeed translated... but were never included in the authoritive translation." (1992, 116)

219 Tāranātha places Ānandagarbha during the reign of King Mahīpāla, who died, according to him, at the same time as the Tibetan King Ral-pa-can, in 838 CE (Chimpa 1970, 284). Tāranātha appears to confuse the Pāla succession, as the first Mahīpāla did not rule until much later, c. 992–1042 CE (Davidson 2002b, 52). There was however, a Gurjara-Pratīhara king named Mahīpāla who came to the throne c. 910 CE (Davidson 2002, 49), which seems the most likely basis for this report. Lessing and Wayman place him during the tenth century, but do not state their reasons for doing so (1978, 24).

220 That is, cause them to take refuge in the Three Jewels, generate the spirit of awakening, and enter into the maṇḍala.

> low born ones who are opposed to the other tantras and who are inclined toward malicious deeds, who have the karmic obstruction of the inexorable sins,[221] and so forth, who adhere to the teachings in the Viṣṇu, the Ḍākinī, and the deviant tantras, who kill, who do not give but take, who tell lies, who "practice" with their mothers and daughters, and who enjoy both suitable and unsuitable foods.[222]

The "Ḍākinī Tantras"—which by Ānandagarbha's time very well may have specifically referred to Yoginī Tantras such as the *Samayoga* and *Cakrasamvara* which highlight the ḍākinī—do indeed contain multiple references to the transgressive practices of the sort that he describes here. However, his argument is disingenuous, as the *Guhyasamāja* is likewise replete with such references. Undoubtedly, for Ānandagarbha, what is "deviant" for others is "skillful means" for his own tradition.[223]

During the tenth century, at the beginning of the "second transmission" of Buddhism to Tibet, king Lha bLa-ma Ye-shes-'od, who ruled in Pu-hrangs in Western Tibet, doubted the orthodoxy of transgressive tantric practices, particularly the sexual rites, violent rituals, and offerings of impure substances described in many of these texts. He sent Rin-chen bZang-po to India to learn if such teachings were orthodox or not.[224] Rin-chen bZang-po confirmed that they were quite popular in India at the time, as he translated several of them, including the *Samayoga* and the *Cakrasamvara Tantras*. Nevertheless, some Tibetans remained suspicious of these teachings. During the eleventh century, the king's grand nephew, Zhi-ba-'od—the younger brother of King Byang-chub-'od who would invite Atīśa to Tibet—would write the following in an open letter: "Although the 'Mother

---

[221] The *pañcānatarīya*, which are: 1) *pitṛghāta*, killing one's father; 2) *mātṛghāta*, killing one's mother; 3) *arhatghāta*, killing an arhat; 4) *tathāgatasyāntike duṣṭicittarūdhirotpādanam*, drawing the blood of a tathāgata with an ill intention; and 5) *saṁghabheda*, causing a schism in the saṁgha. (Rigzin 1986, 343)

[222] Ānandagarbha, *Guhyasamājamahātantrarājaṭīkā*, 2a.

[223] He likewise explains (fol. 4a) that the notoriously erotic Guhyasamāja *nidāna* verse is a skillful means to help practitioners of the Hindu tantras who are addicted to sex "renounce passion by means of passion."

[224] See Karmay 1980a, 154.

Tantras' are excellent, they nevertheless cause many monks to break their monastic vows as a result of not knowing the implications of certain terms. There will not be any contradiction if they are not practiced at all."[225]

Despite his wishful thinking, the "Mother Tantras" did become very popular in Tibet, in spite of (if not because of) their explicit erotic imagery and references to sexual practices. The next section will focus on the nature of this imagery and these practices, and the ways in which they were treated in the Buddhist monastic contexts in which these texts were preserved and disseminated.

To return to the ḍākinīs, they were initially considered to be a class of non-human beings, akin to the rākṣasī demonesses, who were notable for their carnivorous appetite. They were also associated with "perverse" or "heretical" practices. These elements converge in a legend reported by Śubhakarasiṁha and his disciple, Yi-xing, in their *Commentary on the Mahāvairocana-abhisambodhi Sūtra* (T. 1796). In this text, composed during the early eighth century, the ḍākinīs are portrayed as "heretical" sorceresses who are followers of Mahākāla, and who have the nasty habit of killing people in order to consume the concretion that exists in their hearts in order to acquire magical powers. Vairocana manifests in the form of Mahākāla and subdues them. He makes them promise not to kill people, but to consume only the concretion of corpses. He teaches them a special mantra, *hrī hā*, which enables them to locate the bearers of this precious commodity six months prior to their death.[226]

This legend curiously corresponds to the *Cakrasamvara Tantra*, which in several chapters (11, 12, 49) teaches the virtues of consuming this concretion or bezoar (*rocanā*), found in persons "born seven times a man." Such persons can be discovered through the application of Śrī Heruka's quintessence mantra, which contains the ḍākinī mantra.[227] The *Cakrasamvara Tantra* thus appears to advocate the "heretical" practice of magical anthropophagy that so concerned Śubhakarasiṁha.

---

225 Translated in Karmay 1980b, 17; text edited at p. 19.

226 This is a summary of text at T. 1796.39.687b-c. For a translation of this text, see Gray 2005a.

227 This mantra is *oṁ hrī ha ha hūṁ hūṁ phaṭ*. Ch. 12 describes this application of the mantra.

While the *Cakrasamvara Tantra* was certainly not one of the Ḍākinī or Bhaginī Tantras to which Dharmakīrti referred, it may have been influenced by an older text or tradition which might have been so labeled at that time. If so, it is not at all clear that such a text would have been Buddhist; Buddhist texts such as the *Cakrasamvara Tantra* may have been the result of the Buddhist adoption and adaptation of texts and traditions belonging to marginal groups such as the Kāpālikas, who were noted for their involvement with the cult of Mahākāla. This adaptation process is marked in the area of iconography by the Buddhist production of Śaiva images in Kaśmīr during the sixth and seventh centuries,[228] which was probably the same period during which the early Buddhist myths of the subjugation of Śaiva deities were being composed.[229]

The first Buddhist text to portray the ḍākinīs in a manner that is not demonic is the *Samayoga*. This is perhaps the earliest text to propose the well-known "alliterative etymology"[230] for *ḍākinī*, deriving it from the root √*ḍā*, a likely variant of the verbal root √*ḍī*, "to fly."[231] This text describes the ḍākinī as follows:

> *Ḍā* means sky travel, and she who is directly realized in space, that is, who has achieved [the ability] to range all

[228] Regarding these images, see Granoff 1979.

[229] In addition to Śubhakarasiṁha's and Yi-xing's legends of Vairocana's subjugation of the Mahākāla ḍākinīs, there are the more significant myths such as the *Sarvatathāgata-tattva-saṁgraha Sūtra*'s account of Vajrapāṇi's conversion of Maheśvara, discussed in section 2.2 above.

[230] So-called "alliterative etymologies" are not etymologies in the true sense of the term, but are rather punning interpretations based on phonetic similarities between words. Yelle calls such etymologies "fictitious alliterative etymologies." (2003, 50) Regarding this sort of etymology in the *Upaniṣads*, Olivelle argues: "These are clearly not 'folk' etymologies; the authors of these documents were learned men, and these documents themselves demonstrate that the science of grammar had already reached a high degree of sophistication. These men clearly knew the philological etymologies of the terms they deal with, but their quest was not for such common and well-known connections, but for deeper and hidden ones, and they found in the sounds of the names a clue to those connections." (1998, 25) Tantric authors were likewise deeply interested in the hidden connections believed to exist between language and reality.

[231] This etymology was the basis for commentary such as Jayabhadra's gloss of *ḍākinī* as "those who travel in space" (D 4b.3, E 3b.4: *ḍākinyaḥ ākāśagāminyaḥ*). Such commentary surely inspired the Tibetan interpretive translation of *ḍākinī* as "space-goers" (*mkha' 'gro ma*).

> throughout the sky, is called the *ḍākinī*. She who is united with all buddhas by means of all *mudrā* without exception and the great bliss of all without exception is known as the *ḍākinī*. She who is the *ḍākinī* is composed of the buddha elements. The *ḍākinī* who is the self of all buddhas has achieved [the ability to] go everywhere. (JS 151a)

Thus, not only does the *Samayoga* here refrain from portraying the ḍākinīs as demonic, it portrays them as spiritual beings ("composed of buddha elements"); spiritual beings who, moroeover—judging by the erotic language describing their union with the buddhas—are evidently ideal partners for sexual practices.

However, this text does not unequivocally portray the ḍākinīs in this newly positive light, but retains elements of the older vision of ḍākinīs as carnivorous non-human beings.[232] Evidently, the ḍākinīs and yoginīs came to be viewed as dangerous entities that could nonetheless be subdued and used as consorts by intrepid, heroic yogins. Several early Buddhist tantras do in fact describe rituals in which yogins, secreted in isolated places, can summon a *yakṣiṇī* for this purpose. One such text is the *Mañjuśrīmūlakalpa*, a text which appears to have been composed by the eighth century.[233] It contains the following description of one such ritual:

> Now, one who desires to summon a *yakṣiṇī* should take her name and immolate it with Aśoka tree blossoms;[234] she will come and bestow the supreme. She will invariably come at the seventh [immolation] in seven days and will appear as one's mother, one's sister, or one's wife, as [one desires]. Now if she does not come, her head will burst.[235]

---

[232] In a latter section of the text the ḍākinīs are portrayed as evil, and classified with other nefarious non-human beings. See JS 157a, the text of which is translated in section 2.2 above (p. 41).

[233] See Wallis 2002, 9–11, 171–173, for a discussion of the dating of this text.

[234] That is, the flowers of "the tree Jonesia Asoka Roxb. (a tree of moderate size of the leguminous class with magnificent red flowers)..." (Monier-Williams 2002, 113.3).

[235] *Ārya-mañjuśrīmūlatantra: atha yakṣiṇī ākarṣayitukāmaḥ tasya nāmaṁ gṛhya saptāham aśoka-puṣpāṇi juhuyāt / āgacchati varaṁ dadati / saptame saptāhe 'vaśyam āgacchati mātā bhaginī bhāryā yaṁ cārocayati / atha na vāgacchati mūrdhanam asya sphuṭati* (Vaidya 1964, 229,

While the text does not specify what the "supreme" is, the specification that she will arrive in whatever form one desires, including one's mother, sister, and so forth, recalls the notorious passages in the *Guhyasamāja*, *Cakrasamvara*, and other Unexcelled Yoga Tantras suggesting them as ideal partners for sexual union.[236] This passage is preceded by a description of the "zombie" (*vetāla*)[237] rite for reanimating a corpse with a spirit, suggesting the Kāpālika-like charnel ground culture.

An even more explicit account occurs as follows in the *Subāhuparipṛcchā Tantra*:

> With regard to the *yakṣiṇī* rite, it bestows the powers of producing pleasure with mantra. One will succeed with one's mother, mother-in-law, maternal aunt, female friend, daughter, wife, or daughter-in-law. She, being one's mother, mother-in-law, or maternal aunt, is called the supreme achievement, like a wish-fulfilling jewel. One's beautiful friend or daughter is the middling achievement. One's wife or daughter-in-law is the lesser achievement. During the

---

although I read *vāgacchati* in place of *vā gacchati*, following the Tibetan at Tōh. 543, fol. 209b).

[236] This reference to categories of female kinship also occur in a similar passage in the *Subāhuparipṛcchā Tantra*, translated below. I believe that these earlier descriptions of the *yakṣiṇī-sādhana* are direct precursors to the erotic passages in the later Unexcelled Yoga Tantras that likewise make reference to these categories. There are numerous examples of these references, such as *Guhyasamāja Tantra* 5.6–7: "The adept who makes love with his mother, sister, and daughter obtains the great power, the reality of the pinnacle of the Mahāyāna. Making love with the mother of Lord Buddha, he is not defiled. Buddhahood is attained by that wise one who is free of conceptualization." (Matsunaga 1978, 15: *mātṛbhaginīputrīś ca kāmayed yas tu sādhakaḥ/ sa siddhiṁ vaipulāṁ gacchen mahāyānāgradharmatām// mātaraṁ buddhasya vibhoḥ kāmayan na ca lipyate/ sidhyate tasya buddhatvaṁ nirvikalpasya dhīmataḥ//*)

[237] The term *vetāla* has been translated by a wide range of terms from the English necromantic lore, including "demon, ghost, spirit, goblin, vampire (esp. one occupying a dead body)." (Monier-Williams 2002, 1014.3) While it is true that the *vetāla* rite involves summoning a spirit to inhabit a corpse, from which one can then exact a boon, none of these translations seem exactly right—to my knowledge, vampires are not reputed to reanimate corpses. Nor is Davidson's "ghoul" exactly right (2002b, 219), since this term derives from the *ghūl* of Arabic folklore, designating monsters that rob graves and feed on human corpses (Simpson and Weiner 1989, 6:495.3). Rather, the term "zombie" seems most appropriate, since this term derives from an African-Caribbean rite of reanimating a corpse with a spirit. See Davis 1988.

> three times one should worship her with flower garlands, perfumes, butter or sesame oil lamps, sandalwood, scented water, and incense. At night, one should always offer various sacrificial cakes.[238]

Later in the text, one learns the relationship between the adept's female relations and the *yakṣiṇī*. The reader is informed that:

> Although a woman is summoned by the power of mantra across hundreds of leagues of distance, she is not a woman but a *yakṣi* girl (*yakṣīkanyā*, *gnod sbyin bu mo*), who displays herself to the mantrin in that form which he has invoked for the sake of his lust. Insofar as he succeeds in this, it is given to him by the *yakṣi* girl, who, manifesting in the body of that woman, serves his lust throughout the night.[239]

According to Buddhaguhya, the fact that she is a *yakṣiṇī* and not the actual woman for whom the man lusts means that "he who lustfully enjoys her can be one who, in desiring to enjoy another's woman, avoids the faults of perverse incest, and so forth."[240] Apparently, by the eighth century the *yakṣiṇī*s and related non-human females were established as a class of beings to whom the fearless might look for sexual satisfaction, as well as for the possibility of the attainment of magical powers. But truly he would have to be a hero (*vīra*) to undertake such practice. Indeed, at a minimum he would need control of his mind and sexual functions. Thus the adept is warned: "The mantrin, hindering [the flow of] his semen at night, should energetically invoke and give rise to her. Otherwise, those who commence with deluded minds will be quickly destroyed by the *yakṣiṇī*."[241]

These texts do not appear to be exceptions; rather, they appear quite typical of the texts composed during the seventh and early eighth centuries.

---

[238] *Subāhuparipṛcchā Tantra*, 130b. I am indebted to Ronald Davidson for bringing the passages from this text and Buddhaguhya's commentary to light. For a discussion of these passages, see Davidson 2002b, 198, 203, 204.

[239] *Subāhuparipṛcchā Tantra*, 138b.

[240] Buddhaguhya, *Ārya-subāhuparipṛcchā-nāma-tantrapiṇḍārthavṛtti*, 52b.

[241] *Subāhuparipṛcchā Tantra*, 131a.

Another text translated by Śubhakarasiṁha, the *Susiddhikara Sūtra*, contains fascinating traces of the likely Śaiva-inspired cult of the charnel ground, although not with the same level of detail as the *Subāhuparipṛcchā*. For example, chapter eleven describes a ritual procedure for invoking deities with lamps, with different types of lamp oil used for different classes of deities. These include "mantra consorts" (真 言 妃) and "female spirits" (女 仙),[242] which call to mind the summoning procedures described above. Other deities that can be invoked include "heavenly deities" (天 神), such as "Mahākāla, and so forth" (摩 訶 迦 羅 等), and "lower class deities" (下 類 天), such as "the four sisters, Cāmuṇḍā, and so forth"[243] (四 姊 妹 遮 門 茶 等).[244] The text also instructs one to "use the fat of dog flesh when giving rise to zombies (*vetāla*, 吠 侈 羅), and so forth, in a charnel ground,"[245] which locates this text on the fringes of the charnel ground cult, at the very least. Texts such as these imply that the more transgressive Yoginī Tantras are really not as "degenerate" as they have sometimes been portrayed. Rather, they simply continued a trend already present in the earlier tradition, a trend that has been typically ignored, most likely for ideological reasons.[246]

The association between the ḍākinīs, yoginīs, and these dangerous but alluring females appears to have been maintained throughout the extremely

---

242 The term 女 仙 literally means "female immortals," but this translation is not appropriate in this context. Geibel translates this as "female seers" (2001, 169), but this is also inappropriate as it implies that they are human females. Geibel assumes that 仙 here translates a feminine form of *ṛṣi*, although it is not clear that such a form exists. Rather, it seems far more likely that this term here translates one of the many Sanskrit terms for non-human spirits, which is another use of the term 仙 in Buddhist texts. See Soothill and Hodous 1937, 166.1.

243 Cāmuṇḍā is an important Hindu goddess, attested by Bhāvaviveka in his *Tarkajvāla*, composed during the mid-sixth century. See Kapstein 2001, 240, 242–244.

244 *Susiddhikara Sūtra*, T. 893a.18.610b14–18. See also Geibel 2001, 169.

245 *Susiddhikara Sūtra*, T. 893a.18.610b18: (於 寒 林 中 起 吠 侈 羅 等 用 犬 肉 脂). See also Geibel 2001, 169. Note that the term I translate as charnel ground, 寒 林, is a literal translation of *śītavana*, a particularly famous charnel ground in India. See Soothill and Hodous 1937, 370.1.

246 Regarding the tropes of Buddhist "decline" and "degeneration" via the tantras, see Wedemeyer 2001. For a recent example of an attempt at tantric Buddhist historiography employing the "degeneration" trope, see Tsuda 1999, 144–146.

productive period of the composition of Buddhist tantras (seventh through ninth centuries). However, the (non-)human status of such female figures seems to have been ambivalent or mixed. For example, the *Bhūtaḍāmara Tantra* describes a *yoginī-sādhana* which involves the worship of a host of female *non*-human beings, such as *yakṣiṇīs*, celestial nymphs (*apsarasa*), serpent queens (*nāgarājñī*), and so forth. However, several of the yoginī classes appear to refer to *human* females.[247]

The *Cakrasamvara Tantra* likewise presents an ambivalent portrayal of the yoginīs and ḍākinīs. On the one hand, there are numerous indications in the text that the yoginīs are found among human females. Chapters sixteen, eighteen, and nineteen describe their appearances so that the yogin might recognize them. And having done so, chapters fifteen and twenty though twenty-four describe the yoginīs' code syllables, sign language, symbolic gestures and counter-gestures, and "symbolic speech" (*saṁketabhāṣā*) that the yogin needs to know in order to win their confidence and to communicate with them. Collectively speaking, these chapters seem to describe a countercultural yet distinctly human social context.

There are other sections of the text that seem to confirm this human nature and context. Chapter twenty-seven tells us that the "messengers" (*dūtī*), the companionship of whom are essential for the yogins seeking empowerment, "travel from town to town." They thus appear to be a peripatetic class of presumably human renunciant yoginīs. Moreover, chapter forty-one, which describes the twenty-four sacred places of Cakrasamvara, claims that "the ḍākinīs are all-pervasive, in all of the superior seats, and so forth. They are born in land after land, endowed with gnosis in their own places of birth." One might assume that the human females who inhabit these places are the referent here.[248]

On the other hand, following the list of twenty-four sacred places one learns that "the girls of these places are yoginīs who are nondual with

[247] These include the eight *sundarī*, "beautiful women"; the *kātyāyanī*, "middle-aged widows"; and, perhaps, the *śmaśānapraveśinī*, "females who enter the charnel ground," which could refer to human renunciant women, or possibly to the more ghoulish denizens of the charnel ground. Here the term *yoginī* appears to designate a wide range of divine or magical female entities. For a discussion of this text, see Bühnemann 2000, 41.

[248] Though apparently human, some are nonetheless decidedly ghoulish. The reader is informed, for example, that the yoginīs of Kośala are "carnivores who eat human flesh" (CS ch. 41: *piśitāśanā mahāmāṁsāśanāḥ*).

the heroes. They all have passionate forms, and their cessation [occurs] through the power of the mind." The latter part of the verse suggests that these "girls" (*kanyā*) are not human females but something akin to the "*yakṣi* girls" (*yakṣīkanyā*) of texts such as the *Subāhuparipṛcchā Tantra*, girls who are summoned through the power of mantra and the mind, and who are then dismissed afterward by the same means. Hence Bhavabhaṭṭa comments here that "when they—who in the exercise were made manifest by the mind—have been accomplished, then there is [their] cessation through the power of the mind."[249]

Thus, overall the *Cakrasamvara Tantra* exhibits an ambiguity regarding the nature of the female entities—as human versus non-human, as well as real versus imagined[250]—an ambiguity very similar to that exhibited in the Śaiva-Kāpālika tradition which clearly influenced it. Regarding this latter tradition, Sanderson wrote:

> The initiate moved from the domain of male autonomy and responsibility idealised by the Mīmāmsakas into a visionary world of permeable consciousness dominated by the female and the theriomorphic. Often transvestite in his rites he mapped out a world of ecstatic delirium in which the boundaries between actual women and the hordes of their celestial and protean counterparts, between the outer and the inner, was barely perceptible. Intoxicated with wine, itself the embodiment of these powers, he sought through the incantation of mantras and the offering of mingled menstrual blood and semen, the quintessential impurities, to induce the hordes to reveal themselves. Taming them with an offering of his own blood, he received from them the powers he desired. At the same time he was alert to perceive their incarnation in human women and was provided by the tradition with the criteria

---

249 Pandey 2002, 547: *yatra prayojane manaḥ pravṛttaṁ tatsiddhau tato manoveganivṛttiḥ.*

250 We should note that these ambiguities were preserved in the Tibetan tradition as well. For example, at several places in his autobiography 'Jam-mgon Kong-sprul describes meeting "ḍākinī with the body of a human woman" (Barron 2003, 48, 66), suggesting that for this nineteenth century Tibetan master at least, the categories of ḍākinī and human female were overlapping but not identical.

> by which he might recognize their clan-affinities. (1985, 201)

Much of Sanderson's characterization is applicable to the Cakrasamvara tradition as well, no doubt because of the latter's appropriation of elements from the Kāpālika textual and praxical corpus.

The slippage between human and divine or chthonic manifestations of the feminine is evident in the Cakrasamvara tradition's classifications of the "messengers," the female beings who confer the clan fluid in the consecration ceremonies. In commenting upon the "messengers" mentioned in chapter one, Bhavyakīrti proposes a threefold classification scheme of yoginīs who are "natural" (*sahajā*), "born at the yogic power places" (*pīṭhajā*), and "mantra-born" (*mantrajā*).[251] While at least one of these categories, the *pīṭhajā*, appears to refer to human females, the "mantra-born" clearly refers to the (magical) female sexual partners invoked by magical methods such as those described above; and chapter forty-five likewise describes a magical procedure for summoning a (magical) messenger. Moreover, there are several cases where the text portrays the yoginīs as the dangerous non-human beings of the older lore: chapters twenty-one and twenty-two refer to the ḍākinīs and yoginīs as "secret ones" (*guhyakā*), which is an old term for the *yakṣiṇīs*;[252] and chapter thirty-eight threatens the yogin who has broken his commitments (*samaya*) with the terrible fate of being devoured by the ḍākinīs and yoginīs, invoking their old portrayal as nefarious cannibal demonesses:

> Have no doubt that this bad natured one, who is a commitment killer, an evil doer, and a brahmin-slayer, will be eaten by many thousands of ḍākinīs. This deceived, bad natured one, a fool of wicked conduct: I will not rescue him when he is being devoured by the yoginīs. Amidst the secret ones the sacrificial victim is indeed this very adept

[251] SM 8b. See my translation of this passage below in the notes for CS ch. 1.

[252] In the context of ch. 21, Jayabhadra confirms this reference, noting that "**the secret ones** are the yoginīs" (E 25a.4–5: *gukhyakā iti yoginyaḥ*).

> who has fallen from the world of the Buddha, and who harms the guru and the commitments.[253]

These and other references demonstrate that the older model of the yoginīs and ḍākinīs as anthropophagic non-humans or quasi-human cannibals was still powerful when the *Cakrasamvara Tantra* was composed in the eighth century. Perhaps for this reason, the text promises the adept that its root mantra will protect him from these fearsome females. Following the selection of the hero's root mantra in chapter seven, the text states that "the wise know that the root mantra is the abode of all powers, that which pulverizes the hearts of the ḍākinīs." Bhavyakīrti holds that this means that "one draws their hearts forth and completely subjugates them." (SM 16b) The subordination of the ḍākinīs is also promised in chapter twelve to the adept who repeats the hero's quintessence mantra: "In that place where one repeats [the quintessence], all ḍākinīs will be the adept's servants."

This ambivalent portrayal of the ḍākinī and yoginī calls into question the thesis that the Yoginī Tantras, which do focus on female figures, reflect a positive assessment of women, and perhaps even the creative participation of women in the development of the texts and practices of these traditions. Scholars such as Miranda Shaw and Reginald Ray have painted what might be considered a somewhat romantic picture of the role of women in Indian tantric traditions. Shaw has argued that tantras such as the *Cakrasamvara* developed in a social milieu that elevated the spiritual role of women, honoring women in positions of power as gurus.[254] While it is possible that Shaw is correct, the texts themselves do not seem to support her thesis

---

253 My translation; see notes in the full translation in ch. 38 below.

254 Shaw argues that with regard to Yoginī Tantras such as the *Cakrasamvara*: "[S]ince these texts were not created by men in isolation from women, they do not express exclusively male views. These views grew out of communal exploration and practice and proceed from the insights of *both women and men*. Indeed, many of the insights contained in tantric writings can only find their source in practices done by women and men together. The texts openly present tantra as a religious path on which the lives of women and men are closely intertwined. I contend that the extensive descriptions of the interactions and shared practices of women and men are in themselves sufficient evidence that the *yoginī-tantras* are the products of circles consisting of both women and men. Therefore, I include women among the creators of the *tantras* and conclude that the texts reflect the views and interests of women as well as those of men." (1994, 36–37)

unambiguously, and the evidence she supplies is hard to verify.[255] Other scholars of tantric Buddhism have presented a similar ideal apologetic, arguing, from the same slight evidence, that women played positive and powerful roles in the development of tantric Buddhism in India.[256]

The primary sources of evidence cited to support the thesis that women played an important role in the development of tantric Buddhism in India tend to be anecdotal accounts recounted in hagiographic texts. Yet the textual record of Indian tantric Buddhism is largely androcentric, concerned with the needs of men. The portrayal of women in these texts, ranging from positive to hostile, expresses the male perspective. This was noted by José Cabezón, who warned that when we are "examining the textual traditions, we are for the most part examining culture as seen through the eyes *of men*." (1992, 189) Rita Gross corroborates this observation, writing that in the Buddhist tantric traditions "most texts and *sadhana*-s *are* written from the male point of view and *do* treat the woman as if she were an instrument rather than a partner." (1993, 105) Gross attributes this not to a lack of female tantric practitioners, but to the fact that their experiences "have been silenced by generations of androcentric record-keeping and patriarchal social norms." (1993, 91) The degree to which these experiences are recoverable, however, is not at all clear.

---

[255] Wilson has criticized Shaw's work on this basis, arguing that she "overplays her hand in claiming that she has succeeded where other scholars have failed to recover the experiences, voices, and historical agency of the women of Tantric Buddhism." (1996b, 64)

[256] For example, Reginald Ray argues that "the Vajrayana very strongly defines itself as a tradition for both women and men, even though, in sheer numbers, men practitioners and *siddhas* always outnumbered female practitioners and *siddhas*. Much of the Vajrayana's openness to women may be due to its complex and sophisticated psychology, which sees the human traits defined by other traditions and cultures as 'masculine' and 'feminine' as part of both men and women's psychological makeup. Therefore, women and men have the same inherent obstacles to overcome and the same inherent potential for spiritual discipline and enlightenment. All in all, the image of women *siddhas* presented in the traditional literature is highly positive; they are depicted as insightful, dignified, courageous, independent, powerful, and creative—the same qualities that are displayed by male *siddhas*." (1989, 199) Ray's account does not seem to be particularly relevant for the early period in India, and it is debatable if it is an accurate portrayal even of the modern Tibetan tradition. Judith Simmer-Brown, in her 2001 book, also provides a somewhat romantic portrayal of the ḍākinī, but she wisely refrains from speculating about the early Indian tradition, focusing instead on the Tibetan tradition.

There is a long history of androcentricity and misogyny in Indian and Buddhist literature going back to the early period.[257] Tantric Buddhist literature appears to largely conform to this trend. The main exception seems to be the tantric textual passages that instruct the male adept to treat his female consort respectfully and reverentially.[258] Yet even here the texts typically display androcentricity, portraying women as essential for the male adept's spiritual quest while usually remaining silent on women's quests and attainments.[259] This is the case even with texts attributed to female authors, such as Lakṣmīṁkarā's *Advayasiddhi*, which provides the following advice to the male tantric adept:

> One who knows mantra should generate no disgust for anything, for Vajrasattva himself exists as whatever form is before one's eye. The well-equipoised mantrin should not conceptualize where one should go or not go, what one should eat or not eat, and likewise drink or not drink… nor should he have disgust for a woman born of any class (*varṇa*), as she is the Blessed Lady Wisdom (*bhagavatī prajñā*) dwelling in a conventional form.[260]

---

[257] This has been well documented in Paul 1979 and in Wilson 1996a. See also Faure 2003 for an extended critique of Buddhist misogyny.

[258] See Shaw 1994 for many examples of this.

[259] This was a point of strong criticism by Snellgrove, who wrote: "Since all these tantric texts now under consideration have clearly been produced primarily for the benefit of male practitioners, the transference of the whole sexual symbolism to the human body is regularly described in terms of the male, although in theory at least it should also be applicable to the female. In the descriptions of the [Unexcelled Yoga Tantra consecrations]…, the feminine partner known as the Wisdom Maiden (*prajñā*) and supposedly embodying this great perfection of wisdom, is in effect used as a means to an end, which is experienced by the yogin himself. Moreover, once he has mastered the requisite yoga techniques he has no need of a feminine partner, for the whole process is reenacted within his own body. The reverse situation is scarcely suggested, namely that a woman requires a male partner in order to experience the Four Joys and that having mastered the technique, she can do it alone. Thus despite the eulogies of woman in these tantras and her high symbolic status, the whole theory and practice is given for the benefit of males." (1987, 287; insert mine)

[260] *Advayasiddhi* vv. 20, 21, 23: *jugupsāṁ naiva kurvita sarvavastu[ṣu] mantravit / vajrasattvaḥ svayaṁ tatra sākṣād rūpeṇa saṁsthitaḥ // gamyāgamyavikalpaṁ tu bhakṣyābhakṣyaṁ tathaiva ca / peyāpeyaṁ tathā mantrī kuryān naiva samāhitaḥ //… sarvavarṇasamudbhūtā*

This text is written for a male readership, as were virtually all texts, given the fact that the literacy rate for Indian women was almost certainly very low during the early medieval period.

It is possible that Shaw is correct and that centuries of selective preservation of tantric literature in male-dominated monastic institutions eliminated genuine female voices from the literature.[261] There are, in fact, passages in the earliest commentary—that by Jayabhadra—that seem to confirm her thesis. These include Jayabhadra's numerous explanations, many of which are translated below, that the rites described in the text call for an "outer woman" (*bāhyāṅganā*) who is well educated in mantra and tantra. His insistence here is fascinating; the stipulation that the woman be "well educated" suggests a social context in which the female adepts would have been relatively empowered, and perhaps even authority figures in their own right. But his constant insistence that they be *outer women* suggests that the need for actual, empowered women was challenged by others in his tradition. He was likely challenged here by monks who argued for the use of inner visualized consorts rather than actual human women. Jayabhadra was thus likely resisting the Buddhist tendency to efface the presence of actual women, and to reduce them to visualized "inner" presences. It is also possible, although less likely, that he may have been resisting the use of magically summoned, non-human consorts.

As tantric Buddhist practice was incorporated into monastic curricula—as occurred, for example, at Vikramaśīla—the necessity for female companionship was gradually downplayed and even effaced from the actual performance of tantric practices. Jayabhadra's commentary suggests that this process was underway by the ninth century. This tension persisted in later strata of literature, and gave rise to debates concerning the superiority of the different forms of *mudrā*, which will be discussed in section 3.3 below. There was considerable controversy in India during the eleventh century regarding the sexual components of tantric practice, which culminated, in the Tibetan context, in their replacement by non-transgressive symbolic substitutes. Yet at the same time there were also extra-monastic communities of

---

jugup[s]yā naiva yoṣitaḥ / saiva bhagavatī prajñā saṃvṛtyā rūpamāśritā // (Samdhong and Dwivedi 1987, 163).

261 See Shaw 1994, 75–78. See also Gross 1993, 18–24, as well as Davidson's critique of this thesis (2002b, 92).

tantric practitioners, such as those surrounding great saints such as Nāropa, which included important female practitioners, such as his consort Niguma, who were recognized as important teachers.[262] Shaw's case for empowered female practitioners may be more applicable to this relatively later period of the tenth and eleventh centuries. This, of course, was the crucial period when Tibetans were journeying to India.[263] If Shaw's hypothesis is correct, it is possible that this later period is representative of the earlier period as well, for which there are no eyewitness accounts to compensate for the presumed erasure of women from the textual record. Davidson, however, has argued strongly that there is no evidence for this aside from the Tibetan hagiographies, which may reflect more accurately the concerns of Tibetans rather than the actual state of affairs in India.[264]

A number of Yoginī Tantras, particularly the *Caṇḍamahāroṣaṇa Tantra*,[265] advocate respectful treatment for women, at least in the very limited sphere of the sexual yogic practices. This may be comparable to the

[262] Niguma is considered the founder of one of the traditions of "six yogas," *ni gu chos drug*, the popularity of which was exceeded in Tibet only by the set of teachings attributed to Nāropa. See Kapstein 1980, 140–141, as well as his 1992 essay. According to Tibetan sources, another female teacher active at this time includes Subhaginī, also known as Sukhasiddhī (Cuevas 2003, 47).

[263] We should note, however, that while the portrayal of the ḍākinī improves in Tibetan hagiographic literature, it remains somewhat ambivalent, and retains elements of the older portrayal of the dangerous, cannibalistic, quasi-human female. The biography of 'Khyung-po rNal-byor illustrates this nicely. It relates that 'Khyung-po, seeking the "*ḍākinī* of enlightened awareness called 'Niguma'," traveled to Sosadvīpa charnel ground where he encountered her. Rather than greeting him warmly, she threatened him as follows: "How do you know that I'm no cannibalistic witch? When my circle arrive, you'll be our dinner! You better be moving; be quick!" He offered her gold, but when she cast it away, he began to suspect her, thinking "Could she be a cannibalistic witch after all? She's not greedy for gold." (Kapstein 1992, 195–196)

[264] Davidson argues that: "We may conclude, however, from a variety of factors that these [hagiographic] texts are Tibetan reformulations and represent the accelerated involvement of women in esoteric Buddhism in eleventh- to twelfth-century Tibet. This increased involvement may be seen in Tibetan lineage lists and was invoked in an observation made bitterly by Shama Lotsāwa's sister, Shama Machig, to Indian Buddhist men she refused to teach because she was 'from a border country and, even worse (by Indian standards), a woman!'" (Davidson 2002b, 96; insert mine)

[265] See, for example, chs. 6–8 of this text, which are edited and translated in George 1974. Shaw 1994 also includes translations of excerpts of this text.

passages in Mahāyāna texts such as the *Vimalakīrti Sūtra* that argue for the equality of male and female.[266] While rhetoric of this sort might be interpreted as reflecting a more positive outlook toward women, we must also consider the argument of Bernard Faure that the rhetoric of the equality of the male and the female, often combined with an extolling of the latter, not only presupposes but reinforces the assumed inferiority of women.[267] The commitment that the male yogin not disparage the yoginīs[268] seems to derive in part, if not entirely, from the transgressive logic of the tantric sexual rites, which typically involved a higher status male and a much lower status female.[269]

Women and/or the female divinities are also portrayed in the Yoginī Tantras in accordance with Indian gender stereotypes. In particular, they are associated with the left direction, the "sinister" and inauspicious orientation. The *Cakrasamvara Tantra* repeatedly tells us that they favor "heteropraxy" (*vāmācāra*), which, as we learn in chapter twenty-eight, involves favoring the left side of the body, as well as engaging in behaviors that would ordinarily be considered polluting in Indian society, namely commensality with women who would likely be of low or outcaste social status. The association of women with the left is not an arbitrary or value-free association. As Jeffrey Kripal has observed:

> As in many cultures, right and left take on symbolic value in Indian culture. Generally speaking, that which is "right"

[266] See, for example, ch. 7 of this text, in Thurman 1976.

[267] Faure argues that, regarding the rhetorical identification of women with wisdom (*prajñā*) in Mahāyāna and tantric Buddhist literature, "far from extolling wisdom and women as a superficial reading would suggest, this imagery presupposes and reinforces the inferiority of women. Max Weber has already noted that the symbolic abrogation of gender difference usually goes along with a dichotomic system of gender segregation." (2003, 124)

[268] The CS has a particularly weak form of this commitment. Ch. 26 informs the adept that "the master and the mothers of yoga, being adepts in this Tantra, are excellent indeed. They should not be disparaged nor should they be insulted." This commitment seems particularly designed to protect the authority of the male guru, and extends also to his consorts, the "mothers of yoga," as the term "mother," in the context of the circle surrounding the guru, is usually understood to refer to his partner or partners.

[269] Women of untouchable status, such as from the caṇḍāla and ḍomba outcaste groups, are typically valorized in tantric literature. Indeed, these were two of the groups associated with the ḍākinīs in the *Laṅkāvatāra Sūtra*, as noted above.

> is modeled after the established order of *dharma*: it is pure, filled with light, socially acceptable, a model to emulate. That which is "left" is characterized as *adharma*, that which does not conform to the socio-religious order: it is impure, dark, antisocial, evil and in constant need of control. (1995, 48)

The correlation of women with the "left" likely expresses male anxieties. Moreover, the desire to control women and female sexuality is a common feature in the tantras. This suggests that the portrayal of women in these texts was largely generated by men and reflects uniquely male concerns.

Likewise, the tantric "male-female-in-union" sexual imagery largely emphasizes the male perspective, presupposing a male practitioner in whom the female deity is assimilated and subordinated.[270] While there are indeed some meditation traditions that highlight female deities such as Vajrayoginī/Vajravārāhī, and while some contemporary female Buddhists have found these deities to be empowering,[271] it is important to note that Indian *sādhana* texts typically presuppose the male body, implying that these traditions exemplify male-oriented spiritual androgyny, and thus are not genuine reflections of female-oriented religious practice.[272]

As one explores the passages in the Yoginī Tantras, it is very important that one pay close attention to the commentaries on them, for only these provide us with a reliable sense of how they were actually understood

---

[270] This is argued by Herrmann-Pfandt in her 1997 article.

[271] This includes both contemporary Asian and Western female practitioners. With respect to the latter, see Rita Gross' essay, "I will never forget to visualize that Vajrayoginī is my body and mind" (1998, 199–210). With respect to the former, see Kim Gutschow's account of Vajrayoginī practice as conducted by Zangskari nuns. Note, however, that while the nuns are encouraged to practice Vajrayoginī meditation, they are prohibited from performing the rites associated with this goddess, and must call upon the services of monks for the performance of rites such as the *homa* fire sacrifice. See Gutschow 2004, 226–235.

[272] For example, Umāpatideva's *Śrī Vajravārāhī Sādhana* describes a body maṇḍala practice —identical to that of the Cakrasamvara tradition—which includes the penis as one of the points on the body correlated to the maṇḍala. As English notes, "The body point 'penis' poses a problem for the Vajrayoginī tradition in that the body maṇḍala is supposedly conducted by the yogin who has self-generated himself as the goddess Vajravārāhī." (2001, 511 n. 577) Evidently, Umāpatideva presupposed that the practitioner would be male, whose actual sexual anatomy trumps the visualized sexual anatomy of the goddess.

by Buddhists in specific times and places. We might take, for example, the following verse in chapter twenty-three of the *Cakrasamvara Tantra*: "The devoted woman who is beloved by him should be enjoyed by the hero, [like] the earth. Taking her as one's support and ground, worship the binding in union." Shaw interprets this as "honoring both women and the earth as sources of life, energy, and physical and spiritual well-being." (1994, 44) Of course, we do not know the intentions of the author or authors of this text,[273] and it is certainly possible that Shaw's interpretation reflects an early understanding of the text. However, her interpretation is not shared by any of the Indian Buddhist commentators whom I have studied.[274] Bhavabhaṭṭa, writing in the late ninth-century, gives the following interpretation:

> The **devoted woman**, i.e., the yoginī who has the general commitments, who is pleased by a yogin **should be enjoyed by the hero, [like] the earth**. The hero is a champion; his is the hero's enjoyment. The earth is that which holds wealth and treasures. This means that, having advanced upon the earth full of treasure, it is enjoyed by him.[275]

In other words, the yoginī is an object to be approached and enjoyed by the "heroic" yogin, just as a king advances upon and enjoys the earth. This commentary was no doubt the product of a cultural world that was increasingly characterized, as Davidson has argued, by the "idealization of warfare and the apotheosis of kingship."[276] It is perhaps significant that while

[273] Even if authorial intention is recoverable (and this is far from clear), we are severely hampered in the case of the CS by the fact that we know almost nothing about the author or (more likely) authors of the text. At best, we can estimate very roughly its time and place of composition, as noted above. It also seems likely that it was not composed in a normative monastic Buddhist setting.

[274] For Shaw, this fact would not negate but would rather support her thesis, since she argues that the latter Buddhist monastic tradition actively erased evidence of the early participation of empowered women. Of course, the commentators all fall into the category of potential perpetrators of this erasure.

[275] Pandey 2002, 123: *samayinī samānasamayā yoginī saṁtuṣṭā yoginas tasya vīrabhogyā vasuṁdharā syāt / vīraḥ subhaṭas tasyaiva bhogyā vīrabhogyā / vasūni ratnāni dhārayatīti vasuṁdharā / ākramya ratnapūrṇā pṛthvī tena bhujyata iti bhāvaḥ.*

[276] Davidson 2002b, 68. See also ch. 2 of Davidson's work, esp. pp. 68–74.

Shaw's thesis postulates an early gynocentric tradition in India which was later marginalized and erased, she turns to a later Tibetan commentator for support. She quotes a brief passage from the chapter abstract in Sachen Kun-dga' sNying-po's commentary, written during the mid-twelfth century.[277] A more complete comment on this passage occurs later in his commentary as follows:

> As for the **hero's**—i.e., the adept's—**enjoyment**, this enjoyment [serves] as the cause for generating the excellent qualities within the adept's continuum. [One] relies [on that], just as one [relies] on the earth. [One] relies on that because [by so doing] the many excellent qualities arise in the adept's continuum. Regarding the explanation of this, the **support** is the yoginī's vulva (*dharmodaya, chos 'byung*).[278] Since it is the support which gives rise to good qualities in the yogin's continuum, it says **taking her as one's support**. (PG 334.3)

While this text does not objectify women as obviously as Bhavabhaṭṭa's, it does not unambiguously support Shaw's thesis either. Rather, it is a typical example of tantric Buddhism's androcentricity, portraying women as objects and instruments of male pleasure and spiritual needs. As Faure argues regarding tantric Buddhism:

> The utopian quality of this tradition is evident, and the freedom it claims for its female adherents is equally problematic. The real woman is only a means to an end, a kind of "transitional object." She is denied, inasmuch as she has to hide behind a divine mask. Admittedly, this kind of double-role, like that of female mediums, might constitute a form of power, a way to assert one's voice—but always in the name of another, under a false identity. It remains a form of alienation. In short, Tantric ritual offered a role to women, as long as they observed the rule of the game.

---

[277] Sachen lived from 1092–1158 CE. Shaw 1994 (45) quotes Sachen's PG 334.2.

[278] Regarding the interpretation of the term *dharmodaya* as indicating the vulva (*bhaga*), see Bhavabhaṭṭa's commentary, translated in the notes to CS ch. 5 below.

> Admittedly some women, under favorable circumstances, were able to play this game well and turn it to their own advantage, but they remain the exception to the rule, and their success is to their credit as individuals, not as passive followers of some egalitarian teaching. (2003, 126)

Indeed, in either the textual or archeological record, the appearance of Tantra in India seems to be marked *not* with any notable rise in the presence of women in Buddhist institutions, but rather with a decline.[279] Moreover, Davidson may be right in arguing that the rise of tantric forms of Buddhism contributed to this decline.[280] It may not be a coincidence that the passages in the *Cakrasamvara Tantra* that provide the strongest evidence for the active presence of human females, that is, the chapters on the clans of Yoginīs and their characteristics, may derive from non-Buddhist sources, if Sanderson's claims are correct.

Likewise, while tantric Buddhism died out in India, closely related Hindu traditions survived. And we see in these movements a social phenomenon rather similar to what was described in the Buddhist texts. Bholanath Bhattacharya, who conducted field work among tantric Hindu groups in Bengal during the 1970s, describes males who conduct searches for suitable female partners for their *sādhanas* in a (1977) series of articles. Such female partners were typically found among the socio-economically deprived outcaste groups, and were often women forced by economic need to engage in degrading occupations such as prostitution. Interestingly, it is

---

[279] Most notably, the early medieval period saw the disappearance of the order of nuns in India, and with it the possibility for an institutionalized spiritual role for women in Buddhism. Regarding this, see Falk 1989.

[280] Davidson argues: "Our sources suggest that, even while individual women exercised power and authority in political and economic affairs in specific regions during the medieval period, they did not extend that involvement into Buddhist institutions. We have many ways of determining the approximate percentages of women participating in Buddhist activities; particularly important are epigraphic, ethnographic, and textual sources. These sources show a remarkable convergence: women probably constituted between 1 percent and 20 percent of individuals acting in most religious capacities from the medieval period to the present. The data are sketchy, but they indicate that women's numbers precipitously declined during the period of esoteric Buddhism, particularly in high status and authoritative religious positions. Far from being supportive of women's participation, the Mantrayāna was decidedly deleterious to the religious aspirations of those women desiring participation as independent and equal persons." (2002b, 92–93)

precisely women from these same outcaste groups who are valorized in the Buddhist tantras as ideal candidates for consorts. Chapter forty-one of the *Cakrasamvara Tantra* describes a large number of yoginīs present in South India as follows: "At Pullīramalaya and Kanakagiri there are twenty-one thousand women born in caṇḍāla families." Bhavabhaṭṭa notes that they are born as outcastes. Jayabhadra explains that "as for the multitudes of 21,000 accomplished yoginīs, they wander in the form of those who are deprived, yet they abide in the triple wheel."[281]

There is thus a pall of exploitation that lingers over these traditions, as June Campbell has suggested in her (1996) critique of contemporary Tibetan traditions. This is not to say that these relationships are and have always been exploitative, or that there is no possibility for women in these traditions to rise to positions of spiritual authority. On the contrary, we know that this did at times occur—Lakṣmīṁkarā is a perfect example of this. However, Lakṣmīṁkarā evidently represents a small and exceptional minority; her attainment of spiritual authority in the tradition may have been aided by the fact that she was initially of high social status, a princess in fact, and was thus possessed of the social capital (such as literacy) and the economic capital to establish herself as an authority within the tradition. As such, she appears to have been an exceptional figure, as were the Buddhist men who sought to challenge the misogyny that pervaded their cultural traditions.

3.3 Consecration and the Sexual Yogas

The preceding section frequently alluded to, but left open, the question of the sexual practices associated with the *Cakrasamvara Tantra*. The texts of this tradition indicate that some sort of sexual practice is required of the adept. Ascertaining exactly what sort of practice, however, presents a serious methodological challenge. That is, it is probably not possible to conclude from the basis of textual evidence alone exactly what practices were undertaken by a given community. Rather, we are presented with the rhetoric of sexual practices, which reflects at least an *ideal* of practice, even though the exact degree to which this ideal was literally put into practice is unknowable, since it is not possible to assume that textual passages accurately reflect the practices of the communities who created or preserved them.

---

281 See the notes to my translation of ch. 41 below.

However, in the case of the Cakrasamvara and related tantric traditions the epistemological uncertainty is less acute than that faced by scholars of traditions such as Mediterranean Gnosticism, for which much of the evidence is contained in the polemics composed by critics.[282] In the case of this tradition, our evidence largely consists of texts composed by and for initiated members of the tradition. Some of these, as we shall see, are quite specific regarding practices involving sexuality. While the degree to which such practices were actually performed is uncertain, it seems likely that they were performed to some degree, as there also exist criticisms of their *practice* written by members of the tradition. The existence of such criticism strongly suggests that there were Buddhists who interpreted the texts literally and practiced accordingly. It also indicates that there were multiple interpretations of the text, and that its interpretation was a contested issue.

In this section I will seek to shed light on the nature of these practices involving sexuality on the basis of texts in the Cakrasamvara tradition. There are several types of these practices, which fall under the general rubrics of "sacramental practices" and "sexual yogas." The latter, the so-called "sexual yogas"—spiritual disciplines conducted in conjunction with or while engaged in sexual activities—seem to be evidenced only in the context of the later tradition. It is not at all clear if such practices were conducted or advocated by the author(s) of the Tantra itself. For while the Tantra makes numerous references to sexual acts or substances, none of these can be unambiguously taken as descriptions of the complex sexual yogic practices that the later tradition advanced. Rather, the Tantra seems preoccupied with the sacramental consumption of sexual fluids, for the production of which sexual activity was a requisite. Later scholars who wished to read into the text descriptions of the sexual yogas had to do so via exercises of creative commentary.

The notion that sexual fluids have creative power is not unusual.[283] In India, there was long-standing concern regarding their proper use. On the male side, there was anxiety concerning the loss of virility via the loss of

---

[282] See Goehring 2000, 331–334.

[283] There is evidence for the sacrificial consumption of mixed sexual fluids in other cultural contexts. See Goehring 2000, 340–343, for a description of the *agape* practice of the Phibiobite Gnostics as described by Epiphanius.

semen.[284] On the female side, as Wendy Doniger has shown, while female sexuality was rightly invested with great power and potency, there was a tendency to bifurcate women into the benign role of mother, whose milk is a life-giving fluid, and the dangerous and potentially malevolent role of a sexual aggressor, whose reproductive fluid, uterine blood, was viewed with trepidation and treated accordingly as a taboo substance.[285] Women were often viewed as dangerously vulnerable to sexual desire,[286] and the sexual aggression to which they were allegedly prone was personified in the figures of the dangerous females, such as the *yakṣiṇīs* and ḍākinīs,[287] who were particularly notorious for their love of flesh and also their consumption of male sexual fluids, often to the extent that they would "drain" their unfortunate male victims, thereby killing them.[288]

Buddhist and Hindu tantric traditions, following this cultural logic, call for a heroic male adept (*vīra*) to engage these demonic females, and to invert the power dynamic. As Sarah Caldwell has pointed out, the *yakṣiṇīs* were popularly imagined to be sexual vampires, draining and destroying the unfortunate men whom they seduce.[289] Thus, the tantric adept is often

---

[284] See for example the *Bṛhadāraṇyaka Upaniṣad* 6.4.1–10 (Olivelle 1998, 154–157). It compares sexual intercourse to the act of sacrifice, and claims that a man who has this knowledge appropriates the woman's merits, while one who lacks this knowledge loses his merits to the woman. See also White 1996, 339–342.

[285] See O'Flaherty 1980, 33–61. See also White 2003, 68–73.

[286] Diana Paul has argued this with respect to Buddhist literature (1979, 3–50).

[287] This was argued by Gail Sutherland, who observed: "The etiology of the demonic aspect of these yakṣīs and other related female spirits, such as *rākṣasīs* and *nāgīs*, in the folk logic that surrounds their mythology, [is] rooted in abrogations of the feminine nature. Women, it is believed, are defined and compelled by overwhelming reproductive needs that, when denied and truncated, result in their actual transformation into a demonic form. Or as we have seen, when they allow their passions and jealousies to override their fixed social duties, their failure is often depicted metaphorically as a descent into the demonic." (1991, 145)

[288] See White 2003, 72–73. As he notes, a fifth century Buddhist text studied by Michel Strickmann attributes nocturnal seminal emissions to the demonic interference of the Yakṣī named Bhūtī.

[289] See Caldwell 1999, 162–170. These dangerous non-human females are mythic embodiments of the common South Asian belief in aggressive female sexuality that must be controlled in a properly ordered (male-dominated) society. Wendy Doniger (O'Flaherty 1980, 1985; Doniger 1999) has documented this extensively in the South Asian context. Tibetan

warned of the need for mental stability, since being controlled by or overwhelmed with lust here results in death, as the *Subāhuparipṛcchā Tantra* informs us. Instead, he should use his knowledge to extract the powerful sexual substances from the female, taming her in the process. As Gail Sutherland has argued:

> In the Tantric context, the symbolic domestication of the wilderness, which the yakṣa embodies, takes the form of the sexual subjugation of the wild (i.e., erotic) yakṣī by the male practitioner. Her undomesticated sexuality is brought to heel and transmuted into familial goodwill, serving simultaneously and conversely as a metaphor for her actual sexual enslavement by the practitioner. (1991, 147)

Indeed, tantric Buddhism does show a propensity toward the rhetoric of the "family" or "clan" (*kula*), which is, as we shall see, structured around the patriarchal figure of the guru.

While the *Cakrasamvara Tantra* was later interpreted as referring to complex sexual yogic practices, on the surface the text seems largely concerned with the practice of transgressive behavior patterns, involving the acquisition and consumption of substances that are ordinarily considered polluting in many Indian social contexts, including meat, alcohol and other intoxicants, and bodily effluvia. Among these, there is a particular focus on the consumption of meat and sexual fluids. These two are in fact linked in the traditional Indian medical perspective.[290] The *Laṅkāvatāra Sūtra*, for example, provides the following reasons why a yogin should not eat meat: "Since it is related to oneself (*svājanyād*),[291] is a transgression, arises from

culture has likewise portrayed women as sexually aggressive, and has projected this portrayal onto non-human female beings. See Gutschow 2004, 212–218.

[290] According to Ayurvedic theory, the food we eat passes through a sevenfold series of transmutations (including flesh, the third step), before reaching the ultimate step, semen in males, and uterine blood and breast milk in females. See White 1996, 340.

[291] Presumably the point here is that the human body, too, is composed of meat, although the text may be making the point that all living beings are interconnected, an argument the text makes previously via recourse to the concept of the *dharmakāya*. See Vaidya 1963, 104.1–5.

semen and blood,[292] and is terrifying to living beings, the yogin should avoid meat."[293] Several centuries later, the fact that meat is a transgression (*vyabhicāra*) would commend its consumption. But there are further reasons for this as well; evidently the consumption of meat stimulates the production and flow of the requisite sexual fluids that the yogin needs to gather and consume as an essential component of his tantric "commitment" (*samaya*). The *Cakrasamvara Tantra*'s thirty-third chapter opens with the following instructions:

> Furthermore, it is not the case that all are adept in all yogas, capable of feasting to the extent of their ability on fish, flesh, and so forth. One should partake of the five foods, and so forth, with relish, even when they are not present. At night one should always undertake extensive feasting. Then the messenger should be bestowed. Placing one's head in her lap, she is worshipped in the fashion of the nondual hero. Whether or not she is one's mother, sister, daughter, kinswoman, or wife, should one do thus in accordance with the rite, one will be free of all bonds.

One of the primary purposes of this feasting and sexual activity, euphemistically referred to as "nondual hero worship," is the gathering and consumption of the mixed sexual fluids, semen and uterine blood.

The first chapter of the *Cakrasamvara Tantra*, which is often taken by the commentators to be an abstract of the Tantra's contents, dedicates four and a half of its sixteen verses to this process, most of which are apparently derived from two of the older Buddhist tantras which are mentioned in the Tantra. The first of these four and a half verses is verse six, which reads: "The clanswoman indeed should be constantly worshipped at the special occasion, with the central, superior breath, accompanied by scented water." Jayabhadra comments here that:

---

[292] This is undoubtedly a reference to the Ayurvedic theory that conception occurs through the union of male semen and female uterine blood. See Wujastyk 2003, xix.

[293] *Laṅkāvatāra Sūtra* 8.4: *svājanyād vyabhicārāc ca śukraśoṇitasaṁbhavāt / udvejanīyaṁ bhūtānāṁ yogī māṁsaṁ vivarjayet //* (Vaidya 1963, 104).

> Regarding **central**, and so forth, the **central** one is the lotus, which is said to exist in the center. On it is the **superior breath**, which is the placement [there] of the tongue. What occurs with this? It is **accompanied by scented water**, meaning it is accompanied by seminal essence. **Clanswoman** is [an example of] the Tantra's symbolic speech. One **should worship** an outer woman who has the self-nature of Vajravārāhī.[294]

Jayabhadra is not the only commentator to interpret this line in terms of the sacramental production of mixed sexual fluids, removed from the female participant's vulva with the tongue. Kambala likewise explains that

> Regarding **with the central, superior breath**, first, excite the lotus of an eleven-year-old for the sake of alchemy. Second, make pleasure with a twelve-year-old for the sake of the commitments. Third, meditate first on the mantra for the sake of magical power with a menstruating (*puṣpavatī, me tog dang ldan pa*) sixteen-year-old. Fourth, accomplish [the power of] flight (*khecarī*) with a twenty-year-old, who is the embodiment of wisdom. The fifth is the twenty-five-year-old, who is for the sake of consecration. These are indicated in accordance with the process of purification of the five wisdoms, the mirror-like, and so forth. (SN 4b–5a)

The second of these four and a half verses is the eighth verse, "Worship the buddhas and bodhisattvas with one's own seminal drops, with sight and touch, and with hearing and thought," which is intertextually related to a passage in the *Guhyasamāja Tantra*.[295] The final two and a half verses (11c–13) read as follows:

---

[294] E 8a.5–8b.1: *madhyametyādi madhyame bhavatīti madhyamaḥ padma ucyate / tasmin uttamo śvāso jihvāvinyāsaḥ / tena kiṁ bhūtena gandhodakasahitena tu bodhicittasahitenaivety arthaḥ / kulikām iti tantrasamayabhāṣā / vajravārāhīsvarūpāṁ bāhyāṅganā pūjayed iti /*. Note that the Tibetan translation does not translate *jihvā* (see MP 45a). I wonder if this was an oversight, or an instance of self-censorship on the part of the translators.

[295] The verse in question in the CS (ch. 1 v. 8) reads: *svaretobindubhir buddhān bodhisattvāṁś ca pūjayet / darśanasparśanābhyāś ca śravaṇasmaraṇena ca //*. The corresponding passage in the *Guhyasamāja Tantra* is even more erotic: "Through the union of the two organs, one's own

> There is honey and vermilion, mixed with camphor and with red sandalwood. Standing amidst the host, bearing the sign of the universal vajra mark, one should cause him to lick the tips of the thumb and ring finger, always knowing yoga. Consuming it as if it were the beverage *soma*, success is always attained. This should be the five ambrosias, the originator of all powers.

This passage is understood by the commentators as referring to the ritual consumption of sexual fluids in the second "secret consecration" (*guhyābhiṣeka*), with "camphor" (*karpūra*) and "red sandalwood" (*raktacandana*) referring to semen and uterine blood, respectively.[296] This text almost certainly derived from a longer passage in the sixth kalpa of the *Samayoga Tantra*, which contains the following description of the tantric feast (*gaṇacakra*):

> The women who are similar to one's deity who are well prepared, auspicious, and marked with one's insignia (*mudrā*)[297] should be examined in the tantric feast. The human blood that is called the "great blood" is achieved naturally with the powers of reality. Regarding the preparation of the great blood with the vajra water and the vajra, it is well prepared with power (*mthu*), inserted within the vessel of her lotus. The Blessed Lord of great passion, the Tathāgata Vajrasattva, who has the adamantine mind of all buddhas—difficult to surpass is his commitment. The great blood is prepared from uterine blood and the semen, and

---

vajra together with the lotus, one should worship the buddhas and vajrasattvas with one's own seminal drops." *svavajraṁ padmasaṁyuktaṁ dvayendriyaprayogataḥ / svaretobindubhir buddhān vajrasattvāṁś ca pūjayet //* (ch. 7 v. 26, ed. in Matsunaga 1978, 22). The clearly older *Guhyasamāja Tantra* may have influenced the CS here, but it is also possible that these are variants of what might have been an oral traditional text among siddha communities. I thank Dr. Christian Wedemeyer for suggesting this possibility.

296 These are common metaphors, used thus in Hindu texts as well (White 2003, 73, 79).

297 The *mudrā* here appears to be that sort defined at HT II.iv.15: "The *mudrā* is a sign or mark, and by this mark the clan (*kula*) is indicated. Through engaging in meditation with the wrong clan, there will be neither success (*siddhi*) nor one who succeeds." *mudraṇam liṅgaṇāṅkaṁ ca aṅkena lakṣate kulaṁ / vyastakulaṁ bhāvanāyogān na siddhi nāpi sādhakaḥ //*; (my translation from Snellgrove 1959, 2:64; cf. also Snellgrove 1959, 1:103).

> since it arises from great passion, it is called the great blood. Mix the great blood with camphor and red sandalwood. Going amidst the retinue, all of alchemy is gained. For one who has union with one's deity, consuming it as if it were the beverage *soma* from the tip of the thumb and ring finger, success is always attained. (JS 160a)

Surativajra comments on this passage as follows:

> The woman is **well** [prepared], that is, purified through the four [stages of] service and worship (*sevāsādhana*).[298] One visualizes her as one's own goddess, or [adorns her] with one's insignia together with facial ornaments and necklaces.... As for the substance of the tantric feast and the secret consecration, it is **the human blood that is called the "great blood,"** meaning self-arising blood.[299] Why is this necessary? **It is achieved naturally with the powers of reality**, meaning that one achieves the non-conceptual four joys that are devoid of the eighty natures **with the power of reality**—that is, the reality of passion[300] and the reality of entry[301] that are the roots of excellence and that augment life—**naturally**, that is, through the reality of emission.[302] How should one enjoy it? **With vajra water and the vajra**, meaning that the one who has power, through the power of reality, places the five ambrosias—that is, urine, feces, seminal essence, and great blood, together with meat—in a skull bowl, and he

---

[298] *Sevāsādhana* generally refers to the preliminary *sevā* practice of purificatory mantra recitation, together with the *sādhana* involving the ritual and visualization practices in which the deity or deity maṇḍala is invoked. Surativajra may be referring here to the four step *sevāsādhana* creation stage practice of the Guhyasamāja tradition. See Wayman 1977, 41–42.

[299] That is, uterine blood, as opposed to blood flows resulting from illness or injury.

[300] The Tibetan translation reads *kamatatva*, presumably transliterating Sanskrit *kāmatattva*.

[301] The Tibetan reads *beśānatatva*, presumably transliterating Sanskrit *veśanatattva*. It might also be a transliteration of *veṣaṇa*, "service."

[302] Reading *recatattva* instead of *reñjatattva*.

> realizes, in an illusion-like fashion, the commitment of the Blessed Lord Vajrasattva within [the goddess] Rasavajrī.[303]

Surativajra points to the two contexts in which the sexual fluid power-substances were to be generated, within the secret consecration and the tantric feast. The former is of particular significance within the text, and is in fact the only portion of the consecration ceremony that is described in any detail.

According to the commentaries and ritual texts, the Cakrasamvara consecration process follows the general pattern of the Unexcelled Yoga Tantras, which highlight four consecrations.[304] The second consecration is obliquely referred to in the chapter one passage quoted above, which refers to the guru causing the candidate to lick the sexual fluids from the tips of his conjoined thumb and ring finger. It is also described as follows in chapter three:

> The master, well equipoised, should worship the consort. On the second day he should make the drop for the disciples with blood thrice enchanted. Having unveiled his [the disciple's blindfolded] face, he should then show the maṇḍala to the disciple. He should show [the disciple] her in whom is the deity's place.

Jayabhadra explains this passage as follows:

> Immediately after that [i.e., after the preliminary worship of the maṇḍala], one performs all of the consecrations via

---

303 Surativajra, Tōh. 1660, 406a–b.

304 The four Unexcelled Yoga Tantra consecrations are: 1) the "vase consecration" (*kalaśābhiṣeka*), also known as the "master consecration" (*ācāryābhiṣeka*) or "sacred knowledge consecration" (*vidyābhiṣeka*); 2) the "secret consecration" (*guhyābhiṣeka*); 3) the "wisdom-gnosis" consecration (*prajñājñānābhiṣeka*); and 4) the "fourth consecration" (*caturthābhiṣeka*, also sometimes called the "word consecration" or the "name consecration"). The first (vase) consecration is actually a multi-step consecration process which includes all of the consecrations of the Yoga Tantras (cf. Snellgrove 1987, 213–243). These steps of the first consecration are not described in the *Cakrasamvara Tantra* itself, although some commentators read the opening verses of chapter three as referring to them (cf. the notes to my translation of CS ch. 3 below). In the discussion that follows below, we likewise will not be describing the first consecration, nor will we be discussing the fourth; we will rather be focusing on the second and (beginning on p. 116) third consecrations.

the rite celebrated in endless tantras; and as the secret consecration is preeminent, [the master] **should worship the consort**, and so forth, indicates the secret consecration. One's **consort** is an outer woman, well-educated in mantra and tantra, who has the commitments regarding what is to be protected and eaten. **Well equipoised** means that one re-envisions oneself through the yoga of Śrī Heruka, and one recreates her through the yoga of Vajravārāhī, and [both] should be armored with the great armors. **On the second day**, once again one worships the maṇḍala and produces the blessing, and so forth, sets up an abode of bliss, such as a mat, couch, and so forth, either in or near the maṇḍala, and commences with the secret consecration. Regarding **he should make the drop with blood thrice enchanted**, together with an outer woman who has the previously explained characteristics and who is menstruating, he gives rise to sexual joy by means of the process of drinking *soma*, and so forth. Then through the practice of rubbing the vajra and lotus, and so forth, when the [sexual fluids] are flowing, the essence, quintessence, and garland mantras are recited over the blindfolded disciple. Bestow the consecration with the vajra and lotus upon the [disciple's] seven spots—the crown, forehead, both eyes, mouth, throat, and heart. The disciple should consume it as if it were bliss-bestowing ambrosia. Immediately after that, his **face should be unveiled** and he **should be shown the maṇḍala. He should be shown her in whom** is the **deity's place of the lotus**, the place of the secret consecration. This means that he should be shown the outer woman who has the power to bestow consecration.[305]

---

305 E 13a.4–14a.1: *tadanantaraṁ ta[n]trānantanaprasiddhena vidhinā sarvam abhiṣekaṁ nivartyedānī[ṁ] guhyābhiṣekavidhipradhānatvāt / pūjaye[d] mudrām ityādinā guhyābhiṣekaṁ sūcayati / svamudrām iti / bāhyāṅganā mantratantrasuśikṣitā rakṣaṇīyabhakṣaṇīya-samaya-samanvit[ā] / sumsamāhitam iti ātmānaṁ śrīherukayogena dṛ[ṣ]ṭīkṛtya / tāṁ ca vajravārāhīyogena nirmāya mahākavacādibhiḥ kavacayitvā / dvitīy[e] ahaniḥ punar api maṇḍalaṁ sampūjyādhiṣṭhānādikaṁ kṛtvā maṇḍalamadhye maṇḍalasamīpe vā kāṣṭapaṭakhaṭvādi-sukh[ā]śaya[ṁ] saṁsthāpya guhyābhiṣekam ārabhate / raktena trijaptena tilakaṁ tasya kārayed*

The importance and necessity of this second consecration should not be underestimated. Chapter twenty-six lists the commitments (*samaya*) to which the initiated adept must adhere. These represent the behavior patterns that the author(s) of the text sought to reinforce, and thus the values of the tradition. A number of these refer to sexual practices in general, and several to the transfer of sexual fluids that occur in the second consecration and elsewhere. One of these commands is that "one is not hostile in the transfer of fluid." The commentaries leave no doubt that the "fluid" (*srotas*) referred to here is sexual fluid.[306] No doubt this command was necessitated by the fact that sexual fluids (and uterine blood in particular) were viewed as polluting substances in India. This was followed by the injunction: "The wise one should move his little finger." Bhavabhaṭṭa gives the following instructions in explaining the import of this:

> The rite of loving the messenger is indicated by **little finger**, and so forth. The channel called "bird face" (*khagamukhā*), which is like a *bandhūka*[307] flower, should be moved, i.e., stimulated, by the concave space [formed] by the tips of the ring and middle fingers as if around a seed, inserted within the flower. What is the purpose of this? **The messengers**, and so forth, indicate that [it is done in order to

---

iti yathāpūrvoktalakṣaṇānvitā bāhyāṅganā puṣpavatī bhavati tayā saha vā somapānādikrameṇa yathā harṣo jāyate / tathā vajrapadmāsph[ā]lanādikriyayā kṣaraṇāvasthāyāṁ mukhapaṭabaddhasya śiṣ[yasya] hṛdayopahṛdayamālamantroccāraṇaṁ kṛtvā śirasi lalāṭ[e] cakṣurdvaye mukhe kaṇṭhe hṛdaye ca saptasthāne[ṣu] vajreṇa padmena cābhiṣekaṁ dadyāt / śiṣyeṇāpi sukhadattam amṛtam ivākhādayet / tadanantaraṁ mukham udghā[ṭya] darśayen maṇḍalam / padmasya devatāsthānam iti guhyābhiṣekasthānaṁ tatra tāṁ darśayed iti / abhiṣekapradānasamarthīṁ bāhyāṅganāṁ darśayet ity arthaḥ /.

306 According to Jayabhadra, "**not hostile in the transfer of fluid** means that when receiving the seminal essence one should not be angered" (E 27a.3: *akrodhaḥ srotasaṁcāra iti bodhicittagrahaṇakāl[e] 'pratighāta[ḥ] kartavya ity*). Tsong Khapa explains that this means that "one does not generate conduct with hostility when taking up seminal essence with the tongue from a woman's lotus" (KS 142a–b). Vīravajra likewise states that "at the time of taking up the **seminal essence**, one does not give rise to the conception that it is filth" (ST 190a).

307 *Pentapetes phoenicea.*

> stimulate] the descent of the streaming intoxicant which exists within the messenger.[308]

The *bandhūka* flower, brilliant red with six petals and a white stamen, was commonly used, like the lotus, to symbolize the female sexual organ.[309] That direct stimulation, perhaps of the clitoris, stimulates the flow of the desired sexual fluid, suggests that this fluid is not necessarily uterine blood, but rather vaginal secretions. Commentators such as Jayabhadra, however, call for a menstruating woman here,[310] which implies that the resulting fluid would contain traces of blood.

By the ninth century, when Jayabhadra was writing, it is clear that a (presumably human) "outer woman" (*bāhyāṅganā*) was deemed essential for the performance of the consecration ceremonies of this tradition. Jaya-

---

[308] Pandey 2002, 487: *dūtyanurāgaṇavidhim āha kaniṣṭhām ityādi / khagamukhānāḍīṁ bandhūkakusumasadṛśīṁ kusumasadṛśena kiṁbījenānāmikāmadhyamāgrasampuṭanyastena cālayec codayet / kimartham āha dutaya ityādi / dūtīnāṁ samvyasthānaṁ svavasthānaṁ sravanmadatvam /.*

[309] See, for example, the *Caṇḍamahāroṣaṇa Tantra* 6.60 in George's edition (1974, 28), and its translation (1974, 69). See also the discussions at White 2003, 120–121, and Shaw 1994, 155–156.

[310] Terms used for the female's fluid include "[uterine] blood" (*rakta*) and menstual blood (*rajas*). Miranda Shaw argues that these terms in this context denote not uterine blood but rather vaginal secretions, which she argues are "red" with regard to the "endocrinal content of the female sexual fluid." (1994, 158) While Shaw is correct in noting that many texts, including Bhavabhaṭṭa's quoted above, suggest female sexual secretions, her argument is contradicted by some of the commentators. Jayabhadra, for example, explains that the "flower water" (*kusumodaka*) mentioned in CS ch. 42 (which will be quoted below) "is that which arises with a menstruating woman" (D 53b.2: *kusumodakaṁ puṣpavatyā sahotpannaḥ*). The term he uses here, *puṣpavatī*, is a well-known medical term that leaves no doubt that, for Jayabhadra at least, a menstruating woman is called for here. This may be precisely because sex with such a woman was ordinarily deemed polluting and dangerous. The resulting fluid would likely be vaginal secretion "reddened" (*rakta*) by blood. Evidently, there was some slippage here concerning sexual fluids, blood, and milk, which were seen as closely related substances, as Wendy Doniger (O'Flaherty 1980, 43–55) and David White (2003, 92–93) have noted. Yet these and other texts *do* clearly suggest that uterine blood is usually implied by these terms. A decisive example occurs in the *Muṇḍamālā Tantra*, where *kusuma* and *raktacandana* are defined as the blood of a virgin, who by definition has not engaged in sexual intercourse. It occurs as follows: "The flower or blood (*kusuma*) generated from the twining tendrils (*latā*) [of a maiden], who has not had sexual intercourse with a male, is known as the 'self-arisen flower' (*svayambhīkusuma*) or 'red sandalwood' (*raktacandana*), which is to be fed to the great Goddess." (White 2003, 78–79)

bhadra repeatedly states her prerequisite qualities, particularly the need that she be "well-educated in Tantra and Mantra" (*mantratantrasuśikṣitā*). Evidently, this "education" would take place in the context of the social world surrounding the guru. Indeed, the scandalous references to intercourse with one's "mother, sister, daughter" are explained as referring to the women within the guru's retinue, who together with him and his male students constitute the adept's alternate family. In commenting upon chapter twenty-eight's injunction, "One's mother, sister, daughter, and wife are accepted to be messengers," Durjayacandra explains that "the **mother** is the guru's consort, the **sister** one's fellow disciples, the **daughter** she to whom one gives one's oral instructions, and one's **wife** is given by the guru." (RG 294b–295a) This suggests that the female practitioners were assimilated in a family (*kula*) structure centered upon a patriarchal authority figure, the guru. While we know very little about the social context(s) in which such training might have taken place during the ninth century, it most likely would have occurred in the context of the circle of devotees surrounding an established guru. A model here might be the community that surrounded the great guru Nāropa during the early eleventh century at his retreat center, Phullahari. This center was located north of Nālandā, where Nāropa had lived as a scholar before undertaking tantric practice;[311] it might have served as a hermitage of sorts loosely associated with the monastic university. This may have been a venerable pattern, with communities of tantric practitioners having established relationships with some monastic institutions.[312]

The use of the family as a metaphor for Buddhist communities is not peculiar to tantric Buddhism, but occurs throughout the history of Buddhism. Buddhists often portray the monks and nuns, in renouncing their biological families, as joining a new family or lineage, that of the Buddha (*buddhavaṁsa*).[313] As Reinders has argued with regard to Chinese Buddhism:

---

[311] See Roerich 1949, 85. See also Trungpa 1982, esp. xxix.

[312] Stephen Hodge has argued, on the basis of textual and botanical evidence, that the *Mahāvairocana Sūtra* may have been composed in a forest retreat associated with Nālandā monastery. While his conclusions are speculative, they are fascinating, in part because they suggest that there may have been a long established association of tantric practitioners with mainstream Buddhist institutions. See Hodge 1994, 72–74.

[313] Concerning the history of these ideas, see Ruegg 1976 and 1989b.

> [T]he monk's disengagement from the family was simultaneous to his placement in a new pseudo-family, in a pseudo-genetic vertical lineage with ancestors, patriarchs, and sibling-like generations of disciples. This distinction involves time differences and transmission through a lineage. (1997, 257)

Tantric consecration likewise entailed one's entry into an alternative community, a *kula* or clan based not on genetic descent but rather spiritual inclination, hierarchically ranked vis-à-vis the guru who serves as one's father, the source of the spiritual "seed" transmitted to one during the process of consecration and subsequent instruction concerning the details of the theory and practice of the tradition. Through this transmission the disciple enters the guru's lineage and is empowered to learn the intimate details of the tradition's most secret practices, which are symbolically revealed during the third "wisdom-gnosis" (*prajñājñāna*) consecration that follows, in which the disciple, after having his blindfold removed, is instructed in the details of sexual yoga with the consort.

This process of transmission was represented using the symbols and *substances* of biological transmission. This use of biological imagery and materials to construct an alternative community and to represent the transmission of authority therein is not as unusual as it might seem at first glance. Weber noted that charisma could be conceived as an entity transmissible in certain ritual contexts, as follows:

> [C]harisma may be transmitted by ritual means from one bearer to another or may be created in a new person. The concept was originally magical. It involves a dissociation of charisma from a particular individual, making it an objective, transferable entity. In particular, it may become the charisma of office. In this case the belief in legitimacy is no longer directed to the individual, but to the acquired qualities and to the effectiveness of the ritual acts. The most important example is the transmission of priestly charisma by anointing, consecration, or the laying on of hands. (1968, 57)

Semen and blood, particularly menstrual blood, are clearly what could be called, following Marriott, "coded substances," substances that are both transmissible and potentially transformative. Marriott argues that

> persons—single actors—are not thought in South Asia to be "individual," that is, indivisible, bounded units, as they are in much of Western social and psychological theory as well as in common sense. Instead, it appears that persons are generally thought by South Asians to be "dividual" or divisible. To exist, dividual persons absorb heterogeneous material influences. They must also give out from themselves particles of their own coded substances—essences, residues, or other active influences—that may then reproduce in others something of the nature of the persons in whom they have originated. (1976, 111)

This concept of personhood appears to be active in the tantric context, where the transmission of these substances in consecration may have been conceived to do more than just *symbolize* the entry of the disciple into the vajra master's (*vajrācārya*'s) lineage, but to actually effect a transformation in the disciple's person.

Through the consumption of the sacramental fluids, the disciple then would be ritually established with a new family, the family centering around the figure of his guru. Doing so would confer other benefits as well. According to chapter twenty-seven of the *Cakrasamvara Tantra*, "By eating the water of bliss, one's merit is purified and one's sins destroyed." Although the tradition may be androcentric, it is undeniable that it does place great emphasis on female practitioners as essential for the successful completion of the yogin's *sādhana*. His consort in these practices is termed a "messenger," no doubt because it is she who confers the "coded" clan fluid (*dravya*) that confers bliss and success. The *Cakrasamvara Tantra* states in its twenty-eighth chapter that: "His messenger is supreme, divine, energized, and has a companion. Impassioned, she incites the yogic fluid through sexual union. Enamored with the guru's instructions, her aim is to be like the wealth giver."

The *Cakrasamvara Tantra* repeatedly refers to sexual union culminating in the production of sacramental sexual fluids as "worship" (*pūjā*), and it is clearly closely connected to the "worship of the vulva" (*yonipūjā*) that is frequently described in Hindu tantric texts, art, and architecture.[314] This "worship" is also termed the "consort observance" (*vidyāvrata*) or "great observance" (*mahāvrata*). In the *Cakrasamvara Tantra*, it appears that what was called for was sexual intercourse undertaken for the purpose of the production of the mixed sexual fluids for sacramental consumption. Kambala, commenting upon the term "seats of yoga" (*yogapīṭha*) in chapter twenty-six, interprets it as referring to this practice:

> The seats are well-known on earth to be spots within the lotus maṇḍala; by abiding within it there is great bliss, the royal nature of nondual joy. Therefore the lotus seat is supreme: filled with a mixture of semen and uterine blood, one should especially kiss it, and lolling with the tongue take it up. Unite the vajra and lotus, with the rapture of drinking [this] liquor. (SN 40a)

While the *Cakrasamvara Tantra* itself does not appear to directly describe sexual yogic practices of greater complexity than the simple generation and consumption of sexual fluids, the later tradition did read the text as referring to complex sexual practices that involve visualization and manipulation of the subtle body. Obscure passages in the Root Tantra were particularly subject to this sort of commentary. A typical example occurs at the opening of chapter twenty-three, a difficult passage that appears to be describing some sort of sexual practice. The Tibetan master Sachen comments on this both in terms of the postures and signs of sexual love as described in the literature on sexual love (*kāmaśāstra*), as well as in terms of the subtle yogic anatomy of the perfecting stage, as follows:

> From the perspective of the yogin being thus equipoised with her, **binding** refers to the maṇḍala of the Cakrasamvara. **Worship** is the cause of generating passion. One **worships** via the preliminaries of biting, scratching, embracing, kissing, and so forth. From the perspective of the cause of generating passion, that yoginī displays that she is

[314] See White 2003, 109 ff. for examples of these and discussions of their significance. See also Donaldson 1986 regarding the depiction of the *yonipūjā* rite in Orissan temple art.

> impassioned toward the adept. Regarding the actual signs that the yoginī is impassioned toward the adept, **gazing backward** means that the yoginī makes sidelong glances at the adept. The **alteration of her face** means that previously it is white, and later it turns reddish-yellow. **Unchanging bliss** means that her eyebrows quiver and her face is slightly flushed due to the generation of passion that is the cause of the generation of bliss, for the various actions—on the path of practice that achieves bliss which is brought to a climax by scratching, and so forth—quickly give rise to passion. When these **indications** of passion **arise in this way from the ḍākinī**, one **should recognize** that they should be taken to be four [types of] sexual union which give rise to bliss, such as the "swing," and so forth.[315]
>
> Above that ḍākinī's navel are **three lines** like half-moons. Relying on this indication that leads one to recognize her as a ḍākinī, one should know that she is one who gives rise to the gnosis of bliss. Moreover, all of the three worlds are blended together for the adept through the blazing of great bliss that climaxes through the yogic posture (*yantra*) that binds the life force and effort in the empty space of the navel maṇḍala. Also, it is said that "in that very instant, the thoughts of self and other, and likewise earth, water, wind, fire, and space, are all not conceived."[316] **In a moment they return** means that they, having given rise to passion, return to their previous forms and countenance. (PG 334.3–4)

Other commentators, as will be seen below, call for a cultivated experience of sexual orgasm—via the "four joys" (*ānanda*) or "four moments"

---

[315] The "swing" (*dpyang thag*) may refer to a method of intercourse in which the woman is on top, as mentioned in the *Kāmasūtra* (Doniger and Kakar 2002, 64).

[316] Sachen here quotes Kambala's commentary at SN 39a.

(*kṣaṇa*) system of the *Hevajra Tantra*[317]—which involves a controlled ejaculation, moderated by yogic postures (*yantra*) and the placement of seed syllables, followed by the reabsorption of the mixed fluids by the yogin using the technique of reverse urethral suction (*vajrolīmudrā*).[318] For these commentators, it is through such practice that all achievements are attained, including the supreme achievement of awakening. Thus, in commenting upon chapter twenty-seven's description of the ideal adept, Kambala writes:

> **Accustomed to union with a consort** means that through the state of *mahāmudrā* one will effortlessly attain unexcelled, supreme awakening. One will quickly purify clear light and gnosis, and will thus always be considered to be a yogin. Through the application of this meditation, if one stabilizes the jewel of mind, one is blessed, consecrated in a buddha's awakening. Take a sixteen-year-old, and bedeck her with all of the ornaments. Having found one with a beautiful face and large eyes, one should practice the consort observance with her. One should also practice the secret worship in the four moments by means of the great observance. Have no doubt that after six months everything will be achieved. (SN 42a)

The commentators who advocate the sexual yoga practices typically reinterpret the passages dealing with the sacramental consumption of fluids in terms of the more complex yogic practices. Take, for example, the opening of chapter forty-two, which reads as follows:

> Then the hero, having drunk the "flower water" (*kusumodaka*) should recollect this mantra. The adept should thus dance with his consort. At night one should enjoy meat thrice enchanted, and thus drinking with that and offering it, there is this: "May bliss be produced!"

Vīravajra interprets this in terms of sexual yogic practice as follows:

---

317 Regarding this, see Snellgrove 1987, 262–266; and Kvaerne 1975, 109–124, and 1977, 34–36.

318 This technique is discussed at length by David White in his *The Alchemical Body* (1996, esp. 199–202).

> The **hero** and yoginī, being purified by the four [steps of] service and worship (*sevāsādhana*), **having drunk the flower water**—i.e., transmitted uterine blood and semen—into the aperture of the central channel (*avadhūti*), should meditate in concentration upon the upward diversion [of these fluids]. (PD 435b)

Vīrāvajra here reinterprets the "drinking" of the fluid in terms of the subtle yogic anatomy, involving the reabsorption of sexual fluids via reverse urethral suction. Likewise, chapter thirty-six describes the "Great Worship of the Consort" (*mudrāmahāpūjā*). According to Vīravajra, in this the yogin ejaculates, a process that he compares to an oblation into a sacrificial fire. He comments as follows:

> Having thus explained the destruction of the Lord of Death, now I will explain the secret fire sacrifice via the path of passion. **And then** there is stated the **great worship of the consort**, and so forth. The hero and yoginī, having practiced the four [creation stage processes] of worship and means of achievement, make oblations of seminal essence with the ladle of the secret vajra into the fire pit of the lady's vulva: this is what is called the **great worship of the consort**. Should the seminal essence "go" to the joy of cessation [i.e., ejaculation], then in the state of concentration one lays down mantra, i.e., reverses [the flow of seminal essence]. These [practices of the] **worship of the consort** rapidly achieve the twelve ritual actions. (PD 427b)

This passage describes two seemingly contradictory practices. On the one hand, he compares the sexual union to a sacrificial oblation, with the semen as an offering substance, a comparison that is particularly common in Hindu tantric texts, but which is uncommon in Buddhist ones, where typically the adept is instructed not to ejaculate.[319] Yet the second half of

319 See Bharati 1993, 264–265. This is an ancient comparison, present in the *Bṛhadāraṇyaka Upaniṣad* 6.4.3. See Olivelle 1998, 154–155.

this passage appears to imply seminal retention via *mantra-nyāsa*, the laying down of seed syllables for the purpose of obstructing ejaculation.[320]

The *Cakrasamvara Tantra* does contain numerous traces of the older, presumably Hindu-inspired sacramental use of sexual fluids that naturally require ejaculation. White (2003, 109) argues that this is the earlier practice, and that the Buddhist injunction against ejaculation is a later development. The *Cakrasamvara Tantra* appears to be a pivotal text that exhibits traces of both the older Hindu practice as well as the Buddhist transformation of it. One interesting passage in this regard is verse eight in chapter one, "Worship the buddhas and bodhisattvas with one's own seminal drops, with sight and touch, and with hearing and thought." Bhavabhaṭṭa comments that this exemplified what he terms "direct worship" (*sākṣātpūjā*), as follows:

> Outwardly, one should emit seminal essence for the sake of worship in the outer consort, whose defining marks are stated within the Tantra. With the drops which arise in the equipoise of the two, worship the buddhas—that is, the five aggregates such as form, feeling, and so forth, which have been purified and experienced through the mode of eating ambrosia—and the bodhisattvas, the forms of the eye, and so forth. The direct worship is to be observed at the three junctures [of the day]. Thus it is said: "One of firm intelligence should eat the secret semen with eyes wide open. This is the worship of body, speech, and mind with all mantras."[321]

Evidently, the Buddhists who composed and propagated the Yoginī Tantras, drawing as they did from a multitude of sources, Buddhist and non-Buddhist, were engaging in the ritual eclecticism that, according to

---

320 Elsewhere Vīravajra is more specific, arguing that "if one is [about to] 'go' [i.e., ejaculate] at the time of the joy of cessation, then the wind is diverted upward by means of the seal of laughter, i.e., the eight types of *h* sounds." (PD 436b) The eight *h* sounds are the eight seed syllables beginning with *h*, also known as the "laughter mantra," which is introduced in CS ch. 39.

321 Pandey 2002, 23. See the Sanskrit and my comments on it in the notes to my translation of CS ch. 1.

Granoff (2000), was typical of the early medieval period. The relatively simple, Hindu-inspired sacramental rite would ultimately be transformed in its fully-developed Buddhist version, as described by Vīravajra centuries later:

> Regarding the actions of pressing the seals (*mudrā*) of the lotus, at the time of the *joy* which is variegated, the *supreme joy* which ripens, and the [*joy of cessation*] that is devoid of characteristics, **thus one should be furnished with the weapon**. This means that just as one should be furnished with the weapon of yogic postures (*yantra*) involving syllables at the time of bliss, and the weapon of yogic postures involving wind at the time of supreme bliss, at the time of natural bliss one should be furnished with the weapon which turns back conceptualization by means of drawing forth the awareness which is called "unequalled" (*asamasama*), which uproots the subject and object [dichotomy]. (PD 427b)

Vīravajra here presents an elaborate schema of increasingly rarified sexual yoga practice, culminating in the achievement of non-conceptual gnosis free of the subject-object dichotomy, the classic goal of the Yogācāra school of Buddhism.

The *Cakrasamvara Tantra* itself is also marked with signs of the development of the typical Buddhist sexual practice, characterized by the practice of seminal retention. In spite of the passages which indicate sexual union for the purpose of producing the mixed sexual fluids for sacramental consumption, chapter twenty-six lists the following among the commitments that an adept must observe: "[he should] have an excellent churning stick in practice with a woman, yet observe chastity in meditation." Chastity (*brahmacarya*) is understood here to include the practice of sexual union, provided that it is accompanied by seminal retention. Jayabhadra wrote that "**yet observe chastity in meditation** means that, at the time of the trickling of the ejaculate seminal essence, one should observe, i.e., practice, chastity. [This is] the seventh [commitment]."[322] Likewise, chapter twenty-eight informs the reader that "the emanation of Śrī Heruka, noted in all of the

[322] E 27a.2–3: *brahmacaryaṁ tathā dhyāna iti ādhānabodhicittasravaṇakāle brahmatattvaṁ cared ācared ityarthaḥ saptamaḥ* /.

treatises on service, should always be retained." Jayabhadra informs us that this refers to the retention of semen.[323]

This redefinition of chastity was evidently taken by some as a justification for monks engaging in such practices. The Buddhist scholar Tripiṭakamāla felt that the compassionate imperative overrides the *pratimokṣa* monastic vows, evidently providing justification for monks who wished to engage in the "great observance" of sexual union:

> For bodhisattvas who practice the great observance (*mahāvrata*) there are no definite norms; they engage in whatever actions that can perfect the aims of others. Through his passion for all, a bodhisattva may unite with women who are on the road to the bad rebirths; for him "chastity" is that conduct which achieves the unexcelled state in which there is no regard for the *pratimokṣa* vows, and so forth.[324]

This re-interpretation of "chastity" would be supported by passages such as those quoted above from the *Cakrasamvara Tantra*, which were understood to refer to seminal retention in sexual yogic practices. This re-interpretation was highly controversial in Buddhist monastic circles, and, not surprisingly, there was considerable resistance therein to the practice of sexual yogas by monks.

One of the most ardent critics here appears to have been Atīśa Dīpaṁkaraśrījñāna. Not that Atīśa was hostile to the practice of the tantras *per se*. Indeed, according to his Tibetan hagiographies, he was a tantric adept before he was ordained as a monk.[325] Moreover, he was the author of several tantric works, including his important commentary on Lūipa's *Śrī-Bhagavad Abhisamaya*;[326] and he aided Rin-chen bZang-po in the translation of multiple

---

[323] According to Jayabhadra the expression "**the emanation** [of Śrī Heruka]" is also a metaphor for seminal essence (E 31b.2: *nirmāṇam iti bodhicittasyaiva paryāyaḥ*).

[324] Tripiṭakamāla, *Nayatrayapradīpa*, 11b.

[325] See Chattopadhyaya 1967, 71–76.

[326] Regarding this, it can be noted that Richard Sherburne's *The Complete Works of Atīśa* (2000) is not in fact a complete collection of Atīśa's works, but is rather a translation of 27 texts highlighted by the bKa'-gdam-pa order, a grouping that itself excludes his more esoteric works.

tantric texts.[327] Rather, Atīśa was specifically concerned about monks engaging in the second and third "higher" consecrations, which if practiced literally would necessarily violate the vow of celibacy. He wrote in his *Bodhipatha-pradīpa* that:

> Due to the specific prohibition in the *Ādibuddhamahā-tantra*,[328] the secret and wisdom[-gnosis] consecrations should not be received by the celibate. If these consecrations are taken, since those who live celibately and ascetically would be engaging in what is prohibited to them, their ascetic vows would be broken, and they would incur the downfalls which defeat the observant. And as they would certainly fall into the evil destinies, [for them] there would be no success.[329]

In his auto-commentary Atīśa comments that the "higher" consecrations are suitable only for the laity, and insists that they should not be taken by the monks, who would be betraying their root vows, which in his view would have dire consequences. He wrote that:

> Regarding consecrations there are two types: those on which householders rely, and those on which the celibate rely. Those on which the householder may rely include everything taught in the tantras, while the celibate from amongst those should avoid the secret and wisdom-gnosis consecrations. Why should they avoid those two? Celibacy is understood to be one of the virtues which occurs as a point of doctrine, in reliance upon the Buddha's teaching. Those two consecrations are regarded as not being in

---

[327] These include the AU, the *Śrīcakrasamvara-sādhana* (Tōh. 1491), and his own AV commentary. Atīśa also authored and/or translated several *caryāgīti* texts and commentaries (Tōh. 1494–1497). For a complete list, see Tucci 1988, 40–49.

[328] As Vesna Wallace points out (2001, 124), there is no clear passage in the *Kālacakra Tantra* or the *Vimalaprabhā* supporting Atīśa's claim. On the other hand, there are passages in the *Paramādibuddha Tantra* and the *Vimalaprabhā* that contradict him, and describe monks and wandering ascetics receiving these consecrations and being offered consorts for the practice of sexual yoga.

[329] Atīśa, *Bodhipathapradīpa*, 240b–241a.

> accordance with the practice of celibacy. The two consecrations would bring about the end of celibacy, and the end of celibacy would be the end of the Buddha's teaching. And by its ceasing the continuum of merit making would be broken. Since from that basis there would arise innumerable non-virtuous people, the celibate should thus avoid those two [consecrations].[330]

Atīśa's commentary here expresses the understandable anxiety that cenobitic fornication, especially if justified as spiritual practice, could undermine the foundation of Buddhist monasticism, and thus threaten the very existence of the religion, which traditionally centered around the monastic institutions.

While the sexual components of the tantras did not likely originate in the Buddhist monastic context, it seems almost certain that these practices were adopted by some Buddhists in the influential Northern Indian centers such as Nālandā and Vikramaśīla by the time Atīśa was writing in the early eleventh century. Yet they were not completely accepted nor unambiguously integrated into the monastic ritual program. Given their focus on the enjoyment (*bhoga*) of things prohibited to monks, such integration would not have come easily. That the monastic precepts were at times broken in monastic communities by tantric adepts is suggested by the hagiographies of siddhas such as Virūpa[331] and Maitrīpa,[332] who were monks until dismissed from the monasteries for allegedly violating the monastic code.

As Buddhist tantric traditions in India (likely) and Tibet (certainly, with some exceptions) appear to have been dominated by monks, Atīśa's proposed solution of excluding monks from two of the four higher consecrations was probably unacceptable. Thus, rather than excluding monks

---

330 Atīśa, *Bodhimārgadīpapañjikā*, 290a–b.

331 According to 'Jam-mgon A-myes-zhab Ngag-dbang Kun-dga'-bsod-nams (*grub thob brgyas cu rtsa bzhi'i rnam thar*, 6b), Virūpa was a monk at Somapurī prior to his expulsion. Davidson (2002a, 70) reports, on the basis of Grags-pa rgyal-mtshan's *bla-ma rgya gar ba'i lo rgyus*, that Virūpa was the head of Nālandā at the time of his expulsion.

332 According to hagiographical sources, Atīśa was responsible for expelling the siddha Maitrīpa from Vikramaśīla for transgressions related to tantric practice. See Chattopadhyaya 1967, 134–136. Tatz (1988) is critical of this story, but Davidson (2002a, 79 n. 86) argues that sources that contain it are sound.

from these higher consecrations, the consecrations themselves were transformed, with overt sexual practices being replaced by the development of public symbolic performances, and with *karmamudrā* (actual, physical consort) practices conducted privately, if at all. That compromise was possible on this issue is suggested by the Tibetan context, in which the tantras would come to be fully accepted within the monastic ritual programs. The Tibetans adapted the secret and wisdom-gnosis consecrations to the monastic context, removing completely—in public performances of the consecration ceremonies at least—all sexual practice, with the red and white drops being symbolized by neutral substances similar in appearance.[333]

The consecrations thus came to be performed in a symbolic fashion. Moreover, this dichotomy of real versus symbolic ritual performance corresponds to two modes of yoga that were also developed by tantric Buddhist monastic communities. These are practice with an actual physical consort (*karmamudrā*), versus practice with a visualized consort (*jñānamudrā*).[334] For example, Vīravajra, commenting on the term "consort's body" (*prajñāṅga*) in chapter fifty-one, explains that "**consort's body** indicates either the physical consort for lay bodhisattvas, or the reality or symbolic seals[335] for those on the path of liberation."[336] There is some evidence which suggests, however, that the practice tradition of the sexual yogas has still been

[333] For example, at recent consecration ceremonies held in India, yogurt mixed with a red pigment was used to symbolize the mixed sexual fluids; at another held in New York, yogurt mixed with red Gatorade was used. The Cakrasamvara consecration as conducted by Nevārī Buddhists of the Kathmandu valley likewise uses symbolic representations in place of the sexual elements, but not in a manner identical to the Tibetans, suggesting that they developed symbolic forms of the ritual independently. See Bangdel 1999, 3.800–819.

[334] Regarding the *jñānamudrā* qua visualized consort, see Mullin 1996, 70–72.

[335] "Reality seal" (*dharmamudrā*) here probably indicates a mantra, recited in visualization exercises, while "symbolic seal" (*samayamudrā*) may designate a visualized consort or a symbolic consort, namely the *khaṭvāṅga* or skull-staff that is commonly thought to symbolize the consort. See my translation of the longer passage (in which this commentary is embedded) in the notes to CS ch. 51 below.

[336] PD 447b. This idea is further elaborated in the Kālacakra literature, which posits a hierarchy of practitioners, privileging those who avoid actual practice with an embodied consort. According to the *Vimalaprabhā* (ch.4 v. 110): "a *sādhana* with a *karma-mudrā* is for simple-minded Vajrayāna students, a *sādhana* with a *jñāna-mudrā* is for mediocre Vajrayāna adepts, and a *sādhana* with *mahā-mudrā* is for the superior *yogis*" (Wallace 1995 n. 233).

maintained, but has been reserved for the "highest" class of adept, for whom the issue of celibacy may no longer be a central concern.[337]

Often texts on the "sexual" rites employ deliberately vague terminology, such as the term *mudrā*, that leaves one in doubt as to whether an "actual" *karmamudrā* or a visualized *jñānamudrā* is called for. For example, in his *Abhisamayavibhaṅga* Atīśa wrote a description of the third "wisdom-gnosis" consecration which is quite ambiguous in exactly this manner:

> Then, Heruka takes Vārāhī as his *mudrā*, and through being equipoised their winds dissolve. Relying on that, contemplate the experience of the natural (*sahaja*).[338] Then you, a child of the clan (*kulaputra*), unite with the *mudrā* as Heruka, and, depending on that, meditate on clear light, that wisdom which is attained in visionary experience. This is the very essence of the Transcendence of Wisdom (*prajñāpāramitā*) which is the purity of the three consciousnesses,[339] and which is liberation from birth due to the non-existence of body, speech, and mind. This is the ultimate truth which has the characteristic of always appearing completely luminous like the moon, sun, fire, and jewels. Regard [everything] with the eye of wisdom and gnosis, the vision which is beyond the objectification of the other. In this way, do not see anything in and of itself, but *see* the clear light. (AV 197b)

While Atīśa's language is ambiguous here, his use of visionary terminology rather than that of felt bodily experience suggests that the process he de-

---

[337] Mullin notes that at a lecture in India in the 1970s a monk once asked a lama (also a monk) whether a monk who wishes to practice with a *karmamudrā* should disrobe before doing so. Mullin reports that the lama laughed and gave the following enigmatic answer: "No. He just becomes an especially good monk." (1996, 249 n. 17)

[338] There are several possible meanings that *sahaja* could have here, as Davidson has outlined (2002a, 71–72). These include the entire process of sexual yoga culminating in the attainment of *sahajānanda*, or the fundamental state of things (attained via such practice). It might also here imply the relation of *sahaja* to aesthetics, as "*sahaja* is sometimes allied with the aesthetic perception of the incomparable taste of liberation." (2002a, 72–73)

[339] That is, the coarse, subtle, and very subtle levels of consciousness, which relate to the corresponding levels of the taints (*trimala*).

scribes is to be visualized rather than enacted. Though it is not certain if this is what Atīśa intended, it would certainly accord with his strongly stated aim of preserving the monastic practice of celibacy.

Indeed, we see in the Tibetan tradition an interesting move toward a fusion of the visionary and experiential modes of practice of the higher tantric yogas. For example, 'Jam-mgon Kong-sprul recounts the following dream in his autobiography:

> And one morning, as a cheerful sun was rising, I took hold of a dream and made circumambulation around the residence where Lord Pema Nyinjé stayed. On the path I met a *dakini* with the body of a human woman, who approached me with a coquettish air; as I had a clear impression of us as masculine and feminine deities in union, I experienced the four joys in a stable manner. (Barron 2003, 48)

This description of union with a ḍākinī in the form of a human female recalls the older *yakṣiṇī-sādhana*s in which an adept could summon a female spirit for the purpose of prohibited forms of sexual union; in this case, perhaps, the purpose was the experience of the four joys without violating the monastic vows. The fact that this occurred in a visionary dream further displaces it, neutralizing its transgressive character.

It is not surprising that, in the Buddhist monastic context, actual ritual and meditative practices involving sexuality would be downplayed and replaced with symbolic or visualized practices in which the sexual body is removed from public view. But there is also evidence that this was a long-standing tendency within the tradition, which strongly emphasized the imperative for secrecy, and would thus not have approved of the open display, for example, of the Cakrasamvara consecration ceremonies. According to chapter twenty-seven of the Tantra, one should even hide one's identity as an initiated adept, which is signified by the five insignia[340] that one must keep on one's person. The text informs us that: "As for having the five insignia bound, they should be in place at all times, always displayed at night, and concealed during the day." This motif of *tantrika* by night, mild-mannered citizen by day, is elaborated in the hagiography of the tantric Mahāsiddha Saraha who was not a monk, but a brahmin, but as such was

[340] These are a necklace, crest jewel, earring, choker, and the sacred thread.

under at least as much pressure as a monk not to engage in transgressive behavior. The following is his story as recorded by 'Jam-mgon A-myes-zhab Ngag-dbang Kun-dga'-bsod-nams:

> Saraha's class was brahmin, and [he lived] in the town of Roli in Rāḍha[341] in Eastern India. His mother was a ḍākinī. Although the master was a brahmin, Saraha had faith in the Buddhadharma, so he maintained the vows of both a Buddhist and a brahmin. By day he was a practicing brahmin, and by night a practicing Buddhist. He frequented the *gaṇacakra* and also imbibed beer. When the brahmins got wind of this they decided to expel Saraha. The brahmins gathered together and petitioned King Ratnapāla,[342] saying "Is it not your duty as king to uphold the customs in your country? This Saraha, the master of the brahmins of the village Roli of fifteen thousand, by drinking alcohol has fallen from his caste, so let him be exiled!"
>
> The king thought that since he is the master of a village of fifteen thousand, it would not be appropriate to exile him. He went to see Saraha and said, "As you are a brahmin, it is not good that you drink beer."
>
> He replied, "I do not drink beer, but if you do not believe me, assemble all the people and brahmins and I'll swear an oath." The king assembled everyone, and Saraha said, "If I drink beer may my mouth burn!" He drank down boiling oil, but his mouth didn't burn.
>
> The king asked, "Is he not truthful?"
>
> The brahmins replied, "He drinks."

---

341 The text has *radhi*, presumably for Rāḍha, a region in Bengal west of the Gaṅgā.

342 This may refer to the king Ratnapāla who ruled in Assam from 1000–1030 CE. There is not enough evidence, however, to confirm or deny this possible identification. See Kvaerne 1977, 6.

> Once again, he drank molten copper but was not burned, but the brahmins still insisted that he drank beer. So he said, "Let us be thrown into a lake; whoever does not sink does not drink, but whoever sinks is a drinker." Saraha was thrown into the water but did not sink and quickly returned. Still they insisted that he was a drinker. Saraha said, "Place me on a scale. If I am heavier than whatever else [you place on it] then I am no drinker." Saraha became heavy, saying "I do not drink." They placed on it a piece of iron that weighed as much as three men, but Saraha was heavier, and they placed on it a lump of iron weighing as much as six men, but Saraha was still heavier.
>
> The king said, "If he has power like this, it's okay if he drinks." Even the brahmins had faith and bowed down to him, and converting from their own customs they all became Buddhists.[343]

Given the esotericism employed by the tradition, from its inception up to the present day, it is not possible to ascertain to what degree transgressive practices were literally performed. The fact that authors such as Atīśa and King Lha bLa-ma Ye-shes-'od complained about their performance likely indicates that, during the eleventh century at least, some individuals, including monks, were doing so, and that they were attracting attention in so doing. Perhaps fittingly for a tradition based on deliberately obscure texts, the "secret" of the tradition, while always in the process of being revealed, will probably never be exhausted, never be fully revealed, given the infinite possibilities of textual interpretation.[344]

3.4 Mantras and Magic

One of the most important topics covered in the *Cakrasamvara Tantra* is that of the mantras of the major deities. Bestowed upon the initiated adept, the mantras are vocal manifestations of the deities, and their repeti-

[343] 'Jam-mgon A-myes-zhab Ngag-dbang Kun-dga'-bsod-nams, *grub thob brgyas cu rtsa bzhi'i rnam thar*, 12a–b.

[344] For a fuller exploration of the deployment of the trope of secrecy as a means of legitimating changes in the interpretation of the text and the practices it implies, see Gray 2005b.

tion is an essential component of the creation stage meditation exercises in which the adept seeks to actualize an experience of union with the deity. This, we are told, can lead to the ultimate goal of achieving the awakening of a buddha. But the repetition and ritual application of the mantras also lead to the various mundane magical powers (*laukikasiddhi*), and this appears to be one of the major concerns of this scripture, judging by the significant portion of the text dedicated to these topics. Nine of the Tantra's chapters are concerned with the selection of the mantras,[345] while many more detail their ritual and magical applications.

The mantras are an extremely important component of the tradition's ritual and meditative practice. The adept is taught the mantras by his guru in the context of the consecration ceremony, and then he is not only encouraged to recite them, but must make a formal commitment (*samaya*) to do so. As chapter twenty-seven commands, "One should always recite mantra, purifying the body." The adept must also vow not to wantonly disclose the mantras to the uninitiated. Chapter twenty-eight advises that "One should not disclose gnosis, and likewise mantra and *mudrā*, to him [who], along with one's brother or son, is the source of happiness and suffering." This somewhat obscure instruction is understood by the commentators to refer generally to the uninitiated, and particularly to the adept's uninitiated family members, to whom he or she might feel particularly inclined to surreptitiously reveal them.

The Tantra was itself composed to hinder the uninitiated from learning the mantras. It does so by disclosing some of them in less than straightforward ways.[346] The easiest but least effective method employed to hinder casual readers is listing the mantras in reverse order, a method that is not particularly challenging to anyone familiar with the structure of mantras.[347]

---

345 These include: 1) ch. 5, where the consonants of the hero's root mantra are selected; 2) ch. 6, which gives the hero's armor mantras; 3) ch. 7, which selects the root mantra's vowels; 4) ch. 8, which lists the hero's essence and quintessence mantras, and the yoginīs' armor mantras; 5) ch. 25, which states the hero's root mantra; 6) ch. 30, which selects the Trailokyavijaya mantra; 7) ch. 39, which focuses on the laughter mantra; 8) ch. 46, which lists the mantra of the five syllables beginning with *h*; and 9) ch. 48, which gives the heroine's essence mantra.

346 Not all mantras are coded. The mantra of the five *h* syllables is given directly in ch. 46.

347 For example, the hero's essence and quintessence mantra are listed in reverse order in ch. 8, as is the heroine's essence mantra in ch. 48.

A somewhat more complex method occurs in chapters six and eight, where the syllables are given for the hero's and heroine's armor mantras, respectively, but where the reader must assemble the two syllable combinations needed for each mantra. Another strategy taken by the authors of the Tantra was simply to omit the mantra entirely. Both the eightfold "laughter mantra" introduced in chapter thirty-nine, and the heroine's quintessence mantra are not listed or even coded in the text. Both are listed in the commentaries, and while the latter mantra is very well-known, there appears to have been some confusion concerning the former, for which two entirely different versions have been given.

The last and most complex method of encrypting the mantras are the mantra puzzles given in chapters five, seven, and thirty. These puzzles code the mantras' consonants and vowels by assigning them number values, and coding them numerically. Solving the puzzle requires that one compose a chart of the Sanskrit alphabet according to the *varga*s or phonetic classes in which Sanskrit phonemes were organized.

Selecting a mantra in this way was not simply an intellectual puzzle, but also a ritual event. A brief description of the ritual preparation occurs at the beginning of chapter thirty, where we learn that, as in the case of drawing a maṇḍala, one must first select a suitable piece of ground, ritually purify and protect it, and then beautify it with offerings of perfume and incense, flowers, and lamps, after which one can then draw the requisite diagram.

The coded "mantra puzzles" contained in this text are relatively easy to decode if one understands their operative principles. Basically, it is a coding scheme for the letters of the Sanskrit alphabet that operates either by (1) assigning each a number, or (2) graphing them on a table and coding them according to the cell which they occupy. Both systems are illustrated in Table Four.

Table Four: Phonetic Classes

Row #	Column 1	Column 2	Column 3	Column 4	Column 5
1	1. **ka**	2. **kha**	3. **ga**	4. **gha**	5. **ṅa**
2	6. **ca**	7. **cha**	8. **ja**	9. **jha**	10. **ña**
3	11. **ṭa**	12. **ṭha**	13. **ḍa**	14. **ḍha**	15. **ṇa**
4	16. **ta**	17. **tha**	18. **da**	19. **dha**	20. **na**
5	21. **pa**	22. **pha**	23. **ba**	24. **bha**	25. **ma**
6	26. **ya**	27. **ra**	28. **la**	29. **va**	
7	30. **śa**	31. **ṣa**	32. **sa**	33. **ha**	

The consonants are selected in chapter seven either by simply stating the number (e.g., the "thirtieth," which is *śa*), or by stating the column and row (e.g., "the third of the fifth," that is, the third cell of the fifth row, which is *ba*). Sometimes the semivowel row (the sixth) and the sibilant row (the seventh) are selected by name (e.g., "the fourth of the sibilants," which is *h*).

The text deals with consonant conjuncts in a somewhat anomalous way. While we recognize that some syllables are closed, such that we would divide *kalpa* into *kal* and *pa,* in this text the syllables are divided following the vowel, into *ka* and *lpa.* Generally, in the case of conjunct "syllables," such as *lpā* and *gni,* the first consonant, *l* and *g* respectively, are selected with the consonants (in chapter five, for the hero's root mantra), while the additional consonants are selected later with the vowels.

Regarding the vowels, as the chart above indicates, each consonant in Sanskrit is understood to have the vowel short-*a* unless otherwise indicated by a vowel marker. This text also assumes this, and only selects the other vowels, including the *anusvāra* nasalization *ṁ* and the *visarga* unvoiced aspiration *ḥ* when affixed to short-*a,* which are also graphically indicated in Sanskrit. Each "vowel" is assigned a number, and is quite simply selected by number, as illustrated in Table Five.

Table Five: Sanskrit Vowels

1. **a**	2. **ā**	3. **i**	4. **ī**	5. **u**	6. **ū**	7. **ṛ**	8. **ṝ**
9. **ḷ**	10. **ḹ**	11. **e**	12. **ai**	13. **o**	14. **au**	15. **aṁ**	16. **aḥ**

Overall, the selection process is quite simple, provided that one understands these rules. While there are some points where the text introduces ambiguity in order to confuse the uninitiated reader, these are easily resolved through consulting the commentaries.[348] In my translation below, I have literally translated the text, but place the letter or vowel selected in square brackets. Whenever the text varies from the established pattern or introduces other novelties, this is noted and discussed in the notes to the text.

[348] For example, the text refers to the classes (*vargas*) by number, calling, for example, for the "first of the fifth [*varga*]." Normally this would be *p*, the first consonant of the labial class, which is the fifth class counting from the velar class. At times, however, it includes the vowels as the first *varga,* in which case the "first of the fifth" would be *t*.

The selection of the mantras is simply a means to an end, and this end is their employment in ritual and meditative practices. The uses of the mantras in meditative practice are important for the practice tradition, although these are not addressed in any depth in the *Cakrasamvara Tantra* itself.[349] The repetition of mantras (*mantrajapa*) is also extremely important in many of the key ritual practices such as the rites of drawing the maṇḍala and performing the consecrations therein. Here, too, the root text in its treatment of these rites does not provide all of the necessary information, including the mantras that are to be repeated.[350]

One of the major concerns of the *Cakrasamvara Tantra* is the practices employing mantras in magical activities.[351] These invariably involve the repetition of a mantra, either to directly achieve a magical end, such as the pacification of an undesirable condition or the subjugation of another being, or the enchantment of an object that can then be used for achieving such ends. The Root Tantra dedicates a total of sixteen chapters to the description of the ritual applications of the mantras, covering all of the major mantras given in the text.[352]

Generally, the mantras must be repeated a number of times, typically ranging in units of one hundred (or 108), one thousand, or one hundred thousand times. They are repeated silently (mentally) or, sometimes, audibly. According to the commentaries, in a number of the rites such repetition

---

[349] For example, the meditative practices associated with the body maṇḍala, described in section 3.1 above, are referred to in the root text but are not adequately described; nor are the twenty-four seed syllables given in this text adequately described. More details are given in the explanatory tantras, but the fullest descriptions are given in the *sādhanas*.

[350] This information is covered in the ritual texts (*vidhi*) dealing with the respective rite.

[351] See Yelle 2003 for an extended treatment of the magical uses of mantras.

[352] Ch. 9 gives the ritual applications of the hero's root mantra. Chs. 10 and 11 deal with the ritual applications of the hero's essence mantra, and chs. 12 and 14 do so for the hero's quintessence mantra. Ch. 13 treats the ritual applications of the hero's armor mantras. Ch. 35 details a complex meditation involving the "interconnected mantra," a system of generating mantras from a complex visualization of the garland of vowels and consonants while in sexual union with a consort, and ch. 37 details their ritual applications. Ch. 36 describes the use of the syllables of the essence mantras. Ch. 42 presents the applications of the laughter mantra, and ch. 43 presents further applications of the hero's quintessence mantra. Chs. 44 and 45 give applications of the yoginīs' armor mantras, and ch. 46 does so for the five *h* syllables. Chs. 47 and 48 detail the applications of Vajravārāhī's quintessence and essence mantras, respectively.

must be associated with a variety of ritual aids. In some cases, the mantras must be written or inscribed in magical diagrams (*yantra*) on a variety of different substances, often with augments such as the victim's or beneficiary's name.[353] Frequently a variety of ritual implements are required. These include both the objects of enchantment, as well as other accoutrements such as incense, plant substances, skull bowls, charnel ground ash, and so forth.[354]

Mantra repetitions are also employed in the far more standardized system of the six (or more) magical applications (*ṣaṭkarmāṇi*) of classical Indian sorcery, in which the type of ritual action is correlated to specific requisites for the ritual, such as the color of the ritual accoutrements, the time of day and locations in which the rite may be performed, the appearance of the deity that is to be invoked, and so forth. For example, for pacifying (*śānta*), the color white is favored, as is the hour of noon, pleasant locales, and benevolent deities, while for destructive rites (*abhicāra*), the color black is favored, as are inauspicious times (midnight) and places (charnel grounds), and fierce deities.[355] For rites requiring burnt oblations (*homa*), another variable is the shape of the fire hearth, the type of wood burned, and the nature of the oblations used.[356] Such detail is largely absent in the root text, but is given in some of the commentaries.[357]

---

[353] While none of these *yantra*s are described in detail or illustrated in any of the texts that I have seen, I presume that they are similar to the sorts of diagrams depicted and described in Bühnemann 2003.

[354] A number of enchantments of this type are described in ch. 9, as well as in other chapters.

[355] These correlations are discussed at some length by Tsong Khapa in his KS commentary on ch. 9. See my translation of this text (Gray 2017). Classical Indian sorcery is described in depth by Goudriaan (1978, 251–412), and in Türstig 1985.

[356] My notes to the translation below include some descriptions of *homa* rites contained in the commentaries. For a more extensive treatment of Buddhist *homa* rites, see Payne 1991, and the essays in Staal 1983, vol. 2.

[357] I generally have not included such instructions in the notes for this translation, as doing so would have vastly increased the size of this volume. Interested readers may wish to consult my translation of Tsong Khapa's commentary (Gray 2017, 2019), which does describe the magical procedures in greater detail.

4. Texts and Translation

4.1 Texts Employed

The translation which follows is a translation of the Sanskrit version of the *Cakrasamvara Tantra* or *Śrī Heruka Abhidhāna*, based on my edition of the Sanskrit. However, as the Sanskrit sources for this text are incomplete, I also make extensive use of the Tibetan translations and commentaries. There are a number of sources for—but also serious challenges to—the production of an edition of this text. The largest problem is that the surviving manuscripts are all incomplete, due to missing folia in the oldest manuscript. While the lacunae can be partially filled by consulting the surviving Sanskrit commentaries, at this point it is not possible to produce a complete Sanskrit edition of this text on the basis of surviving Sanskrit manuscripts.

In spite of these difficulties, an edition of the text has already been published, namely Shastri Pandey's (2002) edition published by the Central Institute of Higher Tibetan Studies in Sarnath. This edition, while useful, has some serious shortcomings. As a result, at the request of the editors of this series, I have also published in a separate volume my edition of the Sanskrit together with an edition of both Mardo's standard revised translation and the Phug-drag ms. of Sumatikīrti's revised translation. This is available in Gray 2012.

The earliest manuscript of the *Cakrasamvara Tantra* (ms. A in the *sigla* I employ in the notes to this translation)[358] is in Bhujimol script on palm leaves. It is preserved in the collection of the Oriental Institute in Vadodara. Its brief colophon[359] has no date, but there are several features of the script that enable the ascription of an approximate date. The first con-

[358] See the *Conspectus Siglorum* below.

[359] This colophon contains an interesting element, namely the statement of the *Pratītyasamutpādagātha*, occurring there as *ye dharmā hetuprabhavā hetuṁ teṣāṁ tathāgato hy avadat teṣāṁ ca yo nirodha evaṁvādī mahāśramaṇaḥ*. (38a) "This 'Buddhist creed' [is] known in Tibetan as the 'Essence of Relativity dhāraṇī' (*rten 'brel snying po'i gzung*), [and] is used to consecrate images in the Tibetan tradition" (Gyalzur and Verwey 1983, 176–77; bracketed inserts mine). See also Boucher 1991 for a discussion of the consecratory uses of this verse in early medieval India. Its appearance in the colophon of this manuscript is interesting, implying that the text itself was seen as being in need of consecration.

sideration concerns the Bhujimol script itself.[360] It contains the "Nevārī hook" which was in use for a period of about three and a half centuries, from the twelfth through fifteen centuries.[361] Comparison of the script in this text with scripts in other, dated texts suggests that it was written in the mid- to late-twelfth century, making it a relatively early example of this script.[362] The original text would have consisted of thirty-eight double-sided folia, eleven of which are now missing.[363] As a result, out of the fifty-one chapters, there is a total loss of thirteen, and the partial loss of another six.[364]

The other two manuscripts are much later copies of this palm leaf text. Unfortunately, they were made after that manuscript's folia were misplaced, so these also contain the same lacunae. They are on Nepali paper in Devanāgarī script. The one in the Oriental Institute collection (ms. B) is dated N.S. (Nepali *samvat*) 1050, that is, 1930 CE. The manuscript in the Kaiser Library collection (ms. C) has no colophon, but it appears to have been written by the same hand as the former manuscript, and is definitely a twentieth century copy. I have worked from microfilm copies of these three manuscripts, and I have also examined the original manuscripts. As these manuscripts are late copies of ms. A, they do not permit the production of a critical edition. However, they are useful, for there are several points at

---

[360] Lienhard (1988, xviii) explains that the name *bhujiṁmola* means "fly headed," which is probably a reference to its characteristic "hook" at the top of the letters, as opposed to the horizontal line that tops most Devanāgarī letters. It is derived from the ornamental *kuṭila* script.

[361] See Bendall 1992, xxii-xxiii.

[362] There are a variety of different sources for the comparison of different scripts. The examples in Śākya's *Nepāla Lipi Prakāśa* (1974) and Rājavaṁśī's *Prācīna Lipi Varṇamālā* (1959), while generally useful, did not provide a close match to the script in this text. The closest match occurs in the (1992) reprint of Bendall's catalogue. This match is to ms. add. 1686, an 1167 CE palm leaf manuscript of the *Sādhanamālātantra*. See Bendall 1992, 174, and also plate II.3 and the Table of Letters. Both manuscripts contain, for example, an archaic version of the letter *tha*, which does not occur, for example, in the manuscripts described by George (1974), which are of a somewhat later date. On the other hand, the letter *bha* in this text is closer to that contained in Bendall's ms. add. 1693, dated to 1165 CE.

[363] These are the folia numbered 15, 18–22, 28–31, and 36.

[364] The chapters completely lost are 23–29 and 39–44, and the ones partially lost are 18, 19, 22, 38, 49, and 50.

which they provide readings at places where ms. A is unreadable due to damage such as fraying. In these cases, the damage presumably occurred over the past seventy years.

Fortunately, there are other Sanskrit sources that fill in some, but unfortunately not all, of the missing portions of these manuscripts. There are two surviving Sanskrit commentaries that treat the entire root text, Jayabhadra's *Cakrasamvarapañjikā* and Bhavabhaṭṭa's *Cakrasamvaravivṛtti.*[365] Jayabhadra's commentary, as noted above, is the oldest of the commentaries and also one of the historically most important. It is, however, considerably shorter, so while it is invaluable insofar as it does quote the root text, it does jump over large portions of the Tantra. There are two surviving manuscripts of this commentary. The oldest (ms. E) is written in a clear Nevārī script. It is undated, but from the script it appears likely to have been copied during the eighteenth or nineteenth century. Unfortunately, it is incomplete, with the final folia (from chapter thirty-six onward) missing. There is also one additional manuscript (ms. D), which is complete, but which is a later text, dated N.S. 1031, or 1911 CE. It is written in Devanāgarī, but it is less clear and contains numerous mistakes.

Bhavabhaṭṭa's commentary is considerably longer, and also better preserved. It quotes a significant proportion of the root text's verses, often giving several variants, and is thus an indispensable resource for the study of this Tantra. It has been edited by Janardan Shastri Pandey in his (2002) joint edition of both the *Cakrasamvara Tantra* and Bhavabhaṭṭa's commentary. While I have made extensive use of this work, I have also consulted two of the three extant manuscripts. The best extant manuscript (ms. F) is a complete commentary in Bhujimol script on palm leaves. It is undated, but the script seems to date to the fourteenth century. The second manuscript I have consulted (ms. G) is a later copy in Nevārī script on Nepali paper. It is far less helpful as it contains numerous errors. Janardan Shastri Pandey also employed one additional later manuscript to which I did not have access.[366]

---

[365] Additionally, there is Vajrapāṇi's *Laghutantraṭīkā* (ed. in Cicuzza 2001), but as this commentary only covers the first ten and a half verses of CS ch. 1, it does not fill any of these gaps.

[366] This is a copy of the *Cakrasamvaravivṛtti* in the National Archives of Nepal (ms. # 3/720), consisting of 163 folia on Nepali paper. See Pandey 2002, xxix.

These two commentaries cite much, but not all, of the missing portions of the text, and also provide important additional readings for the text that is preserved in the extant manuscripts of the root text. However, there is also one additional important source for the recovery of the missing portions of the Sanskrit text, and that is the *Abhidhānottara Tantra* (AU). As discussed above, the AU is closely related to the *Cakrasamvara Tantra* (CS), and there are fortunately a number of surviving manuscripts of it. In addition, there are also at least four places where the AU overlaps significantly with the text of the CS. These areas of overlap follow a distinct pattern. A single chapter of the AU overlaps with one or more chapters of the CS, each of which contains a core text identical with that in the AU, but often bracketed by one or several verses not found there. It appears that the authors of the AU may have adapted passages from the CS, and, in the process, also resolved some of the problems found in the latter text.[367]

Due to these overlaps, a truly critical edition of the CS will also necessitate a critical edition of the AU. The AU has been partially edited by Martin Kalff (1979), although most of the sections that overlap the CS are not edited by him.[368] For the purposes of this translation, I have examined three AU manuscripts. These include an excellent palm leaf manuscript (ms. H) in Bhujimol script, which is marred only by the absence of several folia. I have also consulted a paper manuscript in Nevārī script dated to 1743 CE (ms. I), as well as the Devānagarī manuscript published by Lokesh Chandra (ms. J). The latter two manuscripts, while more recent, are quite reliable.

---

[367] This is particularly suggested by CS chs. 7 and 8, which respectively end and begin with virtually the same text (ch. 7: *tat sarvavīrasvamātmānaṁ sarvavīrasamāyogaṁ ḍākinījalasamvaram*; and ch. 8: *tataḥ svamātmānaṁ sarvavīrasamāyogam sarvasiddhisamāvahaṁ ḍākinījālasamvaram*). The repetition of this verse in the CS mss. makes little sense, and no doubt for this reason the verse at the end of ch. 7 was deleted in the Tibetan translations. They are resolved into a single line in the *kavacahṛdayabhāvanā* ch. of the AU, namely: *svamātmanaḥ sarvavīrasamāyogaḍākinījalasamvaraḥ* (H 172b.5; I 612a.3; J 281.4: *sarvaśarīra-*). See my note to CS ch. 7 below.

[368] Kalff edited and translated eight chapters of the AU, a small fraction of what is a very large text. Four of these contain text corresponding to five chapters of CS (chs. 16–20). I have been told that a complete edition of the AU has been recently completed as a dissertation at Delhi University, but I have not been able to confirm this, and have not seen this work.

With regard to the four significant instances of intertextuality, the first consists of the overlap of chapters one, two, and three of the *Cakrasamvara Tantra* with the *maṇḍalavidhi* chapter of the *Abhidhānottara*.[369] The second entails a close parallelism between CS chapters five, six, seven, and eight, and two AU chapters.[370] While these sections of the CS Sanskrit text are intact, the AU provides an important additional reading for this text. The third area of intertextuality is much larger and more critical as it provides Sanskrit readings for portions of the Sanskrit missing in the CS mss. It involves a series of nine consecutive chapters of the AU that correspond to a larger group of CS chapters, including chapters eighteen and nineteen, as well as chapters twenty-two through twenty-nine, the text of which largely falls in the missing folia.[371] The fourth and final instance of intertexuality that I have identified consists of an AU chapter that corresponds to CS ch. 30.[372]

[369] See the notes to my translation of these chapters for references to specific points in the AU mss.

[370] CS ch. 5 corresponds to the *mūlamantrakhaṭikoddhāra* ch. of the AU, and CS chs. 6, 7, and 8 correspond to the *kavacahṛdayabhāvanā* ch. of the AU.

[371] The AU's *chomā* chapter corresponds to CS ch. 15, and the *yoginīlakṣaṇa* chapter in the AU is almost identical to CS chs. sixteen and seventeen. The *ḍākinīlakṣaṇa* chapter in the AU corresponds to CS chapter eighteen, most of which is missing in the CS mss. Likewise, CS chapter nineteen, which is also partially lost, is almost identical to the *lāmālakṣaṇa* chapter in the AU. CS ch. 20 likewise corresponds to the *aṅgamudrālakṣana* chapter of the AU. These four chapters of the AU are edited and translated by Martin Kalff in his (1979) dissertation. I have consulted his work as well as the three AU mss. (H, I, J) listed in the *Conspectus Siglorum* below. With regard to the AU chs., I give their names rather than numbers because the chapter numbers vary considerably among the manuscripts. For example, the *aṅgamudrālakṣana-paṭala* is ch. 42 in Kalff's edition, but is ch. 39 in mss. H and J, and ch. 41 in ms. I. Unfortunately, there is also variance in chapter titles. Ms. I confirms Kalff's reading (ms. H is missing a folio here), but in ms. J it is entitled the *chomāpaṭala* (J 220.3). The chapter that follows in the AU likewise corresponds to CS ch. 21. This chapter, strangely, is also entitled *aṅgamudrālakṣaṇa-paṭala* in mss. I (595a.1) and J (221.2). Ms. H is missing a folio here, and Kalff did not edit this chapter. This is followed by the chapter entitled *ḍākinyaṅgamudrā*, which corresponds to CS ch. 22. The AU's *ḍākinīchomālakṣaṇa* ch. corresponds to CS chs. 23 and 24. The next AU ch., entitled *dūtasaumkhyāmbū*, corresponds to CS chs. 26–29. The parallelism is broken by CS ch. 25, a brief restatement of the root mantra.

[372] The *rakṣācaturmukhādhiṣṭhānalipimaṇḍala-catuḥkrodhavajrahūṁkārotpattikhaṭikoddhāra* ch. in the AU, which occurs well after the above section of parallel text, closely parallels CS ch. 30. It also overlaps with several of the opening verses of CS ch. 31.

Janardan Shastri Pandey's (2002) edition is an edition of both the *Cakrasamvara Tantra* itself as well as Bhavabhaṭṭa's commentary. It is a work that I have studied extensively, and about which I have mixed feelings. Perhaps the greatest contribution of this work is its edition of Bhavabhaṭṭa's commentary. This edition is not critical. Pandey and his assistants largely follow the oldest and most reliable manuscript (F), and do not consistently note variant readings. However, their readings are generally sound. I have read extensively through their edition and have compared their readings to the two manuscripts available to me, and I have found relatively few problems. I have noted the points where my readings disagree with theirs.

I have serious reservations, however, with their edition of the *Cakrasamvara Tantra* itself. Here too, the edition is not critical. They are extremely inconsistent in noting variants, doing so only in a small minority of those instances in which they actually occur. They also employ what appears to be a rather liberal editorial policy. In my opinion, they rely far too heavily on the readings present in Bhavabhaṭṭa's commentary, and often emend the root text to agree with it. They also rely heavily on the standard Tibetan translation,[373] and likewise emend the Sanskrit on the basis of it. These emendations are made even when there are additional sources supporting the root text's reading, and usually they do not report readings contrary to their own. These contrary readings are often found in the *Abhidhānottara*, which they seem to have consulted only sporadically, as well as in Jayabhadra's commentary and in alternative Tibetan translations, which they do not appear to have consulted at all. While they were aware of the *Abhidhānottara*, it seems that they largely ignored the alternate readings that it provides. They even ignore it in the cases where it provides the *only* extant Sanskrit reading. In these cases, they seem to prefer "restoring" the Sanskrit by back-translating from the Tibetan.

Thus, the reader of this edition by Pandey, et al., must be aware that it is in no way a reflection of the actual extant Sanskrit manuscripts, since the notes do not consistently provide all of the readings. As a result, it is unfortunately not very useful for scholars with serious interest in the Sanskrit texts of the *Cakrasamvara Tantra*. On the other hand, their edition of the standard Tibetan translation based on multiple recensions of the *bKa'-'gyur* appears to be sound. It is also notable for its reconstruction of the Sanskrit

---

[373] That is, Mardo's revised translation. See section 4.2 below.

of the lost sections. However, given the numerous disparities between the existing Sanskrit and the Tibetan translations of this text, the assumption that the Tibetan translation gives direct insight into the Sanskrit on which it is based appears unsound. Such reconstruction is an approximation at best. This is easily shown in the case of this text; there are numerous cases where the editors chose to reconstruct the Sanskrit from Mardo's Tibetan translation[374] even in places where the Sanskrit of the *Abhidhānottara* or of Jayabhadra's commentary provide a clear reading. Their reconstructions often diverge from the latter sources. By contrast with this, I have herein followed the Sanskrit whenever possible, and have taken the *Abhidhānottara* and the commentaries to be important sources which must be taken into account. I have noted in my translation the places where my readings diverge from those in Pandey's edition.

Regarding the Tibetan translations, while not exactly mirroring the Sanskrit, they do constitute an important resource for the study of this text that cannot be ignored. There were at least two distinct Tibetan translations of this text, both of which survive in three distinct versions. These were made most likely prior to the reproduction of the earliest extant Sanskrit manuscript, which was probably copied during the late twelfth or thirteenth century. The first known translation was that made by Rin-chen bZang-po and the Kaśmīri scholar Padmākaravarman, presumably during the late tenth century when the former was studying in Kaśmīr.[375] This translation was revised twice, but the original version does not appear to be still extant, although it was available to Tsong Khapa in the fifteenth century.[376]

[374] See the discussion immediately below for more on Mardo.

[375] Rin-chen bZang-po (958–1055 CE) studied in India for over a decade, returning to Tibet c. 991 CE. It is not known exactly when he made this translation, but it seems likely that he made it while in India. After his return to Tibet he translated several other works in the Cakrasamvara tradition with Śraddhākaravarman and Atīśa Dīpaṁkaraśrījñāna. His work with the various Indian paṇḍits can be limited in any case to a period of about seventy-five years, since they "are contemporaries of Rin-chen-bzang-po and their activity should therefore be confined to within a very precise time limit: the second half of the 10th century up until about the third quarter of the 11th century." (Tucci 1988, 49) This period can be even more precisely confined to between 975 CE, when he departed for India, and 1055 CE, when he died.

[376] Tsong Khapa refers to this original translation at several points in his commentary. He also refers to what seems to have been an independent translation by Mardo or Marpa Chos-

The best known revised version, which is preserved in the Kangyur section of the Tibetan canon, is that undertaken by Marpa Chos-kyi dbang-phyug, usually known as Marpa Dopa or Mardo (c. 1043–1138 CE),[377] together with Prajñākīrti. Mardo studied the Cakrasamvara tradition in India and Nepal with disciples of the Mahāsiddha Nāropa. In Nepal he translated a number of texts in the Cakrasamvara tradition with the assistance of Sumatikīrti,[378] who was himself responsible for the other revision of the *Cakrasamvara Tantra*. After his return to Tibet Mardo played an important role in the dissemination of the texts and practices of the Cakrasamvara tradition there. I have made extensive use of this version of the Tantra. While I primarily worked from the sDe-dge recension of this text, I have also taken into consideration the variants in other recensions.

A different revision of Rin-chen bZang-po's translation was made by Sumatikīrti. A Kaśmīri, he was a disciple of Nāropa (956–1040 CE), and is depicted as senior to Marpa Lho-brag-pa (1012–1096 CE) in the latter's biography.[379] Sumatikīrti participated in the translation of a number of texts with Mardo, and was himself the author of a short but influential work on the *Cakrasamvara Tantra* entitled *The Intended Import of the Chapters of the Concise Samvara Tantra*.[380] He also revised Rin-chen bZang-po's translation with the help of the Tibetan translator bLo-gros-grags.[381] This version of the text was preserved only in the Phug-brag manuscript Kangyur

kyi dbang-phyug. Neither of these independent works have survived, to my knowledge. See my translation of Tsong Khapa's commentary (Gray 2017).

377 gZhon-nu-dpal writes in his *Blue Annals* that Mardo "seems to have been born when the venerable Mar-pa was about 31. He lived to the age of 95." (Roerich 1949, 383) This would allow us to tentatively assign Mardo the dates of 1043–1138 CE. This Marpa/Mardo should not be confused with Marpa (1012–1096 CE), the famous guru of Milarepa, known variously as Marpa Chos-kyi-blo-gros, Marpa Lho-brag-pa, and as Marpa Lo-tsā-wa ("Marpa the Translator") or simply Marlo.

378 See Roerich 1949, 384.

379 See Trungpa 1982, 106.

380 *Laghusamvaratantrapaṭalābhisandhi*. Tōh. 1411, DT vol. ma, 352a–353a.

381 It is possible that this bLo-gros-grags is Mal-gyo blo-gros-grags, the Tibetan monk who made a second translation of the *Cakrasamvara Tantra*.

discovered in Ladakh,[382] but it is of great significance as it often provides alternate readings, some (but not all) of which accord more closely with the surviving Sanskrit. I have compared both this and the standard translation with the Sanskrit, line-by-line.

A second translation was made by Mal-gyo blo-gros-grags, who also traveled to India. He studied the Cakrasamvara tradition in Nepal with Pham-ting-pa and other disciples of Nāropa.[383] Returning to Tibet he taught Sachen Kun-dga' sNying-po;[384] his translation and lineage thus became the one followed by subsequent members of the Sa-skya school. His translation was not included in the Tibetan canon, but is preserved within this school. While I have not had access to an independent copy of this translation, I have made frequent use of Sachen's *Pearl Garland* (PG) commentary, which is based upon his translation. Finally, in addition to this work, I have also taken into account both Bu-ston's massive and magisterial commentary on the root text, his *Illumination of the Secret Reality* (NS), as well as Tsong Khapa's *Total Illumination of the Hidden Meaning* (KS).

4.2 Translation Methodology

My translation herein is primarily based on the Sanskrit version of the *Cakrasamvara Tantra*. In creating this translation, however, I have made extensive use of Tibetan language sources, which provide important alternate readings as well as essential information concerning the history of the text's interpretation. Generally speaking, while the Tibetan translations are by no means identical to the Sanskrit text, they do closely approximate it. There are, however, two major areas where they diverge from the Sanskrit. The first such area involves non-literal translations, often in response to grammatically or hermeneutically challenging sections of the text. While

---

[382] This edition of the Kangyur was cataloged by Jampa Samten (1992). The manuscripts themselves are preserved in the Library of Tibetan Works and Archives in Gangchen Kyishong, Dharamsala, India. It has also been microfilmed by the Institute for Advanced Studies of World Religions (Carmel, NY), catalogue # Lmpj 016,901.

[383] See Roerich 1949, 382.

[384] Sachen's dates are 1092–1158 CE (see Krapivina 1991). Mal-gyo must have been somewhat older; it seems safe to assume that he traveled to Nepal in the second half of the eleventh century while some of Nāropa's disciples were still thriving, and that he served as Sachen's guru later, during the first half of the twelfth century.

these represent an understandable response to a difficult text, they undermine the soundness of Pandey's "back-translation" methodology.[385] The second major area of divergence involves additional passages not found in the extant Sanskrit texts. Some of this divergence is clearly due to variations found among distinct manuscript recensions. Bhavabhaṭṭa notes that there were at least three renditions of the text at his time. His commentary in several cases attests additional or variant lines found in one or more Tibetan translations but not in the *Cakrasamvara* mss. But there are also additional lines not attested in any of the extant Sanskrit sources, and which may be Tibetan interpolations. The standard Tibetan (Mardo revised) translation contains the most instances of additional text not attested elsewhere. In cases where there is serious divergence between the two, I usually have followed the Sanskrit, but I note the variance.

I have also made use of all eleven of the surviving Indian commentaries. I have privileged Jayabhadra's and Bhavabhaṭṭa's for which the Sanskrit survives. This preference is largely due to the fact that I have spent a great deal of time reading through them, comparing them to the Sanskrit manuscripts and Tibetan translations. But I have also made use of the commentaries that survive only in Tibetan translation, particularly those by Kambala and Vīravajra, which often give helpful explanations of the ritual portions of the text.

Recourse to the commentaries was an indispensable component of the translation process, due to the frequent obscurity of the root text. This obscurity is partly due to deliberate esotericism, and partly due to numerous grammatical errors. The *Cakrasamvara Tantra* is composed in Sanskrit, of the sort typical of Buddhist texts of this period, not the "Buddhist Hybrid

[385] There are numerous cases where the Tibetan renderings are interpretive rather than literal translations, which was undoubtedly essential, given the difficulties of the Sanskrit text. One example occurs in ch. 31, where the text cryptically describes the practice of "hand worship" (*hastapūjā*), in which the deities are visualized on one's hands. The text describes the parts of the hands symbolically, at one point reading "Vajrasattva abides by the tree" (*vajrasattvas tarave sthita*), a text which is ungrammatical, apparently confusing a masculine *u*-stem dative for a masculine or neuter *a*-stem locative. Perhaps in response to this error, the Tibetan translations do not translate literally here "at/on/by the tree," but instead interpretively translate "at/on/by the thumb" (PM 235a: *mthe bor*; SL 124b: *'the bor*), relying on the commentaries. While this translation is not incorrect, it is interpretive. Needless to say, an attempt to back-translate here would yield a novel Sanskrit text that would in no way be a restoration of the "original" text.

Sanskrit" described by Edgerton.[386] While the Sanskrit is often poor, and is particularly haphazard with regard to declension, many of its irregularities are of a sort common to Nevārī manuscripts, often reflecting textual corruptions that inevitably arise when a text is repeatedly recopied by scribes with a limited or non-existent command of Sanskrit.[387] However, in addition to such scribal errors, it seems that the original Sanskrit itself may have been poor, probably composed by a person or persons with imperfect command of the language. Nevertheless, the Sanskrit of this text is still Sanskrit. There is only one case where the text contains vocabulary clearly deriving not from Sanskrit but from later vernacular speech,[388] and also only one case where the text contains a term that is unattested in the common Sanskrit lexicons.[389] Metrical problems also abound. Portions of the text are written in thirty-two syllable *śloka* verse. The meter, however, is irregular, and the syllable count is often violated. This situation has been observed for other Nevārī manuscripts as well, which as a general class do not readily permit

[386] Brough has argued that "Edgerton throughout [his 1953 grammar] rather underestimates the degree of accidental transmissional corruption which our texts may have suffered." (1954, 353) And while Edgerton may be correct that earlier Mahāyāna Buddhist Sanskrit texts are influenced by a Middle Indic vernacular, I see no evidence for this in the later, post-seventh century tantric texts that I have studied. See Edgerton 1953, 1–9.

[387] Common irregularities include the ignoring of *sandhi* rules and confusion concerning the proper endings for the declension of nouns and adjectives. There are also numerous instances where there is a lack of agreement between nouns and verbs, or between nouns and adjectives. The text also frequently breaks up compounds into individual words. Textual corruptions are commonly due to similarities in Nevārī scripts between the letters *c* and *v*, *y* and *p*, *n* and *t*, and *ś* and *s*, as well as to *b* and *v* which are not distinguished in this script; these letter pairs were frequently confused. Moreover, larger errors are not unknown. Particularly common is the loss of subscribed and superscribed marks for vowels and consonants. A full account of the problems commonly found in these manuscripts is provided in Brough 1954. See also George 1974, 14–17.

[388] This instance occurs not in the body of the text itself, but in the titles at the end of chs. 40–48, where in place of the Sanskrit *catvāriṁśa* or *catvāriṁśattama*, "fortieth," the CS mss. read *cāliṁśatimaḥ*, while Bhavabhaṭṭa reads *cālīśatimaḥ*. This is much closer to the forms found in modern languages such as Hindi, Punjabi, and Marathi.

[389] This term, *saṁkulikā*, occurs in CS ch. 37, but is not attested in Monier-Williams' (2002) or Apte's (1965) dictionaries. However, in Pali *sankulikā* means "a cake or sweetmeat" (Rhys-Davids and Stede 1949, 120 col. 1), which corresponds to Sumatikīrti's translation "oil pastry," *snum 'khur* (SL 128a; PM 237a: *snum khur*).

editorial correction for the purpose of restoring the meter.[390] It is simply Sanskrit, albeit of a rather simplified and prosaic variety.

The commentators were well aware of these problems, and often much of their work involved corrections to the grammar of the text. For example, Jayabhadra commented as follows with regard to the incorrectly declined *caturo ratnā*, which occurs at the end of chapter eight: "In the Tantra the grammatical cases are shown haphazardly in order to bewilder everyone. They must be inferred through reference to their meaning."[391]

I have tried to produce a relatively literal translation of the Sanskrit text. Like all translations, it is inevitably interpretative, particularly given the grammatical and semantic obscurity of this text. Many passages in the *Cakrasamvara Tantra* are interpreted by its commentators in a non-literal fashion, even in cases where the text is not particularly challenging. In these cases, I have generally tried to produce a literal translation, but I have provided examples of such commentary in my notes. This I have done selectively, providing only the commentary that seemed to me the most helpful or interesting. To have done otherwise would have utterly overwhelmed the translation with the notes.

In areas where the Sanskrit manuscripts of the root text are incomplete, my translation is based upon the Tibetan translations as well as upon any additional sources, Sanskrit and Tibetan, that shed light on the text. I have not consulted the Chinese translation (1997), as it is a modern work based upon the standard Tibetan translation. While culturally significant, it does not provide any additional information.

---

390 Snellgrove, for example, noted that in mss. of the HT "more than a hundred lines are quite irregular, and although they clearly represent *ślokas* of a kind, it is impossible to see how many of them can ever have been anything but irregular. Thus, where there is a choice of reading, the original one is by no means necessarily the one that would permit correct scansion." (1959, 2:ix) Elder's observations concerning the *Sampuṭa Tantra* are also relevant to the *Cakrasamvara Tantra*: "We must, like Snellgrove, make our confession of leaving very much open in our edition the solution to problems of meter. Essentially, where it occurred, it was *śloka*, but frequently the Pāda reached nine or ten syllables, and occasionally there appears an independent Pāda joined only in sense to a regular line. We think it most likely that mediocre poetical skill is involved in many cases; but we also think that a thorough study of metrical patterns in the *Saṁpuṭa* is necessary in the future." (1978, 34–35 n. 2)

391 E 19b.5: *tantre sarvavyāmohārthaṁ yatheṣṭaṁ vibhaktinirdeśaḥ kṛtaḥ / tadarthavaśād unneyaḥ /*. Many thanks to Dr. George Cardona for his assistance in translating this passage.

While I have striven for consistency in my translation of terms, I do not adhere to such consistency so rigidly as to result in inaccurate or misleading renderings, since Sanskrit and Tibetan terms often have multiple meanings which are not covered by a single word in English. For example, the word *sattva* I usually translate as "being" when it has this sense. However, when appropriate, I also translate it as "hero," as in the case of chapter one, where the term definitely has this sense, as Jayabhadra's commentary clearly indicates. Another important example is *bodhicitta.* When used in its ordinary Mahāyāna sense, I translate this as "spirit of awakening." However, in the Cakrasamvara literature this term is primarily used as a euphemism for semen[392] in the context of the sexual practices; in this context I translate it as "seminal essence," to distinguish it from the ordinary words for semen which are also used in this text and its commentaries. Other terms referring to sexual organs, such as *liṅga* ("penis"), and *bhaga* and *yoni* ("vulva"), I translate literally. However, the commentators frequently use the common Buddhist euphemisms *vajra* and *padma* to refer to the male and female sexual organs, respectively. As these euphemistic terms are so common, I do feel the need to translate them interpretively. Thus, the reader should be aware that in these contexts I leave *vajra* untranslated, and I translate *padma* literally as "lotus."

Other terms have double or triple meanings; these I translate according to the sense in which they are used. A notable example of this is *mudrā*, a complex term with three basic meanings: 1) seal, stamp, or mark; 2) a symbolic hand gesture; or 3) the female counterpart of a god.[393] The term is used in all three of these senses in both the Tantra and its commentaries. In the first case, the Sanskrit term *mudrā*, like the English term "seal" refers not only to an impressed mark (as well as the device for making such), but also to the act of shutting, closing, or locking. *Mudrā* is used in this sense particularly in Vīravajra's commentary, where it refers to the "seals" in the channels of the subtle body that the yogin effects—via the laying down of seed syllables (*mantra-nyāsa*) and/or yogic postures (*yantra*)—

[392] This is, properly speaking, the "white bodhicitta." While the expression "red bodhicitta" (*byang sems dmar po*) is used as a euphemism for female sexual fluid, this expression does not occur in the texts studied here.

[393] This is based upon Saunders' analysis (1960, 5–7). See also the discussion in Gonda 1972.

in order to reverse the flow of semen. A derivative meaning of *mudrā* is mark or insignia, which occurs in the "five insignia," *pañcamudrā*, mentioned in chapter twenty-seven. The term *mudrā* is also used in its well-known sense of a symbolic gesture formed with the hands. In this case, I translate the term "gesture."[394]

Finally, the term *mudrā* can also refer to the women who serve as consorts in tantric ritual practices, such as the "secret" and "wisdom-gnosis" consecrations, and also in the sexual yogas. This is the most common use of the term in Cakrasamvara literature, where I translate the term as "consort." Later Buddhist commentators developed a more elaborate system of four or five such *mudrās*.[395] Among these, only the term *mahāmudrā*, "great seal," occurs in the root text. For example, chapter thirty-three states that "The primordially established great consort (*mahāmudrā*) should be worshipped with great zeal, [as do] men in the Yoga Tantras." The commentators explain that the female consort is referred to here. However, it may be that the term here has the dual meaning typical of the later tradition. As Snellgrove has noted, *mahāmudrā* can refer both to the female partner and to the "absolute truth as realized through her." (1987, 265) Already by the ninth century, the term *mahāmudrā* was used to refer to the gnosis that these practices were thought to produce.[396] The commentators also frequently refer to the actual female consort via the term *karmamudrā*, the technical term used to refer to her in the later scholastic tradition.

A closely related term is *vidyā*, "sacred knowledge," which in this text also has two derivative meanings. It is used as a synonym for *mantra*, in which case I translate it as "spell." It is also commonly used to refer to the female participant in the sexual practices, in which case I translate it also as "consort."

Another term that deserves some comment is *siddhi*. This term is customarily translated as "achievement" or "accomplishment," which is not in-

---

394 See Saunders 1960 for an exhaustive list of tantric Buddhist *mudrā*.

395 These are the *dharmamudrā*, *samayamudrā*, *karmamudrā*, *mahāmudrā*, and *jñānamudrā*. For a discussion of these, see Snellgrove 1987, 265–269.

396 For example, in his comments on CS ch. 28, Jayabhadra glossed the term "gnosis" (*jñāna*) with *mahāmudrā*. See my notes on that ch. below. This interpretation was common by the eleventh century; see my translation of Vīravajra's commentary on the Tantra's opening verses, in section 1.3 above.

correct, if perhaps a bit vague. These are useful translations when speaking abstractly. Tantric Buddhists typically recognize two types of accomplishment, the "ultimate accomplishment" (*lokottara-siddhi*) of awakening, and the "worldly accomplishments" (*laukikasiddhi*), which are various magical powers that tantric meditation and ritual are thought to accrue. The focus of the *Cakrasamvara Tantra* is predominantly on the latter.[397] These are "achievements" in the sense that they are the results of magical operations such as mantra repetition, but they are achievements that manifest as magical powers. I thus generally translate *siddhi* in this text as "power" or "magical power," except in the few instances where the former type may be implied, in which case I use the more generic translation "accomplishment." Note that in so translating I do not mean to imply the ideology of "power" (*śakti*) that is a distinctive feature of tantric Hinduism, for which there is no exact correspondence in tantric Buddhism.[398]

4.3 Technical Notes

In cases where I am translating a technical term, I usually provide the Sanskrit in italics in parentheses at the first instance. But I do not translate or so treat Sanskrit terms that have entered the English lexicon, such as "mantra" and "maṇḍala," except in a few specific instances. One such instance is "karma." As adopted in English, the term "karma" implies the later doctrine of ethical causality advanced by mainstream Indian religions.[399] However, in this text the term is often used in its older sense of a "ritual action." I translate it thus when it is used in this fashion. I also do not translate the term *soma.* Usually designating the plant extract used in vedic ritual, in the context of Cakrasamvara literature it appears to designate the mixed sexual fluids that are produced and used in the rituals described in the text and commentaries.

---

[397] While commentators on the CS argue that the attainment of awakening is the primary purpose of the text, there is little overt discussion of this in the text itself, which is far more concerned with describing techniques for the attainment of mundane powers such as flight, invisibility, and so forth.

[398] Regarding the tantric Hindu concept of power, see Urban 2001b. For a fascinating discussion of the related but not identical ideology of power implicit in tantric Buddhist ritual and ritual discourse, see Beyer 1973.

[399] Regarding the doctrine of karma, see Obeyesekere 2002, and also the essay "How, not What: *Kamma* as a Reaction to Brahminism," in Gombrich 1996, 27–64.

In my translation I use square brackets for two closely related purposes. First, I place in square brackets words in my translation that do not occur in the source texts, but which seem necessary to me to properly render the text in English. Secondly, I also use square brackets to indicate passages in the text which are only attested by a minority of sources. For example, there are instances when the Tibetan translations contain additional lines or verses that are not contained in the Sanskrit. In cases where these additional lines improve the reading of the text, I include them within square brackets. Otherwise, I relegate them to the footnotes. In cases where I add yet additional words to my translation of these passages for the sake of clarity, I indicate these with curly brackets.

I also employ text in bold in a meaningful fashion. In my translations from the commentaries, both in the introduction as well as in the notes to the translation, I indicate the text which is being commented upon in **bold** text. I do so in order to clarify the relationship between the root text and the commentary, which is not always readily apparent, as some of the commentators integrate the text they are explaining into their commentaries.

Within the introductory essay and also in the notes to the translation I have provided numerous translations from primary sources, both Sanskrit and Tibetan. When my translations are based on my readings of Sanskrit manuscripts, I provide the Sanskrit following the translation, since the manuscripts on which they are based are neither widely accessible nor easily read. I also include the Sanskrit of passages of Bhavabhaṭṭa's commentary, even when I am working from Pandey's (2002) edition rather than the manuscripts. This is because the texts published by the Central Institute of Higher Tibetan Studies are not widely distributed, and may not be easily obtained by interested readers. On the other hand, when translating from Tibetan texts that are easily available, such as texts from the canonical collections, I simply give the reference, as anyone who is interested can easily check my translations with the published Tibetan texts.

Part Two

TRANSLATION

1. The Descent of the Maṇḍala

Homage to Śrī Cakrasamvara!

And now I will explain the secret, concisely, not extensively. Union with Śrī Heruka is the means of achieving all desired aims. It is more lofty than the lofty, the binding of the ḍākinīs' network.[1] The hero made of all ḍākinīs, Vajrasattva,[2] Supreme Bliss, always abides in the universal nature,

[1] Jayabhadra explains the compound *ḍākinījālasamvaraṁ* as follows: "As for **the binding of the ḍākinīs' network**, all of the ḍākinīs are positioned in the triple wheel. Their **network** is the assemblage of them; the **binding** of that means that it should be concealed by means of binding." (D 4b.2–3, E 3b.3–4: *ḍākinījālasamvaram iti ḍākinyaḥ sarvās tricakravyavasthitāḥ / tāsāṁ jālaḥ samūhas tasya samvaraḥ samvareṇa gopanīyam ityarthaḥ*) His statement that it "should be concealed/protected" suggests that it may also be a name for a teaching or a text. In ch. 48 below we learn that the "binding of the ḍākinīs' net…was well-spoken by tens of millions of buddhas and also tens of millions of heroes." This is confirmed as well by a somewhat mysterious comment by Vīravajra:

> Regarding **It is more lofty than the lofty, the binding of the ḍākinīs' net**, this is said to be a name. Since this name is a Vajra word, its significance is threefold. It is understood in terms of shape by the bodhisattva Ākāśagarbha, in terms of mantra by Avalokiteśvara, and in terms of reality (*dharma*) by Mañjuśrī. Regarding "shape," it is the **binding** of the four joys through the descent of seminal essence to the Root Wheel. "Mantra" is the **binding** of nonconceptual thought by the insertion of the life-force of the wheels into the central channel (*avadhūtī*) through the inhalation of breath. "Reality" (*dharmatā*) is **binding** with great bliss due to the generation of the gnosis of illusion with regard to emptiness. (PD 355b)

Note that in the two instances where I translate "shape" the text reads first *dbyings* (realm), and then *dbyibs* (shape or form). "Realm" (*dbyings*) is thus an alternate reading here, but I prefer the reading "shape" (*dbyibs*), as it fits the threefold pattern of body, speech, and mind that seems to be operating here. Another possibile interpretation of this line is that the term *ḍākinījālasamvara* could refer to another text, perhaps the JS, in which case the text here is claiming superiority over this earlier Yoginī Tantra. Sachen confirms this possibility, but in the context of ch. 14 below he identifies the *ḍākinījālasamvara* with the *Śrī-Khasama-Āditantra* (PG 325.3), the legendary root text of this tradition. I am indebted to Iain Sinclair for suggesting this possibility.

[2] Jayabhadra glosses Vajrasattva's name as follows: "Since he has capability with respect to the aims of all beings, and since he is endowed with supreme fortitude, he is a **hero** (*sattva*). Since he is unbreakable, he is **adamantine** (*vajra*). He is the **Adamantine Hero** (*vajrasattva*)

the secret that is supreme and delightful.[3] He is the self-arisen Blessed Lord Hero, the binding of the ḍākinīs' network. Arising from the form of sound,[4]

since he guides beings with his adamantine gnosis, the hero who is immovable by anyone such as Viṣṇu or Śiva." (E 4b.3–4: *sarvasattvārthasamarthatvāt sat[tvā]rthaḥ paramadhairyaguṇayogād vā sattva[ḥ] / abhedyatvād vajrajñānena sarvasattvān ūḍhatvād vajrasattvaḥ / sarvair eva harihārādibhir acālyaṁ sattvaṁ yasyeti vā vajrasattvaḥ /*)

[3] Apparently it is Vajrasattva (or the meditator *qua* Vajrasattva) who abides, and the "secret" in which he or she abides is the mystery of the maṇḍala, the "network of ḍākinīs," which is understood to pervade both the universe and the practitioner's body. Jayabhadra comments on this as follows:

> Regarding **secret**, here the word "secret" implies all of the ḍākinīs positioned in the three wheels. [Their network] is secret, mysteriously comprised, and is uniform (*ekarūpaṁ*), due to [their being in] the state of experiential uniformity (*samarasatā*), assembled everywhere throughout the realm of space. It is the palace endowed with the Blessed Lord Śrī Heruka, Vajravārāhī, and so forth. What is it like? It is **supreme**—the best, the highest, the unexcelled—because it is the basis of mundane [knowledge] and supramundane gnosis. How is it delightful? It is **delightful** because the unexcelled worship is pleasing on account of playful activity. Now, it is said to be infinite since it is thoroughly fulfilled. **Always abides in the universal nature** indicates the body or self-form of all who are positioned in the triple wheel, which is the nature of the three realms, in which [they] **always** [abide], i.e., in which they have a state of not being separated [from it] anywhere or at any time.
>
> *rahasya iti rahasyaśabdenātra tricakravyavasthitāḥ sarvaḍākinyo vidhīya[n]te // tasmi[n] raha[s]i saṁkṛtaṁ rahasyaṁ samarasatayaikarūpaṁ sarvākāśadhātusamavasaraṇaṁ // bhagavataḥ śrīherukasya vajravārāhyādisaṁyuktaṁ bhavanaṁ kiṁ viśiṣṭaṁ tad ity āha // paramam iti paramam utkṛṣṭaṁ pradhānam anuttaraṁ // laukikalokottarajñānādhānatvāt // punar api viśiṣṭe ramye anuttarapūjāḥ krīḍākriyayā ramaṇīyatvād ramyaṁ // idānīṁ paryantasampadā anantyatvam āha // sarvātmani sadā sthitaḥ iti sarveṣāṁ traidhātukātmatricakravyavasthitānām ātmakāyaḥ svarūpaṁ vā tasmin sadeti kvacit kadācid api viyogābhāvaṁ sūcayate* (E 4a.1–6)

[4] Bhavabhaṭṭa comments on this as follows:

> Should one ask, from whence did he who is like that arise? [The text reads] **arising**, and so forth. Analyzing that, the deities arise through an origination in the congregation of the vowels and consonants. Whence did they arise? **From the form of sound**— "sound" is simply "word," the subtle [word] in the sense of the substratum. Its "form" or nature refers to the syllable *hūṁ* on its own seat atop the assemblage of vowels and consonants.
>
> *kuta evaṁbhūtaḥ saṁbhūtas tvam ity āha—saṁbhavād ity ādi / samvibhajya devatā bhavanty anena saṁbhava ālikālisamavāyaḥ / tatrāpi kuta ity āha—nādarūpād iti / nādaḥ śabdamātram / tasya pratinidhir daṇḍamātram / tasya rūpaṁ svarūpaṁ yathā svāsane svaravyañjanasamūhas tadupari hūṁkāraḥ* (Pandey 2002, 15–16)

they whose scope is the practice of the commitments come forth,[5] existing in the beginning, middle, and end,[6] difficult to obtain in the triple world.

Listen to what is taught in the Tantra, the yoga that is endowed with mantra repetition, contemplation, and so forth, just like the union of the churned and the churner, along with the knowledge of the rites. The clanswoman[7] indeed should be constantly worshipped at the special occasion, with the central, superior breath,[8] accompanied by scented water.[9] The

---

Evidently this line refers to the generation of the deities from their seed syllables, as this is followed by a typical creation stage generation of the deities from the syllable *hūṁ*. Note that my translation "the subtle [word] in the sense of the substratum" is from the Tibetan (Pandey 2002, 175: *de so so'i rten du 'gyur ba phra mo'o*).

[5] The CS mss. give a plural reading here, with the text *sambhavān nādarūpāt viniṣkrāntāḥ samayācāragocarāḥ*. Bhavabhaṭṭa, however, notes that it should be read as singular, the referent being Vajradhara, the Dharmakāya Buddha (Pandey 2002, 17). Jayabhadra, however, reads it as referring to the plurality of heroes and heroines who inhabit the maṇḍala. This is not a problem for the tradition, which sees the essential nature of Śrī Heruka as pervading the entire triple world. I translate the plural literally here, as I do not wish to disturb the dynamic tension between unity and plurality which the text evidently sets up (as is it understood in the commentarial tradition). Jayabhadra's comments occur as follows: "Regarding they who **come forth from** that **sound** that exists in space, one should know that it is all heroes and ḍākinīs who dwell in the triple wheel who come forth, [just as] diverse speech comes forth from a single sound" (E 7a.6–7b.1: *tasmād ākāśadeśasthān nādāt hīti yasmāt niṣkrāntā iti bahuvacanam ekasmān nādāt / tricakravartinaḥ sarvavīrā ḍākinyaś ca niṣkrānthā iti jñeyatārthaḥ /*).

[6] Jayabhadra explains that this means that he/they exist in mind, speech, and body, and hence in the so-called maṇḍala wheels (E 7b.5–6: *ādimadhyāntasaṁsthitam iti cittavā[k]kāyasaṁsthitam*).

[7] Jayabhadra comments that "**clanswoman** is [an example of] the Tantra's symbolic speech. One **should worship** an outer woman who has the self-nature of Vajravārāhī." (E 8b.1: *kulikām iti tantrasamayabhāṣā / vajravārāhīsvarūpāṁ bāhyāṅganā pūjayed iti*)

[8] I translate this text, *madhyamottamaśvāsena*, following Jayabhadra's commentary, as translated in the next note. This also seems to accord with Bhavabhaṭṭa's gloss (Pandey 2002, 20: *madhyamottamayoḥ śvāsaḥ*). The Tibetan, however, implies two separate breaths (PM 213b: *dbugs 'byin bar ma mchog dag dang*).

[9] Jayabhadra comments here: "Regarding **central**, and so forth, the **central** one is the lotus, which is said to exist in the center. On it is the **superior breath**, which is the placement [there] of the tongue. What occurs with this? It is **accompanied by scented water**, meaning it is accompanied by seminal essence." (E 8a.5–8b.1: *madhyametyādi madhyame bhavatīti madhyamaḥ padma ucyate / tasmin uttamo śvāso jihvāvinyāsaḥ / tena kiṁ bhūtena gandhodakasahitena tu bodhicittasahitenaivety arthaḥ /*) Note that the Tibetan translation does not translate *jihvā* (see MP 45a).

messengers are natural and accomplished, as well as lowly, middling, and lofty.[10] With one's inwardly focused mind,[11] give rise to the achievement of pleasure.[12]

Worship the buddhas and bodhisattvas with one's own seminal drops,[13] with sight and touch, and with hearing and thought.[14] Have no

---

[10] Bhavabhaṭṭa interprets this line as signifying the goddesses of the Cakrasamvara maṇḍala:

> The **messengers** are plural; **clanswoman** and **messenger** are synonyms. Those **natural** ones are the four, ḍākinīs, and so forth, who are equal in nature to the Blessed Lord. Their nature is gnosis. The **accomplished** ones are the eight yoginīs, Yamadāhī, and so forth. The **lowly** ones, who belong to the body wheel, are underworld dwellers. The **middling** ones, who belong to the speech wheel, range on the earth. The **lofty** ones belong to the mind wheel, and rove in the sky. There is thus the worship of the thirty-six yoginīs.
>
> *dūtaya iti bahuvacanam / kulikā dūtaya iti paryāyakathanam / tāḥ sahajā bhagavataḥ prakṛtisamā ḍākinyādayaś catasraḥ / tā iti tasya jñānasvabhāvāḥ / siddhā iti yamadāhyādayo 'ṣṭau yoginyaḥ / adhamāḥ kāyacakragāḥ pātālavāsinyaḥ // madhyamā vākcakragā bhūcaryāḥ / uttamāś cittacakragāḥ khecaryāḥ / ibhyaḥ ṣaṭtriṁśat yoginya eva pūjā iti bhāvaḥ /* (F 23a.2–5; Cf. Pandey 2002, 22–23)

Bhavyakīrti agrees with the correlation of the messengers to the maṇḍala wheels, but also adds:

> **Natural** refers to the natural yoginīs. The yoginīs are threefold, i.e., mantra-born (*mantrajā*), born at the seats (*pīṭhajā*), and natural (*sahajā*); here the **natural** is just an illustration from among these. This implies also the direct realization that is the accomplishment of the threefold yoginīs. With regard to them, the **lofty** is the natural, the **middling** those born at the seats, and the **lowly** the mantra-born. (SM 8b)

[11] Regarding this Bhavabhaṭṭa wrote that "**inwardly focused** means with the mind which has the mode of being Śrī Heruka inseparable from oneself" (F 23b.1–2: *antargateneti svābhinnaśrīherukarūpeṇa cittenety arthaḥ*; Cf. Pandey 2002, 23). He identifies this line as indicating the "imaginative" or "mind-made" (*manomaya*) mode of worship, which is one of the four types of worship referred to in v. 14 below.

[12] Bhavabhaṭṭa comments that "it is held that Śrī Heruka's yogin succeeds through the enjoyment of all pleasures" (Pandey 2002, 23: *sarvakāmopabhogena śrīherukayogī sidhyatīty āśayaḥ*). He argues that this line additionally indicates the "outer" mode of worship, which he defines as follows: "The outer types of worship have the defining characteristic of enjoyment of the sensuous objects such as form, and so forth" (Pandey 2002, 23: *rūpādiviṣayopabhogalakṣaṇā bahiḥpūjāḥ*).

[13] Bhavabhaṭṭa takes this line as referring to "direct worship," as follows:

> Regarding "direct worship," [it is indicated by] **one's own seminal [drops]**, and so forth. Outwardly, one should emit seminal essence for the sake of worship in

doubt that one will be thus liberated from all sins. The state of being a yogin is the supreme purifying merit which destroys sin. The well equipoised adept is successful with mantra repetition, meditative states, and with bliss,[15] and should always protect the commitments. Due to the breaking of the commitments, power will not be gained in the maṇḍala at consecration.

> the outer consort, whose defining marks are stated within the Tantra. With the drops which arise in the equipoise of the two, worship the buddhas—that is, the five aggregates such as form, feeling, and so forth, which have been purified and experienced through the mode of eating ambrosia—and the bodhisattvas, the forms of the eye, and so forth. The direct worship is to be observed at the three junctures [of the day]. Thus it is said: "One of firm intelligence should eat the secret semen with eyes wide open. This is the worship of body, speech, and mind with all mantras."
>
> *sākṣātpūjām āha svareta ityādi bahiḥprajñāyāṁ tantrāntaroktalakṣaṇāyāṁ pūjārthaṁ bodhicittam utpādayet / tasyobhayasamāpattijasya bindubhir amṛtāśvādarūpeṇa viśodhya bhujya buddhān rūpavedanādinapañcaskandhān bodhisattvāṁś cakṣurādi-rūpān pūjayet / evaṁ trisandhyam anuṣṭheyam iti sākṣātpūjā tad āha / guhyaśukraṁ viśālākṣyā bhakṣayed dṛḍhabuddhimān / idaṁ tatsarvamantrāṇāṁ kāyavākcitta-pūjanam iti /* (Pandey 2002, 23)

Interestingly, the Tibetan translators added "mentally" (CP 159a: *yid kyis*) to the last line, to read "One of firm intelligence should mentally eat the secret semen with eyes wide open."

14 Bhavabhaṭṭa explains that "one is liberated through intense engagement with the apprehension, and so forth, of sight, and so forth, through the discipline of the moments through which one realizes the secret of spontaneity. This is the secret worship." (F 24a.5–6: *darśanādināgrāhyādyabhiniviṣṭeṇa mucyate / sahajaguhyavedanakṣaṇayogāt iti guhyapūjā /* Pandey 2002, 24)

15 This translates the Sanskrit preserved in Cicuzza's edition of Vajrapāṇi's commentary, *sidhyate mantrajāpena dhyānena ca sukhena ca* (2001, 40), which corresponds exactly to the Tibetan translations (PM 214b, SL 96a). The CS mss. omit *sukhena ca*, reading instead: *sidhyate japan mantraṁ jāpena dhyānena ca.* Bhavabhaṭṭa reads *sidhyate japamantreṇa jāpena dhyānena ca* (Pandey 2002, 24). The former is preferable for metrical reasons as well as meaning; *japamantreṇa jāpena* seems unnecessarily repetitive. No doubt for this reason, Bhavabhaṭṭa argues that *japamantreṇa* refers to silent mental mantra repetition, while *jāpena* refers to vocalized repetition. He writes:

> As for "repetition," the instrumental augment is elided. It refers to mental employment [of mantra]. With that one contemplates reality (***man****yate dharma-dhātuṁ*) and protects the world (***trā****yate lokadhātuṁ*). One achieves the Śrī Heruka's mantra which is the nature of wisdom and art.... "With repetition" indicates vocal employment [of mantra].

(cont'd)

There is honey and vermilion, mixed with camphor and with red sandalwood.[16] Standing amidst the host,[17] bearing the sign of the universal vajra mark,[18] one should cause him to lick the tips of the thumb and ring finger, always knowing yoga.[19] Consuming it as if it were the beverage *soma*, success is always attained.[20] This should be the five ambrosias, the origina-

---

> *japeti tṛtīyālope sa ca mānaso vyāpāraḥ tena manyate dharmadhātuṁ trāyate lokadhātum iti prajñopāyātmakaḥ śrīherukaḥ mantraḥ sidhyati.... jāpena vāco vyāpāro darśitaḥ* / (Pandey 2002, 24)

One should note that this commentary is based upon the interpretive etymology of *mantra* as "that which protects the mind."

[16] According to Jayabhadra: "This [line] indicates the five ambrosias. As for **honey**, and so forth, **honey** is semen, **vermillion** [is uterine blood], and **camphor** is together with 'great meat.' Additionally, urine is derived from blood, and **sandalwood** is feces. *Raktacandana* is a copulative compound, which is compounded with *yojitaṁ*, i.e., *mixed with* those two." (E 9a.2–4: *idānīṁ pañcāmṛtaṁ darśayate / madhv ityādi madhv ity ceti śukraṁ / raktaṁ / karpūraṁ mahāmāṁsasahitaṁ / puna raktagrahaṇaṁ mūtraṁ / candanaṁ veṭā / raktacandanaṁ ceti dvandva[ṁ] tābhyāṁ yojitam iti samāsaḥ* /) Much of this commentary is based upon a play on words with *rakta*, meaning literally "reddened" or "red," but also denoting "uterine blood" and "vermilion." Jayabhadra interprets *raktacandana* as a copulative compound, which facilitates his analysis of the line into the five component ambrosial substances. While I have translated the text literally, Jayabhadra's interpretation is supported by the reference to the *pañcāmṛta* that soon follows this text.

[17] Jayabhadra explains here that "**amidst the host** means amidst the triple wheel" (E 9a.4: *gaṇamadhye tricakramadye*), that is, amidst the Cakrasamvara maṇḍala. Bhavabhaṭṭa indicates that standing "**amidst the host** means 'in the tantric feast'" (Pandey 2002, 25: *gaṇamadhye gaṇacakramadye*), that is, with the circle of yoginīs at their periodic gatherings.

[18] The CS mss. read here *sarvavajrāṅkacihnadhṛk*. Bhavabhaṭṭa glosses *sarvavajra* as *viśvavajra*, the double or crossed vajra symbol (Pandey 2002, 25).

[19] This line refers to the step in the secret consecration in which the master, in union with the consort, produces a drop of mixed reproductive fluids which, held by the thumb and ring-finger, is placed on the candidate's tongue. This step is also referred to in ch. 3 below. Regarding this, Bhavabhaṭṭa writes that "**knowing yoga** is knowing the yoga of consuming the ambrosia, or is esteemed as [indicating] equipoise by means of mind only. **Always** means that one should eat the five ambrosias together with the assembly of maṇḍala deities." (F 25a.6, G 27b.6–7: *yogavid iti amṛtāśvādayogavit cittamātrasamāpattimānita vā / sadeti māṇḍaleyadevatāpariṣadā saha pañcāmṛtaṁ bhakṣayed ity arthaḥ* /)

[20] Bhavabhaṭṭa comments here: "Regarding ***soma***, and so forth, this *soma* is the beverage of the brahmins, by whom it is drunk. It is the sap of the Kāliṅga creeper, placed in tawny cow hide at the time of sacrifice. By this they are nourished and their merit augmented. Just as *soma* is consumed by the brahmins without doubt, so too is power attained consuming the five ambrosias." (F 25a.6–b.1: *sometyādi viprāṇāṁ yāgakāle kāliṅgalatārasaṁ kapilagocarmaṇi*

tor of all powers. There are the four [types of] worship;[21] thus the yoginīs[22] and heroes are equipoised in the equipoise of the two organs.[23] [This] is the

nidhāya peyaḥ sa ca somas tasya pānaṁ / ta[y]ā puṣyaṁ puṇyavardhanaṁ / viprair yathā niḥsaṁśayaiḥ soma āsvādyate tathā pañcāmṛtam āsvādya siddhiṁ prāpnoti /) He continues, glossing the *pañcāmṛta* by quoting an unidentified source, as follows: "One should not give rise to disgust for feces, urine, semen, or blood; one should always eat these in accordance with the rite. This matter arises from the three secrets." (F 25b.2: *viṇmūtraśukraraktāṇāṁ jugupsāṁ naiva kārayet / bhakṣayet vidhinā nityaṁ idaṁ kāryaṁ triguhyajaṁ // iti*) The "three secrets" (*triguhya*) here are presumably the same as described above by Jayabhadra, namely, the "vajra, lotus, and seminal essence."

[21] Jayabhadra identifies these as the "outer, secret, mind-made, and inner worship," which can also be identified with the four *mudrā*, namely *mahāmudrā, samayamudrā, dharmamudrā,* and *karmamudrā*, and comments "with these four there are the four [types of] worship" (D 12a.5–7: *catuḥ pūjā [i]ti bāhyaguhyamanomayādhyātmapūjā athavā mahāmudrā samayamudrā dharmamudrā karmamudrā tābhiś catasrabhiḥ pūjāḥ catuḥ pūjā*). Bhavabhaṭṭa differs here only in reading "direct worship" rather than "inner worship" (Pandey 2002, 26: *catasraḥ pūjāś catuṣpūjā ity asyārthaḥ bāhyaguhyamanomayasākṣādbhāvabhedena tā uktāḥ*). They see several of the preceding verses as referring to these, as is noted above.

[22] Bhavabhaṭṭa explains that they are the four essence yoginīs (Pandey 2002, 26: *yoginya iti ḍākinyādayaś catasraḥ*). I suspect, however, that it refers to all twenty-four of the yoginīs, and Bhavabhaṭṭa's identification of the four essence yoginīs derived from a desire to reconcile *catuḥpūjā* with the rest of the text. The term *yoginyo* is attested in the CS mss., Bhavabhaṭṭa's commentary, and Sumatikīrti's translation (SL 96b). It is omitted in Mardo's translation as well as in the text as it occurs in Jayabhadra's commentary, and in the parallel passage in the AU mss. This is followed in the Tibetan translation by a line not attested in any of the Sanskrit texts, "doing as one desires" (SL 96b: *ji ltar 'dod par bya ba ste*), and "doing as one mentally desires" (PM 214a: *yid la 'dod pa byed pa ste*), which I have not included in my translation as it does not seem to fit well with the rest of the text.

[23] The CS mss. read here *catuḥpūjā tathā yoginyo vīrā dvayasamāpattisamāpannaṁ*. Bhavabhaṭṭa here reads *vīrādyava-*, i.e., the compound of *vīra* and *advaya-*. He reads this as referring to the yoginīs, despite the fact (as he notes) that it is incorrectly declined if read thus. He comments: "The meaning of the text **the hero's nondual equipoise** is that equipoise of theirs [undertaken] via the method of being nondual with the heroes" (Pandey 2002, 26: *vīrair advayena rūpena samāpattir yāsāṁ tā vīrādvayasamāpattiśabdārthaḥ*). There is, however, a variant text, which I translate in the main text. It is the text which occurs in the AU mss.: *catuḥ pūjā tathā vīrā dvendriyasamāpattisamāpannaṁ* (H 146a.3–4, I 599a.6). This more obviously sexual reading is also attested in Jayabhadra's commentary and in the Tibetan translations (E 9a.4: *tathā dvendriyasamapattisampanne ca*; PM 214a: *dbang gnyis snyoms par 'jug pa yi // snyoms par zhugs pa'ang*; SL 96b: *dbang gnyis snyoms par 'jug pa ni // dbang gnyid sgoms par 'jug pa ni // snyoms par 'jugs pa*). I prefer the latter reading as I suspect the former may be a later, sanitized version of it. Like Bhavabhaṭṭa, I see this text as referring both to the yoginīs and the heroes, and describing the state of union in which they are believed to exist, and in which they are depicted in the maṇḍala.

holding of reality.[24] If the happiness of the divine and human states were taken together, it would not amount to one sixteenth [of that produced] by the adamantine particle.[25] On mountains, in caves,[26] in groves, on riverbanks, or in the primordially established charnel ground, there one should draw the maṇḍala.[27]

---

[24] Bhavabhaṭṭa glosses *tattvadhṛk* as "**holding reality**, i.e., the self-nature which is inseparable from Vajravārāhī" (Pandey 2002, 26: *tathā tattvaṁ vajravārāhyābhinnaṁ svabhāvaṁ dhārayatīti tattvadhṛk*).

[25] The Sanskrit here reads *vajrakaṇikayā*, derived from *vajrakaṇikā*, as Bhavabhaṭṭa informs us. He writes: "Since the **adamantine** is stainless intelligence, and **particle** is subtle, the **adamantine particle** refers to natural gnosis" (Pandey 2002, 27: *vajraṁ nirmalā buddhiḥ tad eva kanikā sūkṣmatvāt vajra ca kanikā ceti vajrakaṇikā sahajaṁ jñānam ity arthaḥ*). The Tibetan translation, *rdor rje 'dzin pa*, is unattested in the Sanskrit texts, with the exception of Jayabhadra's, which appears to read here *vajradhṛk*, "vajra holder." The text here appears to read: "The *vajra* is the Blessed Lord, and one who is focused upon him holds the vajra" (E 9b.6: *vajro bhagavān [taṁ] dhārayatīti vajradhṛk*). He comments on this as follows: "[He] is one who maintains experiential uniformity with all of those who dwell in the triple wheel" (E 9b.6: *sarvatricakravartibhiḥ saha samaikarasadhārī*). This reading of *vajradhṛk* may represent an alternative reading, one which perhaps derives from contamination from v. 14 above.

[26] The Sanskrit here is *gahvara*, which means an inaccessible place, usually a cave, but it can also designate a thicket. Mardo's translation follows the latter, with "thicket" (PM 224a: *tshang tshing*), while Sumatikīrti's text attests both (SL 96b: *tshang tshing phug*). Several of the commentators exhibit a similar indecision.

[27] Indrabhūti wrote the following extensive commentary on this verse:

> Regarding **mountain**, it is a mountain because it arises as a heap of virtues. The **thickets** have various trees with fruits and flowers. The **groves** give rise to various medicines. The **river** refers to the Ganges, and so forth, and its left and right **banks** bring together garden islands and water bearers. The **primordially established charnel ground** is that which is blessed by Śrī Heruka. It should be understood in terms of breath and lack of breath as the place where is halted the conceptualization which has pondered through the eons. **There one should draw the maṇḍala**, by which one should understand the drawing of the colored powder maṇḍala at the time of giving the vase consecration, as well as meditating upon it.
>
> Furthermore, in accordance with the secret and the third [consecrations], the **mountain** is the consort (*vidyā*), whose **thicket** is the intermingled mass of hairs. Or, if we take it as "**caves**," they are the gathering places such as the *pīṭha* and *upapīṭha* in her body. The **groves** are the alchemical sites in the body. The **rivers** flow in the three channels. Their **banks** are all of the body's limbs. **Primordially established** refers to the body produced in the beginning. The **charnel ground** is the place where arises the non-conceptual gnosis. **There one should draw the maṇḍala** means that one should extract and apprehend the essence relying on that *dharmamaṇḍala*.

> In particular, the **mountain** is the central channel (*avadhūti*) in the middle of the body. The **thicket** is the 72,000 channels, and so forth. The **grove** is the realm of seminal essence which cleanses all impurities. The **caves** are terrifying for the dispassionate, since gnosis is difficult to realize for the [practitioners of] the Action and Performance [Tantras]. Also, the **rivers** are the channels frankincense (*sihlaka*), musk (*kastūrī*), uterine blood, and so forth. Their **banks** are the places where the elements gather in the channel wheels. **Primordially established** refers to the self-origination of all of the channels, winds, drops, and syllables. The **charnel ground** is the isolated place conducive to the realization of natural gnosis. **There one should draw the maṇḍala**—its meaning in relation to the latter consecration is that it is done for the sake of extracting the seminal essence of conventional and ultimate unexcelled great bliss.
>
> In accordance with the unexcelled [fourth consecration], the **mountain** is unchanging reality (*dharmatā*), and the **thicket** is the measureless origin of the virtues of a buddha from love and compassion. The **grove** consists of the aids to awakening (*bodhipakṣikadharma*), the six perfections, and so forth. The **river** is the unelaborated emptiness of all things. The **banks** are the intuition free of all extremes. **Primordially established** is reality (*dharmatā*), which has peace and equality, and is relaxed and birthless. The **charnel ground** is the place free of all taints, the eight pure hosts of consciousness. It is taught that **there one should draw the maṇḍala** of the seminal essence of great bliss (*mahāsukhabodhicitta*) for the sake of the unexcelled great secret. (IC 24a–b)

Kambala wrote the following commentary, specifically connecting this passage to its "secret meaning," which concerns the consort with whom the adept engages in sexual yoga:

> The literal interpretation alone of "mountain gorge," and so forth, is easy to understand. Symbolically speaking, they indicate the secret place of the excellent "great lotus" type of consort of the Buddha, hence mountain gorge means an isolated place such as a dense forest.... Also, the female consort is dense with forests of desire, and so forth, and hence her method which is purification serves as a way toward awakening. She is pure because she goes to the supreme limit. The place is the said to be the vulva (*dharmodaya, chos 'byung*), since it is the place of birth of women who have the good qualities of the vajra clan, and so forth, who are praised by all of the buddhas; it is thus isolated. She is the lady of the great bliss of reality, an immovable **mountain**, since she is unmoved by the wind arising from the evil heretics. Since inferior beings cannot strike her depths, she is a **thicket**. Since her cavity is filled with the Victor's ambrosia, [she is] hence a **cave**. Regarding **riverbanks**, she is a river bank since she is on the river of wisdom, vast and profound due to her union of wisdom and art. She is **primordially established**, that is, continually established, as she has abandoned origination and cessation, is fully perfected, and always sky-like. She is a **charnel ground** since she burns the awakening of the disciples, and so forth, with the blazing fire of desire. (SM 6b, 7a)

2. The Procedure of Wheel Worship

The maṇḍala ground should be anointed there with unfallen cow dung,[1] with charnel ground ash together with the five ambrosias.[2] Anointing thus the ground, there the maṇḍala should be undertaken, and truly accomplished [as] a charnel ground.[3] The master who has all good qualities should draw the divine maṇḍala with powdered funeral pyre char together with charnel ground brick. He has the proper knowledge, and understands the Tantra and Śrī Heruka's mantra. He is not angry, is pure and competent, and he understands yoga and is perfected in knowledge. His hair is marked with skulls,[4] his limbs are smeared with ash. His body is decorated

[1] The term *gomaya*, "cow product" here indicates cow dung, as it is cow dung alone for which one can specify the "unfallen" (*apāta*) variety, since urine is not otherwise accessible, and milk (and its products) are not normally evacuated onto the ground. This was understood by the Tibetan translators, who here translated *gomaya* as *lci-ba*, "dung."

[2] In contexts such as this the *pañcāmṛta* are typically the *pañcagomaya*, namely cow dung, urine, milk, butter, and yogurt.

[3] It is not necessary to locate the maṇḍala in a charnel ground. Indeed, this was only one of several possible locations listed at the end the last chapter. However, according to Jayabhadra "**truly accomplished [as] a charnel ground** means that there where the maṇḍala is to be drawn one should visualize the appearance of a great charnel ground" (E 10a.2–3: *śmaśānaṁ tu samācared iti yatra maṇḍalaṁ l[e]khya[ṁ] tatra mahāśmaśānākāraṁ bhāvayed ityarthaḥ /*). Mardo's translation contains an extra line here which is unattested elsewhere: following "truly accomplished as a charnel ground" it adds "by means of visualization in that place" (PM 214a: *gnas de ru ni bsgoms pa yis*). This extra line likely derives from commentary such as Jayabhadra's.

[4] Bhavabhaṭṭa specifies that he has five skulls: "**His hair is marked with skulls**, meaning he has a crest made of five skulls" (Pandey 2002, 29: *kapālaiḥ pañcabhiḥ kṛtaṁ śekharaṁ yena sa kapālakṛtamūrdhajaḥ*).

with ornaments,[5] and it has a bone garland. His hair is formed into one plait,[6] and he wears a bone garland.[7]

Having taken oneself to be Śrī Heruka[8] with a khatvanga staff placed in one's hand, think of Śrī Heruka, and place him in the center of the wheel.[9] Having thus armored oneself, place the fences [in] the directions.

---

[5] Jayabhadra explains that he is ornamented with the "six insignia" (E 10a.6: *ṣaṇmudrā*) of a Kāpālika yogin, which are a necklace, crest jewel, earring, choker, the sacred thread, and ash. See ch. 27 below, which refers to the "five insignia" (*pañcamudrā*) which include the above except for ash.

[6] This is a literal translation of the Sanskrit *ekakhaṇḍīkṛtamūrdhaja*, supported by Bhavabhaṭṭa's comment that this line can refer to the yogin's hair, in particular "a crest made of hair" (Pandey 2002, 30: *keśakṛtamukuṭa*). This evidently refers to the typical hairstyle of the yogin called *jaṭāmukuṭa*, in which the yogin's dreadlocks are twisted into a crest. Another interpretation, however, is that it refers to a skull ornament placed in the hair. Jayabhadra comments that "**hair marked with one-piece** means that there is a skull garland above his forehead. It is also said that the 'one piece' is the supreme lotus case" (E: 10a.6–10b.1: *ekak[h]aṇḍīkṛtamūrdhaja ity anena lalātopari kapālamālākā anenaiva ekakhaṇḍaṁ padmabhāṇḍam uttamam uktaṁ*). The term "lotus case" (*padmabhāṇḍa*) is apparently a poetic metaphor for the head or skull. That is at least the interpretation of the Tibetan translators, who prosaically translated it as *thod pa*, "skull" (see MP 46b). The only problem with this latter interpretation is that it is repetitive, as we have already been told that the yogin's hair is ornamented with skulls.

[7] The text appears to be repetitive here. In v. 5 we are told that he is *asthimālāsaṁsthitaḥ*, while in v. 6 he is described as *asthimālāvalambī*.

[8] Here I follow the Sanskrit text of my own edition, *ātmānaṁ śrīherukaṁ kṛtvā*, the reading which occurs in the extant mss. and which is also supported by Jayabhadra's commentary (E 10b.2) and by the parallel passage in the AU mss. (H 146b.3, I 599b.2, J 238.1), as well as by the Tibetan translations (PM 214a: *bdag nyid khrag 'thung dpal byas nas*; SL 97a: *bdag nyid śrī he ru ka byas nas*). Pandey's edition emends this to *ātmānaṁ śrīherukaṁ dhyātvā* (Pandey 2002, 30), evidently on the basis of Bhavabhaṭṭa's commentary, which alone supports this reading. This may be an explanatory gloss rather than a direct quote.

[9] Here I follow the reading of Jayabhadra and the AU mss., *cakrasya hṛdaye nyaset* (D 13b.2–3, E 10b.3, H 146b.4–5, I 599b.2), which seems to make more sense in the context of maṇḍala construction. The CS mss., Tibetan translations, and Bhavabhaṭṭa give an alternate reading, "place the wheel in his heart" (*cakram asya hṛdi nyaset*). According to Bhavabhaṭṭa this line refers to the creative yogic process of identification with Śrī Heruka and his maṇḍala, via the visualized placement of them in the adept's body. He wrote that "regarding **place the wheel in his heart**, 'his' refers to oneself who has become Heruka. 'In the heart' means that one should place the goddesses such as Pracaṇḍā and the heroes such as Khaṇḍakapāla, and so forth, in one's own body, i.e., in Pullīramalaya, and so forth, which are one's fingernails, teeth, and so forth." (Pandey 2002, 30: *cakram asya hṛdi nyased iti asyeti herukībhūtasyāt-*

Having thus armored oneself, place as well the weapon below.[10] Oneself being equivalent to the wheel,[11] and having made above for oneself a net of arrows and a floating enclosure, one is well-positioned. Thus armed, one who has this armor is unbreakable even by the Thirty-three [deities].[12]

Well-protecting oneself thus, ornamented with *mudrās*[13] and mantras, draw the terrifying maṇḍala which bestows great power. Then, with a corpse thread, or one colored with the great blood,[14] lay out the terrifying

---

manaḥ / hṛdi kāye tato 'yam arthaḥ pracaṇḍādidevīḥ khaṇḍakapālādīṁś ca vīrān svakāye pullīramalayādau nakhadantādau ca nyased iti /)

[10] This refers to the double vajra on which the earth rests. According to Jayabhadra it indicates that "one should imagine that the earth consists of vajras down to the end of the underworld" (E 10.6: *ā rasātalaparyantaṁ vajramayībhūmi[ṁ] parikalpayet*).

[11] This line is almost certainly corrupt in the surviving CS mss. Ms. A reads *cakrasya susamātmānaṁ*, with the syllable *su* partially obscured. This reading is reproduced in both mss. B and C, although both leave a lacuna in place of *su*. Pandey's edition reads *samam ātmānaṁ* (2002, 30), which is clearly a correction, although they do not identify it as such. I provisionally accept this reading, but it should be noted that other readings are possible. There were in fact many alternate translations for this line, as Tsong Khapa shows at KS 52b. Another reading is provided by Jayabhadra who reads the first part of the line as "wheel's weapon" (*cakrasyāstraṁ*). He writes that "**wheel's weapon** means that one should arm oneself, that is, the place of the wheels, with enclosures of weapons" (E 10b.6–11a.1: *cakrasyāstram iti cakrasthaṁ tathātmānaṁ śastrapañjarai kavacayet /*). Note that this is the only extant Sanskrit text which supports the reading in Sumatikīrti's translation, *'khor gnas pa yi bdag nyid mnyam* (SL 97a). This text may ultimately derive from commentary such as Jayabhadra's. Finally, the corresponding passage in the AU reads as follows: *cakrasya svayamātmānaṁ* (H 146b.5–6, I 599b.3, J 238.2), a reading supported by Durjayacandra's commentary (ṘG 253b). This is clearly one of at least two, or even three, possible readings for this line.

[12] The text here reads *tridaśair*, literally "by the three tens," a common short-hand for the thirty-three vedic deities, the chief of whom is Indra.

[13] The term *mudrā* in *mudrāmantrair alaṁkṛtaṁ* could conceivably refer to the five or six insignia of the yogin. However, the commentators take it as a reference to the consort. Bhavabhaṭṭa explains that the *mudrā* is Vajravārāhī (Pandey 2002, 31: *mudrā vajravārāhī*). Jayabhadra comments that "**ornamented with *mudrā* and mantras** means that one is accompanied by a well-trained outer woman" (E 11a.3: *mudrāmantrair alaṁkṛta iti suśikṣitakṛtabāhyāṅganāsahita ityarthaḥ*).

[14] That is, human blood. My translation follows the CS mss., which here read *mṛtakasūtreṇa mahārudhiarañjitena*, which is very close to Mardo's translation, "moistened with great blood" (PM 214b: *ru dhi ra ni chen pos brlan*). Pandey's ed. emends this, on the basis of Bhavabhaṭṭa's commentary, to *mahārudhirārcitena* (2002, 31), "honored with great blood,"

maṇḍala, Heruka's supreme mansion. [It is of] a single cubit, four or eight, [with] four corners all around, bedecked with four doors,[15] adorned with four arches. The mantrin should double [the thread].[16]

Worship[17] the binding of the ḍākinīs' network.[18] Place in the middle of that a lotus with petals and a fully-opened center, endowed with filaments.[19] Place in the center of the lotus the hero who is the terror of Mahābhairava,[20] who is bright and brilliant, and who makes the tremendous noise of very loud laughter.[21] Wearing a skull rosary, divine are his three eyes and four faces. Covered with an elephant hide, his excellent

which is unattested elsewhere and is probably corrupt. The Tibetan translation of his commentary, like Mardo, also reads *brlan* (2002, 218).

[15] This is a translation of the compound *caturdvārasamākīrṇaṁ,* which is a bit unusual, as doors are not typically objects of the actions of "bedecking," "bestrewing," or "covering." Here it is clearly used in the sense of decorating the maṇḍala image.

[16] This refers to the length of cord with which one lays out the maṇḍala. Jayabhadra indicates that "**should double it** means that one produces a thread that is twice as long as the maṇḍala" (E 10b.4–5: *vicared dviguṇam iti maṇḍaladviguṇadairghasūtraṁ vicare[d i]ty abhiprāyaḥ* /).

[17] The CS mss. read *japeḍ* here, a reading which also occurs in the AU mss. (H 147a.2, J 238.4). However, Jayabhadra reads *yajeḍ,* which he and Bhavabhaṭṭa (E 11a.5, Pandey 2002, 32) both gloss as *pūjayeḍ,* which makes more sense, since the term *ḍākinījālasamvara* designates the network of deities who inhabit the maṇḍala. Yet *japeḍ* is also a possible reading, one which suggests the invocation of the maṇḍala's deities through the repetition of their respective mantras and seed syllables.

[18] As Jayabhadra comments, this "refers to all those who are positioned within the three wheels [of the maṇḍala]" (E 10b.5: *ḍākinījālasamvaram iti* / *tricakravyavasthitān sarvān[ī]tyartha* /).

[19] This translation follows the Tibetan, rather than the Sanskrit, which has "lotus" incorrectly declined in the instrumental plural case (*puṣkarais*), and the adjectives declined, correctly, in the accusative singular.

[20] The CS mss. all read *mahābhairavabhīṣaṇam* here. The AU mss., however, read *mahābhairavarūpiṇam,* "who has the form of Mahābhairava" (H 147a.3, I 599b.6, J 238.5–6). Bhavabhaṭṭa gives a third reading which is unattested elsewhere, namely *mahārauravabhīṣaṇam,* "the terror of the Mahāraurava [hell]" (Pandey 2002, 32). See introduction above, p. 9 n. 23.

[21] This compound, *aṭṭahāsamahāravaṁ,* may have Śaiva connotations, since Aṭṭahāsa is an epithet of Śiva.

eyebrows are split by a vajra.[22] His hand wields a khatvanga staff, [and he is] ornamented with a half-hundred garland.[23]

The goddess who stands before him[24] is the truly awesome Vajravārāhī, facing the deity Śrī Heruka,[25] with three eyes and a fierce form. Her

[22] According to Bhavabhaṭṭa, this expression, "split by a vajra," means that "between his eyebrows is a mark. It is a vajra produced with three prongs, below the eyebrows and eyes. Hence it is said, 'between the eyebrows is a vajra mark'." (Pandey 2002, 33: *vajrasambhinnasubhrūḥ bhruvor madhyaṁ varaṭakam / bhruvau netre tayor adhaḥ triśukam iti siddhaṁ vajraṁ tad uktaṁ bhrūmadhyaṁ vajravaraṭakam iti //*; cf. MP 164a) Note that the term I have translated as "mark," *varaṭaka*, which normally designates a small seed or grain, here seems to indicate a mark placed on the forehead, as in the case of the term *tilaka*. This term also designates the center of a vajra, and is thus translated by the Tibetans as *lte ba*, a translation which seems less appropriate in this context.

[23] This refers to the garland of fifty human heads worn by Śrī Heruka. According to Bhavabhaṭṭa, however, it also refers to the "mantra garland in the throat that contains the [fifty] vowels and consonants" (Pandey 2002, 33: *śatamālārdhaṁ tena bhūṣitaḥ / ālikālisambaddhā mantramālā kaṇṭhagateti bhāvaḥ*).

[24] This translates *tasyāgrataḥ sthitā devī*, which is Bhavabhaṭṭa's reading (F 31a.6–b.1, G 33b.5–6), and which is attested by the Tibetan translations (PM 214b: *de 'dun gnas pa'i lha mo ni*; SL 97b: *de'i 'dun na lha mo ni*). It is partially attested by Jayabhadra (D 14b.7, E 11b.3: *tasyāgra-*), and the AU mss. give the close variant *tasyāgratasaṁsthitā mudrā* (H 147a.5, I 599b.7, J 238.7). The CS mss. read "the goddess who stands embraced by him" (*tasyāliṅgatā sthitā devī*). This reading may have resulted from commentarial contamination. For example, Bhavabhaṭṭa explains the line as follows: "**Stands before him** means that she stands embracing [him], face to face. She is a **goddess** as she shines together with the Blessed Lord" (F 31a.6–b.1: *tasyāgrataḥ sthitām iti saṁmukham āliṅgya tiṣṭhatīti sthitā dīvyati bhagavatā saheti devī*).

[25] While the CS mss. here read *śrīherukadevābhimukhāṁ kṛtvā*, there is an interesting variant on this text in Jayabhadra's commentary, as follows:

> As for "facing Mahābhairava," some claim that she should face Maheśvara. That is inappropriate, because it is not relevant and because [the line occurs in] the context of Vajravārāhī as the great consort (*mahāmudrā*). The meaning of this, then, is that Mahābhairava is a Blessed Lord, and she faces him embraced [by him] with body, speech, and mind.
>
> *mahābhairavābhimukham iti maheśvarābhimukh[ed] icchanti kecit / tad anupapannam eva / aprakṛtatvāt / vajravārāhyā mahāmudrāprastāvatvāt / tato 'yam arthaḥ / mahābhairavo bhagavān / tasyābhimukhā kāyavākcittenāliṅgita kṛtvā /* (E 11b.3–5)

This passage highlights a debate in Buddhist circles on the status of the deity Mahābhairava, who originally was a Śaiva deity, the chief deity of the Kāpālikas. Buddhists have often appropriated non-Buddhist deities, and Jayabhadra follows suit, identifying him as a buddha; but clearly this interpretation was resisted by some. Apparently, his opponents were victorious in

skull bowl is filled [with entrails],[26] blood trickles from her mouth. She threatens all of the quarters together with the gods, titans, and humans. The twenty-four ḍākinīs comprising Vārāhī's clan should be worshipped within the wheels and in the directions and the quarters. And here thus one should worship the heroes positioned in the wheels as well. If the adept desires power, he should worship the nondual hero.

Then make the vases, without bases, black [in color], and so forth.[27] They are filled with pearls, gold, and jewels, and with coral, silver, and copper, and with all foods, with skull bowls placed upon them. Then wind their necks with thread, their tips adorned with blossoms. Place eight at the doors, well wound with pairs of cloths. The ninth central vase is wound with a pair of cloths, decorated with gold, silver, jewels, or pearls. One should scatter precious golden ornaments on the maṇḍala. Were one to worship the delightful supreme abode, have no doubt that there will be power. Sprinkling scented water upon oneself while facing everywhere,[28] should one desire the ultimate power, offer one hundred lamps.

---

this case, for at some point following Jayabhadra, the text was revised to *śrīherukadevābhimukhāṁ*. Bhavabhaṭṭa, writing c. 900 CE, cites the revised text, and may possibly have been responsible for the change. Bhavyakīrti, who succeeded Bhavabhaṭṭa at Vikramaśīla, is silent on this matter—despite the fact that he usually follows Jayabhadra closely—perhaps because he was uncomfortable with the older reading. The AU mss. evidently were not revised and preserve the older reading, *mahābhairavābhimukhīṁ* (H 147a.5, I 599b.7, J 238.7). Although it is possible to view (as Jayabhadra does) Mahābhairava as a Buddhist deity, this apparent revision of the text indicates that this interpretation was not accepted by all Indian Buddhists during the ninth century.

[26] The CS mss. here read *kapālāṁ tu saṁpūrṇāṁ*, which is revised in Pandey's edition to *kapālaṁ tv antrasaṁpūrṇaṁ* (2002, 33), on the basis of Mardo's Tibetan translation (PM 214b: *ka pā la ni antras bkang*) and also Bhavabhaṭṭa's commentary. On the other hand, the former reading also occurs in the AU mss. (H 147a.5–6: *kapālāṁ tu saṁpūrṇāṁ*; I 599b.7–8: *kapālāmālāṁ ntu saṁpūrṇāṁ*; J 239.1: *kapālaṁ tu saṁpūrṇāṁ*) This "correction" is probably unnecessary; while the Tibetan translation may be based on an alternate text, it could also be based on commentary such as Bhavabhaṭṭa's.

[27] Bhavabhaṭṭa comments that "the **base** means the [flat] portion made by a potter on a wheel. **Black** means a black portion. The word **and so forth** indicates a spotted [appearance], and so forth." (Pandey 2002, 34: *mūlaṁ cakrāt kulālena kṛto bhāgaḥ / kālaḥ kṛṣṇo bhāgaḥ / ādiśabdāt karburatvādi //*)

[28] Jayabhadra comments here: "**Sprinkling scented water upon oneself** means that one should sprinkle oneself with scented vajra water that has been purified by the mantra. **Facing everywhere** is a quality of oneself—that is, oneself as Śrī Heruka—on account of the Blessed Lord's four faces." (E 12a.4–5: *gandhodakena saṁsicya ā[t]mānam iti mantrapūtena gandha-*

The ḍākinīs in space should all be mentally placed above.[29] The ḍākinīs in the earth realm should be placed everywhere in the maṇḍala. Any ḍākinīs in the underworld should be placed in the underworld.[30] The mothers should all be employed in the directions and quarters.[31] If the adept desires power, he should offer one hundred butter lamps, with flowers, scent, and incense. Worship the heroes and yoginīs who stand in the maṇḍala of Śrī Heruka, with banners of red and likewise yellow, white, black, and tawny brown, well adorned thus with various kinds of wreaths and sundry cloths, with canopies and with curtains. The well-equipoised one should make [offerings][32] with all sorts of food and drink.

---

sahitena vajrodakenātmānaṁ saṁsi[ñc]ed ityarthaḥ / sarvato mukham i[ty āt]maviśeṣaṇaṁ / śrīherukasvayamātmān bhagavataś caturmukhatvāt /)

[29] Jayabhadra writes: "**The ḍākinīs in space should all be mentally placed above** means that they are positioned in the mind wheel, because they move through space with their minds" (E 12b.1–2: *ākāśe ḍākinyaḥ sarvā manasā ūrdhvato nyased iti cittacakravyavasthitā ityathaḥ cittasyākāśagamanasvabhāvatvāt /*). The earth- and underworld-dwelling ḍākinīs correspond to the speech and body wheels, respectively.

[30] In other words, even though the maṇḍala is drawn in two dimensions on the ground, the yogin should visualize it in three dimensions, with the three wheels visualized above, on, and below the earth, respectively.

[31] Jayabhadra explains that "regarding **the mothers in the directions**, those at the four gates are, respectively, Kākāsyā (Crow Face), Ulūkāsyā (Owl Face), Śvānāsyā (Dog Face), and Śūkarāsyā (Pig Face). The four **employed in the quarters** are, respectively, Yamadāhī, Yamadūtī, Yamadaṁṣṭriṇī, and Yamamathanī." (E 12b.4–5: *diśās[u] mātara iti caturdvāreṣu yathākramaṁ kākāsyā / ulūkāsyā / śvānāsyā / śūkarāsyāś catasraḥ / vidiśāsu ca niyojayed iti / krameṇa yamadā[h]ī / yamadūtī / yamadaṁṣṭriṇī / yamamathanīti catasraḥ /*)

[32] The Sanskrit here reads *kuryāt*, and Bhavabhaṭṭa provides the missing object, *pūjāṁ* (Pandey 2002, 36). The Tibetan translations give the interpretative reading *mchod par bya* (PM 215a, SL 98b).

3. The Procedure of Consecration and Fee [Payment]

Thence the adept should first please the master with all things. One who desires power, well equipoised, should worship the guru to the extent of his ability. Having hung sounding bells, decorated with flowers and incense, the adept should sound a melodious bell and drum,[1] and he should make the sound *ha ha.*[2] Worshipping the maṇḍala of all desires, in

[1] This translates my edited text, *ghaṇṭāṁ vādayet susvarāṁ paṭahikāṁ cāpi sādhakaḥ*, which is based upon the readings of the CS and AU mss. Pandey's ed. emends the verb to *nādayet* on the basis of Bhavabhaṭṭa's commentary (2002, 37), but this emendation is unwarranted, as *vādayet*, "to sound, strike," is more appropriate here than *nādayet*, "to make resonant."

[2] Generally, this chapter is thought to describe the performance of the first two of the four Unexcelled Yoga Tantra consecrations, i.e., the vase and secret consecrations, with most commentators emphasizing the latter. A real commentarial tour de force, however, occurs in Indrabhūti's commentary; he interprets the first nine lines of this text in five different ways, in terms of: 1) the vase consecration, which is further divided into the water, crown, vajra, royal, and name consecrations; 2) general Mahāyāna practice; 3) the secret and wisdom-gnosis consecrations, which involve sexual practices with a consort (*karmamudrā*); and finally in terms of internal yogic practices, which he correlates to 4) the *dharmamudrā*, and to 5) the *mahāmudrā* and *samayamudrā*. The passage occurs as follows in a slightly abridged translation:

> At this point, having first completed the foundational rite of pacifying obstacles and the rite of blessing, and having drawn the lines and painted the maṇḍala with colored powder, one propitiates the maṇḍala's presiding deity and ornaments the area. Having well prepared the accoutrements of worship and the sacrificial cakes (*bali*), **thence** how does one **first** worship the guru? Regarding this the glorious Padmavajra has stated: "The first of all worship is respectfully worshipping the guru, the precious vessel of the Buddha, as is stated in the *Śrī[guhya]samāja* and also elsewhere." **Thence the adept first,** since he desires to be consecrated in this Unexcelled Tantra, [worships] **with all things**, i.e., with all of his possessions and pleasing substances. **First** designates the vajra **master**, [whom one worships] in order to achieve the good qualities, since he has the supreme excellence of showing one the good path. **Desiring power** in this context refers to the supreme power of *mahāmudrā*. The **well-equipoised** one, through regarding himself as non-different from the presiding deity, Vajradhara, [performs] the inner and outer **worship** with the many aspects of reality **to the extent of his ability**.... Then, since **first** one has done this so that the master would worship the maṇḍala and bestow consecration, he should commence. The first among the [five] *vidyā* consecrations is Akṣobhya's water consecration. **Having hung bells**, defined in terms of the vase [the ritual locus of the vase consecrations], means that one fumigates it with **incense** of eagle

wood (*Aquilaria agallocha*), and so forth, and ornaments the vase purified by means of purification mantras and the vowels and consonants. **Flowers** means that one has a crown with the emblems of the five clans. **Having hung bells** also means that one has beautified [the vase] by tying silk and cotton cloths to its neck and by ornamenting its mouth with fruit tree [leaves]. It also illustrates binding the crown with hanging silk [strips]. As for **melodious**, one states verses of praise [such as]: "The extremely firm and hard vajra is Lord Amitābha." **Sound**ing the **bell** indicates the vajra consecration in which there is no doubt. **Make the sound *ha ha*** is especially relevant to Vairocana's name consecration. The adept who has the three vows should remain before the vajra master, the very embodiment of Vajrasattva, the sixth [buddha]. The **drum** indicates the great drum, conch, and Dharma roar that exhort the deities to action....

In the manner of the path of the ordinary vehicle, **hung bells** means that one has the monastic vows, and that one excels in going for refuge and in the six perfections. **Flower** means aspiration, **incense** doctrinal engagement, and **decorated** means giving rise to the ultimate spirit [of awakening]. "Very" [*su* of *susvara*] is drawing forth the descent of the outer [i.e., *samayasattva*], while **melodious** is the descent of the inner, the descent of gnosis [i.e., *jñānasattva*]. **Bell**, and so forth, means abiding by the vows and commitments, and **sound**ing is identifying with the deity. The **adept** is the guru, and **sound**ing the **drum** is proclaiming the Dharma. Making **the sound *ha ha*** is giving rise to joy upon seeing the maṇḍala.

If we take this in the manner of the secret and third [consecrations], the **hung bell** is the naturally present twelve-year-old girl. The **melodious** one is the mantra-born sixteen-year-old woman. **Bell** ringing is the field-born eighteen-year-old woman, and **drum** beating the twenty-year-old consort who arises from gnosis. They are all worshipped, **decorated with flowers and incense**. ***Ha ha*** indicates that the adept has achieved joy and the [corresponding] moment.

As for the *dharmamudrā*, the **hung bell** is the couple who manifest as the deity. The **flower** is the left channel, the **incense** the right channel, and it is the central channel that is **decorated** by them. **Melodious** is the sound of the insertion of the wind into the central channel (*dhūtī*) in the place of the channels. The **bell** is **sound**ed though union with the vajra. The **adept** achieves natural bliss through having the three cognitions [i.e., limited, extensive, and immeasurable] of the couple. **Drum** beating is the bliss set in motion by the woman. ***Ha ha*** is the bliss of joy and the moment conducted to the place of great bliss by means of the upward return of the drop.

From the perspective of the *mahāmudrā* and *samayamudrā*, **hung bell** is the crown's *haṁ* held upside down. The **flower** is the left channel (*lalanā*), and **incense** is the right channel (*rasanā*). **Decorated** means insertion into the *dhūtī*. "Very" is the state of excitation of all channels, and **melodious** the earnest control of the life-force. The **bell** is movement of the lower wind by means of the fury fire (*caṇḍālī*). **Sound**ing refers to the secret blazing and dripping [of the drops]. The **adept** is the yogin who has the yogic postures (*yantra*) of the essential points in the

accordance with the rites, he should cover with a cloth the face of these lads,[3] and place them [before the maṇḍala] with their palms full of flowers. Then, circumambulating, the well-equipoised adept should enter the pleasing palace, resting his body to the south.[4] Then the flower in the palm should be cast above the maṇḍala, and he should be assigned to that clan on which his flower falls.[5] He may be shown the seats of Śrī Heruka, and so forth.[6]

> body. **Drum** beating is the suppression of the wind of the four elements. **The sound *ha ha*** is the emergence of the laughter of gnosis by means the upward blazing of natural bliss. (IC 32b–33b)

Note that in this text *karmamudrā* refers to the outer consort, *dharmamudrā* refers to the visualization of oneself and one's consort as the deity couple, and *mahāmudrā* and *samaya-mudrā* refer to internal yogic processes. For a good introduction to the consecrations, see Snellgrove 1987, 213–277.

[3] The singular actor implied by this sentence is the master, while "these lads" whose faces are bound (*mukhaṁ teṣāṁ tu putrakānāṁ*) are presumably the younger male disciples for whom he is performing the consecration ceremony.

[4] Regarding the meaning of this, Bhavabhaṭṭa writes: "The oral instruction is that one casts it facing south. Or, [one worships it] by circling the Blessed Lord clockwise, in the manner of worshipping a sacred site (*caitya*)" (2002, 39: *dakṣiṇābhimukhaḥ kṣiped ity upadeśaḥ / bhagavato dakṣiṇāvartena caityavandanākrameṇa vā*). Thus, either one casts the flower facing south, or one does so facing right following the usual respectful protocol. Kambala gives a somewhat different interpretation, arguing that one faces different directions for the sake of different powers:

> Regarding **resting to the south**, [cast the flower] from the eastern door of the maṇḍala for the sake of liberation, gnosis, being free of disease, the powers of the sword and underground [travel], and attaining a kingdom as a lord of the Earth. [Cast] from the southern door of the maṇḍala for the sake of eternal peace, auspiciousness, glory, gifts of wealth or grain, being free from disease, alchemy, or the production of gold. [Cast] from the western door of the maṇḍala for the sake of an increase of sons, grandsons, and so forth, enticing people, augmenting, pacifying, perfecting, summoning, and controlling. [Cast] from the northern door of the maṇḍala for the sake of averting and defeating enemies, and cutting off the life of the malicious to preserve the Teaching. (SN 12a)

[5] The CS mss. here read *yasmin patati tatpuṣpaṁ kulaṁ tatra vinirdiśet*. This is supported by the AU mss., with *tasya* in place of *tatra*, which is a better reading (I 600a.9, J 240.7–241.1). Pandey's edition inexplicably reads *maṇḍalasyopari pated yatra tatkulaṁ tasya vinirdiśet* (2002, 39), taking *maṇḍalasyopari* from the previous line and deleting *puṣpa*. No annotations are present explaining this radical change; it has no basis in the commentaries or even the Tibetan translation. My translation follows my own reading of the CS and AU mss.

[6] The Sanskrit on which this sentence is based is *śriherukādiṁ pīṭhaṁ darśayet*, which occurs only in the CS mss. The term *pīṭha* here is best understood as "throne" or "seat," in reference

The master, well equipoised, should worship the consort.[7] On the second day he should make the drop for the disciples with blood thrice enchanted. Having unveiled his [blindfolded] face, he should then show the maṇḍala to the disciple.[8] He should show her in whom is the deity's place.[9]

---

to the deities' positions in the maṇḍala. Pandey's edition revises this, without explanation, to *darśayet śriherukādipīṭhā ācāryo nāma nirdiśen.* The latter line appears to be based upon Mardo's revised translation, *slob dpon gyis ni ming bstan no* (PM 215b), which is not attested in any Sanskrit text. Evidently Pandey, et al. are back translating from Tibetan to Sanskrit, without providing any indication of such, despite the fact that the CS mss. contain a viable alternative.

[7] She is described by Jayabhadra as follows: "One's **consort** is an outer woman, well educated in mantra and tantra, who has the commitments regarding what is to be protected and eaten" (E 13a.5–6: *svamudrām iti / bāhyāṅganā mantratantrasuśikṣitā rakṣaṇīya-bhakṣaṇīya-samayasamanvit[ā] /*).

[8] These verses refer to the secret consecration, described by Jayabhadra as follows:

> **On the second day**, once again one worships the maṇḍala and produces the blessing, and so forth, sets up an abode of bliss, such as a mat, couch, and so forth, either in or near the maṇḍala, and commences with the secret consecration. Regarding **he should make the drop with blood thrice enchanted**, together with an outer woman who has the previously explained characteristics and who is menstruating, he gives rise to sexual joy by means of the process of drinking *soma*, and so forth. Then, through the practice of rubbing the vajra and lotus, and so forth, when the [sexual fluids] are flowing, the essence, quintessence, and garland mantras are recited over the blindfolded disciple. Bestow the consecration with the vajra and lotus upon the [disciple's] seven spots—the crown, forehead, both eyes, mouth, throat, and heart. The disciple should consume it as if it were bliss-bestowing ambrosia. Immediately after that, his **face should be unveiled** and he **should be shown the maṇḍala.**
>
> *dvitīy[e] ahaniḥ punar api maṇḍalaṁ saṁpūjyādhiṣṭhānādikaṁ kṛtvā maṇḍalamadhye maṇḍalasamīpe vā kāṣṭapaṭakhaṭvādisukh[ā]śaya[ṁ] saṁsthāpya guhyābhiṣekam ārabhate / raktena trijaptena tilakaṁ tasya kārayed iti yathāpūrvoktalakṣaṇānvitā bāhyāṅganā puṣpavatī bhavati tayā saha vā somapānādikrameṇa yathā harṣo jāyate / tathā vajrapadmāsph[ā]lanādikriyayā kṣaraṇāvasthāyāṁ mukhapaṭabaddhasya śiṣ[yasya] hṛdayopahṛdayamālamantroccāraṇaṁ kṛtvā śirasi lalāṭ[e] cakṣurdvaye mukhe kaṇṭhe hṛdaye ca saptasthāne[ṣu] vajreṇa padmena cābhiṣekaṁ dadyāt / śiṣyeṇāpi sukhadattam amṛtam ivākhādayet / tadanantaraṁ mukham udghā[ṭya] darśayen maṇḍalam /* (E 13b.1–6)

[9] This translates the somewhat ambiguous and ungrammatical text *yo yasya devatāsthānaṁ tatra tāṁ darśayet.* Jayabhadra, in place of *yo yasya,* reads *padmasya,* commenting upon it as follows: "**He should be shown her in whom** is **the deity's place of the lotus**, the place of the secret consecration. This means that he should be shown the outer woman who has the

Then, afterwards, one bows correctly[10] and circumambulates once more the palace, as well as the master, beginning from the left. Saluting the maṇḍala and the guru in accordance with the rite, then make an offering to the guru,[11] presenting[12] the fee declared by the Tathāgata: a hundred thousand gold [pieces], and a variety of treasures; also one hundred pairs of clothing, and even elephants, horses, and territory; earrings, bracelets, necklaces, and an excellent ring; a golden sacrificial thread, and also one's wife and daughters, servants and maids, or even one's sister, should be offered, bowing. The intelligent one should give himself with all of [his] things to the guru, [saying,] "Henceforward I am given over to you as a servant." Doing thus the ritual procedure, [things] are well settled by the adept.

On account of that the ḍākinīs and mothers of yoga are pleased with him, along with Ḍākinī, Lāmā, Khaṇḍarohā, and Rūpiṇī. The adept should wander the whole world with these ḍākinīs. There is no doubt regarding anything done by that adept. Were he to be accomplished in this yoga, [the adept will have the powers of] being unhindered in the three worlds, invisibility, [traveling in] the underworld,[13] resurrection,[14] flight, foot unguent,[15] and alchemy. The adept will always without fail be born as he wills, and will take on many forms, and will travel by means of space. He destroys all

---

power to bestow consecration." (13b.6–14a.1: *padmasya devatāsthānam iti guhyābhiṣekasthānaṁ tatra tāṁ darśayed iti / abhiṣekapradānasamarthīṁ bāhyāṅganāṁ darśayet ity arthaḥ /*)

[10] According to Jayabhadra, "**correctly** means with a nonconceptual mind" (E 14a.1: *samyag iti nirvikalpena manasā /*).

[11] This text is a bit unclear. According to Tsong Khapa, the consecrated disciple first circumambulates both the maṇḍala and the guru, and then salutes them both. Following this, he offers the prescribed fee to the guru. See KS fol. 31a.

[12] This translates *niryātya*, which occurs in the CS and AU mss. (I 600b.2, J 241.3) and which corresponds to the Tibetan translation, *dbul*. Pandey's ed. reads *nirjātya*, which is based on one source, Bhavabhaṭṭa's commentary (2002, 40).

[13] This is a very interpretive translation of the item *bila*, "cave, hole, pit," which is understood by commentators such as Tsong Khapa to refer to the power more commonly called *patālasiddhi*, "the power of [moving] in the underworld."

[14] Here I follow Bhavabhaṭṭa's gloss of *uttiṣtha* as "causing the dead to rise, [or] knowledge of killing, i.e., [the power of] slaying" (Pandey 2002, 42: *uttiṣṭheti mṛtotthāpanam, niṣūdanajñānaṁ māraṇaṁ*). The former interpretation seems more likely to me.

[15] That is, the power of rapid travel bestowed by an unguent applied to the feet.

beings through the yoga of a single glance, above all the ḍākinīs, and gives rise to the state of being a yogin in an instant.

The yogin who has not seen the maṇḍala, and yet longs for the state of being a yogin, [is like one who] punches at the sky, or drinks the water of a mirage. This yoga is the most excellent, the highest among all yogas, which can kill anyone, gods, titans, or men. The adept who has been taught all tantras, and who has been initiated in the maṇḍala, will go forth, conquering. Smiling,[16] looking, hand-holding, coupling, and so forth:[17] one should be initiated in that, the supreme of all tantras. This king of maṇḍalas does not occur, nor will it occur, in the *Tattvasaṁgraha*,[18] *Samvara*,[19]

---

[16] The Sanskrit text here reads "hiding" (*gopya*), varying from the Tibetan reading "laughing/smiling" (Tibetan *rgod pa*, =Sanskrit *hāsya*) which is the usual member of this list. *Gopya*, which occurs before *īkṣaṇa* ("looking"), does make some sense here, as we might have a variant list of the levels of increasing intimacy, which here are hiding (coyness, perhaps?), looking, hand-holding, and coupling. On the other hand, all of the Tibetan translations of the Root Tantra and the commentaries have *rgod pa* ("laughing"), which is most likely a translation of *hāsya*, the much better known member of this list. *Gopya* would thus seem to be a late variation, if it were not for the fact that Devagupta, who normally follows Kambala closely, reports (in some Tibetan editions of his text) both *sbas*, the equivalent of *gopya*, and *rgod pa*, the equivalent of *hāsya* (interestingly, this occurs only in the Beijing Tengyur, SS QT 39.2; the sDe-dge edition has only *rgod pa*, SS DT 81a). While he offers no explanation for this, it may mean that he was aware of manuscripts containing both variants. Bu-ston reports that the Sanskrit here reads **gosya*, which has been variously translated as "hiding," "playing," and "laughing" (NS 68a). While there is always a possibility of misreading, **gosya* does seem to be suspiciously midway between *hāsya* and *gopya*. This suggests that the original read *hāsya*, which was later miscopied as *gosya* (a possibility that would not be as unlikely in some scripts as it would be in Devanāgarī), which in turn was "corrected" by a later copyist to *gopya*. This verse may be a later addition to the text, as it does not occur in the corresponding passage in the AU mss.

[17] These are generally understood by the commentators to refer to four classes of tantras, namely the "ritual action" (*kriyā*) class, which corresponds to "looking"; the "performance" (*caryā*) class, which corresponds to "laughing/smiling"; the "yoga" class, which corresponds to "hand-holding"; and the "unexcelled yoga" (*anuttarayoga*) class, which corresponds to "coupling." See, for example, Devagupta's commentary at SS 81a.

[18] This is the well known *Sarvatathāgata-tattvasaṁgraha-nāma-mahāyāna-sūtra*, Tōh. 479, T. 882, 865, 866.

[19] In the literature of this period the term *Samvara* typically, as here, refers not to the *Cakrasamvara Tantra*, but to the *Sarvabuddhasamayogaḍākinījālasamvara-nāma-uttaratantra* (Tōh. 366).

Guhyasamāja,[20] or *Vajrabhairava*.[21] Everything whatsoever, spoken or unspoken, exists in Śrī Heruka.

[20] That is, the *Sarvatathāgatakāyavākcittarahasya-guhyasamāja-nāma-mahākalparāja* (Tōh. 422, T. 885).

[21] While it is impossible to identify this text on the basis of this name alone, it may refer to one of the texts studied and translated in Siklos 1996.

4. *The Procedure Called "The Nonduality of the Heroes and Yoginīs"*

Thence the ḍākinīs pervade the worlds:[1] Mahāvīryā ("Great Energy"), Cakravartinī ("Wheel Turner"), Mahābalā ("Great Strength"), Suvīrā ("Excellent Heroine"), Cakravarmiṇī ("Armed with Wheels"), Śauṇḍinī ("Barmaid"),[2] Khaṇḍarohā,[3] Cakravegā ("Wheel's Velocity"),[4] Khagānanā ("Bird Face"), Hayakarṇā ("Horse Ears"), Subhadrā ("Extremely Good"), Śyāmādevī ("Dark Goddess"), Surābhakṣī ("Lush"), Vāyuvegā ("Wind's Velocity"), Mahābhairavā ("Great Terrifier"), Airāvatī,[5] Drumacchāyā ("Tree Shade"), Laṅkeśvarī ("Lady of Laṅka"), Kharvarī ("Dwarfess"), Vīramatī ("Hero's Resolve"), Mahānāsā ("Big Nose"), Prabhāvatī ("Lumi-

[1] The following is a list of the twenty-four ḍākinīs or goddesses of the Cakrasamvara maṇḍala, who, together with their consorts, constitute its mind, speech, and body wheels. For a complete synopsis of their correlations to the pilgrimage places and body parts, see Table One in section 3.1 of the introduction above. Jayabhadra remarks here: "Regarding **thence the ḍākinīs pervade the worlds**, the names of the ḍākinīs who are positioned in the triple wheel are stated one by one. They are stated in reverse order, [beginning] with Mahāvīryā, and so forth." (E 14a.4–6: *tataḥ ḍākinyo bhuvanāni vijṛmbhayantīti tricakravyavasthitānāṁ ḍākinīnāṁ pṛthakpṛthagnāmā[n]i kathante / mahāvīryetyādinā vilomena kathitaṁ*)

[2] The term *śauṇḍiṇī* designates a female who produces or sells alcoholic beverages, as is reflected in the Tibetan translation, *chang 'tshong ma*, "she who sells beer."

[3] Probably best left untranslated, following the example of the Tibetan texts; this name is evidently a compound, consisting of *khaṇḍa*, "broken, cleft, piece, portion," and *roha*, "rising, mounting, ascending," which is also translated into Tibetan as *dum skyes ma*.

[4] Bhavabhaṭṭa explains here that "all [eight of] them—Cakravegā, Khaṇḍarohā, Śauṇḍinī, Cakravarmiṇī, Suvīrā, Mahābalā, Cakravartinī, and Mahāvīryā—are white, and [constitute] the body wheel" (Pandey 2002, 44: *cakravegā khaṇḍarohā śauṇḍinī cakravarmiṇī suvīrā mahābalā cakravartinī mahāvīryety etāḥ sarvāḥ śuklā iti kāyacakram*).

[5] Airāvatī in Indian mythology is the spouse of Airāvata, Indra's elephant, who supports the eastern quarter. The name of this goddess is undoubtedly derived from this older figure. According to Bhavabhaṭṭa: "Regarding Airāvatī, Mahābhairavā, Vāyuvegā, Surābhakṣī, Śyāmādevī, Subhadrā, Hayakarṇā, and Khagānanā, they are red, and [constitute] the speech wheel" (Pandey 2002, 44: *airāvatī mahābhairavā vāyuvegā surābhakṣī śyāmādevī subhadrā hayakarṇā khagānanety etā raktā iti vākcakram*).

nous One"), Caṇḍākṣī ("Fierce Eye"), and Pracaṇḍā ("Fury");[6] they are the achievers, the twenty-four ḍākinīs previously established. [Within body, speech, and mind, they are inside just as they are outside.][7] The syllables *hūṁ hūṁ phaṭ* are affixed to the end of the mantras which are utterances of each one's name.[8]

Seeing this excellent yoga supreme, the others are like worm[-infested] straw.[9] The syllable *oṁ* is a lamp everywhere.[10] It is the giver of the

[6] Bhavabhaṭṭa comments: "Regarding Pracaṇḍā, Caṇḍākṣī, Prabhāvatī, Mahānāsā, Vīramatī, Kharvarī, Laṅkeśvarī, and Drumacchāyā, they are dark blue, and [constitute] the mind wheel" (Pandey 2002, 44: *pracaṇḍā caṇḍākṣī prabhāvatī mahānāsā vīramatī kharvarī laṅkeśvarī drumacchāyety etāḥ kṛṣṇā iti cittacakram*).

[7] Mardo's and Mal's translations add these two additional lines here not attested in the Sanskrit mss. or in Sumatikīrti's translation. These are: *sku gsung thugs kyi dbus su ni // ji ltar phyi rol nang de bzhin /* (PM 216a). These lines are also quoted in Kambala and Devagupta's commentaries (SS 81a, SN 13a), and probably reflect a genuine textual variant.

[8] This line, and the one below about the syllable *oṁ*, obliquely indicate the mantras of the goddesses. According to Jayabhadra: "Thus, in all cases the **utterances of each one's name**, and so forth, refer to sixty mantras which join the terminal *hūṁ hūṁ phaṭ* with the utterances of each one's name, i.e., [the names of] of the twenty-four ḍākinīs and also of the [twenty-four] heroes, the four [essence yoginīs], Ḍākinī, and so forth, and the eight [guardians], Kākāsya, and so forth." (E 13b.6–14a.1: *evaṁ sarvatra svanāmoccāraṇetyādinā caturviṁśariḍākinīnā[ṁ] vīrāṇāṁ ca ḍākinyādicatasṛṇāṁ ca kākāsyādyaṣṭānāṁ ca svanāmoccāraṇai[r] hūṁ-hūṁ-phaṭ-kārāntayojitaṣaṣṭimantrā bhavanti /*) The Tibetan translation of the commentary also adds, correctly, that *oṁ* is added to the beginning of each mantra. See MP 49b.

[9] Jayabhadra explains this slightly obscure comparison as follows: "**Seeing the best, supreme yoga, the others are like worm[-infested] straw** means that should some other see Śrī Heruka's supreme yoga, he is like worm-infested straw, i.e., in the manner of grass" (E 14a.1–2: *dṛṣṭvā yogavaraṁ śreṣṭhaṁ ghuṇam anya[t] palālavad iti amū śrīherukayogavaraṁ dṛṣṭvā anya[t] palālavat tṛṇaviśeṣavat ghuṇaniḥsāram ityarthaḥ /*). He further comments: "If these previously mentioned good qualities are attained just by having engaged in the rite of consecration, how much more [can be attained] by means of constant cultivation by means of repetition, contemplation, and so forth? This is stated to show the greatness of the Tantra." (E 14a.5–6: *abhiṣekavidhivartitamātreṇa ete yathoktaguṇā siddhā bhavanti / kiṁ punaḥ japadhyānādibhiḥ sadābhyāsavaśen[e]ti tantrasya māhātmya[ṁ] darśayitum āha /*)

[10] The CS mss. A and C here read *oṁkāra dīpakāḥ sarve siddhidaṁ sarvakāmikaṁ*. In place of *sarve* ms. B reads *sarva*, which Pandey understands as being in compound with *siddhidaṁ* (2002, 45). This is clearly the most grammatically plausible reading. However, it does not accord with the Tibetan translations, which clearly do not read *sarva-* in compound, but appear to read it as a stand-alone pronoun declined in the dative or locative case, reading that "the syllable *oṁ* is a lamp," either "for all" or "everywhere" (PM 216b: *oṁ ni kun la gsal byed de*; SL 100a: *oṁ ni thams cad gsal byed de*). It appears that here, as occurs often in this text, *sarve* is ungrammatically declined as a masculine or neuter *a*-stem noun in locative singular

powers, all that is desired. They are perfected ones (*siddhas*) who have reached the state of being a hero, having seen the maṇḍala in the house. Knowing thus, one should always meditate on the powers taught by the Tathāgata.

---

case. This, at least, appears to be the reading of the Tibetan translators and the Indian pandits who assisted them.

5. The Procedure of Selecting the Letters of the Root Mantra

Thence in the origin of things,[1] in the corolla, is the universe,[2] indestructible and propitious. The mantrin should write in accordance with the rite, gathering into one all things.[3] Here are the mantra's syllables. Having prepared the vowels and consonants, they are completed in classes, and should be discerned as being four and four.[4] On the chart the supreme sage[5]

---

[1] My translation of *dharmodaye* is based upon Bhavabhaṭṭa's gloss, which is *sarveṣāṁ dharmāṇāṁ udayaḥ*. He also notes that "the *dharmodaya* does not differ in meaning from the vulva" (Pandey 2002, 48: *athavā dharmodayo bhaga ity anarthāntaram*).

[2] Bhavabhaṭṭa explains that it is "**the universe** because it is all letters" (Pandey 2002, 48: *viśvaṁ viśvavarṇatvāt*). Bhavabhaṭṭa further explains: "Due to the implication of [the term] **corolla**, [here the term] **universe** means endowed with the universal lotus. [Moreover,] it is not just a universal lotus; it is a universal lotus within the *dharmodaya* in which [the letters] should be arranged." (Pandey 2002, 48: *viśvaṁ viśvapadmānvitaṁ karṇikāhatatvāt / na kevalaviśvapadma dharmodayāntarviśvapadme vā prastared iti sambandhaḥ*) In other words, within the inverted triangle (*dharmodaya*) is the corolla of lotus petals, within which is the chart containing all letters. This is "the universe" if one accepts the widespread Indian metaphysical belief that reality is linguistically structured.

[3] As Bhavabhaṭṭa comments, "**all things**, the actuality of vowels and consonants, are **gathered into one**, which is a figure of speech for their tabular representation in forty-nine cells" (*sarvadharmā akārādikakārādirūpā ekatvena saṁgṛhyante aneneti / tad evonapañcāśatakoṣṭhakaṁ bhuvanaṁ prastāra iti paryāyau /*). This refers to the alphabetical chart by which the mantra is coded. See my comments on this in the introduction.

[4] As Bhavabhaṭṭa informs us (Pandey 2002, 49), "four and four" refers to the eight classes of vowels and consonants, which consist of the class of the sixteen vowels, the five classes of five consonants, i.e., the velar, palatal, retroflex, dental, and labial, and the final two classes, the semivowels and sibilants, each of which has four members, for a total of forty-nine letters in eight classes. The fiftieth, *kṣ*, is not shown, which is indeed the case, as *kṣ* is not coded as a single letter in this text, but rather as a conjunct.

[5] "Supreme sage" (*munisattamaṁ*) is attested in all of the CS and AU mss. (H 166a.1; I 608b.4; J 269.3) and in the standard Tibetan translation (PM 216b: *thub pa mchog*). It is also attested by Bhavabhaṭṭa, who corrected it to *munisattamaḥ* (Pandey 2002, 49). There is, however, a variant, "the seven sages" (*munisaptaḥ*), attested in Jayabhadra's commentary, as well as in the SL revision and Mal's translation (SL 100b, PG 310.3: *thub pa bdun*). Jayabhadra comments are as follows: "**The seven sages on the chart** means that there are seven

should draw forth the hero[6] who stands there, who is the means of achieving all desired aims.

That which is the fifth of the fourth [**n**], and also that which is the fifth of the fifth [**m**].[7] That which is the fourth of the fifth [**bh**], and that which is the third of the first [**g**]. Thus as well the twenty-ninth [**v**],[8] and that which is first of the fourth [**t**]. That which is the fourth of the semivowels [**v**], and also the second of them, too [**r**]. Take here the thirtieth [**ś**], and likewise the twenty-sixth [**y**], drawing them all out, and likewise half a half a hundred [**m**]. Take then the thirty-third [**h**], the first of the first [**k**], the third semivowel [**l**], and also the third of the first [**g**].[9] The thirty-second as

---

classes bounded by the syllables *ka* and *ha*" (E 15a.2: *prastare munisapta iti kakārādi-hakāraparyantāḥ saptavargā bhavantītyarthaḥ /*). This, however, creates a problem, since the previous two lines clearly indicate that there are eight classes. He solves this by reinterpreting the previous line, as follows: "**Should be discerned as being four and four** refers to the eight-lined mantra" (E 15a.1–2: *catuś catur vijñeyam iti mantrapadāny aṣṭau bhavantītyarthaḥ*). This is an ingenious but unlikely solution. Interestingly, the Tibetan translation of this text has apparently been revised, reading *thub pa mchog*, with entirely different commentary upon it. See MP 50a.

[6] As Jayabhadra notes, "the word **hero** refers to the mantra, due to the singular nature of the teaching and teacher" (E 15a.2–3: *tatra stham uddhared vīram iti deśyadeśakayor ekamūrtitvād vīraśabdena mantra uktaḥ /*).

[7] Thus begins the coding for the mantra's consonants. See my introductory section 3.4 for the rules that govern this process. I also provide here the consonants in bold font within square brackets. Although this chapter contains some verbs, most of the selected letters are simply listed. I represent this in the translation, and do not try to render it in complete sentences.

[8] The CS mss. here read "thus as well the twenty-third" (*trayoviṁśas tathaiva ca*), which erroneously codes *ba*, a letter commonly confused with *va*. Bhavabhaṭṭa's commentary and the AU mss., however, have the correct reading.

[9] The last three consonants selected here (*k*, *l*, and *g*) form part of the word ***kalpāgni*** in the final root mantra. As explained in section 3.4 of the introduction (esp. p. 134), this text deals with syllable divisions and consonant conjuncts in an anomalous way. Firstly, it divides syllables following the vowel. Thus here *kalpa* is divided as *ka lpa*. Secondly, while the first consonants of conjuncts are selected in the main chapter which selects the consonants of a given mantra (as here chapter 5 is selecting the consonants of the hero's root mantra), additional consonants within the conjunct are selected later with the vowels (chapter 7 for this mantra). Thus, for *kalpāgni*—since the syllable divisions are considered to be *ka lpā gni*—here in chapter 5 the first consonants of each syllable are selected (*k*, *l*, and *g*), and then later in chapter 7, when the non-*a* vowels are selected, the latter consonants (*p* and *n*) of the conjunct syllables are selected (see p. 188). For the final, completed hero's root mantra, see my note 3 to chapter 25 (p. 263).

well [**s**], and that which is the fifth of the fourth [**n**], that which is fourth of the fifth as well [**bh**], and the first of the semivowels [**y**]. That which is third of the second [**j**], the first of the third [**ṭ**], the fifth of the fifth [**m**], and the first of the first [**k**], too. Likewise, the eleventh [**ṭ**] and the sixteenth [**t**] are also [selected by] the wise.[10]

The first of the third [**ṭ**], and likewise the twenty-sixth [**y**], that which is third of the fourth [**d**], and the second sibilant [**ṣ**]. That which is first of the first [**k**], and thus the twenty-seventh [**r**]. And again the twenty-eighth [**l**], the third of the first [**g**], and the fourth of the fifth as well [**bh**]. Take then the thirty-first [**ṣ**], and also thus the fifteenth [**ṇ**]. Likewise the twenty-fifth [**m**], and the second of the first, too [**kh**]. Likewise the twenty-sixth once more [**y**], and also the thirty-second letter [**s**]. The last of the sibilants [**h**],[11] and the thirty-second once again [**s**]. The fourth of the fifth [**bh**], and the third of the second as well [**j**]. The fourth of the fifth [**bh**], and also the third sibilant [**s**]. The twenty-seventh once more [**r**], and also the first semivowel [**y**]. Likewise the twenty-first again [**p**], and that which is the second semivowel [**r**]. Thus once more the thirtieth [**ś**], and that which is the first of the fifth [**p**].

The first of the sibilants also [**ś**], and thus the syllable *dya*,[12] too. That which is the first of the fourth [**t**], and that which is the first sibilant [**ś**]. Likewise the twenty-eighth [**l**], and the second of the first, too [**kh**]. The first of the third [**ṭ**], and also that which is the third of the first [**g**]. The fourth of the fourth [**dh**], and that which is the second semivowel [**r**]. The

[10] Following this, the CS mss. read *prathamasya prathamaṁ*, "the first of the first," coding the second consonant in the conjunct *-otka*, but this is an anomaly unattested elsewhere, as it violates the pattern of the text, namely, that subsequent consonants in a conjunct are coded with the vowels (as mentioned in the previous note).

[11] All CS mss. here read *ūṣmāṇām trayam eva ca* (though Pandey does not report this). The correct reading, *ūṣmāṇām antam eva ca*, is preserved in Jayabhadra's (E 15a.5) and Bhavabhaṭṭa's commentaries (Pandey 2002, 52), and in the AU mss. (H 166b.2–3, I 608b.9, J 270.3), and is also attested by the Tibetan translations (PM 217a: *u ṣmā ṇā yi tha ma nyid*; SL 101a: *u ṣma yi ni tha ma nyid*).

[12] The reading *dyakāram* occurs in all CS mss. except for C, which omits it. It also occurs in Jayabhadra's commentary (D 21a.4.; E 16a.2), Bhavabhaṭṭa's commentary (Pandey 2002, 53), and the AU mss. (H 166b.5; I 609a.1; J 270.5), as well as in the Tibetan translations. For some unexplained reason, Pandey's ed. emends this to *dyākāram*, which makes no sense, as this syllable *dya* is being used to code the compound *paraśupāśodyata-* ("wielding an axe and noose") in the mantra.

fifth of the third as well [**ṇ**]. The syllable *vyā* is called the "hero."[13] That which is the fourth of the first [**gh**], and indeed thus the eighth also [**j**]. That which is the fifth of the fourth [**n**], and the fifth of the fifth as well [**m**]. Likewise the twenty-seventh [**r**], and the fourth of the fourth, too [**dh**]. The twenty-seventh once again [**r**], and likewise the twenty-sixth as well [**y**]. Take the twenty-fifth [**m**] and also the thirty-third [**h**]. The fourth of the fourth [**dh**], and the fifth of the fifth [**m**]. The fifth of the fourth as well [**n**], and also the first of the first [**k**]. Likewise the twenty-seventh [**r**], and the fourth semivowel, too [**v**]. Thus the twenty-first [**p**], and also the second sibilant [**ṣ**], and likewise the twenty-sixth [**y**].

[The *kara kara* mantra:][14]

> Make! Make! Do! Do! Bind! Bind! Terrify! Terrify! Incite! Incite! *hrauṁ hrauṁ hraḥ hraḥ pheṁ pheṁ phaṭ phaṭ!* Burn! Burn! Cook! Cook! Eat! Eat! Seize! Seize for him who is draped with a garland of greasy, bloody entrails! Threaten! Threaten the snake or serpent that resides in the seven underworlds! *ākaḍḍha ākaḍḍha hrīṁ hrīṁ jñauṁ jñauṁ kṣmāṁ kṣmāṁ hāṁ hāṁ hīṁ hīṁ hūṁ hūṁ kili kili sili sili cili cili dhili dhili hūṁ hūṁ!*[15]

---

[13] This line (*vyākāraṁ vīram ity āhūḥ*) is contained in all CS mss. and is also attested in Bhavabhaṭṭa's commentary. Mardo's revised translation, however, reads "thence taking the letter *byā*" (PM 217a: *yi ge byā ni de nas blang*), and Sumatikīrti's is almost identical to this, reading *bya* instead of *byā* (SL 101a: *yi ge bya ni de bzhin blang*). This seems to be based on a genuine textual variant, corresponding to the Sanskrit preserved in the AU mss. (J 270.7: *vyākāraṁ tatoddhṛtya*; H 166b.6, I 609a.3: *vyokāraṁ tatoddhṛtya*). The text *tatoddhṛtya* is undoubtedly the result of improper *sandhi* across the vowel hiatus, and should be corrected to *tata uddhṛtya.*

[14] The extant CS mss. select the consonants and vowels only for the eight line mantra (*aṣṭapadamantra*), and omit selection of the *kara kara* mantra, which Jayabhadra explains is "an addendum to the mantra garland" (E 16b.3: *karakareti mālāmantropanyāsa*). The CS mss. here simply list the *kara kara* mantra following the selection of the former eight-lined mantra's consonants. The Sanskrit text is followed precisely in Sumatikīrti's translation. Mal's translation, and also all of the Indian commentaries, also omit selection of this mantra. Mardo's translation, however, does select the *kara kara* mantra. In so doing it seems to be following the AU, which likewise selects it. Here I follow the root text in reproducing, rather than selecting, this mantra.

[15] This is the mantra with translatable portions translated. In Sanskrit it occurs as follows: *kara kara kuru kuru bandha bandha trāsaya trāsaya kṣobhaya kṣobhaya hrauṁ hrauṁ hraḥ*

The mantra of the king of spells[16] obviates all [other] means of achievement;[17] other than this there is nothing greater within the three worlds. Knowing Śrī Heruka's mantra, one should forsake all the others, which are like worm[-infested] straw.

---

hraḥ pheṁ pheṁ phaṭ phaṭ daha daha paca paca bhakṣa bhakṣa vasarudhirāntramālāvalambine gṛhṇa gṛhṇa saptapātālagatabhujaṅgaṁ sarpam vā tarjaya tarjaya ākaḍḍha ākaḍḍha hrīṁ hrīṁ jñauṁ jñauṁ kṣmāṁ kṣmāṁ hāṁ hāṁ hīṁ hīṁ hūṁ hūṁ kili kili sili sili cili cili dhili dhili hūṁ hūṁ. Where the CS mss. and also Bhavabhaṭṭa's commentary read *cili cili* (Pandey 2002, 58), the AU mss. read *hili hili* (H 169a.1, J 274.7; I omits), and Mardo's translation follows suit. It is important to note, however, that the Tibetan tradition appears to follow the latter, reproducing the *hili hili* version in ritual texts.

16 The term *vidyārājā* is incorrectly declined in the root text as *vidyārājasya*. Jayabhadra comments upon it as follows: "the **spells** (*vidyā*) are the ḍākinīs positioned in the three wheels; their king (*rājā*) is the **king of spells**. This refers to his mantra." (E 16b.4: *vidyārājasyeti vidyā tricakravartitaḍākinyaḥ tāsāṁ rājā vidyārājaḥ tasya mantra ityarthaḥ /*)

17 The CS mss. here read *sarvasaṁtrāsavaritaḥ*, "devoid of all terrors," which is meaningful, but unattested elsewhere. Jayabhadra (D 21b; E 16b.4–5), Bhavabhaṭṭa (Pandey 2002, 58), and the AU ms. (I 610a.4) read *sarvasādhanavarjitaḥ*, which I have followed here (H omits; J 274.7: *sadhānavarjitaḥ*). One should also note that there is some variation here in the Tibetan translations. Sumatikīrti reads *bsgrub pa thams cad rnam pa'o* (SL 101b), which confirms the *sarvasadhāna* reading. Mardo reads *bya ba thams cad rab sgrub pa'o* (PM 218b), "achieves all ritual actions," which is another variant not attested elsewhere. Regarding the meaning of *sarvasādhanavarjitaḥ*, Jayabhadra comments that "**obviates all [other] means of achievement** means that it is accomplished through recitation alone" (D 21, E 16b.5: *sarvasādhanavarjita iti paṭhitamātreṇa siddha ityarthaḥ*).

6. The Procedure of Selecting the Hero's Six Armor [Mantras]

Aside from this, there are the twenty-two syllable essence and seven syllable quintessence.[1] The eighth seed from the *y* class is thus [embellished] with the twelve ornaments. Taking the intervening syllables [yields] the six limbs spoken by Śrī Heruka.[2] Each syllable is positioned through unification with the six heroes,[3] endowed with the syllables *oṁ*, *namaḥ*, *svāhā*, *vauṣat*, *hūṁ hūṁ*, and *phaṭ*. The essences should be known by the adept.[4]

---

[1] These are given below in chapter eight.

[2] Jayabhadra explains this cryptic passage as follows:

> The **eighth seed from the *y* class** is the letter *h*. **Thus with the twelve ornaments** means that one should arrange twelve "seeds," i.e., the letter *h*, embellished with the twelve ornaments, excluding the neuter ones. [These are:] *ha hā hi hī hu hū he hai ho hau haṁ haḥ*. **Taking the intervening syllables** means excluding the second, fourth, sixth, eighth, tenth, and twelfth. [The result] is the six limbs spoken by Śrī Heruka. These are the six limbs of Heruka.
>
> *yavarg[āc] cetyādim aṣṭamaṁ bījaṁ hakāraḥ / māt[rair] dvādaśabhiḥ tatheti napuṁsakavarjitai[r] dvādaśamātrair virājitāni hakārabījāni nyaset / ha hā hi hī hu hū he hai ho hau haṁ haḥ iti / akṣarāntaritaṁ kṛtveti / dvitīya-cathurtha-ṣaṣṭhāṣṭa[ma]-daśama-dvādaśāni varjayitvā ṣaḍaṅga[ḥ] herukocyata iti herukaṣaḍaṅgam ityartha /* (E 16b.6–17a.2)

Once the syllables listed by Jayabhadra are excluded, the six that remain are *ha hi hu he ho haṁ*. Evidently the "neuter" vowels are the dental and retroflex vowels (*ṛ*, *ṝ*, *ḷ*, and *ḹ*), which are the four excluded from his list.

[3] Jayabhadra comments: "Through attendance to the indivisibility of the support and the supported, or from reference to the ultimate, there is the **unification of the six heroes**. This refers to the syllables *oṁ* and so forth." (E 17a.2–3: *ā[lambālambana]yor abhedopacārāt paramārthato vā ṣaḍvīrasamāyoga iti ṣaṇṇāṁ vīrāṇāṁ samāyogā oṁkārādayaḥ /*) The beginning of this comment is corrupt in the Sanskrit; my tentative reading is based on the Tibetan *rten dang brten pa po dbyer med pa'i tshul gyis sam* (MP 51a).

[4] In the Sanskrit *jñeyaṁ hṛdayāni tu sādhakaḥ*, both *jñeyaṁ* and *sādhakaḥ* are incorrectly declined. Jayabhadra corrects it as follows: *sādhakena jñeyānītyarthaḥ* (E 17a.4–5)

The first is known as the heart,[5] and the second as the head. Give the third to the crown, let the fourth be the armor. Let the fifth be the eye, and the sixth is said to be the weapon.[6]

---

[5] Jayabhadra comments here, linking the armor mantras themselves to their respective body parts and "heroes," as follows:

> **The first is known as the heart** means *oṁ ha*, which is Vajrasattva in the heart. **And the second the head** refers to *namaḥ hi*, Vairocana in the head. **Give the third to the crown** means *svāhā hu*, Padmanarteśvara on the crest. **Let the fourth be the armor**: by the sign "armor" is meant *vauṣaṭ he*, through which there is Śrī Heruka on the shoulders. **Let the fifth be the eye**, meaning *hūṁ hūṁ ho* which is Vajrasūrya in both eyes. **And the sixth is said to be the weapon**, namely *phaṭ haṁ*, Hayagrīva, the weapon on all limbs.
>
> *prathamaṁ hṛdayaṁ caiveti oṁ ha ity anena vajrasattvo hṛdaye / dvitīyaṁ tu śiraḥ smṛta iti namaḥ hīty anena vairocanaṁ śirasi / tritīyaṁ tu śikhā[ṁ] dadyād iti svāh[ā hv] ity anena padmanarteśvaraḥ śikhāyām / caturtha[ṁ] kavacaṁ bhaved iti kavaca-rūpeṇa vauṣaṭ ha ity anena śrīherukasya skandhayoḥ / pañcamaṁ tu bhaven netram iti hūṁ hūṁ ho ity anena vajrasūryaś cakṣurdvaye / ṣaṣṭhasyā[s]tram ucyata iti phaṭ haṁ ity anena hayagrīvaḥ sarvāṅg[ās]tram /* (E 17a.5–17b.2)

[6] All of the CS mss. here read *ṣaṣṭhamaṁ tv astram ucyate*, which is a viable reading. Without alerting the reader, Pandey emends this to *ṣaṣṭhasyāstram ucyate* (Pandey 2002, 61), evidently on the basis of Bhavabhaṭṭa's commentary. While this reading is also found in Jayabhadra's commentary, as shown in the previous note, it is not a superior reading; the text in the CS mss. follows the pattern of the previous lines, declining the numeral in the same case as the body part or the implement to which it corresponds.

7. The Procedure of Selecting the Mantra

Next, the second syllable[1] is supplied with the thirteenth of the vowels [**mo**]. The sixth syllable is graced with the eleventh vowel [**te**]. The seventh syllable is furnished with the fourth vowel [**vī**], and the wise provide the eighth syllable with the eleventh vowel [**re**]. Taking the ninth syllable, it is likewise furnished with the second vowel [**śā**]. The twelfth syllable is also joined by the second vowel [**hā**]. Taking the twenty-first thus, it is joined with the second vowel and the esteemed fourteenth [**lpā**].[2] Taking the fifteenth syllable and receiving the twentieth syllable, they are joined to the third vowel [**gni**]. The fifteenth of the vowels likewise distinguishes the sixteenth syllable [**saṁ**]. The third vowel is connected with the seventeenth syllable [**ni**], and the eighteenth syllable is endowed with the second of the vowels [**bhā**].

The twenty-first syllable is linked with the second of the vowels [**ṭā**].[3] The twenty-third syllable is linked with the fifth vowel [**ku**]. The thirteenth of the vowels is linked with that, the twenty-fourth syllable [**ṭo**]. Taking the first of the first, it is conjoined with the twenty-fifth syllable [**tka**].[4] The

---

[1] Regarding the numbering of the syllables, here the "second" refers to the order of the syllables in the mantra, as selected in chapter five. Only those syllables that have vowels other than short *a* are selected here in this chapter, since that vowel is assumed in Sanskrit unless otherwise noted via vowel markers. As an aid to the reader, I will include each entire syllable selected in this chapter, with consonants and vowels, in square brackets.

[2] That is, the twenty-first consonant on the chart (*p*) is joined to the second vowel (*ā*), both of which are conjoined with the fourteenth (partial) syllable (*l*) selected in ch. 5, to form the final conjunct syllable *lpā*. The next line, which codes the fifteenth syllable, is likewise formed. See introduction (p. 134), and ch. 5 n. 9.

[3] The CS mss. here read "the twenty-first syllable is linked with the letter *ā*" (*ākārasvarasaṁyuktam ekaviṁśatimākṣaram*). This line violates the pattern of the chapter by indicating the vowel directly rather than giving coding it by number; it may thus be a later alteration. Jayabhadra's commentary codes it in the normal way, reading: "The twenty-first syllable is linked with the second of the vowels" (E 18a.4: *svarāṇāṁ dvitīyenaiva saṁyuktam ekaviṁśatyakṣaram*). This reading also occurs in the AU mss. (H 169b.3; I 610b.2; J 276.2), and is most likely the oldest variant. I follow this latter reading in my translation.

[4] That is, *k* is added to *ta* to form the conjunct *kta*.

first of the third,[5] which should be the twenty-sixth letter, should be distinguished by the second vowel [**ṭā**].[6] The twenty-eighth as well is honored with the fifteenth [**daṁ**]. The twenty-ninth syllable should be endowed with the first of the third, endowed with fire, a portion below, and provided with the second vowel [**ṣṭrā**].[7]

The thirty-first syllable is supplied with the second vowel [**rā**], and the thirty-second syllable is endowed with the thirteenth vowel [**lo**]. Let the thirty-third letter be endowed with the sun [**gra**].[8] The thirty-fourth is accompanied by the fourth of the vowels [**bhī**]. It is the means of achieving all desired aims. The thirty-seventh, which is the means of achievement prescribed by the ḍākinīs,[9] is endowed with the fifth vowel [**mu**]. The thirty-eighth as well is provided with the second vowel [**khā**]. Have no doubt that this is the very means of achieving all deities. The forty-second is likewise endowed below with the burning portion[10] by the adept [**sra**]. The forty-

---

5 This line, *tṛtīyasya prathamaṁ tu*, is unnecessary as it was already selected in chapter five. It is not found in the Tibetan translations. It is, however, attested in Bhavabhaṭṭa's commentary (Pandey 2002, 64), Jayabhadra's commentary (E 18a.6), and also the AU mss. (H 169b.5; I 611a.3; J 276.3). The AU mss., however, omit coding for the twenty-sixth syllable, reading *tṛtīyasya prathamaṁ tu svaradvitīyasya tu tad bhavet*, which at least is not repetitive.

6 The CS mss. here read *dvitīyasvareṇa bhedayet*, "should be distinguished (or split) by the second vowel." An alternate reading occurs in Jayabhadra's commentary (E 18a.6), *dvitīyasvareṇa yojayet*, "should be joined with the second vowel." Yet another variant occurs in Bhavabhaṭṭa's commentary (Pandey 2002, 64), *dvitīyasvarasaṁyuktaṁ*, "endowed with the second vowel." Pandey's edition emends the text to accord with the latter reading, without listing the variants.

7 That is, the twenty-ninth syllable (*ṣ*) is provided with the letter *ṭ* and then with "fire" (*r*), and *ā*. This, together with the preceding syllable, forms the word *daṁṣṭrā*.

8 "Endowed with the sun," *bhāskareṇa saṁyuktaṁ*, is one of several ways that this text codes the *r*-affix.

9 Bhavabhaṭṭa here comments: "As for **ḍākinīs**, the ḍākinīs' means of achievement is all mantras. Now, having visualized the **thirty-seventh**, the letter *m*, as a single image of the true sun upon the victim's head, the *yakṣa*, and so forth, are subjugated—this is the **means of achievement**. Prescribed by the ḍākinīs means authorized by the ḍākinīs." (F 51a.3–4: *ḍākinīti ḍākinīnāṁ sādhanaṁ samagro mantraḥ / athavā saptatriṁśan makāraḥ kevalasamyagarkasaṁkāśaḥ sādhyaśirasi dhyāto yakṣādīn vaśatīti sādhanam / ḍākinīsmṛtaṁ ḍākinīsaṁmatam /*; cf. Pandey 2002, 65).

10 "Endowed with the burning portion below," *dahanena tu saṁyuktam adho bhāgena*, is another way the text codes the *r*-affix.

third letter is supplied with the fifth vowel [**bhu**]. The forty-fifth is also supplied with the second vowel [**bhā**]. The fifth vowel is also connected with the forty-sixth [**su**]. It is worshipped by all heroes. The forty-seventh is also provided with the second vowel [**rā**]. It is esteemed as the supreme Vajrasattva.

The fifty-first is likewise thought to be most splendid[11] through the fifth vowel [**śu**]. The fifty-second is likewise provided with the second vowel [**pā**]. Have no doubt that this is the very means of achieving all deities. Thus again the fifty-third is supplied with the thirteenth vowel [**śo**]. The syllable *dya* is extracted from the fourth class.[12] The fifty-sixth syllable is provided with the sixth vowel [**śū**]. It permanently destroys enemies.[13] The fourth semivowel is supplied with the second vowel. Likewise let the fifty-ninth syllable have the fifteenth, the means of achieving all powers [**ṭvāṁ**].[14] The sixty-first letter is endowed with the second vowel, too [**dhā**]. The wise know thus.[15] The sixty-second thus as well is supplied with the third vowel [**ri**]. It is considered to be the supreme of the ḍākinīs. The sixty-third furthermore is endowed with the eleventh vowel [**ṇe**]. It is the most splendid syllable.

---

[11] The reading *śobhanaṁ* ("splendid") is attested by Bhavabhaṭṭa (Pandey 2002, 66), the AU mss. (H 170a.5; I 611a.8; J 277.3), and also the Tibetan translations (PM 219a: *mdzes pa mchog ni yin par 'dod*; SL 103a: *mdzes par mchog ni yin par 'dod*). The CS mss., however, all read *bhojanaṁ*, a corrupt variant not reported in the Pandey edition.

[12] This is in reference to the fifty-fourth syllable of the mantra, which is *dya*. In the CS ms. A, this syllable is partially obscured by insect damage; it appears to be a *d* in conjunct with a *y*, but it is not possible to ascertain if it is a *dy* conjunct or a *ddy* conjunct. I read the latter, *d-dyakāra*, since it is necessary given the fact that it is preceded by *caturthavargā[d]*. Pandey follows Bhavabhaṭṭa in reading *d-dakāra*, which does not make sense, since *dya* was selected in ch. 5. The former reading, while repetitive, is not contradictory. This selection is omitted in the Tibetan translations, and also does not occur in the AU mss.

[13] Bhavabhaṭṭa glosses this, saying "**It permanently destroys enemies** because it is victorious over the enemy of the afflictions" (Pandey 2002, 67: *dhruvaṁ śatrunikṛntanam iti kleśaśatru-jayāt*).

[14] This and the previous line code the fifty-ninth syllable, *ṭvāṁ*.

[15] The CS mss. here read *evam eva vidur budhāḥ* (A; B, C: *budhaḥ*). This is supported by the AU ms. (J 277.6), and by mss. H (170b.2) and I (611b.1) which read *budhā* due to *sandhi*. Bhavabhaṭṭa, however, attests another reading of the root text, *evam eva vidur varāḥ* (Pandey 2002, 67), which is closer to the Tibetan translations (PM 219b, SL 103a: *'di nyid mchog ni yin par bshad*). Pandey's edition of the root text (2002, 67) follows Bhavabhaṭṭa's reading here.

The sixty-fifth as well is thus split by Vajrasattva[16] [**ghra**].[17] The sixty-sixth syllable is equipped with the third vowel [**ji**]. It is the giver of power, that is, great liberation, in all affairs, [as] the Tathāgata stated.[18] The sixty-seventh syllable is endowed with the second vowel [**nā**]. Have no doubt in all of the yoginīs' affairs. Next is the sixty-eighth; attach the letter *b* to it. Put it down in the portions below [**mba**]. The seventy-first syllable is also endowed with the second vowel [**rā**]. Have no doubt that it is the splendor of all syllables.

The seventy-fourth is likewise equipped with the second vowel [**hā**]. It is the primal power drawn from the mouth of the Tathāgata. The seventy-fifth is [endowed] with the sixth vowel, too [**dhū**]. It is the supreme yoga, and also the best among all yogas. The seventy-sixth also has the second vowel. Let it be split by the sun, and attach the letter *v* there [**mvrā**]. There

---

[16] The CS mss. here read "The sixty-forth as well is thus split by Vajrasattva, and is provided with the second vowel" (*catuṣaṣtis tathā caiva vajrasattvena bheditaṁ dvitīyasvarayojitaṁ*). This is hopelessly corrupt, as the sixty-fourth syllable, *vyā*, was selected in the fifth chapter. While it does have the second vowel, long *ā*, it is the sixty-fifth, *gh*, that is "split by Vajrasattva," i.e., provided with an *r*-affix, to yield the *ghra* of *vyāghra*. This is evidently an old corruption, as there is considerable variation here among the Tibetan translations; see Tsong Khapa's discussion in my translation of his KS commentary (Gray 2017). The AU seems to have the best reading here, with "The sixty-fifth as well is thus split by Vajrasattva" (H 170b.3: *pañcaṣaṣti tathā caiva vajrasattvena bheditaḥ*; I 611b.1–2, J 277.7: *-bheditaṁ*). It correctly locates the *r*-affix with the sixty-fifth syllable, and makes no mention of the second vowel, *dvitīyasvarayojitaṁ*, which would have been incorrect in the context of the sixty-fifth syllable and superfluous in the context of the sixty-fourth. Bhavabhaṭṭa correctly reads *pañcaṣaṣṭi*, but incorrectly preserves *dvitīyasvarayojitaṁ*. One could hypothesize an earlier text that might have read something like *catuṣaṣtiṁ tathā caiva dvitīyasvarayojitam / pañcaṣaṣtis tathā caiva vajrasattvena bheditaḥ*, but I feel the most consistent and probably oldest reading is that preserved in the AU, while the CS text most likely became contaminated by commentary on the sixty-fourth syllable.

[17] Pandey's edition makes a serious emendation here without providing any explanation. It adds *idaṁ bījaṁ paraṁ divyaṁ* (2002, 68), which does not occur in the CS mss. or the commentaries, and is evidently a hypothetical reconstruction based on one of the Tibetan translations (PM 119b: *sa bon 'di ni lha rdzas mchog*). It follows this with *siddhidaṁ mokṣadaṁ mahat*, again based on the Tibetan (PM 119b: *grub sbyin thar pa sbyin chen po*). This does occur in the Sanskrit, in the next verse, describing the sixty-sixth syllable.

[18] CS ms. A here reads *siddhidaṁ mokṣadaṁ mahat sarvakāryeṣu tathāgata idaṁ bravīt*, with minor variation in mss. B and C. Pandey's edition, however, reports that *siddhidaṁ* does not occur in this mss. It also transfers *mokṣadaṁ mahat* to the preceding verse, apparently out of a desire to produce an edition that accords with Mardo's translation.

is none other more splendid. Possessed of the seventy-seventh, attach there the syllable *dha* [**ndha**]. It is held to be splendid by the ḍākinīs. The seventy-eighth is also endowed with the second vowel [**kā**]. It is believed to be the ultimate cause. The eighty-first letter is distinguished by that which follows the fourth [**pu**].[19] It is that which produces the primal power and promotes all powers. The eighty-second letter is likewise endowed thus with the second vowel [**ṣā**].[20]

The wise know[21] that the root mantra is the abode of all powers, that which pulverizes the hearts of the ḍākinīs.[22] The power from reciting the king of spells of the deity Śrī Heruka is complete.[23] With the syllable *oṁ* joined at the beginning and *hūṁ hūṁ phaṭ* at the end, the root mantra achieves all desired aims. This is the self nature of all heroes, the unification of all heroes, the binding of the ḍākinīs' network.[24]

---

[19] That is, the vowel which follows the fourth vowel (*ī*), namely *u*.

[20] This ends the selection of the "eight line mantra" (*aṣṭapadamantra*). As in the case of ch. 5, Mardo's translation continues with vowel selection for the *kara kara* mantra, evidently following the *Abhidhānottara*. This is omitted in the CS mss., the Indian commentaries, and the other Tibetan translations, and is not translated here. It is covered, however, in my translation of Tsong Khapa's commentary (Gray 2017).

[21] Here again (see note 15 above) Pandey's edition of the root text emends *vidur budhāḥ* to *vidur varāḥ*, on the basis of Bhavabhaṭṭa's commentary.

[22] Jayabhadra comments here: "As for **pulverizes the heart of the ḍākinīs**, just by reciting this mantra all of the terrible ḍākinīs, and so forth, are terrified" (E 18b.6–19a.1: *ḍākinīnāṁ hṛdarśanam iti ayaṁ mantra uccaritamātreṇa sarvā bhayaṁkarā ḍākinyādayaḥ t[r]āsam āpadyante*). Note that his text is corrupt, reading *hṛdarśanaṁ* rather than *hṛdayamardanaṁ*, which is also attested in the AU mss. (H 172b.4; I 612a.2; J 281.3). Bhavyakīrti repeats Jayabhadra's comments, and then adds: "I, Bhavyakīrti, hold that **pulverizing the hearts** means that one draws their hearts forth and completely subjugates them." (SM 16b)

[23] The CS mss. here read *śrīherukadevasya vidyārājapaṭhitasiddhi amoghanī*, which is ungrammatical but understandable, and corresponds with the Tibetan translations (PM 221a: *dpal ldan khrag 'thung lha rig rgyal // bklags pas grub pa don yod pa*; SL 104a: *dpal ldan khrag 'thung lha rigs rgyal // klags pas grub pa'i don yod pa*). For some reason, the Pandey edition omits *amoghanī* and replaces it with *ayaṁ mantraṁ*, evidently on the basis of Bhavabhaṭṭa's commentary. But this emendation makes no sense, as in his commentary *ayaṁ mantraṁ* follows *mūlamantraḥ* in the next verse. It also occurs thus in the AU mss. (H 172b.5, I 612a.2, J 281.4).

[24] These last lines, *tat sarvavīrasvam ātmānaṁ sarvavīrasamāyogaṁ ḍākinījālasamvaram*, are very close to the first verse of the next chapter, and they correspond to the single verse which occurs in the AU mss. (H 172b.5–6; I 612a.3; J 281.4); the AU passage which corresponds

to CS chs. 7 and 8 is in fact included within a single chapter. It is thus debatable with which chapter this line most properly belongs. That is, does it describe the root mantra, completed in ch. 7, or Śrī Heruka's essence and quintessence mantras, revealed in ch. 8? The Tibetan translations place this only at the beginning of ch. 8; for this reason, no doubt, the Pandey edition drops these lines from its edition of ch. 7. However, Jayabhadra's comments suggest that these lines may be more appropriate here, in reference to the root mantra: "**Thus one's own self is the union of all heroes, the binding of the ḍākinīs' network** means that Śrī Heruka himself and also [his] mantra are the self-nature of all ḍākinīs who are arranged in the three wheels [of the maṇḍala]" (E: 19a.2: *evaṁ svamātmānaṁ sarvavīrasamāyogaḍākinījālasamvaram iti śrīherukātmako 'pi mantras tricakravyavasthitaḥ sarvaḍākinīsvabhāva ityarthaḥ*). Interestingly, he has *mantra* declined in the singular case, not dual as we would expect if this referred to the essence and quintessence mantras of ch. 8. Given the loose use of declensions in these texts, this is not a definitive argument, but as the proper location of these lines is questionable I have decided to follow the CS mss. and preserve these lines in both the seventh and eighth chapters.

8. The Procedure of Selecting the Reversed Yoginī Mantras[1]

Thence one's own nature[2] is the unification of all heroes, the producer of all powers,[3] the binding of the ḍākinīs' network.[4]

hā svā raṁ mva sa la jā nī ki ḍā
ṭ pha hūṁ hūṁ kaṁ ru ru he he jra va śrī oṁ[5]

The king of spells' essence has not arisen nor will it arise.

ṭ pha hūṁ hūṁ ha ha hrīḥ oṁ[6]
ṭ pha hūṁ hreṁ hrīṁ hāṁ oṁ[7]

---

[1] This translates the title preserved in the CS mss., *viparītayoginīmantroddhāravidhipaṭalo 'ṣṭamaḥ*. A more extensive title is preserved in Bhavabhaṭṭa's commentary and the Tibetan translations, namely "The Method of Selecting the Reversed Essence and the Six Yoginī Mantras," (Pandey 2002, 74: *viparītahṛdayaṣaḍyoginī-vajravārāhī-mantroddhāravidhipaṭalo 'ṣṭamaḥ*; PM 221a: *go bzlogs pa'i snying po dang rnal 'byor ma drug gi sngags btu ba'i cho ga'i le'u ste brgyad pa'o*; SL 104b: *go bzlogs pa'i snying po dang // rnal 'byor ma drug gi sngags btu ba'i cho ga'i le'u ste // brgyad pa'o*)

[2] *Svam ātmānaṁ*. Bhavabhaṭṭa comments that "**one's own nature** refers to 'one's own mind'" (Pandey 2002, 73: *svātmānam iti nijaṁ cittam ityarthaḥ*).

[3] This line is not attested in the Tibetan translations or commentaries; the translation and several of the commentaries have the alternate line "is said to be the Cakrasamvara," (PM 221a: *'khor lo bde mchog yin par 'dod*).

[4] In support of the proposition that these lines are more suitable here, rather than at the end of chapter seven with reference to the root mantra, Durjayacandra comments as follows: "**the union of all heroes, the binding of the ḍākinīs' network** signifies the essence and quintessence and are declined as neuter, [i.e., since *hṛdaya* and *upahṛdaya* are neuter nouns]" (RG 275a: *dpa' bo thams cad mnyam sbyor ba // mkha' 'gro ma yi dra ba'i sdom pa ste / snying po dang nye ba'i snying po dang rtags la brten nas ma ning gi rtags su byas pa'o /*).

[5] This is Heruka's essence mantra, with the syllables given in reverse order. In normal order it reads: *oṁ śrī vajra he he ru ru kaṁ hūṁ hūṁ phaṭ ḍākinījālasamvara svāhā*. Note that the mantra as usually given, in Bhavabhaṭṭa's commentary, for example (Pandey 2002, 73), reads *ḍākinījālasamvara*, not *ḍākinījālasamvaraṁ*, as given in this chapter's reverse mantra coding.

[6] This is Heruka's quintessence mantra, which in normal order is: *oṁ hrīḥ ha ha hūṁ hūṁ phaṭ*.

[7] These six syllables, in reverse order, are *oṁ hāṁ hrīṁ hreṁ hūṁ phaṭ*. These are then linked to the six syllables listed next to form the the six yoginīs' armor mantras (*ṣaḍyoginīkavacamantrāḥ*).

The syllables *vaṁ*, *yoṁ*, *moṁ*, *hrīṁ*, and also *hūṁ* and *phaṭ*, are enumerated. They are famed as the six yoginīs.[8]

hā svā ye nī ca ro vai jra va oṁ[9]

The great spell of the ḍākinīs has not arisen, nor will it arise. On the earth there are four treasures.[10] The mantra garland[s] are supreme,[11] the great spell of the ḍākinīs, and the King of Spells, Heruka.[12]

---

[8] Jayabhadra lists the six yoginīs' armor mantras (*ṣaḍyoginīkavacamantrāḥ*) and correlates them to their respective yoginīs and body parts as follows:

> *Oṁ [vaṁ]* is Vajravārāhī in the navel. *Oṁ hāṁ yoṁ* is Yāminī in the heart. *Oṁ hrīṁ moṁ* is Mohanī at the throat. *Oṁ hreṁ hrīṁ* is Saṁcālanī in the head. *Oṁ hūṁ hūṁ* is Trāsanī at the crown. *Oṁ phaṭ phaṭ* is Caṇḍikā, whose form is excellent weapons in all of the limbs.
>
> *oṁ vajravārāhī nābhau / oṁ hāṁ yoṁ yāminī hṛdaye / oṁ hrīṁ moṁ mohanī vaktre / oṁ hreṁ hrīṁ saṁcālanī śirasi / oṁ hūṁ hūṁ trāsanī śikhāyāṁ / oṁ phaṭ phaṭ caṇḍikā sarvaṅge sastrarūpā / ṣaḍyoginīnāṁ hṛdayam /* (E 19a.6–19b.2)

Note that Jayabhadra adds the syllable *oṁ* to the beginning of all of the mantras except for Vajravārāhī's, which begins with *oṁ*.

[9] This mantra is generally identified by the Indian commentators as the Blessed Lady Vajravārāhī's quintessence mantra. Durjayacandra, however, identifies it as her essence mantra, and he is followed by the Tibetans. In proper order it reads: *oṁ vajravairocanīye svāhā*. Usually a *hūṁ hūṁ phaṭ* is also inserted, yielding *oṁ vajravairocanīye hūṁ hūṁ phaṭ svāhā*.

[10] Jayabhadra identified these as follows: "The four mantras, which are treasures, are the mantra garland, and the essence, quintessence, and armor mantras of the Blessed Lord and Blessed Lady" (E 19b.4–5: *catvāro mantrā evaṁ ratnānīti bhagavato bhagavatyāś ca mantramālāhṛdayopahṛdayakavacamantrāś ca*). With regard to the incorrectly declined *caturo ratnā*, he observes that "in the Tantra the grammatical cases are shown haphazardly in order to bewilder everyone. They must be inferred through reference to their meaning." (E 19b.5: *tantre sarvavyāmohārthaṁ yatheṣṭaṁ vibhaktinirdeśaḥ kṛtaḥ / tadarthavaśād unneyaḥ /*)

[11] The Sanskrit here is declined as accusative singular, but the referent is evidently dual, i.e., the two mantra garlands which are named immediately afterward.

[12] Bhavabhaṭṭa has a somewhat different interpretation of this line. He identifies the mantra garland with Śrī Heruka's eight line mantra, and the King of Spells with the *kara kara* mantra. The ḍākinīs' great spell he identifies with "the mantra of Vajravārāhī, and so forth" (Pandey 2002, 74: *vajravārāhyādimantraḥ*).

9. The Procedure of the Ritual Actions of the Root Mantra

Next I will explain the root mantra's supreme ritual actions, in successive order.[1] Whatever might exist in the triple world, all of those things will be achieved in an instant, and one will undertake all ritual actions.[2] One causes all serpent deities (*nāga*), all gods, all *yakṣas*, and all races[3] to die immediately through recollection. One dispels clouds, causes rain to fall and holds it back.[4] One dries up the oceans, causes a river to flow backwards,

[1] Descriptions of many of the rituals to which this chapter succinctly refers are contained in my translation of Tsong Khapa's commentary on this text (Gray 2017). Here I will add notes to supply additional information to aid in understanding of the present text only.

[2] Most of this *pada* is lost due to fraying of ms. A. Ms. A fol. 8a ends with the text *sarvaṁ ka-*, and the rest is missing as it is in the obliterated portion of fol. 8b. The reading *sarvaṁ* is also attested by Bhavabhaṭṭa. Ms. C, which seems to have been copied when the damage was less extensive, reads *karma* at the end of the *pada*. The *pada* is reconstructed in the Pandey ed. as *sarvakarmāṇi karoti*. This reconstruction of the Tibetan seems unlikely, given the portions of the *pada* that do survive. But given the fact that the Sanskrit here is incomplete, I translate here the Tibetan as preserved in Mardo's and Sumatikīrti's revised translations, namely *las rnams thams cad byed pa'o* (PM 221a; SL 104b: *las rnams thams cad byed pa po*).

[3] Bhavabhaṭṭa comments that *sarvayonayaḥ* refers to "fierce humans," *krūrā mānuṣāḥ* (Pandey 2002, 76), which implies that the term *yoni* is used here in its sense of "race, stock, class," and so forth. See Monier-Williams 2002, 858 col. 2.

[4] Jayabhadra gives a non-literal interpretation of this line, in accordance with sexual yogic practices, as follows:

> With regard to **dispelling clouds**, and so forth, first the literal meaning is apprehended, and later there is the following meaning. **Dispelling clouds** in the state of the vajra and lotus subdues the ḍākinī. **Causing rain to fall** [occurs] via the flow of seminal essence, and **holding it back** is immobilizing it with seals (*mudrā*).
>
> *meghān trāsayatītyādi prathamaṁ yathārtha gṛhyate paścād ayam arthaḥ / vajrapadmāvasthāyāṁ meghān trāsayati ḍākinīvaśī-karoti / varṣāpayati bodhicittadhārayā nivārayati sthāpayati saha mudrābhiḥ /* (D 19b.4–5; E 20b.6–7)

and restrains Indra.[5] Through one hundred thousand repetitions of this mantra one can cause the earth to quake, and climbing a tree one will go wherever one desires.[6]

One can steal all mantras[7] and steal all powers. One can draw out blood and furthermore cause it to flow. One can assume many thousands of forms. One can be visible as one desires, and one can be invisible when one wishes. One can reduce palaces, trees, spires, and so forth, to dust.[8] Poison

---

[5] Bhavabhaṭṭa explains that "one **restrains** [Indra], the Lord of the sentient and insentient, from deeds that are not to be done" (Pandey 2002, 76: *cetanācetanādhipatīn akāryakāraṇān niṣedhayatītyarthaḥ*).

[6] Jayabhadra comments here: "**Climbing a tree one will go wherever one desires** means that one mounts the magical diagram together with the consort, and becomes a space traveler together [with her]" (E 20b.2–3: *vṛkṣam āruhya yatr[e]cchati tatra gacchati / vidyayā saha yantram āruhya satrākāśagāmī bhavati /*).

[7] Jayabhadra explains that "**steal all mantras** means that one who has ascended all magical diagrams can cause anything spoken in isolation within the triple world to be exclaimed within his own place" (E 20b.3–4: *sarvamantrān apaharatīti trailokye kecit svasthāne yad rah[e] vadanti sarvayantrārūdha evaṁ kathayati /*).

[8] The exact meaning of the compound *prāsādadrumaśikharādīṁś* is interpretable. The Tibetan translation *khang bzangs dang shing gi rtse mo la sogs* implies that there are two items, *prāsāda* (palaces) and *drumaśikhara* (tree tops). Bhavabhaṭṭa's comments on the "interpretable" meaning here implies that it is structures that are being named here; perhaps *drumaśikhara* designates a tower or spire. He writes that "**palaces**, and so forth, shows that even structures, and so forth, are destroyed. **And so forth** refers to stone, rock mountains, and walls. Thus there is the ability to destroy structures." (Pandey 2002, 77: *prāsādetyādinā sughaṭitasyāpi vighaṭanaṁ darśitam / ādiśabdāt pāṣāṇaśailaprākārādayo darśitāḥ / iti sughaṭitavighaṭanasāmarthya /*). Note that the inclusion of stone and rock mountains breaks the pattern of structures. Were it the case that *drumaśikhara* designated a well-known type of structure I would follow the Tibetan. Since this is not the case, however, I have simply translated this line as a simple list of three high or imposing objects. In this I follow Jayabhadra's analysis, as well as Bhavabhaṭṭa's "definitive" explanation, each of which breaks the compound into three components which are then explained in a non-literal fashion. Jayabhadra, as is usually the case, explains the compound in terms of sexual practices, as follows: "Regarding **reducing palaces, trees, spires, and so forth, to dust**, the palace is the lotus because it is the abode of all buddhas. The tree is the vajra because it has masculine form. The spire is the tip of the nose of the lotus." (D 27b.4–6, E 20a.6–b.1: *prasādadrumaśikharādi cūrayat[ī]tyarthaḥ prāsādaḥ padma sarvabuddhānām āśrayatvāt / drumo vajraḥ puṁ[sa]rūpatvāt śikharaḥ padmanāsādīvīnāṁ[?]* [Tib. MP 53a: *padma'i sna rtse = *padmanāsāgraḥ*]) Bhavabhaṭṭa, as is often the case, takes a more chaste and sublimated position:

> As it is that in which the mind is settled (*prasīdati*), the **palace** (*prāsāda*) is the body. The **tree** (*druma*) is the flow that flows, the impermanence [of] the texts and teachings that is perception. The **spire** is the mind, and the term **and so on**

can be turned into ambrosia, and ambrosia into poison. *Soma* can be turned into milk, and milk into *soma*.[9] One can steal all scents.[10] One can travel wherever one wishes. The superior man is one who consorts with women who gather the *soma* emitted in the course of the mouth-eagle.[11] No one

> refers to entities (*dharmāḥ*). **Reduce to dust** is to analyze with the sword of wisdom. Here the statement of these four recollections illustrates emptiness.
>
> *prasīdaty asmin mana iti prāsādaḥ kāyaḥ / dravatīti druḥ / āgamaśāsanam anityam iti na tuk / drur eva drumo vedanā / śikharaṁ cittam / ādiśabdād dharmāḥ / cūrṇayati prajñāśastreṇa vibhajyate / itaś catasro 'nusmṛtaya uktā ity śūnyatā darśitā.* (Pandey 2002, 77)

Note that the Sanskrit of the passage explaining *druma* appears to be corrupt; see CP 181a.

[9] Bhavabhaṭṭa comments that ***soma*** is liquor and **milk** is water (Pandey 2002, 77). Jayabhadra however, identifies *soma* with the seminal essence which is like milk (MP 53a–b; the Sanskrit text is corrupt here).

[10] According to Jayabhadra: "One **steals** the **scents** of the five ambrosias. One transfers them wherever one desires. One can transfer them elsewhere, such as into the food of brahmins, and so forth." (E 21a.3–4: *pañcāmṛtagandhāpahāri kārayati / yatrecchate tatra saṁkrāmayati / tata gandham anyatra brāhmaṇādibhojane saṁkrāmayati /*) This dirty trick would not be appreciated by brahmins (or anyone else for that matter), since the five ambrosias are bodily effluvia including feces.

[11] This term, *mukhagaruḍa*, evidently refers to a position in which a woman is seated, squatting, with her legs spread and knees erect, a position depicted on certain Indian temples that Donaldson has identified with the Kaula *rajapāna* ceremony (See Donaldson 1986). That this is the case is made clear by the commentators. Jayabhadra, for example, wrote:

> As for **mouth**, and so forth, one **consorts with women who gather** that very ***soma*** which is **emitted**, just as the garuḍa, in moving itself, causes its two wings to move, moving on its **course** with its **mouth** like the king of the garuḍa birds. This means that, having taken the seminal essence with one's mouth, one should deliver it into the mouth of the goddess.
>
> *mukhetyādi mukhena garuḍarājavat yānagamanaṁ sṛṣṭikṛd iti gamanātmake garuḍaḥ pakṣadvayaṁ calayati tadvat somasaṁga[ma]str[ī]ṇāṁ samā[c]arati mukhena bodhicittam ādāya devatāmukhe deyam ity arthaḥ /* (E 20b.4–6)

Bhavabhaṭṭa connects *mukhagaruḍa* with the human anatomy, writing that "[it is] a *garuḍa* because it is like a *garuḍa*, since the two arms move like birds' wings" (Pandey 2002, 78: *garuḍo garuḍavad bāhudvayasya pakṣavaccālanāt*). Tsong Khapa is a bit more specific in his description. Relying on these and other comments he wrote that "*mukhagaruḍa* is an inverted way of sitting such that the knees are lifted up, the lotus is expanded, and the channel which has the uterine blood within it is opened" (KS 91a).

will steal the splendor (*lakṣmī*) that he has in his hand. Being thus endowed with the rite, the fruition of all the powers will arise.[12]

Through recollection one can kill, cause fire to flare up, cause the underworld to split open, or cause a thunderbolt to be cast down. Through recollection one can cause lightning to flash, and can cause the images of all deities to dance.[13] By repeating the mantra once, holding the name of him who is to be acted upon, he will surely be killed in an instant.

There will be enjoyment of all of the worlds without exception. Take as one desires; the Blessed Lord ordained no observance, no conduct[14] nor fasting. Acts should be undertaken by means of this ritual method as desired. If the fervent one one repeats it once, one hundred million will be killed. If repeated peacefully, they will be revived. Repeated once over charnel-ground char, whomever it strikes will immediately fall down.[15] Whomever is struck

---

[12] Indrabhūti interprets this entire verse both in terms of internally visualized yoga and the yoga of external union with a consort, as follows:

> [The passage] from **mouth-eagle** up until **fruition** refers to the time and accoutrements of worship of the consort (*vidyāpūjā*). Additionally, as for the inner worship of the path of yoga, the **eagle** (*garuḍa*) is the [syllable] *haṁ* in the crown, and the **mouth** is the fury fire. Their **course** is the manifold appearance of all things. **Emission** is their arising as bliss and emptiness. ***Soma*** is seminal essence, and **gathering** is visualizing its blazing and trickling. The **goddess** is the fire of gnosis, who **consorts**, i.e., revels in the central channel. If we take it from the perspective of the path of the *dūtī*, **eagle** is the penis (*liṅga*), and **mouth** is the opening of the channel called "Crow's face" (*kakāsyā*). This is the **course** to the simultaneity (*sahaja*) of all things. **Gathering** is enjoying, and ***soma*** is seminal essence. **Consorting** is the action of uniting at the time of equipoise. Furthermore, **eagle** is the bliss of the drop, and the **course** is extending the arms. The **mouth** faces downward, and **emission** is taking without giving the conventional seminal essence. Moreover, **eagle** is the natural joy (*sahajānanda*), **emission** is the joy of cessation. ***Soma*** is **gathered** as the supreme joy (*paramānanda*), and is seminal essence eaten as ambrosia. The **goddess** is the consort, with whom one consorts for the sake of bliss in the major and minor points in the body. The **superior man** is he who accomplishes the worship of the consort. (IC 46b–47a)

Note that Indrabhūti's text reads "goddess" (*lha mo*) in place of "women" (*strīṇāṁ*).

[13] That is, images or "idols" (*pratimā*) made of stone, metal, and so forth.

[14] Bhavabhaṭṭa comments that "conduct" (*caryā*) means "having the form of a tantric renunciant, and so forth" (Pandey 2002, 1.79: *caryā avadhūtādirūpatā*).

[15] Jayabhadra here comments:

by enchanted ash will be immediately seized by a goblin (*piśāca*). The name of whomever one writes at night with charnel ground char on a tablet or a mat will be seized by a great astral spirit.[16] Whomever is struck by a once-enchanted *atimukta* creeper[17] will come at once with the speed of the wind. Whomever is hit with a once-enchanted pebble will be immobilized, and will go wherever one wishes. If one enchants bdellium[18] once, and uses it as incense, one will cause all beings to become entranced.[19] Covering one's mouth with one's once-enchanted hand, one will drive out the sting of the death (*kāladaṣṭaṁ*).[20] [Evil spirits] will be arrested with once-enchanted water sealed by the ḍākinīs' seal.[21] With once-enchanted *karavīra*[22] creepers one can transfer to a womb wherever one wishes.

> Here the oral instruction on **charnel ground char** is stated [as follows]: Cutting a branch on the southern side of a Vibhītaka tree (*Terminalia bellerica*) with a caṇḍāla's axe, incinerate it in a charnel ground at night on the fourteenth day of the waning fortnight. Extinguish it with donkey urine, and taking its char and ash, place it well. Then, doing the rites of speaking the mantra, its effect is not hindered.
>
> *śmaśānāṅgāreṇety [a]tropadeśa ucyate / vibhītakivṛkṣasya dakṣiṇadigśākhāṁ caṇḍāla-kuṭharādinā chedya kṛṣṇacaturdaśyāṁ rātrau śmaśāne saṁdahya kharamūtreṇa [ni]r-vāṇya tadaṅg[ā]rāṇi bhasma gṛhītvā saṁyaksthāpayet / tadanantara[ṁ] mantrokta-vidhayaḥ kāryā tatphalam anivārtitaṁ bhavati /* (E 21b.2–5; D 29a.4–7)

16 The *mahāgraha*, i.e., Rāhu, is a demonic astrological entity which would "seize" the sun or moon during eclipses.

17 *Gaertnera racemosa*, a creeper with white fragrant flowers.

18 That is, *guggula*, the fragrant resin from trees and shrubs of the *Balsamodendron* genus.

19 The Sanskrit here reads *sarvasattvān āveśayati*, which could mean "cause all beings to become entranced (or possessed)," or "cause all beings to approach." I have selected the former meaning following the Tibetan translation, *'bebs par 'gyur*, which is used when translating the former sense (see PM 222a). Vīravajra provides a clear explanation of this as follows: "[The text] 'fumigate with great bdellium' means that one mixes alcohol with equal amounts of the four hooves of a he-goat, human fat, and feces. If one fumigates [with it], the ḍākinīs possess all sentient beings." (PD 382a)

20 I am translating this term figuratively, understanding *kāla* as a reference to death. Bu-ston (NS 107a) and Tsong Khapa (KS 93b) interpret this as the bite of the venomous black snake (*sbrul nag po*).

21 The Sanskrit (*ḍākinīmudrāmudritasya sakṛj japtenodakena stambhayati*) does not indicate what is arrested by the operation. My interpretation is based on Vīravajra's explanation, which occurs as follows:

One who longs for power without knowing the gnosis of Śrī Heruka is threshing chaff, and is bereft of this mantra. This man will not obtain power nor happiness. If a yogin desires the state of being a yogin without knowing this mantra, his efforts are in vain, nor will he attain any result. The practitioner of desire (*kāmācāra*)[23] is given the fruit of all the powers of mantra. He who is adept in mantra and *mudrā* knows that which was extolled by the Sugata, that enjoying the enjoyable—that is, food and drink such as the *caru* oblations,[24] with the savors, and so forth—is the means of achieving all powers.

> As for **sealed by the ḍākinīs**, draw the previously explained magical diagram on charnal ground cloth with an *atimukta* shoot. At its center draw the triangular [letter] *e*, in the three corners of which draw [the syllables] *a*, *ma*, and *hūṁ*, in the center of which one should write four times "Protect so-and-so." Bind it to the beneficiary's throat. Enchant water with the eight-line [mantra], and insert the evil spirit's name in the heart of a simulacrum of the evil spirit. If one pounds it again and again with [that] water and casts it away, the evil spirit will be immobilized. (PD 382a)

Mardo's translation, in place of "immobilized" (*stambhayati*), reads "expelled" (PM 222a: *gtong par byed*), while Sumatikīrti's reads "released from immobilization" (SL 105b: *reng pa grol bar byed*). Both of these appear to be interpretive translations that accord with Vīravajra's explanation.

22 The sweet oleander, *Nerium odorum*.

23 Bhavyakīrti defines this term as follows: "*kāmācāra* is the enjoyment of all objects of desire. He who conducts himself immodestly day and night is a **practitioner of desire**." (SM 18b)

24 In the vedic context, *caru* is a porridge made of rice and other grains, used as an oblation in some vedic rituals. Here, however, it appears to refer to the consecrated offerings consumed in the context of the tantric feast (*gaṇacakra*). Vīravajra, in the context of ch. 28 below, explains that they are offerings corresponding to the five senses. In the context of ch. 31 below, Bhavabhaṭṭa equates them with the five ambrosias, and explains that they are eaten from a single vessel.

10. The Achievement of the Triple Body and the Procedure of the Ritual Actions of the Essence Mantra

Next I will explain the triple body in accordance with the nondual union with Śrī Heruka, through mere knowledge of which they succeed. Have no doubt regarding this.[1] I proclaim gnosis (*jñāna*) when one

[1] Bhavabhaṭṭa provides excellent commentary on the first section of this chapter dealing with triple embodiment theory. I will follow each verse with his corresponding commentary.

> He whose nature is the triple body is Śrī Heruka. If one were to form the question, "What is the triple body?"—for indeed the word **next** has this meaning—[it indicates] that you ask "What is the triple body?" The response to this is **I will explain the triple body.** How does this come about? **In accordance with nondual union with Śrī Heruka**—this means that the triple body is that to which Śrī Heruka is undoubtedly, nondually united. Animating from the first to the last, the triple body is preeminent; this shows that here especially the triple body is that which is to be achieved. By what means [is it achieved]? **Through mere knowledge**, i.e., through direct awareness or realization only. The word "mere" is a delimiter. **They succeed** refers to the yogins [who] strive for the reality body (*dharmakāya*), and so forth. **Have no** [doubt] **regarding this**, i.e., there is no **doubt** regarding whether or not this success will occur.
>
> *kāyatrayātmakaḥ śrīherukaś cet kāyatrayam eva kiṁ tad iti svayaṁ kṛte praśne athaśabdaḥ tato 'yam arthaḥ kāyatrayaṁ kiṁ tad iti pṛcchasi cet kāyatrayaṁ vakṣya iti prativacanaḥ / kiṁ bhūtam ity āha śrīherukādvayayogata iti śrīheruko 'dvayenāsaṁśayena yujyate yatra tat tathā kāyatrayam / prathamāntān trasilā kāyatrayaṁ viśiṣṭaṁ kāyatrayam eveha sādhyam iti darśayati / yenetyādi vijñātamātreṇāvabuddhamātreṇa sākṣāt kṛteneti yāvat mātraśabdo 'vadhāraṇe / sidhyante sidhyanti dharmakāyādikaṁ yogino 'bhilaṣantītyarthaḥ nātreti nāsyāṁ siddhau bhavati na bhavatīti saṁśayaḥ /* (F 61a.3–b.1;G 60a.4–9)

I provide here my own edition since Pandey's edition falters around a particularly obscure portion of the text. This is the portion which I tentatively translate "animating from the first to the last," based on ms. G's text *prathamāntān trasilā*, reading *-lā* as a verbal particle "giving" and *trasi* as the compound form of *trasin*, "possessing movement." Ms. F, however, reads here *prathamāntā tusilā*. Pandey reads *prathamāntāttasil* (2002, 82). This reading is difficult to evaluate since no variants are listed, but this is clearly *not* the reading in the two manuscripts I have consulted, and Pandey et al. have consulted only one additional ms. It is not at all clear what this reading might mean. The Tibetan is no help here, as it only transliterates the term in question as *ta shi la* (CP 184a). Pandey's edition of the Tibetan

becomes adept in the bodies of the reality body.[2] I proclaim communal enjoyment (*sambhoga*) when one becomes adept in the bodies of the communal enjoyment body.[3] I teach the manifestation body when one

---

(2002, 353) emends this to the unwieldy and incorrectly constructed **tasil'i*, apparently to accord with their reading of the Sanskrit.

[2] Bhavabhaṭṭa continues:

> As for the means of achieving the **reality body**, as it is "reality" and also a "body" it is the "body of reality." It is the victors whose body this is. **When one has become** their **adept** then there is success, and **I proclaim gnosis.** I characterize and define the gnosis which is the reality body as being free of singularity and plurality, always being the scope of the tathāgatas, and being the natural clear light. The reality body is the totality, the Victor's own form. Thus it is said to be not singular nor multiple, it manifests as the basis of the great perfection which benefits self and other. It is neither existent nor non-existent. It is sky-like and experientially uniform. Its nature is difficult to understand. It is stainless and unchanging, auspicious and unequalled. It is pervasive yet unadulterated (*niṣprapañca*). I bow down to that very potential for self-knowledge as the peerless reality body of the victors.
>
> *dharmakāyasādhanam āha dharmetyādi dharmaś cāsau kāyaś ceti dharmakāyaḥ śarīraṁ yeṣāṁ te tathā jināḥ / teṣāṁ sādhako yadā bhavati sidhyati tadā jñānaṁ pravādāmy aham / jñānaṁ dharmakāyam ekānekavirahitaṁ tathāgatagocaraṁ prakṛtinityaṁ prakṛtiprabhāsvaraṁ pravibhajya niścinomi / sa ca dharmakāyo jinasvarūpa iti samudāyaḥ / tathā cāha / yo naiko nāpy anekaḥ svaparahitamahāsampadādhārabhūto / naivābhāvo na bhāvaḥ kham iva samaraso durvibhāvasvabhāvaḥ // nirlepanirvikāraṁ śivam asamasamaṁ vyāpinaṁ niṣprapañcam / vande pratyātmavedyaṁ tam aham anupamaṁ dharmakāyaṁ jinānām // iti /* (F 61b.1–5; G 60a.9–b.4; cf. Pandey 2002, 82)

[3] Bhavabhaṭṭa continues:

> As for communal enjoyment, one who has a charming body when engaging in Dharma teaching has the **communal enjoyment body**, being one for whom the scope of the bodhisattva is a continuous course. Regarding **communal enjoyment**, [the state of being] a buddha or bodhisattva is enjoyed and made one's own through true accomplishment. Moreover, having for oneself the powerful, true, and beneficial fruit which is supramundane and inconceivable, one extends it amidst the assembly in various ways, as this is the delight of those of great wisdom. The sound of the continually proclaimed true Dharma is extended through all of the worlds by the buddhas. I bow down here to that communal enjoyment body which is exists as the great sovereignty of the Dharma.
>
> *saṁbhogam āha sambhogetyādi asecanakavigrahādiyukto dharmadeśanāṁ yadā karoti tadā saṁbhogakāyo bodhisattvagocaraḥ pravāhanityaḥ sambhoga iti / buddhabodhisattvaḥ samyakpratipattyā bhujyata ātmasāt kriyata iti sa tathā / tathā cāha / lokātītām acintyāṁ sukṛtasatphalām ātmano yo vibhūtiṁ / parṣanmadhye vicitrāṁ pratha-*

becomes adept in the bodies of the manifestation body.[4] Have no doubt that gnosis, communal enjoyment, and manifestation will be attained. Do not doubt that one will achieve the lofty nature of Śrī Heruka.[5]

Listen, you who are adept in the secret, as I will explain the essence of this mantra.[6] By repeating the essence one will fly ten million leagues, going and returning. One can assume many thousands of forms. Ascending palaces, trees, or houses, one can travel ten million leagues together with a

---

> *yati mahatāṁ dhīmatāṁ prītihetoḥ // buddhānāṁ sarvalokaprasṛtam aviratoccārasaddharmaghoṣam / vande sambhogakāyaṁ tam aham iha mahādharmarājyapratiṣṭham iti /* (F 61b.5–62a.3; G 60b.4–8; cf. Pandey 2002, 83)

[4] Bhavabhaṭṭa continues:

> As for "manifestation," the **manifestation body** is a continuous series which is common to all beings. Thus it is said that, on account of the ripening of beings' [karma], it appears in some places, luminous like a flame in complete awakening in the wheel of Dharma, and again elsewhere it manifests cessation. I bow down to the manifestation body which does not set out in a single form, but which by means of all forms and strategies pervades the ten directions, removing the fears of the three realms of existence, which is the great aim of the sages.
>
> *nirmāṇam āha nirmānetyādi sarvasattvasādhāraṇaḥ prabandhanityo nirmāṇakāyaḥ / tathā cāha / sattvānāṁ pākahetoḥ kvacid analam ivābhāti yo dīptamānaḥ saṁbodhau dharmacakre kvacid api ca punar dṛśyate yaḥ praśāntaḥ // naikākārapravṛttaṁ tribhavabhayaharaṁ viśvarūpair upāyair vande nirmāṇakāyaṁ daśadigantagataṁ taṁ mahārthaṁ munīnām // iti /* (F 62a.3–5; G 60b.8–61a.2)

[5] The CS mss. here read *śrīherukamāhātmānaṁ siddhyate* (A, C; B: *-mātmānaṁ*), which should presumably be revised to *śrīherukamahātmānaṁ*. Bhavabhaṭṭa's commentary provides a slightly different reading, namely *śrīherukasvātmānaṁ siddhyante*, "they achieve the self-nature of Śrī Heruka" (Pandey 2002, 83). A rather different reading occurs in Jayabhadra's commentary, namely *śrīherukasamo bhavati*, "one becomes the same as Śrī Heruka" (E 22a.5).

[6] This verse reads *asya mantrasya hṛdayaṁ vakṣāmi śṛṇu tvaṁ guhyasādhakaḥ*. I read *tvaṁ guhyasādhakaḥ* as vocatives connected with the imperative *śṛṇu*, despite the fact that they are declined in the nominative case. I follow Bhavabhaṭṭa in reading *guhyasādhaka* as a compound. He explains the term as follows: "**adept in the secret** means he [who] accomplishes the secret, the triple body, which is the reality of mind, and so forth, and [who] is perfected among yogins" (Pandey 2002, 84: *guhyasādhaka iti / cittādisvarūpaṁ kāyatrayaṁ guhyaṁ sādhayati yogiṣu niṣpādayatīti sa tathā /*). Mardo's translation divides *guhya* and *sādhaka*, seeing the former as the object of *vakṣāmi*, and the latter as a vocative (PM 222a: *gsang ba bshad kyis sgrub po nyon*). Sumatikīrti's translation, however, omits *guhya* and reads *sādhaka* as plural (SL 106a: *bshad kyis sgrub pa po rnams nyon*).

ḍākinī.[7] Travelling in space, one will return again. One can be visible as one desires, and one can be invisible when one wishes. One can take on immature, youthful, or elderly forms as one wishes. One can take on the forms of the elephant, water buffalo, gayal ox, tiger, lion, bull, rabbit, cat, or camel, as one wishes. One can take on the forms of the peacock, cock, goose, duck, crane, owl, hawk, vulture, or crow, as one wishes. One can assume the form of that which one desires. One can steal speech and steal hearing. One can plunder sight and plunder his sense of smell.[8] One can snatch the tongue. One can draw out the blood of whomever one wishes, or immobilize him.

---

[7] The Sanskrit here reads the singular *ḍākinyā saha*. Mardo's text reads the plural, *mkha' 'gro ma rnams dang lhan cig* (PM 222b), while Sumatikīrti reads "together with the yoginīs" (SL 106a: *rnal 'byor ma rnams dang*).

[8] The Sanskrit here reads *ghrāṇaṁ*, which can indicate the "sense of smell" or the "nose." The Tibetan translations followed the later, translating it as *sna* (PM 222b, SL 106b).

11. The Procedure of Characterizing the Seven-lived One

Now above all I will speak of the power that the adept should attain, through which there is rapid engagement in power by means of eating only.[1] The person who goes perspiring a pleasant fragrance, speaking the truth, blinks after a long time, is not angry, and who has fragrant breath in his mouth, is one who is born as a man for seven lives.[2] Eating him, there is

[1] Literally "eaten" (*prāśita*), I have translated this as "eating" since translating it as a past passive participle here seems awkward in English. Note that the Tibetan translates this as *bsten pa*, "devotion," which may be based upon the Sanskrit *prasita*, or the misreading (intentional or unintentional) of the former for the latter. Bhavabhaṭṭa reads here *ghrāṇitamātreṇa* (Pandey 2002, 85), "through smelling only," which appears to be a creative misreading to render the text less transgressive, although it may also be a genuine textual variant, as *prāśita* and *ghrāṇita* are not dissimilar in scripts such as Bhujimol.

[2] These are the characteristics of a "person born seven times a man," who, according to Jayabhadra, is "one characterized with the defining marks of a sacrificial victim" (E 22a.6: *yasya puruṣasyetyādi paśulakṣaṇaṁ lakṣitaṁ*). He is evidently a person of the brahmin class, as we learn in ch. 32 below. Chapter 65 of the AU gives an expanded list of this person's qualities:

> Furthermore, I will explain that which comes into existence within the one born seven times. There are various conventions regarding the victim. He has a divine form and is charming. He has a divine body, is glorious, truly a king among victims. He is soft-spoken and takes delight in the sugatas. His hair is long, his eyes wide and red, shaped like lotus petals. There is sweat on his body. He is always stung by bees. His limbs are divinely, pleasantly scented, or scented like camphor. The stench of his feces and urine is potent, and his speech should be unimpeded. He is gentle with his hands and feet, and has the scent of an *utpala* lotus. He is free of wrinkles and grey hair. His body is oiled, and he is fond of women. He will have concretion in his heart, head, or navel. He must be one with a sevenfold shadow, who has a goose's gait, and a compassionate disposition. He is always devoted to the Three Jewels, and is thus possessed of generosity and ethical discipline.
>
> *athānyaparaṁ vakṣye saptajanmāntarodbhavam / vividhāṁś ca paśusamayā divyrūpāṁ manoramām / divyakāyavapuḥ śrīmān rājā vai paśumadhyagam / priyāvādī saugatarato dīrghakeśāṅkuras tathā / viśālanetrā raktākṣāḥ padmapattradalākṛti / prasvedaṁ tasya kāyeṣu bramarair bhakṣate sadā / divyagandhasugandhāṅgo vā karpuragandhikāḥ / viṇmūtragandhakaṁ bhūryā vācā askhalitā bhavet / hastapādaiś ca mṛdutā utpalagandhanāṁ tathā / valipalitanirmukto snigdhāṅgo vanitāpriyaḥ / hṛdaye mastake nabhau rocanaṁ tasya bhaviṣyati / saptachāyo hansagatiko karuṇāśayato bhavet /*

the concretion in his heart.[3] Taking this, make a drop with one hundred repetitions of Śrī Heruka's essence mantra. One will fly up and travel tens of millions of leagues. Just through eating one will become one who has knowledge of the triple world. One will travel five hundred million [leagues] and return in a day and a night. One will have a divine body. One who knows Śrī Heruka's essence will be given whatever he desires.[4]

> *triratnabhaktiḥ satataṁ dānaśīlair yutas tathā //* (H 185a.6–185b.5; I 618b.1–4; J 303.3–304.2)

The text "He must be one with a sevenfold shadow, who has a goose's gait, and a compassionate disposition" occurs in Mardo's translation (PM 222b), but is not attested elsewhere.

[3] "Eating him" translates the Sanskrit preserved in the CS mss., which is *taṁ bhakṣayitvā,* the latter term being a gerund derived from the 10 P. root √*bhakṣ*, "to eat, drink, devour." There is, however, a great deal of variance here, no doubt due to the transgressive nature of this text. Mardo's revised translation, perhaps following commentary such as Vīravajra's (see note 4 below), reads *bsten* (PM 222b), "to serve," while Sumatikīrti reads *bsnams* (SL 106b), "to seize, grasp, or smell," perhaps following Bhavabhaṭṭa, who, as in the case of the first verse (see note 1 above), reads "smelling," *ghrāṇayitvā* (Pandey 2002, 86), an unattested verb form that is almost certainly derived from the nominal *ghrāṇa*, and modeled on *bhakṣayitvā*, for which it is clearly an emendation.

"Concretion" translates *rocanā*, a medicinal concretion or bezoar-stone found within the organs of animals. This text is transgressive in calling for a concretion derived from a human being. Regarding this, Bhavyakīrti wrote:

> With regard to taking the concretion, it is not just taking his concretion; the explanation of heretics. Is this not suitable to be taught in a Yoginī Tantra? This is not the case, however, since there are instructions to eat medicinal substances such as cow products in all of the Yoga Tantras such as the *Śri Guhyasamāja*, as well as in those of the heretics. Since these involve taking it from a corpse, is it not heretical? How are the Yoga Tantras and Yoginī Tantras different with regard to the explanation that the *rocanā* is taken by oneself from the corpse of one born seven times a man? Some [say that] the Yoga Tantras were taught by the Tathāgata, and the Yoginī Tantras were taught by Māra. I myself am unclear about this. However, it should be understood in accordance with the following explanation: "When two things have the same fault, both having the same fault in meaning, investigating it in such a case, it is not suitable to settle on one of them" (SM 19a).

[4] Vīravajra comments here:

> Knowing these signs of [one born human for] seven lives, one should serve him with reverence so long as he lives, and pray "May I attain my power when he dies." As soon as he dies, one should take the concretion that is in his heart, repeat one hundred times the appropriate [mantras] such as Śrī Heruka's essence and quintessence [mantras]. If one forms it into a drop on one's forehead, one will soar into the sky and travel ten million leagues. If one forms it into a drop on one's heart,

one will know others' minds. If one forms it into a drop on one's eye, one will attain the divine eye. If one forms it into a drop on one's ear, one will attain the divine ear. If one forms it into a drop on one's foot, one will gain the power of speedy feet. You should refer to the *Abhidhānottara*. Simply through this sort of service one will become a buddha endowed with knowledge of the three worlds. As for [travelling many] leagues, if one eats the flesh of the seven-lived, one will be able to go and return fifty [koṭis of] leagues—a worldly power. If one eats his heart, one will attain the meditative states and a formless body, which are common powers. (PD 385a–b)

12. The Procedure of the Ritual Actions of the Quintessence

Next I will explain the quintessence which perfects all powers, [whereby] one can accomplish in an instant everything, whatever might exist in the triple world.

ṭ pha hūṁ hūṁ ha ha hrīḥ oṁ[1]

This is the quintessence of the essence. With one hundred thousand repetitions of this mantra one can even cause the triple world to tremble. One can summon gods, titans (*dānava*), *yakṣas*, demons (*rākṣasa*), celestial musicians (*gandharva*), and centaurs (*kinnara*).[2] One can dry up rivers, oceans, ponds, and so forth, or immobilize them. In that place where one repeats [the quintessence], all ḍākinīs will be the adept's servants. Enchanting water with this, if one rinses one's eyes [with it] one will recognize the one born seven times. Those whose life is exhausted will appear as if dead; the long-lived will appear to be full of life. Enchanting the eyes with mantra, he whom one sees will be immobilized.

Take the skin of the sole of the foot of the corpse of a hero, pulverize[3] it with human blood, and insert antimony[4] in the middle of the ball.[5]

---

[1] In proper order, Śrī Heruka's quintessence mantra is: *oṁ hrīḥ ha ha hūṁ hūṁ phaṭ*.

[2] I have translated here in accordance with the CS mss., all of which read *devadānavayakṣa-rākṣasān gandharvakinnarān ākarṣayati*. This omits the serpent deities (*nāga*), which occur in the Tibetan translation between the *rākṣasa* and *gandharva*. Pandey's edition emends the CS mss.' reading to *devadānavayakṣarākṣasanāgagandharvakinnarān* (2002, 87), apparently to bring it into accordance with the Tibetan.

[3] The Sanskrit mss. here read *piśya* (A, C) and *pisya* (B), but clearly *piṣya* should be read here, as attested by Bhavabhaṭṭa (Pandey 2002, 88) and by the Tibetan (PM 223a, SL 107b: *btags*).

[4] That is, *srotoñjana*, which is kohl—or the black, powdered, calcined antimony commonly used as a cosmetic in India.

[5] Bhavabhaṭṭa comments that "**in the middle of the ball** means that one should make a ball from these [ingredients]" (Pandey 2002, 88: *golakamadhya iti / tatpiṇḍīkāryam iti bhāvaḥ /*).

Saturate it with realgar,[6] bovine concretion, saffron, and blood. Dry it in the shade and encase it in the three metals,[7] and also make it habitable.[8] It is, moreover, prepared during the Puṣya lunar mansion; ensure it is made during Puṣya.[9] Putting it in Śrī Heruka's mouth,[10] cover his mouth with one's left hand. Furthermore, one should repeat [the mantra] one hundred and eight times. From that moment one is rendered invisible without any shadow. As one cannot even be seen by gods, how much less [is the chance of being seen] by humans? Taking it out of one's mouth, one will be visible.[11] This pill of the power of flight[12] was taught in this Tantra by the hero himself.

With this mantra, the quintessence of Śrī Heruka's essence, make a substitute skull devoid of flesh for his head, and rub it with the tip of one's

---

[6] That is, *arsenic disulphide*, a naturally occurring red-colored mineral.

[7] Jayabhadra notes, somewhat ambiguously, that "**the three metals** are gold, silver, copper, and so forth" (E 22b.2–3: *triloha iti suvarṇarajatatāmrādi*).

[8] The CS mss. lack any text corresponding to the Tibetan *yang lhag par gnas par byas la*, which occurs in all of the translations (SL 107b, PG 321.3; PM 223a: *yang de lhag par gnas pa*) as well as in Kambala's commentary (LS 29a). The verb *adhivāsya* is attested by Bhavabhaṭṭa (Pandey 2002, 88). To "make it habitable" means to consecrate it, as Kambala and Devagupta inform us (LS 29a, SS 98a). This no doubt refers to the rite of *adhivāsana* in which a deity is invoked into an object that is being consecrated.

[9] Bhavabhaṭṭa qualifies this, stating "**during Puṣya**, and also during any other auspicious lunar mansion" (Pandey 2002, 88: *puṣyena ceti anyenāpi śubhanakṣatrādinā*). The CS mss. read *punaḥ puṣyasādhita[ṁ] puṣyeṇa ca kārayet*. Pandey omits *puṣyasādhita[ṁ]*, but reports that it is attested by the Tibetan (2002, 88).

[10] According to Bhavabhaṭṭa, "**Śrī Heruka's**, and so forth, means that the Śrī Heruka yogin should put in his own **mouth** the pill which has within it the maṇḍala's wheels, and repeat [the mantra] as is stated" (Pandey 2002, 88: *śrīherukasyetyādi / śrīherukasya yogī tām antargatāṁ maṇḍalacakrām gulikāṁ svamukhe prakṣipya yathoktaṁ japet /*).

[11] According to Tsong Khapa, this rite involves placing the pill in the mouth of a corpse while repeating the mantra and fumigating it with bdellium. After the repetition, the corpse, *qua* Śrī Heruka, expells the pill, which makes one invisible if one puts it in one's own mouth. One becomes visible again by expelling it. See KS 101b–102a, as well as my translation of this text (Gray 2017).

[12] This text appears to link the powers of invisibility and flight, both here as well as in ch. 13 below (p. 215).

forefinger.[13] His blood will be drawn out. By rubbing it with the left it will return again.[14] If, enchanting with mantra, the skull is struck with one's fist, the head of him whose name one utters will ache.[15] Calling the mantra to mind, fill the skull with milk and he will be relieved.

Enchant cow concretion and form it into a drop. He whom one sees will be bound. Enchanting one's forefinger, he at whom one brandishes it will instantly fall down. If one strikes the earth with one's foot repeating the mantra, he whose name [one utters] will instantly perish. If one sprinkles enchanted water on the earth, one will restore him to life again. If one brandishes one's mantra-enchanted forefinger at as many as one thousand, they all will become injured and immobilized.[16] With a word one can

---

[13] The Sanskrit here reads *anena mantreṇa tarjanyāgreṇa śiraḥkapālanirmāṁsopadhiṁ kṛtvā nirmathati*. The term *upadhi* usually means "foundation, base, material thing" or "fraud." Here it appears to mean a "base" for sympathetic magic, standing in for the victim, as Bhavabhaṭṭa explains: "The substitute is the body, which is fleshless, just as the substitute is. Having made, i.e., causing, the victim's body to be like this, one rubs it." (Pandey 2002, 89: *upadhiḥ śarīram, nirmāṁsaś cāsāv upadhiś ceti sa tathā / tathābhūtaṁ sādhyaśarīraṁ kṛtvā kārayitvā nirmathati nirmathnāti /*) Note that the Tibetan translations have no equivalent to *upadhiṁ*. Tsong Khapa explains that as one rubs it one imagines that it is the skull of the victim's head (KS 102b).

[14] Jayabhadra explains this obscure passage as follows:

> As for **with the tip of the forefinger**, and so forth, this refers to drawing out blood. The procedure for this is as follows: Taking a human skull, the mantrin who has performed the prior service instantly utters the syllable *hūṁ* while in union with Vajrarudra. Khaṇḍarohā, with a sword in hand, issues from the deity's right nostril. Visualize that she pierces in five places the head of him who is named, and that the skull fills with streams of his blood.
>
> *tarjanyagreṇetyādinā rudhirākarṣaṇam āha / tatrāyaṁ kramaḥ / naraśira[ḥ]kapālam ādāya kṛtapurvasevāmantrī jhaṭiti vajrarudrayogāt hūṁkārocāraṇa / devasya dakṣiṇa-nāsāpuṭ[ā]ntarāt / khaṇḍarohā śastrahastā niścārya tayāḥ yasya nāmnā pañcasthāne śirovedhaṁ kārāyitvā tadrudhiradhārabhiḥ kapālaparipūrṇa bhāvayet /* (E 22b.3–5)

[15] The CS mss. here read *śiro vedanā bhavati*, a reading confirmed by Jayabhadra (E 22b.6: *śiro vedanaṁ*). The Tibetan translations read "his brain will burst" (PM 223b: *de'i klad pa 'gas par 'gyur*) and "his brain will sicken" (SL 107b: *de'i klad pa na bar 'gyur ro*).

[16] All CS mss. here read *sarve duṣṭā stambhitā bhavanti*, which I have interpreted as referring to all of the thousand at whom one brandishes the enchanted finger. It could also possibly mean "all of the wicked [among them] will become immobilized." The Tibetan translations lack anything corresponding to *duṣṭā*, reading only *de thams cad gnon par 'gyur ro* (PM 223b, SL 108a), which is likely a translation of *sarve stambhitā bhavanti*. Pandey's edition emends *duṣṭā* to *draṣṭāraḥ*, with no justification (2002, 89).

release them. Enchanting one hundred times the [crematory] ash of a caṇḍāla,[17] he whom it strikes will take on the form of whatever being one thinks. Enchanting one hundred times the ash of a sacrificial fire, he whom it strikes will not be seen even by the gods. Should one strike him with seven-times enchanted water, he will be seen again.

Binding the conjoined skull seals, repeat [the quintessence mantra] without breathing. He whose name the fierce one [utters] will instantly become mad.[18] As many as one thousand people will be maddened. One can mentally release them. Enchanting one's hair crest ten times, bind it up. All the ḍākinīs whose name [one utters] will come. Go to an empty house and tie up one's hair crest which has been enchanted one hundred times. Opening one's eyes, one will be invisible as long as one repeats [the mantra]. Releasing it, one will be visible again. Enchanting [gravel] with[in] a skull bowl,[19] cast it above, below, and in the directions and quarters. All of the gods, titans, *yakṣas*, demons, celestial musicians, centaurs, and even the great serpents (*mahoraga*) will be bound.

---

[17] That is, a member of the caṇḍāla outcaste group.

[18] Kambala explains here:

> Place the magical diagram (*yantra*), augmented with the name of whomever [is the victim], within the **conjoined skull seals**—i.e., conjoined skull [hemispheres]—of a rabid dog, together with the five intoxicants. **Repeat** [the mantra] seven times **without breathing**, then bind and seal them. Should one conceal it together with his name in a charnel ground, he will **become mad**. (SN 29b)

[19] The CS mss. here read *sakaroṭam abhimantrya*. Pandey's reading of *śarkaroṭāṁ* (2002, 89) appears to be based on Mardo's translation of *gseg ma* (PM 223b), i.e., *śarkara*, "gravel." Bhavabhaṭṭa's commentary attests *śarkoṭa* (Pandey 2002, 90), which is clearly corrupt or based on a misreading, which he glosses as *śarkarā*. But this commentary is actually not on this verse but on the section below on controlling water. *Sakoṭaṁ* is attested in Vīravajra's commentary, as *thod pa dang bcas pa*, "with a skull" (PD 387b). This, however, leaves unstated the actual substance which is enchanted within the skull bowl. I follow the Tibetan texts in inserting "gravel" here. Sumatikīrti's text is particularly helpful, as it includes both the skull bowl and gravel, perhaps as an interpretive gloss. It reads: "Pour gravel within a skull bowl and enchant it" (SL 108a–b: *thod pa'i nang du bseg ma blugs la mngon par bzlas te*). One should note, however, that Vīravajra would have one use mustard seeds here:

> Regarding **with a skull bowl**, should one draw a magical diagram within a skull bowl, and **cast** mustard seeds, as was previously explained, **above, below**, and **in the** ten **directions**, [then] the sky-dwellers, i.e., the **gods** and **celestial musicians**; the surface dwellers, i.e., the ***yakṣas*** and **demons**; and the underworld dwellers, i.e., the serpent deities and **titans**, **will be bound**. (PD 387b)

One can steal all the yogas of the ḍākinīs. Seeing a woman or man sleeping in his or her bedroom, if one repeats the mantra one hundred times one can cause him or her to be stuck [there]. [He or she] is released with one's mind. If one enchants [gravel] with[in] a skull bowl[20] and casts it into rivers, they are forced to flow upstream.[21] With the skull bowl one can also immobilize the waves. One can cause them to turn mentally. Should one repeat it one thousand [times] gazing above, one can suppress a tremendous storm. If one makes one thousand repetitions facing an enemy army, when one enters into battle and is struck by a hundred weapons, pain will not arise, nor will one be cut by one thousand weapons.[22] One will develop an adamantine body.

---

[20] Here again the CS mss. read *sakaroṭaṁ*, revised by Pandey to *śarkaroṭāṁ* on the basis of Bhavabhaṭṭa's commentary, as noted above. With regard to the Tibetan translations, Sumatikīrti's reads "skull bowl" (SL 108b: *thod pa*), and Mardo's reads "with gravel" (PM 224a: *gyo mog dang bcas pa*). Vīravajra here again reads "with a skull bowl," commenting as follows: "Regarding **with a skull bowl**, should one write the magical diagram within a skull bowl, and place it into a river, it will be **forced to flow upstream**" (PD 387b).

[21] All of the CS mss. read here *pratikūlaṁ vāpayati*, which does not make much sense. Pandey emends this to *pratikūlaṁ vāhayati* (2002, 89), "cause to flow upstream," which makes more sense and is also idiomatic. It also accords with the Tibetan translation, *rgyun phyogs las bzlog ste 'bab par 'gyur* (PM 223b; SL 108b: *rgyun phyogs las ldog ste 'bab par 'gyur*).

[22] The Tibetan translations omit the number of weapons here.

13. The Procedure of the Applications of the Armor Mantra

Next I will explain the ritual action[s] of the armor [mantras] in accordance with their regular order. [One will attain] all those things one's mind fancies, whatever might exist in the triple world. Should one proceed on the road just repeating the armor [mantras], there will be no fear of brigands or tigers, nor will one be seen.[1] Nor will one be seen entering into the harem of a royal palace if one is repeating the armor. One will take that which one likes and depart. One will not even be seen by the gods.

He whom one touches with an armor-enchanted hand will be immobilized as if impaled. Even the thirty [gods] will not be able to move him. Should one repeat the mantra and strike him with one's foot he will be released. Forming a thrice-enchanted drop with one's own blood or semen, all those with whom one speaks, whom one sees, or who see [oneself], will have their blood drained. Everyone will come down with fever in whichever house one repeats it one thousand times filled with ferocity. If one sprinkles water enchanted five times, they will recover.

One will steal the speech of him at whose face one gazes, repeating [the mantra]. If one repeats it a thousand times standing near a river or a pond, one can walk on the water.[2] One will walk on the water as if it were firm ground. Entering the water, one can stay in the river or even in the ocean. Should one repeat it one thousand [times] rubbing both hands, the yoginīs will be subdued. The yoginīs have various forms; they are famed as Ḍākinī, Lāmā, Khaṇḍarohā, and Rūpiṇī. They will all become one's faithful servants.

Make cloth during the lunar conjunction of Puṣya. One's body covered with it, should one repeat it ten thousand times, one will thence-

[1] The text *na dṛśyate vā* occurs in all CS mss. here, but it is omitted by Pandey (2002, 91), despite the fact that it is also attested in the Tibetan translation (PM 224a, SL 108b).

[2] The Sanskrit here reads *udakopari vrajet*, which I've translated here. Mardo's Tibetan reads "one can stay on the water" (PM 224a: *chu'i steng du gnas*), but Sumatikīrti has the correct translation (SL 109a: *chu'i steng du 'gro*).

forth be realized. One's body covered with it, one will be invisible in space for a thousand leagues. One will go wherever one desires. With it one will travel over the earth and the ocean. One will arrive via the upward flow.[3]

One should experience[4] everything, whatever comes naturally within the path of the sense powers, as being composed of buddhas, through the yoga of ultimate equipoise.[5] Gathering the sap of the coral tree,[6] enchant it

---

[3] Bhavabhaṭṭa comments here:

> **Arrive via the upward flow** omits the *s*-[stem of the] etymological derivation, [i.e. *strotas*]. It means that one comes, having crossed over the currents of a river, against the flow. The yogin, when he immobilizes the seminal essence within the jewel [energy center, at the tip of the penis], directly arrives **upwards**, i.e., at the natural (*sahaja*). This is understood to be the inner meaning.
>
> *ūrdhvasrotenāgacchatīti nairuktaḥ sakāralopaḥ / vilomena nadīpravāhān atikramyāgacchatītyarthaḥ / maṇyantarbodhicitte sthirīkṛte yogī ūrdhvaṁ sahajaṁ srotena sākṣād āgacchati pratyetītyarthāntaram* / (F 66b.1–2; G omits)

The Pandey edition errs here; where ms. F clearly reads *ūrdhvasrotenāgacchati*, Pandey et al. read *ūrdhvasrote tā gacchati* (2002, 92). Ms. G omits this passage, and the edition lacks notation indicating the basis for this reading. This reading may have been influenced by the Tibetan translation of the root text, which here reads *steng du rgyud du 'gro bar 'gyur ro* (PM 224b). Note that the root CS mss. here all read *ūrdhvaśrotrenāvāgacchati*, which is clearly defective. Based on Bhavabhaṭṭa's commentary I emend this root text to *ūrdhvasrotenāgacchati*. Pandey's edition strangely emends this root text to *ūrdhasrotago vā gacchati*.

[4] I interpret *vahet* here in its sense of "to experience, feel." The Tibetan, however, reads *'gyur* (PM 224b, SL 109a), perhaps for *bhavet*, "should be."

[5] The Sanskrit here reads *yad yad indriyamārgatvaṁ yāyāt tat tat svabhāvataḥ / paramāhitayogena sarvam buddhamayam vahet //*. I follow Bhavabhaṭṭa in reading *tat tat* in reference to *sarvaṁ* (Pandey 2002, 93). Bhavyakīrti comments here:

> Regarding **One should experience everything, whatever comes naturally within the path of the sense powers, as being composed of buddhas, through the yoga of ultimate equipoise**—"whatever" is explained as referring to all of the realms of the world without exception. That which is of **the path of the sense powers** is analyzed with wisdom (*shes rab, prajñā*) by means of both direct perception (*mngon sum, pratyakṣa*) and inference (*rjes su dpag pa, anumāna*). Whatever is realized **comes naturally. Through the yoga of ultimate equipoise** in this sort of reality or nature, that is, through the application of art and wisdom, **everything should be experienced as being composed of buddhas**, meaning that all things should be regarded as the reality of the buddhas. This is because, as was said by the scions of the Victor, "These three worlds are mind only." That is, everything exists as mind only. (SM 19b; Bhavyakīrti here quotes directly from the third chapter of the *Ārya-Pratyutpanna-buddhasaṁmukhāvasthitasamādhi-nāma-mahāyānasūtra*, Tōh. 133, DK mdo sde vol. na, 15a.)

(cont'd)

one thousand times. He for whom one forms it into a drop will turn into a tree. He is restored if one sprinkles him with water enchanted seven times. Taking the fresh dust of an elephant's foot,[7] enchant it one thousand times. Whomever is struck by it will become an elephant.

Vīravajra also comments as follows on this verse:

> Regarding **One should experience everything, whatever comes naturally within the path of the sense powers, as being composed of buddhas, through the yoga of ultimate equipoise**: if we take this in terms of the three yogas of attaining power, it refers to the three concentrations. To achieve power on the creation stage one conceives the six **sense powers** as the six heroes (*sems dpa', sattva*), and one regards form, and so forth, which **come within the path of the** corresponding **sense powers**, as the goddesses Rūpavajrā, and so forth. Also in the context of meditative equipoise, one visualizes the worship of Rūpavajrā, and so forth. This occurs **through the yoga of ultimate equipoise**. Through the experiential unity of direct perception and inference (*mngon rjes ro mnyam pa*), **everything should be experienced as being composed of buddhas**. In terms of the attainment of the secret consecration: form, and so forth, which **come within the path** of **whatever** arises as nonconceptual cognition, are taken as the nature of that bliss which is the reality of joy, ultimate joy, and natural joy. Also in the context of meditative equipoise, just as form is devoid of the eighty natures, so the [apprehension] of the reality of the three joys in sound, scent, taste, and touch is **the yoga of ultimate equipoise**. Why is this? It is due to the experiential unity of direct perception and inference. Therefore, the fruit of all yogas is to be **composed of buddhas**. Through the attainment of the wisdom-gnosis consecration, one understands that **whatever** is of **the sense powers** such as vision, and so forth, is empty, and the objects which **come within** their **path** are taken as their nature, which is emptiness. Understanding the nature of great bliss at the occasion of the equipoise which seals [the realization] that the nature of great bliss is the reality of the joys in all things: this is **the yoga of ultimate equipoise**. This is due to the experiential unity of direct perception and inference. (PD 389b–390a)

[6] *Pārijāta* (*Erythrina indica*).

[7] The Sanskrit here reads *hastipādasadyadhūliṁ*, which might be amended to read *hastipāda-sadyodhūliṁ*, as translated here. Mardo's translation reads *glang po che'i rkang mthil dang bsgrub bya'i rdul* (PM 224a), "dust formed on an elephant's foot," implying *sādhya* rather than *sadyo*. Sumatikīrti's translation, however, reads *glang po che'i rkang rjes kyi sa rdul* (SL 109b), "dust of an elephant's footprint," attesting neither variant. Pandey's edition here reads *hastipāda-talasthāṁ dhūliṁ* (2002, 93), but provides no support for this reading.

14. The Procedure of the Donkey-Form Yoga for Becoming Śrī Heruka

Next I will explain the spiritual discipline (*sādhana*) whereby the adepts attain the essential yoga of the donkey form,[1] for the sake of the cessation of the movement of the mind.[2] As for the yoginīs, Lāmā, Rūpiṇī, Ḍākinī, and Khaṇḍarohā are the yoginīs.[3] They have desirable forms and donkey-shaped, bloody faces. They are invested with the ḍākinīs' trident.[4]

---

[1] The term *yogātmā* might be literally rendered "essence of yoga." I translate it as "essential yoga" since the *-ātmā* termination seems to have a laudatory function here. Vīravajra provides a commentary which refers to the Cakrasamvara origin myth, in which the three wheels of the maṇḍala are correlated to the triple world, as follows:

> **The essential yoga of the donkey** means that, in order to discipline those who range in the underworld, one assumes the appearance of the donkey, Śrī Heruka's animal form, with the host which is a reflection of Vairocana's manifestation body. To discipline those who range on earth, one assumes the appearance of a manifestation body reflection which is a human form. And to discipline those who range in space, one gives rise to a host which have aerial manifestation body forms. One should have no doubt as this is stated in the *Saṁcāra*. (PD 391a)

There is a reference to Heruka's donkey form in ch. 16, v. 14 of the *Yoginīsaṁcāra* (see Pandey 1998, 145, 350), but Vīravajra is not directly quoting this text here.

[2] Bhavabhaṭṭa comments that "**movement of the mind** refers to mastery of the mind, since it is the achievement of its cessation. How [is this achieved]? [By means of] **the essential yoga of the donkey form**." (Pandey 2002, 94: *manovego manorājyam tasya nivṛttiḥ siddhitvāt / kuta ityāha gardabhākārayogātmeti*) Kambala interprets this in terms of the perfecting stage yoga practice, as follows: "**For the sake of the cessation of the movement of the mind** means that one who has the proper procedure turns back the **movement of mind**, i.e., all wrong views and obscurations, and quickly transforms into a dreamlike, purified body, and is thereby free of movement and is indestructible." (SN 33b–34a)

[3] Jayabhadra gives the following brief account of the *sādhana* to which this chapter refers:

> Regarding the yoginīs, Rūpinī, and so forth, one should regard them as beasts, through dependence on the visualization yoga. It is said that that the yoga of the donkey is excellent. The following is the oral instruction concerning it. For the sake of consecration, one should present the maṇḍala as follows. [It is] surrounded on the outside by the Cakravāḍa [mountain range]. Within it, in the middle of an eight-petalled lotus, is the syllable *hūṁ* surrounded by the vowels and consonants.

(cont'd)

If successful, one will foresee the end of one's life, and also the length of one's life.[5] In that the yogin should see [himself] as an excellent donkey.[6]

On the four petals in the cardinal directions are both essence and quintessence mantra sets. On the four petals in the ordinal directions are skull bowls filled with blood. On the twenty-four spokes are the forty-eight mantras of Khaṇḍakapāla, and so forth. Within the root thread are the eight mantras of Kākāsyā, and so forth. At the four gates are the four respective lines of the Śumbha mantra. At both of the walls is the root mantra. At the gates of the outer wall and the eight junctions of the turrets there are the armor mantras. On the Cakravāḍa [mountains] is the Blessed Lady's root mantra. Outside of that, it is surrounded by the great armor seed syllables, [such as the *pūṁ* of] Pullīramalaya, and so forth, like a pearl necklace. Produce an image of the donkey form, made of rice paste, and place it in the middle of the wheel, and rub it with sesame oil and red sandalwood paste, and its mouth trickling blood. Contemplate the yoga of the donkey, through the steps stated in the Tantra. Lamps blaze in the four ordinal directions by means of the visualized mantra stated here. Should one, having performed the preliminary worship, gaze at the image continually reciting the mantra, he will appear there. This is the oral instruction.

yoginīrūpiṇītyādinābhimatayo[gā]lambyena tā paśu nirīkṣayet / tathāpi gardabha-yog[a]syādhikyam āha / tatrāyam upadeśakramaḥ / yathābhiṣek[ā]rthamaṇḍalaṁ bahi-cakravāḍaparyantaṁ tathaivoddharet / tatrāṣṭadalapadmaki[ṁ]jalkamadye ālikāli-parivṛtto hūṁkāraḥ / caturṣu diśāpatreṣūbhayahṛdayopahṛdayau / caturṣu koṇapatreṣū kapālāni rudhirapūrṇāni / caturviṁśatyareṣu khaṇḍakapālād[y]-aṣṭacatvāriṁśat-mantraḥ / mūlasūtrābhyantare kākāsyādy-aṣṭau mantrāḥ / mūlasūtrād upari dvāra-catuṣṭaye śumbhamantrasya yathākramaṁcatvāri padāni prākārobhayato mūla-mantrāḥ / prākārabahidvāre śirasi aṣṭaniyūthasandhiṣu kavacamantrāḥ / cakravāḍ[e] bhagavatyā mūlamantraḥ / tadbahī rasm[y]ākāreṇa pullīramalayādimahākavacabījaiḥ parikṣ[i]pyate / cakragarbhe śālipiṣṭamayīṁ gardabhākārāṁ pratikṛtiṁ kṛtvā saṁsthāpya tailāraktakair abhyaṅgaṁ sravadrudhiramukhaṁ gardabhayogaṁ tantrokta-krameṇālambya caturṣu koṇeṣu dīp[ān] prajvālyābhimatamantreṇāta uktena / pūrva-kṛtasevanānan[t]aramantram āvartī pratikṛtiṁ paśyet tatra darśyate / ayaṁ upadeśaḥ / (D 31b.7–32a.5; E 23a.3–b.6)

[4] The Sanskrit here is somewhat inconsistent, alternating between singular and plural declensions. Given the plural context of the passage, I have translated it accordingly.

[5] The term *dīrghāyuṣaṁ* means "longevity" or "long life," but this does not translate well into English as the object of the verb "to see" (*paśyet*).

[6] The Sanskrit here, *asmin tu sugardabho yogī paśyet*, is rather ambiguous. "In that" (*asmin*) apparently refers to the image in the center of the maṇḍala at which the yogin gazes. Bhavabhaṭṭa commented that "**in that** means when one is undertaking the ritual procedure" (Pandey 2002, 95: *asminneva vidhāne kṛte satītyarthaḥ*). Bhavabhaṭṭa also understood *sugardabho* both as glossing *yogī* as well as being the object of the verb *paśyet*, despite its nominal declension. This is because the yogin is viewing his past life, as Bhavabhaṭṭa's next line makes clear: "As for **excellent donkey**, should it truly be the case that the yogin was previously a donkey,

Then he will be seen as he was before, as a donkey or even an elephant. The yogin sees here his form in a previous life, any of which he can invoke.[7] Should there be a power-bestowing person who was a man for seven lives,[8] a sacrificial cake fire sacrifice should be made with him,[9] so the adept will succeed.[10] One will ascend hundreds of thousands of leagues in an instant.

This supreme mantra-yoga[11] is the best, as it achieves the ḍākinīs' yoga.[12] Whoever repeats the sign of yoga will succeed within a month.[13] The secret of the Tantra[14] is the supreme essence of the mantra. This yogin

---

then he will see himself as a donkey" (Pandey 2002, 95: *sugardabha iti suṣṭhu yadi pūrvaṁ gardabho bhavet yogī tadā gardabham ātmānaṁ paśyet*).

[7] The Sanskrit in ms. A here reads *yasya yasya tu yo jātim āvahet pūrvajanmani tasyaiva tad dṛśyate rūpaṁ dṛśyate iha yoginā*. Pandey is sound in deleting the first *dṛśyate*, but he misreads *yoginā* as *yoginī*, probably misled by ms. B which does read *yoginī* (2002, 94). Ms. C, however, also reads *yoginā*, and this reading is supported by the Tibetan translation *rnal 'byor pas* (PM 225a). Note as well that the Tibetan translations lack any equivalent to *āvahet*. Both texts read a form of the verb "to be" (PM 224b: *gyur ba dag*; SL 110a: *'gyur ba dag*). In addition to the verb *mthong ba* that both attest, Mardo's text also reads *snang bar* (PM 225a), as if translating the additional *dṛśyate*.

[8] Bhavabhaṭṭa comments: "Through this it is easy to see the one born seven times" (Pandey 2002, 95: *anena saptajanmano darśanaṁ sulabham ityāha*).

[9] Jayabhadra comments here that "making a sacrificial cake with him means that he should be eaten" (D 32a.5–6, E 23b.6: *tena baliṁ kṛtveti bhakṣayītvety arthaḥ*). Note that Jayabhadra's reading of *tena baliṁ kṛtvā* is different from that of the CS mss., which is *tena balihoma kartavyaḥ*.

[10] Bhavabhaṭṭa comments: "**sacrificial cake fire sacrifice** means eating; **should be made** means will be making. In making a sacrificial cake fire sacrifice with him, one becomes a yogin." (Pandey 2002, 195: *balihomo bhakṣaṇaṁ kartavyaḥ karisyan / tena balihomaṁ kariṣyan yogī bhavati*)

[11] This translates *mantrayogavaraḥ*. The Tibetan translations read a different order, namely *rnal 'byor sngags mchog* (PM 225a, SL 110a).

[12] According to Bhavabhaṭṭa, this is "the *yoga* by which one achieves a vision of previous lives" (Pandey 2002, 96: *yogas tena pūrvajanmadarśanasādhakaḥ*).

[13] In the Sanskrit, the term *yoganimittaṁ* is the object of the verb *japet*. This may be an oblique reference to the mantra. The Tibetan, however, reads its as instrumental, as "whoever repeats with a sign of yoga" (PM 225a: *rnal 'byor mtshan mas gang zlos pa*). Devagupta comments that "**whoever repeats with a sign of yoga** means repeating with a conch rosary" (SS 104b).

[14] The Sanskrit here reads *rahasyam etat tantrasya*. The Tibetan translation reads "this secret Tantra" (PM 225a: *de ni gsang ba'i rgyud 'di yin*).

who knows by means of reality has no doubt regarding this.[15] The hero Heruka obtains the binding of the dākinīs' network.[16]

---

[15] This section, which literally reads as praise for the essence mantras and associated yogas, is interpreted by Vīravajra in terms of the perfecting stage fury fire meditation practice:

> **This supreme mantra-yoga is the best** refers to the Donkey Heruka of the perfecting stage, which is as is stated in the *Four Seats*: "The two sides of right and left are said to be the sun and moon. One should know that the donkey's form is like a flower of a banana tree, abiding for liberation in the center of the navel, [on] a lotus [like] a bull's hoof." The *rasanā* on the right and the *lalanā* on the left are the kindling cords, and the central *avadhūtī* channel is the firestick, and the fury fire drop in the navel is the kindling. If one kindles it with the wind of indestructible space and the winds of the left and right [channels], there will just be the heat of wind-fire. Moreover, this wind of the left and right [channels] is the **supreme mantra, the best. Achieves the ḍākinīs' yoga** means that the navel's fury fire heat ascends space since it goes to the space maṇḍala in the head. **Achieves yoga** refers to its kindling by the wind of the right and left. **Whoever repeats the sign of yoga** means that one sees the [following signs]: the smoke-like, as earth dissolves into water; the mirage-like, as water dissolves into fire; the firefly-like, as fire dissolves into wind; the lamp-like, as wind dissolves into consciousness; the sky-like, as consciousness dissolves into space. **Repeats** refers to the insertion of the life-force into the *avadhūtī*. **Will succeed within a month** means that by means of the method of kindling fury fire in the wheel with the firestick, **this secret of the Tantra, the mantra's quintessence, is supreme**. That is, the **secret of the Tantra** is the insertion of the life-force and energy into the *avadhūtī* from the channel which is like a bull's hoofprint, which is the nose of the right and left channels. Since the seminal essence descends from that, giving rise to the nonconceptuality of joy, ultimate joy, and natural joy, it is **supreme**. [The yogin] **who knows by means of reality**, and so forth, means that by inserting the three winds into the *avadhūtī* the conditions of conceptualization are removed, and nonconceptuality is generated. At that time, having abandoned the obscurations, one knows the three times, past, future, and so forth. Furthermore, as it states in the *Four Seats*: "Immovable, unconfused, unmanifest, free of the five obscurations, one manifests as Heruka." **The yogin has no doubt regarding this** means having no doubt concerning the generation of the nonconceptual bliss of seminal essence when the winds are inserted into the bull's hoofprint-like [channel nexus] which is a "laughing face" in the center of the navel's manifestation wheel. (PD 392a–b)

The Tibetan translations of the root text verses embedded in this commentary at times diverge from the Sanskrit; I have kept my translations from the Sanskrit. The text quoted, the *Four Seats* (*gdan bzhi*), may be the *Śrīcatuḥpīṭha-mahāyoginītantrarāja* (Tōh. 428–30), though I was unable to locate the quoted passages during a search of these texts.

[16] This translates the text *eṣate heruko vīro ḍākinījālasamvaraṁ* (Pandey, CS ms. B; CS mss. A and C read *ḍākinījālasamvaraḥ*). The Tibetan translations, however, give different readings, all of which seem to attest a Sanskrit reading of *te* or *ete* as "these." As a verb, *eṣate* is

not the standard form, which is *eṣati*. It is read as such, however, by Bhavabhaṭṭa, who glosses it as *prāpnoti* (Pandey 2002, 96). Note that his comments here are misunderstood in the Tibetan translations, which take *eṣate* as the instrumental plural of the pronoun *etad*. Mardo's translation reads "all these are stated in the *ḍākinījālasamvara*" (PM 225a: *mkha' 'dro dra ba'i sdom par ni // de dag thams cad brjod pa yin*), which is presumably a reference either to this text or to another such as the JS. Sumatikīrti, however, reads "these things taught by me are the *ḍākinījālasamvara*" (SL 110a: *nga yis de rnams bstan pa ni // mkha' 'gro dra ba'i bde mchog yin*). Sachen gives the following commentary on this: "These methods of achieving the seven-lived one were taught by me, the Blessed Lord Śamvara who is the very yogin of this sort, [as I] taught the *ḍākinījālasamvara*, i.e., the *Śrī-Khasama-Āditantra*" (PG 325.3).

15. The Procedure of the Syllabic Signs

Now, the secret signs occur in all sanctuaries.[1] Have no doubt that he who knows the secret signs will succeed by means of reality. *Ḍā* is known to mean "person," and *ḍī* "woman." *Pu* means "restraint,"[2] and *su* "eating."

[1] The Sanskrit here is *sarvasamvareṣu*. The term *samvara* is used in its derivative meaning of a "sanctuary," i.e., a community that is somehow enclosed or set apart from the larger social world that surrounds it. In this case, it is a *secret* community, and the secret signs given in this chapter are meant to provide one the bases for the maintenance of this secrecy. This interpretation is supported by several of the commentaries. According to Bhavabhaṭṭa: "**In all sanctuaries** means those sanctuaries which are to be protected for all people, and which are to be hidden from the disciples (*śrāvaka*), and so forth" (Pandey 2002, 97: *sarvasamvareṣv iti sarveṣāṁ puruṣādīnāṁ śrāvakādibhyo gopanīyānāṁ samvarā rakṣaṇāni, teṣu tadartham ityarthaḥ* /). Vīravajra interprets the *samvara* in terms of communities of yoginīs, as follows:

> **Now...in all sanctuaries** refers to those which are to be established by the three [classes of *dūtī* ("messenger" or "consort")]: 1) those born of gnosis, the factors for achieving the body, speech, and mind wheels; 2) those born at seats (*pīṭha*); and 3) those born of mantra. As [CS ch. 1] states, "the messengers are natural and accomplished, as well as lowly, middling, and lofty." Moreover, since the manifestation bodies exist without interruption in the twenty-four places in Jambudvīpa, when they saw that the time had arrived to discipline yogins, the buddhas and bodhisattvas who are born of gnosis arrived in female form, and taught [the meditation techniques of] quiescence (*śamathā*), insight (*vipaśyanā*), and the concentration of the four joys (*caturānandasamādhi*). Or, it refers to all of the heroes, and so forth, who were born in the twenty-four places, and who, since they possess it as their own acquisition, are accomplished in the concentration of bliss. Or, it refers to the yoginīs who have been consecrated and have the mantras, and who by means of yogic postures (*yantra*) send [their life-force] into the *avadhūtī*, giving rise to the meditative states (*dhyāna*) and undefiled bliss. Thus, one should first know their colors, shapes, and behavioral patterns, and then their syllabic and verbal signs, and the signs pertaining to eyes and lips. (PD 392b–393a)

[2] All three CS mss. read *pu* here. Pandey emends this to *ṣu* on the basis of Bhavabhaṭṭa's commentary (2002, 97), although that text does not provide a clear testimony. Ms. F does read *ṣu* (69a.6), but ms. G appears to read *pu* (67a.1), and the Tibetan translation of Bhavabhaṭṭa's commentary also reads *pu* (CP 189b). The syllables *pu* and *ṣu* are easily confused, but this does appear to be an old variant. Mardo reads *pū* here (PM 225a), and Sumatikīrti reads *pi* (SL 110a). *Śāśvatavajra reads *pū* (TV 290b), Vīravajra and Jayabhadra read *spu* (PD 393b; MP 189b). However, Indrabhūti reads *su* (IC 62b); and the parallel passage in the AU, moreover, reads *sa* (I 591b.6, J 210.2; H omits due to missing folia). Nevertheless,

Mā is indeed known to mean "mother," and *yo* "wife."[3] *Bhī* is likewise "sister," and *vī* is renowned as meaning "girlfriend." *Lu* means "daughter," and *strī* should be known as "blood."[4] *So* is "drinking *soma*," and *pe* likewise means "beverage." *Hī* is "meat,"[5] and *bha* "eating." *Bhū* indicates a "meeting place" (*melāpaka*), and *pī* likewise a "charnel ground."[6] *Dū* is known as a "corpse,"[7] and *ḍī* is understood to mean "yoginī."[8] *Ga* moreover designates

while several possibilities are attested, Pandey's emendation here seems unsound, since *pu* is attested by many more sources.

[3] The CS mss. read *yo* here, as do the AU mss. (I 591b.6, J 210.2). Bhavabhaṭṭa's commentary reads *ye* (Pandey 2002, 97), although its Tibetan translation reads *yo* (CP 189b), as do the commentaries of *Śāśvatavajra (TV 290b) and Indrabhūti (IC 62b). Mardo reads *yā* (PM 225a), and Sumatikīrti *ya* (SL 110a). Pandey's emendation of the text to *ye* does not seem sound.

[4] The CS mss. and the AU mss. (I 591b.6, J 210.3) read *strī*, a reading confirmed by Bhavabhaṭṭa (Pandey 2002, 97). Sumatikīrti reads *tri* here (SL 110a), while Mardo reads *śrī* (PM 225a).

[5] The CS mss. read *pī* here, as do the AU mss. (I 591b.7, J 210.3), a reading close to the *pi* in the Tibetan translation of the AU (327a). Bhavabhaṭṭa's commentary in the Tibetan translation reads *phī* (CP 190a), but his Sanskrit text reads *hī*. This is supported by *Śāśvatavajra (TV 290b), and by Vīravajra who reads *hi* (PD 393b). The Tibetan translations both read *he* (PM 225a, SL 110b), as does Indrabhūti (IC 63a). I have followed Bhavabhaṭṭa's reading here, as *pī* is not well attested in the CS commentarial tradition.

[6] The syllable *pī* is well attested in the CS mss. and commentaries. The parallel passage in the AU, however, reads *śī* (I 591b.7, J 210.4), although its Tibetan translation reads *pi* (AU 327a). The AU may have been emended here to remedy the repetition of *pī*. I suspect that the texts of the CS were emended for the same reason in the case of "meat" above.

[7] There is great variation concerning this sign. The CS mss. here read *dū*, which may be a corruption of *hū*, the reading preserved in Bhavabhaṭṭa's commentary (Pandey 2002, 98). Yet the Tibetan translation of the AU reads *du* (327a), as does Vīravajra (PD 393b). The AU mss., however, read *prī* (I 591b.7, J 210.4). Mardo reads *dhu* (PM 225a), and Sumatikīrti *bhu* (SL 110b), a reading also found in the commentaries of *Śāśvatavajra (TV 290b) and Indrabhūti (IC 63a). I have retained the reading of the CS mss., which is attested by the greatest number of additional sources.

[8] The CS mss. here read *hī*, as do the mss. of Bhavabhaṭṭa's commentary (F 69b.5; G 67a.8: *ha*), which Pandey reads as *dhī* (2002, 98), apparently out of a desire to accord with Mardo's text and the Tibetan translation of this commentary, both of which read *dhī* (PM 225a, CP 190a). Sumatikīrti reads *dhi* (SL 110b). The AU mss. read *ḍī* (I 591b.7, J 210.4), a reading supported by *Śāśvatavajra (TV 290b) and Indrabhūti (IC 63a). Vīravajra reads *di* (PD 393b). I suspect that *ḍī* is the best reading here, in part due to the old interpretive etymology deriving the term *ḍākinī* from the verbal root *ḍī*, "to fly," as well as the belief that ḍākinīs and yoginīs possess the power of flight. I have thus included it in my translation.

the "Lāma," and *trī* indeed is "Rūpiṇī."[9] *Kū* is understood to mean "Ḍākinī," and *hā* "Khaṇḍarohā." *Ja* refers to "both shanks,"[10] and *ka* the "pair of forearms." *Bha* is a salutation, and *su* functions as "welcome."[11]

[*Mī* is "fish,"[12] *bha* "eating,"[13] *bhyo* "fasting,"[14] and *pe* "Is it drinkable?"[15] *Ga* means "Is {he or she} approachable?"[16] *Ka* means "desirable."[17]

---

[9] The CS mss. and Bhavabhaṭṭa here read *trī*. The AU mss., however, read *strī* (I 591b.7, J 210.4). Mardo and Sumatikīrti read *stri* (PM 225a, SL 110b). Indrabhuti reads *tri* (IC 63a), and *Śāśvatavajra *stri* (TV 290b). *Trī* seems to be the best reading, as *strī* would be repetitive.

[10] The *jaṁgha*, or lower legs.

[11] Both the CS mss. and Bhavabhaṭṭa's commentary conclude the listing of signs here. However, the AU mss. continue with a longer list, as do the Tibetan CS translations and the commentaries of *Śāśvatavajra, Vīravajra, and Indrabhūti. I suspect that the shorter list was the original text of the CS, but that some later CS mss. may have incorporated the longer text of the AU, as I will argue below. I will translate this additional text next in square brackets, on the basis of the AU mss. and the Tibetan CS translation and commentaries.

[12] Mardo and Sumatikīrti give *mi* (PM 225a, SL 110b), but the AU mss. read *mī* (I 591b.8, J 210.5).

[13] This line, *bha iti bhakṣaṇam*, occurred earlier in the CS mss. In the AU mss., however, it was omitted there and occurs here instead. Its repetition here suggests that this additional AU text was appended to the CS text in some mss., without concern for the resulting repetition.

[14] This line, *bhyo abhakṣaḥ* (I 591b.8; J 210.5: *-abhakṣa*), is omitted by Mardo, and conflated with the previous line by Sumatikīrti, who reads "*bhyo* is eating" (SL 110b: *bhyo zhes bya ba bza' ba yin*). It is accurately represented by *Śāśvatavajra (TV 290b: *bhyo zhes pa mi za ba'o*). Vīravajra comments that it means "consecrating and eating the five ambrosias" (PD 393b).

[15] This is Mardo's reading (PM 225a) of a sign for which there is no consensus. Sumatīkīrti reads *byi* (SL 110b), the AU mss. read *mā* (I 591b.8; J 210.5: *mo*), and the AU translation reads *phyo* (327a). *Śāśvatavajra reads *sya* (TV 290b), and Indrabhūti *phe* (IC 63a). Moreover, while the Tibetan translations read "beverage" or "drinking" (*btung ba*), the AU mss. read "Is it drinkable?" (I 591b.8–9, J 210.5–6: *mo iti peyāpeyam*). I believe that the most likely reading here is *pe*, given its similarity to verbal derivatives from the root *pā*, "to drink."

[16] This is another question employing gerundives, as in the previous case. The AU mss. read *ga iti gamyāgamyam* (I 591b.9, J 210.6). The Tibetan translations capture the sense of the question but still do not translate it properly (PM 225a: *gha ni bgrod dang bgrod min yin*; SL 110b: *ga zhes bgrod da bgrod med yin*; note Mardo also gives *gha* in place of *ga*). The gerundive is correctly translated in *Śāśvatavajra's commentary (TV 290b: *ga zhes pa bgrod bya dang bgrod bya ma yin pa'o*). The question appears to be whether or not the person is "approachable" for sexual purposes, which is one of the senses of the term *gamya*. This seems to be Indrabhūti's interpretation. He wrote, also reading *gha*, "*gha* refers to the two embracing for the purpose of practice" (IC 63a: *gha ni spyod pas gnyis 'dzin dag pa'o*).

Sa means "virtuous woman,"[18] *ra* "slut,"[19] and *du* "wicked woman" (*duścāriṇī*). *Su* means "beautiful woman" (*subhagā*), and *na* "ugly woman" (*durbhagā*). *Sa* means a "committed person" (*samayī*), and *a* an "uncommitted person" (*asamayī*). *Ā* means "has come" (*āgataṁ*), and *ṇa* means "has not come" (*anāgataṁ*).[20] *So* means a "virtuous master."[21]] Heroes and sisters should know every single one of these syllabic signs. [These should not be communicated to those who lack faith. They should be communicated to those who are devoted to the pleasing, supreme commitments.][22]

---

[17] The AU here reads *ka iti kāmyam* (I 591b.9; J omits). Sumatikīrti's text concurs (SL 110b), but Mardo reads *kā* (PM 225a).

[18] All three Tibetan translations have the abstract reading "not going to another" (PM 225a, SL 110b, AU 327a: *sa zhes bya ba gzhan mi 'gro*). Tsong Khapa clarifies this, commenting that it means "a woman who does not consort with another man" (KS 113b). The AU mss. read *sati* (I 591b.9) and *sabhī* (J 210.6). The former, which should probably be read as *satī,* seems most likely, as it accords with the Tibetan translation. The latter is an unattested term, but it may refer to a woman associated with a gaming hall, one of the later meanings of *sabhā.* *Śāśvatavajra also gives a feminine reading, namely *dam ma* (TV 290b), "excellent" or "excellent woman."

[19] That is, *raṇḍā* (I 591b.9, J 210.6), a disparaging term with force more or less equal to that of the English translation. Mardo translates this as "widow" (PM 225b: *khyo med ma*), which is another meaning of *raṇḍā*, but one less likely in this context, given its juxaposition with *satī.*

[20] The Tibetan translations read *na* (PM 225b, SL 110b), evidently due to a failure to recognize the retroflex nasal.

[21] The AU mss. here read *sajjanaḥ ācāryaḥ* (I 592a.1, J 210.7), which I have translated. The Tibetan translations read "attachment" (PM 225b, SL 110b: *chags pa*), but this is clearly due to a misinterpretation of *sajjana.* The translation of *Śāśvatavajra's commentary gives the correct and very literal translation "excellent person" (TV 290b: *skye bu dam pa*).

[22] This additional text does not occur in the CS mss., but occurs in widely varying forms in the translations and the AU mss. As Sumatikīrti's text here is superior, I have translated it in brackets above (SL 110b: */ dad pa dang mi ldan pa rnams la sbyin par mi bya'o // dam tshig gi mchog yid du 'ong ba la // dgos pa dang ldan pa rnams la sbyin par bya'o /*). Mardo's translation is less consistent, reading: "[They] should be communicated to the devoted and undevoted. [They] should be communicated to the devoted, those who benefit the pleasing, supreme commitments." (PM 225a: *gus pa dang mi gus pa la sbyin par bya ba dam tshig gi mchog yid du 'ong ba phen 'dogs par byed pa ste gus pa la sbyin par bya ba'o*). The two AU mss. differ somewhat here, as follows. I 592a.1–2: *bhakṣī bhakṣaṁ pradāpayet dīkṣākāleṣu yoginām abhiṣekāditaḥ parāṁ paramasamayāmanojñopakārakānāṁ bhakṣābhakṣāya pradātavyam.* J 210.7–211.1: *bhakṣyābhakṣyaṁ pradāpayet dīkṣākāleṣu yogīnām abhiṣekāditaḥ parāparamasamayāmanojñopakāranāṁ bhakṣyābhakṣyāya pradātavyaṁ.*

16. The Procedure of Examining the Characteristics of the Seven Yoginīs

Next I will impart here for the adept[1] the secret of what should and should not be enjoyed.[2] Those who are to be enjoyed[3] reside within the supreme commitments, and are pleasing assistants.[4] The adept may attain power merely through recognizing that which is to be communicated to the

[1] As is so often the case the text declines the term *sādhaka* in the nominative case, when it should be, in this case, in the dative singular, *sādhakāya*, as Bhavabhaṭṭa informs us (Pandey 2002, 100). Sumatikīrti's text has the defective reading *khro med ma* (SL 110b).

[2] Here I translate the Sanskrit *atha guhya bhakṣyam abhakṣyaṁ vai pravakṣyāmīha sādhakaḥ*. There is some variance here regarding *bhakṣyam abhakṣyaṁ* ("what should and should not be enjoyed"). This is attested in commentaries such as Vīravajra's (PD 394a: *de nas bza' dang bza' min bya*) and Durjayacandra's (RG 281a: *de nas / gsang ba'i bza' dang bza' min bshad /*), as well as Tathāgatarakṣita's (UN 227b). Mardo's translation (PM 225b: *de nas skal ldan skal ldan min*) seems to be based upon a (mis)reading of *bhavyam abhavyaṁ*. On the other hand, there is another well attested variant. This replaces *bhakṣyam abhakṣyaṁ vai* with *mahāsiddhiṁ*, and it is preserved in Bhavabhaṭṭa's commentary. It is also attested in Sumatikīrti's translation (SL 110b) and Mal's translation (see PG 326.3), as well as the commentaries of Kambala (SN 35a) and Indrabhūti (IC 63b). I prefer the former reading not only because it is what actually occurs in the text, but also because it is the most consistent reading when read in the light of the second half of this verse. Pandey revises the text to accord with Bhavabhaṭṭa's reading (Pandey 2002, 100).

[3] The CS mss. give variant readings. Mss. A and C read *bhaktyāḥ*, while ms. B reads *bhakṣyāḥ*. This latter reading is supported by the parallel passage in the AU (J 211.1: *bhakṣyā*; I 592a.2: *bhakṣā*). The *bhakṣyā* reading is attested by Vīravajra (PD 294a: *bza' bya*), while the *bhakṣāḥ* reading is attested as *bza' ba* in the commentaries of Durjayacandra (RG 281a), Tathāgatarakṣita (UN 227b), and Indrabhūti (IC 64a). The *bhaktyāḥ* reading is supported by Sumatikīrti (SL 11a: *dad pa rab dang ldan pa*). Pandey (2002, 100) emends this to *bhavyāḥ* on the basis of Mardo's Tibetan translation (PM 225b: *skal ldan*), but as this reading is unattested elsewhere, this emendation is unwarranted.

[4] Bhavabhaṭṭa explains: "It is the yoginīs who are **pleasing assistants**, from whom there is pleasing assistance for the adepts" (Pandey 2002, 100: *manojñopakāro yebhyaḥ sādhakānāṁ bhavati te manojñopakārakā yoginījanāḥ*).

devotee,[5] the secret class distinctions[6] of the yogin[ī]s who are nondual with the hero.[7]

A woman who is pale like the lotus root, with long eyes like lotus petals, who always prefers white clothing, who exudes the fragrance of fresh sandalwood, and who delights in assemblies of sugatas: she should be known as one born into the clan lineage. The woman who is like refined gold, who prefers red and yellow garments, who has the scent of jasmine and campaka [flowers],[8] is one who ought to be a companion to the heroes. She who is dark blue like the Indīvara lotus,[9] who prefers wearing indigo clothing, and

---

[5] Here again the texts vary concerning the reading of *bhaktāya* vs. *bhakṣāya*. The CS mss. read *bhaktāya pradātavyaṁ* here, as does Bhavabhaṭṭa's commentary (Pandey 2002, 100). This reading is supported by both Mardo's translation (PM 225b: *gus pa nyid la*) and Sumatikīrti's translation (SL 111a: *dad pa can la*), as well as by the commentaries of Durjayacandra (281a) and Tathāgatarakṣita (UN 227b). However, the reading *bhakṣāya pradātavyaṁ* occurs both in the AU mss. (I 592a.2, J 211.1) and in Jayabhadra's commentary (D 32b.3, E 24a.3). Given the age of these latter sources, this appears to be a genuine variant.

[6] I translate here the text preserved in the CS mss., which is *varṇabhedaṁ tu yaṁ guhyaṁ*. Pandey emends this to *varṇabhedaṁ tu pragṛhya* on the basis of Mardo's translation (PM 225b: *de nas rigs kyi dbye gzung na*), but this emendation is unwarranted as this text is unattested elsewhere. This line is only commented upon in two of the Indian commentaries, but both support the CS reading (RG 281a: *kha dog dbyes bas gsang ba gang*; IC 64a: *rigs kyi bye brag gsang ba dang*). Sumatikīrti gives a very different reading, namely "color, scent, and so forth" (SL 111a: *kha dog dri la sogs pa dang*). This verse does not occur in the AU; it appears to be a linking verse unique to the CS. Note that *varṇabhedaṁ* could refer generically to the yoginī classes, or more specifically to the color differences that are one of the major features for distinguishing them.

[7] Bhavabhaṭṭa comments as follows: "Regarding hero, and so forth, except for **nondual with the hero,** I will explain that knowledge of the colors, and so forth, of the yoginīs' people, by which one **may attain** realization of the **powers**" (2002, 100: *vīretyādi vīrādvayaṁ vinā yoginījanānāṁ yena varṇādinā jñānena siddhisākṣātkāram āpnuyāt tat pravakṣāmīti sambandhaḥ* /). Note that in the CS mss. *yoginaḥ* is declined in the masculine gender. The translations and the commentarial tradition, however, take this as referring to the female yoginīs, who after all are the focus of this chapter.

[8] The Sanskrit here reads *jāticampakagandhā ca*, a reading confirmed by the Tibetan (PM 225b: *dzā ti tsam pa'i dri dang ldan*). This is rendered by Pandey as *jātivatyekagandhā* (2002, 101). *Jāti* is the jasmine (*Jasminum grandiflorum*), and *campaka* refers to the yellow, fragrant flowers of the tree *Michelia campaka*.

[9] *Nymphaea stellata* or *cynea*. The CS mss. here all read *sarvendīvaraśyāmā*. However, the corresponding passage in the AU reads *yā ca indīvaraśyāmā* (I 592a.4, J 211.5), which not only makes more sense but fits the pattern of the text; Mardo's translation also corresponds to this reading, with *gang zhig utpal ltar sngo bsangs* (PM 225b). The text here is undoubtedly

who is scented like the indigo Utpala lotus,[10] is indeed a companion of the hero Rudra.[11]

The woman[12] whose skin is the color of white lotus petals, and who always has the scent of lotus root,[13] is one who thus has a hero's resolve.[14] A woman who is red and pale yellow, whose shapely figure is red garbed,[15] and who smells like jasmine[16] and utpala lotus, is one born into the vajra

corrupt, but the corruption is quite old, as it is attested in Sumatikīrti's translation (SL 111a: *thams cad ud dpal sngo sangs ma*).

[10] *Nymphaea caerulea.*

[11] This line, as one might expect, caused considerable difficulty for Buddhists. The reading *vīrarudrānugā hi sā* itself is confirmed by the corresponding passage in the AU mss. (I 592a.5, J 211.5). The Tibetan translations, however, have different readings. Sumatikīrti's translation (SL 111a) and Mal's translation (PG 327.2) read *dpa' bo bzang* and *dpa' bo bzang po*, respectively. This reading is supported by Jayabhadra, who comments: "**A companion of the Hero Bhadra** means one born in Śrī Heruka's clan" (E 24a.4–5: *vīrabhadrānugā iti śrīherukakula-sambhūtetyarthaḥ* /). Mardo's translation reads *dpa' bo dran*, a reading unattested elsewhere, unless *dran* was altered from *drag*, the Tibetan translation of *rudra*. Here, as in ch. 2, reference to a Śaiva deity was replaced by "Śrī Heruka," but here the original reading is preserved in the root text. This replacement does occur, however, in Bhavabhaṭṭa's text, where *śrīherukānugā* occurs in its place (2002, 101). Pandey emends the root text in accordance with Bhavabhaṭṭa. I believe, however, that this emendation is unwarranted, unless the editor seeks to complete the incomplete Buddhist adaptation of this text.

[12] Mardo's translation adds that she is beautiful (PM 225b: *mdzed ma*), but this added text in absent both in the CS and AU mss. Pandey adds *sundarī caiva* in brackets here (2002, 101). Sumatikīrti's translation also glosses *nārī* here, but differently: in his text, she is "very pure" (SM 111a: *shin tu rnam dag*).

[13] While the lotus root is not strongly scented, it is colored with a pale off-white hue, and thus fits the pattern of the text.

[14] This term *vīramatī* is the name of one of the twenty-four goddesses listed in chapter four above. According to Bhavabhaṭṭa it designates a yoginī who is of Vīramatī's clan (Pandey 2002, 101: *vīramatīkulānugā*). Other commentators, however, correlate these to the male deities' clans, in this case Amitābha's. See Kambala's commentary translated in note 19 below.

[15] The CS mss. read *raktavastrasvarūpiṇī*, which I emend to *raktavastrasurūpiṇī* on the basis of the AU mss. and the Tibetan translations. This reading is supported by Sumatikīrti's translation (SL 111a: *gzugs bzang gos ni dmar ba dang*), and also by Vīravajra (PD 395a: *gos dmar*), the only commentator who cites this line. Pandey emends this line to *raktavaktra-surūpiṇī* (2002, 101) on the basis of Mardo's translation (PM 225b: *gzugs bzang kha ni dmar ba dang*), but the emendation from *vastra* to *vaktra* is unwarranted as it is unattested elsewhere. The AU mss. read here *raktavarṇasurūpiṇī* (I 592a.5–6; J 211.6).

[16] That is, *mallikā* (*Jasminum zambac*).

clan.[17] A woman who is yellow and dark blue, who prefers wearing white clothing, and who has the scent of śirīṣa blossoms,[18] is known to be a companion of the tathāgatas. A woman who is of reddish hue, who wears clothes of that color, and who always smells of camphor, is a companion of Vairocana's clan.

Seven are the yoginīs' clans spoken by me.[19] They always take pleasure in heteropraxy,[20] and each has her own gesture and color.[21] Here the clans' magic syllables occur in six classes.[22] [Each one] forms her own

---

[17] Jayabhadra (E 24a.5) and Bhavabhaṭṭa (Pandey 2002, 101) both interpret this as referring to Vajravārāhī's clan.

[18] This translates the text preserved in the AU, *śirīṣapuspagandhā* (J 211.7; I defective), on which Sumatikīrti's somewhat garbled translation appears to be based (SL 111a: *shrī shi dri yi me tog ldan*). The CS mss. here read *śirasipuspagandhā*, which appears to be defective, but could be translated as "who has the scent of flowers on her head." This latter reading is supported by the Tibetan, *mgo la me tog dri dang ldan* (PM 225b). The flowers of the śirīṣa tree (*Acacia sirissa* or *Mimosa lebbeck*) are white, which accords well with this passage.

[19] Kambala associates the seven yoginī clans with the masculine deities, and correlates these to Indian social groupings. It is not clear how these actually correlate to the clans listed in this chapter. He writes: "Vairocana is said to [correlate to] the brahmin [class]; Ratna [-sambhava] should be known to be the caṇḍāla. Amitābha is the lord of the dancers, and Amogha[siddhi], who has the vajra, with the dyers. The ḍombis are [associated] with Akṣobhya, and one should recognize the sixth, Vajrasattva's, as the kshatriya class. The seventh is the shudra [class], which gives rise to the universal clan of Heruka." (SN 35a)

[20] This is my translation of *vāmācāra*, literally "the conduct of the left." While much of this conduct involves observing a preference for the left in one's behavior, it goes beyond this to include a wider range of behavior that is best labeled "heteropraxic" in the Indian social context. Rendering *vāma-* as *hetero-* is not inappropriate here, as the left is the inauspicious side in Indian discourse.

[21] The CS mss. here read *hy ete svamudrāvarṇalakṣaṇāḥ*, but all other sources attest the reading *hy ete svamudrāvarṇasaṁkulāḥ*, including Bhavabhaṭṭa (Pandey 2002, 102), the AU mss. (I 592a.7–8, J 212.2: *-saṁkulā*), as well as the Tibetan translations (PM 226a: *'di dag rang rgya'i mdog gis khyab*; SL 111b: *'di dag rang gi mdog gis khyab*).

[22] This translates *kulavidyākṣarāṇi ṣaḍvarṇāni bhavantīha*. The first line is translated correctly in Sumatikīrti's text (SL 111b: *rigs kyi rig pa'i yi ge yang*), but is defective in Mardo's (PM 226a: *rigs kyi rjes su 'dir 'gyur ba*). Both incorrectly translate *varṇa* as "color" (PM 226a: *'di la kha dog drug tu 'gyur*; SL 111b: *kha dog drug tu 'gyur ba yin*). Regarding the meaning of this, Vīravajra explains as follows: "The **syllables** displayed by them are divided into **six classes**. As for their **own gestures,** they form the gestures of the six clans, such as the vajra and wheel gestures. It is said that since the seventh clan is the *dharmadhātu-vārāhī* [clan], it is pervasive." (PD 395a) In other words, Vīravajra resolves the tension between the seven clans and the six classes of syllables by arguing that there are six basic clans with distinctive

gesture and speaks the speech that arises in her own lineage. A woman who always goes to the left or from the left is [one of] the yoginīs.[23] She speaks by means of her left hand,[24] and looks gazing to the left.

He who eagerly speaks with women[25] is understood to be committed. Should he solicit a woman, he addresses her using the seed syllables of [their][26] clan. He does not disregard the actions of their clan, and does not set aside that which is enjoined in the treatises of their own [tradition]. He repeats the spell of their clan; he is thus understood as being committed.

---

colors, syllables, gestures, and so forth. Vajravārāhī's clan is the seventh, and pervades all of the others, and thus apparently lacks these distinguishing features. Regarding the "clans' magic syllables," Durjayacandra identifies them with the six yoginī armor mantras listed in chapter eight. See RG 281b.

[23] This translates the CS text *vāmena yāti yā nārī yoginyo vāmatas sadā*, which is the basis of Mardo's translation (PM 226a: *g-yon nas 'gro ba'i bud med gang // rnal 'byor ma la'ang g-yon la brtag*), and which is also supported by Bhavabhaṭṭa (2002, 102). This text is rather ungrammatical. Durjayacandra comments on it as follows: "Regarding **always...from the left**, one should understand that those women who are consorts, and who are 'always...from the left,' meaning that they **go to the left** of others, are yoginīs" (RG 282a). However, there is another reading which makes more sense grammatically. This is the reading in the AU, which replaces *yoginyo* with *yogināṁ* (I 592a.8, J 212.3). This text would thus read: "A woman who goes to the left is always to the left of the yogins." This text is attested by Sumatikīrti's translation (SL 111b: *g-yon las 'gro ba'i bud med gang // rnal 'byor pa'i g-yon la brtag*). It appears that both versions of the text were attested in the CS tradition.

[24] CS ms. A reads *vāmahastaprabhāṣī*, which undoubtedly refers to the yoginīs' sign language. Nevertheless, there is an alternate reading, *vācāmahatprabhāṣī*, "She speaks with an impressive voice." It is attested in the AU mss. (I 592a.8; J 212.3), Bhavabhaṭṭa's commentary (Pandey 2002, 102), and also Mardo's translation (PM 226a: *skad ni chen por rab smra ba*). On the other hand, *vāmahastaprabhāṣī* is attested in the parallel passage in the *Samvarodaya Tantra* (Tsuda 1974, 103) and also Sumatikīrti's somewhat defective translation (SL 111b: *lag pa g-yon gyis mtshan pa dang*).

[25] CS ms. A reads *strīṇāṁ hṛṣṭaprabhāṣī*, a reading also attested in the AU mss. (I 592a.9; J 212.3) and the SU (Tsuda 1974, 103). Pandey emends this to *strīṇāṁ hṛṣṭaprahāṣī* ("eagerly laughs with women") on the basis of Bhavabhaṭṭa (2002, 102), but this revision is unwarranted as it is only attested in one source. The Tibetan translations also support *prabhāṣī*, with their readings of *rab smra ba* (PM 226a) and *sgra smra ba* (SL 111b).

[26] The Sanskrit text and Tibetan translations do not provide gender specific pronouns here. In my interpretation, the clan affliliation applies both to the adept and to the *yoginī* he is soliciting, since purpose of the chapter is to aid him in finding a *yoginī* with the same clan affiliation that he received when he was initiated. I thus insert "their" here and throughout the remainder of this passage to indicate this mutuality.

When saluting one always bows with one's body to the left.[27] One should speak with women, being truthful indeed. One should dig one's left big toe into the earth and draw with one's foot.[28] One should scratch one's head with one's left hand, looking askance.[29] Recollecting one's own consort, she is suitable for that adept.[30] Pointing with a finger to one's cheek, chin, or nostril, and glancing obliquely and repeating the mantra once, examine the consort (*vidyā*).[31] The yoginīs who have the commitments truly go to the real thing.[32]

---

[27] This translates *vāmāṅgapraṇataḥ sadā*. Mardo's translation, *g-yon pa'i lus kyis rtag tu 'dud* (PM 226a), implies a different interpretation, namely, "always bows with the left [side] of one's body."

[28] The CS mss. here read *vāmāṅguṣṭha nikhanyā su bhūmau saṁlikhyate padā*. The AU mss., however, read *vāmāṅguṣṭhaṁ nikhanyāt tu* (Kalff 1979, 377), which makes more sense, and fits the pattern of the text. This text is missing in extant mss. of Bhavabhaṭṭa's commentary, although Pandey "reconstructs" the text on the basis of Mardo's translation to read *vāmāṅguṣṭhalikhanyā subhūmau*. The Tibetan translations do not help here, as they lack any term corresponding to *nikhanyā / nikhanyāt / likhanyā*.

[29] The Sanskrit here reads *śiraḥkaṇḍūyanaṁ kuryāt tiryagdṛṣṭvā vāmapaṇinā*. Presumably *vāmapaṇinā* refers to the action of *śiraḥkaṇḍūyanaṁ kuryāt*.

[30] The CS mss. here read *svavidyāsmaraṇaṁ tasya sādhakasya viṣaye hitā*. A feminine object is suggested by *viṣaye hitā*, as it is likewise suggested by the AU mss. reading, *svavidyāsmaraṇaṁ tasya sādhakasya viṣaye hi sā* (I 592b.2, J 212.6). Bhavabhaṭṭa, however, reads *hitam* (Pandey 2002, 103), while the ST reads *hitaḥ* (Tsuda 1974, 103). *Svavidyā* here might mean "one's own [mantric] spell," but according to Bhavabhaṭṭa, "**One's own consort** means that one should see her as just like one's own chosen deity" (Pandey 2002, 103: *svavidyāṁ sveṣṭadevatām iva tāṁ paśyed iti bhavaḥ*).

[31] Bhavabhaṭṭa explains that the term *mantra* here refers to the *vidyārāja* mantra (Pandey 2002, 103). The *vidyāṁ* qua object of the verb *nirīkṣayet* is clearly the female yoginī, as was the case above.

[32] In the Kaula context *sadbhāva* is the *amṛta* emitted by the yoginīs. See White 1998, 190.

17. The Procedure of the Signs, Gestures, and Perambulant Forms of All Yoginīs

Thence the yoginīs and ḍākinīs are difficult to obtain,[1] as they are the source of the five ambrosias.[2] Yāminī,[3] Trāsanī,[4] Kāminī,[5] Bhīmā,[6] [Rūpā],[7] Saṁcārā,[8] and Bhāsurā[9] are the seven assembled ḍākinīs. Their characteris-

[1] This line, *durlabhā yoginīnāṁ tu ḍākinīnāṁ*, is awkward when literally translated ("the difficulty of obtaining of the yoginīs and ḍākinīs"). Jayabhadra rephrases it as *durlabhā yoginyo ḍākinyaś* (E 24b.3), which is the way in which I translate it. Jayabhadra comments that "they are easily attained through mastery of the five ambrosias" (E 24b.3–4: *pañcāmṛtābhyasena sulabhā bhavantīty abhiprāyaḥ*).

[2] The CS mss. here read *pañcāmṛtasadbhāvāt* ("as they are the reality of the five ambrosias"). This is also attested by Bhavabhaṭṭa (Pandey 2002, 104). Jayabhadra (E 24b.3) gives the variant *-sambhavāt* ("as they are the source…"), which I believe is a better reading. It corresponds with the Tibetan translations *yang dag 'byung* (PM 226a), *yang dag byung* (SL 112a), and *yang dag par 'byung* (PG 328.2). It is also closer to the AU reading, *samudbhavā* (I 592b.3, J 213.1). I suspect that this term was transformed to *sadbhāvāt* due to the proximity of this term in the last verse of the preceding chapter. These ideas are also related, as the yoginīs and ḍākinīs are indeed the source (*sambhāva*), for the yogin, of the "real thing" (*sadbhāva*) or essential clan fluid that bestows power.

[3] *Yāminī*, "she who is the night."

[4] *Trāsanī*, "she who is terrifying."

[5] *Kāminī*, "she who is impassioned," is also attested in Bhavabhaṭṭa's commentary (Pandey 2002, 104) and in Sumatikīrti's translation (SL 112a). Here the AU mss. (I 592b.3; J 213.1) read *kānanī*, "she who is of the forest," which corresponds to Mardo's *nags tshal ma* (PM 226a).

[6] *Bhīmā*, "she who is formidable."

[7] *Rūpā*, "she who is shapely." *Rūpā* does not occur in the CS mss., but it is attested by Bhavabhaṭṭa (Pandey 2002, 104), the Tibetan translations (PM 226a: *gzugs*; SL 112a: *gzugs can*) and also the AU mss. (I 592b.3, J 213.1). It is also necessary to complete the list of seven.

[8] *Saṁcārā*, "she who transits."

[9] *Bhāsurā*, "she who is radiant."

tics will be stated here.[10] Rūpikā,[11] Cumbikā,[12] Lāmā,[13] Parāvṛttā,[14] Sabālikā,[15] Anivartikā,[16] and Aihikīdevī[17] are known as the seven ḍākinīs.

She may gaze passionately, and furrows her brows. First she assumes a form, and later she abandons it.[18] She is known to be Rūpikā, who is nondually served by the hero.[19] She [who]—whether it is desired or not—embraces and kisses a child, should be known to be Cumbikā, the ḍākinī who destroys sin. She who has a frowning face that looks askance, who

[10] Bhavabhaṭṭa states that "there are also different names that are closely related with them" (Pandey 2002, 105: *tāsāṁ sānvayaṁ nāmāntaram apy āha*), which seems to indicate that these two sets of seven names are closely related, if not synonymous, i.e., that they refer to the same general set of seven classes of yoginīs/ḍākinīs. According to Sachen, these two sets of ḍākinī's names are, respectively, their "worldly" and "transcendent" name arrangements (PG 328.2–4).

[11] *Rūpikā*, "she who is beautiful."

[12] *Cumbikā*, "she who is a kisser."

[13] *Lāmā* is not a Sanskrit term, and is most likely a term borrowed from another language. P.C. Bagchi has suggested that it derives from the Tibetan *lha mo*, "goddess" (1939, 50–51).

[14] *Parāvṛttā*, "she who returns."

[15] *Sabālikā*, "she who is with child."

[16] *Anivartikā*, "she who does not turn back."

[17] The name *Aihikī* appears to derive from *aihika*, an abstract term derived from *iha* meaning "of this world, terrestial." See Monier-Williams 2002, 235.1.

[18] This translates the AU text, *rūpaṁ saṁharati prāk paścān nyāsaṁ karoti ca* (I 592b.4–5; J 213.3). The term *nyāsaṁ karoti* is attested in Sumatikīrti's translation (SL 112a: *'jog par byed pa*). However, the CS mss. here read *nāsaṁ*, which might be corrected to *nāśaṁ* on the basis of Mardo's reading (PM 226b: *'jig par byed pa yin*), and translated as "first she appropriates and later she destroys [her] form." This reading seems to make less sense, but it is the reading adopted by the Tibetan commentators. According to Bu-ston, "at first her form is beautiful, and confers benefit, but later it is ugly, destroying, i.e., suppressing" (NS 135a). The terms he uses, *rjes su 'dzin pa* (*anugraha*) and *tshar gcod pa* (*nigraha*), are terms for magical procedures, which may be implied here.

[19] The CS mss. here are partially obliterated, with only ms. B reading *-sevitaṁ*. This reading is supported by the AU mss., which read *vīrādvayasevitaṁ* (I 592b.6, J 213.5), which I have translated here, assuming that *-sevitaṁ* should be declined as *-sevitā*. Bhavabhaṭṭa, however, gives the reading *vīrādvayasevitum*, which he explains means that she is one who serves (*sevinī*) the nondual hero (Pandey 2002, 105: *vīrādvayasevitum iti vīrādvayasevinītyarthaḥ*). Following Bhavabhaṭṭa, we might translate this line as "She is Rūpikā, who is known to nondually serve the Hero." While both readings are ungrammatical, the former is less so, and it thus seems the most likely reading to me.

threatens with her raised brows,[20] and who aside from this is the terrifier of breath should be called Lāmā. Pigs, *śarabha*[21] deer, cats, jackals, goats,[22] and Śiva's snakes[23] will all be frightened on account of her. She is indeed known to be Parāvṛttā. She who, being delighted, laughs,[24] and moreover having gone does not return, and who is openly impassioned and laughing, is known to be Khaṇḍarohā.

She is distraught, and whomever she touches—with her hand, a clod of earth, her foot, the hem of her garment, or with a stick of the āru tree[25]—will not live. She should be recognized as Anivartā, who is infamous as one not to be invoked. She who laughs, mutters, weeps, or suddenly flies into a rage is known to be Aihikā. [She is the goddess who always has a cheerful

[20] The text here is deficient in the CS mss. due to the fraying of the folio in ms. A. I follow here the reading in AU ms. I, *bhruvotkṣepais tarjayanti* (I 592b.6–7; J 213.5–6: *bruvotkṣeppā*). Pandey's edition reads here *brūkṣepe*, and does not explain the source or reasoning for this text (2002, 105).

[21] The term *śarabha* originally designated a species of deer, but the term is also applied to the young elephant as well as to a mythical mountain dwelling beast. The Tibetan translations seem to incline toward the latter meaning but vary in its interpretation; Mardo's revision reads *dred* (PM 226b), the red bear (*Ursus isabellinus*), Sumatikīrti's reads *seng ge*, the lion (SL 112a).

[22] The CS mss. here read *-sṛgālādyā*, which makes no sense in this context; the AU mss. read *-śṛgālājā*, which corresponds to the Tibetan *ce sbyang ra* (PM 226b, SL 112a).

[23] Regarding the interpretation of *śivāhayā* as "Śiva's snakes," see Kalff 1979, 280–81. It is based upon its analysis as *śiva+ahayaḥ* (masc. nom. pl. of *ahi*), with the observation that *-aḥ* terminations are frequently transformed to *-ā* in Buddhist Sanskrit texts. It does make more sense than the Tibetan translation, "jackals, goats, and horses" (*ce sbyang ra dang rta dag dang*), which ignores *śivā*, probably because they read *śivā* as "jackal" and *hayā* as *hayāḥ*, "horses" (which is redundant since *śṛgāla*, mentioned in the same line, also means jackal). Pandey emends the line to read *varāhaśarabhamārjaraśṛgālādyā ajā hayā* to accord with the Tibetan translation, but this is inappropriate as it retains the defective *ādyā* termination.

[24] This translates the Tibetan (PM 226b: *rgod pa*; SL 112a: *dgod pa*). The CS mss. here are damaged due to fraying, but the AU mss. here read *sahate* (I 592b.8, J 213.7). Note that *hasate*, which is attested by the Tibetan translations *rgod pa* and *dgod pa*, is repeated below, and makes more sense in this context than *sahate*.

[25] Ms. A is damaged here; it reads *vā-x-kāṣṭena*, with the damaged syllable appearing to be *ru*. This reading is suppored by AU ms. I, which reads *cārukāṣṭena* (I 592b.8; J 214.1: *vāsakāṣṭena*, misreading *ru* as *sa*). Pandey reads *vā kāṣṭena* here, seemingly unaware of the damaged syllable or the AU parallel text (2002, 105). He was probably influenced here by the Tibetan translations, which read simply "with sticks" (PM 226b, SL 112b: *shing dag gis*). The name *āru* refers to the tree *Lagerstroemia regina*.

countenance,[26] and converses with Buddhists, and who is known as one born in the Vajra clan.][27]

One should recognize the emblem in the ḍākinīs' clan that is honored by the hero.[28] A skull, an axe, a tusk, a wheel, armor, a banner, a sword, and a terrible [knife][29]—counting them, they are known as the eight that are famed as the emblems of the clans.[30]

---

[26] This translates the Sanskrit preserved in the AU mss., *prahasitavadanā* (I 592b.5, J 213.3–4). The Tibetan translations here read "saluation" (PM 226b, SL 112b: *gsong por smra ba*), but this reading seems to make less sense in this context.

[27] The text in brackets does not occur in the CS mss., but occurs both in the AU mss. (I 592b.5, J 213.3–4) and in Mardo's and Sumatikīrti's translations (PM 226b, SL 112b).

[28] The CS mss. here read *ḍākinīnāṁ kule mudrāṁ vīrasevituṁ lakṣayet*, which Pandey renders as *ḍākinīnāṁ kulānīha mahāvādīni lakṣayet* (2002, 106), despite the fact that *mahāvādīni* is attested nowhere, and *mudrā* is attested in all sources, including Mardo's Tibetan (PM 226b). Bhavabhaṭṭa reads *kulamudrā*, and the reading *kūlānīha* occurs in the AU mss. (I 592b.9, J 214.1), where it makes sense, as the AU omits *mudrāṁ*, and thus needs an object for the verb. Bhavabhaṭṭa reads *mudrā*, but does not seem to know what to do with it. He glosses the infinitive *sevituṁ* as *vīrasevinī*, as above; I translate the term as "honored" here because the *mudrāṁ* does not appear to be the human consort, but rather the inanimate emblems listed in the next verse. Bhavabhaṭṭa also glosses *lakṣayet* as *jānīyāt*, which is one of the two meanings of this verb (2002, 107).

[29] There is considerable divergence among the various sources here. I have translated the reading of the CS mss., which is *kapāla-paraśu-daṁṣṭrāś cakra-kavaca-dvaja-khadga-saṁtrāsanī saṁkhyā[ḥ] cāṣṭamī smṛtāḥ kulamudrāprakīrtitāḥ*. Regarding *saṁtrāsanī*, I follow Bhavabhaṭṭa's gloss of it as *kartrī* (2002, 107). Sachen, however, glosses it as *vajra* (PG 329.2). Bhavabhaṭṭa's text is identical to this, except that he reads *kacadhvaja* ("hair banner") which he glosses as *muktakeśatā* ("the state of having loose hair"; Pandey 2002, 107); this, however, is not a hand implement, and it also is problematic in that this list has only seven items. He also cites an alternate text that has five items, reading *kapāla-paraśu-daṁṣṭrāś ca khadga-saṁtrāsanī caiva*. This is almost identical to the AU reading, which is *kapāla-paraśu-daṁṣṭrā khadga-saṁtrāsanī caiva* (I 592b.9, J 214.1–2). Jayabhadra does not quote the full list, but he does state that it has five items, which indicates that this was likely the original list, writing "As for the five—**skull**, and so forth—each one is as one wishes" (E 24b.5: *kapālādīni pañca pratyekaṁ yatheṣṭam eva*). He also glosses *trāsanī* as *vajra*. The Tibetan translations have alternate readings. None of the three attest *kavaca* or anything like it, and all three (PM 226b, SL 112b, PG 329.2) read *drung* ("conch"), seemingly reading *śaṁkhā* in place of *saṁkhyāḥ*. Mardo reads *vajra*, and reads *saṁtrāsanī* with *khadga* as "terrible sword" (*ral gri kun tu sgrag byed nyid*). Sumatikīrti omits *vajra*, and seems to take *saṁtrāsanī* as a separate item.

[30] According to Kambala, the eighth deity is Vārāhī. They hold these implements in their right hands. In their left hands they hold khatvanga staffs and skull bowls filled with uterine blood and semen. See SN 35b, 37b. Tsong Khapa generally follows Kambala's commentary, but identifies the eighth goddess as Narteśvarī (KS 119a).

18. The True Procedure of the Colors, Characteristics, and Signs of All Yoginīs

Now, moreover, I will explain the supreme state[1] of the ḍākinīs, whereby one correctly discerns the ḍākinīs who abide by the commitments.[2]

The woman who is reddish golden is redolent with the scent of lotus. Although her look is naturally placid, it is accompanied by an impassioned appearance. The woman whose fingernails are reddened, and likewise her eyes,[3] and who has drawn lotuses in her house, is one who is born into the clan of Padmanarteśvara.

She who has a trident between her eyebrows, and has a body which is dark blue and pale, is ever intent upon the Vajra clan. She should always honor the vajra drawn in her house. The vajraḍākinī born into Śrī Heruka's clan is known to appear with a trident[4] and also a spear on her forehead. Her eyes are red as well as reddish-yellow,[5] and her feet and hands are likewise red. She constantly exhibits affection for and is intent upon a goat or a chicken, and she always worships the vajra sign in her house. There is no doubt that she is a ḍākinī born into Śrī Heruka's clan.

---

[1] The CS mss. read *paramaṁ padaṁ*, emended by Bhavabhaṭṭa to *paraṁ padaṁ* (Pandey 2002, 108), which corresponds to the Tibetan translation *mkha' 'gro mchog gi go 'phang* (PM 226b). Sumatikīrti's text, however, has *mkha' 'gro rnams kyi mtshan nyid ni* (SL 112b), which corresponds with the AU mss., which read *ḍākinīnāṁ tu lakṣanaṁ* (I 593a.1, J 214.3).

[2] The paragraph breaks in this chapter reflect the groupings of yoginī clans according to Tsong Khapa. See KS 119b–121b.

[3] Mardo omits the text that her eyes are reddened, and adds here that she "loves all men" (PM 227a: *de bzhin skye bo kun la brtse*). This text is unattested elsewhere.

[4] The AU mss. here read "lance" (H 133a.1, I 593a.3–4, J 214.6: *śūla*). The Tibetan translations, however, read "trident" (PM 227a, SL 113a, PG 331.2: *rtse gsum*), corresponding to the Sanskrit *triśūla*.

[5] The AU mss. read *raktākṣo gaurā ca* (H 133a.1, I 593a.4; J 214.6: *raktākṣau*), which is apparently a defective line missing two syllables. The Tibetan translation (PM 227a, SL 113a: *mig dmar mdog ni dmar ser yang*) suggests an emendation, namely *raktākṣ[ī] [rakta]gaurā ca.*

On her forehead or hand a wheel is visible. Swarthy as a [rain] cloud, she always wears a silk headband. She is a woman of perfected good fortune and exemplary virtue.[6] The wheel drawn in her house is constantly worshipped. She is a ḍākinī born into Vajravārāhī's clan, and is proud of her power. She is dark as black kohl, and buck-toothed.[7] She is constantly cruel, contrarian,[8] and courageous. She always takes pleasure in bathing, and is not one of many words. The auspicious vajra drawn in her house is constantly worshipped. She who is born in Vajravārāhī's clan is [one of] the fifteen thousand.[9]

She is yellow like gold, and hairy, with unmoving eyes.[10] On her forehead or hand a vajra is visible. She always maintains a state of royalty, and she is haughty and truthful. She is scented with jasmine perfume. The great vajra in her house is continuously worshipped. She is a supreme lady of great yogins,[11] born into Khaṇḍarohā's clan.

She is ever fond of meat, is lean, and has the color of black kohl. She has the form of a lance on her forehead, and takes delight in cruel deeds. She always goes to the charnel ground, and she is fearless and free of disgust.[12]

---

[6] That is, *sādhvī paratarā* (Pandey 2002, 110), correctly translated by Sumatikīrti (SL 113a: *mchog tu bden pa*). Mardo reads here that she has "exemplary happiness" (PM 227a: *mchog tu bde ba*), which may represent a very old misprint.

[7] The Tibetan translations add that her teeth are white (PM 227a, SL 113a, PG 331.3). The Sanskrit preserved in the AU mss. omits this information.

[8] The Sanskrit reads merely *vāmā*, which Bhavabhaṭṭa glosses as "she delights in illicit affairs" (Pandey 2002, 110: *vāmeti asatpade ratā*).

[9] Bhavabhaṭṭa explains that "**fifteen thousand** refers to the fifteen thousand yoginīs" (Pandey 2002, 110: *sahasrāṇi daśapañcakam iti pañcadaśasahasrāṇi yoginya ityarthaḥ*).

[10] All of the Tibetan translations agree that she has "unmoving eyes" (PM 227a, SL 113a, PG 331.3: *mig mi g-yo*). The AU mss., however, give the variant reading *tathārūpīkṣī* (I 293a.7; J 215.4: *tathārūpikṣī*).

[11] The Sanskrit here reads *mahāyogīśvarī parā*, literally "supreme lady of great yogins." The Tibetan translations, however, read *rnal 'byor ma yi dbang phyug mchog*, "supreme lady of great yoginīs" (PM 227a; SL 113b).

[12] This translates *nirghṛṇā* (H 133b.3), which can mean "cruel" or "ruthless," but which also means "free of aversion or disgust." The Tibetan translations are not particularly clear here, but seem to point to the latter interpretation. Mardo's revised translation reads *rtsog med* (PM 227b), which Tsong Khapa glosses as *btsog med*, "free of filth" (KS 121a). Pandey also notes that Mardo's text reads *rtog med*, "free of conceptual thought," in some editions (2002, 427). However, Mal and Sumatikīrti read "free of purity" (PG 331.4: *gtsang sbra med*;

She has a lance on her forehead,[13] and the skull drawn in her house is worshipped. She is a ḍākinī born into the clan of the deity Śrī Heruka.

She is a woman who is cloud-colored and has uneven teeth. She always [delights in] cruel deeds, and bares her left incisors. The axe drawn in her house is always worshipped. Have no doubt that she is a ḍākinī born in Vināyaka's clan.[14] These characteristic[s] of the troop of ḍākinīs born into Heruka's clan[15] were stated for the sake of benefiting the adepts.

SL 113b: *gtsang med*). The idea, perhaps, is that she is free of conceptions of purity and impurity, i.e., free of aversion or disgust.

[13] This translates the Sanskrit preserved in the AU mss., namely *yasyā lalāṭe śūlaṁ* (H 133b.3, I 593b.1, J 215.6–7). However, the Tibetan translations all indicate here that she has a "drop" (*thig le*) on her forehead (PM 227b, SL 113b, PG 331.4). I follow the former for it merely has the fault of being repetitive, while the latter has the fault of contradicting the previous assertion that she has a lance drawn on her forehead.

[14] Literally meaning "remover," *vināyaka* is a name of Gaṇeśa. Bhavabhaṭṭa comments that Vināyaka refers to Vighnāri, "foe of obstacles" (Pandey 2002, 110), which is another name for Gaṇeśa. Vighnāri or Vighnāntaka is also a tantric Buddhist deity usually depicted as trampling Gaṇeśa. See Heller 2001. Bu-ston comments that *vināyakakulodbhūtā* means one born into the clan of the Vināyaka Samvara (NS 139a: *rnam par 'dren pa bde mchog gi rigs las byung ba'o*).

[15] According to Bhavabhaṭṭa, the text here, *ḍākinīgaṇasya herukakulodbhavā*, is incorrectly declined. He glosses *herukakulodbhavā* as *herukakulasambhavasya*, declining it with *ḍākinīgaṇasya* (Pandey 2002, 111).

19. The Procedure of Pointing Out the Gestures of the Yoginīs

Furthermore, I will explain the defining marks of the lāmās, through which the adept can recognize their actual physical characteristics.[1] Her face appears round,[2] and she has long, hairy eyebrows on her ever-bearded face. She is well dressed, clean, gentle, imperturbable, and truthful, and always delights in the true Dharma. She should be known as a sister of the heroes. The lotus gesture[3] should be presented, or perhaps the turtle gesture.[4] It is

---

[1] The first seven verses of this chapter are missing in the CS mss. due to a missing folio, but the Sanskrit can be restored using the parallel passage in the AU and quotations in the commentaries of Jayabhadra and Bhavabhaṭṭa. The Sanskrit preserved in these sources for this verse reads *ataḥ paraṁ pravakṣāmi lāmānāṁ tu lakṣanam / samyagaṅgāvayavaṁ sādhakaḥ /.* On the basis of the Tibetan translation, Pandey adds *jānīyād yena* before *sādhakaḥ* (2002, 112). I also follow the Tibetan here in translating this additional text.

[2] Pandey adds here the term *vistīrṇaṁ* (2002, 112), on the basis of Mardo's translation *yongs rgyas par* (PM 227b). This addition appears unwarranted as it is not attested elsewhere.

[3] Vīravajra describes the *padmamudrā* as follows: "As for the hand gestures, the yogin binds together the thumbs and little fingers, and extends [the other] fingers [around them]; this is **the lotus gesture**" (PD 397b). Kambala gives a complementary description: "Regarding **the lotus gesture**, both hands are presented [as if] surrounding a lotus" (SN 38a). Bhavabhaṭṭa describes it succinctly as follows: "curling the fingers toward the palm is the **lotus gesture**" (Pandey 2002, 112: *añjaligatāṅgulikuñcanāt padmamudrā*).

[4] Three seemingly divergent explanations of the *kūrmamudrā* are given by our commentators. According to Vīravajra: "The yogin sets his left hand face downward (*kha spub tu byas pa* [presumably meaning with the palm facing downward]), and covers it with his right hand, placing the right fingers between the left fingers; this is **the turtle gesture**" (PD 397b, 398a). This appears to describe a gesture in which, with both palms face downward, the right hand is placed over the left, and the fingers are intertwined. Bhavabhaṭṭa writes: "Spread out and raise one's right hand; the left, contracted, should be placed on top of it; this is the **turtle gesture**" (Pandey 2002, 112: *dakṣiṇaṁ hastaṁ prasāryoddhṛtāṁ kṛtya ca tadupari vāmaṁ cākuñcitaṁ sthāpayed iti kūrmamudrā*). This is similar to the above, but reverses the placement of the hands, and does not call for the intertwining of the fingers. Kambala, however, describes it as follows: "**The turtle gesture** is joining the palms of both hands" (SN 38a). I am inclined to accept the former explanations, since they better approximate a turtle, and also because the *mudrā* Kambala describes sounds more like the better known *añjalimudrā.*

held that [displaying] an antelope hide or a water-vessel is her counter gesture.[5] The tenth is her lunar day, and a lotus is drawn in her house. This is characteristic of women[6] who are lāmās.

She has prominent lips and large, reddish yellow eyes. She is wealthy, fortunate, and auspicious, and yellow like the campaka flower. Her fangs are neither too long nor too short.[7] She prefers variegated clothing. On her forehead are three lines reaching up toward the part of her hair. She laughs and is pleased, seizes the road and stays [there].[8] She always takes delight in tales of death in battle.[9] Seeing such a wanton one, display the lance gesture and exhibit the dance in which the left foot is drawn up.[10] It is held that turning to the left is her counter gesture. The eighth and fourteenth lunar

[5] Vīravajra clarifies these obscure counter gestures as follows: "The yoginī, in response to the lotus gesture, forms the antelope gesture, [also known as] the Avalokiteśvara gesture, which is placing the left fist over the left breast. In response to the turtle gesture, she places the vajra fist over her knee; this is the Maitreya gesture." (PD 398a)

[6] The AU mss. here read *striyānāṁ* (H 134a.3, I 593b.5, J 216.5–6), "of women," in an unconventional declension, and this reading is supported by the Tibetan translations *bud med rnams kyi* (PM 227b; SL 114a: *bud med kyi*). Bhavabhaṭṭa gives the variant *śriyānāṁ*, "of the glories," which Pandey accepts (2002, 113); but this makes less sense, and is unattested elsewhere.

[7] This translates the text preserved in the AU, *dīrghādīrghakarālā ca* (I 593b.5, J 216.6; H 134a.3: *dīrghādīrghau karālā ca*). The term *karālā* means "terrible" or "dreadful," but it primarily refers to fearsome teeth or fangs, from its root meaning "gaping, cleaving." This reading is attested in two of the Tibetan translations (SL 114a: *mche ba ring min thung ba min*; PG 332.2: *mche ba ring min thung ba min pa dang*). Pandey's edition refers to the AU, but apparently misreads this line as *dīrghādīrghakarā*; it rejects this reading and instead "restores" the Sanskrit from Mardo's revised translation, which omits *mche ba*, resulting in the text *nādīrghā nātidīrghā* (2002,113).

[8] This passage (*mārgam ākramya tiṣṭhati*) is difficult to interpret. It could simply mean that she "treads upon the road and stays [there]," perhaps meaning that she is peripatetic, continually traveling and periodically stopping at places along the way. The Tibetans, however, translated *ākramya* as *rnam par gnon pa*, suggesting that they interpreted the term in its sense of "to seize, attack, or invade." Sachen comments that "when she meets a man traveling on the road, she seizes and obstructs him" (PG 332.2), suggesting banditry or worse. This seems to accord with her martial character, indicated by the text which follows.

[9] Here I follow the Tibetan (PM 227b: */g-yul du 'chi ba rnams kyi ni/ /gtam dag la ni rtag tu dga'/*). However, the Sanskrit *saṁgrāme mṛtakānāṁ tu kathāsu ramate sadā* could also be read as "She always takes delight in battle and tales of death."

[10] According to Vīravajra, "The yogin extends his left forefinger, displaying the **lance gesture**, and displays the **dance** in which **the left foot is drawn up**" (PD 398a).

days are attributed to her. There is continual worship of the lance drawn in her house. This is characteristic of the Lokeśvarī lāmās.

Her cheeks appear ever sunken, and she is reddish golden and always has greenish yellow eyes. Her hair is curled and her head turbaned. She appears to have a single line extended across her brow. Moreover, she has a long neck and is tall,[11] and she always prefers red clothing. She laughs, sings, and also becomes instantly excited. Her mind wavers, and she is particularly attracted to quarrels. Seeing such a wanton one, display the spear gesture.[12] Then the second gesture, that of the bell,[13] should be eagerly presented. It is held that turning to the left is her counter gesture.

She is short with thick calves, always prefers yellow garments, and drapes cloth over her shoulders. Seeing such a wanton one, display the wheel gesture.[14] Then the second gesture, that of the conch,[15] should be eagerly presented. It is held that turning to the left is her counter gesture. The fourteenth is her day, and a vajra is drawn in her house. This is characteristic of the Śrī Herukī lāmās.[16]

---

[11] The Tibetan translations lack any text corresponding to *coccā* ("and is tall"); they also lack any alternate readings here.

[12] The CS mss. here read *vajraṁ śaktim vā mudrāṁ* ("vajra or spear gesture"), but the *vajra* is probably a later interpolation, unattested in the AU mss. or Tibetan translations. Regarding the spear gesture, Bhavabhaṭṭa comments that "one should brandish one's index finger, pressing all the other fingers with the thumb; this is the **spear gesture**" (Pandey 2002, 115: *aṅguṣṭhena śeṣasarvāṅgulisamākramaṇād ūrdhvīkṛtāṁ tarjanīṁ dhārayed iti śaktimudrā*). Vīravajra adds some additional information: "Extending the forefinger from the fist of the right hand is making the **spear gesture**" (PD 398a).

[13] Vīravajra explains: "Cupping the hand over the left knee is displaying the **bell gesture**" (PD 398a).

[14] The CS mss. here read *cakramudrāṁ*, a reading which is supported by the AU mss. (H 134b.6, I 594a.2, J 217.6) and the Tibetan translations (PM 228a, SL 114b: *'khor lo'i phyag rgya*). Pandey emends this to *mukhamudrā* ("mouth gesture") on the basis of Bhavabhaṭṭa's commentary (Pandey 2002, 114–15), but this is inappropriate as this reading is unattested elsewhere. According to Tsong Khapa, "one should display the **wheel gesture**, in which one joins the tips of the thumbs and forefingers, and 'opens,' i.e., extends, the other fingers" (KS 123a).

[15] According to Bhavabhaṭṭa, "one should contract the three fingers, the little finger, and so forth, of the left hand facing up, and join and then extend the index finger and thumb; this is the **conch gesture**" (Pandey 2002, 115: *uttānavāmakarakanīyasyādyaṅgulitrayaṁ saṁkocya tarjanyaṅguṣṭhau saṁyojya prasārayed iti śaṅkhamudrā*).

[16] That is, those who belong to Śrī Heruka's clan.

All of her limbs are hairy, and her eyes are dark yellow. She is dreadful,[17] deformed, and terrible, with a large mouth and large teeth.[18] She is black colored, and has a large lower lip,[19] sunken eyes, and a broken nose. Always conversant with the celestial musicians,[20] she is cloud-colored and charming. Seeing such a wanton one, display the serpent deity gesture.[21] The second gesture, that of the spear, should be presented eagerly. It is held that turning to the left is her counter gesture. The eleventh is her day, and a tusk is drawn in her house. This is characteristic of the Vajravārāhī lāmās.

---

[17] The Sanskrit here reads *karālā* (H 135a.2; I 594a.3, J 218.2: *karāla*; A, B, C: *karālī*). All of the Tibetan translations here read "thick" (PM 228a, SL 115a, PG 332.4: *sbom*), which may be due to contamination from the previous section.

[18] The CS mss. here read *sthūlāsyā sthūlavaktrā*, which is redundant as *āsya* and *vaktra* are more or less synonymous, meaning "mouth." The line is also metrically defective, missing one syllable. Pandey emends the line to *sthūlāsyā sthūlavaktrakā* to restore the meter, but this does not eliminate the redundancy (2002, 115). The AU mss., on the other hand, read *sthūlāsyā sthūlavaktrakajā* (J 218.2; I 594a.4: *-vaktrajāḥ*; H 135a.2: *-vaktragāḥ*), which eliminates the redundancy, since *vaktrajā* (lit. "that which arises in the mouth") means "teeth." While the Tibetan follows the CS reading (PM 228a: *kha che*), I believe that *sthūlavaktrajā* is the best reading here.

[19] The text here, *lamboṣṭhī*, is correctly translated by Sumatikīrti (SL 115a: *mchu 'phyang*), but rendered by Mardo as "hanging belly" (PM 228a: *gsus pa glo zhing*).

[20] This is a literal translation of *gandharvakuśalā*. The Tibetan translations are not literal here. Mardo reads "skilled in song" (PM 228a: *glu la mkhas pa*), while Sumatikīrti elaborates "she is a dancer with songs of the body(?)" (SL 115a: *lus kyi glu dang gar byed ma*).

[21] According to Bhavabhaṭṭa, to form the *nāgamudrā*: "One should raise the left hand, and place the right elbow upon it. Hold the right hand with the elevated thumb and forefinger, and contract the other three fingers. This is the **serpent deity gesture**." (Pandey 2002, 115: *vāmaṁ hastam uddhṛtīkṛtya tadupari dakṣiṇaṁ kaphoṇiṁ nidhāyāṅguṣṭhatarjanīsamutthāpanād aṅgulitrayam ākuñcya dakṣiṇahastaṁ dhārayed iti nāgamudrā*)

20. The Procedure of the Symbolic Hand Gestures of the Yoginīs

Now above all I will explain the left-handed signs, whereby one may discern one's true brothers and sisters. Should she show the left hand, it is to say "I salute [you]." Should she show her ring finger, it is to say the proper salutatory response. Should she slap her belly, it is to say "We are hungry." Should she show her brow, it is to say "I come from space." Should she place her finger in her mouth, that is to say "I am eating." Should she loll her tongue, this means "I have eaten."

Should she touch her knee, that is to say "I am exhausted." Should she touch her fingertips, that is to say "I have rested." Should she gnash her teeth, that is to say "I am eating flesh."[1] Should she show a frown, that is to say "I am bound." If she displays the "eagle" (*garuḍa*),[2] this is to say "I am free." If she shows a fist, display the trident (*paṭṭiśa*)[3] to her. If she indicates her hair, gaze with a strange [expression].[4] If she displays her fingernail, show her your khatvanga staff.[5]

---

[1] The CS mss. are corrupt here due to the fraying of ms. A, but the AU mss. here read *māṁsaṁ bhakṣayāmi* (H 135b.3, I 594a.9, J 219.2). Mardo's translation only attests *bhakṣayāmi* (PM 228b: *bza'yi*), but Mal and Sumatikīrti's translations also attest *māṁsaṁ* (PG 333.2: *sha za'o*; SL 115b: *sha za ba*). *Śāśvatavajra glosses *māṁsaṁ bhakṣayāmi* as the fiendish threat "I will eat your flesh" (TV 295a).

[2] According to Jayabhadra: "**If she displays the 'eagle'**" means that she repeatedly moves about, i.e., shakes, both of her arms which are bent in the manner of wings" (E 25a.1–2: *garuḍa[ṁ] darśayet yā [t]v iti pakṣāk[ā]reṇa vakrīkṛtabāhudvayo para[ṁ]paraṁ vidhūn[o]ti kampanta ityarthaḥ*). According to Bhavabhaṭṭa, "*garuḍa* is the tip of the nose" (Pandey 2002, 117: *garuḍam iti nāsikāgram*), but this seems less likely to me, given the association of the *garuḍa* with the movement of the arms evidenced in the commentaries on ch. 9, and also given the common association of freedom with the flight of birds.

[3] According to Bhavabhaṭṭa the "**trident** [gesture] involves indicating the forehead, bound with a hero's cloth, with one's left hand" (Pandey 2002, 117: *paṭṭiśam iti vīrapaṭabandhākāreṇa vāmahastaṁ lalāṭe darśayet*). Tsong Khapa states that it involves "touching three fingers to one's forehead, in the manner of a skull" (KS 124b).

[4] This translates the Sanskrit *keśān darśayed yā tu vikṛtaṁ ca nirīkṣayet*, which occurs in both the CS and AU mss. (H 135b.5, I 594b.1–2, J 219.4). This order is evidenced in Sumati-

Display [the gesture of] two fangs[6] to her who shakes her limbs. If she indicates one hand with the [other] hand, this is to say "The sacrificial cake should be eaten." If she shows her right hand, it is to say "Do thus!" She touches her ear so as to say "Stay." If she touches her fingernail with her fingernails, it is to say "The corpse is being conducted [here]."[7] If she scratches the earth, it is to say "Today I will enter the maṇḍala."[8]

If she touches her chin,[9] it is to say "Protect my son."[10] If she scratches the earth with her left thumb, it means "The elder protects me."[11] If she

kīrti's translation (SL 115b: *skra ston pa ni rnam par khro*), but it is reversed in Mardo's, which also connects it with the response of displaying the khatvanga staff (PM 228b: *rnam par 'gyur ba bltas nas ni // gang zhig skra ni ston pa la // kha tvāṁ ga ni de la bstan*). Mal follows the order of the Sanskrit, but has no equivalent to *vikṛtaṁ ca nirīkṣayet* (PG 333.2). Bhavabhaṭṭa explains that this means "gazing with a frown" (Pandey 2002, 117: *vikṛtaṁ ceti bhṛkuṭyā nirīkṣaṇasya vikṛtatvam*).

[5] The Tibetan translations and the AU mss. omit the yoginī's sign of displaying the fingernail (*nakhaṁ darśayed yā tu*) but do give the yogin's countersign that follows. Bu-ston, however, notes that this line occurs "in two [versions] of the Indian text" (NS 143a).

[6] According to Bhavabhaṭṭa, "one should place two Vajra fists by both sides of the mouth, raising up both little fingers, [making] **two fangs**, i.e., the gesture of two fangs" (Pandey 2002, 117: *kanīyasīdvayam ucchrity āsyabandhadvaye vajramuṣṭidvayaṁ nyased iti daṁṣṭrādvayaṁ dve daṁṣṭre yasyāḥ sā dvidaṁṣṭrā mudrā*). The "vajra fist" is a fist made by bending both the thumb and forefinger, touching the tip of the forefinger to the thumb's knuckle, and grasping the top joint of the thumb with the other three fingers.

[7] This translates my reading of the Sanskrit in the CS mss. Ms. A is damaged here, missing two syllables, reading *mṛta nīyate x x ktaṁ bhavati*. Pandey reconstructs this as *mṛtā nīyatety uktaṁ bhavati*, but this accounts for only one of the missing syllables. I read here *mṛto nīyate ity uktaṁ bhavati*, which accounts for the extra missing syllable (the failure to take *sandhi* into account is a common error). This reading seems to correspond to Mardo's translation, although Mardo strangely reads "corpse" in the instrumental case (PM 228b: *shi yis khyer*). The AU mss. read here "Death is certain" (H 135b.7, I 594b.3, J 219.6: *mṛtyo[r] niyatam*). This reading is supported by Mal's translation (PG 333.3: *shi bar nges*). Sumatikīrti's translation may be a garbled version of this (SL 115b: *'chi bar brjod par 'gyur*).

[8] According to Jayabhadra, "**maṇḍala** means an assembly of the committed" (D 33b.7, E 25a.2: *maṇḍalam iti samayimelāpaka ityarthaḥ*).

[9] This translates the Sanskrit *cibukaṁ*, attested in Mal's translation (PG 333.3: *kos ko*). Sumatikīrti's translation reads *ko sko*, a variant spelling of the term *kos ko*, "chin" (SL 115b). Mardo, however, reads "breast" here (PM 228b: *nu ma*).

[10] The Sanskrit here, *putro me rakṣitavyam*, is improperly declined in all mss., but would translate thus if declined *putro me rakṣitavyaḥ*.

opens her eyes, she would be saying "Do thus!" Should she scratch her knuckles,[12] this means "Lying in bliss." Any of these whatsoever may be displayed for the messengers.

---

[11] The Sanskrit here, as above, is improperly declined as *gurujano me rakṣitavyam*. The Tibetan translates this line as "the elder protects me" (PM 228a: *bla ma'i skye bos nga srungs*). This actually corresponds to the reading in the AU mss., which is *gurujano me rakṣati* (I 594b.4, J 220.1). This not only makes more sense, but it is also likely the original reading. I suspect that the text *gurujano me rakṣitavyam* reflects influence from the previous line.

[12] The CS mss. here read "should she lick her knuckles" (*parvāṇi lehayed yā tu*). Mardo and Mal here read "touch" rather than "lick" (PM 229a, PG 333.3: *reg pa*). The AU mss. here read the variant *lekhayed* (I 594b.5; H omits; J 220.2: *leṣayed*)—literally meaning "should cause to scratch," although the causative sense may not be implied here—which would roughly correspond to the Tibetan *reg pa*. Bu-ston indicates that *'bri bar byed pa* (a literal translation of *lekhayed*) is the equivalent reading here (NS 143b), indicating that *reg pa* is an interpretive translation.

21. The Procedure of the Characteristics of the Visual Body Gestures

Next I will explain the characteristic[s] that are the great secret of vision. One should show one's head to the woman who touches her crown. One should show one's cheek to her who shows her forehead. One should show one's tongue to her who shows her tooth. If she displays her lips, show her [one's] chin.[1] Show [one's] belly to her who touches her neck. If she shows her hands, show her one's forearm. Point out the earth[2] to her who displays her buttocks.[3] Should she display her breasts, show her one's chin. Show one's navel to her who shows her belly.

Should she display her secret,[4] show her one's penis. One should show one's anus to her who shows her thigh. If she displays her knee, show her one's shank. Display the sole of one's foot to her who displays her feet. Should she show her finger,[5] show her one's fingernail. Should she point to the earth, point out the sky to her. Point out the sun to her who indicates

[1] While this sentence follows the same grammatical pattern as the others, in this and several other instances below I translate the relative clause as a conditional clause in order to relieve somewhat the passage's repetitiveness.

[2] The Sanskrit texts here all read *pṛthvīṁ*, which Bhavabhaṭṭa explains refers to the "earth touching gesture" (Pandey 2002, 119: *bhūsparśamudrā*), the gesture in which, in seated position, one rests one's upper right arm on one's right knee and touches the ground with the tip of one's fingers. The Tibetan texts indicate that it is the back (*rgyab*, *pṛṣṭhaṁ*) that is indicated here, which very well may represent a genuine textual variant.

[3] The Sanskrit here, *trikaṭikā*, is a bit obscure; *kaṭi* or *kaṭikā* refer to the hips or buttocks, but the prefix *tri* (three, triple) makes the referent obscure. According to Bhavabhaṭṭa, "*trikaṭikām* is a [textual] difficulty connected to the two buttocks" (Pandey 2002, 119: *trikaṭikām iti sphigdvayasambandhigranthiḥ*). The Tibetans translated this literally as "triple waist" (PM 229a: *sum rked*) and "waist" (SL 116a: *bsked pa*).

[4] This, as Bhavabhaṭṭa informs us, is her *dharmodaya* (Pandey 2002, 119), which he identified with the vulva (*bhaga*) in the context of ch. 5 above.

[5] The Tibetan translations here read *sor tshigs*, "finger joint."

the sky. If she indicates a river,[6] point out the ocean[7] to her. Have no doubt here regarding the ḍākinīs' body gestures; with them one should always display the true vision, [to which] the secret ones[8] proceed.

[6] Bhavabhaṭṭa explains that this is the "**river** gesture, which is gesturing with the hand in the air in the shape of a river" (Pandey 2002, 119: *hastenākāśe nadyākāreṇa rekhādānābhinayā nadīmudrā*).

[7] According to Bhavabhaṭṭa, this is the "**ocean** gesture, [which is made] with the two hands fluttering in space" (Pandey 2002, 119: *ākāśe vepamānena hastadvayena samudramudrā*).

[8] According to Jayabhadra, the "secret ones" (*guhyakā*) are the yoginīs, which is fascinating since this is a term for the *yakṣa* class of spirits (E 25a.4–5: *gukhyakā iti yoginyaḥ*). This term was mistranslated by the Tibetans as "secret" (PM 226a: *gsang ba*). This final verse was omitted in Sumatikīrti's text.

22. The Procedure of the Characteristics of the Distinctive Limb Gestures

Furthermore, I will explain the distinct limb gestures,[1] whereby one's brother or sister may be recognized, without doubt.[2] If she shows one finger, it is to say "Welcome." As for showing two fingers,[3] this is to say "[You are] truly welcome." These are famed as the gestures of the limbs of all yoginīs.[4] One should know the eye gesture, [in which] the finger[s] of both [hands] are shown,[5] and the forefinger is somewhat bent.[6] She to whom the mantrin

---

[1] The CS mss. can be read here as *ataḥ paraṁ pravakṣyāmi aṅgamudrāviśeṣataḥ*, which I have translated above, or as …*aṅgamudrā[ḥ] viśeṣataḥ*, which would be translated as: "Furthermore, I will explain above all the limb gestures." I follow Kambala in choosing the former reading, as the Tibetan translation of his commentary clearly indicates the compound here (SN 38b: *yan lag phyag rgya'i khyad par ni*). Bhavabhaṭṭa attests this reading, but also states that there is an additional text which reads here *athātaḥ saṁpravakṣyāmy aṅgamudrā yathāvidhiḥ* (Pandey 2002, 121). The term *yathāvidhiḥ* occurs in the AU mss. (I 595a.2, J 221.3), and also in one of the Tibetan translations (PM 229a: *cho ga bzhin*), while another points to both (SL 116a–b: *yan lag ji bzhin phyag rgya mchog*). This reading is also viable, translated as: "Further, I will explain the limb gestures in accordance with the procedure."

[2] The CS mss. are corrupt here, reading *yena vijñāyate bhrāta bhagiṁ vā viśeṣataḥ*. A better text is preserved in the AU mss., namely *yena vijñāyate bhrātā bhaginī vā na saṁśayaḥ* (I 595a.2, J 221.3). I believe that the second *viśeṣataḥ* here is an erroneous substitution based upon the preceding line. The Tibetan translations both attest *na saṁśayaḥ* (PM 229a: *the tshom med 'gyur ba'o*; SL 116b: *the tshom med ba'o*).

[3] According to Bhavabhaṭṭa, it is the index and middle fingers that are shown (Pandey 2002, 121: *tarjanīmadhyamayor darśanena*).

[4] The CS mss. here read *etā sarvayoginyaḥ aṅgamudrāprakīrtitāḥ*, which is supported by the Tibetan translations (PM 229a, SL 116b). In place of *etā sarvayoginyaḥ*, AU ms. I reads *mudrā pātraṁgīnāṁ* (I 595a.3), and ms. J reads *mudrātaṁ yoginīnāṁ* (J 221.4), both of which appear to be corrupt readings.

[5] At this point the CS ms. is missing five folia. The following is derived from the parallel passage in the AU and from the commentaries, in consultation with the Tibetan translations. Significant variants will be noted as they occur.

[6] Bhavabhaṭṭa comments here: "The **eye gesture should be known** as that gesture in which one should indicate with—i.e., form a pointer with—the middle and index fingers of both hands. The remaining fingers are contracted, and the index fingers bent slightly." (Pandey

shows this will instantly come under his control for as long as he lives, have no doubt.[7]

Should she show a middle finger, show her a forefinger. If she displays her ring finger, show her one's tongue. If she shows the trident [gesture], present to her the lance [gesture].[8] Should she display her head, show her the part of one's hair. If she points to the ground, show her one's mouth.[9] Should she frown, indicate the part of one's hair. If she shows her teeth, show her one's lips. [If she shows her neck, show her one's mouth.][10] If she shows her forehead, show her one's eye. These are proclaimed to be the gestures of the limbs of all yoginīs; with them one should display the true vision, [to which] the secret ones proceed.

2002, 121: *dvābhyāṁ jyeṣṭhātarjanībhyāṁ hastadvayagatābhyāṁ sūcyaṁ sūcīkṛtvā śeṣāṅgulisaṁkoce kiṁcit kuñcitā tarjanī yasyāṁ sā tathā mudrā tāṁ netramudrāṁ vijānīyāt*) This translation follows the Sanskrit in the AU mss. (I 595a.3, J 221.4–5), Bhavabhaṭṭa's commentary, and Sumatikīrti's translation (SL 116b). Mardo's instructions for the gesture differ slightly, reading "the left middle finger is extended, and the forefinger contracted slightly" (PM 229b: *g-yon gyi gung mo brkyang pa la // cung zad mdzub mo bskum pa ni*).

[7] Bhavabhaṭṭa's commentary adds an additional line here: *mudrā potaṅginīnāṁ yāvajjīvaṁ na saṁśayaḥ* (Pandey 2002, 122). This likely reflects a genuine textual variant, but I have not included it in my translation, as it is unattested elsewhere, it is repetitive, and it is seemingly defective. As noted above (p. 248 n. 4), the text *mudrā pātraṁgīnāṁ* does occur in one AU ms. (I 595a.3), although not at this point in the text.

[8] This translation is based upon Jayabhadra's commentary: "The **trident** [gesture is made with one's fingers] on the forehead in the shape of a trident. **Present** [to her] the **lance** [gesture] —i.e. touching little finger and thumb—with the three remaining fingers in the shape of a lance." (E 25a.3–4: *paṭṭiśam iti lalāṭe paṭṭiśākāreṇa / śūlam iti kaniṣṭhāṅguṣṭhābhyāṁ sparśena śeṣāṅgulitrayaṁ śūlākāreṇa darśayet*)

[9] The AU mss. here read *medinīṁ darśayed yā tu vaktraṁ tasyāḥ pradarśayet* (H 137a.3, I 595a.5; J omits). Mardo's translation, however, reads "If she points to the ground, indicate the sky" (PM 229b: */ gang zhig sa ni ston byed pa // de la mkha' ni bstan par bya /*); but Sumatikīrti's translation supports the Sanskrit reading (SL 116b: */ gang zhig svo ni ston byed pa // de la kha ni bstan par bya*). Although *svo* may be erroneous, *kha* corresponds directly with Sankrit *vaktra*. While Mardo's translation may represent a genuine textual variant, I suspect that *mkha'* may be an erroneous substitution for *kha*, perhaps under the influence of the similar passage in ch. 21 above (*bhūmiṁ pradarśayed yā tu ākāśaṁ tasyā pradarśayet*). Despite the preponderance of evidence in support of the *vaktra/kha* reading, Pandey emends the text to read *ākāśaṁ* here (2002, 122).

[10] This sentence is present in all of the Tibetan translations (PM 229b, SL 116b, AU 331b), but is not attested in the surviving Sanskrit texts.

23. The Procedure of the Characteristics of the Ḍākinīs' Signs and Insignia

Now I will explain the ḍākinīs' characteristic[s] whereby the heroes recognize their heroic sister from afar.[1] The devoted woman who is pleased with him[2] should be enjoyed by the hero, [like] the earth.[3] Taking her as one's support and ground, worship the binding in union[4] (*yogasamvara*).[5]

---

[1] The AU mss. read *ataḥ paraṁ pravakṣāmi ḍākinīnāṁ tu lakṣaṇaṁ / jñāyate dūrato yena vīrāṇāṁ vīrabhaginī //* (H 137a.5–6, I 595a.7, J 222.3). The first *pada* is attested by Sumatikīrti (SL 116b: *de nas gzhan yang*), but Bhavabhaṭṭa gives the alternate text *athā[taḥ] sampravakṣāmi* (Pandey 2002, 123), attested by Mardo (PM 229b: *de nas yang dag bshad bya ba*). For the second *pada* Mardo and Sumatikīrti both read "play of the ḍākinīs" (PM 229b: *mkha' 'gro ma yi rnam rol pa*; SL 116b: *mkha' 'gro ma yi rnam rol ni*). This reading, however, is unattested elsewhere, while *lakṣaṇa* is attested by several of the commentators (RG 295b, TV 296a, PD 400a). The expression *vīrāṇāṁ vīrabhaginī* in the fourth *pada* is ambiguous; I have followed Bhavabhaṭṭa's gloss of *vīrāṇāṁ* as *vīrair*. Sumatikīrti supports this interpretation (SL 117a: *dpa' bo yis*), but there is no support for Mardo's translation *dpa' mo* (PM 229b).

[2] Jayabhadra's commentary here appears to read: "**The devoted woman who is pleased with him** is the hero's yoginī who is the outer, physical goddess loved by that adept with all things, and who is not in another's power and does not know another man." The Sanskrit of Jayabhadra's commentary here is corrupt; my tentative reading, made in consultation with the Tibetan translation (MP 56a) is as follows: *anuraktā samayī yasyeti / yasya sādhakasya bāhyāṅga-devatā sarvabhāvena sneh[ā] 'parvaśā 'nyapuruṣ[ā]jñānā vīrasya tasya yogin[ī] /* (E 25a.5–6).

[3] This line is clarified via recourse to the commentaries. Bhavabhaṭṭa, for example, writes in a somewhat clearer fashion that "The **devoted woman**, i.e., the yoginī who has the general commitments, who is pleased with a yogin **should be enjoyed by the hero, [like] the earth**. The hero is a champion; his is the hero's enjoyment. The earth is that which holds wealth and treasures. This means that, having seized the earth full of treasure, it is enjoyed by him." (Pandey 2002, 123: *samayinī samānasamayā yoginī saṁtuṣṭā yoginas tasya vīrabhogyā vasuṁdharā syāt / vīraḥ subhaṭas tasyaiva bhogyā vīrabhogyā / vasūni ratnāni dhārayatīti vasuṁdharā / ākramya ratnapūrṇā pṛthvī tena bhujyata iti bhāvaḥ*).

[4] Vīravajra provides a richer explanation, as follows:

> The phrase **the devoted woman who is pleased with him** indicates the procedure for propitiating the yoginī. The devoted yoginī is the charming one who is loved. How is she propitiated? The phrase **should be enjoyed by the hero, [like] the earth** [shows that she] is the *karmamudrā* who is the ground which gives rise to the harvest of meditative states and concentrations. As it says in the *Samayoga*,

> "The magic of women is much greater than all [other] magic" [JS 151a]. Regarding **taking her as one's support and ground**, she is taken as the basis through the bestowal of the monastic and bodhisattva vows (*samvara*) and the mantric commitments. Then **worship the binding** (*samvara*) of the wheels of the yogin's body. (PD 400a–b)

According to Jayabhadra: "The **ground** is the goddess well-trained in tantra and mantra. **Taking her as one's support**, one should **worship the binding in union**, i.e., the *mahāmudrā-yoga.*" (E 25b.1–2: *medinī tantramantrasuśikṣitāṁ devatām ādhāraṁ kṛtvā yogasamvaraṁ mahāmudrāyogaṁ yajet pūjayed ity artha*)

[5] It is difficult to determine the translation of the term *yogasamvara*, which might be rendered as "binding in union" or "supreme bliss in union." In settling on the former I follow the Tibetan translation, *sdom pa*. Both translations could be justified with reference to the commentary of Bhavabhaṭṭa, who explains it in terms of perfecting stage yogic practices:

> **Union** (*yoga*) is that by which art and wisdom, when they are not harmonized, are bound. *Sam* is bliss, regarding which there is the supreme bliss of union or **supreme bliss in union**, which one should worship. After the supreme joy (*paramānanda*), when one returns to the village of the sense powers from the sense objects, and depends upon that bliss alone that is solely mind, then one attains the joy of cessation, which is such in so far as the sense powers turn away from their objects. When that comes to an end, then one attains the natural joy (*sahajānanda*) which arises from and is completely filled with the bliss that abides in rapture, and is the reality of nonconceptual wisdom. One is realized through stabilizing the seminal essence within the jewel [i.e., the *maṇicakra*]; one needs the great instructions for the sake of self-realization. On account of this, the lotus feet of the reverend true guru should be pleased. Therefore, since one binds the conceptual mind, there is **binding**, which is natural joy. Through the **union** of art and wisdom there arises the gnosis which accords with both of these. One should know that it is from precious wisdom and art alone that there is born this priceless gnosis.

> *yogaḥ prajñopāyau vaiṣamyātmanaḥ samvṛṇoty aneneti saṁbandhaḥ / saṁ sukhaṁ yogasya samvaro yogasamvaras taṁ yajet / ādatte paramānandānantaraṁ viṣayebhya indriyagrāmo nivartate manomātraṁ sukhamātram ālambate yadā tadā viramānandaḥ / tataś ca viṣayebhya indriyavirāmo viramaḥ / tasyaiva paryantabhūto nirvikalpajñānasvarūpo niratiśayasukhaparipūrṇas tajjaś ca sahajānandas tam ādatta iti samudāyārthaḥ / sa ca maṇyantargatabodhicittasthirīkaraṇena pratīyamāno 'py upadeśaṁ mahān tam apekṣate svapratītaye / tadathaṁ sadgurubhaṭṭārakacaraṇakamalam eva prasannīkāryam / ataḥ saṁkalpātmanaḥ samvṛṇotīti samvaraḥ sahajānandaḥ / prajñopāyayogena tayor eva tādṛśaṁ jñānam udeti / yābhyāṁ jñānam amūlyaṁ jāyate tau prajñopāyāv eva ratnabhūtāv iti jñeyam /* (Pandey 2002, 123–124)

My translation "conceptual mind" follows the Tibetan (Pandey 2002, 462: *rnam par rtog pa'i yid*).

Gazing backward,[6] the alteration of her face, the knitting of her brow, and her unchanging countenance[7]—the various [indications][8] that thus arise from the ḍākinī should be quickly recognized.[9] Thrice lined and circular, they should be known through their turning and transformations.[10] The ḍākinīs, truly going, return in an instant.[11] One should recognize their sign.

[6] Bhavabhaṭṭa glosses the term *vilomataḥ/vilomena* as follows: "It is said that going against the grain (*vilomataḥ*) is a characteristic of the ḍākinīs. Abandoning looking forward, they gaze backward." (Pandey 2002, 124: *ḍākinīlakṣaṇam āha vilomeneti / pūro nirīkṣaṇaṁ vihāya paścānnirīkṣaṇaṁ vilomanirīkṣaṇam*) The reading *vilomataḥ* occurs in the AU mss. (H 137b.1, I 595a.8, J 222.4). This is preceded in Pandey's edition by the line *eṣāṁ hi ḍākinīnāṁ tu*, which appears to be a back translation from a line that occurs only in Mardo's translation (PM 229b: *'di dag rnal 'byor ma rnams kyi*), and is unattested elsewhere.

[7] This expression, *śāśvataṁ mukham*, is attested in two of the AU mss. (H 137b.1, I 595a.8) as well as in Bhavabhaṭṭa's commentary (at least in my reading). However, the other AU ms. reads *sukham* (J 222.5), a reading supported by the Tibetan CS translations. Pandey reads or emends Bhavabhaṭṭa's commentary to *sukham* (2002, 224). While *m* and *s* are very similar in Bhujimol and Nevārī scripts, the oldest ms. of Bhavabhaṭṭa's commentary, ms. F (82a.1), clearly reads *mukham*, as it lacks the "tail" hanging from the lower left portion of the character which distinguishes *s* from *m* in this variety of Bhujimol script, and ms. G (77a.3) even more clearly reads *mukham*. Both of these instances are distinct from the word *sukhaṁ* which occurs on the preceding folio of each ms. The Tibetan translation of the commentary (as well as all of the other commentaries except for one) attests *mukham* with the translation *rtag tu bzhin* (CP 198b). The reading *mukham* may make much more sense here, since the verse is listing the yoginī's facial indicators. However, "her unchanging countenance" seems to contradict the previous indication, "the alterations of her face." The *sukhaṁ* reading is also venerable. One commentator, Tathāgatarakṣita, does attest to *śāśvataṁ sukham*, "unchanging bliss," glossing it as "the reality (*tattva*) which indicates outer and inner great bliss" (UN 230a). This is thus an old alternate reading.

[8] That is, the signs or indications which are non-verbal, such as the previously listed facial indicators, as Bhavabhaṭṭa informs us (Pandey 2002, 224: *tatheti tathābhūtam avāggocaram ityarthaḥ*).

[9] According to Tsong Khapa, these facial indicators show that the yoginī is "pleased with" the yogin (KS 127b: *rjes su chags pa, anuraktā*), that is, favorably inclined toward him. Vīravajra interprets these signs as indicators of inner yogic processes, saying that they "indicate the time of joy" (PD 400b: *dga' ba'i dus mtshon pa yin no*).

[10] This very obscure text has given rise to speculation. Vīravajra informs us that the "outer interpretation" of this line is that it refers to circular lines drawn or marked on the yoginī's forehead (PD 400b). Tsong Khapa agrees with this placement, holding that they occur "at or on the *ūrṇā*" (KS 128a: *mdzod spu na*), i.e., at the swirl of hair between the eyebrows. Sachen, however, locates them elsewhere on the body, explaining that "it is said that above the navel of that ḍākinī are **three lines** that are like semi-circles, and thus are **circular**" (PG 334.4). Bhavabhaṭṭa does not specify a location, but merely interprets the entire line as indicating

the circularity of the lines, writing: "Thence **transformed**, those **three lines** that have the form of going and returning thus **turn**. Should one ask again, what is it is like, it is **circular**, because it is ring-shaped." (F 82a.4: *ato vikṛtāḥ tisro rekhā gamanāgamanarūpā ye te tathā āvartāḥ / punaḥ kīdṛśa ityāha parimaṇḍalā kuṇḍalāḥ*; cf. Pandey 2002, 124) For the "inner interpretation" of this and the following line, see Kambala's commentary below, which explains in terms of the inner anatomy of the subtle body (note that he does not comment upon the text *trirekhā parimaṇḍalā*, although his mention of "the three worlds" [*'jig rten gsum po*, **triloka*] may reflect an alternate reading [or a variant] of *trirekhā*). Sachen's placement of the lines (see above) may also reflect an inner yogic interpretation of this sott.

[11] Kambala gives an interpretation of this puzzling section in terms of internal yogic processes, as follows:

> Regarding **turning and transformations**, "turning" means reversing [the flow of] seminal essence in order to achieve perfected bliss. [This is done] by means of the yogic posture (*yantra*) which binds the life-force and vital energy, [drawing forth] the perfected great bliss and igniting [the fury fire] which blazes within the navel maṇḍala. The mantrin who inserts [these] into the empty central [channel] mixes together the three worlds. In that very instant, the conceptions and perceptions (*rtog tshor*) of self and other, and likewise earth, water, wind, fire, and space, are all not conceived. [They] **return in an instant,** i.e., one experiences bliss. (SN 39a, with the assistance of Devagupta's explanatory glosses at SS 109a–b)

Sachen cites Kambala's commentary, and then continues: "[They] **return in an instant** means that, having given rise to passion, they return to their previous forms and countenance" (PG 334.4).

First, the speech uttered [by her] is interrupted, and her mouth gapes,[12] opened in the shape of a vajra.[13] Then her voice is again always embellished with the tone of the cuckoo.[14] In her house there should be [the following] sign[s]: the form of a vajra, together with a mirror, and the form of a sword, together with a mirror. The flag-staff, [that is,] intercourse, should always

[12] This is a particularly perplexing passage. The AU mss. here read *prāguktārthasamarpaṇe*; while this is consistent with the AU translation (331b), it diverges from the sources concerning the CS. Most of the CS translations and commentaries attest two lines here dealing with her voice and mouth. Two lines to this effect are cited in Bhavabhaṭṭa's commentary, namely *nirarthakaṁ vacanaṁ khaṇḍitam* and *prāggirāṁ vadanakhaṇḍitaṁ* (Pandey 2002, 124). Pandey takes these as alternative readings, and accepts the latter on the authority of Mardo's revised translation, which has only one line here, namely *sngar bzhin gdong ni 'jig gyur pa* (PM 229b). Pandey makes up the extra line by back-translating from Tibetan another line present in this translation which is not attested elsewhere, namely *rnam pa de lta de yi de* (PM 229b). I, however, am not inclined to accept this back-translation; I would rather accept the latter line from Bhavabhaṭṭa that is also attested in multiple other sources. A close variant occurs in the translations of Sumatikīrti and Mal, where we read, respectively, *sngar tshig gi ni nyams pa yin* (SL 117a), and *sngar bshad tshig nyams pa* (PG 334.4), which diverge only in *sngar* (*bshad*), "previously uttered," which corresponds to the AU's *prāgukta*. Most of the commentaries do not comment on this line; two do, however, and they confirm the reading in Mal's and Sumatikīrti's texts. These include Tathāgatarakṣita's (UN 230a) and rTag-pa'i rDo-rje's (TV 297a) commentaries. On the basis of this evidence, I propose the emended text *prāguktagirāṁ khaṇḍitām*. Although *nirarthakaṁ vacanaṁ khaṇḍitam* ("her speech is interrupted, bereft of meaning") seems more meaningful to me, it is not possible to ignore the preponderance of evidence supporting *prāguktavacanaṁ khaṇḍitam*. This emendation makes Bhavabhaṭṭa's reading for the other line redundant; as a result, I adopt there the AU reading, *vadanaṁ ca khaṇḍitaṁ tasyā*, which corresponds exactly with Sumatikīrti's text, *de yi gdong ni 'jigs 'gyur ba* (SL 117a), as well as with Mal's (PG 334.4). What exactly does this mean? According to Tathāgatarakṣita, both of these lines indicate that she is hare-lipped (UN 230a). This reading, however, does not make much sense in the context of a description of the yoginīs' facial indications. It seems more likely that this text indicates a temporary transformation of her face and voice, rather than a permanent disability.

[13] The Sanskrit here reads *vajrākṛtir iva sphuṭam*, which I interpret as referring to her face (*vadana*) from the previous line. The Tibetan here translates *sphutaṁ* as "clear" (PM 229b, SL 117a, PG 335.1: *gsal ba*). The Tibetan translators may have been reading it in reference to *svara* in the following line, although it is difficult to see how a "voice" could have the "form of a vajra."

[14] This translates the Sanskrit *svaraḥ kokiladhvanivyaktaṁ tasyāḥ sadaiva hi*. The Tibetan translations are far less clear, translating *vyaktaṁ* as *lta bu* (PM 229b, SL 117a). The second line of each also reads *gsal ba*, which makes little sense here, although Sumatikīrti's text is closest to the Sanskrit (SL 117a: *gsal bar de ni rtag tu 'gyur*; PM 229b: *mchog tu gsal bar de'i de nyid*).

be known by means of a mirror.[15] These signs should be known [by him whose] form is accomplished.[16] She who is endowed with these characteristics should be recognized as being the supreme ḍākinī.

---

[15] The term *dhvajaśaktiḥ*—a compound of *dhvaja* (flag) and *śakti* (staff, spear, or power)—was taken by the commentators as referring to the conjoined (*saṁpuṭa*) male and female sexual organs. Jayabhadra rather cryptically comments here as follows: "**The flag-staff should always be known** refers to her power on that flag, i.e., the penis: this is **intercourse. By means of a mirror** means that the flag-staff is known, i.e., realized, by her gazing at a mirror incessantly." (E 25b.2–4: *dhvajaśaktiś ca jñāyate nityam iti / dhvaje liṅgaṁ tasmin śaktir yasyā iti saṁpuṭa darpaṇena jñeyam iti anavatara[ṁ] darpaṇa[ṁ] nir[ī]kṣamāṇayā tasyā dvajaśaktijñeyaṁ avaboddhavyam ityarthaḥ*) Kambala provides an abstract but poetic commentary on these implements, clearly associating them with meditative and yogic processes, as follows:

> **In [her] house**, and so forth, is easy to understand. In addition, [it refers to] the **vajra** inserted within the lotus: truly meditating on emptiness, everything is sky-like. Misknowledge, and so forth, are suddenly [seen to be] faults of conceptualization arising from conceptualization. The mind, naturally pure clear light, is regarded as **mirror**-like, and all things as if reflections. They are clear and pure like the sky. The **sword** cuts away the afflictions; it is very sharp in achieving the aims of sentient beings. Hoisting [them] by means of merit like a **flag**, the **staff** pierces the afflictions. The mind is one-pointed, and with its pinnacle of flame the yogin [undertakes] **intercourse** (*sampuṭa*), achieving bliss. [This] clarifies the symbolic implements. (SN 39a)

[16] I base this translation on Bhavabhaṭṭa's comments: "**These signs should be known** summarizes [the text above]. How is it that **with these,** and so forth, the yogin knows these things? It is said that his **form is accomplished**, i.e., it is he who is meditatively habituated to the nature of the ḍākinīs' marks." (Pandey 2002, 125: *jñeyāni cihnāny etāni ity upasaṁharati / ata āha ebhir ityādi / katham evaṁ bhūtāni tāni yogī jānātīty āha kṛtarūpo hi / yato 'bhyastaḍākinīcihnasvarūpaḥ saḥ /*)

24. The Procedure of the Symbolic Speech of the Four Classes

Now I will explain the secret signs [indicated] by means of an alternate language, through which a brother or sister is known by the adept, without a doubt.[1] *Potaṅgī* is the respectful salutation. *Pratipotaṅgī* is the respectful reply. *Gamu* means "I go," and *lumba* "I come." "Body" (*dehaṁ*) means "town,"[2] and *gṛhānaṁ* means "a wooden vessel" (*caṭuka*).[3] *Bīrāṇāṁ*[4] is the heart as well, and *kauravā* means death.[5] "Bell" (*ghaṇṭā*) means the

---

[1] The adept, *sādhako*, is presumably the logical subject of this act of knowing, but the term is incorrectly declined in the nominative, given the passive verb *jñāyate*. Mardo's revised translation, *sgrub po la* (PM 230a), reflects a different interpretation, taking it to be the indirect object of *pravakṣyāmi*.

[2] The word *dehaṁ* literally means "body." According to the Sanskrit preserved by Bhavabhaṭṭa, this means "town" (Pandey 2002, 127: *nagaraṁ*), a reading supported by Mardo's translation (PM 230a: *grong khyer*). While this line is not preserved in the AU mss. that I have consulted, both Sumatikīrti's revised translation and also the AU translation attest a variant, "eat!" (SL 117b: *zos*; AU 331b: *zas*).

[3] This follows the reading in the AU mss. (H 137b.6, I 595b.2–3; J 223.2: *catukam*) as well as Bhavabhaṭṭa's commentary (F 83a.6; G 78a.5: *caṭakam*). Pandey reads here *vaṭukam* (2002, 127), but this reading is not supported by the two mss. that I have consulted. They are omitted in Sumatikīrti's translation. Note also that the reading *gṛhānaṁ* is supported by all of the Sanskrit mss. but one (G 78a.5, H 137b.6, I 595b.2–3; J 223.2; F 83a.6: *gṛhāṇāṁ*). As above, these two terms are reversed in Mardo's translation (PM 230a). Mardo translates *gṛhānaṁ* as "take!" (*zung zhig*), apparently reading the imperative *gṛhāṇa*.

[4] There is significant variation here. Bhavabhaṭṭa attests *bīrāṇāṁ*, which is supported by the Tibetan transliterations *bīrāṇa* (PM 230a), *biraṇām* (SL 177b), and *piraṇaṁ* (AU 332a). The AU mss. read *dhāraṇaṁ* (I 595b.3, J 223.2; H 137b.6: *dhāraṇakaṁ*), and Bhavabhaṭṭa lists *kāraṇaṁ* as a variant (Pandey 2002, 127). One should note that this was mistakenly included in Pandey's edition along with *bīrāṇāṁ*, which they read as *vīrāṇāṁ* (2002, 126).

[5] This text, *kauravā māraṇaṁ*, is preserved in Bhavabhaṭṭa's commentary (Pandey 2002, 127). They are reversed in the AU mss. (H 138a.1, I 595b.3: *māraṇaṁ kauravā*; J 223.3: *māraṇaṁ kauraṁvā*), and the Tibetan translations follow suit, taking *māraṇaṁ* as code for *kauravā*. However, *kauravā* is not particularly meaningful; they translate it as "a bad or evil word/utterance" (PM 230a: *smra ngan*; SL 117b, AU 332a: *sgra ngan*), which may be a reading of *krūraravā*.

corolla [of the lotus],[6] and *ali* the "head."[7] *Karaṇa* means the belly, and *vārā-haṁ* hair.[8] *Śravaṇa* indicates the ears. [There are] "the place of ambrosia" (*amṛtasthāna*) and "the churning stick" (*manthāna*).[9]

"Encounter" (*samāgamaḥ*) designates a man, and "cover" (*tālikā*) the ḍākinīs. "Hell" (*narakaṁ*) means the maṇḍala, and "such and such" (*amu-kaṁ*) the charnel ground, and *kākhilā*[10] the gate. "Blow-hard" (*śvasana*)

[6] Once again, the Tibetan translations reverse the reading preserved in the Sanskrit, taking *karṇikā* as code for *ghaṇṭā*, bell.

[7] The Sanskrit here reads *śiro 'liḥ*, which according to the pattern thus far should mean that *śiro* is a code word for *ali*. Mardo's translation omits this line, but it is interpreted thus in Sumatikīrti's translation as well as the AU translation, both of which read "*śiro* means a falsehood" (SL 117b, AU 332a: *shi ro ni brdzun no*). This seems to be based upon a reading of *ali* as *alīka*. Bu-ston, however, takes the opposite interpretation, arguing that "*ali* designates the head" (NS 150b), an interpretation also followed by Tsong Khapa (KS 130a–b). This interpretation seems to make more sense, since the signified here seem to be largely body parts, coded by words that are often nonsensical.

[8] The Sanskrit occurs in the AU mss. as *karaṇam udara[m] vārāhaṁ keśaḥ* (H 138a.1, I 595b.3, J 223.3). The term *udaraṁ*, however, is omitted in Bhavabhaṭṭa's commentary; he equates *karaṇaṁ* with *varāhakeśa*, pig's hair (Pandey 2002, 127). This is also the reading taken in Mardo's translation. Sumatikīrti's text is a bit scrambled, equating *karaṇa* with "hair" and then just translating *varāha* as "pig" (SL 117b). Clearly, one version of the CS omitted *udaram*, but I believe that there was also another rendition which preserved it like the AU mss. This is attested in the other CS commentary (aside from Bhavabhaṭṭa's) which comments on this, namely Indrabhūti's. He wrote: "***kar[a]ṇa* means the belly**, meaning that it is the unelaborated, natural gnosis of the essence of the middle way which is reality itself. ***Vārā[ha]* is the hair**, meaning experiential unity in the various *samādhis* [states of concentration]." (IC 68a–b: */ karṇa ni lte ba ste / chos nyid dbu ma'i snying po sprod med lhan cig skyes pa'i ye shes su shes pa'o // pā rā ni sgra ste / sna tshogs du ma ting nge 'dzin du ro gcigs pa'o /*) I follow this latter line of interpretation because it makes more sense, preserving the trend of symbolically alluding to parts of the body.

[9] It is difficult to judge here which term is the signifier and which is the signified, as both are valid Sanskrit terms that can be read as euphemisms for the sexual organs. Tsong Khapa, unlike the SL translators but like the AU translators, takes *amṛtasthāna* to be the signifier here (KS 130a–b). Buston seemingly takes the opposite interpretation, writing "*manthāna* is the place of ambrosia, which signifies that the vajra rubs within the lotus, the place of ambrosia" (NS 150b). The pattern of the text seems to break down here, as *manthāna* and *amṛtasthāna* clearly signify complementary but distinct entities, the "vajra" and "lotus," or male and female sexual organs.

[10] The AU mss. read *kākhilā* (H 138a.2, I 595b.4, J 223.4), a reading supported by Mardo's translation (PM 230a). Bhavabhaṭṭa reads *kampilyā*, a reading supported by Sumatikīrti's translation (SL 117b).

indicates a brahmin,[11] and "enclosure" (*paridhi*)[12] the kshatriya. "Abstention" (*virati*)[13] designates the vaishya, "cruel" (*krūra*)[14] the shudra, and "outsider" (*antastha*)[15] the caṇḍāla. *Paṅgulikā*[16] indicates a house, and

[11] The word *śvasana* means "blowing, hissing, panting, breathing," and so forth, which calls to mind common caricatures of the brahmins. Since the term does seem to be used here humorously, I have translated it with the English term "blow-hard," which has similar humorous connotations.

[12] Literally meaning "enclosure, fence, protection," the term *paridhi* evokes the protective functions attributed to the kshatriya or warrior aristocracy.

[13] The association of the term *virati* ("resignation," "abstention," etc.) with the vaishya at first seems counter-intuitive, as they are usually associated with abundance and wealth. They are also, however, considered "food" for the "eaters" of the higher classes, the brahmins and kshatriyas. In other words, they are producers of food and wealth for others, and are thus expected to abstain from enjoying the fruits of their labor. See Smith 1994, 46–48.

[14] A word with many meanings, ranging from "wounded" to "cruel," "fierce," "harsh," and "inauspicious," it is not difficult to see the reason for the association of the term *krūra* with the shudras, the "servant" class excluded from the vedic tradition.

[15] Literally meaning "positioned at the end, limit, or boundary," *antastha* (AU mss. H 138a.3, I 595b.4, J 223.5) is a natural descriptor for outcaste groups such as the caṇḍāla, whose dwellings literally were positioned at or outside of the "limit or boundary" of towns and villages. Bhavabhaṭṭa's commentary here reads *antaḥ*, "end, limit," a reading supported by Sumatikīrti's text (SL 117b: *yan ta*). The AU reading, however, is supported by Mardo (PM 230a: *anta stha na*) and Indrabhūti (IC 68b: *an ta sta*), and also makes more sense.

[16] The mss. of Bhavabhaṭṭa's commentary that I have read both clearly read *paṅgulikā* (F 84a.3, G 78b.4; Pandey here reads *aṅgulikā*), a term which, if it has any meaning at all, probably means "cripple." There is considerable variance here, however. The AU mss. read *pāntalikā* (H 138a.3, I 595b.4; J 223.5: *patalikā*), and the Tibetans translations transliterate the term as *pa shu li ka* (PM 230a; AU 332a), while Sumatikīrti's text reads *a li ka li phyugs so* (117b), evidently taking the syllables *alikali* to designate *paśu*, i.e., "livestock," "beast," or "sacrificial victim."

"sister" (*bhaginī*) a ḍākinī.[17] Liquor (*medaka*) is water, and "the astrological mansions" (*gṛhāṇi*) is [a sign] for the seals.[18]

Touching the teeth with the tongue means "I am hungry." "Bearing scent" (*gandhavāhinī*) indicates thirst.[19] [If asked] "Whence?" (*kutaḥ*), [answer] "Coming from such and such a place."[20] "Ray of light" (*kiraṇa*) means a flower, and *tulamba* means laughter.[21] "Cleaving" (*daraḥ*) indicates the teeth. "Rain" (*vṛṣṭi*) means restraining,[22] and "satisfaction" (*tripti*)

---

[17] Here again there is variance regarding the identification of the sign and the signified. The AU mss. read *bhaginī* first (H 138a.3, I 595b.4: *bhaginyā ḍākinī*; J 223.5: *bhaginā ḍākinī*), seeing the former as designating the latter, which reading is also supported by Mardo's translation (PM 230a: *bha gi ni mkha' 'gro ma'o*), while Bhavabhaṭṭa inverts the order (Pandey 2002, 128: *ḍākinī bhaginī*), which inversion is followed by Sumatikīrti and the AU translation (SL 117b: *ḍa ki na ni sring mo'o*; AU 332a: *ḍā ki ni sring mo'o*). I accept the former interpretation, as *bhaginī* is commonly used as a code word for *yoginī* and *ḍākinī* in this text.

[18] Bhavabhaṭṭa here has *mudrāṇāṁ*, "of the seals," which is close to the AU mss.' reading, *trimudrāṇāṁ*, "of the three seals" (H 138a.4, I 595b.5; J 223.5: *timudrāṇām*). The Tibetan translations attest *mudrita*, "sealed" (PM 230a: *phyag rgyas 'debs pa'o*; SL 117b: *phyag rgyas btab pa'o*; PG 335.4: *phyag rgyas btab pa*). According to Sachen, this means that "I have you as my lord" (PG 335.4: *nga la bdag po khyo yod ces pa'i don no*), presumably indicating that the speaker is "bound" to the addressee. The AU translation, however, gives a very different reading, "urination" (AU 332a: *rdo rje chu gtong ba'o*, lit. "emission of vajra water"), which probably resulted from a misreading of *mudrā* as *mūtra*, "urine."

[19] The Sanskrit here reads *tṛṣṇā gandhavāhinī*. Mardo's translation (PM 230a) takes the latter term as a signifier for the former, as does Tsong Khapa (KS 130b), and I am inclined to follow this interpretation, given the fact that hunger was indicated just previously. Both Sumatikīrti's translation and the AU translation, however, take *tṛṣṇā* as the code term for *gandhavāhinī* (SL 117b: *krishna ni dris bsgo ba'o*; AU 332a: *trishna ni dris bsgo pa'o*). Buston comments that this thirst is "thirst for placing sentient beings on the path" (NS 151a: */ tṛṣṇa tri sgo ba'i ming ste / sems can lam la gzhug par sred pa'o /*).

[20] Bhavabhaṭṭa (Pandey 2002, 128) interprets *kuta āgamanaṁ amukasthānāt* as a question followed by a response. He takes *kuta āgamanaṁ* as the question followed by *amukasthānāt*, but I follow the alternate reading provided by all three translations, which interprets *kutaḥ* as the sign, and *āgataḥ amukasthānāt* as, presumably, the generic answer.

[21] All three translations take *tulamba* as the sign here. Bhavabhaṭṭa argues that *lamba* is the sign and *tu* a conjunction (Pandey 2002, 128), but I find this unlikely, as this chapter is otherwise devoid of conjunctions or any other grammatical features, generally just juxtaposing the sign with the signified.

[22] Here again I follow Bhavabhaṭṭa's interpretation; the translations are a bit garbled here. The AU translation is the most consistent, taking *danta* ("teeth," from the previous set) as a sign for *vṛṣṭinirodhanaṁ*, "cessation of rain" (AU 332a). Sumatikīrti's translation takes *dantaṁ* as a sign for *vṛṣṭi*, omitting *nirodhanaṁ* entirely (SL 117b), while Mardo takes *nirodha* as a

means an entreaty (*vijñapti*). *Dhuryu* means "outside," and "fond of mist" (*dhūmapriyā*) refers to a cloud. "Summit" (*sānu*) means mountain, and "streams" (*saritaḥ*) means rivers.[23] "Finger" (*aṅguli*) refers to the limbs. "Mouth" (*vadana*) means "face."[24] [The term] "stripe" (*rājikā*) indicates the tongue, and "withholding" (*adāna*) the teeth. [The term] "troop" (*paṅkti*) refers to a flag, and a "chanter" (*chandas*) is a rosary.

"Moving" (*cāla*) means the wind,[25] "beast" (*paśu*) refers to wild animals (*mṛga*),[26] and "they go" (*yānti*) indicates the maṇḍala. "A pair" (*samaṁ*)[27] means a crossroad, and *phalguṣaṁ* a living being. The "great syllable" (*mahākṣaraṁ*) is the great corpse.[28] *Ga* is a goat,[29] and *na* a human.[30] *Go* is a

---

sign for *vṛṣṭinirodhanaṁ* (PM 230a: *ni ro dha ni char 'bab pa zlog pa'o*), which is absurd as it reads *nirodha* both as the signifier and part of the signified. Pandey emends to *vṛṣṭinirodhanaṁ nirodhaḥ* (Pandey 2002, 128), to accord with Mardo, but this is not attested elsewhere.

23 Here both terms (*saritaḥ* and *nadyaḥ*) are in the nom. pl. declension.

24 The text here juxtaposes *vadana* and *mukha*, continuing the pattern of using synonyms or synecdochical terms to refer to each other.

25 Following this, Mardo's translation adds an additional line, "carrying along (*pravaha*) means a boat" (PM 230b: *pra ba ha ni gru'o*). Pandey back-translates this into Sanskrit, but this is unwarranted as this line is not attested in any of the other translations or commentaries.

26 The term *mṛga* is usually translated as "deer," but here the term may refer to a wider range of animal species. The Tibetans translated this here with *ri dvags*, which usually refers to deer or antelope but which also, like *mṛga*, can refer to a wider range of wild animals.

27 The reading *samaṁ* is clear in the older mss., both Bhavabhaṭṭa's (F 84b.3, G 79a.3) and the AU ms. H (138b.1). The newer AU mss., however, read *sasaṁ* (I 595b.7, J 224.1), which is likely a misrecognition of *samaṁ*. This latter reading is, however, supported by the Tibetan translations (PM 230b: *sva saṁ*; SL 118a: *sha sa*). The letters *m*, *ś*, and *s* are often mistaken for one another in these mss.

28 All of the extant Sanskrit mss. here read *mahāsavaṁ*, "great corpse." All of the Tibetan translations, however, read *phyugs chen po'o* (PM 230b, SL 118a; AU 332b), "great sacrificial victim," presumably a translation of *mahāpaśuṁ*. The difference in meaning between these variants, however, is slight.

29 The AU mss. read "*ga* is a goat" (I 595b.7, J 224.1: *ga chāgalaṁ*; H 138b.1: *vāgavaṁ*), which is supported by all three Tibetan translations (PM 230b, SL 118a, AU 332a: *ga ni ra skyes so*). Bhavabhaṭṭa's commentary, however, reads *mahāpaśu chāgalaṁ*, "the great sacrificial victim is a goat," which is unattested elsewhere.

30 There are two variants here. The AU mss. read *na* (H 138b.1, I 595b.7, J 224.2), a reading supported by Sumatikīrti's translation (SL 118a.2). Bhavabhaṭṭa reads *nā* (F 84b.5, G 79a.5), as does Mardo (PM 230b).

bull, and *ma* is a buffalo. *Bhā* means "eating," and *hā* is its synonym (*paryāyāḥ*).[31] [The term] *adhyakā*[32] refers to royal officials.[33]

Touching the breast means dwelling in the forest,[34] and touching the mouth means "[I have] eaten." Touching the teeth means "[I am] satisfied," and *ho* is sometimes its synonym. *Hrī* means "shame."[35] In touching the void (*śūnyaṁ*),[36] "Let's engage in sexual union"[37] is meant. In touching the

---

31 That is, a synonym for *bhā*, also meaning "eating."

32 The expression *adhyakā* is attested in Bhavabhaṭṭa's commentary (F 85a.2), along with the variant *asyakā* (G 79a.8). These mss. do not read *appakā* as reported by Pandey (2002, 128), who again follows the reading in Mardo's translation, *apba ka* (PM 230b). This may have resulted from a misreading of the variant attested in the AU mss., *āvyakā* (H 138b.2, I 595b.8, J 224.1). The *adhyakā* reading is also attested in several Tibetan translations (SL 118a: *a dya ka*; AU 332a: *adhya ka*), and in Indrabhūti's commentary, "*adhya* refers to the king of self awareness" (IC 68b: *adhya ni rang rig pa'i rgyal po'o*).

33 Here I translate *rājapuruṣa* ("royal attendants or ministers"), which occurs in two of the three AU mss. (I 595b.8, J 224.3) and is also attested by both of the Tibetan translations. The other AU ms. reads *rājasparṣano* (H 138b.2–3), a variant spelled correctly in one of Bhavabhaṭṭa's mss. (F 85a.2: *rājasparśanaḥ*); the other (G 79a.8) reads *rājaspalana iti*; neither reads *rājasparśe* as reported by Pandey (2002, 128). Both translations, however, support the *rājapuruṣa* reading (PM 230b, SL 118a: *rgyal po'i skyes bu'o*), and *rājapuruṣa* is also reported in Bhavabhaṭṭa's commentary. I suspect that *rājasparśanaḥ*, "touching the king," results from a mistaken substitution under the influence of the text which follows this.

34 The first part of this sentence, "touching the breast," is attested in one Tibetan translation (PM 230b: *brang la reg pa ni nags na gnas pa'o*), but not in all Tibetan translations, as this line does not occur in the AU. Bhavabhaṭṭa does quote the second half of the line, *vanaṁ sthiti* (Pandey 2002, 128).

35 "Shame" is in fact the meaning of the word *hrī*, making this more a prosaic definition than a secret code. This Sanskrit word, however, may not have been well known in the social context in which this code may have been employed, and thus it might have functioned as code in such a context.

36 The *Śrī Herukābhyudaya* has in place of "the void" (*stong pa, śūnyaṁ*) "the secret" (HA 19a: *gsang ba*), a term sometimes used in this text to refer to the vulva. Tsong Khapa comments that this refers to "touching the void within the loins" (KS 131a: *'doms kyi bar stong pa la reg na*). According to Indrabhūti, "touching the void of the female sex organ (*chos 'byung, dharmodaya*) refers to the expansion of the experiential elements (*khams, dhātu*) by means of the sexual union, blazing, and trickling" (IC 69a).

37 The Sanskrit here, *maithunaṁ kuruṣva*, is conjugated in the second person imperative singular, but as *maithuna* (sexual union) is an action that requires two people, I presume that the speaker is asking the addressee to have sex with her. A more literal translation would be "You engage in sexual union [with me]," but I prefer the less literal translation as it is also less awkward.

thigh,[38] "[Do it] thus from above!" is implied.[39] It is not [done] from below.[40] [These] gestures, counter gestures and secret signs are characteristic of the four classes[41] of the hero's wives.[42]

---

[38] There is an ancient tradition in India associating a woman's touching or displaying of her thigh with sexual intercourse. During the vedic horse sacrifice (*aśvamedha*), prior to the sexual union of the queen and the dead horse, the horse is circled by women who (according to the *Śrauta Sūtra of Āpastambha*) "tying up the right side of their hair and loosening the left, slapping their right thighs and fanning with their hems,...go around the horse three times to the right" (20.17.13, translation in Jamison 1996, 67). Another verse from this same rite describes a woman showing the thigh as a sign that she is interested in sex: "When the gods have favored the man with a star-marked, stiffened (penis), the woman displays with her thigh, like eye-witnesses to the truth" (*Vājasaneyi Saṁhitā* 23.29, translation in Jamison 1996, 71).

[39] Mardo's revised translation here reads: "In touching nothing 'it is not' is meant. In touching the thigh 'You have sexual intercourse!' is implied." (PM 230b: */ stong pa la reg pa ni med do zhes pa'o // brla la reg pa ni mai thu na gyis shig pa'o /*). Pandey emends the Sanskrit to accord with this (2002, 127). The only problem with this reading is that it is not attested anywhere else. The extant Sanskrit in Bhavabhaṭṭa's commentary and the AU mss. reads *śūnyaśparśane maithunaṁ kuruṣveti / ūrusparśane ūrdhvena evam iti* (H 138b.3, J 224.3, Pandey 2002, 128; I 595b.8: *mithunaṁ*), which is supported by the other two translations (SL 118a, AU 332a), and by Indrabhūti's CS commentary (IC 69a). Parallel textual passages also occur in three other explanatory tantras: the *Vajraḍākā* (VD 20b: *stong pa la reg pa ni me thu na las gyis shig pa'o // brla la reg pa ni da lta gyis shig pa'o zhes*); the *Ḍākārnava* (DM 208a: *stong pa la reg pa/ 'khrig pa'o brla la reg pa ni / de ltar da ltar gyis zhes par /*); and the *Śrī-Herukābhyudaya* (HA 19a: *gsang bar reg na 'khrig pa'o // brla la reg na gyis zhes pa'o /*). While all of these translations vary somewhat from the Sanskrit quoted above, they all correspond with it in associating "touching the void (or secret)" with sexual intercourse. I believe that Mardo's association of it with "it is not" (*med do, nāsti*) resulted from an interpolation of the term *nāsti*, under the influence of the term in the next line. Such an interpolation is in fact evidenced in the AU mss., which just before the quoted line read *nāstīti śūnyaṁ* (H 138b.3, I 595b.8; J 224.3: *nāstiti śūnya*).

[40] Bu-ston explains here: "As for **touching the thigh**, [it means] 'I should be below; you should do it from above.' **Thus**, in this way it should be done. Do it as the uppermost, that is, in the unobjectifying *samādhi* of all things. **It is not [done] from below**, meaning doing other than this is not one of the gestures, counter gestures, or signs. These explanations of the definitive meaning are the esoteric instructions of Padmavajra." (NS 152b) Bu-ston here follows and expands upon the briefer comments contained in Padmavajra's commentary on the *Ḍākārnava* (Tōh. 1419, 219b–220a).

[41] According to Bhavabhaṭṭa (Pandey 2002, 129), this refers to the four essence yoginīs (Ḍākinī, Lāmā, Khaṇḍarohā, and Rūpiṇī), and presumably the yoginī classes associated with them.

[42] Here I follow both the Sanskrit *vīrabhāryā* (I 595b.9, J 224.4; H omits due to ms. damage) and one of the Tibetan translations (SL 118a: *dpa' bo'i btsun mo*); the other two translations read "stated by the hero" here (PM 230b: *dpa' bos gsungs pa*; AU 332a: *dpa' bo'i gsung gi*), on the basis of which Pandey provides the reconstruction *vīrākhyā* (2002, 127). This may represent a genuine textual variant, or it may be a misreading of *bhāryā* as *bhāṣya*.

25. The Procedure of Completely Hiding the Root Mantra

Now, one is furnished with the end of the eight, which was hidden[1] out of desire for the aims of all, and on account of sentient beings of little faith and with deluded, ignorant minds.[2] With respect to that, the mantra clearly stated by the heroes and yoginīs is as follows:

1) Homage to the Blessed Lord, the Lord of Heroes,
2) Who is like the world-ending conflagration,
3) Endowed with a crest of dreadlocks,
4) Whose mouth is terrible, with awful projecting fangs,
5) Splendid with a thousand arms
6) Wielding an axe, lasso, upraised spear, and khatvanga staff,
7) Wearing a tiger hide,
8) And who has a great smoky-dark form.[3]

---

[1] That which is hidden, the commentators tell us, is the root mantra; it is hidden via the mantra coding of chs. 5 and 7. Bhavabhaṭṭa informs us that **eight** refers to "the eight mantras [derived] from the eight-lined [mantra]" (Pandey 2002, 130: *aṣṭeti aṣṭapadatvād aṣṭau mantrāḥ*). That is, each of the mantra's eight "lines" becomes a mantra when preceded by *oṁ* and concluded with *hūṁ hūm phaṭ*. According to Vīravajra: "**end of the eight**—i.e., end of the eight line [mantra]—means that *hūṁ hūṁ phaṭ* **is joined** to the end of each line…[thus yielding, for example:] *oṁ namo bhagavate vīreśāya hūṁ hūṁ phaṭ*" (PD 286b, 287a).

[2] Bhavabhaṭṭa comments here: "**sentient beings of little faith** refers to disciples (*śrāvaka*), who have little faith on account of being merely self-disciplined and pacified. It is **hidden** in order to protect it from those who are evil due to having a **mind**—i.e., an intellectual faculty—characterized by the **ignorance** of the degenerate heretics. This is the intended import here." (Pandey 2002, 130: *hīnādhimuktisattvam āśayo yasya sa tathā śrāvakasyāpy arthāyetyarthaḥ / sa hi svadamaśamamātrārthitvād dhīnādhimuktiḥ kutīrthyānām ajñānaṁ tatra cittaṁ buddhis tad arthena etenāsadbhyo rakṣaṇārthaṁ gopitā ity abhisandhiḥ*)

[3] The eight-lined mantra occurs as follows: *oṁ namo bhagavate vīreśāya / mahākalpāgnisannibhāya / jaṭāmakuṭotkaṭāya / daṁṣṭrākarālograbhīṣaṇamukhāya / sahasrabhujābhāsurāya / paraśupāśodyataśūlakhaṭvāṅgadhāriṇe / vyāghrājināmbaradharāya / mahādhūmrāndhakāravapuṣāya /*

Make! Make! Do! Do! Bind! Bind! Terrify! Terrify! Incite! Incite! *hrauṁ hrauṁ hraḥ hraḥ pheṁ pheṁ phaṭ phaṭ* Burn! Burn! Cook! Cook! Eat! Eat! Seize! Seize for him who is draped with a garland of greasy, bloody entrails! Threaten! Threaten the snake or serpent that resides in the seven underworlds! *ākaḍḍha ākaḍḍha hrīṁ hrīṁ jñauṁ jñauṁ kṣmāṁ kṣmāṁ hāṁ hāṁ hīṁ hīṁ hūṁ hūṁ kili kili sili sili cili cili dhili dhili hūṁ hūṁ.*[4]

---

[4] This is the mantra with translatable portions translated. In Sanskrit it occurs as follows: *kara kara kuru kuru bandha bandha trāsaya trāsaya kṣobhaya kṣobhaya hrauṁ hrauṁ hraḥ hraḥ pheṁ pheṁ phaṭ phaṭ daha daha paca paca bhakṣa bhakṣa vasarudhirāntramālāvalambine gṛhṇa gṛhṇa saptapātālagatabhujaṅgaṁ sarpam vā tarjaya tarjaya ākaḍḍha ākaḍḍha hrīṁ hrīṁ jñauṁ jñauṁ kṣmāṁ kṣmāṁ hāṁ hāṁ hīṁ hīṁ hūṁ hūṁ kili kili sili sili cili cili dhili dhili hūṁ hūṁ.*

26. The Procedures of Inspecting the Disciple, and the Vows[1]

Furthermore, having known Śrī Heruka's mantra, which does not exist in the triple world, all [other] mantras should be disregarded. The messengers are placed in the usual or reverse order.[2] My messengers are omnipresent, always bestowing power above and below.[3] These messengers bestow all powers,[4] always looking, touching, kissing, and embracing.[5]

---

[1] This chapter is among the folia missing from the CS mss. Fortunately, the Sanskrit is almost entirely recoverable from Bhavabhaṭṭa's and Jayabhadra's commentaries, as well as from the AU mss., which parallel the text beginning from verse six. Any significant variants among these sources and the Tibetan translations are noted below.

[2] Jayabhadra identifies the messengers with the twenty-four "heroines" listed in chapter four, in reverse order. He comments: "**The messengers are placed in the usual or reverse order**. This means that while Mahāvīryā, and so forth, were previously stated in reverse order, they should be arranged in the usual order." (E 25b.5–6: *anulomavilomena dūtayaḥ samvyavasthitā iti pūrva[ṁ] mahāvīryādayo vilomena nirdiṣṭāś cān[u]lomena vinyased ityarthaḥ /*)

[3] Durjayacandra interprets this both in terms of the maṇḍala's three wheels, which correspond to the triple world cosmos, as well as to the types of powers, as follows: "**Below** is the underworld, and **above** is the heavens. From these two one should also assume the middle, [the surface of the earth]. How are these—the above, the below, and the middle—relevant? They refer to those accomplished women (*dngos grub ma, siddhāḥ*) who range in space, range on the earth, and range in the underworld. It also refers to the higher and lower powers." (RG 287a–b)

[4] This translates the Sanskrit as preserved in Jayabhadra's commentary: *taṁ dūtīṁ sarva-siddhidaṁ* (E 26a.1). Bhavabhaṭṭa's text reads "this messenger bestows power for the sake of all beings" (Pandey 2002, 483: *taṁ dūtī sattvārthasiddhidam* [note that this chapter occurs at the start of the second volume of Pandey's edition]); but this reading is unattested elsewhere. I suspect *sattvārtha* was added in place of *sarva* to deepen the Buddhist character of the text. Bhavabhaṭṭa also notes that the text is improperly declined here, correcting it to the nominative plural *tāḥ dūtayaḥ*, "these messengers."

[5] Jayabhadra makes it clear that there is a causal connection between these actions and the messengers' ability to "bestow all powers," as follows: "Here this means that the messengers who exist there, in the seats of yoga [such as] fields and subsidiary fields, bestow power by means of kissing and embracing" (E 26a.2–3: *atrāyam arthaḥ yāvanti kṣetropakṣetrāṇi yoga-pīthāni tatra vyavasthitā dūtyaḥ siddhidā / cumbanāvagūhanād etāḥ*). Note that those four activi-

Especially at the seats of yoga,[6] as long as there are bands of yoginīs[7] then there are those who produce all powers, it is said. The real thing should by all means be offered[8] [to them]; it is never otherwise. One's mother, sister, daughter, or even one's wife can serve as messengers. Should she bestow the mantra to him, this procedure is always remembered by him.[9]

Now[10] I will explain the commitments difficult to obtain in the Yoga Tantras. Going left-wise, a man or woman proceeds to [his or her] desired power. Those who stay in houses and fields should be recognized, even if far away. There is no other yoga than Heruka's.[11] The master and the mothers

---

ties (looking, touching, kissing, and embracing) are also traditionally understood to characterize the four classes of Tantra. I thank our editor, Dr. Thomas Yarnall, for pointing this out.

[6] Kambala comments here as follows, interpreting *yogapīṭha* in terms of internal yogic anatomy: "The seats are well known on earth to be spots inside the lotus maṇḍala; by abiding within it there is great bliss, the royal nature of nondual joy. Therefore the lotus seat is supreme; filled with a mixture of semen and uterine blood, one should especially kiss it, and lolling with the tongue take it up. Unite the vajra and lotus, with the rapture of drinking [this] liquor." (SN 40a)

[7] The Sanskrit here reads *yogasaṁghātāḥ*. A *saṁghāta* is a band or company of travellers, and so forth, and *yogasaṁghātā* might be translated as "a band of yoga [practitioners]." According to Bhavabhaṭṭa, a *yogasaṁghāta* is "a community of yoginīs" (Pandey 2002, 484: *yogasaṁghātā iti yoginīsamūhā ityarthaḥ*).

[8] The surviving Sanskrit text is vague here, reading *dātavyaṁ sarvasadbhāvaṁ*. Jayabhadra's comments make it clear that it is offerings to the yoginīs that are implied here: "**Should be offered**, and so forth, means that having seen that committed yoginī, one should display the secret signs for drinking, eating, and the *caru* oblations" (E 26a.4: *dātavyam ityādi samay[in]ī[ṁ] tāṁ yoginī[ṁ] dṛṣṭvā bhakṣabhojyacaruchomakādīn da[r]śyād ityarthaḥ /*). The phrase *sarvasadbhāvaṁ* is awkward, declined as it is in the singular. Bhavabhaṭṭa glosses *sarva* as *sarvathā* (Pandey 2002, 484), "by all means," which I have followed in my translation.

[9] Bhavabhaṭṭa unpacks this somewhat cryptic text as follows: "Should the yoginī give the yogin his mantra, then accepting her he should achieve, i.e., be established in, power. The procedure and methods of mantra are remembered by him, as this is his aim." (Pandey 2002, 484: *yasmai yogine yoginī mantram ātmānaṁ dadyāt sā gṛhītvā siddhiṁ sādhayed iti samarpayet, tasya mantanayavidhiḥ smṛtaḥ tasya tadarthatvāt /*)

[10] With this verse the parallel passage in the AU mss. begins.

[11] This line, *nā herukasya paro yoga*, is attested in Jayabhadra's commentary (E 26b.1: *nā herukas tu paro yoga*), the AU mss. (H 138b.6, I 596a.1: *nā herukasya paraṁ yoga*; J 224.6: *...para yoga*), and two of the Tibetan translations (SL 119a, AU 332b: *he ru ka las 'byor gzhan med*). There is, however, a variant reading preserved in Bhavabhaṭṭa's commentary, "Śrī Heruka's yoga is supreme" (Pandey 2002, 485: *śrīherukaparo yoga*), which is attested in Mardo's translation (PM 231a: *he ru ka dpal rnal 'byor mchog*). Jayabhadra clarifies the

of yoga, being adepts in this Tantra, are excellent indeed. They should not be disparaged, nor should they be insulted. They should be worshipped with devotion,[12] these eight, Kākāsyā, and so forth,[13] who truly promote devotion and faith.[14]

The protection of the commitments, moreover, is always the cause of the powers.[15] Do not be stupefied by lust[16] through union with another goddess.[17] [One should] be free of duality,[18] unobstructed,[19] occupied with

---

former reading as follows: "**There is no other yoga than Heruka's** means that there is no other yoga superior to Herukayoga" (E 26b.1: *nā herukas[ya] paro yoga iti herukayogād anyaḥ uttamo yogo nāstītyarthaḥ*).

[12] The two older AU mss. (H 139a.1, I 596a.2) and both mss. of Bhavabhaṭṭa's commentary (F 88b.4, G 82a.2) read here *bhaktitaḥ*, "with devotion." Pandey emends this to *śaktitaḥ* (2002, 485), "to the best of one's ability." This emendation is made on the basis of the Tibetan translations, which here read *nus pa yis* (PM 231a, SL 119a, AU 332b), despite the fact that the Tibetan translation of the commentary reads *gus pa yis*, i.e., *bhaktitaḥ* (2002, 607). One AU ms. (J 224.7), however, does read *śaktitaḥ*, suggesting that both are legitimate variants.

[13] Bhavabhaṭṭa's commentary preserves this text, *kākāsyādayo 'ṣṭau hy ete*, which is supported by both CS translations (PM 231a: *kā ka'i gdong sogs brgyad po ni*; SL 119a: *kā gdong la sogs brgyad 'di dag*). The AU mss. here read *aṣṭau ḍūtyo hy ete*, "these eight messengers" (H 139a.1, I 596a.2).

[14] All extant Sanskrit mss. here read *bhaktiśraddhāvivardhikāḥ* (Pandey 2002, 485, H 139a.1, I 596a.2, J 224.7, E 26b.4), a reading supported by all of the Tibetan translations except for Mardo's, which reads *grol dang dad pa 'phel byed pa* (PM 231a), apparently misreading *bhakti* as *mukti*.

[15] Here the text begins the accounting of the eight special commitments of the Cakrasamvara tradition. According to Jayabhadra, "**The protection of the** previously stated **commitments** concerning heteropraxis is the first [commitment]" (E 26b.4–5: *pūrvoktavāmācārādi-samayānāṁ pālanaṁ prathamam /*).

[16] This is a translation of *kāmavimohitaḥ*, preserved in Bhavabhaṭṭa's commentary (Pandey 2002, 486). The AU mss. have a variant text that is probably corrupt, *hṛdā vikalpaiḥ kāmalo-lupāḥ*, "those greedy for lust with their heart, due to conceptualizations."

[17] Jayabhadra notes: "Avoiding **union with another goddess** is the second [commitment]" (E 26b.5: *anyadaivatāsaṁyogavarjanaṁ dvitīyaḥ*).

[18] Jayabhadra here comments: "**Free of duality** means that one should be free of separation between self and other; [this is] the third [commitment]" (D 36a.4–5, E 26b.5: *advaita[ṁ] svaparavibhāgarahito bhaved iti tṛtīyaḥ*).

[19] Jayabhadra gives the following rather unhelpful commentary: "**Unobstructed** means that one is not obstructed; [this is] the fourth [commitment]" (E 26b.5–6: *apratihata iti na*

the performance of the commitments,[20] have an excellent churning stick in practice with a woman,[21] yet observe chastity in meditation.[22] One is not [to be] hostile in the transfer of fluid.[23] These are the eight supreme com-

---

pratihanyata ityarthaḥ caturthaḥ /). Bhavabhaṭṭa comments that it means that one is "firmly oriented toward liberation" (Pandey 2002, 486: *dṛḍhādhimokṣatvaṁ*). It is hard to see how this is a commitment, however. Indrabhūti gives a more typical explanation: "**Unobstructed** means that one should not show to others nor proclaim the secrets of the substances or accoutrements of worship, or the setting and procedure of the *gaṇacakra*, [all of which] should be concealed" (IC 72a).

[20] Jayabhadra comments: "**Occupied with the performance of the commitments** means that one should be occupied with desire for that practice with the goddesses, by virtue of which one comes to be occupied with the practice of the commitments; [this is] the fifth [commitment]" (E 26b.6–27a.1: *samayācāraceṣṭitam iti samayo devyaḥ tā[ḥ] s[a]mācāraḥ icchā tatra ceṣṭāvyā yāto yasya samayācāraceṣṭitaḥ pañcamaḥ /*).

[21] This line has at least two variants. I have translated the reading attested by Jayabhadra's commentary and the AU mss., *nārīcaryāsumanthānaḥ* (E 27a.1: *nārīcaryāsamanthānaḥ*; H 139a.2, I 596a.3, J 225.1: *nārīcaryāsumanthāna*). This reading is supported by Durjayacandra's commentary, in which the compound is glossed as follows: "Regarding the statement **practice with a woman**, and so forth, the goddess who has the [previously] explained characteristics is the 'woman.' In practice [with her] one has the **churning stick**, which is the means of achieving power." (RG 288b) However, Bhavabhaṭṭa's commentary provides another reading, *nārīśvaryā samanthānaḥ* (F 89a.3–4), which might be translated as "have a churning stick with a woman who is a lady." This reading is attested in the Tibetan translations of the CS and the AU, the other commentaries, and even the translation of Jayabhadra's commentary. I suspect that both are legitimate variants, which do not differ greatly in meaning. As Bhavabhaṭṭa comments: "Having a **churning stick** means that one has mastery in rubbing the vajra and lotus with the yoginī; [this is] the sixth [commitment]" (F 89a.4–5, G 82b.1: *samanthāna iti yoginīvajrapadmasphālane tatraiśvaryam eva ṣaṣṭham*; cf. Pandey 2002, 486, which omits *padma*).

[22] According to the commentators this seventh vow deals with the retention of semen. Jayabhadra states: "**Yet observe chastity in meditation** means that, at the time of the trickling of the ejaculate seminal essence, one should observe, i.e., practice, chastity; [this is] the seventh [commitment]" (E 27a.2–3: *brahmacaryaṁ tathā dhyāna iti ādhānabodhicittasravaṇakāle brahmatattvaṁ cared ācared ityarthaḥ saptamaḥ /*).

[23] I read here the Sanskrit in my edition, *srotasaṁcāre* (*srotasaṁcāra* after *sandhi*). The AU mss. read *śrotasamcāre* (I 596a.3, J 225.2; H 139a.2–3: *srorthasaṁcāre*). Bhavabhaṭṭa's and Jayabhadra's commentaries read *śrotrasaṁcāra*, but this is clearly corrupt; the Tibetan translations attest *srotas*, "fluid, flow" (SL 119a, AU 332b: *rgyun gyi kun tu spyod*; PM 231a: *sbubs su kun tu spyod*). What does this mean? According to Jayabhadra, "**not hostile in the transfer of fluid** means that one should not be angered when receiving the seminal essence" (E 27a.3: *akrodhaḥ śrotasaṁcāra iti bodhicittagrahaṇakāl[e] 'pratighāta[ḥ] kartavya ity*). According to Tsong Khapa this refers to "practicing without hostility at the time of taking up the seminal essence from the woman's lotus" (KS 142a–b). Tsong Khapa follows this with a

mitments[24] which should be known by adepts, since they always exist in the means of achievement (*sādhana*).[25] They are common to all tantras,[26] and should not be broken without [good] reasons.[27] They are apprehended through faith alone, not by the hand nor by the eye. This is not to be brought to light, as it is a secret. It should be vigorously concealed.[28]

The wise one should move his little finger; the messengers are positioned.[29] Now there are three types of adepts: the pure, the impure, and the

---

quote from Vīravajra, namely that "at the time of taking up the bodhicitta, one does not give rise to the conception that it is filth" (ST 190a, quoted by Tsong Khapa at KS 142b; Tsong Khapa's text has the correct reading *btsog pa'i 'du shes*; the ST reads *bcog pa'i 'du shes*). Regarding this practice of fluid transfer, see White 1998 and 2003.

[24] The mss. of Jayabhadra's commentary and the AU mss. here read *aṣṭau samayā parāḥ*, while the translations imply the reading *aṣṭau samayācārāḥ*, which does in fact occur in Bhavabhaṭṭa's commentary (Pandey 2002, 486). While the latter reading is possible, the former appears to make more sense.

[25] In other words, their practice is an intrinsic component of this Tantra's spiritual discipline, or *sādhana*.

[26] Literally speaking this is not the case; these are special commitments peculiar to this tradition. Jayabhadra resorts to the notion of secrecy to resolve this, as follows: "**Common to all tantras** means that this is the secret of all tantras. While this secret is implied, those who know other tantras do not know it." (E 27a.4–5: *sāmānyaṁ sarvatantrāṇām iti etad rahasyaṁ sarvatantrāṇām iti eta[d] eva rahasyaṁ abhisaṁdhānam anyatantravido na vidanti /*) In other words, they are the "secret" of all tantras, which is only explicitly revealed here.

[27] I am indebted to Dr. Thomas Yarnall for suggesting this translation. Jayabhadra and Bhavabhaṭṭa comment that "**without [good] reasons** [refers to reasons established] by means of knowledge such as direct perception, etc." *nirhetubhiḥ pratyakṣādibhiḥ pramānaiḥ* (E 27a.5–6; Pandey 2002, 487).

[28] The Sanskrit here reads *gopanīyaṁ prayatnataḥ* in all extant sources, a reading supported in two of the Tibetan translations (SL 119a, AU 332b: *rab tu 'bad de sba par bya*). Mardo's translation, *rab tu 'bad de bstan par bya* ("should be vigorously disclosed") is clearly mistaken.

[29] Jayabhadra comments here that:

> **The wise one should move his little finger** means that he has union with the goddess at the time of worshipping the goddess. But if a woman who is well educated in Mantra and Tantra has not been obtained, then cultivating some other uncultivated woman, she should be worshipped. **The messengers are positioned** means that at that very time all of the messengers are pleased by the wise one, i.e., the yogin.
>
> *kaniṣṭhāṁ cālayed dhīmān iti devīpūjākāle devatāyogavān ity arthaḥ / atha vā mantratantrasuśikṣitā yadi na labhyate itarām apy aprākṛtaṁ kṛtvā pūjāyed iti /*

(cont'd)

mixed.[30] There are the aspirant, the purified one, and the illuminating virtuous man.[31]

---

dūtayaḥ samavasthitā iti eva tatkāl[e] dhīmato yoginaḥ sarvā dūt[a]yaḥ suprasannā bhavantītyarthaḥ / (E 27b.1–3)

Bhavabhaṭṭa gives more specific instructions concerning the sexual practice implied here:

> The rite of loving the messenger is indicated by **little finger**, and so forth. The channel called "bird face" (*khagamukhā*), which is like a *bandhūka* flower, should be moved, i.e., stimulated, by the concave space [formed] by the tips of the ring and middle fingers as if around a seed, inserted within the flower. What is the purpose of this? The **messengers**, and so forth, indicate that [it is done in order to stimulate] the descent of the streaming intoxicant which exists within the messenger.
>
> *dūtyanurāgaṇavidhim āha kaniṣṭhām ityādi / khagamukhānāḍīṁ bandhūkakusumasadṛśīṁ kusumasadṛśena kiṁbījenānāmikāmadhyamāgra-saṁpuṭanyastena cālayec codayet / kimartham āha dutaya ityādi / dūtīnāṁ samvyasthānaṁ svavasthānaṁ sravanmadatvam* / (Pandey 2002, 487)

This passage, then, is connected with the transfer of vital fluid. This connection is made most clearly by Kambala who wrote that it is taken up by the tongue, and serves as the basis for the generation of great bliss for one engaged with the power of alchemy (*rasāyāna*) (SN 40b).

30 These three, the *śuddha*, *aśuddha*, and *miśra*, presumably correspond respectively to the *viśuddha*, *ārādhaka*, and *dīpako guṇavān naraḥ* in the next line.

31 Jayabhadra describes these as follows:

> **The aspirant, the purified one, and the illuminating virtuous man** refers to the three types of yogins. The aspirant has not given rise to inspiration (*pratibhā*), the purified one has given rise to competence. The illuminating one is middling, having given rise to a little inspiration, and awakening for the sake of self and others. In addition, the aspirant worships the deity through the discipline of *mantrayoga*. The illuminating one who is virtuous and who knows the meaning of the treatises is like a lamp, and is able to accomplish the aims of all beings.
>
> *ārādhako viśuddha dīpako guṇavān nara iti yogintridhā vidyate / ārādhaka ity anutpannapratibhāḥ viśuddha ity utpannasamarthaḥ dīpaka iti madhyadīpakaḥ kiṁcid utpannapratibhāḥ svaparārthabodhakaś ca atha vā ārādhakaḥ mantrayogābhyāsena devatārādhakaḥ / guṇavān śāstrārth[jñāna]dīpaka pradīpavat sarvasattvārthakriyāsamarthaḥ* / (E 27b.3–6)

27. The Procedures of the Conduct, Observances, Worship, and Sacrificial Cakes[1]

Now, the hero who has the conduct and observances[2] is the adept of all yoginīs. Knowing [the yoginīs'] characteristic distinction[s],[3] one rapidly engages the power[s]. The messengers travel from town to town.[4] [As for their] physical characteristic[s], the messengers are a sword blade[5] that purifies and augments merit. The adept obtains powers by being well associated with the messenger.[6] They are achieved quickly even without [mantra]

[1] Like the previous chapter, this chapter also falls in the lacuna of the CS mss., but is recoverable from Bhavabhaṭṭa's and Jayabhadra's commentaries, as well as the parallel passage in the AU, which includes everything but the first verse.

[2] This text, *caryāvratavīraḥ*, is my reconstruction from Bhavabhaṭṭa's commentary. The Pandey edition reconstructs it from this same source as *vīracaryāvrataṁ*, "the hero's practice and observance" (2002, 487). This reading corresponds with Mardo's translation (PM 231b); mine corresponds with Sumatikīrti's (SL 119b). Bhavabhaṭṭa writes here: "There is exclusive engagement in the **practice**, i.e., the practice of yoga, and the **observance** of this [practice]. What is done and by whom it is to be undertaken? It is **the hero**, and so forth." (F 89b.1, G 83a.7–8: *caryā yogacaryā tasyā vratam ekāntena pravṛttiḥ / sā ca kiṁ kṛtvā kena vā caraṇīyetyāha vīra ityādi /*; note that the Pandey ed. misreads *pravṛttiḥ* as *pravṛtteḥ*)

[3] Bhavabhaṭṭa clarifies that the "**characteristic distinction[s]** [are] the yoginīs'" (Pandey 2002, 487: *yoginīnāṁ lakṣaṇabhedaṁ*).

[4] I have translated the text preserved in Jayabhadra's commentary, *grāme grāme vrajanti ca dūtayo* (E 27b.6). Bhavabhaṭṭa (Pandey 2002, 488) and the AU mss. (H 139a.5, I 596a.5, J 225.4), read *vrajan tasya*, which appears to be an incorrectly declined present participle.

[5] Jayabhadra here comments: "**The messengers are a sword blade**, i.e., they are like a sword blade in that they are difficult to overcome" (E 28a.1: *dūtayaḥ asidhārāṁ ceti dūt[a]yo 'sidhārāsamā durārādhyā ityarthaḥ*).

[6] The grammar of this line, *sādhakaḥ siddhim āpnoti susaṁparkād dūtayas tathā*, is a bit garbled; emending *dūtayas* to *dūtyās* would correct this. In any case, the meaning is clear. Bhavabhaṭṭa restates the line as follows: "Through association with—i.e., viewing, and so forth—the messenger, the adept obtains power" (Pandey 2002, 489: *dūtidarśanādisaṁparkād sādhakaḥ siddhim āpnoti*). Bhavabhaṭṭa reads *saṁparkād* here, but Jayabhadra and the AU mss. read *susaṁparkād*, which is supported by the Tibetan translations (PM 231b: *legs 'grogs pas*; SL 119b, AU 332b: *legs 'dres pa*).

repetition, meditation, and worship. And if adepts who have mantras and gestures engage in worship, "this worship is not supreme"[7] is the fixed opinion of the teaching.[8]

The adept of the pleasures of the messengers' path[9] has power as his highest object. And endowed with spells (*vidyā*)[10] and mantra, he should always eat the *caru* oblation.[11] The adept who is well equipoised [by means

[7] This line, *etat pūjā paraṁ nāsti*, presents an interpretive challenge in that *paraṁ* is declined in the neuter nom. sing. case, while *pūjā* is fem. nom. sing. However, given the frequent slippage in gender and number, this is less problematic than the translation (following the Tibetan) "there is no other worship than this" (PM 231b, SL 119b, AU 332b: *'di las gzhan pa'i mchod med de*), which makes less sense in the context of this verse.

[8] That is, *śāstrasya niścayaḥ*. Bhavabhaṭṭa glosses *śāstrasya* as *śrīsamvarākhyasya yoginītantrasya*, "the Yoginī Tantra known as the *Śrī Samvara*" (Pandey 2002, 489). Tsong Khapa adds that the practice being extolled here is the "inner" or internal practice of mantra repetition, and so on, presumably excluding the outer forms of these practices. See KS 146a.

[9] Unlike the AU mss., which here read *dūtīmārgaratānāṁ tu sādhakaḥ* (H 139b.1, I 596a.7, J 225.6), which I have translated above, Bhavabhaṭṭa's commentary reads *dūtīmārgaratā nityaṁ sādhakāḥ*, "adepts who always take pleasure in the messengers' path" (Pandey 2002, 489). While this is a viable reading, it is not attested elsewhere. Most likely, this reading resulted from the transposition of the *nityaṁ* in the following line. Devagupta comments here:

> The path to the messenger, and so forth, is the path to awakening. It purifies all of the infinite afflictions, as the afflictions are adventitious. For example, if one who is deluded—in the same way that the sky is obscured by snow or smoke—clears this away, he will become a Vajradhara in this very life. But if one undertaking this [methodology] abandons it, and adheres to another yoga, such as the practice of the disciples, the Action Tantras, and so forth, then, since he is deluded, even though he desires power, he will never attain power or even happiness. (SS 121a; cf. SN 49a)

Note that this explanation is embedded in the commentary on ch. 28 in both Devagupta's and Kambala's texts, where it is apparently out of place.

[10] The term *vidyā* here could also indicate the consort, as it often does. I translate it as "spell" here due to its juxtaposition with the term *mantra*.

[11] Bhavabhaṭṭa comments: "The *caru* oblation, and so forth, is said to be a special characteristic of worship, and the word **and** means in conjunction with worship. **He should eat the *caru* oblation** as food together with the yoginīs, **always**, i.e., for a long time without interruption." (Pandey 2002, 489: *ārādhanaviśeṣam āha cāruṁ cetyādi / cakāra ārādhanasamuccaye / carum ekatra bhojanaṁ yoginībhir bhojayen nityaṁ sādaraṁ nirantaraṁ dīrghakālaṁ ca /*)

of being engaged with all yogas][12] should have intercourse with all social classes,[13] and should not discriminate with regard to food. Indivisible in their true nature, the messengers have two means of achievement.[14] While one should practice both,[15] the messengers truly have only one.[16] Through connection with them one is impelled toward power.[17] [There are the

---

[12] This line, *sarvayogapravṛttasya*, occurs only in Bhavabhaṭṭa's commentary, and is attested only in one of the translations (SL 119b: *rnal 'byor kun la 'jug pa yis*). It is likely a variant which occurred in a minority of available editions of the text.

[13] As this section of the text deals with prohibitions against ordinary discriminatory behavior, it makes the most sense that the injunction to "have intercourse" (*ācaret*) with "all classes" (*sarvavarṇebhyaḥ*) would refer to the social classes, the area where such discrimination ordinarily occurs. Bhavabhaṭṭa comments that this refers to commensality, the practice of communal eating which is normally prohibited between the social classes. He writes: "**intercourse with all social classes** means that one should eat together with all classes" (Pandey 2002, 489: *ācaret sarvavarṇebhya iti sarvair varṇaiḥ sahaikatra bhuñjītetyarthaḥ*). Bhavyakīrti likewise understands this in terms of social discrimination, but discrimination regarding the special tantric clans, writing "**should have intercourse with all classes** means that one should eat, and so forth, with all of the classes which arise from the clans of Akṣobhya, and so forth; this is Bhavya's understanding" (SM 25a). But it should be noted that the tantric clans were commonly associated with the social classes, as was seen in the context of ch. 16 above.

[14] According to Jayabhadra, "**two means of achievement** indicates the means of achievement of both worldly and ultimate power" (E 28a.3: *dvau sādhanam iti laukikalokottara-siddhisādhana ityarthaḥ*).

[15] Here I translate the text as it occurs in Bhavabhaṭṭa's commentary, *dvividhau sādhayec caiva* (F 92a.3). The AU mss. read *dvividhau caraṇasyaiva*, "practicing in the two ways" (H 139b.3, I 596a.8, J 226.1). The Tibetan translations all read "when practicing in the procedure of power" (PM 231b, SL 119b, AU 332b: *dngos grub cho ga la spyod tshe*). Jayabhadra's commentary is garbled here, but it appears to support the Tibetan reading, which probably represents a genuine textual variant.

[16] As one would expect, Jayabhadra takes "only one" to refer to the means of achievement (*sādhana*). He comments as follows: "The **only one** is Śrī Heruka's yoga; this demonstrates its superiority" (E 28a.4: *eka eva śrīherukayoga ity ādhikyaṁ darśayati*).

[17] Bhavabhaṭṭa's commentary appears to attest two versions of the line. The first version is embedded in the commentary with only a few words present, but has been hypothetically reconstructed in Pandey's edition as *pracoditā siddhayas tu sādhanasannikarṣataḥ* (2002, 490), largely on the basis of Mardo's translation. Interestingly, in this case the edition emends the reading of Mardo's translation, *rang dga' nyid* (PM 231b), to *rab bskul nyid* (2002, 619) to conform to Bhavabhaṭṭa's reading; however, Sumatikīrti's text makes it clear that *rab dga'* is the best reading here. Bhavabhaṭṭa also quotes, in full, another version of this text, *pracoditāḥ siddhes tāsāṁ sannikarṣakāraṇatvāt* (Pandey 2002, 490). I translate *pracoditāḥ* as singular in order to accord with the singular *sādhayet* in the previous verse. "Impelled toward power" is a

accomplished places of the domains—here the ḍākinīs gather. Positioned there, one should perform {mantra} repetitions, and enjoy the *caru* oblation all together. Positioned there, they frolic.][18]

He is well enchanted with the consecrations obtained from the gurus' lineage succession,[19] has spoken truly with the messengers, and is accus-

---

loose, interpretive translation of *praceditāḥ siddhes*, which might also be read as "impelled by power" (*praceditāḥ* and the rest of the passage is separated by a sizable chunk of commentary, making this reading hypothetical). The AU mss. have a variant reading *pratibodhitāḥ* (H 139b.3, I 596a.8; J 226.1: *pratibodhikā*). Following this, all three mss. suffer an extensive ellipsis, omitting the rest of the verse. Regarding the translations, Sumatikīrti's and Mardo's are close, reading *rab dga' nyid dang dngos grub nyid* (SL 119b) and *rang dga' nyid dang dngos grub ni* (PM 231b). The AU translation reads *byang chub phyogs kyi dngos grub ni*, "the power which is an aid to awakening" (AU 332b). Regarding the second line, Sumatikīrti here reads *sgrub pa dag dang nye ba'o* (SL 120a, following an intervening verse); Mardo reads *sgrub pa dag dang nye ba ste* (PM 231b); and the AU translation reads *sgrub pa dag dang nye ba dang* (AU 332b). While *nye ba* could translate *sannikarṣa*, the reading *sgrub pa dag* differs from the Sanskrit text preserved in Bhavabhaṭṭa's commentary. While Pandey back-translates from the Tibetan, yielding *sādhanasannikarṣataḥ* ("through connection to the means of achievement"), I adhere to the reading that is actually preserved, *tāsāṁ sannikarṣakāraṇatvāt*, since it makes more sense that connection to *them*, i.e., the messengers, would be the cause of empowerment.

[18] The text in square brackets is preserved only in Sumatikīrti's translation (SL 119b–120a) and in Bhavabhaṭṭa's commentary. This text begins with what Bhavabhaṭṭa terms an "additional verse" (*granthādhikyam*), which he gives as follows: *kṣetrasthānāni siddhāni ḍākinyo 'tra ca saṁgatāḥ / tatra sthito japaṁ kuryād ekatra carum āharet /* (Pandey 2002, 490). This text is then followed by the additional bit of text *krīḍante tatrasthā*, regarding which Bhavabhaṭṭa notes: "It is said that this text as well should be put down [here], as it is essential" (Pandey 2002, 490: *krīḍante tatrasthā iti grantho 'yam evam avatāraṇīyaḥ hṛdayakṛtety āha*).

[19] This is a translation of *guruparvakramaprāptair abhiṣekaiḥ sumantritaḥ*, preserved in Jayabhadra's commentary. Bhavabhaṭṭa reads *guruparvakramāt praptābhiṣiktaṁ*, which he explains as follows: "One has obtained the consecrated [state], i.e., consecration, from the uninterrupted succession of those links, i.e., lineage of gurus, which has the special form of water, and so forth" (F 92b.3–4, G 85a.1–2: *guruparva guruparamparā te 'nāyātāḥ kramād udakādirūpā viśeṣāḥ / taiḥ prāptābhiṣiktam abhiṣekaḥ /*). My reading differs from Pandey's (2002, 490), which appears to have several errors here. Bhavabhaṭṭa then lists three alternatives for the concluding portion of this text: *sumantritaṁ* ("well enchanted"), *suyantritaṁ* ("well restrained, well fettered"), and *samanvitaṁ* ("well endowed"). I follow the former since it is also attested in Jayabhadra's commentary. For some reason, Pandey emends this text to *guruparvābhiṣiktaṁ ca suyantrasamanvitam* (2002, 490), but this does not accord with either Bhavabhaṭṭa's commentary or the Tibetan translations (PM 231b, SL 120a, AU 332b), all of which support *sumantritaḥ* (*sngags legs ldan*) as well as *krama* (*rim*).

tomed to union with a consort.[20] Produced from the cause of perfect gnosis,[21] the nature of mind[22] arises at dawn.[23] One should put into practice the

[20] Jayabhadra comments that this means "being accustomed to union with an outer woman," presumably again meaning a real woman rather than an internally imagined consort (E 28a.6: *[mudr]āsaṁyogaśīlaś ceti bāhy[ā]ṅganāsaṁyogaśīla ityarthaḥ*). Kambala comments here:

> **Accustomed to union with a consort** means that through the state of *mahāmudrā* one will effortlessly attain unexcelled, supreme awakening. One will quickly purify clear light and gnosis, and will thus always be considered to be a yogin. Through the application of this meditation, if one stabilizes the jewel of mind, one is blessed, consecrated in the Buddha's awakening. Take a sixteen-year-old, and bedeck her with all of the ornaments. Having found one with a beautiful face and large eyes, one should practice the consort observance (*vidyāvrata, rig pa'i brtul zhugs*) with her. One should also practice the secret worship, in the four moments, by means of the great observance (*mahāvrata, brtul zhugs chen po*). Have no doubt that after six months everything will be achieved. (SN 42a)

[21] This text, *saṁpūrṇajñānahetujaṁ*, is preserved in Jayabhadra's commentary, and corresponds to Mardo's translation *legs rdzogs ye shes rgyu skyes pa'o* (PM 231b). Jayabhadra comments upon it as follows: "**produced from the cause of perfect gnosis** refers to the cause or instrument of the wisdom which is preeminent and complete. The Blessed Lord Vajrarudra is produced from that." (D 38a.6–7, E 28b.1–2: *jñānahetujam iti jñānasya prakarṣaparyantasya hetuḥ kāraṇaṁ / bhagavān vajrarudra tasmāj jāto bhavatītyarthaḥ /*) The Tibetan translation of this commentary reads Śrī Heruka rather than Vajrarudra (MP 58a), which is probably yet another case of Śaiva elements in the texts being replaced by Buddhist terms. However, the reading Vajrarudra is also attested in Vīravajra's commentary (ST 191a), which no doubt was written in dependence upon an unaltered copy of Jayabhadra's Sanskrit text. There is also another variant here, *saṁpūrṇajñānadehajā*, "produced from the body of perfect gnosis." This occurs in a somewhat garbled form in Bhavabhaṭṭa's commentary (Pandey 2002, 491; note that the editors of this text include not only the probably corrupt text but also Bhavabhaṭṭa's commentarial gloss in their CS edition). While this variant is not attested in any of the CS or AU translations, it is also attested in Durjayacandra's commentary (RG 291b: *yongs rdzogs ye shes lus las skyes*).

[22] That is, *cittātmā*, which in Bhavabhaṭṭa's analysis is "the nature of mind, being that which has the mind only as its nature or reality" (Pandey 2002, 491: *cittātmā bhavati / cittamātram evātmā svarūpaṁ yasya sa tathā /*).

[23] Jayabhadra comments somewhat cryptically here that "the nature of mind, i.e., the one who has the *mahāmudrā-yoga*, arises at the end of the night" (MP 58a; the Sanskrit text is corrupt here). Other commentators connect this line more clearly with perfecting stage practice, particularly the emergence of the magic body and the realization of clear light. Vīravajra writes: "**Produced from the cause of perfect gnosis** is the generation previously visualized. **The nature of mind arises at dawn** is meditation on clear light which goes beyond joy, supreme joy, and natural joy." (PD 406b)

weapons which are extensions of the limbs[24] and the body's places, completing the body.[25] One should always recite mantra, purifying the body. One should show the places of yoga.[26] Do not tread upon the weapons.[27] The devoted man should not revile [others].[28] Do not overstep the dedicated ones.[29] Produce bliss together with them,[30] having the aim of libera-

---

[24] Bhavabhaṭṭa's text here reads *atyaṅgāni ca śāstrāni* (F 93a.4, G 85a.9). The reading *atyaṅga*, "that which surpasses the limbs," is supported by Jayabhadra's commentary (E 28b.3) as well as by the Tibetan translations (PM 231b: *yan lag las 'das mtshon cha rnams*; SL 120a: *nyid lag las 'das mtshon cha ni*); it is misread by Pandey as *abhyaṅgāni* (2002, 491), which makes no sense in this context.

[25] Jayabhadra comments here: "All body parts must be covered with nets of weapons" (E 28b.3–4: *sarvaśarīrāṇi śastrapañjaraiḥ prachādayed ityārthaḥ*), which clearly refers to the process of *kavacamantranyāsa*, the placement of the armor mantras. Bhavabhaṭṭa has a less likely but more Buddhist explanation, interpreting the line as a reference to insight meditation (*vipaśyanā*) techniques: "**Completing the body** means that one should meditate upon emptiness, dividing the body into portions, such as the aggregates of form, and so forth, by means of the weapon of wisdom" (Pandey 2002, 491: *sakalīkṛtya vigraham iti prajñāśastreṇa skandhādirūpaṁ śarīraṁ khaṇḍaśo vibhujya śūnyatāṁ bhāvayed iti bhāvaḥ*).

[26] Jayabhadra glosses *yogasthānāni* very cryptically, writing "**one should show the place**, i.e., the woman, **of yoga**, i.e., concentration" (E 28b.5: *yogasthānāni darśayed iti yogasya samādhiḥ sthānam aṅganā tāṁ darśayet*). Tsong Khapa expands upon this as follows: "The **yoga** is the concentration of great bliss, and **the place** from which that is generated is the woman" (KS 147b).

[27] Jayabhadra gives alternate interpretations for this line: "**Do not tread upon the weapons** means that one should not step upon the previously described armors, and so forth. Or it means that one should not tread upon the weapons, i.e., the messengers who are like weapons. Or, the 'weapons' are signs for self and other." (E 28b.6–29.1: *śāstrāni na laṅghayed iti evaṁ yathoktakavacādikaṁ nākramed ityarthaḥ / atha vā śastravat śāstrāṇi dūt[ī na] laṅghayet / atha vā śastrāṇi svaparayo[ḥ] cihnāni /*)

[28] The inserted word "others" is not present in the text, which in fact does not specify who is the object of the action of reviling. The Sanskrit reads, in both Bhavabhaṭṭa's and Jayabhadra's commentaries, *nākrośet samayī naraḥ*. Presumably this means the committed yogī should not revile anyone; as Jayabhadra writes: "**The devoted man should not revile** means abuse should not be done at any time" (E 29a.1: *nākrośe[t] samayī naraḥ sarvadā ākrośo na kartavya iti*). One should note that two of the Tibetan translations read the committed one as the object of this prohibited abuse (PM 231b, AS 332b: *dam tshig can la khro mi bya*). Sumatikīrti's translation is ambiguous, but it seems, like the Sanskrit, to read the *samayī* as the agent rather than the object of this action (SL 120a: *dam tshig can gyi khro mi bya*).

[29] According to Bhavabhaṭṭa the "**dedicated ones**" (*abhiyuktān*) are "those dedicated to Śrī Cakrasamvara" (Pandey 2002, 492: *abhiyuktān nātikramed iti śrīcakrasamvarābhiyuktān*). Devagupta explains a bit more fully: "Regarding the **dedicated ones**, should one treat contemptuously the guru who bestows consecration in [the tradition of] this *Samvara Tantra*, his

tion as well as the aim of that,[31] undertaken by means of the practice of the commitments.

One engaged in wandering is released.[32] Always naked at night, one should ever be black and red.[33] Wearing a garment [made] from a living being's body,[34] [he is ornamented with a choker, an armlet, an earring, a sacred thread, a garland of heads around his neck, a girdle,[35] and also with {anklets that produce} growling sounds.[36] He has a crest of dreadlocks

---

disciples, or the messengers, by virtue of whom one attains the supreme [state], then one will destroy in a single instant the store of merit accrued by giving rise to the spirit of awakening over a billion eons" (SS 115a).

[30] According to Bhavabhaṭṭa, "**them** refers to the yoginīs, and **bliss** to the bliss of sexual pleasure, and so forth" (Pandey 2002, 492: *tābhiṛ iti yoginībhiḥ / sukhaṁ suratādisukham*).

[31] This text is preserved in Bhavabhaṭṭa's commentary, and is explained by him as follows: "**Having the aim of liberation as well as the aim of that** means that one who has both the aim of emancipation and the aim of bliss should sleep together with them, doing the things stated in the treatises on sexual love (*kāmaśāstra*)" (Pandey 2002, 492: *muktyarthī tadarthī ceti mokṣārthi sukhārthī ca ceṣṭitaṁ kāmaśāstroktaṁ kṛtvā tābhiḥ sārdhaṁ supyād iti saṁbandhaḥ*). This reading is attested in both of the Tibetan translations. There is also a variant text present in Jayabhadra's commentary and the AU mss., namely "having one's own aim and the aim of that" (E 29a.4: *ātmārthī ca tadarthī*; H 139b.3, J 226.2: *ātmārthī tadarthī ca*; I 596a.8: *ātmārthi tadarthī ca*).

[32] According to Jayabhadra, "**one engaged** as a yogin, **wandering** with a heroic mind, **is liberated**, i.e., is one who is liberated as he wishes" (E 29a.6: *vairiś cittam eva bhramaṇayogi-ceṣṭita mucyate / yatheṣṭamukto bhavatītyathaḥ*).

[33] Devagupta comments: "**Always naked at night** means that at night one should worship the consort. **Black** should be taken in reference to [oneself in] Heruka's form, and **red** to [the consort] in Vajravārāhī's." (SS 115a) Tsong Khapa provides a commentarial gloss indicating that one visualizes oneself as Heruka and one's consort as Vajravārāhī (KS 148a).

[34] That is, as Bhavabhaṭṭa explains, "it should be understood that one should make a **garment** out of animal hide" (Pandey 2002, 493: *prāṇyaṅgavāsasāvāsam iti carmāmbareṇa vāsaṁ kuryād iti jñeyaṁ*).

[35] Bhavabhaṭṭa notes that "**the sacred thread** and **girdle** are made of hair" (Pandey 2002, 492: *brahmasūtraṁ mekhalā ca keśaracite*). Tsong Khapa further states that they are composed of the hair of executed thieves (KS 148a).

[36] This is, presumably, because they are adorned with bells or some other noise maker. Bhavabhaṭṭa explains that "**growling** refers to an anklet together with the sounds of that" (Pandey 2002, 492: *ghurghurā nūpuraṁ tasyā ravās taiḥ*).

marked with strips of cloth, and adorned with artificial hair, and so forth.[37] He has a vajra and lotus,[38] a skull-staff, and a *ḍamaru* drum that makes the sound *hūṁ*. All heroes and yoginīs are adorned with the three armors.[39]][40]

One whose aim is bliss should foster bliss.[41] Renounce the sacred thread; purity depends upon Śrī Heruka.[42] As for having the five insignia bound,[43] they should be in place at all times, always displayed at night, and concealed during the day.[44] [Knowledge of the ritual actions should be well

---

[37] Bhavabhaṭṭa explains that this refers to "a plume [or chowrie], and so forth, made from the hair of others" (Pandey 2002, 492: *mithyākeśādyalaṁkṛtam iti anyakeśacāmarādiracitam ityarthaḥ*).

[38] According to Bhavabhaṭṭa, "the **lotus** is a skull marked with a **vajra**" (Pandey 2002, 492: *vajralāñchitaṁ padmaṁ kapālaṁ*).

[39] Bhavabhaṭṭa explains that these are "the three armors which are situated in the three wheels" (Pandey 2002, 492–3: *tricakravartinyaḥ kavacatrayaṁ*), which evidently refers to the heroes and yoginīs who dwell in the three wheels, together with their respective sets of armor mantras.

[40] This bracketed text is only attested in Bhavabhaṭṭa's commentary and the sDe-dge recension of Mardo's revised translation; it is absent in all of the other four recensions that I have consulted (i.e., the Beijing, sNar-thang, Phug-brag, and sTog Palace). My translation is based both upon the Sanskrit partially preserved by Bhavabhaṭṭa (Pandey 2002, 492–3) as well as the Tibetan translation (PM 232a). Note that the Pandey edition (2002, 492) back-translates from the Tibetan to fill in the gaps, i.e., the portions of the text on which Bhavabhaṭṭa did not comment.

[41] Jayabhadra clarifies: "One should produce the bliss of sexual pleasure" (E 29b.2: *surata-sukhaṁ kuryāt*).

[42] Regarding this line, Jayabhadra comments that "the **sacred thread,** and so forth, means that one abandons the purity decreed in the traditions of the sages (*ṛṣismṛti*), and **depends upon Śrī Heruka** means that one is observant of all [rules of] purity, worldly and ultimate" (E 29b.2–3: *yajñopavītādi ṛ[ṣ]ismṛtivihitasauca[ṁ] parityajya śrīherukādhiṣṭhāna sarvalauki[k]a-lokottarasauca ācarito bhavatīty arthaḥ*).

[43] Jayabhadra explains that "the five insignia are the necklace, crest jewel, earring, choker, and the sacred thread" (E 29b.4: *pañcamudrā rucaka-śiromaṇi-kuṇḍala-kaṇṭhikā-yajñopavītāḥ*). These five are also listed in both Mardo's and Sumatikīrti's translations, with the addition of *thal ba*, "ash" (PM 232a, SL 120a–b). This text is defective, however, in listing six items; it is not attested in any Sanskrit text, and is likely an interpolation deriving from commentary such as Jayabhadra's.

[44] The latter half of this verse, *ratrau tu prakaṭaṁ nityaṁ divā guptaṁ ca kārayet*, is preserved in Bhavabhaṭṭa's commentary (F 94b.4, G 86b.2). While it does not occur in the AU mss., it is attested in both translations (PM 232a, SL 120b) and in numerous other commentaries. Note that my reading differs from Pandey's (2002, 493–4).

hidden, and fatigue should be removed and avoided. Purity is known to be threefold, and it exists in one's own {mental} continuum.[45]][46]

Drawing attention to social class or lack thereof,[47] and tying up the hair in a crest, and so forth,[48] are to be avoided. The messengers are the first purity, and the second is acknowledged to be *soma*. Eating the *caru* oblation together is said to be the third purity. Gradually attaining purification through the protection of the purities, whence will power not arise?

That which is stated in the *Tattvasaṁgraha*—and is likewise stated in the *Samvara*,[49] is proclaimed in the *Guhya Tantra*[50] as well as in the *Śrī Paramādya*,[51] as well as in the *Mahābhairava*[52]—bestows the powers of [mantra] repetition, observance, and so forth. Here[53] the mantrin brings

---

[45] Here Bhavabhaṭṭa clarifies: "**exists in one's own continuum**, i.e., in one's own mind" (Pandey 2002, 494: *svasrotasi svacitte vyavasthitam iti*).

[46] This verse is preserved in Bhavabhaṭṭa's commentary, and it is attested in Mardo's translation (PM 232a) and partially in Sumatikīrti's (SL 120b). It is omitted, however, in the parallel passage of the AU, and is not attested in most other commentaries.

[47] Bhavabhaṭṭa comments here: "Those with **class** are the brahmins, and so forth; those **lacking** it are those of the lowest class" (Pandey 2002, 494: *varṇā brāhmaṇādayaḥ / avarṇā antyajāḥ*).

[48] According to Jayabhadra, "the expression **and so forth** indicates that other worldly practices are to be avoided" (E 29b.6: *ādiśabdāt anyalaukikācāravarjitāḥ*).

[49] Bhavabhaṭṭa comments that here "**the *Samvara*** refers to the *Samvara Appendix*" (Pandey 2002, 494: *samvara iti samvarottare*), which is most likely a reference to the *Sarvabuddha-samayoga-ḍākinījālasamvara-uttaratantra* (Tōh. 366). This is confirmed by Śūraṅgavajra in his AU commentary (SC 210a). The AU mss. here read *cakrasamvare* (H 140a.1, I 596b.2, J 226.5), which is meaningful there, but nonsensical here. The Pandey edition mistakenly adopts this reading.

[50] Ordinarily this is identified with the *Guhyasamāja Tantra*, but according to Bhavabhaṭṭa this refers to the "*Guhyakośa*, and so forth" (Pandey 2002, 494: *guhyatantra iti guhya-kośādau*). The name *Guhyakośa* was apparently used for the "Secret Nucleus" (*gsang ba'i snying po*) Tantra preserved in the rNying-ma rGyud-'bum (Tōh. 832, *rnying rgyud* vol. kha, 110b–132a; Kaneko 1982, #187). See Davidson 2002b, 422.

[51] The name *Śrīparamādya* (Tōh. 487, 488; T. 244) is attested by all translations, including the AU, which read *dpal mchog dang po*, as well as by CS ch. 30, where *paramādya* occurs in a similar list. All extant Sanskrit mss. here read *haritantre*, which may be an alias for this text.

[52] This may refer to one of the texts studied in Siklos 1996.

[53] Bhavabhaṭṭa clarifies that "**here** means in the *Śrī Cakrasamvara [Tantra]*" (Pandey 2002, 495: *iha tu śrīcakrasamvare*).

[those powers] forth in an instant through meditation alone. He should undertake purity with the pleasures of the path of yoga. It is not possible to speak—with one [mouth only]—about the merit that would derive from the purities. It is the expanse of the adept's good qualities, [for which] not [even] a [hundred] thousand mouths[54] [would suffice].

The knowledge of Śrī Heruka is the purified means of achieving all qualities. By drinking the water of bliss, one's merit is purified and one's sins are destroyed.[55] Freed of all sins,[56] the superior man, who practices through contact or even intercourse,[57] has a purified body that is free of illness, is purified of all sins, and obtains the glory of being a tathāgata. In life after life one is born in the Tathāgata clan, and one becomes a righteous king, [a universal monarch].[58]

---

[54] Bhavabhaṭṭa here reads "one thousand" (Pandey 2002, 495: *ekasahasrān*), a reading matched by Sumatikīrti's revised translation (SL 120b: *stong phrag gcig pa'i gdong*). The AU mss., however, read "one hundred thousand" (H 140a.3, I 596b.3: *ekaṁ śatasahasrān*; J 226.7–227.1: *ekaśatasahasānanā*), a reading matched by Mardo's revised translation (PM 232a: *stong phrag brgya yi gdong*).

[55] This is a translation of the text preserved in the AU mss., *saukhyāmbuprāśanāt puṇyaṁ pavitraṁ pāpanāśanam* (H 140a.3–4, I 596b.4, J 227.1), which corresponds to Sumatikīrti's translation (SL 120b). There is an alternate reading preserved in Bhavabhaṭṭa's commentary, which corresponds to Mardo's translation (PM 232b), namely "The adept's drinking of the water of bliss is the nature of nondual yoga; it purifies and destroys sin" (F 96a.3–4: *sādhakasya ca saukhyāmbuprāśano 'dvayayogātmā pavitraṁ pāpanāśanam*). I suspect that *'dvayayogātmā* is a commentarial interpolation, and that the AU preserves the older reading here.

[56] This line, *sarvapāpavinirmuktaḥ*, is preserved in Bhavabhaṭṭa's commentary (Pandey 2002, 495) and attested in Sumatikīrti's translation (SL 120b), but it is not attested elsewhere. It may be an interpolation, a redundant one added perhaps for emphasis.

[57] The AU mss. preserve here the reading *bhāvanāt* (H 140a.4, I 596b.4, J 227.1), "through meditation," which is appealing, as the context of this passage is the sexual yogas, implying here that one may practice either through "contact," i.e., actual engagement in sexual yoga, or "meditation," i.e., visualized simulation of the same. However, this reading is not attested elsewhere. It may, however, be an emendation made to justify the celibate version of this yoga. Bhavabhaṭṭa here reads *saṁbhāṣaṇād*, "through intercourse" (Pandey 2002, 495), which in Sanskrit as in English has the double meaning of verbal communication as well as sexual union.

[58] The term *cakravartī* is attested only in the AU mss. (H 140a.5, I 596b.5, J 227.2–3: *cakravartiṁ*). Bhavabhaṭṭa does not comment on this line, and Pandey "reconstructs" it in a manner which conflates it with the following line (2002, 496).

Always worshipping thus, one should offer sacrificial cakes with devotion.[59] They should be given [by the yogin in accordance with the ritual procedure] for the sake of his desired ritual action. On [the tenth day of] the waning fortnight, and on that of the waxing fortnight, the Vajradevīs[60] should be worshipped quickly and energetically with spirits and meats. They are worshipped by the devoted man who has come to take delight in Śrī Heruka. When they are contented they confer boons, and he reaches the state of being in the hands of those supreme ones.[61] [One who has the nocturnal observance should offer sacrificial cakes, naked with one's hair let down, and united with Śrī Heruka. Thence the mothers are pleased.][62]

---

[59] The parallel passage in the AU mss. ends here. The last three and a half verses (or fourteen lines) of this chapter are preserved completely in Tibetan translation, and the Sanskrit is partially preserved in Bhavabhaṭṭa's commentary, where one and a half verses (or six lines) are completely preserved, and another verse (four lines) is partially preserved. The last verse of the chapter is available only in Tibetan translation. Text translated exclusively from the Tibetan is here enclosed in square brackets.

[60] Bhavabhaṭṭa here reads *vajradevyaḥ*, which corresponds to Sumatikīrti's *rdo rje lha mo* (SL 121a). Mardo's text, on the other hand, reads here *rdo rje phag mo*, "Vajravārāhī" (PM 232b).

[61] This is a literal translation of the Sanskrit *tāsāṁ karasthāni yato varāṇām*. The Tibetan translations differ somewhat, with *de rnams lag gnas mchog rnams so* (PM 232b) and *de rnams la gnas mchog ster byed* (SL 121a), both of which lack the verb and read "supreme" as modifying "state."

[62] This last verse is translated on the basis of Mardo's revised translation: */mtshan mo brtul shugs can gtor ma/ /skra grol gcer bur gyur pas sbyin/ /śrī he ru ka'i bdag nyid du/ /sbyor des ma mo rnams mnyes 'gyur /* (PM 232b). Sumatikīrti's text differs slightly from this: */mtshan mo brtul shugs can gtor ma / /skra grol gcer bur gyur pas sbyin/ /śrī he ru ka'i bdag nyid shes / /sbyor bas ma mo rnams mnyes 'gyur /* (SL 121a).

28. The Procedures of the Inner Fire Sacrifice and Class Oneness[1]

Indeed, worthy of worship and with a purified nature, one should worship the hero who has come forth from *nirvāṇa*,[2] as well as oneself,[3] and through that all beings are worshipped.[4] One should worship all heroes and the yoginīs,[5] the animate and inanimate. Those who are on the brothers'

---

[1] As is the case with the previous two chapters, the folia covering this chapter are missing from the extant CS mss., but the Sanskrit is preserved in the parallel passage in the AU, as well as in Jayabhadra's and Bhavabhaṭṭa's commentaries. Significant differences between these sources and the Tibetan translations will be noted below.

[2] Jayabhadra glosses this as follows: "One should worship **the hero who has come forth from nirvāṇa**, i.e., who is in the state immediately following the bliss of ultimate sexual pleasure" (E 30a.1: *nirvānanirgata iti / paramasuratasukhāvasthānantaraṁ vīraṁ ca pūjayed ityarthaḥ /*). Bhavabhaṭṭa comments that "**nirvāṇa** refers to the joy of cessation—by not apprehending the objects of the outer perceptual powers. Immediately after that, departing with resolution, abiding, one should **worship** him—i.e., one's own mind that abides in natural joy—by means of the concluding worship." (Pandey 2002, 498: *nirvāṇaṁ nirgataṁ vīram iti / nirvāṇaṁ viramānando bahirbuddhiviṣayānupalambhāt / tato 'nantaraṁ niścayena gataḥ sthitaḥ taṁ pūjayed iti pratipattipūjayā ātmānaṁ cittaṁ sahajānanandasthitam /*)

[3] This line, *pūjayec caivam ātmānaṁ*, is preserved in the AU mss. (I 596b.5, J 227.3; H 140a.6: *ātmānaḥ*). Bhavabhaṭṭa's commentary attests *pūjayed* and *ātmānaṁ* (2002, 498); this was missed by Pandey, as it is embedded in commentary. Instead, he adds *yaḥ sādhakaḥ* (2002, 498), which is not attested anywhere.

[4] I translate here the text which occurs in the AU mss. and Jayabhadra's commentary, *pūjitaṁ tena sarvasya jagataḥ* (E 30a.2–3, H 140a.6, I 596b.5–6, J 227.3–4), which I suspect was the original reading here. Bhavabhaṭṭa's commentary reads *sarvabuddhādipūjitaṁ* (Pandey 2002, 498), "all buddhas, and so forth, are worshipped," which corresponds to Mardo's translation (PM 232b: *sangs rgyas sogs kun mchod pa yin*). This appears to be a later emendation, perhaps to give the text a more Buddhist appearance.

[5] This line, *dpa' bo kun dang rnal 'byor ma*, which occurs in all translations (PM 232b, SL 121a, AU 333b), does not occur in the AU mss. and is not cited by Jayabhadra. It is attested by Bhavabhaṭṭa, but he only quotes a portion of the line, *sarvavīrasya* (Pandey 2002, 498). As a result, it is not clear whether the yoginī(s) are singular or plural, or the agent or object of the action of worship. I read them as plural objects, since the line is embedded in a list of beings who are to be worshipped.

course[6] stay together in the confluence of *soma*.[7] One should not disclose gnosis, and likewise mantra and *mudrā*, to him [who], along with one's brother or son, is the source of happiness and suffering.[8] One should use the *caru* oblation as food, and always observe of the commitments. Then there is purification.[9] One should not give the mantra to anyone whatso-

[6] Jayabhadra explains that this refers to "one who practices yoga together with one who has been initiated into the same maṇḍala, and so forth" (E 30a.3–4: *ekamaṇḍalādipraviṣṭaṁ saha yogācārī*).

[7] Bhavabhaṭṭa analyzes this compound as follows: "Those who abide equally there in **confluence** or union with ***soma***, i.e., seminal essence, are those who **stay together in the confluence of *soma*"** (Pandey 2002, 498: *somena bodhicittena saṁgamo yogas tatra samatayā sthitāḥ somasaṁgamasaṁsthitāḥ*). According to Devagupta: "**Staying together in the confluence of *soma*** means entering into union with a consort. ***Soma*** is liquor, and is also the camphor of bliss, which always naturally gives rise to clear light." (SS 120b)

[8] Jayabhadra comments here that this means that "[this] gnosis, i.e., *mahāmudrā*, and so forth, and also mantra and gesture, are not disclosed in the company of worldly ones such as one's brother, son, and so forth" (E 30a.4–5: *laukikabhrātṛputrādibhiḥ sārdha[ṁ] jñānaṁ mahāmudrādikaṁ mantramudrāṁ ca na prakāśayed ityarthaḥ*). Regarding the interesting line, "along with one's brother or son, is the source of happiness and suffering," Vīravajra clarifies:

> The **brother** is well known in the world, and the son protects his blood relations. Since **together with** them there arises the nature of worldly happiness and the three and eight types of worldly suffering, one is on account of this despised. Therefore, one should not disclose to them **the mantra,** i.e., the *gaṇacakra*, the ***mudrā***, i.e., the drinking of *soma*, and the **gnosis**, the messenger's purities. (PD 412a)

The three types of suffering are: 1) the suffering of suffering, *duḥkhaduḥkha*; 2) the suffering of change, *vipariṇāmaduḥkha*; and 3) the suffering of conditioned states, *saṁskāraduḥkha*. The eight types of suffering are the sufferings of 1) birth, 2) old age, 3) sickness, 4) death; and suffering due to 5) separation from desired things, 6) contact with repulsive things, 7) seeking but not finding desired things, and 8) the five aggregates.

[9] Vīravajra explains that this verse describes the sort of person to whom gnosis, and so forth, may be disclosed:

> To whom may they be disclosed? As [the text] states, "[to him who] eats the purifying ***caru* oblation** and who **always observes the commitments**." Regarding the purifying *caru* oblation, it refers to the *gaṇacakra*'s five sensual objects (*pañcakāmaguṇa*, which correlate to the five senses). "Always observe the commitments"—i.e., the commitments of eating—means that the five sensual objects are enjoyed by one free of the eighty natures. (PD 412a)

The eighty natures (*aśītiprakṛti*) in the *Guhyasamāja* system are mental states which serve as obscurations to the realization of the three clear lights, and are divided into 33 feminine, 40 masculine, and 7 neuter forms. For a complete list, see Wayman 1977, 185–88.

ever,[10] nor should one destroy the oral instructions.[11] The oral instructions should be given appropriately to those who abide by the commitments. One should not, deluded by lust, abandon one's messenger and consort with another. One who is always attached to the messenger[12] should enjoy liberation,[13] even if he has transgressed.[14]

---

[10] Kambala qualifies this: "**One should not give the mantra to anyone whatsoever**, i.e., to sentient beings who are not fully developed. 'Give' refers to bestowing consecrations." (SN 49a)

[11] Bhavabhaṭṭa comments: "**Nor should one destroy the oral instructions** [means] one who has been solicited should never bestow the consecration, and so forth, due to avidity" (Pandey 2002, 499: *upadeśaṁ na vināśayed iti / sakṛd upayācito na tṛṣṇayā sekādikaṁ dadyāt /*).

[12] Jayabhadra and the AU mss. here read *dūtīraktaṁ* (D 40b.6, E 30a.6; H 140b.3, J 227.6: *dūtīraktā*; I 596b.7: *dūtiraktā*), as translated here; this also corresponds to the Tibetan translation (PM 233a: *pho nya rtag zhen thar pa*; SL 121b erroneously reads *zhes* instead of *zhen*). Bhavabhaṭṭa, however, gives an alternate reading, *dūtīrakṣā*, "the protection of the messenger." Interestingly, while the surviving mss. of Jayabhadra's commentary clearly read *dūtīrakta*, his commentary is suggestive of the latter reading, as follows: "**always attached to the messenger** means that, in the context of sexual pleasure, the outer woman should be armored by the great armors, and so forth" (E 30a.6–30b.1: *dūtīrakta sadā mokṣa iti suratāvasthāyāṁ bāhyāṅganā mahākavac[ā]dibhiḥ kavacayitavyetyarthaḥ*).

[13] Here I follow the AU mss.' reading of *mokṣaṁ* (H 140b.3, I 596b.7, J 227.6), which I take as the object of *bhojayet*. Bhavabhaṭṭa and Jayabhadra, however, read *mokṣa* (E 30b.1, Pandey 2002, 500), which suggests the alternate translation, "Being attached to the messenger is always liberation." The problem here is that *bhojayet* then lacks an object. The Tibetan is grammatically vague here and does not resolve this question.

[14] In the context of this verse the concept of transgression is a bit problematic, as it implies the transgression of infidelity condemned in the previous verse. Jayabhadra appears to interpret this "transgressing" in terms of the rules for finding an appropriate consort, as follows: "**Should enjoy [liberation], even if he has transgressed** means that...should she not be well educated, then becoming intimate with a good and fortunate woman, one should enjoy her" (D 40b.7–41a.1, E 30b.1–2: *atikramo 'pi bhojayed iti...na ca suśikṣitā bhavet / subhagā bhadrāṅganā / tāṁ saṁstutya bhojayed ityarthaḥ /*; both texts contain a corrupt portion, cf. MP 59b). Bhavabhaṭṭa appears to interpret the "overstepping" as being *too* attached to the messenger, arguing that this inordinate respect must be suspended during the practice of sexual yoga: "**Even transgressing one should enjoy** refers to those who hold respect for the messenger. When one is [engaged] in sexual pleasure with them, one should not act respectfully toward them. Even by means of grasping her hair, and so forth, one should enjoy the bliss of sexual pleasure." (F 99a.1–2, G 90a.1: *atikramyāpi bhojayed iti dūtyā gauravagṛhitā iti tābhiḥ saha surate tāsu na gauravaṁ kuryāt/ kacagrahaṇādināpo tāḥ suratasukhaṁ bhojayet*; Pandey misreads *atikramyāpi* as *atikramyā 'pi* [2002, 500]) His reference to hair pulling brings to mind the unconventional sexual techniques described in the *Kāmasūtra*, such as biting, scratching, slapping, and so forth. See Doniger and Kakar 2002, 45 ff. Lastly, Kambala's commentary gives a different reading which drops the notion of transgression, as follows:

One should not revere nor be preoccupied with sex with those of lesser birth.[15] One's mother, sister, daughter, and wife are accepted to be messengers.[16] Asceticism is destroyed by all means, thus there are the powers of the wheel.[17] One should draw forth [*soma*] together with the ultimate.[18] Thus there is the determination by means of fluid.[19]

"Through attachment to the messenger there is liberation; therefore, one should enjoy even by means of bliss, because all bliss is truly that very ambrosia which arises from the vulva" (SN 49a).

[15] Jayabhadra reverses the normative Indian social taxonomy, arguing here: "**One should not revere nor be preoccupied with sex with those of lesser birth**; regarding 'birth,' this means that the clans of brahmins, and so forth, should not be acknowledged. Why? Since they are not suitable receptacles for the supreme yoga, one should not show respect for them." (E 30b.2–3: *satkāraṁ ca na vai kuryāt janmahīnarate 'sthitā iti janmeti brāhmaṇādikulaṁ na grāhya kiṁtu paramayogasyāpātratvāt tatrādaro na kartavya ityarthaḥ*) Bhavyakīrti clarifies that the "clans of brahmins" refers to the clans of heretics (*tīrthika, mu stegs*), and he then adds, "I, Bhavyakīrti, hold that one should not revere those who are preoccupied by sex with those who do not know the commitments, and so forth" (SM 27a–b). I translate here the text preserved in Jayabhadra's commentary. An alternate text is preserved in the AU mss., *janmahīnena susthitān* (H 140b.3; I 596b.8: *sustitāḥ*; J 227.7: *saṁstitāḥ*), "[do not revere] those who are well-positioned on account of inferior birth status." This reading makes sense if one assumes the anti-brahmin bias exhibited by figures such as Jayabhadra. Jayabhadra's translation accords with Sumatikīrti's and the AU's translation (SL 121b, AU 333b: *skye gnas dman la mi gnas la*), except that the Tibetan lacks an equivalent to *rata*.

[16] Durjayacandra identifies these familiar figures as women of one's substitute family within the circle of relations centering upon the guru, writing "the **mother** is the guru's consort, the **sister** one's fellow disciples, the **daughter** she to whom one gives one's oral instructions, and one's **wife** is given by the guru" (RG 294b–295a).

[17] Here I translate the text preserved in the AU mss., *cakrasya siddhayas tathā* (H 140b.4, I 596b.8, J 228.1), which corresponds to Sumatikīrti's translation (SL 121b: *'khor los de bzhin grub pa la*). Bhavabhaṭṭa's commentary preserves an alternate reading, *cakraṁ vā* (F 99a.4, G 90a.5), which corresponds to Mardo's translation (PM 233a: *'khor lo'am de bzhin grub pa la*). Note that Pandey reads *vakraṁ vā* here, despite the fact that both mss. F and G clearly read *cakraṁ*. The "powers of the wheel" refers to the powers attained through the practice of the yoga of maṇḍala visualization, which is described at length in Kambala's (SN 49b ff.) and Devagupta's (SS 121b ff.) commentaries.

[18] Bhavabhaṭṭa explains that "the **ultimate** is seminal essence together with uterine blood" (F 99a.6, G 90a.6: *uttamaṁ bodhicittaṁ rajo 'nvitaṁ yat*; cf. Pandey 2002, 500). Jayabhadra, confirming this, further explains: "Conceptual thought should not be produced in the procedure of drawing forth *soma*" (E 30b.5: *somākarṣavidhau vikalp[o] na kartavyaḥ*); this also seems to imply that he understands being "together with the ultimate" (*cottamaṁ sārdhaṁ*) to refer to a state of mind, one which is non-conceptual (*nirvikalpa*). Kambala, however, reads this line differently, in accordance with Sumatikīrti's translation, which reads "together

In the world there is always heteropraxy. One should advance with the left foot forward. Proceeding with the left hand, showing respect with the left half [of the body],[20] [her] body embraced from the left,[21] and presenting libations and eating with the left [hand]: the adept who is devoted to the commitments does not destroy but fulfills [this] observance.[22] Through practice in the committed clan, one eats the *caru* libation together

---

with the ultimate, middling, and inferior" (SL 121: *mchog dbus tha ma lhan cig dgugs*), and interprets them, as in the case of ch. 1, in terms of the three classes of messengers, who correlate to the three levels of the triple world as well as to the maṇḍala's three wheels (SN 51b). It is thus possible that "ultimate" here refers to the messenger who is the yogin's partner in this procedure.

[19] Here I follow David White in translating *dravyam* as "fluid" rather than "substance" (its more common translation). As White notes, "as a derivative of the root *dru*, 'flow, run,' *dravyam* may in fact be read as a gerundive, as 'that which is to, which ought to flow,' which is entirely appropriate in the contexts in which it is used in Tantric sources" (White 2003, 275 n. 36). This is certainly one of these contexts; Bhavabhaṭṭa explains that "the **fluid** is seminal essence, and taking it up without objection is the **determination**" (Pandey 2002, 500: *dravyaṁ bodhicittaṁ tasya niravadyagrahaṇaṁ niścayaḥ*). Again, this seems to imply that the yogin's ability to consume the sexual fluids, the "substance" of the yoginī's clan, is an important matter, bearing in mind that not showing disgust or anger in this context is one of the commitments listed in ch. 26 above.

[20] The AU mss. here read *vāmārdhaparipūjakaḥ* (H 140b.5, I 596b.9), which I have translated here, as it makes the most sense, referring presumably to the gestures, and so forth, by which the adept communicates with the yoginīs. Bhavabhaṭṭa has the variant *vāmordhvapratipūjakā*, "showing respect with the left elevation [or the elevation of the left]." Regarding this, Bhavabhaṭṭa comments: "The word *elevation* designates the vajra, by which there is worship by the yogin of the intended object, the yoginīs" (Pandey 2002, 501: *ūrdhvaśabdena vajraṁ tena yoginīnāṁ pratītyāśayaṁ pūjakā yoginaḥ*). This reading, however, is not attested elsewhere, and seems less likely to me. The two Tibetan translations both read "showing respect by means of the conduct of the left" (PM 233a, SL 121b: *g-yon gyi spyod pas rab mchod byed*), which does not precisely correspond to either Sanskrit reading.

[21] Unfortunately, Jayabhadra and Bhavabhaṭṭa do not comment on this line, and the AU mss. give variant readings. The oldest ms., however reads *vāmagūḍhagātras tu* (H 140b.5), which I emend to *vāmavigūḍhagātras tu*, since *vigūḍha* corresponds to the Tibetan translations *'khyud pa* (PM 233a) and *rnam par 'khri* (SL 121b).

[22] Here I translate *sādhakaḥ samayatatparaḥ*, the reading preserved in the AU mss. (H 140b.6, I 597a.1; J 228.2: *samayatatparaparaḥ*) and attested by Sumatikīrti's translation (SL 121b: *sgrub pa po ni dam tshig brtson*). A variant text preserved by Bhavabhaṭṭa, *kṛtatatparaḥ* (Pandey 2002, 501), does not make as much sense, as *kṛta* indicates a completed action, while *tatparaḥ* indicates an ongoing engagement in or dedication to something.

with [others]. [This is] known as practice in the five classes, and [also in] the four classes.[23] Practice in the one clan is revered for the yogic powers.[24]

Should one make a triangular maṇḍala [and offer] beef, horse meat, dog meat, and [meats] of various others,[25] even the Buddha will be permanently destroyed.[26] Furnished with *mudrā* and mantra, this indeed is the enjoyment of the heroes.[27] The emanation of Śrī Heruka,[28] noted in the

---

23 I translate here a hybrid reading, *pañcavarṇasamācāraś caturvarṇaś ca kīrtitaḥ*, that corresponds to both Tibetan translations (PM 233a, SL 121b). The text *pañcavarṇasamācāraś* occurs in Bhavabhaṭṭa's commentary (Pandey 2002, 501); the AU mss. read instead *bāhyamaṇḍalasamācāraś* (H 140b.6, I 597a.1, J 228.3). The text *caturvarṇaś ca* occurs in the AU mss. (J 228.3; H 140b.6: *caturvarṇa-*, last syllable omitted due to missing folio; I 597a.1: *caturvarṇa*), while Bhavabhaṭṭa here reads *acaturvarṇaś*. Bhavabhaṭṭa reads *kīrtitaḥ* (Pandey 2002, 501), while the AU mss. read *prakīrtitaḥ* (I 597a.1, J 228.3). Regarding this, Kambala comments: "Regarding **practice in the five classes**, since the Mahāratna clan can be subsumed into the Akṣobhya clan, they are classified in terms of **four classes**" (SN 52a).

24 Kambala comments that "there is also the ultimate, the **practice in the one clan** of the lord of the mind" (SN 52a).

25 Jayabhadra explains that "**of various others** indicates the employment of the peacock or cock" (E 31a.6: *citriṇām iti mayūrasya kurkuṭasya vā grahaṇaṁ*).

26 Jayabhadra offers the following commentary on the oblation ceremony briefly described here:

> As for **beef**, and so forth, it is the instruction on the annihilation of those who injure many beings. As for the process regarding this, the procedure ordained in the fire sacrifice instructions is as follows: Make a triangular fire pit, and kindle a fire with mustard seeds, and so forth, using the paraphernalia and substances of a fierce oblation, according to the rules stated for that. Imagine that Khaṇḍarohā enters [the victim's] right nostril and exits from his anus. With an adamantine hook and knife in hand she summons the victim, rendered naked and confused. Imagine that he is completely shattered, and that the requisite meat—the beef, and so forth—is the victim's flesh. [Say] "so and so must die," with the pride of one accompanied by a great fierce one, and offer sacrifice with the root mantra.
>
> *gomāṁsetyādinā satabahusattvāpakāriṇāṁ teṣāṁ vināśārtham upadiṣṭaṁ tatrāyaṁ krama // homopayikāvihitavicāraṇa // t[ri]koṇakuṇḍa[ṁ] kṛtvā k[rū]rahomopakaraṇadravyeṇa taduktavidhānena kaṭukatailādibhiḥ prajvālya khaṇḍarohā dakṣiṇanāsāpūṭena praveśya pāyunirgatāṁ dhyātvā tayā vajrakuśakarttikāgṛhītahastayā nagnakṛtaṁ vihvalībhūtaṁ sādhyam ākṛṣya tayaiva khaṇḍakhaṇḍī{kṛtaṁ}vicintya gomāṁsādiyathāvihitamāṁseṇa tasya sādhyasya māṁsam iti vicintya mahākrodhānvitenāhaṁkāreṇāmukaṁ mārayed iti mūlamantreṇa juhuyād iti /* (E 31a, with an emendation from the similar passage at F 100a.4, G 90b.9, in curly brackets)

27 Jayabhadra comments: "It is held that **the heroes** praise that **enjoyment** which is **furnished with**, i.e., attended by, an outer woman who is made of ***mudrā* and mantra**, well

treatises on service,[29] should always be retained. As for protection by means of all ritual actions, this is accomplished without obstruction. There is no other [way] whatsoever.

His messenger is supreme, divine, energized, and has a companion.[30] Impassioned,[31] she incites the yogic fluid through sexual union.[32] Enamored with the guru's instructions, her aim is to be like the wealth giver.[33]

---

educated in mantra and tantra" (E 31b: *mantramudrāmayī mantratantrasuśikṣitā bāhyāṅganā tayā [samo]p[e]tasahita yad bhojanaṁ tad vīrāṇāṁ praśastaṁ bhavatīty abhiprāyaḥ*).

[28] According to Jayabhadra, "[the expression] **the emanation of Śrī Heruka** is a metaphor for seminal essence" (E 31b.2: *nirmāṇam iti bodhicittasyaiva paryāyaḥ*).

[29] This translates the reading preserved in the AU mss., *upacāraśāstravilakṣitaṁ* (J 228.5; I 597a.2: *upacārasarvaśāstravilakṣitaṁ*). There is no alternate Sanskrit text preserved. However, in place of *vilakṣitaṁ*, "noted, observed," the Tibetan translations read *spang*, "abandoned" (PM 233a, SL 122a). I follow the former reading, since the latter reading makes less sense, especially as it seems to directly contradict the line which follows.

[30] According to Jayabhadra, "she **has a companion** means that she is not one who goes to another. She who is like this is **divine**." (E 31b.3: *sahāyānvitā aparagamanā evaṁ bhūtā divyā bhavati*)

[31] "Impassioned" (*suraktā*) is the reading preserved in Jayabhadra's commentary (E 31b.3), and corresponds to the two translations (PM 233a: *kun nas chags*; SL 122a: *chags pa'i*). The AU mss. here read "dispassionate" (I 597a.3, J 228.6: *araktā*), a reading also found in Bhavabhaṭṭa's commentary.

[32] That is, *ratisaṁyogād*, preserved in both Jayabhadra's and Bhavabhaṭṭa's commentary (E 31b.3–4; Pandey 2002, 502). The AU mss. read *ratisaṁbhogād* (I 597a.3, J 228.6), which could likewise translate as "through sexual union" or "though sexual pleasure." Regarding *yogadravya*, Jayabhadra writes that "the **fluid** of yoga—i.e., of concentration—is that which is to be eaten" (E 31b.4: *yogaḥ samādhidravyaṁ bhakṣaṇīyaṁ*).

[33] Commenting on this line, Jayabhadra writes: "Thus, one who practices with [this] aim as stated is like Śrī Heruka" (E 31b.6: *evaṁ yathoktārthacārī śrīherukasamo bhavati*). Bhavabhaṭṭa explicitly identifies the "wealth giver" (*dhanada*) with Śrī Heruka and describes the wealth he gives as follows:

> Now, having that as one's aim means striving to obtain it. Here wealth is faith, and so forth; as it is said, there are "wealth of faith, wealth of wisdom, wealth of learning, wealth of energy, wealth of happiness, wealth of concentration, and wealth of memory." The **wealth giver** is he who bestows these, i.e., he who is established through the accomplishment of the aim of the impassioned ones. This refers to Śrī Heruka, and those who are like him.
>
> *ataḥ tad arthayantīti tadarthāḥ / itaś ca dhanaṁ śraddhādi / tathāha śraddhādhanaṁ prajñādhanaṁ śrutadhanaṁ vīryadhanaṁ prītidhanaṁ samādhidhanaṁ smṛtidhanaṁ ceti tad dadāti kāminām athasampādanān niyatam iti dhanadaḥ śrīherukas tatsamāḥ* (Pandey 2002, 503)

29. The Procedures of the Messenger's Defining Marks and the State of Empowerment

Now, moreover, one should know that which is taught regarding the messengers' characteristics, whereby one correctly discerns the ḍākinīs who are devoted to the commitments. In a moment one sees the brother, father, and even the Lord himself. She has a thick tongue, tawny eyes, is rough,[1] and has tawny hair.[2] One who is equal with regard to all of the powers,

---

[1] Bhavabhaṭṭa glosses this as "**rough** to the touch" (Pandey 2002, 504: *karkaśī sparśane*).

[2] Kambala takes this list of qualities as a starting point for a lengthy exposition of the qualities of the different types of messengers. It is not entirely clear how they break down into separate types; I read the text in terms of five different types, and number accordingly in my translation. (Tsong Khapa, however, groups it into four types; see KS 158a–b.) Kambala writes:

> Regarding **thick tongue**, (1) her face is broad and her breasts expansive. Her face is also short, and her hair short. She smells and tastes like an elephant, and is haughty. In short, she is very well known. (2) Her body is tall and her face long, and her hands and feet are likewise long. She smells and tastes like fish, and exudes [sexual] fluid. Her vagina is long and like a [crescent] moon. Her breasts are equal, greenish blue, and firm. (3) Her limbs are small and her hair fine. Her vagina is small, and her hair coarse. She speaks with ease and her nose is high. Her neck is long but not too long. Her body is beautiful like a white lotus. Her body always exudes a ravishing fragrance. Her eyes and glance are like those of a deer, and she has a deer's neck and deer's belly, and a waist like the king of deer's. She is auspicious, and has the scent of a lotus. Regarding **tawny eyes**, (4) "tawny" means slightly reddened, and her hands and feet are also red. She exudes the scent of jasmine. This woman who takes pleasure in the company of the sugatas bestows power. Her body is expansive, as are her breasts. Her hair is wound, and she has a goose-like gait. She speaks with ease. Her face is round and not very long, and there are three folds [of fat] across her belly, which hang from the center. [Thus] is she known. As for **rough**, (5) her limbs are rough, and she curses like Indra. Her hair is wound and sorrel colored. Her complexion is bad, and she is devoid of breasts, like a man. She has the scent and taste of fermented rice. She is radiant and anointed with fermented rice. She always takes pleasure in alcohol. She has perfected the practice of the commitments, and exerts herself in examining her thoughts. She is a fan of alcohol that is particularly delicious, with which she gets very intoxicated. In addition, her [sexual] fluid is copious. (SN 56a)

always intent upon [mantra] repetition and observance, and endowed with recollection, is connected to the state of the messenger, and so forth.[3] The twenty-four ḍākinīs[4] bestow the fruit of enjoyment and liberation.

Always repeat the root mantra which is the means of achieving all desired aims. [It pacifies all devils][5] and is the gift of the fruit of yogic play. The mantra arises suddenly in the triple world, in everything mobile and immobile. Endowed with the mantra and the consort,[6] the adept is entirely focused on power.[7] Devoid of the consort, the mantra will not be present for the embodied.

One will be awakened through constant practice in the nature of the exercises of heat.[8] Those who disparage [this] great yoga (*mahāyoga*) that is

---

[3] According to Jayabhadra, "**connected to the state of the messenger** refers to the mantrin who is endowed with the messenger on account of the continual practice of yoga. **And so forth** here means that he is devoted to the vows regarding what is to be protected and what is to be eaten." (E 32a.2–3: *dūtyādipadānvitam iti / an[ā]ratayogābhyāśena dūtīsaṁyuktaṁ / ādiśabdo 'tra rakṣaṇīyabhakṣaṇīyasamvarasthito mantrī /*)

[4] Here I translate *caturviṁśatiḍākinyaḥ,* as preserved both in Jayabhadra's commentary (E 32a.2) and also in one ms. of Bhavabhaṭṭa's commentary (G 92a.5). The AU here reads *caturviṁśativīraḍākiny[aḥ]* (J 229.1), "twenty-four heroes and ḍākinīs," while another Bhavabhaṭṭa ms. reads *caturviṁśaparā ḍākinyo* (F 101b.6), which corresponds to all of the Tibetan translations (PM 233b, SL 122a, AU 334a: *mkha' 'gro ma mchog nyi shu bzhi*). I have translated the former, as I believe that both *vīra* and *parā* are later interpolations.

[5] This line (*bdud kun rab tu zhi bar byed*) is present in both Tibetan translations (PM 233b, SL 122b), but is not attested in any of the surviving Sanskrit texts or Indian commentaries.

[6] According to Bhavabhaṭṭa, the term *mudrā* here indicates the goddess (*devatā*) or consort (Pandey 2002, 505).

[7] This text, which is omitted in the AU, is reconstructed from the following text in Bhavabhaṭṭa's commentary: *siddhitatparaḥ sa sādhako bhavati* (Pandey 2002, 505). While this accords with the Tibetan translations (PM 233b: *sgrub pa po ni dngos grub brtson*; SL 122b: *sgrub byed bsgrub la brtson dang*), Pandey ignored this text and devised instead the following reading: *siddhyabhiyuktaś ca sādhakaḥ* (2002, 505).

[8] Jayabhadra defines "heat" (*uṣma*) as "the power of yoga" (*yogabala*), and also connects it to the four "aids to penetration" (*nirvedhabhāgiya*) of the "path of application" (*prayogamārga*), described by Asaṅga in the *Mahāyānasūtrālaṁkāra* (ch. 14 following v. 26, see Bagchi 1970, 91), as follows: "**Exercise of heat** is a metaphor; heat, peak, tolerance, and world triumph should be realized in accordance with reality" (E 32a.5: *uṣmākriyayā ity upalakṣaṇa / uṣmāmūrdhākṣāntyagradharmādayo yathārthatvā [bo]ddhavyā /*). Bhavabhaṭṭa, however, connects it to success in the magical rites such as pacifying (*śāntika*), enriching (*pauṣṭika*), destroying (*abhicāra*), and so forth (Pandey 2002, 506).

the means of achieving all desired aims will, after passing through one hundred dog wombs, be born among the caṇḍālas.[9] [It is] just as if someone whose aim was butter were to churn water with confidence: butter would not be produced, only physical pain [would result]. Those who have resorted to other yogas, due to the motive of [earning] a livelihood, uphold or even revere them in error and in vain.

One should select the land in which the heroes who uphold great yoga dwell, even if it is in a land of caṇḍālas and barbarians. Through that I always exist in order to benefit sentient beings.[10]

---

[9] That is, an outcaste and generally despised social group.

[10] Bhavabhaṭṭa expands on this last line as follows: "**I always exist** for the sake of the benefit of those **sentient beings** who are connected with **that** land which is blessed with the yogins of Śrī Heruka" (Pandey 2002, 506: *tasyeti śrīherukayogyadhiṣṭhitasya deśasya sambandhino ye sattvās teṣām anugrahārthaṁ nityaṁ tiṣṭhāmi*).

30. The Procedure of Mantra Selection Bound in the Muraja Drum

Now[1] above all I will speak of the chart that is very hard to obtain, through mere knowledge of which there is rapid perfection of the powers. Having anointed the level, pleasing piece of ground with sandalwood, it is rubbed with perfume and filled with a flower arrangement. It is covered with rows of lamps, and has pleasing incense and fragrance. Having done everything oneself, one should undertake the binding of the directions. Then, having made the *muraja* drum binding,[2] the nine lines and a circle,[3] write down the whole class of letters,[4] well placed within the chart. One should select the hero who stands there, the means of achieving all desired

---

[1] As Jayabhadra informs us in commenting upon the chapter's first word—"**now**, and so forth, [indicate] that one should select the *śumbha-niśumbha* mantra" (E 30a.6: *athetyādinā śumbhaniśumbhamantram uddharet*)—this chapter encodes a mantra. As in the case of ch. 5, the actual mantra is given below, at the end of the chapter. Unlike chs. 5 and 7, however, both consonants and vowels are encoded here.

[2] Jayabhadra comments here: "**Then, having made the *muraja* drum binding** means that one should draw [a grid] with forty-nine squares in the shape of a *muraja* drum" (E 30a.6–b.1: *murajabandha[ṁ] tataḥ kṛtveti murajākāra unapañcāśa[t]koṣṭhayuktaṁ likhet*). A *muraja* is a large drum, not unlike a kettle drum.

[3] The Indian commentators who comment on this line (Kambala, Devagupta, and Durjayacandra) do so in a cryptic fashion. A clearer explanation is given by Sachen as follows:

> One scatters flowers at the edge [of the piece of ground] which one has anointed with alcohol and the five nectars while repeating the mantra of the Four-Faced [deity]. **Then, having made the *muraja* drum binding** means that one should make the four-faced drum. How is that done? According to the *Khaṭikā*, first draw an outer circular line, and within it make the **nine lines**, that is, draw the forty-nine square [grid]. At the edge of that, draw the eight lines which are the drum's fastening cords. (PG 346.1)

[4] Here I interpret x-*mātra* as meaning "the whole class of x," which in this case would designate all forty-nine letters of the Sanskrit alphabet written on a 7x7 grid. The Tibetan translations here is "the last letter" (PM 234a: *yi ge phyi mo*; SL 123a: *yi ge phyi ma*), which would appear to be a translation of *varṇāntaṁ*, which *may* represent a genuine textual variant, but which makes less sense.

aims.[5] The classes of letters are completed both via the normal and reverse orders.[6]

The sage, having entered into the calculation of this, should take the thirty-second square [**s**],[7] which is distinguished by the fifth [**u**]. Taking half of half of a hundred [**m**], it is distinguished by the twenty-fourth [**bha**]. The thirty-sixth square [**n**][8] is distinguished by the third square [**i**]. Taking the thirty-second [**s**], it is distinguished by the fifth square [**u**]. Taking the twenty-fifth [**m**], it is linked to the twenty-fourth [**bha**]. Taking the thirty-third [**h**], it is illumined by the fifteenth square [**ṁ**], and is endowed with the fifth [**u**]. [And endowed with the twenty-second (**pha**), there is also the twenty-seventh (**ṭ**).][9] The first line, which is held to be magnificent and supreme, is stated.

---

[5] As noted above in the context of ch. 5, the term "hero" (*vīraṁ*) is used to refer here to the *mantra*, which is viewed as being inseparable from the deity himself.

[6] According to Sachen: "**The normal order** means that the vowels are placed in the grid in clockwise order, while the **reverse order** means that the consonants are placed on the grid beginning with *ha* in counterclockwise order" (PG 346.2). Tsong Khapa, however, argues against this, and states that the consonants also are placed on the grid in the usual order. He is, however, not able to come up with a convincing explanation of *vilomena*, "in reverse order." See KS 161a–b. If Tsong Khapa is correct, "normal order" (*anuloma*) refers to the normal order of counting the letters, i.e., starting from *a* or *k*, while "reverse order" (*viloma*) refers to the two cases where the text explicitly calls for counting backwards from *h*.

[7] That is, counting from *k*. Some of the numbers given for consonants presume that one count the vowels, as will be noted below. One should also note that the text, here and below, incorrectly codes the letter *s* for the names *śumbha niśumbha*, no doubt due to the assimilation of *s* and *ś* in colloquial speech. The proper spelling, however, is given in the mantra at the end of the chapter.

[8] That is, the thirty-sixth counting from *a*; if we exclude the vowels and subtract 16, we get 20, the number which usually encodes *n*.

[9] This translates an additional half-verse that is absent in both the CS mss. and the parallel passage in the AU, but is preserved in Bhavabhaṭṭa's commentary as follows: *dvāviṁśati-samāyuktaṁ saptaviṁśatim eva ca* (Pandey 2002, 509), with the "twenty-seventh" counting from *a*. Both Tibetan translations have a close variant of this, namely: "And endowed with the twenty-second, there is also the eleventh" (PM 234a, SL 123a: */ nyi shu rtsa gnyis pa dang ldan // bcu gcig pa yi mtshan pa'o /*), with "the eleventh" also coding *ṭ*, counting from *k*. Most likely, this is a later interpolation, added to reflect the fact that the first line of the mantra does indeed contain the syllable *phaṭ*.

The nineteenth from the square [**g**] is endowed with the son of fire [**r**], and is distinguished by the third square [**i**].[10] The eighth seed from the semivowel class [**h**] is endowed with the thirty-sixth square [**na**]. Then one will have the syllables. Moreover, this line as well is the means of achieving all desired aims. Taking next the self-arisen [**h**], it is conjoined with the fifth square [**u**], and is adorned above with a drop [**ṁ**]. The second line, which is called the means of achieving all [desired aims], is stated.[11]

The nineteenth square [**g**] is distinguished by the twenty-seventh [**r**], and conjoined with the third [**i**]. Taking the thirty-third [**h**], it is endowed with the second [**ā**] and twentieth squares [**n**]. It is constituted as magnificent and supreme. The twenty-first square [**pa**] is likewise endowed with the twenty-sixth [**ya**]. The well-equipoised one should select again the twice-repeated word. Next, take the first among the squares via the reverse order [**h**]; it is endowed with that which is the end of the fourth [**u**], and is illumined by the fifteenth [**ṁ**]. The third line is spoken for the sake of morality, wealth, desire, and liberation.[12]

Take the seed which is the second square [**ā**], the thirty-third from the square [**na**], the twenty-sixth [**ya**],[13] and also the thirty-third [**h**]. [The latter] is illumined by the thirteenth square [**o**]. The adept [selects] the tenth square via the reverse order [**bha**]. [Select] the nineteenth from the square [**ga**], and likewise the twenty-third from the square [**b**],[14] which is

---

[10] As was the case in ch. 7 above, the text incorrectly codes for the semivowel *r* and the vowel *i* instead of for the retroflex vowel *ṛ*.

[11] This translates the text in the AU mss., *sarvārthasādhanaṁ nāma* (H 174b.6, I 613a.3; J 285.1: *sarvārthasādhanaṁ nāmaṁ*), which is supported by Sumatikīrti (SL 123b: *don kun bsgrub ces bya ba*). The CS mss. read *sarvārthasādhakaṁ*, and Bhavabhaṭṭa reads *sarvakāmārthasādhakaṁ nāma* (Pandey 2002, 510), a reading supported by Mardo (PM 234a: *'dod pa'i don kun sgrub byed yin*).

[12] The placement of this statement regarding "the third line" follows the order in the AU mss., Jayabhadra's and Bhavabhaṭṭa's commentaries, and the Tibetan translations. In the CS mss. this statement occurs just above, before the coding for the syllable *huṁ*.

[13] Bhavabhaṭṭa's commentary includes the additional line "the fourth line is spoken" (Pandey 2002, 511: *caturthaṁ padam ucyate*). It is not included in the CS or AU mss., or in the Tibetan translations. Jayabhadra does quote a portion of this text (E 33a.6–b.1: *catutho pado*; D 44b.3: *catutho padā*), but not in this context. He quotes it in place of the reading "the third line" (*tṛtīyaṁ padaṁ*) contained in all of the other sources.

[14] As in the case of chapter 5 above, the text incorrectly codes the letter *b* rather than *v*, no doubt due to confusion of the two letters. The correct number should be twenty-nine, which

linked to the second square [**ā**]. It is adorned above with a drop [**ṁ**]. Taking next the lord of the earth [**va**], the learned one should once again distinguish the eighth [**j**] with fire [**ra**]. The syllables *hūṁ phaṭ* are affixed to the end [of the mantra].

This mantra is called the "Conquest of the Triple World" (*trailokya-vijaya*), and it is ornamented with four lines. The syllable *oṁ* illumines all, and the syllables *hūṁ phaṭ* are affixed to the end. This univeral monarch king of spells (*vidyārājacakravartī*) mantra does not occur, nor will it occur, in the *Tattvasaṁgraha, Paramādya, Samvara,* [*Guhya*{*samāja*}], or *Vajra-bhairava.*[15] It is endowed with the four fierce ones[16] and is complete with the eight forms,[17] for the sake of protecting this maṇḍala, especially from all

---

is in fact present in one of the AU mss. (J 285.6: *ekonatriṁśatikoṣṭhakāṁ*). The other two mss. incorrectly have the numbers thirty-nine and nineteen (H 175a.4–5: *ekonacatvāriṁśamaṁ koṣṭhakā*; I 613a.6–7: *ekonaviṁśatikoṣṭhakāṁ*).

[15] These refer to well-known Buddhist tantras, as noted in chs. 3 and 27 above. These refer to well-known Buddhist tantras, as noted in chs. 3 and 27 above. Note that the text *guhye* here occurs only in the CS mss., and does not occur in the AU mss., the Tibetan translations, or Bhavabhaṭṭa's commentary.

[16] According to Durjayacandra:

> **Endowed with the four fierce ones** should be explained as being Ṭakkirāja, Nīla-daṇḍa, Mahābala, and Acalanātha. The first three are white, green, and red, and the fourth is blue and red. They have fierce faces with barred fangs, and have skull garlands and their right legs extended. They tread upon the four Māras, and are terrifying, with human bone ornaments. In their fury, blazing with radiant light, they are embraced by their own consorts of light. They gaze with fierce gazes, and with two of their six hands they form the gesture of victory on their foreheads. With their remaining four hands they hold, respectively, a hammer, cudgel, trident, sword, bell, skull, vajra, brandish the index finger, and hold a tiger skin. They have three eyes and fierce forms. This completes the four fierce ones. (RG 299a–b)

[17] According to Durjayacandra: "**The eight forms** indicate the messengers who exist in the Commitment Wheel, from Yamadāhī, and so forth, through Yamamathanī" (RG 299b). Vīravajra gives a more equivocal explanation: "**Complete with the eight forms** refers to the mantra which has the eight fierce kings. Or, it refers to Vairocana, and so forth. Or, it refers to the eight, Kākāsyā, and so forth." (PD 195a) The last option accords with Durjaya-candra's. The first, presumably, refers to the *aṣṭakrodharāja* of the Māyājāla tradition, which includes, in addition to the four previously mentioned in Durjayacandra's quote, the following four deities: Yamāntaka, Aparājita, Hayagrīva, and Amṛtakuṇḍalī. See the *Māyājāla-mahātantrarāja* (Tōh. 466), 99b–100a. There are several lists of eight deities beginning with Vairocana, such as the *Sampuṭa Tantra*'s Vajrasattva maṇḍala which centers upon Vajradhara surrounded by Vairocana, Ratneśa, Amitābha, Amoghasiddhi, Locanā, Māmakī, Pāṇḍarā,

of the wicked ones. Were such a one to merely obtain it, he would undoubtedly die. Uttering it in union with the wheels, one will give rise to the fruit of all powers.

[The Trailokyavijaya mantra:]

> *oṁ śumbha niśumbha hūṁ hūṁ phaṭ phaṭ*
> *oṁ gṛhṇa gṛhṇa hūṁ hūṁ phaṭ phaṭ*
> *oṁ gṛhṇāpaya gṛhṇāpaya hūṁ hūṁ phaṭ phaṭ*
> *oṁ ānayahobhagavān vajra hūṁ hūṁ phaṭ phaṭ.*[18]

---

and Tārā (Bhattacharyya 1949, 37). Identical or close variants also occur in the Akṣobhya and Mañjuvajra maṇḍalas (Bhattacharyya 1949, 34–35).

[18] Note that I have provided the etymologically correct readings, with the retroflex nasal, for the terms *gṛhṇa* and *gṛhṇāpaya.* The text incorrectly codes the dental nasal, and the mss. are inconsistent in their readings. Note as well that there is considerable variance concerning the terminations of the mantras. Mss. A, F (107a.2), and G (95b.9) consistently read *hūṁ hūṁ phaṭ phaṭ.* The AU mss. consistently read *hūṁ hūṁ phaṭ* (H 175b.2–3, I 613b.1, J 286.3–4). CS ms. B reads *hūṁ hūṁ phaṭ phaṭ* after the first three, and *hūṁ hūṁ phaṭ* after the last, while CS ms. C reads *hūṁ hūṁ phaṭ phaṭ* for the first two lines, and *hūṁ hūṁ phaṭ* for the last two. Mardo's translation reads *huṁ hūṁ phaṭ* after each (PM 234b). Sumatikīrti's translation reads *hūṁ phaṭ* after the first three, and *hūṁ hūṁ phaṭ* at the end of the fourth line (SL 124a). Tsong Khapa, however, reads *huṁ huṁ phaṭ* at the end of each line (KS 166a). While the text itself codes *huṁ phaṭ,* I follow CS ms. A and Bhavabhaṭṭa in reading *hūṁ hūṁ phaṭ phaṭ.*

31. The Procedure of the Rites of Eating, Fire Sacrifice, and the Sacrificial Cakes, and the Hand Signs

Then the destruction of all,[1] arising from the vajra, is held [to be accomplished] with the great meat. It[2] is the dreadful destroyer of all the cruel ones.[3] Should one thus perform without hesitation the rites of eating, fire sacrifice, and sacrificial cakes with the meats of dogs and pigs, and also with [the meat] of those that have copper [colored] crests,[4] everything without exception will be achieved, and all kingdoms will be subdued.

By whom is the skull of the relics of the reality body disparaged, arising as it does from the tripartite cause of conch, mother-of-pearl, and pearl?[5] The hero who has a skull garland and who is adorned with a half moon is regarded as one who is born as the heroes' hero.

---

[1] The Sanskrit here reads *sarveṣāṁ nāśanaṁ*, which is translated here. The Tibetan translations read "terrifier" (PM 234b, SL 124a: *'jigs byed*).

[2] Bhavabhaṭṭa glosses the pronoun *etat* here as "meat oblation" (Pandey 2002, 514: *māṁsa-homaḥ*), indicating that the text is here describing an *abhicārahoma* rite, which itself is the "dreadful destroyer."

[3] This verse occurs as follows in the CS mss.: *tato mahāmāṁsena sarveṣāṁ nāśanaṁ vajrajaṁ smṛtam / etat sarvakrūrāṇāṁ nāśako dāruṇas tathā //*. As Bhavabhaṭṭa indicates (Pandey 2002, 514), this verse is an intertext of *Guhyasamāja* 15.78: *tato mahāmāṁsena sarveṣāṁ nāśanaṁ vajrajaṁ smṛtam / eṣo hi sarvakrūrāṇāṁ nāśako dāruṇaḥ smṛtaḥ //* (Matsunaga 1978, 77). Many thanks to Dr. Alexis Sanderson for his assistance in translating this verse.

[4] According to Jayabhadra this refers to domestic chickens (*khyim bya*). See MP 61b. Both Sanskrit texts of Jayabhadra's commentary contain a major ellipsis spanning from the end of ch. 30 to the middle of ch. 32.

[5] This verse attempts to challenge the alleged impurity of skulls, and employs both an overt Buddhist and a covert Hindu strategy for defending the use of skulls in Buddhist ritual. The overt Buddhist strategy is associating it with the relic cult, which focuses upon such physical, crematorial remnants, although it is a bit peculiar, as ordinarily it is the form body (*rūpa-kāya*), not the reality body (*dharmakāya*), that is connected with physical relics. The text also associates skulls with "pure" and auspicious substances that are similar in appearance. This may be a covert reference to *Atharva Veda* 4.10, which connects pearl and mother-of-pearl with the bones of the slain asura Vṛtra. See Whitney 1962, 161–162. If so, this is interesting, given the long association of the study of the *Atharva Veda* with Śaiva groups such as the Pāśupatas. Regarding this, see Bisschop and Griffiths 2003. (Many thanks to Dr. Joseph

The adept should display the five secret signs with his left hand. This indeed is the abode of the heroes, the procedure of the secret signs. All beings are born from the left, as is the triple world with all things animate and inanimate. Vajrasattva abides by the tree,[6] and Vairocana likewise by the creeper.[7] Padmanartaka abides by the guru,[8] and by the current the Hero,[9] the bestower of all powers. The imperishable body of Ākāśagarbha[10] [abides] by the little finger. Hayagrīva's abode is at the fingernails. These are the principles which arise from the left of all heroes. On the palm of the hands are Śrī Heruka and Vārāhī, eager for union. On the back [of the hand] are all ḍākinīs; they should be placed on the hand. This is the union of all lovers. Worship the supreme hero by means of the rules of ritual.

Walser for bringing this article to my attention.) Bhavabhaṭṭa comments: "Just as conch, and so forth, is purifying for vedic brahmins, likewise the skull is as well" (Pandey 2002, 515: *yathā śaṅkhādayo vaidikānāṁ pavitrās tathā kapālam api*). Note that the reading *dharmakāya-śarīrāṇāṁ* occurs in the CS mss., and is also attested by the Tibetan translation (PM 234b: *chos kyi sku yi lus can gyi*; SL 124b: *chos sku'i lus can gyi*). However, Bhavabhaṭṭa and AU ms. J (288.5) have the variant text *dharmajñānaśarīrāṇāṁ*. Regarding this, Bhavabhaṭṭa comments: "Gnosis or understanding is by means of the emptiness of elements, aggregates, and so forth. It is the yogins whose bodies or self-natures consist of that." (Pandey 2002, 515: *dharmajñāna-śarīrāṇām iti dharmāṇāṁ skandhādīnāṁ śūnyatādinā jñānaṁ bodhas tad eva śarīraṁ svarūpaṁ yeṣāṁ te tathā yoginām*)

[6] This translates the Sanskrit *vajrasattvas tarave sthitaḥ*. Here *tarave* is the dative of *taru*, and it follows the pattern of the dative *gurave* below. The masc. *u*-stem dative is likely used here in place of the locative due to a confusion owing to its similarity to the locative of masculine and neuter *-a* stem nouns. Pandey reads *tanave* here (2002, 516), but this is mistaken as ms. F clearly reads *tarave* (F 109a.5) in agreement with the CS mss. The more defective ms. G, however, does read *taneve* here (G 97b.4), probably due to confusion between the graphs for *r* and *n*, which are similar in Nevārī script. The Tibetan translations here read "thumb" (PM 235a: *mthe bor*; SL 124b: *'the bor*), but this is clearly an interpretive translation. Bhavabhaṭṭa, following Jayabhadra, glosses "in/on the tree" as "on the thumb" (F 109a.5: *tarave 'ṅguṣṭhe*; D 58b.5: *tarave aṅguṣṭ[he]*).

[7] Bhavabhaṭṭa glosses "by the creeper" as "by the index finger" (Pandey 2002, 516: *latāyāṁ tarjjanyāṁ*).

[8] That is, by the middle finger. Bhavabhaṭṭa also identifies Padmanartaka with Padma-narteśvara (Pandey 2002, 516: *gurave madhyāṅgulau padmanartakaḥ padmanarteśvaraḥ*).

[9] That is, Śrī Heruka abides by the ring finger (Pandey 2002, 516: *dhārāyām anāmikāyāṁ vīraḥ śrīherukaḥ*).

[10] Bhavabhaṭṭa identifies Ākāśagarbha with Vajrasurya (Pandey 2002, 516).

Earth is said to be Locanā, and water Māmakī. Fire is said to be Pāṇḍarā, and wind is famed as Tārā. Cumbikā is likewise transcendent in the void.[11] In the middle [of the hand] is the abode of all heroes.[12] The sage should commit them to the back [of the hand].[13]

This secret should not be brought to light; it should be zealously concealed. The hero should thus symbolize, and should commence with the *caru* oblation in one place. [This is] the union of all heroes, the binding of the ḍākinīs' network.[14]

---

[11] Bhavabhaṭṭa comments here: "**Cumbikā** is another name for Vajravārāhī. **In the void** means in emptiness, which refers to purification in emptiness. Through that she is **transcendent**. One should know the [other] ḍākinīs, up to Vajravārāhī, who correspond to the Transcendences of generosity, discipline, patience, effort, and meditation." (Pandey 2002, 517: *cumbiketi vajravārāhyā aparaṁ nāma / saiva śūnye śūnyatāyām / śūnyatāviśuddhyetyarthaḥ / ataḥ pāramitā iti / yā dānaśīlakṣāntivīryadhyānapāramitā-ḍākinyādayo vajravārāhyantāḥ krameṇa jñeyāḥ /*)

[12] Bhavabhaṭṭa comments: "Regarding **in the middle is the abode of all heroes**, it is known that in the middle one should see the playful abode through the vajra songs of all heroes, and so forth. The pure place of the heroes' play is in the middle of the hand." (Pandey 2002, 517: *madhye tu sarvavīrālayam iti / madhye sarvavīrāṇāṁ vajrapadādīnām ālayaṁ krīḍanaṁ paśyed iti jñeyam / sarvavīrakrīḍāsthānaviśuddhyā karamadhyam iti bhāvaḥ /*)

[13] Bhavabhaṭṭa explains: "**The sage should commit them to the back** of his [hand], which means that all deities should be seen on the back of the hand or in a reflected image. This particularly means that they should be visualized on or at the back of the hand." (Pandey 2002, 517: *pṛṣṭhe tasya visarjayed budha iti / karapṛṣṭhe vā sarvadevatā darpaṇapratibimbe tatpaśyed ityarthaḥ / tena karasyopari pṛṣṭhe ca bhāvayed iti viśeṣārthaṁ*)

[14] Bhavabhaṭṭa comments: "Through the procedure of the five ambrosias, and so forth, one should eat the *caru* oblation from one vessel without dividing it [into portions]. The fruit of eating [thus] the *caru* oblation is, it is said, **the union of all heroes, the binding of the ḍākinīs' net**; that is, the state of being Heruka." (Pandey 2002, 518: *anena pañcāmṛtādividhinā carukam abhakṣam ekapātragataṁ bhuñjītetyarthaḥ / carubhogaphalam āha sarvavīrasamāyogaḍākinījālasamvaram iti herukatvaṁ bhavatītyarthaḥ*)

32. The Procedures of the Animal Sacrificial Victims, the Means of Achieving the Zombie, and the Creation Stage

Henceforth is related the fellowship[1] of feasting, through the correct application of which there is rapid engagement in power. Even the summoning of the sacrificial victims is achieved via the aforementioned procedure. The sacrificial victims are thus five, with the donkey, the man, tortoise, camel, jackal, and horse, and so forth.[2] These sacrificial victims are limbs of power in the maṇḍala which is the means of attaining power. From among the classes the brahmin is the sacrificial victim.[3] From among the four-footed the elephant is stated. From among the winged there is likewise the goose, and from among the lower animals the turtle is stated.[4] [And there

---

[1] This term, *melaka*, implies communal participation, in this case, in the act of feasting.

[2] There are, of course, six items in this list. The Tibetan translations each have five, but differ. Mardo omits the man (PM 235a), and Sumatikīrti omits the donkey (SL 125a). These could represent genuine variants, but are most likely the results of attempts to reconcile the number with the list. The use of the term "and so forth" (*ādi*) suggests that this may be an open list. Durjayacandra lists all six, and includes a seventh, the "fox," although the translators may have here translated the same word, *śṛgāla*, twice. See RG 301b. Note that the number five here may be quite arbitrary, a reference to the lists of five sacrificial victims contained in vedic literature, such as the *Śatapatha Brāhmaṇa*, which are the man, horse, bull, ram, and he-goat. Only the first two of these reappear in this list. See Smith 1994, 250–1.

[3] The Sanskrit texts here read *varṇānāṁ varṇataḥ paśuḥ*. Here *varṇataḥ*, "from the class(es)," appears to be a corruption, as it is redundant following *varṇānāṁ*. The Tibetan translations differ here, with Mardo's text reading "from among the classes the supreme class is the victim" (PM 234b: *rigs rnams las ni rigs mchog phyugs*), and Sumatikīrti's text reading "among the four classes the brahmin is supreme" (SL 125a: *rigs bzhi rnams la bram ze mchog*). I follow Bhavabhaṭṭa, who glosses *varṇataḥ* as brahmin, as follows: "among humans, from the class—i.e., from among the classes—the brahmin is the sacrificial victim" (Pandey 2002, 520: *manuṣyāṇāṁ madhye varṇato varṇebhyo brāhmaṇaḥ paśuḥ*).

[4] This is a tentative reading of the CS mss., emended to *kacchapa ucyate* from either the reading *kacchapar ucyate*, in which *sandhi* is incorrectly applied, or *kacchapa rucyate*, which could be read as *kacchapo rocyate*, "the turtle is pleasing." I adopt the former reading, as it presumes less, and follows the pattern of the text. Note, however, that the latter reading may be supported by Sumatikīrti's reading, "the turtle is supreme" (SL 125b: *ka tsha pa mchog*);

are] those whose mouths are moved by the gods.[5] These are reckoned to be the sacrificial victims in the maṇḍala which is the means of achieving power. [By means of] the crow, heron, jackal, the twice-born,[6] the prime minister,[7] the curlew, swan, and the kādamba goose, there is the desired achievement of the rites of feasting, fire sacrifice, and sacrificial cakes.[8]

The confident one should, with mantras, offer the oblation of a porridge of black dog's milk with black lentils and rice into the mouth of a

---

Mardo's reading for this *pada* is redundant (PM 135b: *dud 'gro rnams las dud 'gro phyugs*). Bhavabhaṭṭa reads here *kacchapanirjataḥ* (Pandey 2002, 520), which makes less sense.

[5] This line, *devānāṁ mukhacālanaṁ*, is rather obscure. On the pattern of the preceding line we would expect that one member of a larger class be selected, presumably as the ideal sacrificial victim of the class. Hence we would want to read "among the gods" there is "*mukhacālana*," literally "that whose face shakes" or "that whose face is caused to move," or simply "the shaking of the face/mouth/beak." This does not, of course, correspond to any known deity, and thus perhaps this line cannot be interpreted in the light of the preceding lines. Bhavabhaṭṭa, for example, interprets it as referring to yet another group of animal victims: "As for **those whose mouths are moved by the gods**, it is the goat, water buffalo, and chicken whose mouths are moved, i.e., their mouths are caused to move, referring to the goat, and so forth. By whom are their mouths caused to move? The gods, titans, and so forth, play by means of diverse forms." (Pandey 2002, 520: *devānāṁ mukhacālanam iti chāgalo mahiṣaḥ kukkuṭāś ceti mukham cālayatīti mukhacālanaṁ chāgalādayaḥ / keṣāṁ mukhacālanam ity āha dīvyanti nānārūpeneti devā dānavādayaḥ /*) I am not sure which natural feature brings together these three very different animals; perhaps it is the *unnatural* fact that they are undoubtedly the animals which to this day remain the most common victims of sacrifice in India.

[6] According to Sachen, "the twice-born is the parrot, as it is first an animal, and then later utters human speech" (PG 349.1: *skye gnyis ni ne tsho ste dang po dud 'gro yin la phyis mi'i skad smra bas so*).

[7] According to Sachen, the "prime minister" is the owl (PG 349.1).

[8] The Sanskrit here reads *-siddhir bhavati kāminī*, with *kāminī* ("having passion") modifying *siddhiḥ*. The Tibetan reads "achieves desires" (PM 235b: *'dod pa dag ni 'grub par 'gyur*) and "achieves the desired aim" (SL 125a–b: *'dod pa'i don ni 'grub par 'gyur*). Sachen comments on this passage as follows: "Having consecrated the flesh of those [animals] as ambrosia, one eats them, and furthermore one also forms the charred substance of fire sacrifice into cakes [offered] to the worldly and transcendent ones. Then one will achieve all three." (PG 349.1–2) Presumably by "all three" he refers to the rites of feasting (*bhakṣa*), fire sacrifice (*homa*), and sacrificial cakes (*bali*). I translate *kāminī* loosely as "desired" here, following the Tibetan, as it does not make much sense to attribute passion to an abstract noun such as *siddhiḥ*.

corpse.[9] The ultimate adepts[10] should sacrifice up to as many as one hundred and eight times.[11] Then the dead person[12] stands up and says, "I am [your] servant." [Regarding the powers of traveling in] the underworld, resurrection,[13] the sword, as well as benefiting or destroying,[14] the pill,[15] eye ointment, [finding] treasure,[16] or foot unguent, and also alchemy: one of

---

[9] Bhavabhaṭṭa comments here:

> Regarding the great ghost *sādhana*, performing the preliminary service with the Śumbha and root mantras, one who has obtained the [proper] omen takes a corpse which is intact and not putrid. At midnight, in a charnel ground, one undertakes a fire sacrifice with mantra in its mouth with [a porridge of] unbroken rice and black lentils, ground with the milk of a black dog.
>
> *mahāpretasādhanam āha kṛṣṇetyādi / sumbhamantreṇa mūlamantreṇa ca pūrvasevāṁ kurvat labdhanimitto 'kṣatam apūtikaṁ śavam ādāya śmaśāne 'rdharātre kṛṣṇaśunī-dugdhamrakṣitaiḥ sākhaṇḍataṇḍulaiḥ kṛṣṇair māṣaiḥ tasya vaktre tenaiva mantreṇa homaṁ kuryāt /* (Pandey 2002, 521)

Jayabhadra adds that this rite should be performed alone during the waning fortnight (E 35a.1: *kṛṣṇapakṣe kevalaṁ... homaṁ kuryāt*). A much more lengthy description of this *sādhana*, with more specific details concerning the time and place of performance and the type of corpse to be used, and so forth, is contained in Vīravajra's commentary (PD 422a ff).

[10] This translates *sādhakottamaiḥ*, which I presume is the agent of *hotavyaṁ*. It is possible, however, that this means something like "accomplishing the last of these." There is no parallel to this in the Tibetan translation.

[11] The Sanskrit here, *śatam aṣṭottaraṁ yāvat*, could be read as either 108 or 800, although the former interpretation is followed in both translations (PM 234b, SL 125b) as well as in Durjayacandra's (RG 302a) and Vīravajra's commentary (PD 422a). Tsong Khapa, however, explains that it should be performed as many as 108 or 800 times (KS 171a).

[12] I translate here *preta*, which originally meant a deceased or dead person, or the ghost or evil spirit of a dead person. In this case it evidently refers to the corpse reanimated by a spirit of this sort. The term *preta* here does not have the specifically Buddhist sense of the "hungry ghost" which constitutes one of the six realms of rebirth in the Buddhist cosmos.

[13] As in the case of ch. 3 above, I follow Bhavabhaṭṭa in interpreting *pātālottiṣṭha* as a reference to two separate powers: traveling in the underworld and resurrecting the dead.

[14] The Sanskrit *nigraha* can mean restraining, subduing, taming, punishing, or destroying, but the last meaning is indicated by Bhavabhaṭṭa, who writes that it means "destroying the wicked" (Pandey 2002, 521: *nigraham iti duṣṭamardanam*). It is also indicated by the Tibetan translation "annihilation" (PM 235b, SL 125b: *tshar gcod*).

[15] According to Sachen, "the pill is bestowed by the tongue of the corpse" (PG 349.3).

[16] Bhavabhaṭṭa provides the correct reading here, *nidhāna*, which is supported by the Tibetan translations (PM 235b, SL 125b: *gter*). The CS mss. here all read *vidhāna*.

[these] powers being bestowed, it will not go otherwise.[17] Invoking the messengers above and below, have no doubt regarding this Tantra.

One[18] should produce that which is emaciated in the cattle pen,[19] and likewise ashes,[20] a dried head, and thence that which is made of the great conch, and that which is unbroken of the turtle.[21] [He has][22] four faces, and from four to as many as one hundred thousand hands. He has a

---

[17] That is, one can ask the *preta* to bestow one of these powers. According to Kambala, the adept "gives it water, and then [states]: 'Excellent, great hero! I have achieved an excellent observance of Vajrasattva. Bestow upon me a power of great bliss.' It gives that one [power] which is desired in the adept's mind, and then goes to its own place." (SN 62b)

[18] The text now shifts, with no transition, to the topic of the creation stage *sādhana*. Sachen connects the two topics as follows: "Since these powers are achieved by generating oneself as the deity, [the text] expounds the third general topic [of the chapter], the actual secret of the path, namely, the creation stage deity yoga at the time of invoking the zombie powers" (PG 349.3).

[19] This translates *goṣṭhotpalikāḥ*, a reading which occurs in CS ms. A and which is confirmed by Jayabhadra's commentary (E 35a.3: *goṣṭha utpalakā*). Both mss. of Bhavabhaṭṭa's commentary read *goṣṭhopelikāś* (F 113a.4, G 100b.2), which Pandey reads as *goṣṭhopalikāś* (Pandey 2002, 521). I take *utpalikāḥ* to be derived from *utpala*, "fleshless" or "emaciated." Bhavabhaṭṭa comments that this refers to "the dried cow products of a cattle pen" (Pandey 2002, 522: *goṣṭhaśuṣkagomayāḥ*); that is, it means dried cattle dung.

[20] The Sanskrit here reads "residues" (*śeṣāḥ*), which Jayabhadra glosses as "ash in particular" (E 35a.3–4: *bhasmaviśeṣaṇa*), ash, of course, being the preeminent residue and a frequent referent of the term *śeṣa*, as ash is the residue left over following the rite of burnt oblation.

[21] There are numerous explanations of this cryptic verse, the least complex taking them to be simply ritual implements used in the zombie *sādhana*. They are exhaustively discussed by Buston (NS 206a–b) and Tsong Khapa (KS 171b–172b). The explanation taken by Kambala and Devagupta is that it is a cryptic reference to the generation of the habitat maṇḍala, namely Mt. Sumeru resting upon the five elemental disks. He writes: "Dung is [the element] earth, and **ash** is water. The **dried head** is fire, and **thence** should be taken to be fire. These are intended to refer to the maṇḍalas of the four great elements. **That which is made of the great conch** is that which arises as the great mountain. Thus it is stated." (SS 137a–b) This is followed by a lengthy description of the visualization of the elemental wheels and Mt. Sumeru. Additionally, Jayabhadra takes "turtle" as a reference to a skull bowl (E 35a.4), while Devagupta takes this as a reference to the generation of the deities from an egg (SS 139a–b). The Tibetan translations add an additional line here that is not attested in the Sanskrit, namely "power is rapidly bestowed" (SL 125b: *myur du dngos grub sbyin 'gyur yin*) or "then power is bestowed" (PM 135b: *'di de dngos grub sbyin 'gyur zhing*).

[22] That is, Śrī Heruka. Jayabhadra comments here that "[the text] **four hands**, and so forth, demonstrates the majesty of the Blessed Lord Śrī Heruka." (E 35a.4–5: *catu[r]bhujetyādinā bhagavataḥ śrīherukasya māhātmya[ṁ] darśayati*)

white body and Bhairava's form,[23] and Vajravārāhī, who has his color and weapons,[24] gazes at him. The hero has a garland of skulls, and his body is anointed with ash and is adorned with [the five] insignia.[25] He has a dreadlock crest and a hooked lance. His powerful fangs jut out, and he [takes] the great ghost as his seat.[26] Knowing thus, the adept yogin should visualize all of the deities in accordance with the rite at all times.[27] Thus there will be the desired accomplishment[28] of the particularly good qualities.

---

[23] That is, *bhairavākāraṁ*, which could also be translated "having a terrifying form," although the reference to the Hindu deity Bhairava, whom Śrī Heruka subdued according to his origin myth, is striking. The Tibetan translations also add that he is "very fierce" (PM 235a, SL 125b: *khro bo che*).

[24] Bhavabhaṭṭa explains: "She bears a vajra, skull bowl, and so forth, and here she has four faces. The Blessed Lord is white, so the Blessed Lady is also white." (Pandey 2002, 522: *vajrakapālādidhāriṇīṁ / itaś caturmukhatvam asyāḥ / bhagavān śuklo bhagaty api śuklā*)

[25] This translates the text preserved in Jayabhadra's commentary, *mudrādehavibhuṣitam iti pañcamudrābhiḥ* (E 35b.1–2), which corresponds to the text of both Tibetan translations (PM 235b, SL 125b: *phyag rgya yis ni sku la brgyan*). The CS mss. have the variant text *pañcamudrādigātraṁ*. As Jayabhadra indicates, this line is undoubtedly a reference to the five insignia listed in ch. 27, namely the necklace, crest jewel, earring, choker, and the sacred thread. Note that Pandey's attempt to reconstruct this text as *mudrādibhuṣitagātraṁ* (2002, 522) on the basis of the CS text and the Tibetan, while more grammatical, is likely incorrect.

[26] Jayabhadra writes that "having **the great ghost as his seat** means that he treads upon the Lord of Beings" (D 45b.6, E 35b.2: *mahāpretāsanam iti bhūt[a]patim ākrantaḥ*). "Bhūtapati" (MP 62b: *yi dags gyi [sic] bdag po*) is a common name of Śiva. Note that both mss. here read *bhūtāvipatim ākrantaḥ*, which I have emended to the above text.

[27] Here I translate the text as it occurs in the CS mss.: *tato jñātvā vidhivad yogī bhāvayet sarvadevatāṁ / sadā kālaṁ tu sādhakaḥ /*. There is, however, a variant text, partially preserved in Jayabhadra's commentary. It reads "thence the mantra should be known" (D 45b.6–7, E 35b.2), which corresponds more closely to the Tibetan translations. Mardo's text reads: "Knowing that mantra, the adept should meditate at all times" (PM 235b: */ sgrub pa po yis dus rtag tu // sngags de shes nas bsgom par bya /*). Sumatikīrti's text reads: "The adept should always meditate knowing the deity of mantra" (SL 125b: */ das nas rtag tu sgrub pa po // sngags kyi lha ni shes nas bsgom /*). One might surmise that there was a variant Sanskrit text that might have read something like *tato jñātvā mantraṁ bhāvayet sadā kālaṁ sādhakaḥ*.

[28] This translates *siddhir bhavati kāminī*, following the Tibetan interpretation as above.

33. The Reverential Procedure of Secret Worship

Furthermore, it is not the case that all are adept in all yogas, capable of feasting to the extent of their ability on fish, flesh, and so forth. One should partake of the five foods, and so forth, with relish, even when they are not present.[1] At night one should always undertake extensive feasting. Then the messenger should be bestowed.[2] Placing one's head in her lap, she is worshipped in the fashion of the nondual hero.[3] Whether or not she is one's mother, sister, daughter, kinswoman, or wife, should one do thus in accordance with the rite, one will be free of all bonds.

Then the mantras are accomplished, until the end of the world.[4] Assuming the master's form, I, the adept, take the worship. Have no doubt

---

[1] Jayabhadra comments here that "**One should partake of the five foods even when they are not present** means that when there is nothing to serve as the five ambrosias, then one should visualize whatever food one has as the essence of the five ambrosias" (D E 35b.3–4: *avidyamāne 'pi kartavyaṁ pañcakhādyakā iti / yadā pañcāmṛtasamārūpaṁ nāsti tadā yadbhakṣaṁ tatpañcāmṛtatvena parikalpayed ity abhiprāyaḥ*).

[2] This translates the CS mss.' text, *dūtīṁ ca tato dadyāt*, which corresponds to the Tibetan translations (PM 236a, SL 126a: *de nas pho nya rab sbyin zhing*). Bhavabhaṭṭa gives a reading based on what is likely corrupt text, *dūtī ca tato 'dyāt* (Pandey 2002, 524). According to Durjayacandra: "Regarding **then the messenger should be bestowed**, and so forth, as was shown in ch. 26, it refers to that messenger who is explained to be the **mother, sister**, and so forth, stated below. Regarding her, the guru should bestow and commit the second consort to the disciple who is to obtain the secret and the consort." (RG 302b) This refers to the wisdom-gnosis consecration, and the "second consort" refers to the "sister" consort whom the guru has prepared for the disciple. The "mother" or first consort is the guru's own consort who aids him in consecrating the disciple.

[3] The Sanskrit here, *svotsaṅge śiraḥ kṛtvā*, is ambiguous, and could be translated "placing the head on one's lap." I have chosen the less obvious of the two possible interpretations based on the commentaries. According to Vīravajra: "As for **messenger**, one should embrace her who has the perfected qualities of a messenger. The disciple should place his head between the left one's thighs. Regarding **worshipped in the fashion of the nondual hero**, that is Heruka's nondual worship, and she is bestowed for the sake of that." (ST 197b) Tsong Khapa, commenting on this commentary, notes that "*the left one* is the messenger, and placing one's head between her thighs means placing the head of the vajra in her lotus" (KS 175a).

[4] That is, *yāvadāhūtasaṁplavaḥ*, the reading preserved by Bhavabhaṭṭa, with *āhūta-* a variant of the more common *ābhūta-*, which Bhavabhaṭṭa glosses as "until the end of the afflictions"

that the heroes' place[5] is indeed the consort (*mudrā*). The well-equipoised adept should sing, dance, and so forth.[6] So long as all embodied ones are not intent upon knowledge of yoga, they roam through cyclic existence, hastening toward dissatisfaction and grief. The adept should thus worship the consort with all things. The contemptuous ones who desire that which is unworthy of the worshipped will burn.[7]

The primordially established great consort (*mahāmudrā*) should be worshipped with great zeal, [as is done by] men in the Yoga Tantras.[8] Later

(Pandey 2002, 525: *yāvadāhūtasaṁplava iti yāvad āhūtānāṁ kleśānāṁ saṁplavo nyathābhāvaḥ*).

[5] The literal translation of *āsanaṁ*, following the Tibetan (PM 236a, SL 126a: *stan dag*), would be "seat." However, *āsanaṁ* is probably used loosely in the sense of "dwelling," "encampment," and so forth. Bhavabhaṭṭa glosses it as "place" (Pandey 2002, 525: *sthānaṁ*). Bhavyakīrti comments that "**seat** refers to [the place of] eating and drinking" (SM 33a). This makes sense, given the commitment the adept must take to eat together with his consort.

[6] Jayabhadra comments here as follows: "Regarding **well-equipoised**, and so forth, one should know forms of song and speech which are [performed] via a non-vulgar method" (E 35b.4–5: *susamāhita ity aprākṛtarūpeṇa gītavādyādīnā[ṁ] prayogo vijñeyaḥ*). Bhavyakīrti expands on this, attacking the conventions of dance and love poetry, of which he is obviously not a fan, as follows:

> I, Bhavyakīrti, hold that gazing is false, raising the arms is false,…as are the sexual arts of the god of love. Comparing oneself to a bee and a woman's face to a lotus is false. Whispering in the ear about beauty and not having a man is false. These are all completely false. As it is said, "I state that if one is moved by utterance of all sorts, then, alas, one is defeated by the god of love's fool. If one does not understand this, what can be done?" If one investigates the objects of singing, dancing, and so forth, it is not the case that they all have equal [value]. (SM 33a–b)

His curmudgeonly attitude seems far from the spirit of those who composed this text!

[7] This is a tentative translation of the text preserved in the CS mss., *pūjitāpūjyam icchanti nirdahanty apamānitā*. I read *apamānitā* as *apamānitāḥ*, i.e., as the plural subject of the plural verbs *icchanti* and *nirdahanti*. I also read *pūjitāpūjyam* as a compound of *pūjitā* and *apūjyam*. Note that Bhavabhaṭṭa preserves a different reading, *pūjitāḥ pūjayati*, and he glosses *pūjayati* as *pūjyaḥ*, which he explains, somewhat confusingly, means *pūjakaḥ*, which has the opposite meaning (Pandey 2002, 526). The negative *apūjyam* is not attested in the Tibetan translations, but it makes more sense to me; otherwise, it is difficult to account for the dire fate that is predicted here.

[8] Vīravajra explains:

> Regarding what is done first, the **consort** who arises in the clans such as the Ratna [clan], which are famed for the achievement of power, **should be worshipped with zeal** by the yogin as is done by **men in the Yoga Tantras** such as the Śrī

one should assume the heroism of the heroes.[9] As for the adept who [travels in] the underworld and resurrects [the dead],[10] having thus done the worship, have no doubt that [this] adept will attain without trouble anything whatsoever in accordance with all ritual actions, [such as the powers of] pacifying, enriching, subjugation, summoning, killing, expelling, and so forth, and even crushing and immobilizing, and likewise inciting enmity,[11] destroying and conferring benefit.[12]

> Guhyasamāja, and so forth, in an isolated and pleasing place. [The text] means thus. As for the import of that, the following is stated for the sake of clarification. Regarding what is done first, one takes [a consort]—the **mother, sister**, and so forth, who has the perfected qualities of the **great consort**, and so forth—and one draws the maṇḍala of this very Śrī Cakrasamvara in an isolated and pleasing [place]…, and visualizing oneself in the form of the deity of one's own clan, one maintains this day and night, and throughout an entire night one should thus worship **with great zeal**. (ST 197b–198a)

[9] Bhavabhaṭṭa comments here that "having previously torn asunder conceptualization, then **one should assume** the nonconceptuality of the hero's mind" (Pandey 2002, 526: *paścād vīravīratvam ācaret iti / pūrvaṁ vikalpaṁ vihāya tato vīrasya cittasya nirvikalpatvam ācaret /*). Tsong Khapa, commenting on Vīravajra's explanation of the previous line, explains here: "**Later**, i.e., after one has entered the clear light by first practicing in that way, then rising up from disappearance in the two clear lights, **one should assume the heroism of the heroes**, that is, one manifests the body of a buddha via the stage of integration using the adamantine concentration. One should abide being adorned with all of the good qualities." (KS 176b)

[10] As in the case of chs. 3 and 32 above, I follow Bhavabhaṭṭa in interpreting *pātālottiṣṭha* as a reference to two separate powers: traveling in the underworld and resurrecting the dead.

[11] In place of "inciting enmity" (*vidveṣa*), both Tibetan translations read "breaking, cleaving" (PM 236a, SL 126b: *dbye [ba]*). I find the CS mss.' reading more convincing, since *vidveṣa* is a well known magical operation, and "breaking" seems redundant given the various other destructive operations listed.

[12] Both Tibetan translations omit "conferring benefit" (*anugraha*). The Sanskrit has these last three in the locative case, *vidveṣe nigrahe 'nugrahe*, a fact which is not reflected in my translation or in the Tibetan translations.

34. The Procedure of Summoning via the Fire Sacrifice of the Nondual Messenger

Next [there is] the extensive procedure known as the wheel of the ḍākinīs' network,[1] the component spokes [of which] one should employ.[2] This—that is, any ritual action whatsoever—is rapidly [achieved] by the adept, have no doubt.[3] All of the heroes and ḍākinīs should be placed upon

[1] Jayabhadra comments that this "forms the nature of the triple wheel, or it means that one should worship the triple wheel" (E 35b.6–36a.1: *tricakrātmako vā tricakraṁ pūjayet*). Bhavabhaṭṭa explains:

> **Next**, immediately following the statement of reverential worship, [the text] "I will explain **the extensive procedure known as the wheel of the ḍākinīs' network**" is to be examined. That which is the ḍākinī has the nature of the ḍākinīs, and the network is net-like because it binds the sea monster of the afflictions, and so forth. Their wheel is that which is called the maṇḍala.
>
> *atheti pūjāsatkārakathanānantaram / ḍākinyajālacakrākhyavidhivistaraṁ vakṣya iti draṣṭavyam / ḍākinīnāṁ bhāvo ḍākinyaṁ tad eva jālavaj jālaṁ kleṣamakarādi-bandhanāt tasya cakraṁ maṇḍalaṁ tad ākhyāti* (Pandey 2002, 527)

[2] The text "the component spokes [of which] one should employ" (*sakalāreṣu niyojayet*) is contained in all three CS mss. but is omitted from the Tibetan translations. It is likely a commentarial gloss, but is evidently a rather old one, as it is attested in Jayabhadra's commentary, albeit in a somewhat scrambled form: "As for its component parts, these are the parts in the spokes" (E 36a.1: *kalāvayava / sa cāsau [a]re[ṣ]u kalā ca*).

[3] This is my reading of the lines *yatkiṁcit karmāṇi sā kṣipraṁ sādhakasya na saṁśayaḥ*. Following commentators such as Kambala and Devagupta, I take the pronoun *sā* as referring back to *cakrākhyaṁ vidhivistaraṁ*, despite the fact that it is incorrectly declined, and I also read, in brackets, the necessary verb. Kambala comments as follows: "All of these ritual applications of mantra and *yantra*—which are called 'the extensive wheel of the ḍākinīs' net'—are achieved by the adept, have no doubt" (SN 65a). Bhavabhaṭṭa, perhaps as either a direct quotation or commentarial gloss, gives the missing verb *siddhyati*, which appears to be a late, derivative passive form of the verb √*sidh*. He also glosses *sā* as referring to the goddess Khaṇḍarohā (Pandey 2002, 527), but this interpretation is unattested elsewhere.

the lotuses. One should likewise place[4] the purified point[5] between the eyebrows.

Then one with the hero's parching mouth should sacrifice the oblation[6] in the fire.[7] Offer [quickly and energetically][8] five sacrifices with beef

[4] The CS mss. and Bhavabhaṭṭa read *nikṣipeta*, the second person plural optative conjugation. The text may have shifted from the usual third person singular for metrical reasons, i.e., to add another syllable. Jayabhadra, however, here reads *nikṣet*, "one should pierce."

[5] This is an interpretative translation of *avadhūtapadaṁ*, a word which is associated by the commentators with the *avadhūti*, the central channel of the Buddhist subtle body. Several texts do in fact attest *avadhūtipadaṁ*, "the place of the central channel," including Bhavabhaṭṭa's as well as Mardo's translations, the latter of which here reads *avadhūtī'i gnas* (PM 236b). But since the CS mss. and also Jayabhadra read *avadhūta*, I do not translate it in that manner. My translation, "purified," is derived from an extension of the root meaning of *ava+√dhū*, "to shake off or down," with *avadhūta* meaning by extension "shaken off" and perhaps "purified," which is in line with its nominal meaning of an "ascetic," i.e., one who has shaken off all worldly attachments. Kambala thus comments here that "because the taint of conceptualization has been shaken off, it is 'of the central channel'" (SN 65a: *rnam par rtog pa'i sdig bskyod pas na avadhūti'i ste*). Jayabhadra in a similar vein comments on the line as follows: "**Likewise** pierce **the purified point between the eyebrows** means that on the forehead there is a perfected point or place which is purified by the light rays of the vajra garland. This perfected [point] refers to [the state of] having a third eye, which should be regarded as being between the eyebrows, i.e., on the forehead." (E 36a.2–3: *nikṣet bhruvo[r] madhye 'vadhūtapadaṁ tatheti / lalāṭe vajramālāraśmibhir avadhūtaṁ niṣpannapadaṁ sthānaṁ tad avadhūtaṁ saviṣamanayanaṁ tad bhruvo[r] madhye lalāṭe darśayed ity arthaḥ*)

[6] "Oblation" is a loose translation based upon Mardo's translation, *bza' ba* (PM 236b), "food." The CS mss. read *nāmnaṁ* (A) and *nāmraṁ* (B, C), which may be corruptions derived from *annaṁ*. Bhavabhaṭṭa here reads *nānyaṁ*, "none other," which is attested by Sumatikīrti's translation, *gzhan du min* (SL 126b). Bhavabhaṭṭa comments, however, that "none other" refers to beef (Pandey 2002, 527: *nānyaṁ padārthaṁ gomāṁsam eveti bhāvaḥ*).

[7] The word *ucchuṣma*, "parching," is a common designation for *agni*, the ritual fire. Bhavabhaṭṭa comments: "**The hero's parching mouth** means a mouth filled with ferocity. **One** who is characterized by that **should sacrifice**." (Pandey 2002, 527: *vīrocchuṣmaṁ mukhaṁ krodhāviṣṭaṁ mukhaṁ tena lakṣitaḥ san juhuyāt tataḥ iti*) Jayabhadra comments: "**The hero's parching**, and so forth, relates the fire sacrifice [that achieves] all ritual actions. **One should sacrifice** the meat having assumed the **parching** [state] of the **Hero**, Śrī Heruka, i.e., being in a state of impassioned ferocity." (E 36a.3–4: *vīrocchuṣmetyādinā sarvakarmikahoma[ṁ] kathayati / vīrasya śrīherukasya ucchuṣmakṛte rāg[a]krodhāvasthāyāṁ māṁs[aṁ] juhuyā[d] dhomayet /*)

[8] Both the CS mss. and Bhavabhaṭṭa here read *gomāṁsarudhireṇāśu*, which both also follow with the defective text *pañcahutayaḥ*. Jayabhadra preserves the full second line, reading *gomāṁsarudhireṇa pañcahutiṁ dadyād yatnataḥ*, "Offer energetically the five sacrifices with beef and blood," which corresponds with both Tibetan translations (PM 236b: */ go māng sa*

and blood, and then offer nine sacrifices.[9] In the blazing eater of oblations there is the fire-garlanded ocean. Then one should see [there] the wheel facing in all directions.[10] There is the four-faced Lord of Heroes, and thus the hero's abode with the heroes.[11] On the petal[s] are the four messengers,[12] the nondual bliss of the wheels' heroes.[13] Bestow Khaṇḍarohā

---

dang ru dhi ra // 'bad pas bsreg bya lnga dag bya /; SL 126b: */ go ma sa dang ru tir bcas // 'bad pas bsreg bya lnga dag dang /*). Jayabhadra, however, also attests *āśu*, in his following commentary: "Then after that, in accordance with the ritual action [to be accomplished], **one should energetically offer five sacrifices with beef and blood**, **quickly,** i.e. speedily" (E 36a.5–6: *tataḥ paścād yathākarmānurūpeṇa gomāṁsa[rudhi]reṇa / āśu śīgh[r]aṁ pañcahutiṁ dadyāt yatnata iti*).

[9] Jayabhadra recommends here that one should "assuming the deity's identity, **then offer nine sacrifices**" (E 36a.6: *devatāhaṁkāreṇa navāhutiṁ tato dadyāt*).

[10] According to Jayabhadra, the "wheel" here indicates the triple wheel or Cakrasamvara maṇḍala:

> Making thus the oblations in the mouth of the deity Agni in accordance with the ritual action [to be achieved], this is a reference to the rite of making offerings to the deities residing in the triple wheel. **Then one should see the wheel facing in all directions** means that within the [fire-]pit one should visualize the triple wheel, i.e., with the palace and the wall, and [the deities] with their respective colors, [number of] arms, and implements.
>
> *evam agnidevatāmukhe āhutiṁ kṛtvā tricakrasamanviteṣu devatāhutividhim āha / tata ityādi / paśye[c] cakraṁ sarvatomukham iti / kuṇḍamadhye yathā tricakraṁ / kūṭāṅgāraprākārasahitaṁ / svavarṇabhujamudropetaṁ dhyāyet /* (E 36b.1–3)

According to Bhavabhaṭṭa, "**facing in all directions** refers to the four gates [of the maṇḍala], and through that, the four faces, i.e., Śrī Heruka" (Pandey 2002, 528: *sarvatomukham / caturdvāratvāc caturmukhaṁ śrīherukam /*).

[11] The "four-faced Lord of Heroes" is, of course, Śrī Heruka. According to Kambala: "**With the heroes** means through the yoga of oneself as the deity. The Hero's abode is the palace together with [the rest of the setting]." (SN 65b) Note that the Sanskrit here, *vīrair*, is attested in all available sources, including Bhavabhaṭṭa's commentary. Pandey, however, emends the text to *vīravīrālayaṁ* (2002, 528), presumably to accord with Mardo's translation, "and thus the abode of the heroes and heroines" (PM 236b: *dpa' bo dpa' mo'i gnas de bzhin*). The equivalent to *vīrair* or *vīra-* is omitted in Sumatikīrti's translation (SL 126b).

[12] According to Kambala: "**On the petal are the four messengers** means that on the four petals of the corolla of the lotus are the four, Ḍākinī, and so forth" (SN 65b); that is, the four essence yoginīs, Ḍākinī, Lāmā, Khaṇḍarohā, and Rūpiṇī.

[13] This translates Bhavabhaṭṭa's reading *cakravīrādvayasukhaṁ*. The CS mss. have the metrically defective reading *cakravartivīrādvayasukhaṁ*, while the Tibetan translations read "the nondual bliss of all heroes" (PM 236b: *dpa' bo kun dang gnyis med bde*; SL 126b: *dpa' kun*

outside, and view them in the center of [their respective] wheels, residing with their own forms.[14] He should successively make the Three Wheels radiant.[15] This is the accomplishment of all powers. Have no doubt that that which was taught succinctly in the *Ocean of Spells* in the manner of the hero is achieved here through nondual union with the messenger.

---

gnyis su med bde ba). Bhavabhaṭṭa comments on his reading as follows: "The **wheels' heroes** are situated in the triple wheel [maṇḍala], and exist by means of the experience of true bliss that is nondual with the hero" (Pandey 2002, 528: *cakravīreti tricakragatā vīrādvayasat-sukhānubhavena sthitā iti bhāvaḥ*).

[14] Jayabhadra comments: "**Bestow Khaṇḍarohā outside** refers to the aim of accomplishing all ritual actions" (E 36b.4–5: *khaṇḍarohāṁ bāhyato dadyād / sarvakarmaprasādhanārtham ityarthaḥ*). That is, one can focus on a particular deity for the purpose of accomplishing particular ritual aims. Bhavabhaṭṭa further comments that "**with their own forms**—that is, in accordance with the ritual action [to be achieved] when pacifying, and so forth—one should view, i.e., visualize, them with forms that are white, and so forth" (Pandey 2002, 528: *svarūpair karmānurūpaiḥ śāntikādau śuklādirūpair darśayed bhāvayet*).

[15] Here I translate the text preserved in Jayabhadra's text, *tricakrodbhāsaṁ*. The prefix "three" (*tri-*) is not attested elsewhere. The CS mss. read *te cakrodbhāṣaṁ*, and Bhavabhaṭṭa reads *te cakranirdiṣṭaṁ*. The reading *te cakrodbhāsaṁ* is attested by Mardo's translation (PM 236b: *'khor lo 'di dag gsal bar ni*), while Bhavabhaṭṭa's reading is attested by Sumatikīrti's translation (SL 127a: *'khor lo 'di dag bstan pa ni*). I suspect that *te* is a misreading of *tri-*, albeit an ancient one, since it is not appropriate for a pronoun to correlate to a noun contained within a compound. Pandey's edition contains a reading for this verse which includes both variants, *cakrodbhāṣaṁ* and *cakranirdiṣṭaṁ*, perhaps on account of editorial indecision, as these are not attested together anywhere. Jayabhadra comments here: "**He should successively make the three wheels radiant** means that the fire-pit should be made in the shape of the triple wheel [maṇḍala] successively, i.e., by not violating the order of the rites of pacification, and so forth" (E 36b.6–37a.1: *eṣa tricakrodbhāsaṁ kuryāt yathākramam iti / etat [ku]ṇḍaṁ tricakrākāraṁ kuryāt yathākramaṁ śāntyādividhikramānatikrameṇa /*).

35. The Procedure of the Nondual Ritual Action and the Method of Cheating Black Death

Now[1] I will successively explain[2] the excellent and supreme ritual action that depends upon the [ritual] process,[3] the worship that has the nature of nondual union, and the disclosure of these mantras that yield success when applied to the corresponding ritual actions. Revolve the mantra—which [corresponds to] the color, messenger, and so forth—with the speed of an arrow.[4] The interconnected mantras are separated by means

[1] Jayabhadra comments: "**Now**, and so forth, relate the procedure of repeating mantra and meditating in accordance with the ritual action [to be accomplished]" (E 37a.2–3: *idānīm ata ityādinā karmānurūpeṇamantroccāraṇadhyānavidhiṁ kathayati*).

[2] Pandey's edition omits "I will explain" (*vakṣāmi*), most likely because Bhavabhaṭṭa omits it. It is, however, contained in all three CS mss., and it is attested in Mardo's translation (PM 236b). It is, however, omitted from Sumatikīrti's, so it very well may represent a variant text.

[3] This translates the text preserved in the CS mss., *yathānukramalambitaṁ*. Bhavabhaṭṭa preserves the text *yathākramalakṣitaṁ* (Pandey 2002, 530), "as indicated by the process," a reading supported by the Tibetan translations (PM 236b: *ji bzhin rim kyis mtshon pa te*; SL 127a: *ci bzhin rims kyis mtshan byas te*).

[4] There are several interpretations of *varṇadūtyādi*. Vīravajra interprets *varṇa* both in terms of "color" and "social class," as follows:

> **Mantra** [here] is connected to the yogic postures and the wind that is the inhaled breath. As for the successive **disclosure of these mantras** of the four ritual actions, pacifying is white, enriching yellow, controlling red, and destroying black. This is the **color** of the syllables. Pacifying is the kshatriya class, enriching the vaishya class, controlling the brahmin class, and destroying the shudra class. This is the [social] distinction of the **messenger**. **And so forth** refers to the water maṇḍala for pacifying, the earth maṇḍala for enriching, the fire maṇḍala for controlling, and the wind maṇḍala for destroying. (PD 425b)

Kambala interprets *varṇa* as "letter," as follows:

> **The letters** refers to the vowels and thirty-three consonants; the **messengers** are the yoginīs who are the nature of the channels; **and so forth** is taken to be a reference to the twenty-four heroes. Their **mantra revolves with the speed of the arrow**. Arrow refers to wind, and with that speed they move, i.e., revolve. (SN 66b)

of placement.[5] Then the garland of seed syllables is taken, and the syllable *hūṁ* is affixed at the end.

---

[5] Jayabhadra comments here that:

> **Separated by means of placement** means that, in the procedure of pacification, in one's mouth there are mantric syllables that enter within with the form of a linked chain. They are discharged from the urethra, and again enter the goddess' womb through the vagina. [Then] they proceed from the goddess' mouth to one's own mouth. In the fierce rites, it is distinguished by their procession from one's own mouth to the goddess' mouth.
>
> *praveśena tu bheditā iti śāntividhau svamukhād antapraviṣṭāni mantrākṣarāṇi śṛṅkhalādāmarūpāṇi / vajramārgeṇa sṛṣṭāni punar api padmamārgeṇa devatāgarbhapraviṣṭāni / devatāmukhāt svamukham kramaḥ / k[ru]ravidhau tu svamukhād devatāmukhakrameṇeti viśeṣaḥ* / (E 37a.5–b.1)

Vīravajra concurs with the view that this rite involves a real or imagined coupling, writing:

> If one repeats the **mantra, revolving** it as if **with the speed of the wind**, for pacifying and enriching it revolves by entering the male's mouth from the female's mouth, and then entering the female's navel from the male's navel. For controlling and destroying, it revolves by entering the female's mouth from the male's mouth, and then entering the male's navel from the female's navel. Through the entry and revolution of this **interconnected mantra** there is the [mantra] **garland.** (PD 425b–426a)

Finally, Kambala comments: "**The interconnected mantras** refers to the assembly of the vowels and consonants. **Separated by means of placement** refers to their placement at the heart, throat, navel, and head." (SN 66b)

Should the victim be restrained, he will not proceed one step.[6] There is envelopment through the state of being enveloped[7] and binding with the adamantine chain.[8] And one should also separate them with the vajra,[9] so

---

[6] Vīravajra interprets this and the following text as describing ritual actions employing the goddess Khaṇḍarohā with eight different implements. He describes this first one in some depth as follows:

> Regarding **should the victim be restrained, he will not proceed one step**, one should assume the form of Māra the Lord of Death (*mṛtyupatimāra*) and draw the magical diagram (*yantra*) of the eight line mantra on charnel ground cloth with poison and blood, and write the name *mṛtyupatimāra* in the middle. If you place the *yantra* in a *liṅga* and pierce it with the eight light rays of the mantra, he will be unable to go even a single step, i.e., he will die. What are the eight light rays? They are that which **envelop**; that is, since the white and red light rays of adamantine particles emanate as an impediment, he will not proceed a single step. This is the first. (PD 426a–b)

The term *liṅga* here refers to a symbolic sacrificial effigy employed in Buddhist exorcism rituals. In the Tibetan context it is often an anthropomorphic image on paper. See Kohn 2001, 73–86.

[7] According to Jayabhadra: "**Enveloping through the state of being enveloped** means: through the procedure of pointing out the analysis of mantras, and so forth, [the mantra,] *oṁ*, and so forth, has *oṁ* at the end, i.e., is enveloped through the state of being enveloped. [It is:] *oṁ devadattāya svāhā oṁ*." (E 37b.3–4: *sampuṭaṁ sampuṭībhāveneti / mantra-vyākaraṇādinirdiṣṭakrameṇa / oṁkārādi / oṁkārāntaṁ sampuṭaṁ sampuṭībhāveneti / oṁ deva-datta svāhā oṁ iti /*) "Devadatta" here stands in for the name of the victim inserted into the mantra, as "Devadatta" is the Sanskrit equivalent of the generic name "John Doe." The practice of mantric enveloping (*sampuṭa*) entails the creation of mantras which are palindromes or near palindromes, often surrounding a victim's name. See Yelle 2003, 24–28.

[8] According to Vīravajra, this relates to the second ritual action to which this chapter alludes, as follows:

> The goddesses of the light rays return, and regarding the method of conquering untimely death, one holds a khatvanga staff with one's left hand, and taking up a skull with the five ambrosias with one's right hand, one applies the ambrosia which is the offering substance to one's own mouth. Thus one diverts untimely death and augments one's life. Likewise, the eight goddesses, who bind with the adamantine chain, emanate and bind the Lord of Death. Therefore, one conquers untimely death, and engages in the intercourse (*saṁputa, zhal tu sbyor ba*) that is worship with ambrosia (*amṛtapūjā, bdud rsti'i mchod pa*). This is the second. (PD 426b)

[9] Vīravajra interprets this text as a reference to the third ritual action, as follows:

> **Separate them with the vajra** means that one emanates the goddess who wields a vajra, who defeats—i.e., returns again to—the Lord of Death. Having conquered

that they flutter like peacock feathers.[10] Then one should also summon with a hook.[11] Likewise, with regard to agitating, there is the mace.[12] With regard to devouring, the vajra was stated.[13] For piercing, the arrow is employed.[14] Applying the khatvanga staff to the limb is also the cheating of

---

the untimely death, one holds a khatvanga staff and draws forth from the "face" the offering substance of the ambrosial worship. This is the third. (PD 426b)

[10] Jayabhadra comments that "**so that they flutter like peacock feathers** means that one should visualize them as being so closely contiguous that they appear like closely packed peacock feathers floating" (E 37b.5–6: *picchavad bramayet tatheti picchakabramaṇanirantaraṁ yathādṛsya tathā nirantaraṁ bhāvayet*). Vīravajra interprets this text as a reference to the fourth ritual action, as follows: "Likewise, one emanates a mass of feathers of the five adamantine colors, and one summons the victim. This is the fourth." (PD 426b)

[11] According to Vīravajra, this refers to the fifth ritual action, summoning by means of the goddess who wields a hook. (PD 426b) Jayabhadra elaborates as follows: "**One should summon with a hook** means that when summoning is desired then one should set down a magical diagram in the house, and augmenting the mantra, then one should summon the victim by means of Khaṇḍarohā holding a hook in her hand" (D 49a.1–3, E 37b.6: *ākarṣayed aṅkuśen[ev]eti yadā ākarṣaṇam abhimataṁ tadā yantra[ṁ] bhavan[e] nyāset mantra[ṁ] vidarbhyāṅkuśagṛhītahastayā khaṇḍarohayā ākarṣayed ityarthaḥ*). With regard to "in the house," it is not clear if the *yantra* is to be placed in the victim's house or one's own house. Note that the incomplete ms. E ends with folio 37; all translations from Jayabhadra's commentary that follow will be derived from the more recent and somewhat less reliable ms. D and/or the Tibetan translation.

[12] Vīravajra comments that "summoning wielding the mace is the sixth" (PD 426b). Jayabhadra elaborates: "**Likewise, with regard to agitating, there is the mace** means that when agitating an army, and so forth, is desired, then one should agitate all armies, and so forth, by means of Khaṇḍarohā holding a mace" (D 49a.3–4: *[kṣ]obhaṇe muṣalaṁ tatheti yadā sainyādikṣobhaṇam abhimataṁ tadā muṣalagṛhītayā khaṇḍarohayā sarvasainyādikaṁ kṣobhayet*).

[13] Vīravajra comments that "devouring with the vajra mouth is the seventh." (PD 426b) Jayabhadra elaborates: "**With regard to devouring, the vajra was stated**—devouring is eating, so such-and-such should be eaten by means of [Khaṇḍarohā] holding a vajra, meaning that he should be eaten with the method of cruelty" (D 49a.4–6: *grasa[ne] vajram evoktam iti grasane bhakṣaṇe vajragṛhītayā amukaṁ bhakṣayed iti krūravidhinā bhakṣyed*).

[14] Jayabhadra comments that "**for piercing, the arrow is employed** by Khaṇḍarohā with an arrow in her hand" (D 49a.6: *vidhane [i]ti śarayojitaṁ kāṇḍhastayā khaṇḍarohayā*). Vīravajra writes that "binding with the arrow is the eighth" (PD 426b), but this translation probably resulted from a translator mistaking *vedhane* for *bandhane.*

black death.[15] The skull bowl offering vessel is the weapon employed at the mouth.[16]

---

[15] This is a literal translation of *kālamṛtyu*. The Tibetan translation *dus min 'chi ba*, "untimely death," is figurative and accurate.

[16] With regard to this concluding verse, Vīravajra writes:

> Having thus emanated the goddess wielding the eight implements, there is victory over the lord of untimely death. Having completed the ritual actions, once they are collected again, imagine that one wields a **khatvanga staff** with one's left hand, and with one's right one [one holds] to one's **mouth** a **skull bowl** with the **offering** substance of the five ambrosias along with a white, five pronged vajra. Drinking the offering substance of the five ambrosias is how it is **employed**. (PD 426b)

36. The Procedure of Summoning the Reality Worship

And then there is the great worship of the consort that is famed as the laying down of mantra. Have no doubt that this worship of the consort rapidly achieves power.[1] The application of the mantra to the two signs is the nonduality of the ḍākinī and hero.[2] For immobilizing a consort there is the ritual action of eating. Thus one should be furnished with the weapon.[3]

---

[1] According to Vīravajra, this "great worship of the consort" is an internalized fire sacrifice performed via sexual yoga. He comments as follows:

> Having thus explained the destruction of the Lord of Death, now I will explain the secret fire sacrifice via the path of passion. **And then** there is stated the **great worship of the consort**, and so forth. The hero and yoginī, having practiced the four [creation stages of] service and worship (*sevāsādhana*), make oblations of seminal essence with the ladle of the secret vajra into the fire pit of the lady's vulva: this is what is called the **great worship of the consort**. If the seminal essence "goes" to the bliss of cessation, then in the state of concentration one lays down mantra, i.e., one reverses [its flow]. These [practices of the] **worship of the consort** rapidly achieve the twelve ritual actions. (PD 427a)

[2] Vīravajra explains that "**the application of the mantra to the two signs** means that, as is stated in the *Saṁcāra*, one should turn back the seminal essence within the secret vajra and vulva by means of the mantra of the two syllables *dhi* and *vya*" (PD 427a). The syllables are given in the extant text of the *Yoginīsaṁcāra*, ch. 8 v. 4, as *dyā* and *vyā* (Pandey 1998, 78).

[3] This translates two lines which are present in all CS mss., but which Pandey omits (2002, 533), evidently because they are omitted in Mardo's translation and are not commented upon by Bhavabhaṭṭa. They are, however, attested in Sumatikīrti's translation and several of the commentaries. The first line is clearer and better attested. The CS mss. read *mudrāstambhe 'danakarma*, which differs somewhat from the Tibetan translation (SL 127b: *phyag rgya gnon pa'i las rnams ni*). The CS mss.' reading is confirmed by Jayabhadra, who comments: "**For immobilizing a consort there is the ritual action of eating**, i.e., for the immobilization of another's consort one should undertake the ritual action as if eating" (D 49b.3–4: *mudrāstambhe adanakarmeti paramudrāstambh[e] adanavat bhakṣaṇavat karmārabhet*), a comment repeated by Vīravajra in one of his commentaries (ST 200a). This does not shed light on the "ritual action of eating." Tathāgatarakṣita, on the other hand, writes: "**Immobilizing a consort** means that one immobilizes yoginīs who are committed to other doctrinal systems. **The ritual action of eating** indicates the repetition of fierce mantra, and seizing with a vajra. These statements indicate the rites of Khaṇḍarohā." (UN 238b) The second line is less clear. The CS mss. read *avayojyā tu vai tathā*. This is likely corrupt, and unfortunately Jayabhadra does not comment upon it. Sumatikīrti reads *de bzhin mtshon cha nyid dang sbyar*

Moreover, the mantrin should be endowed as well with the essences of the ḍākinīs.[4] The wise one should churn the yoginī,[5] one's body purified as is desired.[6]

(SL 127b), and this is also attested by Vīravajra (PD 427b: *mtshon cha dang sbyar ba*). I tentatively emend the Sanskrit to *astayojyā tu vai tathā*. What does this mean? Vīravajra, the only commentator who explains it, interprets these lines as he does the rest of the chapter, in terms of sexual yoga, as follows:

> Regarding the actions of pressing the seals (*mudrā*) of the lotus, at the time of the *joy* which is variegated, the *supreme joy* which ripens, and the [*joy of cessation*] which is devoid of characteristics, **thus one should be furnished with the weapon**. This means that just as one should be furnished with the weapon of yogic postures (*yantra*) involving syllables at the time of bliss, and the weapon of yogic postures involving wind at the time of supreme bliss, at the time of natural bliss one should be furnished with the weapon which turns back conceptualization by means of drawing forth the awareness which is called "unequalled" (*asamasama*), which uproots the subject and object [dichotomy]. (PD 427b; note that I read *lus* as *las*)

[4] Jayabhadra comments: "**Moreover the mantrin should be endowed with the essences of the ḍākinīs** means that he can thus perform the ritual procedure by means of the essence mantras of the ḍākinīs" (D 49b.4–5: *ḍākinīnāṁ yojayet mantr[ī] hṛdayabhis tathaiveiti ḍākinīnāṁ hṛdayamantrai[r] vā tathā vidhiḥ kāryaḥ*). Vīravajra is more specific about how these are used: "**Moreover the mantrin should be endowed as well with the essences of the ḍākinīs** means that he should turn back the seminal essence with the essence [mantras] of the heroes and heroines as well" (PD 427b).

[5] Bhavabhaṭṭa here reads *yoginīr*, in the correct case but plural, while the CS mss. read *yogino*, in the incorrect case but singular. The Tibetan translations do not indicate the plural here, although this is hardly definitive as the plural marker is often dropped. I have translated it in the singular as it would hardly be possible for the mantrin to "churn" (*manthayed*) more than one yoginī at a time.

[6] Kambala comments: "**Churning the yoginī** means being equipoised [in sexual union]; as for **the wise one**, i.e., one learned in the rite, his **body** is **purified**, i.e., he is liberated from the subject-object [dichotomy]. **As is desired** means that the hero, having taken one among the mother, daughter, and so forth, who have the [proper] clan [affiliation] and discipline, should embrace her." (SL 69b)

Knowing the procedure of the worship of the hero,[7] energetically perform the ritual action. The mantrin, distinguishing as he wishes, should employ the counter [ritual actions].[8] One should augment the elements of action with regard to the aims of destroying and benefiting. Divided by means of the divisions of reality, they are applied to the paths of the channels.[9] Execute the aim of the application,[10] whereby one will swiftly overpower gods, titans, and men.

---

[7] The CS mss. here read *vīrapūjām ayaṁ*, "this worship of the hero," which is plausible despite the fact that *ayaṁ* is in the wrong case and gender. Bhavabhaṭṭa reads *vīrapūjādvayaṁ*, "nondual worship of the hero," but this reading is unattested elsewhere. The extant copy of Jayabhadra's ms. reads *vīrapūjācittaṁ*, but the following commentary as well as the translation (*cho ga*) make it clear that *cittaṁ* here is a corruption of *vidhiṁ*. The corrected commentary reads as follows: "**Knowing the procedure of the worship of the hero, energetically perform the ritual action** means that having performed the worship of the hero by means of the procedure stated here, later one should undertake the ritual action" (D 49b.5–6: *vīrapūjā[v]i[dhi]ṁ jñātvā karma kurvīta yatnata iti atroktena vidhi[nā] vīrapūjāṁ kṛtvā paścāt karma samārabhet /*). The reading of *vidhiṁ* here is attested by Sumatikīrti's translation (SL 127b: *dpa' bo mchod pa'i cho ga shes*) as well as several other commentaries.

[8] The reading *viparītāni yojayet* is preserved in both Jayabhadra's and Bhavabhaṭṭa's (Pandey 2002, 533) commentaries. According to Jayabhadra: "**The mantrin, distinguishing as he wishes, should employ the counter [ritual actions]** means that the mantrin, having distinguished or isolated accordingly the ritual action, employs the [appropriate] counter ritual action" (D 49b.7–50a.1: *vibhajya svecchayā mantr[ī] vipar[ī]tā niyojayed iti tat karmānurūpato vibhajya pṛthak kṛtvā vipar[ī]tāni karmāni mantrī niyojayatīty arthaḥ*).

[9] Jayabhadra comments: "It is those mantras which are **divided**, i.e., separated, into **divisions** of multitudes of ritual actions through the states of things. They are **applied to the paths of the channels**, i.e., in the paths of the vajra and lotus." (D 50a.2–4: *tatt[v]abhed[e]ṣu nāḍimārgeṣu yojitā iti tattvānāṁ karmaprasarāṇāṁ bhedā teṣu bheditā[ḥ] pṛthakṛtā mantrās te nāḍīmārgeṣu vajrapadmamārgeṣu yojitaḥ*)

[10] Mardo's revised translation has an additional line here, "internally in the same manner as externally" (PM 237a: *phyi rol ji bzhin nang de bzhin*). This line is not attested elsewhere.

37. The Procedure of Inner Mastery

Now above all I will explain the means of overpowering the body.[1] The interconnected mantras are applied to each one of the ḍākinīs.[2] That which has been eaten is vomited up; the food should be vomited at the conclusion of the repetition. At the conclusion of seven nights it should be applied to food and drink.[3] Through this they will be under one's power for as long as one lives, have no doubt. Drinking reddish clarified butter, it should be vomited at the conclusion of the repetition. Then one should anoint one's own face with it. Should one be angered, through looking [at someone he or she] shall always be brought under one's power.

Preparing a cake[4] with rice flour and smeared with sesame and sesame

---

[1] I am translating *vigraha* as it is understood in the commentarial literature. Jayabhadra, for example, wrote: "**Now**, and so forth, connects with **I will explain**, the object of which is showing the ritual applications such as controlling, and so forth, which are the means of achieving the subjugation, and so forth, of people such as women, and so forth, whose bodies are overpowered" (D 50b.1–2: *idānīm athetyādinā vaśyādiprayogaṁ darśayati vigraha śarīra[s]yākrānta stryādi jagat teṣāṁ sādhanaṁ vaśīkaraṇādikaṁ tad vakṣyām[ī]ti saṁbandaḥ*).

[2] Jayabhadra comments here: "Combining both root mantras into one, the ḍākinīs are unified. This has the aim of making them apparent." (D 50b.3–4: *anyonyavalitā ma[ntr]ā iti ubhayo mūlamantrāv ekīkṛtya ḍākinya[ś] [c]aika[t]ra yojitā iti sa evārtho vispaṣṭīkṛtaḥ /*) This is undoubtedly a reference to the similar passage in ch. 35, where the syllables of the mantras are visualized as the ḍākinīs/yoginīs of the maṇḍala who are localized within the body. Interestingly, while this chapter primarily deals with ritual actions for controlling others, Bhavabhaṭṭa comments that it has healing applications as well. He comments as follows, taking the "interconnected mantras" to refer not to the two root mantras of the divine couple, but rather to three mantras, since he divides the hero's root mantra into two components, the eight line mantra which he terms the root mantra and the *kara kara* mantra which he calls the king of spells (*vidyārāja*): "Taking the three—root mantra, king of spells, and ḍākinī mantra—as one, one achieves healing efficacy" (Pandey 2002, 535: *mūlamantro vidyārājo ḍākinīmantraś ca trayam ekatrīkṛtya bhaiṣajyaṁ sādhayed ityarthaḥ*).

[3] Bhavabhaṭṭa provides a more elaborate explanation: "Having cleansed [oneself by] **vomiting up that which was eaten**, eating that one should again vomit it. Mix it with raw camphor, enchant it with the three mantras for **seven nights** and at the three divisions of the day [i.e., dawn, noon, and dusk]." (Pandey 2002, 535: *bhuktam udgīrṇaṁ prakṣālya punas tad bhakṣayitvā vamet / apakvakarpūramiśraṁ kṛtvā mantratrayeṇa saptarātrīs trisaṁdhyaṁ japet /*)

[4] This translates *saṁkulikā*, a word not attested in Sanskrit lexicons; however, in Pali *sanku-*

oil, the mantrin should use it as food. [He or she will] always be in one's power for as long as one lives, so long as one does not relinquish the ritual action, that is, [the ritual action of] causing [him or her] to always eat regurgitated black sesame seeds along with black mustard seeds. Pulverize kuṣṭha root[5] discharged from the anus,[6] a finger nail, and an intestinal worm, and mix it with one's own blood and semen. Should it be used as an unguent with [his or her] food, drink, eye ointment, and clothing, have no doubt that [he or she will] thus be in one's power for as long as one lives.

In the oblations of beef, the deity is anointed with the blood of the sacrifice. From that moment on [the deity] comes under one's power. If it does not come, it dies. Imagining that the meat is before him,[7] the sage should sacrifice it. Offering the sacrificial cake at the end of the sacrifice, the triple world will be summoned in an instant. There should be success after seven nights.

The characteristics of one's personal commitments and conduct, difficult to obtain in the three worlds, should always be zealously protected with the hidden mantras. The unfortunate will neither see nor apprehend the hidden meaning, but it will be attained [even] by adepts of trifling merit on account of my being pleased [with them].

---

likā means "a cake or sweetmeat" (see Rhys-Davids and Stede 1949, 120 col. 1). This clearly corresponds to Sumatikīrti's "oil pastry" (SL 128a: *snum 'khur*; PM 237a: *snum khur*).

[5] The aromatic root of *Costus speciosus* or related species.

[6] I have translated the reading preserved in CS ms. A, *kuṣṭhaṁ cāpānasaṁmuktaṁ*. This is very close to the reading preserved in Bhavabhaṭṭa's commentary, *kuṣṭhaṁ cāpānamuktaṁ tu* (F 121a.1; G 106a.8: *cāpānāmuktaṁ ta*). Pandey's edition emends this to *kuṣṭhaṁ cāpānayuktaṁ tu* (Pandey 2002, 536), presumably to make it accord with Mardo's translation, *ru rta bshang ba dang ldan* (PM 237b), which makes less sense. Interestingly, CS mss. B and C read *cāpānasaṁyuktaṁ*, which corresponds to the Tibetan; but these are simply copies of ms. A, which indicates that this reading is erroneous. Bhavabhaṭṭa comments that "one should prepare *kuṣṭha* root which has emerged seven times from the anus" (Pandey 2002, 536: *kuṣṭhaṁ saptavārāpānanirgataṁ kāryam*), meaning, presumably, either a piece of root which has been passed through the digestive tract by being swallowed whole and excreted, or, perhaps, inserted in and removed from the anus seven times.

[7] The commentators make it clear that the referent of "him" (*tasya*) is not "the "sage" (*vicakṣaṇaḥ*). Jayabhadra comments that "**before him** means before Śrī Heruka or, literally, at his mouth" (D 51a.3–4: *tasyāgrata iti śrīherukasyāgre vā śabdān mukhe vā*). Bhavabhaṭṭa comments that "**before him** means either [before] a painting or image of Śrī Heruka, at his mouth, or in front of or behind [him]" (Pandey 2002, 536–37: *tasyeti agrata iti śrīherukapaṭasya tatpratimāyā vā tanmukhe vā pūrvāparayoḥ*).

38. The Procedure of the Yoginīs' Place and the Heroes' Secret Abode[1]

Next are the secret signs, and also the physical characteristics of the ḍākinīs, as well as the heroes' physical distinctions.[2] The Lord of Heroes, the heteropraxical adept,[3] does not write [this Tantra]—nor should he

---

[1] This is a translation of the Sanskrit title as preserved in Bhavabhaṭṭa's commentary, *yoginī-sthānaguhyavīrālayavidhipaṭalo* (Pandey 2002, 541). *Yoginīsthāna* is attested by Sumatikīrti's translation, which reads *rnal 'byor ma'i sa* (SL 129b). Mardo's translation here reads "the place for achieving the yoginī(s)" (PM 238a: *rnal 'byor ma'i sgrub pa'i sa*). On the other hand, **heroes' secret abode** is attested by Mardo (PM 238a: *gsang ba'i dpa' bo'i gnas*), while Sumatikīrti has the radically different reading "mantra" (SL 129b: *gsang ba'i sngags*).

[2] According to Jayabhadra, "the **physical distinctions** are the [body] colors, [number of] faces and arms, [types of] implements, and so forth" (D 51a.4–5: *aṅgabheda varṇamukha-bhujāyudhādaya[ḥ]*). Each of the Tibetan translations add a different additional line that is not attested in the CS mss. or in the commentaries of Jayabhadra and Bhavabhaṭṭa. These are: "I will thus explain…" (SL 129b: *de bzhin du ni bshad par bya*), and "that is the achievement to be achieved" (PM 237b: *grub par gyur pa de 'grub 'gyur*).

[3] The expression *vāmācāras tu sādhakaḥ* ("the heteropraxical adept") declines with *vīreśvaraḥ* and should thus likewise be taken as describing the *yogin*. This reading is attested by Mardo's translation (PM 237b: *g-yon pa'i kun spyod sgrub pa pos*). Bhavabhaṭṭa has another reading here, which he explains as follows: "'Well-concealed by the **heteropraxical**' means that the secret signs, and so forth, are thoroughly concealed by the heteropraxical Śrī Cakrasamvara yogins" (Pandey 2002, 538: *vāmācārasugopitam iti vāmācāraiḥ śrīcakrasamvarayogibhiḥ suṣṭhugopitaṁ chommakādi*). This reading is also attested in Sumatikīrti's translation (SL 128b: *g-yon pa'i kun spyod legs sbas pa*).

recite it—in front of anyone at all.[4] [If] a mantrin recites madly the ḍākinīs characterized by secrecy,[5] I do not look upon him.

Have no doubt that this bad natured one, who is a commitment killer, an evil doer, and a brahmin-slayer, will be eaten by many thousands of ḍākinīs.[6] This deceived, bad natured one, a fool of wicked conduct—I will not rescue him when he is being devoured by the yoginīs.[7] Amidst the secret ones the sacrificial victim is indeed this very adept who has fallen from the world of the buddhas, and who harms the guru and the commitments.

I will favor him who protects the Tantra—which is the awesome teaching of Śrī Heruka—with good looks and the company of the ḍākinīs. The gurus authorize and the adepts conceal, and [if] he is always dear to the yoginīs, [then] have no doubt that success is his. The adept who becomes a hero is the commander flying through the triple world. He becomes worthy

---

[4] In these lines, the CS mss. read *vīreśvaraṁ*, making "Lord of Heroes" the object of the actions of writing and reciting. However, both Jayabhadra and Bhavabhaṭṭa read *vīreśvaraḥ*, taking him as the agent of the actions. Bhavabhaṭṭa supplies the missing object of these actions—it is "[this] Tantra." He also glosses *vīreśvara* as the *yogī* (Pandey 2002, 538), who presumably must keep this commitment, regarding which Jayabhadra explains: "**the Lord of Heroes does not write** means that the Blessed Lord does not see those who throw off their commitments; and likewise with regard to **nor should he recite**, and so forth" (D 51a.5–6: *na ca likhyati vīreśvara iti sama[y]o[ttīrṇ]aṁ na paśyati bhagavān ityarthaḥ na paṭhed ityādi yathā*).

[5] I translate Bhavabhaṭṭa's reading, *guhyalakṣaṇaḍākinīḥ* (Pandey 2002, 538), which has the "ḍākinīs" as the object of the verb "recite." This likely refers to the ḍākinīs' mantras; Mardo's translation reads *sngags rnams* (PM 237b), reading "mantras" instead of "mantrin."

[6] The Sanskrit here appears to be somewhat garbled, and my translation here most closely follows the Tibetan, which takes "many thousands of ḍākinīs" (PM 237b: *mkha' 'gro stong phrag du ma yis*; SL 128b: *mkha' 'gro stong phrag du ma yi*) as agents of the action of the action of "eating" (*za*). The surviving Sanskrit, however, places the ḍākinīs as the objects of this action. The CS mss. read *ḍākinīsahasram anekadhā bhakṣayan asau durātmakaḥ*, with a present participle derived from the causative stem (i.e., "causing to be eaten") that declines with the "evil-natured one." Bhavabhaṭṭa's commentary reads *bhakṣyam*, which declines with *ḍākinīsahasram*, who are thus what are "to be eaten." These readings clearly reverse the intended meaning of the text, which is to scare the adept into keeping his commitments by listing the terror that will befall him if he does not do so, i.e., consumption by ferocious ḍākinīs. This threat is repeated (almost) correctly in the next verse.

[7] The Sanskrit here reads *nāhaṁ tasya paritrātā bhakṣamāṇasya yoginībhiḥ*. We would expect here *paritrāmi*, in parallel with the previous line *nāhaṁ tasya paśyāmi* ("I will not look at him"), rather than a misplaced and oddly declined past passive participle. Bhavabhaṭṭa glosses *paritrātā* with *durātmanaḥ*, indicating that it is the "evil-natured ones" who are [not] rescued. But for this reading to work we would need the pronoun *mayā* rather than *ahaṁ*.

of worship everywhere; the adept is one who strives to be a hero. The yogas come forth for him, and he has the lineage tradition. Seeing the master who is a hero and who upholds Śrī Heruka's observances, seeing and being enraptured with this mantra, the adept should utter seven times the supreme hero root mantra, distinguished by the syllables *oṁ* and *hūṁ*.

Bowing down to them with zeal, all the buddhas, and so forth, are worshipped. Have no doubt that the great hero is always playful. Vajravārāhī resides in their hearts in a form nondual with the [great hero] and the yoginīs.[8] Through the vision of the merit of that well-born living being, the ḍākinīs abide with impassioned eyes[9] everywhere, at rivers, ponds, and the ocean,[10] on mountains, and at crossroads, waterholes, wells, empty houses, and alleys.

The great hero plays at ease in the charnel ground of great terror,[11] likewise ranging in space and in the underworld, in the company of many dreadful zombies and great mighty ones (*mahābala, stobs chen po*). In a hollow,[12] a cave,[13] or a secret [spot][14]—in these places the men of mystery[15] and the yoginīs sport with the adept upon the earth.

---

[8] The CS mss. here read *teṣāṁ hṛdisthavārāhyā mahāvīrayoginyam advayarūpataḥ*, which I emend to *teṣāṁ hṛdisthavārāhī mahāvīrayoginyadvayarūpataḥ*. Bhavabhaṭṭa here reads *hṛdisthavīrāḥ yoginyam advayasthitam*, which omits reference to Vajravārāhī, who is attested in both Tibetan translations. It seems that *mahāvīra* is an interpolation, and that the extra syllable in the remainder of the verse, the unusual *-am* suffix with *yoginy*, should be dropped to yield *yoginyadvayarūpataḥ*.

[9] According to Bhavabhaṭṭa, "they have **impassioned eyes** because of passion at the sight of him who upholds Śrī Heruka's observance" (Pandey 2002, 541: *saṁraktanayanāḥ / śrīherukavratadhāridarśanānurāgād iti*).

[10] Following this text, CS ms. A is missing four folia (as are the copies based upon it, mss. B and C), which covers the text through ch. 44. The translation up to there will be based upon the Tibetan translations and the Sanskrit text preserved in the commentaries. Any significant variants will be noted as they arise.

[11] PM 238a: *'jigs pa chen po dur khrod du*; SL 129b: *'jigs pa chen po'i dur khrod gnas*.

[12] That is, *kuhare*, "in a cavity, hole, hollow," which Bhavabhaṭṭa glosses as *bile*, "in a cave, hole, pit" (Pandey 2002, 541).

[13] That is, *gahvare*, which means "in an inaccessible place," i.e., a cave, thicket, or wood. Here Bhavabhaṭṭa glosses it as *parvatodare*, "in a mountain cavity" (Pandey 2002, 541). Regarding this, see ch. 1 ns. 26–27 above.

[14] That is, *guhye*, which Bhavabhaṭṭa glosses as *gahane vane*, "in a dense forest" (Pandey 2002, 541).

[15] That is, *gūḍhamānuṣya*, or *gsang ba'i mi* (Pandey 2002, 541, 751).

39. The Procedure of Vision and Loud Laughter

Now, have no doubt that the yogin of great power,[1] displaying through laughter the eightfold mantra[2] for him, imparts it. The unbearable ḍākinīs terrify with many kinds of awesome sounds. If that hero is frightened, he trembles and runs away.[3] But if the hero is not frightened, then held by the left hand he will be led by them to their abode, together with the ḍākinīs. Through devotion and desire for Śrī Heruka,[4] one is conducted

[1] Bhavabhaṭṭa glosses *mahāsiddhiyogī* as "Śrī Heruka's yogī, with regard to the great power, i.e., the accomplishment of *mahāmudrā*" (Pandey 2002, 542: *mahāsiddhiyogī mahāsiddhau mahāmudrāsiddhau śrīherukayogī*).

[2] While we might take *mantraṁ aṣṭavidham* to be a single "eightfold mantra," Jayabhadra and Bhavabhaṭṭa interpret them in terms of two separate mantras of the divine couple, each of which has eight component parts. Bhavabhaṭṭa states: "The **mantra** here is *kili kili cili cili sili sili dhili dhili*, which is eightfold laughter by means of that mantra and the rest of the king of spells [mantra]. There is also eightfold laughter by means of the goddess' mantra, namely *hā hā he he ho ho hūṁ hūṁ*." (Pandey 2002, 542: *mantraś cātra kili kili cili cili sili sili dhili dhili iti vidyārājasya śeṣo mantras tenāṣṭavidho hāsaḥ / hā hā he he ho ho hūṁ hūṁ iti devīmantreṇāpy aṣṭavidhau hāsaḥ /*) Regarding the mantras themselves, other commentators such as Jayabhadra read the first mantra as *kili kili sili sili hili hili dhili dhili* (MP 65b), which he calls the "four aspects of the hero's root mantra" (D 51b.1: *vīramūlamantrasya caturvidhaṁ*). The Sanskrit text of Jayabhadra's commentary agrees with Bhavabhaṭṭa's on the second mantra, the "ḍākinī's root mantra" (D 51b.2: *ḍākinīmūlamantra*), but the Tibetan translations of both texts differ from the reading given in the Sanskrit texts, with *ha hā he hai ho hau huṁ hūṁ* (MP 65b, CP 225b).

[3] The Sanskrit here, *vidravanti*, is plural, but I translate it in singular as the Sanskrit is only preserved in fragments, and the Tibetan does not indicate plurality here.

[4] Here I translate Mardo's *he ru ka dpal gus 'dod pas* (PM 238a), which corresponds to text in Bhavabhaṭṭa's commentary that I would emend to *śrīherukabhaktikāmena*. Here Pandey reads *śrīherukaśaktikāmena*, which is the reading preserved in ms. F (124a.5). Ms. G, however, reads *mukti* here (G 108b.5). The Tibetan translation of this text, *he ru ka dpal chags 'dod pas* (CP 226a), does attest *bhakti*. Bhavabhaṭṭa comments here: "**Through devotion and desire for Śrī Heruka** means with desire for communion with Śrī Heruka" (F 124a.5, G 108b.5, Pandey 2002, 543: *śrīheruka[bh]aktikāmeneti śrīherukasaṁghābhilāṣeṇa*). On the other hand, the *śakti* reading is attested in Vīravajra's commentary (PD 431a), which suggests an alternative reading, "through desire for Śrī Heruka's power." This line is not attested in Sumatikīrti's translation, which varies significantly from the reading in Mardo, Bhavabhaṭṭa, and the other commentaries.

to the aerial state (*khecarīpada*). Always delighting [them],[5] one will go to the Land of Bliss (*sukhāvatī*). [For] the adept who has a mantra body, nowhere is there old age or death.[6]

---

[5] *rtag tu mngon par rtse byed de* (PM 238a). Pandey's reconstruction here, *tatrābhrato nityam* (Pandey 2002, 543), is likely incorrect as it does not take into account the causative sense which is implied by the Tibetan, and which also accords with the text as a whole, in which the adept's spiritual welfare is dependent upon pleasing the yoginīs. Based on the Tibetan translation, I would suspect that something like *abhirāmayaya nityaṁ* was the Sanskrit reading here.

[6] I have translated Bhavabhaṭṭa's reading, *na jarāmṛtyu[ḥ] sarvata sādhako mantravigrahaḥ* (Pandey 2002, 543). Mardo reads instead: / *sgrub pa po ni sngags lus can* // *'khor bar 'chi dang rga ba med* / (PM 238a), "[For] the adept who has a mantra body, there is no old age or death in *saṁsāra*." Bhavabhaṭṭa comments: "Regarding **nowhere is there old age or death**, since old age and death arise from conceptualization, when that is abandoned, those [too] are abandoned. How is conceptualization abandoned? [It is abandoned] because **the adept has a mantra body**, i.e., he has the nature of mantra, which is the immediate cause or self-nature of all things." (Pandey 2002, 543: *na jarāmṛtyu sarvatreti tayor vikalpajatvāt / taddhānau taddhānir iti bhāvaḥ / vikalpahānir eva kuta ity āha / sādhako mantravigraha iti / mantraḥ sarvadharmasvarūpasākṣātkaraṇam / tadātmakatvād iti bhāvaḥ* /) Vīravajra explains the entire latter half of this chapter as follows:

> **If the hero is not frightened**, he is **held by the left hand** and **led** to each of **their abodes**, i.e., the twenty-four [pilgrimage] places. He makes love **with the ḍākinīs**, and it will be as if he was in the **Land of Bliss**. If he desires to go to Akaṇiṣṭha, then, **through the power of Śrī Heruka**, that passionate yogin **is conducted to the state of ranging in space**. If he is not conducted to that abode, then the **adept** who has heard the sound of the eight laughs obtains that **mantra body** which is the inconceivable transformation of cyclic existence's old age and death, and he brings all ḍākinīs into his power. If we apply this to the perfecting stage, the [text] indicates the following: When art and wisdom are equipoised, the wheel of wind diverts [the seminal essence] upward by means of the eight *h*-[syllables]. At the time of joy, and so forth, the many terrible sounds such as the breathy laugh and violent breath are irresistible. With regard to them, if the hero fearlessly inserts the life force into the central channel, then it is conducted to the crown, the natural abode of seminal essence—this is designated by the words **left hand**. Then, delighted by constant bliss with the ḍākinīs, i.e., the thirty-two channels, it is as if one is [in] the Land [of Bliss], which is Jālandhara at the crown. Thus, conducting it to the abode of the space wheel in the head through desire for the power of Śrī Heruka, the adept has a mantra body of diverted wind which crosses the four rivers of birth, sickness, old age, and death. (PD 431a)

40. The Procedures of Subjugating the Five Social Classes, and Mahāmudrā

Next I will explain [the method] by which a mortal can be brought under one's control.[1] It is achieved within a month by the hero who abides by the procedure of mantra yoga. For this[2] there are pieces of flesh, with intoxicants, together with fish and flesh. The Lord of Heroes,[3] who has all states,[4] gives the extensive power[5] to the adept after seven days.[6] At night one is occupied with fire sacrifice.[7] If one prepares one hundred and eight [fire sacrifices] through the three divisions of the day, within seven days one

[1] Jayabhadra comments that "generally, it is said that [this is for] the subjugation of kings, and so forth" (D 51b.2–3: *sāmānyena rājādīnāṁ vaśīkaraṇam āha*).

[2] Jayabhadra comments: "**For this** means for the fire sacrifice. All fire sacrifices [fall into] two types, outer fire sacrifice, and [the internal] fire sacrifice in the body. And hence it is endowed **with fish and flesh** as is stated." (D 51b.4–5: *asyeti homasya sarvahomā dvividhaḥ bāhyahomaṁ kāyahomaś ca / ata evoktamatsamāṁsayutasya ceti*)

[3] The Lord of Heroes is Śrī Heruka, as Jayabhadra informs us (D 51b.6: *vīreśaḥ śrīherukaḥ*).

[4] Jayabhadra comments: "**has all states** refers to the states of being angered or pleased" (D 51b.5–6: *sarvāvastho 'pi ruṣṭatuṣṭāvastho 'pi*).

[5] Jayabhadra preserves the text here as *dadāti vipulāsiddhiṁ*, rather than as *mahāsiddhiṁ pradadāti*, which is the Pandey edition's reconstruction from the Tibetan text (2002, 544).

[6] Bhavabhaṭṭa comments here: "**After seven days** means that once one performs one hundred and eight oblations for three months through the three divisions of the day [i.e., dawn, noon, and dusk], then, by means of the fire sacrifices over seven days, the power which is to be accomplished is **given to the adept**" (Pandey 2002, 544: *māsatrayaṁ trisaṁdhyam aṣṭottaraśatāhutidānaṁ vidhāya tataḥ saptāhahomena sādhyasiddhiṁ dadāti sādhakāya*).

[7] Jayabhadra writes here: "**At night one is occupied with fire sacrifice** means that the fire sacrifice in the body should be by all means performed at night" (D 51b.7: *niśihomaparāyaṇa iti avaśyam [e]va rātrau kāyahomaḥ kārya[ḥ]*). Bhavabhaṭṭa provides the following symbolic interpretation: "Since **night** designates wisdom, it means that one should sacrifice endowed with wisdom" (Pandey 2002, 544: *niśihomaparāyaṇa iti / niśā prajñāsāṁketakatvāt / prajñāyukto juhuyād iti bhāvaḥ /*).

will subjugate a king together with his army. With half,[8] one [subjugates] a great hero,[9] and with half of that,[10] a minister is brought under one's power. With regard to vassal lords (*sāmanta*), one should sacrifice thirty-two [times] through the stages of sacrifice.[11]

For a brahmin, one should sacrifice twenty [times] over seven days. For a kshatriya, one should sacrifice seven [times], and for a vaishya, five [times]. For a shudra, sacrifice three [times], and for an outcaste, once. Should the hero practice for one month through the stages of the social classes, the adept equipped with mantra[12] will summon all beings.[13] The hero, depending upon the previous procedure, will attain his desire. He will be like a lord of love on earth, [or] one of glory and great fortune, [or] he will become an adept pleasing to the ḍākinīs, have no doubt.[14]

---

[8] According to Bhavabhaṭṭa, "**with half** means with fifty-four fire sacrifices" (Pandey 2002, 544: *ardhena tv iti catuḥpañcāśatāhutibhiḥ*).

[9] This text is lost in the Sanskrit; Sumatikīrti here reads *dpa' bo chen po* (SL 130a), which is attested by Vīravajra, who explains that this indicates the crown prince (PD 431b). On the other hand, Mardo reads *dpa' bo blon po*, "hero minister" or "hero and minister" (PM 238b).

[10] That is, "twenty-seven [sacrifices]" (Pandey 2002, 544: *tadardhena tv iti saptaviṁśatyā*).

[11] According to Bhavabhaṭṭa, "it is established that **one should sacrifice through the stages of sacrifice** means that sacrifices should be according to the divisions of the social classes" (Pandey 2002, 545: *homayed āhutikramād iti varṇakrameṇāhutayo deyā iti pratipādayati /*).

[12] Here I follow Sumatikīrti's text, *gsang sngags ldan pa'i sgrub pa pos* (SL 130b), attested in Vīravajra's commentary (PD 432a: *sngags dang ldan pa'i sgrub pa pos*). Mardo's text reads "the adept who has the power of mantra" (PM 138b: *sngags kyi nus pa sgrub pa pos*).

[13] Vīravajra comments here: "**Should the hero practice for one month through the stages of the social classes** means that if one is not successful after a week, then should one continue by means of the procedure of continuing for a month, they will be subjugated. **The adept equipped with mantra**—i.e., the adept equipped with the mantra "Subjugate! Ho!" (*vaśaṁ kuru ho*)—will subjugate all beings such as the kshatriya, and so forth." (PD 432a)

[14] Vīravajra comments here:

> If one **depends upon** this [method of] inner and outer fire sacrifice, then one **will attain** whatever one desires of the twelve ritual actions, such as this procedure of subjugation. **Like a lord of love on earth** means that he attains the [state of] a universal monarch among men, or becomes one who has **glory and great fortune**. This means that he becomes a universal monarch among the gods, such as Indra. Or, the adept pleases the thirty-six ḍākinīs, and thus attains the supreme power which is like that of Śrī Cakrasamvara. (PD 432a)

The Pandey edition's reconstruction of this last verse is highly problematic (2002, 545).

41. The Procedure of Laying Down the Maṇḍala of the Twenty-four Syllables

Now, adepts[1] know the excellent, supreme ritual action,[2] through which [one can master] subjugating, summoning, inciting hatred, killing, expelling, befogging, immobilizing, and likewise staking, stealing speech, blinding, causing impotence,[3] and shape changing. The adept always achieves these twelve great ritual actions. Have no doubt that the adept has success through recollection.[4]

The ḍākinīs are all-pervasive, in all of the superior[5] seats, and so forth. They are born in land after land, endowed with gnosis in their own places of birth.[6] They are the ḍākinīs known as the mistresses of the

---

[1] Jayabhadra comments here: "**Now**, **ritual action**, and so forth, shows that the perfected yogin has the aim of achieving all ritual actions" (D 52a.1–2: *atha karmetyādinānena niṣpannasya yoginaḥ sarvakarmasiddhyatha[ṁ] darśitaṁ*).

[2] According to Vīravajra, this is the magical diagram of the syllables (PD 432a: *akṣarayantra, yi ge'i 'khrul 'khor*), that is, the "maṇḍala of twenty-four syllables" which is the subject of this chapter, namely, the seed syllables which correspond to the deity couples of the outer and inner maṇḍalas (the maṇḍala as mapped across the body of the practitioner, and the landscape of India and the Himalayas).

[3] That is, *ma ning nyid du bya ba* (PM 238b, SL 130b), which Pandey reasonably reconstructs as *ṣaṇḍhatvakaraṇa* (2002, 546), "causing a state of impotence" or "causing the state of being a eunuch."

[4] Bhavabhaṭṭa glosses this as follows: "There is recollection, i.e., thinking only, of these great actions, whereby success in these arises" (Pandey 2002, 546: *eteṣāṁ mahākarmaṇāṁ smaraṇaṁ cintāmātraṁ tato jāyate teṣāṁ siddhiḥ*).

[5] Bhavabhaṭṭa preserves the reading *sarvottareṣu* (Pandey 2002, 546), and Jayabhadra attests *sarvottameṣu* (D 52a.3), both of which correspond to Mardo's translation *thams cad bla ma'i* (PM 238b). Sumatikīrti's text reads "in the northern and eastern/in the northeastern [seats, etc.]" (SL 130b: *shar dang byang gi*), which may be a translation of *pūrvottareṣu*.

[6] That is, *svayoniṣu*, which Bhavabhaṭṭa glosses as "in their own familes (or castes)" (Pandey 2002, 547: *svajātiṣu*). The idea seems to be that they are born in "land after land" (*yul dang yul du, deśe deśe*) among various social classes.

adamantine maṇḍala.[7] [They are:][8] in Kulutā[9] and [Maru],[10] in Sindhu and Nagara,[11] in Suvarṇadvīpa and Saurāṣṭra,[12] in Gṛhadevatā and Pretapurī,[13]

[7] As Jayabhadra explains, they are the "**mistresses**, preeminent ones, **of the adamantine maṇḍala**, i.e., in Śrī Heruka's maṇḍala" (D 52a.4–5: *vajramaṇḍalaṁ śrīherukamaṇḍalaṁ tatra nāyakāḥ pradhānā[ḥ]*).

[8] The text here lists the twenty-four pilgrimage sites, in reverse of the usual order. For the usual order, as well as the correspondences to the deities, the seed syllables and bodily parts, and the constituents, see section 3.1 in the Introduction above. Jayabhadra comments here: "The [places] beginning with Pullīramalaya are taken in reverse order, in all directions and quarters" (D 52a.6–7: *pullīramalayaprabhṛtayo vilomanaṁ sarvadiśavidiśā[su] gṛhyante*).

[9] The places and their correspondences to the deities are listed in many places. See for example the *Pīthādiyoginī* chapter of the AU, edition and translation in Kalff 1979. Both Kulutā and Maru are classified as the "secondary charnel grounds" (*upaśmaśāna*). Kulutā is located on the upper Beas River in the Kūlū region in Himachal Pradesh. This is confirmed by Bu-ston, who wrote: "Regarding Kulutā, in a cave in Kūlū (*gnyung-ti*) in the hinterlands of Garzha, there is a place of practice which has a knee-like stone liṅga and yoni, in a trench dug in a pit" (DS 57).

[10] The Sanskrit text here is not preserved, and the Tibetan translations list the variant *mgon pa* (PM 239a, SL 130b), which is unattested elsewhere. Several verses down, however, *marudeśe* is attested by Bhavabhaṭṭa (Pandey 2002, 548). The region of Maru included modern Marwar, in the Jodhpur region of Rajasthan, but also encompassed the northwestern portion of Gujarat (see Sircar 1971, 97). Bu-ston, however, identifies it with a region in the Indian foothills of the Himalayas, in contemporary Himachal Pradesh, writing: "Regarding Maru, just north of Jālandara in a cave there is a stone yoni" (DS 57).

[11] Sindhu and Nagara constitute the "charnel grounds" (*śmaśāna*). Sindhu is a province in what is now southern Pakistan, surrounding the Indus river. Nagara, or Nagarahāra, was a region in the Northwest encompassing modern Jalalabad in Afghanistan. See Sircar 1971, 293.

[12] Suvarṇadvīpa and Saurāṣṭra are classified as the "secondary meeting places" (*upamelāpaka*). Suvarṇadvīpa, "the Golden Isle," is famous in Indian literature, and is usually located in Southeast Asia (see Sircar 1971, 23). Bu-ston clearly does not know exactly where it is located, writing only that it is "the small island of the king of Golden Isle" (DS 57). Saurāṣṭra is the region in Western India roughly equivalent to the Kathiawar peninsula in Gujarat. See Sircar 1971, 94, 94.

[13] Gṛhadevatā and Pretapurī are classified as "meeting places" (*melāpaka*). Gṛhadevatā corresponds to no known place; the term literally means "household deity." Bu-ston claims that "in a brown willow grove in Khotan is a place of practice named after a heart-like stone liṅga" (DS 57). This identification, however, is clearly speculative. Alexis Sanderson has argued that this list derives from a Śaiva/Kāpālika text, the *Tantrasadbhāva*, which in *adhikāra* 16 lists not only the twenty-four places, but also a category of deities that corresponds to each. The deity class that corresponds to Saurāṣṭra is the *gṛhadevatā*; Sanderson thus concludes that the Buddhists derived this list from this or a similar source, but mistakenly included *gṛhadevatā* as a place name in place of *samudrakukṣi*, "seashore," the only name in the *Tantrasadbhāva* not

in Himālaya and Kāñci,[14] in Lampāka and Kaliṅga,[15] in Kośala and Triśakuni,[16] in Kāmarūpa and Oḍra,[17] in Mālava,[18] Devīkoṭa,[19]

---

included in the Buddhist Yoginī Tantras. See Sanderson 1994, 95; and 99–100 n. 20. Ronald Davidson, however, has questioned this argument, suggesting that such lists may have in turn been generated under Buddhist influence. See Davidson 2002b, 211.

Bu-ston locates Pretapurī in the region of Pu-hrangs in Tibet, where, "in the middle of a valley, [there] is a stone liṅga the size of a large man. A hot spring emerges at its base." He adds, "Some say it is China" (DS 57).

[14] Himālaya and Kāñci are classified as "secondary *chandoha*" (*upacchandoha*). "Himālaya" generally refers to the mountain range of the same name, but there was considerable controversy regarding exactly which mountain could be identified with this site. Bu-ston writes here: "Himālaya is the snow mountain; some identify it as a stone liṅga of about a cubit in a river at Kailash. Some identify it as Tibet in general." (DS 56) Other Tibetans identified it with Mt. Kailash. Regarding this controversy, see Huber 1990.

Kāñci is the well-known city, once called Conjeeveram and now again known as Kanchipuram, in Tamil Nadu. See Sircar 1973, 17–18.

[15] Lampāka and Kaliṅga together constitute the *chandoha* pilgrimage places. Lampāka corresponds to the modern Laghman region in Afghanistan, centered around a river valley northwest of Jalalabad and northeast of Kabul. See Sircar 1971, 35. Bu-ston gives a correct but rather vague description, as follows: "Lampaka is a very isolated place of practice in the mountainous hinterlands of Garlok on the bank of a raging river" (DS 56). Garlok was the Tibetan term for the region in Northwest India which was, by the 11th century, controlled by Muslim Turks.

Kaliṅga is the region on the east coast of India roughly extending from Purī in Orissa south to the Kṛṣṇā River in Andhra Pradesh. See Sircar 1971, 91. Bu-ston (DS 56) incorrectly identifies it as being southwest of the Vajrāsana at Bodhgaya, rather than southeast as it actually is.

[16] Kośala and Triśakuni are the "secondary fields" (*upakṣetra*). Kośala is the kingdom in north-central India, now in Uttarpradesh, with its capital at Ayodhyā. I have not been able to locate Triśakuni, but Bu-ston provides a fascinating though perplexing identification: "Triśakuni is in the land of *stag-gzig*, in the valley which brings together the rivers Gaṅgā, Ganti, and Sarupa" (DS 56). The place name *stag-gzig* points to the northwest. However, the rivers mentioned all point to north-central/northeast India. *Ganti* most likely refers to the Gumpti or Gomatī, a tributary of the Gaṅgā which flows south through Kośala, joining the Gaṅgā east of Vārāṇaṣī, while *Sarupa* may refer to the river variously called the Sarabhu/Sarayū/ Sarju/Gogra, another tributary that runs south through Uttarpradesh. This suggests a location in the vicinity of the old kingdom of Kośala. Regarding these rivers, see Hoey 1907.

[17] Kāmarūpa and Oḍra are designated as the "fields" (*kṣetra*). Kāmarūpa is the famous pilgrimage site in Assam in Eastern India. Oḍra is an old form of the name Oḍiśā, the region now called Orissa in eastern India. See Sircar 1971, 167 ff.

[18] Mālava was an important polity in Western India, centered on the Mālava plateau north of the Narmadā river valley. The group of four beginning here (Mālava, Devīkoṭa, Rāmeśvara, and Godāvarī) are designated as "secondary seats" (*upapīṭha*).

Rāmeśvara,[20] and Godāvarī,[21] and in Arbuda,[22] Oḍḍiyāna,[23] Jālandhara,[24] Pullīramalaya,[25] and so forth.[26]

---

[19] Sircar identifies Devīkoṭa with Bangarh in the Dinajpur district in Bangladesh (1971, 112; 1973, 83). According to Bu-ston: "Devikoṭi, the 'Goddess Fort' to the east of Varendra [in northern Bengal], has the temple of Devikoṭi, which is about 4 krośa [8 miles] from the town 'Pañcapa,' to the south of Gro-mo" (DS 55–56). Gro-mo, it should be noted, was located in the vicinity of eastern Sikkim and western Bhutan (*bod rgya tshig mdzod chen mo*, 1.408), which supports Sircar's identification. However, other Tibetan sources point to Kāmākhyā in Assam (Ferrari 1958, 102). Templeman argues for this latter location (1999, 192).

[20] Rāmeśvara is most likely Setubandhu Rāmeśvara in the Ramnad distinct in Tamil Nadu. Sircar notes that there is also another site with this name at the confluence of the Banas and Chambal rivers in east-central Rajasthan (1973, 94). Bu-ston's vague account agrees with the former. He wrote that "Rāmeśvara has a stone liṅga established in the town of the eastern king Rāmeśvara which was named after its resemblance to a horse's mane" (DS 55).

[21] While Godāvarī's location is uncertain, it is presumably on the Deccan plateau in south-central India, somewhere near the river of this name, which drains the plateau flowing to the southeast. According to Bu-ston: "Regarding Godavarī, the 'Gift Supreme,' an offering of milk was made by a white cow in cattle country; afterward, digging there, a liṅga of Maheśvara appeared. It is near the Vindhya Mountains. It is a two-and-a-half month journey from Vajrāsana, and by offering there miraculous springs arise." (DS 55)

[22] Arbuda corresponds to Mt. Abu, a predominantly Jain pilgrimage site located about 100 kilometers west of Udaipur (Davidson 2002b, 209). The final group of four beginning here (Arbuda, Oḍḍiyāna, Jālandhara, and Pullīramalaya) are classified as the "seats" (*pīṭha*) of this tradition.

[23] Oḍḍiyāna is undoubtedly the most famous of tantric Buddhist pilgrimage sites, and while there was much debate over its location, in part due to confusion with Oḍra, it has now been definitively established as being the contemporary Swat valley, as Kuwayama has shown on the basis of inscriptional evidence. See Kuwayama 1991, and Davidson 2002b, 209.

[24] As Davidson notes, "Jālandhara-pīṭha, where the goddess Mahāmāyā (Vajreśvarī) is worshipped in the modern town of Kangra...was probably a Gaddi tribal site before Brahmans and Śaiva sādhus took possession" (2002b, 209). Bu-ston comments:

> Jālandhara, west of Guge, has a great city in a valley which brings together three rivers, the Shavaru [Sutlej] River of Tholing, the Pipashana [Beas] River of Garsha [a region northwest of Gartok] and the Merave [Ravi?] River of Shiladze [?]. Near there is a stone liṅga which is as if turned downward, and which has an orifice on one side. Near there is a *kṣetrapāla*, the goddess Jvālāmukhī, who is self-generated on the stone, lying prone. A temple was erected there. Elsewhere, a few miles from there, is a waterfall at the base of a vertical rock cliff which has one hundred rock cavities which are places of practice, one hundred springs, and one hundred nearby trees. The heretics bathe there. (DS 55)

The girls of these places are yoginīs who are nondual with the heroes.[27] They all have passionate forms, and their cessation [occurs] through the power of the mind.[28] The six yoginīs[29] are in Kulutā, and the

---

Kangra is very close to the Beas River, but it is not particularly close to the Sutlej or Ravi, which flow through separate valleys to the south and north, respectively.

[25] Pullīramalaya has not been located. Bu-ston positions it as follows: "To the east, in the south of Bengal, is the place of the river of lake Malaya" (DS 54). However, as Davidson notes, "its name (*malaya*) seems to indicate that it was located in South India and was probably a Buddhist name for all or part of the Agastya Malai, the southernmost mountain range of India and very close to the fabled Buddhist pilgrimage site of Potalaka" (2002b, 209). Perhaps it was in the vicinity of the district of Puliyagudi, located east of Devar Malai.

[26] The term "and so forth" (Pandey 2002, 547: *pullīramalayādayaḥ*) here is significant, for it made possible the identification of alternate pilgrimage places as the tradition was transmitted to Nepal and the Himalayan regions, Tibet and Mongolia.

[27] This translates the Tibetan: */ yul 'di dag gi bu mo gang // dpa' bo gnyis med rnal 'byor ma /* (PM 239a; SL 131a: *-gnyis su rnal 'byor ma*). Bhavabhaṭṭa partially preserves the Sanskrit with the reading "girl who nondually pervades the hero" (*kanyā vīrādvayavyāpinī*), which he corrects in his commentary: "The **girls**, since they thus abide everywhere, are those who have the natural disposition of being pervaded in a nondual manner by the heroes, Khaṇḍakapālī, and so forth." (Pandey 2002, 547: *kanyāḥ sarvadā tathaivāvasthitatvād vīraiḥ khaṇḍaka-pālyādibhir advayatvaṁ vyāptaṁ śīlaṁ yāsāṁ tās tathā*) Note that this correction only applies to the plural case; it is interesting that he also changes the "girls" from the active agents of pervasion (*vyāpinī*) to passive recipients of it (*vyāptaṁ*). The term "girl" here (*kanyā*) also means "virgin" and "daughter," and reflects the tantric predilection for young women and girls as consorts.

[28] Bhavabhaṭṭa comments here: "When they—who in the exercise were made manifest by the mind—have been accomplished, then there is [their] **cessation through the power of the mind**" (Pandey 2002, 547: *yatra prayojane manaḥ pravṛttaṁ tatsiddhau tato manoveganivṛttiḥ*). This interpretation—which (evidently) sees the "yoginīs" as objects of worship mentally conjured by the yogin in his practice, and then brought to an end when he is done—does not seem fully consonant with the rest of this text, which appears to imply that the yoginīs do exist in these places as human females. But this may be a residue of the older practice of *yakṣī-sādhana*, in which the adept would summon a non-human female as a consort. See my discussion of this in the Introduction above. Note that the *nivṛtti/nivṛttayaḥ* reading is not attested in the Tibetan, which here reads simply *'jug pa* (PM 239a: *'jug pa yis*; SL 131a: *'jug pa yin*). Bhavabhaṭṭa's commentary here reads *manoveganivṛttaya iti* (Pandey 2002, 547). I read this as *-vṛttayaḥ*, more in line with Sumatikīrti's translation, and declining with *kāmarūpiṇyo*. For some reason, Pandey reads it as the dative singular - *vṛttaye*, I think to bring it in closer accordance with the instrumental reading of Mardo's translation.

[29] According to Jayabhadra, "the **six yoginīs** are [the six armor goddesses,] from Vajravārāhī, and so forth, ending with Caṇḍikā" (D 52a.7–b.1: *ṣaḍyoginyo vajravārāhyādicaṇḍikāntāḥ*).

(cont'd)

six mothers[30] are in the land of Maru. The lāmās[31] are in the land of Sindhu, and the clan leaders[32] are in Nagara. In Lampāka and Saurāṣṭra are the clan goddesses.[33] In Pretapurī is Rūpinī together with the Mahākālā ḍākinīs.[34] It is said that Sabālikā[35] is at the Himālaya mountain[36] and Kāñci.

That is, the goddesses Vajravārāhī, Yāminī, Mohanī, Saṁcālanī, Trāsanī, and Caṇḍikā. They are discussed in the notes to ch. 8 above.

[30] The term "six mothers" (*ṣaḍmātarāḥ*) does not have an obvious Buddhist reference, and calls to mind instead the six mothers or yoginīs of the Śaiva Kubjikā traditions. Regarding these, see White 2003, 228–29. Bhavabhaṭṭa explains that they "have the form of the seven mothers" (Pandey 2002, 548: *saptamātṛrūpāḥ*), linking them to the much better known cult of the seven mothers. Jayabhadra comments that "the **mothers** are Kākāsyā, and so forth" (D 52b.1: *mātaraḥ kākāsyādyāḥ*). That is, without resolving the numerical contradiction, he identifies them with the eight guardians of the doors and quarters, namely: Kākāsyā, Ulūkāsyā, Śvānāsyā, Śūkarāsyā, Yamadāhī, Yamadūtī, Yamadaṁṣṭriṇī, and Yamamathanī.

[31] Jayabhadra explains that "the **lāmās** are the fierce yoginīs who belong to the lāmā class" (D 52b.1–2: *lāmā tv iti lāmājātīyā ugrayoginyaḥ*). This may refer only to the first class of lāmās listed in ch. 19, the "lāmās who are women" (*striyānāṁ lāmānām*), or perhaps it may refer to all of the classes.

[32] Jayabhadra explains that "the **clan leaders** are the four ḍākinīs" (D 52b.2: *kulanāyikā ḍākinyaś catasraḥ*). That is, the four essence yoginīs, Ḍākinī, Lāmā, Khaṇḍarohā, and Rūpiṇī.

[33] Vīravajra simply states that the clan goddesses are the goddesses of the respective places. However, he gives Saurāṣṭra and Suvarṇadvīpa, in the proper order, rather than Lampāka and Saurāṣṭra, which are out of order (PD 434a). Tathāgatarakṣita, however, comments that the clan goddesses are the seven goddesses listed in ch. 17, namely: Rūpikā, Cumbikā, Lāmā, Parāvṛttā, Sabālikā, Anivartikā, and Aihikīdevī (UN 241a).

[34] There is considerable variance here. The reading *mahākālā ḍākinī* is preserved in Jayabhadra's commentary, and appears to be attested, in a corrupt form, in Mardo's translation (PM 239a), which, rather than *nag chen mo* reads *nags chen la*, "in the great forest," adding an additional site which is unattested elsewhere. According to Tsong Khapa (KS 202a), Rin-chen bZang-po's original translation here read *nag mo che*, which is an overly literal translation of Mahākālā. Mardo emended this slightly to *nags che la*, perhaps out of discomfort regarding this apparently Śaiva name. There is also one other variant, preserved in Bhavabhaṭṭa's commentary, which is *mahākanyā ḍākinī*, "great virgin ḍākinī," which is also attested in Sumatikīrti's translation (SL 131a: *bu mo*). According to Bhavabhaṭṭa, this refers to "ḍākinīs belonging to Rūpiṇī's class who have girlish forms" (Pandey 2002, 548: *pretapuryāṁ mahākanyā ḍākinī saha rūpinīti kanyārūpā ḍākinī rūpiṇījātīyāḥ*). I believe that *mahākanyā* is a later emendation of Mahākālā, made again in order to efface the text's overtly non-Buddhist elements. Jayabhadra emends the grammar here, writing: "With regard to the referent of *together*, it [should be in] the third [case], namely, [together] with the **Mahākālā**—i.e., the Mahābhairava—**ḍākinīs**" (D 52b.2–3: *mahākālā mahābhairavaḥ ḍākinībhir iti sahārthe tṛtīyā*). There is a venerable association between the deity Mahākāla and the ḍākinīs. Regarding this, see Gray 2005a.

In the region of Pañcāla, Gṛhadevatā, and Kaliṅga[37] are those who uphold the observance.[38] The carnivores[39] are in Kośala, and the vajraḍākinīs are in Pretapurī.[40] In Sthūleśvara[41] and Triśakuni are those born in Khaṇḍarohā's clan. At Pullīramalaya and Kanakagiri[42] there are twenty-one thousand women born in caṇḍāla families.[43]

---

35 Sabālikā is one of the seven consecration goddesses listed in ch. 17.

36 That is, at the "Snow Mountain" or "Himālaya mountain" (*himādrau*), as preserved by Bhavabhaṭṭa (Pandey 2002, 548).

37 The Sanskrit here, as preserved by Bhavabhaṭṭa, reads *pañcālaviṣaye gṛhadevatā kaliṅge ca vratadhāriṇyaḥ*, which should be translated "In the region of Pañcāla are the household deities (*gṛhadevatā*) and in Kaliṅga are those who uphold the observance," which would actually make more sense, as *gṛhadevatā* is not a place name, but a class of deities. Bhavabhaṭṭa glosses it, however, as "in Gṛhadevatā" (Pandey 2002, 548: *gṛhadevatāyāṁ*) in order to accord with the standard interpretation that it is one of the twenty-four pilgrimage sites. Tathāgatarakṣita, on the other hand, interprets these two lines separately, i.e., as if Gṛhadevatā were a deity [class] rather than a place (UN 241b). This line may indicate, however, that Pañcāla was originally the correct site in the list. Pāñcāla is in fact a place in India. According to Sircar, it was a region located in what is now southern Kaśmīr and western Punjab, i.e., in Pakistan (1971, 201–2). Regarding this, Jayabhadra writes: "Pañcāla is a land which is a place of the accomplished ones which is other than the seats, subsidiary seats, and so forth" (D 52b.5: *pañcāla iti pīṭhopapīṭhādibhyo 'nyatra ca siddhasthānadeśaḥ*).

38 That is, Śrī Heruka's observance, according to Bu-ston (NS 243a).

39 Bhavabhaṭṭa notes that the carnivores are "those women who eat the great meat [i.e., human flesh]" (Pandey 2002, 548: *kośale piśitāśanā mahāmāṁsāśanāḥ*).

40 I am not sure why Pretapurī is repeated here. Regarding the vajraḍākinīs, they are perhaps are equivalent to the "Mahākālā ḍākinīs," but this is not addressed in the commentaries I have consulted. Bhavabhaṭṭa simply comments that they are "the yoginīs who have nondual gnosis born in Pretapūrī" (Pandey 2002, 548: *pretapuryāṁ vajraḍākinya iti / pretapurīsaṁbhūtā yoginyo 'dvayajñānāḥ*).

41 Although listed as a place name in Bhavabhaṭṭa's commentary (Pandey 2002, 548: *sthūleśvarādiṣu*), Sthūleśvara does not correspond to any place known to me, nor have I located any commentary addressing it. Mardo translates it literally as *sbom dbang phyug* (PM 239a); Sumatikīrti has the probably corrupt *bsgom pa dbang* (SL 131a).

42 Evidently there is a place named "Kanakagiri" in Chamarajanagar district, Karnataka, near Mysore, at which is located a Jain sacred site of this name. But as this name, meaning "Golden Mountain," seems quite generic, there may have been multiple sites so named. Nevertheless, given its apparent association with Pullīramalaya, a location in South India seems likely, as noted above.

43 That is, born as outcastes (*antyajāḥ*), as Bhavabhaṭṭa notes (Pandey 2002, 548). Outcaste women in general—and those of the caṇḍāla outcaste group in particular—are valorized in

However many there may be at other additional [places], they are Śrī Heruka's yoginīs. They are the ladies of the maṇḍala for him, the great churner[44] Śrī Heruka. These twenty-four ḍākinīs pervade everything,[45] the animate and inanimate. This commitment[46] of the ḍākinīs is indeed the transformative meditation.[47] Meditative states, and so forth[48]—anything whatsoever—should be brought to completion on the surface of the earth.[49] [If] one is always heteropraxical, naked, and equipoised at night, [then] all heroes and yoginīs, who are born from the hero, are delighted.[50] The self-

tantric Buddhist literature as ideal consorts. Jayabhadra comments here: "As for the multitudes of 21,000 accomplished yoginīs, they wander in the form of those who are deprived, yet they abide in the triple wheel. They are to be joined again in reverse order to the places, Pullīramalaya, [and so forth,] beginning with Pracaṇḍā." (D 52b.6–53a.1: *vistarās tv ekaviṁśatisahasrāḥ siddhayoginyaḥ / t[e] cy[u]tarūpeṇa bramanti / tricakravartinyas t[u] punaḥ pullīramalayapratisthāneṣu pracaṇḍāprabhṛtayo yathāvilomena yojanīyāḥ*)

[44] That is, *mahāmanthānaḥ*, a reading preserved in both Jayabhadra's (D 53a.2) and Bhavabhaṭṭa's commentaries. Bhavabhaṭṭa explains: "the great churner is that which has the nature of wisdom and art" (Pandey 2002, 549). The term *mahāmanthāna* here does imply sexual union, which is often compared to the acts of churning milk or igniting fire by rubbing a fire-stick. Pandey ignored this reading, and reads *mahāyogaḥ* in his edition of the root text (2002, 548). This is evidently a back-translation from the Tibetan *sbyor ba che* (PM 139a).

[45] Jayabhadra preserves the text "pervade everything" (*sarvavyāptaṁ*), as is translated here. Both Tibetan translations here read "pervade the triple world" (*-'jig rten gsum*) instead (PM 139a, SL 131b).

[46] Bhavabhaṭṭa glosses *samaya* here as "instruction," *upadeśa* (Pandey 2002, 549).

[47] *Nirmito bhāvitaḥ*, as preserved by Bhavabhaṭṭa, which is translated into Tibetan as *sprul pa'i bsgom pa* (SL 131b) and *sprul pa sgom pa* (PM 139a). Regarding this, Vīravajra comments: "As for the **commitment of the ḍākinīs**, the commitment of this adept who binds the *yantra* [i.e., who puts into effect the special yogic postures] which produce the twelve ritual actions is the **meditation** on the wheels of **transformation**" (PD 434b–435a). This expression appears to refer to the perfecting stage meditation on the inner body maṇḍala.

[48] Bhavabhaṭṭa comments that "**meditative states, and so forth** refers to the any of those things that are connected to the ḍākinīs' mantras, gestures, and so forth" (Pandey 2002, 549: *dhyānādi yāni kāni cin mantramudrādisambandhāni tāni ḍākinīnām eva*).

[49] Jayabhadra comments here that "**completion** means uniting the churner and the churned by means of an extraordinary method, i.e., with an outer woman" (D 53a.5–6: *pūrṇāyāṁ cāprākṛtarūpeṇa manthāmanthānayogyaṁ bāhyāṅganāyā*).

[50] According to Vīravajra, the term "heroes" refers to the visualization of the twenty-five heroes (i.e., Heruka and the twenty-four heroes of the three wheels), "yoginīs" refers to the thirty-seven goddesses (Vajravārāhī, the four essence yoginīs, the twenty-four yoginīs of the three wheels, and the eight guardian goddesses), and their being "delighted" refers to the medi-

emergent worship should be performed with offerings of gesture and dance.[51] Everything is achieved without exception by means of the worship of the left.

---

tative concentration of the four joys once one has inserted the life-force into the central channel (PD 435a). The Sanskrit, preserved in Bhavabhaṭṭa's commentary, is: *sarvavīrā yoginyaś ca vīrasambhavā tuṣyanti.* The Tibetan translations differ, reading "all men or left ones and all yoginīs proceed to the Hero" (PM 239a: *skye pa'am gal te g-yon pa kun // rnal 'byor ma kun dpa' bo 'gro*) and "all men or left ones, heroes, and yoginīs are delighted" (SL 131b: *skyes pa 'am gal te g-yon pa kun // rnal 'byor ma dang dpa' bo dgyes*). Both translations attest elements of the Sanskrit. Bu-ston glosses *dpa' bo 'gro* as *dpal he ru kar 'byung ba kun* ("all who are born from Śrī Heruka"), i.e., *vīrasambhavāḥ.* Sumatikīrti's translation attests *tuṣyanti,* which is omitted in Mardo's translation.

[51] Bhavabhaṭṭa comments here: "**The self-emergent worship should** always **be performed with offerings of gesture**, i.e., by means of union with the deity, **and dance**, but not the ordinary [type], as well as with seminal essence together with uterine blood. This is said to be the purification of worship." (Pandey 2002, 549: *mudrā devatāyogas tena nṛtyopahāraḥ / na punaḥ prākṛtatvena / tena nityaṁ pūjā kāryā svayaṁbhuvā ca rajonvitena bodhicittena / iti pūjāviśuddhir uktā*) Vīravajra comments on these lines as follows: "In [the state of] the joy of cessation, one should worship the deities of the aggregates, sense elements, and sense media, as is stated [in ch. 1], **worship the buddhas and bodhisattvas with one's own seminal drops**" (PD 435a).

42. The Procedure of the Laughter Mantra and the Magic of the Yoginīs' Forms

Then the hero, having drunk the flower water,[1] should recollect this mantra.[2] The adept should thus dance[3] with his consort. At night one should enjoy meat thrice enchanted,[4] and thus drinking with that and offering it,[5] there is this: "May bliss be produced!"[6] Having touched [her],[7]

---

[1] The basic meaning of *kusuma* in the compound *kusumodaka* is "flower," but it has a secondary meaning, "uterine blood," which is clearly implied here. Jayabhadra comments: "**Flower water** is that which arises with a menstruating woman" (D 53b.2: *kusumodakaṁ puṣpavatyā sahotpannaḥ*). Bhavabhaṭṭa comments: "**Having drunk flower water,** i.e., seminal essence together with uterine blood, then one **should dance** to vajra song **together with** one's **consort**" (Pandey 2002, 551: *kusumodakaṁ rajonvitaṁ bodhicittaṁ pītvā tato nṛtyaṁ vajrapadena kuryāt mudrayā prajñayā saha*).

[2] Jayabhadra comments that "**this mantra** refers to the root mantra or the seven syllable mantra" (D 53b.2–3: *idaṁ mantraṁ mūlamantraḥ saptākṣaramantro vā*). Regarding the latter mantra, see ch. 8 above.

[3] Mardo translates *rtag tu* here (PM 239b), evidently misreading *nṛtyaṁ* as *nityaṁ*, and leaving the verb without an object. Sumatikīrti's text omits this line entirely.

[4] Bhavabhaṭṭa here reads *triyantritam* (Pandey 2002, 551), "thrice bound," which may make sense in the context of the internal sexual yogic procedures described by Vīravajra, but does not make as much sense in the literal context of this passage, which seems to call for enchantment of the meat (*trimantritam*) as indicated by the Tibetan translations (PM 239b: *lan gsum bsngags*; SL 131b: *sngags gsum bya ba*).

[5] Jayabhadra explains that "**thus offering it** means offering to her who abides in the triple wheel" (D 53b.3: *tathā [dattv]eti tricakravartinyā dattvā*).

[6] This translates the text preserved in Bhavabhaṭṭa's commentary, *anena pītvā tathā dattvā idam astu sukhāvaham* (Pandey 2002, 551), which differs somewhat from both Tibetan translations, which appear somewhat garbled here. According to Bhavabhaṭṭa, *idaṁ* here refers to a mantra, which includes the command *astu sukhāvaham.* He gives two versions of the mantra: *oṁ astu sukhāvahaṁ hūṁ* ("Oṁ May Bliss be Produced Hūṁ"), and *oṁ sukhāvahaṁ hūṁ* ("Oṁ Production of Bliss Hūṁ") (Pandey 2002, 551). This mantra is evidently used to consecrate the food offerings described in this chapter. Bhavabhaṭṭa comments: "The five ambrosias, and so forth, are employed having been enchanted with this" (Pandey 2002, 551: *pañcāmṛtādikaṁ cānenaivābhimantrya prayoktavyam*).

Mahākālī,[8] who truly observes chastity (*brahmacāriṇī*), laughs,[9] with laughter and gestures at the beginning and end.[10] She is a celebrated woman with

---

[7] Regarding "touching," Bhavabhaṭṭa's text here reads *pṛṣṭvā* (Pandey 2002, 551), which I emend to *spṛṣṭvā* on the basis of the Tibetan translations "having been touched" (PM 239b: *reg nas*) and "together with touch" (SL 131a: *reg dang lhan cig*). Who or what is being touched? According to Kambala: "Touching refers to the supreme greatness of the lotus. One should unite one's vajra with that which is like a red lotus by means of mental generation." (SN 72b) According to Vīrāvajra:

> **Thrice enchanted** refers to joy, supreme joy, and natural joy, and the mantra which protects one's mind. At the time of these three joys, one attains physical and mental bliss by means of the water of conventional seminal essence. Having thus summarized, I will extensively explain this. **Thus drinking and offering** means that having "drunk" the woman's uterine blood and the hero's seminal essence via upward diversion; **offering** refers to the joy of cessation [i.e., ejaculation]. (PD 436a)

In other words, the hero takes up the combined seminal fluids via urethral suction and sends them into the central channel, experiencing the joys. Apparently he then offers it to the goddesses in his internal body maṇḍala, as well as to his consort as an oblation, i.e., by ejaculation.

[8] This reading, *mahākālī*, is preserved in Jayabhadra's commentary (D 53b.3–4), as well as in Vīravajra's (PD 436a). Bhavabhaṭṭa provides an alternate reading, *mahākulī* (Pandey 2002, 551). The latter reading is almost certainly a transformation of the former, presumably made in order to efface text that evokes a Hindu deity. Here the transformation is defective, for the substition of the vowel *ā* with *u* transforms the feminine reading *mahākālī* into the masculine reading *mahākulī*, "he who belongs to a great clan," which Bhavabhaṭṭa defines as "one who has the great vow, i.e., the yogin who practices [that]" (Pandey 2002, 551: *mahākulī mahāvratī caryāyogītyarthaḥ*). This masculine reading is clearly out of place in the context of this passage. There is also another reading, preserved only in Tibetan, namely "great mistress" (PM 239b, SL 131b: *gtso mo che*), which differs from the previous two but confirms that the figure being described here is female. Jayabhadra notes that "Mahākālī is, in truth, Vajravārāhī" (D 53b.3–4: *mahākālī satyena vajravā[rā]hī*).

[9] Vīravajra explains: "**Touch** is the joy brought about by the contact of the apertures of the central channel (*avadhūtī*). **Mahākālī** refers to the consort who is visualized to be Vajravārāhī, who is pervaded by bliss—[this refers to] the supreme joy. **Observes chastity** by means of bliss means that she observes celibacy by the sealing of bliss in the [state of] natural joy which is mental bliss." (PD 436a) Here he evidently reads *sukhena brahmacāriṇī* (*bde bas tshangs par spyod pa*) instead of *satyena brahmacāriṇī*.

[10] This text, *ādyante*, is preserved in Jayabhadra's commentary (D 53b.4–5). Vīravajra explains that the "laughter and gestures" are "salutations [performed] **at the beginning and end** [of an encounter]" (ST 202b). While this is attested in both Tibetan translations, Bhavabhaṭṭa's text has the alternate text "to be achieved" (Pandey 2002, 551: *sādhyaṁ*), which is also found in several other commentaries. Kambala explains that "it is great gnosis that is to be accomplished" (SN 72b). The line might then be translated as "accomplished with seals of

a haughty glance.[11] At night or during the day[12] one should make laughter[13] with that.[14]

Listen truly, hero, to the action of form that is the essence.[15] Then [there is her] dance[16]—tears arise and her body hair stands on end due to

laughter." Vīravajra's other commentary adopts this interpretation, arguing that it means that "if one is [about to] 'go' [i.e., ejaculate] at the time of the joy of cessation, then the wind is diverted upward by means of the seal of laughter, i.e., the eight types of *h* sounds" (PD 436b). That is, as was explained in the context of ch. 39 above, the seminal essence can be diverted into the central channel by means of the yogic seals (*mudrā*) which are the seed syllables visualized within the appropriate channels.

[11] Jayabhadra explains here: "It is the **celebrated woman**, i.e., the distinguished outer woman, who has the haughty look" (D 53b.7: *saṁdṛṣṭagarvā [v]iśiṣṭā bāhyāṅganā sā yaśasvinī bhavati*). Vīravajra comments that "**she is celebrated** for her **haughty glance** means that she should wink with gestures of the eye" (PD 436a).

[12] Bhavabhaṭṭa comments: "**At night** means during the bliss of cessation, which has the nature of the setting of the savor of conceptualization from the outer sensory field. **During the day** refers to the natural [joy] which in nature is simply self-awareness. **Or** implies the inclusion of joy and supreme joy." (Pandey 2002, 552: *rātrāv iti bahirviṣayavikalparasāstaṁgamasvarūpe viramānande / ahani svasamvinmātratāsvarūpe sahaje vā ānandaparamānandayoḥ samuccayārthaḥ /*).

[13] Jayabhadra explains here that "**laughter** is a metaphor…for the bliss of great sexual pleasure in which all indulge, which one should produce day or night" (D 54a.1–2: *hāsyam ity upalakṣaṇa…sarvasevamahāsuratasukhaṁ rātrā[v] ahani vā kūryād iti sambandhaḥ*).

[14] Bhavabhaṭṭa explains that "**with that** means with *kili kili*, and so forth, and with *hā hā*, and so forth" (Pandey 2002, 551: *aneneti kilikilītyādinā hāhetyādinā ca*). That is, with the two eight-syllable "laughter mantras" discussed in ch. 39 above.

[15] This text, minus one word, is preserved in Bhavabhaṭṭa's commentary as *rūpakarma yat tac chuṇḍaṁ [śṛṇu] vīra yathāsthitam*. The term *śuṇḍa* means elephant musk and also liquor; Bhavabhaṭṭa glosses it as "the secret" (*guhyaṁ*), and it is non-literally translated in this way in the Tibetan (PM 239b, SL 132a: *gsang ba*). He also glosses *rūpakarma* as "the **action**, i.e., performance, of **form**, i.e., one's own nature" (Pandey 2002, 552: *rūpetyādi rūpasya svarūpasya karma kriyā*). The Tibetan translations, however, read "form and action," interpreting *rūpakarma* as a *dvandva* compound. I read *vīra* as vocative and *yathāsthitam* as an adverb, in opposition to Bhavabhaṭṭa who reads it as "in accordance with the heroes, i.e., the tathāgatas" (Pandey 2002, 552: *vīrais tathāgatair yathāsthitam*). Vīravajra, on the other hand, glosses this text as follows: "Listen, you hero Vajrapāṇi who accords with the secret method of diverting the seminal essence" (PD 436b).

[16] Jayabhadra indicates that the dance is performed by the consort, as follows: "Regarding the **action of form**, when the adept has been seen and accomplished by the goddesses, they produce unprecedented forms and actions. One displays this action and counter action. Dance, and so forth, is the goddess' action." (D 54a.2–4: *rūpakarmetyādinā sādhak[o] dṛṣṭa-*

devotion. [Not] mounting with one's vajra,[17] there is thus worship [when they] are naked. This is the sequence of the host of gestures of all ladies of the left.[18] One should perform before the universal one[19] a marvelous dance with exhalations, exhortations, laughter, and ecstatic frenzy.[20] One should recollect the gestures and laughter mantra.[21] The eightfold laughter, *hā hā*

---

siddho dev[ī]bhyo 'pūrvar[ū]pa[k]riyā kurvanti / tatkarma pratikarma ca darśayati nṛtyādi dev[ī]kriyā) As above, the Tibetan translations have "always" in place of "dance," apparently due to a misreading of *nṛtyaṁ* as *nityaṁ*.

[17] Jayabhadra preserves this text, which he explains as follows: "**Not mounting with one's vajra**, and so forth—this is the adept's action" (D 54a.4: *vajrasyālaṅghanam ityādi sādhaka-kriyāḥ*). This reading roughly corresponds to the Tibetan translations (PM 139b: *rdo rje la ni 'gom mi byed*; SL 132a: *rdo rje sogs ni 'gom mi byed*). This and two other variants are attested by Bhavabhaṭṭa, who comments: "**Mounting with the vajra** means that the vajra is extremely erect. In [another] text there is: **not mounting with the vajra**, which means that since I or the previous one have been thoroughly mounted, thus there is a rest from sexual passion. In [another] text, 'supporting' [with the vajra] means that having conveyed their action, the vajra is obtained by the yoginī." (Pandey 2002, 552: *vajrasyetyādi laṁghanam atiśayaḥ vajrotthānam ityarthaḥ / alaṁghanam iti pāṭhe aśeṣeṇa ahaṁ pūrvo vā laṁghyati ratiśayārtha eva / ālambanam iti pāṭhe prāpaṇam tatkriyā yoginyā ca vajraprāpaṇam /*)

[18] These are, as Bhavabhaṭṭa informs us, the yoginīs (Pandey 2002, 552). This text, *vāmeś-varīṇāṁ sarveṣāṁ*, is confirmed in Sumatikīrti's text (SL 132a: *g-yon pa'i dbang phyug tham cad kyi*). Mardo has the variant "ladies of love" (PM 239b: *'dod pa'i dbang phyug tham cad kyi*), presumably from *kāmeśvarīṇāṁ*.

[19] The text *viśvāyāḥ* is preserved in Jayabhadra's commentary (D 54a.5), and I take it as modifying *purataḥ* and referring to the yoginī(s), on the basis of Bhavabhaṭṭa's commentary: "**One should perform** one's own display, with characteristics such as **exhalations**, and so forth, **before** them, i.e., in front of the yoginīs who previously undertook a performance" (Pandey 2002, 553: *recakādibhir viśeṣeṇa svayaṁ darśanaṁ purataḥ pūrvakriyākāriṇīnāṁ yoginīnām agrataḥ kuryāt*). Bu-ston explains that this term (*sna tshogs*) refers to the adept's actions (NS 247b), but it is difficult to reconcile this interpretation with the grammar of the surviving Sanskrit.

[20] Jayabhadra here preserves the text *tāṇḍavair*. As he informs us, *tāṇḍava* is a style of dance characterized by wild and ecstatic motion (D 54a.5: *tāṇḍavair iti nṛtyaviśeṣaḥ*). The Tibetan texts have here *sgeg pa* (PM 239b; SL 132a: *sgeg*), "sensual enjoyment" or "flirtation," on the basis of which Pandey back-translates here *śṛṅgāra*. This Tibetan translation appears to be interpretive, perhaps due to the erotic qualities of *tāṇḍava* dance.

[21] Bhavabhaṭṭa here reads *hāsamudrām anusmaret* (Pandey 2002, 553), which differs somewhat from the Tibetan "mantra and *mudrā*" (PM 239b, SL 132a: *phyag rgya sngags*). However, by *hāsa* clearly ch. 39's laughter mantra should be understood.

he he, [and so forth,] is the ultimate love of the universal lady.[22] In their vicinity [one utters] the syllables *hā hā.* A tear falls—through this one will become their love, having well deployed meditative concentration and mantra. In conjunction with bliss, the yoginīs' and yogins' body hairs bristle, and so forth.[23] One should [not] mount with the vajra [those] who are fixed upon the left.[24]

---

22 As Bhavabhaṭṭa explains, "these syllables are extremely beloved by the yoginī" (Pandey 2002, 553: *viśveśvaryāḥ paraṁ priyā iti ete varṇā yoginyā atiśayena priyāḥ*).

23 Bhavabhaṭṭa preserves the Sanskrit *yoginīnāṁ yogināṁ,* which differs somewhat from the Tibetan, "mistresses' and heroes'/heroines'" (PM 239b: *gtso bo rnams dang dpa' bo ni*; SL 132a: *gtso bo rnams dang dpa' mo kyi*).

24 That is, *yā vāmāparikalpitāḥ,* which according to Bhavabhaṭṭa designates the yoginīs (Pandey 2002, 553). As before, Bhavabhaṭṭa sees "mounting with a vajra" (*vajralaṁghana*) as an action which one should do, while the Tibetan translations hold that it should not be done (PM 239b, SL 132a: *rdo rje 'gom par mi bya ba*).

43. The Procedure of Accomplishing the Ritual Actions of the Quintessence [Mantra]

Now I will explain the glance[1] of the man who is nondual with the hero, who knows the procedure of classifying the [sacred] places, and who always delights in meditation. The ḍākinīs see, even from afar, the places of the commitments, at crossroads, in houses, at the abodes of heroes, or on mountains. One is liberated through ritual action with the consort, for whom there is the naked worship.[2] Casting away[3] clothing or other [garb], one should touch and make love with the consort by means of that.[4]

[1] The Sanskrit here is *avalokaṁ*, as preserved in Bhavabhaṭṭa's commentary (Pandey 2002, 554). This is correctly translated by Sumatikīrti (SL 132a: *gzigs pa*), but apparently misinterpreted by Mardo as a proper name, Avalokiteśvara (PM 239b: *spyan ras gzigs*).

[2] There is some variance here among the texts concerning the verb. My translation follows most closely Sumatikīrti's translation, which reads *yongs su grol* (SL 132b), a reading also supported by Vīravajra, and which may be a translation of *parimucyate*. Bhavabhaṭṭa's reading is very close to this, with *paramucyate*. Mardo's text here reads "the holy station" (PM 239b: *go 'phang dam pa*), which does not fit at all, since it lacks a verb. Regarding this text Vīravajra comments: "Regarding **worship** with the **naked consort**, the yogin who is nondual with the consort **is liberated through** that very **ritual action** of worship" (PD 237a–b).

[3] This translates Bhavabhaṭṭa's text, *prakṣipya*. The Tibetan translations read "covered" (PM 239b: *bkab pa*) and "filled" (SL 132b: *bkang nas*), which make less sense. Bhavabhaṭṭa, however, does gloss it with "wearing," *paridhāya* (Pandey 2002, 554). Vīravajra comments on this entire sentence as follows: "*covered with another [sort of]* **clothing** means one is sky-clad, and **touching** that physical **consort** (*karmamudrā, las kyi phyag rgya*), one engages in **making** the **love** of physical and mental bliss" (PD 437b).

[4] This translation is based on the Sanskrit preserved by Bhavabhaṭṭa. The term *kāmayet* means to "love" or "make love with" the consort. This reading is supported by Vīravajra's commentary, as noted above. The Tibetan translations differ here, reading "one should not be touched by desires" (SL 132b: *'dod pa rnams kyi reg mi bya*) and "one should not be covered by desires" (PM 139b: *'dod pa rnams kyis gos mi bya*). Bhavabhaṭṭa comments here: "**one should touch and make love with the consort by means of that** means that one should be blissful by means of that ritual action" (Pandey 2002, 554: *kāmayet mudrāṁ tena saṁspṛśed iti tena karmaṇā sukhī syād ityarthaḥ*).

Having thus let down one's hair, commence with all ritual actions.[5] Bind the directions with the root mantras, and with others, that is, with the four.[6] While worshipping, one should not be seen even by the hosts of gods in heaven.[7]

One should toss up a handful of flowers. If the flowers, flying,[8] do not fall and are not seen there on the ground, then one will subjugate the thousand ḍākinīs[9] who dwell there.[10] One will summon the Lord of Speech[11] and the Mother,[12] and one will gradually know the divine speech, as well as the course of the heavenly bodies. He who recalls the essence and quintessence

---

[5] According to Bhavabhaṭṭa, "all ritual actions" refers to "eating/enjoyment, and so forth" (Pandey 2002, 554: *sarvakarma bhojanādi*).

[6] This text, *mūlamantrais tathā cānyair digbandhāś caturbhis tathā kuru*, is preserved by Bhavabhaṭṭa (Pandey 2002, 555), who explains that "with the four" refers to "the four line Śumbha mantra" (2002, 554), the mantra selected in ch. 30 above. The reading *caturbhiḥ* is also attested by Jayabhadra (D 54a.7). Bhavabhaṭṭa also gives another reading, however, "turning to the binding of the directions" (*digbandhāvartayaṁs tathā*), which corresponds more closely with the Tibetan (PM 240a: *phyogs bcing bar ni 'jug pa yis*).

[7] The passive optative singular *dṛśyeta* is used here, with no stated subject, but presumably it is the adept. One engages in the rites of binding the directions for this very purpose, to create a magically protected ritual arena. The agent here is clear, *dividevagaṇair api*, about which there is some confusion in the Tibetan texts. Mardo has the defective reading "even by the hosts of gods and gods" (PM 240a: *lha dang lha yi tshogs kyis kyang*), obviously missing the locative sense of *divi*. Sumatikīrti's text reads "even by the hosts of gods and titans" (SL 132b: *lha dang lha min tshogs kyis kyang*).

[8] Bhavabhaṭṭa comments that "**flying** means that it [the handful of flowers] should be moving in space, i.e., positioned in the atmosphere" (Pandey 2002, 555: *sa ca khecarī khecaro 'ntarīkṣasthaḥ syāt*).

[9] That is, *mkha' la 'gro ba* (PM 240a, SL 132b), which is usually a translation of *ḍākinī*.

[10] Jayabhadra explains here: "Having enchanted with enchantments a **handful of flowers**, one should **toss** it into space. If it does not fall to the ground, then one will be able to have all in one's service." (D 54b.2–4: *yadābhimantreṇābhimantr[ya] puṣpāñjalim ākāśe kṣipeta / bhūmau na patati tadā sarvasevakarttavyaṁ śakta iti*) Bhavabhaṭṭa adds that it is with the seven syllable mantra, i.e., Śrī Heruka's quintessence (see ch. 8), that the flowers are enchanted (Pandey 2002, 555: *kusumāñjaliṁ saptākṣarajaptaṁ*).

[11] That is *vāgīṣa*, whom Bhavabhaṭṭa identifies as Bṛhaspati, the preceptor of the gods (Pandey 2002, 555).

[12] Bhavabhaṭṭa glosses "mother," *mātaraṁ*, as "the Goddess of Speech," *vāṇī*, i.e., Sarasvatī.

will not be seen by gods or men,[13] in the underworld,[14] in towns or forests, cities or crossroads, at a tree, at the home of a hero, or in space. Through that the adept always stays in these places.[15]

Visualizing sevenfold syllables, red colored, on top of a tree, one will cause even the mountains[16] to bow down without breaking, not otherwise. Placing it on one's body, one should recline on a grass mat on the ground. Should one repeat the sevenfold mantra one hundred and eight times, all of the deeds one desires will manifest in one's dream.[17] One will bring about the destruction of untimely death,[18] annihilation, or any other deeds. Having repeated the mantra over a sword, water, one's thumb, a lamp, or a mirror, one will cause the descent of the divinatory image (*prasenā*) by means of the yoga of oneself [as the deity].[19] One who has meditated[20] and who repeats it seven times[21] will reveal the auspicious and the inauspicious.

---

[13] Jayabhadra explains that "**not seen by gods or men** means that one is not interrupted by gods or men" (D 54b.4–5: *na dṛśyate devamānuṣair iti na devamānuṣair bhidyate*). Jayabhadra gives a singular verb here. Bhavabhaṭṭa gives the verbs in the plural, i.e., *smaranti* and *dṛśyante*. He glosses the former as "repeating" (Pandey 2002, 555: *japanti*).

[14] "Underworld" (*pātala*) is the first item in the list in Bhavabhaṭṭa's commentary, and it is attested in Sumatikīrti's commentary, although somewhat displaced, occurring with the things learned from the divine preceptors in the previous verse (SL 132b). Instead of this, Mardo reads "large town" (PM 140a: *grong rdal*).

[15] As before, Bhavabhaṭṭa gives the plural forms here, i.e., *tiṣṭanti sādhakāḥ* (Pandey 2002, 556).

[16] Bhavabhaṭṭa reads here *bhūdharān*. The term *bhūdhara*, "that which supports beings," usually means the earth, but here it cannot, being declined as plural. Bhavabhaṭṭa glosses the term here as "stone mountains" (Pandey 2002, 556: *śilāśailān*).

[17] Vīravajra comments that this is a "dream shown by the deity" (PD 438a), suggesting that it is a form of divination that is being described here. The next line, however, suggests that in the dream one can actually effect ritual actions.

[18] Jayabhadra comments that "**the destruction of untimely death** means that one clears away untimely death and increases one's lifespan" (MP 67a). Here ms. D preserves the text *apamṛtyuhataṁ naṣṭaṁ* (D 54b.6), but the commentary is garbled.

[19] Bhavabhaṭṭa comments: "**Having repeated** [the mantra] one hundred and eight [times] **over a sword**, and so forth, **one will cause the descent of the** luminous **divinatory image**" (Pandey 2002, 556: *khadgādau cāṣṭottaraśataṁ japtvā prasenaṁ jyotiṣam avatārayet*). The *prasenā* or *pratisenā* is a method of divination which probably reached India via Tibet. It involves the ritual preparation of a smooth surface into which either the yogin or a virgin girl gazes and sees divinatory images. This rite is also described in literature associated with the *Kālacakra Tantra*, and is discussed and described in stanzas 27–34 of the *Sekoddeśa* (ed. in

Now, the seven syllable mantra is set down and divided.[22] It is visualized within the solar [maṇḍala], and one should repeat it one thousand times. In an instant [the area] afflicted by disease, the size of a thumb, will appear crystalline.[23] The disease will be broken, have no doubt. One will be free of disease, as if it were the autumnal moon.[24]

Orofino 1994b, 63–64). Giacomella Orofino has written an article on this rite (1994a). Nāropā, in his *Śekoddeśaṭīkā*, states that the rite can be carried out using the same "supports" listed here, and adds "the sun, moon, and eyes" (1994a, 612). Typically, the rite is carried out with a virgin girl whose eyes are blindfolded. Vīravajra describes the rite as follows:

> **Repeating the mantra**, one applies the magical diagram of the seven syllable [mantra] (*saptākṣarayantra*) to the **sword**, to **water**, **one's thumb**, **a lamp or a mirror**, and **the divinatory image should** clearly **descend**. If one arranges the seven syllable magical diagram over the eyes of a virgin girl and **repeats** the mantra **seven times**, **the auspicious and inauspicious will be revealed**. (PD 438a)

[20] That is, *dhyātaḥ*, as is preserved in Jayabhadra's text, not *vibhāvya*, as Pandey back-translates (2002, 556). Jayabhadra comments here that "**one who has meditated**, and so forth, indicates the alleviation of illness" (D 54b.7: *dhyāta ityādinā vyādhyupaśamaṁ darśayati*), but this connection is not apparent to me, since the passage so clearly deals with divination. The text here is probably corrupt, with the commentary on *dhyātaḥ* mixed up with the commentary on *atha*, which begins the next paragraph, where the issue of disease comes up. As Bhavabhaṭṭa notes, "by **now**, and so forth, the alleviation of illness is stated" (Pandey 2002, 557: *athetyādinā vyādhiśāntim āha*).

[21] "Seven times" is indicated in Mardo's translation (PM 240a: *lan 'dun*), and supported by Vīravajra as noted above. Sumatikīrti here reads "one hundred times" (SL 133a: *lan brgya*).

[22] Jayabhadra here uses a passive construction, declining *saptākṣaramantro* with *japto*, which works well with the *bheditaḥ* attested by Bhavabhaṭṭa. Bhavabhaṭṭa attests an active construction, which he explains as follows: "**having set down the seven syllable mantra** means having written or visualized [it]" (Pandey 2002, 557: *aptākṣaraṁ mantraṁ vinyasya likhitvā dhyātvā vā*).

[23] I translate here an additional line, *kṣaṇād aṅguṣṭhamātram*, which occurs in Bhavabhaṭṭa's commentary, and which is attested in Sumatikīrti's translation (SL 133a) but not in Mardo's. Regarding this, Bhavabhaṭṭa comments: "**in an instant**...**the size of the thumb** means that one should visualize in his [i.e., the sick person's] heart wisdom that is like stainless crystal the size of the thumb" (Pandey 2002, 557: *kṣaṇād aṅguṣṭhamātram iti tasya hṛdi cāṅṣṭhaparimāṇaṁ vimalasphaṭikasamaṁ vijñānaṁ dhyāyāt*). Jayabhadra likewise comments: "Should one produce in the heart the wisdom which is blazingly radiant like **crystal**, the size of the thumb, then one will be healthy" (D 55a.3–4: *hṛdaye aṅgu[ṣṭha]mātraṁ spaṭikanirmalaṁ jvalatbhāsurākāravijñānam ārabhet sustho bhavati*). Vīravajra comments upon this more clearly, as follows: "Place the **seven syllable** magical diagram **in the middle of the solar maṇḍala** on the palm of the hand. Visualize that the syllables radiate **light like a crystal** rosary, and imagine that from the syllable *kaṁ* in the heart there is the **disease** as a black

Place the wheel in the lunar [maṇḍala] on the left hand.[25] The crystalline syllables,[26] [which] should appear in five forms, are placed on all diseased [areas]. Visualizing the syllables in the moon disk, have no doubt that fever, astral spirits, epilepsy, leprosy, severe pain, and so forth, and also all diseases [caused] by poison consumption, will be dispersed throughout the ten directions.[27]

At night in a secret place, beef should be pulverized with the three sweets.[28] Should the mantrin perform eight thousand[29] fire sacrifices know-

---

form with yellow hair in the heart. By means of [the mantra] *oṁ jala dośāya phaṭ*, it melts down to **the size of the thumb**, and one is free of disease." (PD 438a)

[24] That is, as if it were the cool, dry season, when the illnesses acquired during the rainy season often dissipate. Jayabhadra notes that "by **autumnal**, and so forth, the removal of poison is indicated" (D 55a.4–5: *śaratkāla ityādinā viṣāpahāraṁ kathayati /*).

[25] Bhavabhaṭṭa comments here: "Visualize a lunar disk on the left hand, in which there is a wheel [divided into] nine cells [i.e., a center surrounded by eight 'petals']. In its center is *oṁ*, to the east *hrīḥ*, to the south *ha*, to the west *ha*, to the north *hūṁ*, and again in the middle *hūṁ*. In the four corners is *phaṭ*. This is the seven syllable mantra." (Pandey 2002, 557: *vāmahaste śaśibimbaṁ vicintya tatra navakoṣṭhaṁ cakraṁ tasya madhye oṁ pūrve hrīḥ dakṣiṇe ha paścime hṛa uttare hḷaṁ punar madhye hūṁ konacatuṣṭaye phaṭ / iti saptākṣaro mantraḥ*) This is evidently an example of the "seven syllable magical diagrams" to which commentators like Vīravajra refer. Note that the syllables given in the Sanskrit here differ in several cases from the actual mantra. The Tibetan translation (2002, 795) gives the "correct" reading, which I follow in my translation.

[26] This translates a line found in Sumatikīrti's translation (SL 133a: *gzugs lnga ru ni snang bar bya*), but not in Mardo's. It is also attested by Jayabhadra, who comments: "**Five forms** means that when producing the five-squared moon maṇḍala, a nine-squared [maṇḍala] is generated" (D 55a.5–6: *pañcarūpam iti śaśimaṇḍal[e] pañcakoṣṭh[e] kriyamāne navakoṣṭhā jāyate*). This presumably means that the moon maṇḍala consists of five squares arranged in a cross-like pattern, with four squares organized around a central square in the cardinal directions, in the classic maṇḍala pattern. This, in turn, implies nine squares, namely the four squares in the ordinal directions that are produced if you "square" the cross-shaped maṇḍala. Many thanks to Dr. Thomas Yarnall for suggesting this possibility.

[27] Jayabhadra comments: "Placing this [*yantra*] on the head of one who has consumed static or dynamic poison, should one visualize that all bodies are free of poison through streams of ambrosia proceeding from it, then he or she will be healthy" (D 55a.6–55b.1: *etat sthāvarajaṁgamaviṣagrastasy[a] śirasi vinyasya tadamṛtadhārābhi[ḥ] sarvaśarīraṁ nirviṇībhūtaṁ dhyāyet svastho bhavati /*). The terms "static" (*sthāvara*) and "dynamic" (*jaṁgama*) refer to different classes of poisons. Regarding these, see Wujastyk 2003, 139–146.

[28] According to Bhavabhaṭṭa, "**the three sweets** are molasses, honey, and crystallized sugar" (Pandey 2002, 559: *trimadhuraṁ guḍamadhuśarkarāḥ*).

[29] This is the text preserved in the Tibetan translation. Vīravajra moderates this, claiming that one need only perform 108 sacrifices (PD 438b).

ing the seven syllable mantra, in the morning he will obtain a thousand measures of gold.[30] Through ten thousand fire sacrifices, one obtains an excellent country. Moreover, a king of mantra is born in whatever place to which he directs his thoughts. Have no doubt regarding this.

One pacifies with [the color] white,[31] and one kills instantly with black. With red one subjugates and summons in a moment. With yellow, all are subdued—this is the fixed opinion of the teaching. With yellow, one subdues an army with its boats, war machines,[32] and elephants. Just by contemplating the white, the dead are revived. One who has been devoured by one hundred great serpents is also quickly revived. Seeing one who is unconscious due to poison, he is roused and wakened. Seeing one's hand, fever, astral spirits, and epilepsy are terrified.[33] If one makes a fist while gambling or fighting,[34] and always mentally repeats [the mantra], so long as one does not relax one's fist, one will accomplish everything one undertakes. Even if one's enemy wields a weapon in his hand, so long as one does not relax one's fist, the weapon will not be able to strike oneself.[35] Thus all deeds are accomplished, with leaves, flowers, fruit, betel nut, and food.[36]

The first is physical union, the second is power, the third is speech, and the fourth is not objectified.[37] Have no doubt that these are achieved

---

[30] The measure here (Tib. *srang*, Skt. *pala*) is equal to approximately one ounce.

[31] This section is based upon the colors associated with the various magical operations, which govern the colors of the deities invoked, of the substances used, and so forth.

[32] That is, *yantra* (PM 240b, SL 133b: *'khrul 'khor*), which in this context probably refers to war machines, such as siege engines and the like.

[33] Tsong Khapa notes that "they are **terrified**, i.e., destroyed, by the sight of the wheel drawn on the mantrin's left hand" (KS 212b, reading *'jig* as *'jigs*).

[34] This translates Mardo's *rgyan po g-yul du* (PM 140b). Pandey, however, notes that several editions of the Tibetan canon here read *g-yul gyi dus su*, "when fighting," omitting any reference to gambling (2002, 799). Sumatikīrti's text here reads *rgyal po*, which is clearly corrupt.

[35] Vīravajra comments here: "If one places the magical diagram on the palm of one's left hand, and one makes a fist while in battle, one will not be injured by [any] weapon" (PD 438b).

[36] Viravajra explains that this is "the [rite of] subjugating. Fruit, flowers, betel nut, and food, and so forth, are sacrificial substances for the inner fire sacrifice. If one enchants them with the seven syllable [mantra], or if one mentally binds them with magical diagrams with [the victim's] name added at the middle, he or she will be subjugated." (PD 438b–439a)

[37] Sachen explains these four in terms of a hierarchy of practitioners, as follows:

by this king of mantras, on the earth, among the trees, and at the seashore. One will be able to benefit and harm the animate and inanimate beings of the three realms.

With regard to **the first is physical union**, and so forth, if the superior person visualizes the arrival of those things that he desires by means of the **union** of himself and the deity, then he achieves them by means of meditative concentration. Thus, **second**ly, the middling person does so by means of **power**, i.e., the repetition of the seven syllable mantra. The **third**, **speech**, means that the beginner, inferior person does so by repeating [the mantra] in conjunction with magical diagrams with augmented words. The **fourth** person, the **non-objectified**, succeeds by means of the seven syllable [mantra] without the necessity of the first, second, or third [methods]. (PG 368.2)

44. The Procedure of the Six Yoginīs' Ritual Actions with the Seven Syllable [Mantra]

Now, the messenger is achieved[1] by those who are endowed with the seven syllable [mantra],[2] with which a ritual action, having been begun, is quickly achieved in an instant. One should set down the six yoginīs in the middle of one's hand,[3] as the wheel wherein the six abide[4] by means of the procedure of the seven syllable [mantra]. Visualizing that which has his form together with an impelling [augment] on one's left [hand], and reciting the king of mantras,[5] he to whom one displays one's hand will be summoned.[6]

---

[1] Bhavabhaṭṭa preserves the verb here, *samāsādhya*, which is attested by Sumatikīrti (SL 135a: *grub pa*). Mardo here reads "depending on the messenger" (PM 241a: *pho nya la brten*). Sumatikīrti also describes the messenger as "difficult to obtain" (SL 135a: *rnyed dka'*).

[2] As the chapter's title informs us, this is not the hero's seven syllable mantra, but the six yoginīs' seven syllable mantra, which is: *oṁ hāṁ hrīṁ hreṁ huṁ hūṁ phaṭ* (Pandey 2002, 560). This differs from the mantra given in ch. 8 in that one additional syllable is added, *huṁ*.

[3] The text indicating that they are set down "in the middle of the hand" occurs in Sumatikīrti's text (SL 135a: *lag pa'i dbus su*), and is attested also by Vīravajra (PD 439a). It does not occur in Mardo's translation.

[4] This translates Bhavabhaṭṭa's Sanskrit, *ṣaṭsaṁsthitaṁ cakraṁ* (Pandey 2002, 560), which is very close to Mardo's translation (PM 240a: *'khor lor legs par gnas pa drug*). Sumatikīrti adds that the wheel has six spokes (SL 135a), information which is confirmed in Kambala's (SN 75a) and Vīravajra's (PD 439a) commentaries.

[5] Bhavabhaṭṭa explains:

> Visualizing the six-spoked wheel on one's left hand, place the six syllables, i.e., *oṁ* in the middle, and *hāṁ hrīṁ hreṁ hūṁ phaṭ* on the five spokes. Visualize that the victim is being led by a net of light rays from that in the form of a hook, reciting the mantra **together with** the **compelling [augment],** "*oṁ hāṁ hrīṁ hreṁ hūṁ phaṭ* summon so-and-so," which is together with the wheel [on] the hand. Seeing the hand directly, **he will be summoned.**
>
> *ṣaḍāracakraṁ vāmakare vicintya tatra madhye oṁ pañcāreṣu hāṁ hrīṁ hreṁ hūṁ phaḍ iti ṣaḍakṣarāṇi vinyaset / tatkiraṇajālenāṅkuśākāreṇa nīyamānaṁ vibhāvya sādhyaṁ tasmai karaṁ cakrānvitam / oṁ hāṁ hrīṁ hreṁ hūṁ phaṭ devadattam ākarṣayeti codanāvitaṁ mantram āvartayan sākṣāt karaṁ darśayaṁs tam ākarṣayatīti samudāyārthaḥ* (Pandey 2002, 560–61)

[6] This passage has an apparent flaw. If a person was close enough for one to show him one's

One should mix together and examine red sandalwood powder, black mustard seeds, and salt in the victim's footprint. Kneading it with both hands, one should sacrifice it to the yoginīs; at night, reduce it to ash in a caṇḍāla fire or a charnel ground fire.[7] Facing the victim, one should commence with this yoga. As soon as one repeats [the mantra] one hundred times, he will be summoned with that.[8] When one achieves this application the victim's very self, as well as his wealth and men, will be brought under one's control.[9] I do not say otherwise.

Taking that very powder, burn it with powdered iron, and wrap it in charnel ground cloth.[10] Enchant it seven times, and dig the earth at a crossroad to the depth of eight inches. One should hide it there together with the name of one's enemy. He whose name one states will be quickly overcome. Enchanting that very powder, he may be restored again by energetically [washing it] with pure milk.[11] Have no doubt regarding the achievement

---

hand, there would be no need to summon him. Vīravajra resolves this by introducing the notion that one constructs a mannequin of the victim, to whom one shows one's hand, as follows: "If one sets down on one's hand the magical diagram of seven syllables, and augments it with the mantra of the six yoginīs on the six spokes of the wheel, then one should make an image of the individual one wants to subjugate, and enchant it with the mantra. If one presses [one's left hand] to the heart of the image and **displays** one's left hand to it, **he will be summoned** immediately." (PD 439a)

[7] Kambala indicates that this designates a charnel fire for the corpse of a caṇḍāla (SN 75a).

[8] Kambala explains: "**With that** ash one makes an image of the victim, and one draws the wheel on a sheet of birch bark, and positions it facing [the image]. If one visualizes him being drawn forth and falling down senseless calling his name, and repeats [the mantra] one hundred and eight times, he will be summoned." (SN 75a–b)

[9] This translates Mardo's text (PM 241a: *bsgrub par bya ba'i bdag nyid dang // nor dang skye bo dbang du 'gyur /*), which Tsong Khapa expands upon as follows: "One will bring under one's control **the very self** of **the victim**, i.e., the object of the ritual action of summoning, who is a lord of wealth, **his wealth,** and the **men** of **his** retinue" (KS 214a). There is a variant text preserved in Sumatikīrti's translation, "the very self of the Lord of the Earth [i.e., the king], as well as his wealth, becomes one's own" (SL 135b: *sa'i* [emended to *sa yi*] *bdag po bdag nyid dang // nor yang bdag tu 'gyur ba yin*).

[10] That is, *dur khrod ras* (PM 241a). Sumatikīrti's text reads "charnel ground soil" (SL 135b: *dur khrod sa*), which is probably a corruption as this makes less sense with the verb *btum*, "to wrap."

[11] Bhavabhaṭṭa here preserves the text *śucikṣīreṇa pratyānayanam*, and this is confirmed by Jayabhadra (D 55b.3: *śaucakṣīraḥ*). Bhavabhaṭṭa glosses *śucikṣīreṇa* as "with cow's milk" (Pandey 2002, 561: *gavyena kṣīreṇa*). The Tibetan translation, *ba yi 'o ma* (PM 141a, SL 135b), is

of this. One should take this powder, bind it with charnel ground cloth together with the five intoxicants,[12] and also write the name of one's enemy. If one repeats [the mantra] one hundred times and hides it in a charnel ground, then the victim will become insane. By taking it out he is released. Should one take it out, and wash it energetically with cow's milk, he will be revived again—have no doubt that this will be achieved.

---

probably based on commentary such as this. Bu-ston explains that in this ritual application a wheel is drawn with this enchanted powder, and that "if one energetically washes **with pure milk** the powder of this wheel, then the victim is restored again" (NS 255b).

[12] Bu-ston explains that "the five intoxicants" (*myos byed lnga*) refers to the root, stem, leaves, flowers, and fruit of the *datura* plant, a powerful and very toxic hallucinogen (NS 255b).

45. *The Six Yoginī Ritual Actions and the Summoning of the Power of Speech*

Next there is the excellent and supreme ritual action which is the means of achieving the powers of speech.[1] Assemble one hundred and eight red *karavīra*[2] flowers and rinse them thoroughly with cow's milk.[3] Cause them to be enchanted one hundred times, and with each enchantment hit the head of the penis with a flower. The well-equipoised one should do thus day after day for a week.[4] After eleven days, take the flowers and go to a great river and cast them in one by one. Apply an enchantment to each of them successively. [If] the final flower in the river is carried upstream, grasp it, together with [some] water, and drink it without touching it with one's teeth. [This] is the means of achieving the power of speech divulged in the secret Tantra.[5]

---

[1] Bhavabhaṭṭa comments here: "**Supreme ritual action** should be understood as being connected to the six syllable mantra. Through the mantra *oṁ vaṁ yoṁ moṁ hrīṁ hūṁ hūṁ phaṭ* there is the ritual action which is **the means of achieving power** in that." (Pandey 2002, 563: *karmavaraṁ ṣaḍakṣaramantrasambandhi bhavatīti jñeyam / oṁ vaṁ yoṁ moṁ hrīṁ hūṁ hūṁ phaḍ iti mantras tasya karma tatsiddhiprasādhakam*) The six yoginī mantra syllables occur in ch. 8 above as *vaṁ*, *yoṁ*, *moṁ*, *hrīṁ*, *hūṁ*, *phaṭ*. Bhavabhaṭṭa adds *oṁ* as well as an additional *hūṁ* here.

[2] A variety of oleander, *Nerium odorum.*

[3] Pandey omits one line here, *prakṣālayet yatnataḥ*, which is attested in all CS mss. and is partially attested in Bhavabhaṭṭa's commentary (2002, 563: *yatnataḥ*). This emendation is probably based on Mardo's translation, which omits the verb corresponding to *prakṣālayet*. It is attested, however, in Sumatikīrti's translation (SL 136a: *'bad de ba yi 'o mas dkru*).

[4] Bhavabhaṭṭa indicates that the mantra should be repeated daily at the three junctures of the day—dawn, noon and dusk (Pandey 2002, 563).

[5] This is a more or less literal translation of *guhyatantre vinirgatā.* The singular reading here, *guhyatantre*, presumably indicates either this CS text or the legendary *Abhidhāna* from which it derives. Durjayacandra, however, advances a different interpretation, understanding *tantra* here as "continuum." He comments that "Regarding **arisen in the secret continuum**, the secret continuum is the triple body. Regarding that which arises in that, it arises as the meaning of that, hence it is *arisen in the secret continuum.*" (RG 312a) His commentary is a

Binding the vulval seal,[6] the mantrin should repeat [the mantra] one hundred and eight [times], facing the victim. Positioned on the victim's abdomen, the wise one should cause the little finger to move, his mind positioned on the three junctures of a day. Even [if one is] a brahmin-slayer, Śakra, and so forth, come under one's power after seven days.

Making an image of the victim,[7] its form is anointed with red sandalwood powder and the three spices,[8] and smeared with beeswax. The adept pierces it with a copper needle in the secret place.[9] The wise one should heat it for seven days with smokeless acacia charcoal.[10] Having enchanted a hundred times, one can then immediately summon the king and his vassal lord,[11] along with his high priest, harem, and retinue.

Write [the mantra] on a leaf of birch bark with the lac and concretion of a corpse,[12] adding the name[13] of the king together with his court. Repeat

---

bit opaque; I presume that he is referring to some sort of gnosis or secret understanding of the triple body.

[6] According to Durjayacandra this refers to a magical diagram that one draws in order to effect the ritual. He writes: "One **binds the vulval seal**, i.e., a triangle that is white like an autumnal cloud, surrounded by a universal lotus in space, meaning that one draws this wheel with lac and red sandalwood on the cloth of a ghost (i.e., a charnel ground cloth). One should place it in the heart of an image of the victim, and also visualize it in her vulva. [There] one **should cause the little finger**, i.e., the vajra, **to move**." (RG 312a) Bhavabhaṭṭa reads here *yoginīyogamudrāṁ*, which is no doubt a euphemistic misreading, but also attests *yonimudrāṁ* (Pandey 2002, 565). Pandey follows the former reading (2002, 564), despite the fact that *yonimudrā* occurs in all CS mss. as well as Jayabhadra's commentary (D 55b.4) and many of the commentaries such as Durjayacandra's and Kambala's (SN 75b). It is also attested in Mardo's translation (PM 141b).

[7] According to Jayabhadra, the image is made of beeswax (D 55b.5: *atra si[kth]akena pratikṛtiṁ kṛtvā*).

[8] According to Monier-Williams' dictionary the *trikaṭuka* are black and long pepper and powdered ginger (2002, 458 col. 1).

[9] That is, in the genitals.

[10] That is, *nirdhūmair khadirāṅgārais*, smokeless charcoal of the Khadira tree, *Acacia catechu*, a tree with a resinous wood.

[11] The term *sāmanta*, present in the Sanskrit mss., is not attested in Mardo's translation. Sumatikīrti's text here reads *blon bcas*, "together with his minister(s)" (SL 136b).

[12] The text here, *pretālaktakarocanayā*, is somewhat ambiguous. Most commentators read *alaktaka*, "lac," here. It of course makes sense that *rocanā* is derived from a corpse, but it is difficult to see how lac, which is derived from an insect, could be acquired from a corpse.

(cont'd)

it facing him [i.e., the victim], and burn it for the sake of success on a fire of acacia wood in an abode of corpses. So long as the beeswax is heated but does not melt, the king along with the universal monarch[14] is summoned.

The adept compounds dust from the victim's feet, and also red sandalwood, with charnel ground remnant ash,[15] and [warms it vigorously][16] with smokeless acacia charcoal. Grinding that powder with both hands, immolate it; there is power as soon as it is immolated. Having taken this powder of hers, bury it; she[17] [then] is stupefied, rendered senseless, afflicted,[18] and even beguiled. [She] will come with the speed of the wind and throw herself

---

Sumatikīrti apparently reads the same word twice in its translation *dur khrod ras la sen rtsi dang, 'gi haṁ dag gis bris nas ni* (SL 136b), "drawing with lac and concretion on a funeral cloth," which may have entailed the reading of *laktaka*, a dirty cloth or rag. Mardo omits all reference to *pretālaktaka*, reading only "with concretion" (PM 141b).

[13] This translates the Tibetan *ming dang spel nas* (PM 241b, SL 136b). The Sanskrit here, *nāmavidarbhitaṁ*, contains the unattested verb form *vidarbhita*, which may be a corruption of *vardhita*.

[14] The text *sacakravartinam* is a bit odd, as a cakravartin is a superior type of king, not a figure separate from the king.

[15] The CS mss. here clearly read *śmaśānocchiṣṭabhasmasya*, which corresponds precisely with Mardo's translation *dur khrod lhag ma thal bas* (PM 241b–242a). For some reason Pandey emends this to *śmaśānotsṛṣṭaṁ bhasma* (2002, 565). Note that while *bhasmasya* is technically incorrect, this text often declines *-an* stem nouns as *-a* stems, as in the case of *karmasya* below.

[16] This text occurs in Mardo's translation (PM 242a: *rab tu 'bad pas bsro bar bya*), but does not occur in the Sanskrit mss. or in Sumatikīrti's translation.

[17] It is not clear from the text who is the victim of this operation. The feminine singular pronoun *tasyāḥ* and feminine singular declensions (*mūrcchitā cetanarahitā kliṣṭāś caiva vimohitā*) suggest a feminine singular object. Vīravajra states that through this ritual application "either a male or female, as is appropriate" (PD 440a), may be stupefied, and so forth, but that its primary application is summoning a woman to serve as a "messenger" (*dūtī*) or "sacrificial victim" (*paśu*), which he comments refers to a female renunciant (*saṁcāriṇī*; PD 440b: *kun spyod ma*). Bhavabhaṭṭa likewise comments that the "sacrificial victim" could be a man or a woman (Pandey 2002, 566: *puruṣaṁ striyaṁ vā*). Obviously, the other option of turning the object of the rite into a messenger (*dūtī*) could only apply to a female.

[18] The CS mss. here read *klīnāś*, which is clearly corrupt. On the basis of the Tibetan translation *nyon mongs pa* (PM 242a; SL 136b: *nyon mongs*), it seems likely that *kliṣṭā* should be read here.

upon the adept. [She] should be made into a sacrificial victim[19] or a messenger. Thus indeed is a messenger captured by means of the ritual action.[20]

Taking a forearm's measure of moist *karavīra* creeper, and inscribing it with mantras with regard to whatever is to be attained,[21] cast it into a blazing funeral fire, and quickly seize it; so long as it is not consumed, circumambulate[22] the fire, recollecting the sevenfold enchantment with the spell. In a moment a truly excellent, comely woman will come with the speed of the wind.[23]

A red *karavīra* flower, enchanted by the adept one hundred times during the Puṣya conjunction, is smeared with cow concretion, and that flower is placed in water. Descending into a river, one stands in the water up to one's navel. Positioned within one's cupped hands, once it is enchanted thus one thousand times with the spell, drink it together with the water filling both of one's hands. Then through this there will be power; the power of speech is attained. One may surely summon the king or queen with one's mind. The gods, titans, and men will be instantly brought into one's power. Fervent, one may kill them with a word. The adept controls, overthrows, and suppresses with just a word. With a word he may immobi-

---

[19] As noted just above, Vīravajra interprets *paśu* here as referring to a *saṁcāriṇī* (PD 440b: *kun spyod ma*), evidently referring to a female renunciant or perhaps a woman with whom one has an affair.

[20] This translation represents my interpretation of this half-verse, *tato vai karmasya dūtīgrahaṇam eva ca*, taking the incorrectly declined *karmasya* as an instrument of the action of *dūtīgrahaṇam*. Some of the commentators, however, read *karmasya* as modifying *dūti*. Devagupta claims that this refers to an *anumṛtā*, a woman who "follows [her husband] into death" by casting herself into his cremation fire (SS QT 71.5). Kambala's commentary agrees here, providing the additional information that *anumṛtā* entails a situation in which a "woman and man are immolated together" (SN QT 206.5). This could be a reference to using a human victim as a sacrificial oblation.

[21] Bhavabhaṭṭa explains that "this means that one writes this [six yoginī] mantra with the augment of the name of [him] who [is the operand]" (Pandey 2002, 566: *yasya nāmavidarbhaṇena mantraṁ tam evābhilikhyetyarthaḥ*).

[22] The Sanskrit, *bhrāmayet*, means to wander, roam, circulate, revolve. The Tibetan translations interpret it as "circle" (PM 242a: *bskor na*; SL 137a: *bsgor nas*), presumably meaning that one should circle the fire until the creeper is consumed.

[23] That is, *varastriyāṁ vā svarūpiṇīṁ*. The Tibetan translations read "a comely man or woman" (PM 242a: *skye pa'am bud med rang gzugs can*) and simply "women and men" (SL 137a: *bud med dang skye pa dag*). These may be based on a misreading of *varastriyāṁ* as *narastriyāṁ*.

lize rivers, vehicles, war machines,[24] the ocean, elephants, horses, and likewise clouds, people, or even birds. With a word one brings about everything, whatever one desires with one's mind. The application of attraction is the means of bewitching all women.

Taking a red *karavīra* blossom, carry it off. Having enchanted it seven times with the spell, cause it to be deposited in the middle of her vulva. Having enveloped it, put that flower in the secret places. The mantrin who has the yoga of nondual gnosis should repeat it one hundred and one times. From among those flowers, the one positioned in the middle of the vulva should be taken by the adept. She who is struck by the flower will come into one's power in an instant. She is agitated and rendered senseless, under the power of another in all of her limbs and joints; she comes under one's power instantly and her confidence is thwarted. This power of confidence is the production of unfailing subjugation.[25]

---

[24] That is, *yantra*, which again seems to refer to the devices used in warfare (cf. p. 348 n. 32 above).

[25] According to Vīravajra, this procedure is used to secure a physical consort (*karmamudrā, las kyi phyag rgya*). Part of the treatment this female candidate is to receive is "purification by means of the four [types of] service and worship" (PD 421a: *bsnyen sgrub bzhis sbyangs*). However, it is clear that this rite is fundamentally coercive.

46. The Procedure of Ritual Actions with the Five *ha* Syllables

Next, there is the accomplishment of all ritual actions through the five *ha* syllables, through mere knowledge of which there is rapid engagement in power. One should rub one's hands[1] on which are the five syllables, *haṁ hau ho hai haḥ*.[2] Drawing blood[3] from his mouth with a [word of] command, one's foe dies instantly. Should one anoint the skull that is the receptacle of one's own blood[4] with the blood of one's ring finger,[5] as soon as it dries the victim perishes. Should one, angered and with reddened eyes,

---

[1] The CS mss. clearly read *haste*, while Bhavabhaṭṭa reads the dual accusative *hastau* (Pandey 2002, 569), which makes more sense. He also explains that these can be either written or visualized, as follows: "Vizualize or write directly a five-spoked wheel on both hands, and visualize or write there the five syllables. Then one should rub them." (2002, 569: *pañcāraṁ cakraṁ hastayor vicintya sākṣād vā vilikhya tatra pañcākṣarāṇi vicintya vilikhya vā tau mṛdnīyād iti samudāyārthaḥ*)

[2] This is the reading of all three CS mss., which is confirmed by Mardo's translation (PM 242b). Bhavabhaṭṭa, however, reads *hā hī hai hau haḥ* (Pandey 2002, 569). There are also a number of other variants. Sumatikīrti's text here reads *he ho hu haṁ ha* (SL 137b), Kambala reads *ha hi hu he ho* (SN 76a), and Durjayacandra reads *haṁ hūṁ ho he ha* (RG 312a). Pandey emends the text to accord with Bhavabhaṭṭa's commentary without noting the CS mss.' reading. I have preserved the CS reading, which, since it is supported by Mardo's translation, is the best attested text.

[3] The CS mss. and Bhavabhaṭṭa are missing the verb here corresponding to the Tibetan *khrag 'dzag cing* (PM 242b, SL 137b). Jayabhadra, however, provides the missing word, with *rudhiram uddhṛtya*. Bhavabhaṭṭa's text preserves a variant here, which in the mss. reads *rudhiram udvasya* (F 138b.2, G 119b.1), "removing blood," although this is emended by Pandey to *rudhiram udvamya*, "emitting blood" (Pandey 2002, 570).

[4] The CS mss. here read *svaśoṇitakapālastham*, which is supported by the Tibetan translation *rang gi khrag ni thod gnas pa* (PM 242b, SL 137b). Bhavabhaṭṭa here reads *śvaśoṇitam*, "dog blood" (Pandey 2002, 569), but this is undoubtedly a corruption due to the widespread confusion concerning the ligatures for *ś* and *s*.

[5] Bhavabhaṭṭa glosses *anāmikā*, "ring finger," as *anapatyā*, a "childless woman," whose "blood" is uterine blood, *rajaḥ* (Pandey 2002, 569, 570: *anāmikā anapatyā tasyā rudhiraṁ rajaḥ*).

repeat [the syllables] excitedly, the king will quickly be killed, along with his army and his mount.

Make an offering of the ḍākinī sacrificial cake, with cat, mongoose, dog,[6] crow, crane, and jackal;[7] there is no doubt that in this Tantra this quickly yields power. Make a cord from the hair of rabbit, and so forth, and enchant it a thousand times; he around whose neck it is bound will become like that.[8] Having enchanted one's hand one thousand times with *karavīra* blossoms, and employing each syllable,[9] touch a pregnant woman. One transfers the embryo, and in release [from it] there is liberation.[10] Whomever is admonished is killed and then caused to live again.

---

[6] The item "dog" (Skt. *śvāna*, Tib. *khyi*) is omitted in Mardo's Tibetan translation, but occurs in the CS mss. as well as in Sumatikīrti's translation (SL 138a).

[7] That is, offerings are made of the flesh of these animals. Jayabhadra wrote that "it is said that the flesh of the **cat**, and so forth, is known to be valued by the ḍākinīs" (D 56a.1–2: *mārjarādimāṁsaṁ ḍākinīnāṁ praśastam iti darśayaty āha*). Note that the Tibetan (PM 242b, SL 138a) translates *jambukā* ("jackal") as *wa* ("fox").

[8] In other words, according to Vīravajra, one can take on the form of the animal whose hair is used for the enchanted necklace (PD 442a).

[9] That is, having enchanted one hundred thousand times for each letter, for a total of five hundred thousand times. Bhavabhaṭṭa explains that "immediately after the five hundred thousandth repetition, then there is the ritual application" (Pandey 2002, 570: *ekaikākṣaraṁ saṁyojyeti pañcalakṣajāpād anantaraṁ tataḥ karmayoga iti bhāvaḥ*). Jayabhadra expands this even further, calling for the use of the seven syllable mantra, and repeating three times for a total of three oblations, as follows: "As for [employing] **each syllable** [of] the seven syllable mantra, having first sacrificed thrice with one hundred thousand repetitions for the measure of syllables, afterwards [one repeats it] one thousand and eight [times]" (D 56a.2–4: *saptākṣaro mantra ekaikākṣaram iti akṣāpramāṇalakṣajāpena prathama trīṇi hutvā paścād aṣṭasahasrāṇīti saṁbandhaḥ*).

[10] This appears to be a magical procedure for inducing abortions. I take *garbha* here to indicate an embryo or fetus, rather than the womb, as the Tibetan *mngal* indicates (PM 242b, SL 138a). Here I follow Bhavabhaṭṭa, who comments as follows on this cryptic text: "**In release there is liberation** means that when her body is released by means of one's hand, then there is the liberation which is the discharging of the embryo" (F 139a.1, G 119b.6: *mukte mokṣa iti kareṇa tasyā śarīre mukte garbhatyāgo mokṣaḥ*). Note that Bhavabhaṭṭa's text clearly reads *garbhatyāgo* in both mss. available to me (F 139a.1, G 119b.6), while Pandey here reads *garbhasrāvo* (2002, 570).

47. The Procedure of All Ritual Actions of the Sarvabuddhaḍākinī Mantra

Now I will explain [the mantra of] all ḍākinīs that is in the heart,[1] the mere utterance of which gives rise to the fruition of all powers.[2] Then, repeating the ḍākinīs' great spell, one brings all of the social classes under one's control.[3] Through constant repetition great glory is generated.[4] Produce a stake made of human bone, six finger's breadths long and enchanted one hundred and eight times. The lineage of him in whose door it is infixed

[1] Bhavabhaṭṭa explains this somewhat cryptic statement as follows: "The essence in the heart of that—i.e., Vajravārāhī's *sarvaḍākinī* essence mantra of all ḍākinīs—is Vajravārāhī's quintessence mantra. It is *oṁ vajravairocanīye svāhā*." (Pandey 2002, 572: *sarvaḍākinīvajravārāhīhṛdayamantraḥ tasya hṛdi hṛdayam / vajravārāhyā upahṛdayamantraḥ ityarthaḥ / oṁ vajravairocanīye svāheti*) This is supported by the next chapter, which identifies *oṁ sarvabuddhaḍākinīye vajravarṇanīye hūṁ hūṁ phaṭ svāhā* as her essence mantra.

[2] Although statements such as this are probably best understood as extolling the greatness of the text and its mantras, here Vīravajra provides ritual instructions for the achievement of "all powers," as follows:

> One draws a wheel with eight spokes as the base of the magical diagram. One should place [the syllable] *ho* in the center, *oṁ* on the eastern [spoke], *suva* to the north, *suja* to the west, *supi* to the south, *ro* to the southeast, *ca* to the southwest, *nī* to the northwest, and *ye* to the northeast, and place *hūṁ*, *hūṁ*, *phaṭ*, and *svāha* at the four gates in a counterclockwise fashion. Then place it in the heart of the *liṅga*, and **through the mere utterance** of the mantra the twelve **powers** are generated. (PD 442a–b)

The term *liṅga* here refers to a symbolic sacrificial effigy employed in Buddhist exorcism rituals. In the Tibetan context it is often an anthropomorphic image on paper. See Kohn 2001, 73–86.

[3] Vīravajra explains: "If one, with the **ḍākinīs' great spell**, inserts the magical diagram for controlling in the heart of the five classes, they will be **under one's control**" (PD 442b).

[4] Vīravajra explains: "As for the second ritual action, if one produces a magical diagram for enriching, **great glory is generated**" (PD 442b).

will be cut off.[5] If one implants it in his field, in his cattle pen, and in his place for buffalo, elephants, and horses, it will be the end of him.[6]

Now, one who wants to control the king or the royal minister would be wise to make a likeness [of him] out of clay, eight finger's breadths long, and have it set at the royal gate. Should one, on the first day, immolate three thousand citron flowers mixed with [other] blossoms,[7] he will be subjugated. With this mantra one can bring about operations [causing] invocation,[8] stupefaction, inciting hostility,[9] bewitching,[10] theft of speech, and also [those causing] muteness and dispelling.

A man who wishes to become a woman should assemble flowers from a human corpse, *kākaṇḍakī* fruits,[11] the skin, nails, and so forth, [from] the

---

[5] Vīravajra explains: "As for the third ritual action, if one hides a magical diagram for expelling within the interior of a **stake made of human bone**, and **enchants** it **one hundred and eight times** with the mantra, he **in whose door** one hides it will be expelled" (PD 442b).

[6] Vīravajra explains: "As for the fourth ritual action, if one hides a magical diagram for annihilating within his **field**, his wall, **and in his place for water buffalo**, and so forth, he will be ruined" (PD 442b).

[7] This translates the text as preserved in the CS mss., *prathame dine trīṇi mātuluṅgapuṣpāṇi kusumamiśrāṇi sahasraṁ juhuyāt.* Bhavabhaṭṭa only attests one portion of this text, reading *mātuluṅgakusumāṇi*, which is not a significant difference as *puṣpa* and *kusuma* are synonymous. The Tibetan translations, however, differ significantly. Mardo's translation reads: "Should one, on the first day, undertake 100,000 fire sacrifices with citron flower and fruit and mixed blossoms" (PM 243a: *nyin zhag dang po la ma tu lung ga'i me tog dang 'bras bu rnams dang ku su ma bsres pas sbyin sreg brgya stong byas na*). Sumatikīrti's reads: "Should one, on the first day, undertake 100,000 fire sacrifices with citron fruit and mixed blossoms" (SL 138b: *nyin zhag dang po la ma tu lung ka'i 'bras bu dang // me tog bsres te sbyin bsreg brgya stong byas na*). Vīravajra here reads: "citron flowers mixed with safflowers" (PD 442b: *ma tu lung ga'i me tog dang / le brgan rtsi'i me tog dang bsres te*), which suggests the reading *kusumbha* rather than *kusuma.*

[8] The CS mss. here read *mantreṇāvāhanaṁ*, with *āvāhanaṁ* translated in Tibetan as *dgug pa* (PM 243a, SL 138b, PD 442b). Pandey's emendation here to *ākarṣaṇa* (2002, 572) is unnecessary.

[9] In lieu of "inciting hostility" (*dveṣaṇa*) the Tibetan translations here read "destroying" (PM 243a, SL 138b, PD 442b: *gnon pa*). These three texts also read "dessication" (*skems pa*), which is not attested in the Sanskrit.

[10] That is, *mohana*, referring to the magical act of bewildering the victim, rendering him or her vulnerable to manipulation by the enchanter.

[11] *Diospyros tormentosa*, a species native to Eastern India, the fruit of which is edible but astringent. See Tanaka 1976, 259.

feet[12] of one who is ravenous,[13] and divide them into equal portions. Pulverize them with rabbit blood, and form them into eleven shade-dried pills. Then on a good day[14] bind them to one's hand. He on whose head the powder is applied on the twelfth day will become a woman.

Now, a man who wants to become a dog should place a piece of meteoric iron[15] in the skull of a mongoose. Repeat [the mantra] eight thousand times over seven nights. On the seventh day, balance[16] it with saffron. Enchant the powder eight hundred times and immolate it. He on whose head this ash is applied will become a dog. With regard to his restoration, undertake at night [or] twilight a great ḍākinī worship [ceremony].[17] Offer the sacrificial cake, and then he will return to his original nature.

One who wishes to become substantial or insubstantial should immolate one hundred and eight golden fruits.[18] One will become substantial or

---

[12] While *pādau* is declined as nominative or accusative rather than genitive—and is thus in apposition to *carmanakhādi*—I translate it as genitive on the basis of the translation (PM 243a: *rkang pa'i 'og gi pags pa*; SL 138b: *rkang pa'i 'og gi sen mo*). Note that "skin" is attested in the former and "nails" in the latter.

[13] That is, *bubhukṣitasya*, attested in Sumatikīrti's translation (SL 138b: *bkres pa'i*). Mardo reads instead "of a crow" (PM 243a: *khva'i*), which is apparently an interpretive translation. Bhavabhaṭṭa comments that "ravenous one" refers to a crow (Pandey 2002, 574: *bubhukṣitaḥ kākaḥ*).

[14] Vīravajra comments that this means a day during the Tiṣya lunar mansion (PD 443a: *skar ma rgyal gyi zhag*). Note that while *skar ma rgyal* is usually a translation of *tiṣya*, it has also been used to translate the *puṣya* lunar mansion.

[15] The CS mss. read *puṣyaloha*, translated into Tibetan as *rgyal gyi lcags* (PM 243a; SL 138b: *rgya lcags*). Vīravajra explains that this is "a piece of iron which fell as a thunderbolt" (PD 443a). Regarding its relation to the *puṣya* lunar mansion, perhaps it refers to meteoric iron that fell during such a time period. Bhavabhaṭṭa glosses *puṣyaloha* as *lohakīṭa* (Pandey 2002, 574), "iron worm," which perhaps refers to a type of insect.

[16] This expression, *samaṁ kṛtvā*, means to pulverize it with (presumably an equal amount of) saffron, according to Jayabhadra, who comments: "pulverize it together with saffron" (D 56a.6–7: *kuṁkumena saha cūrṇi[ṁ] kṛ[tvā]*).

[17] Vīravajra here calls for the well-known *gaṇacakra* rite, to which the appellation *ḍākinīṁ mahatīṁ pūjāṁ* presumably refers (PD 443a).

[18] Jayabhadra explains that *kanakaphala* refers to the fruit of the *datura* or thorn-apple plant (D 56a.7: *kanakaphalānīti dhathuraphalāni*).

insubstantial. If one immolates yellow myrobalan[19] [fruit], one will return to one's original nature.

Now, one who wishes to give rise to an omen[20] should immolate the abode of the great *śakuna* bird.[21] On the seventh day, an omen will arise. With regard to restoration, immolate chaff and it will be terminated.

Taking hairs of a cat during a lunar eclipse, immolate them with the mantra and the name of [the victim]. Taking that ash, he upon whose head one causes it to be bestowed will turn into a cat. If one repeats [the mantra] again, he will return to his original nature. Taking and enchanting a cord of crow sinew, he around whose neck it is bound will become a crow. Likewise one may become one who has the form of a crow, pigeon, peacock, heron, owl, or a vulture. Making and enchanting a cord of cow's hair, he around whose neck it is tied will become a cow. Taking and enchanting a sinew cord of whatever living being, he around whose neck it is bound will become like that. Making and enchanting a cord of any quadruped whatsoever, [he around whose] neck it is bound will have that form. When [the cord] is released he is liberated. Enchanting grain, cast it upon the home of a wealthy man. Consecrating oneself with the remainders, in seven days all [of his] grain will be drawn forth.

---

[19] That is, *harītakā* (*Terminalia chebula*).

[20] The CS mss. here read *athotpādaṁ*, which does not make a great deal of sense in this context. Pandey emends this to *athonmādaṁ* (2002, 573) on the basis of Mardo's translation (PM 243a: *de nas smyo bar bya bar 'dod na*), reading *smyo ba* as *unmāda*, "insanity." Sumatikīrti reads *de nas blo bur pa rnams bskyed par 'dod na* (SL 139a), which is also unclear. But an improved translation occurs as follows in Vīravajra's commentary, with contextual information added: "If one wishes to suddenly give rise to an ill omen in one's enemy's household" (PD 443a: *dgra bo'i khyim du blo bur du ltas ngan bskyed par 'dod na*). Clearly, *utpāda* should be emended to *utpāta*, "omen," which corresponds to these translations and commentaries, and which also makes better sense in the context, particularly since the spell involves the immolation of the nest or dwelling of the *śakuna* bird, which is associated with prognostication.

[21] According to Jayabhadra, this is the owl (D 56a.7–b.1: *mahāśakunavāsa ulūka*). According to Vīravajra, it is the crow or the owl (PD 443a).

48. The Procedure of the Maṇḍala of the Hidden Abode of All Heroes and Ḍākinīs

Next I will propound that which is auspicious for all ḍākinīs, the essence of all the yoginīs which is the means of achieving all desired aims, the mere recollection of which shakes the entire triple world, as does its mere subsequent recollection, and also the correct progression of the powers.

hā svā ṭ pha hūṁ hūṁ ye nī rṇa va jra va
ye nī ki ḍā ddh bu rva sa oṁ[1]

The power of reciting this mantra is the auspicious accomplishment of all ritual actions. This is the famous mantra of all yoginīs, namely the ḍākinīs, yoginīs, khaṇḍarohās, lāmās, and so forth.[2] Whatever ritual actions occur in the triple world—in the underworld, in heaven, or even moreover in the mortal world—this mantra should accomplish all of them. Other than this there is no greater means of achieving any power whatsoever. This is the unexcelled, through which is shown the approaches to the divine.[3]

I will explain the abode of all ḍākinīs, concisely but not extensively. One should draw the divine mountain, on which appears a variety of flowers and fruit, and always visualize on top of that the ḍākinīs, and likewise the lāmās, the yoginīs and khaṇḍarohās,[4] and indeed the heroes' hero.[5]

---

[1] This is Vajravārāhī's essence mantra, with the syllables given in reverse order. In normal order it reads: *oṁ sarvabuddhaḍākinīye vajravarṇanīye hūṁ hūṁ phāt svāhā.* This identification is supported by Jayabhadra, who writes: "**Next**, and so forth, indicates the Blessed Lady's essence mantra" (D 56b.1–2: *athetyādinā bhagavaty[āḥ] hṛdayamantr[aṁ] n[i]rdiśati*).

[2] This translates the Tibetan reading, *mkha' 'gro rnal 'byor ma rnams dang // khaṇḍa ro hā lā ma sogs* (PM 243b; SL 139b: *lā ma sogs*). The Sanskrit here, *ḍākinānāṁ yoginām tu khaṇḍa-rohālāmādayas tathā*, is declined erratically.

[3] This translates the Sanskrit *divyopāyapradeśakaḥ*, which is the CS mss. reading, attested by Bhavabhaṭṭa, who glosses *divyopāya* as plural (Pandey 2002, 576: *divyān upāyān pradiśatīti divyopāyapradeśakam*). The Tibetan translations, however, read "the means of achieving all ritual actions" (PM 243b, SL 140a: *las rnams thams cad bsgrub byed yin*).

[4] The term *khaṇḍarohā* can designate a specific goddess or a generic class of goddesses. The term is given in plural above, indicating the latter case. Here it is declined as singular, which

Hā hā he he[6]—the twenty-four heroes are the binding of the ḍākinīs' network. And likewise there are:[7] Vajrasattva (Adamantine Hero), Vairocana (Illuminating), Padmanarteśvara (Lotus Lord of the Dance), Śrī Vajraheruka (Glorious Adamantine Heruka), Ākāśagarbha (Space Womb), and also Hayagrīva (Horse Headed).[8] There are also Ratnavajra (Precious Vajra), Mahābala (Great Strength), Virūpākṣa (He who has Misshapen Eyes), and Bhairava (Terrifier).[9] There is also Vajrabhadra (Adamantine Goodness), Subhadra (Extremely Good), Vajrahūṁkāra (Adamantine Syllable *Hūṁ*), Mahāvīra (Great Hero), Vajrajaṭila (Adamantine Hair Crest), Aṅkurika (Sprout), and Vajradehaka (Adamantine Body). There is also Vajraprabha (Adamantine Light), Amitābha (Immeasurable Light), Surāvairiṇa (He who has Enmity through Liquor),[10] Vikaṭadaṁṣṭriṇa (Dreadful Fangs), Kaṅkāla

---

seems out of place, as it is in the context of a list of generic goddess classes declined as plural. For the sake of consistency, I translate it here also as plural.

[5] Jayabhadra here gives an expanded account of the visualization: "[One should] **draw the divine mountain**, meaning the wind, [fire, water,] and *mahendra* [maṇḍalas], the turtle, the universal vajra, and the universal lotus, atop of which is the mountain with the seven clans, surrounded by subsidiary mountains. Visualize **on top of that** the three wheels, and so forth, as is revealed in the context of the perfecting stage." (D 56b.2–4: *likhitvā parva[t]aṁ divyān iti anilāvāyu mahendre ka[c]chapa viśvavajraviśvapadmopari saptakulaparvata[ṁ] pariveṣṭitaṁ anuparvataṁ dhyātvā tadupari tricakrādi niṣpattikramasūcitaṁ*) Note that the square brackets in the translation in this note indicate words not in the Sanskrit text (which is corrupt and possibly incomplete) but found in the Tibetan translation (MP 67b-68a).

[6] Jayabhadra explains that "***hā hā he he*** is said to be the great mantra which is the cause of the deity" (D 56b.4–5: *hā hā he he ceti devatākāraṇamahāmantra[ḥ] kathitaḥ*). The Tibetan translation identifies it as "the great mantra of divine pride" (MP 68a: *lha'i nga rgyal gyis sngags chen po*). Bhavabhaṭṭa comments as follows: "As for ***hā hā he he***, the heroes who are the twenty-four heroes are characterized by laughter" (Pandey 2002, 577: *hā hā he he ityḥadi hāsopalakṣitāṁś caturviṁśativīrāṇāṁ vīrān ityarthaḥ*).

[7] As in the case of ch. 4, Jayabhadra explains that "then the naming of the twenty-four heroes is related in reverse order" (D 56b.5–6: *tataḥ caturviṁśativīrāṇā[m] abhidhāna[ṁ] kathitaṁ vilomena*). See Table One in the Introduction for a complete list of the deities.

[8] While *grīva* means "neck," horse-headed is probably the best translation, as both van Gulik (1953, 10) and Kohn (2001, 17) have argued.

[9] Jayabhadra glosses "Bhairava" here as "Mahābhairava" (D 56b.6: *bhairava mahābhairava*).

[10] The Tibetan translates this name as "enemy of the gods" (PM 244a: *lha yi dgra*; SL 140a: *lha yi sgra*), as if translating *suravairī*.

(Skeleton), Mahākaṅkāla (Great Skeleton), and Khaṇḍakapālin (Broken Skull), and so forth.[11]

The entire world is completely pervaded by the twenty-four heroes. The heroes' ḍākinīs, the yoginīs Pracaṇḍā, and so forth, should be seen as positioned in the wheels. He who is adept in all rites[12] and who desires power should always, well-equipoised, visualize himself as consisting of the three wheels. By means of what was previously taught and the established method, worship the binding of the ḍākinīs' network,[13] which is indeed the great wheel that is the abode of all powers, and which was well-spoken by tens of millions of buddhas and also tens of millions of heroes. Each one of the yoginīs is attended by [a retinue] amounting to ten million. Among the yoginīs are Ḍākinī, Rūpiṇī, Khaṇḍarohā, Lāmā, and so forth, the auspicious accomplishers of all powers.

---

[11] Regarding the iconography of these heroes, Bhavabhaṭṭa explains:

> Since the eight [heroes] from Khaṇḍakapālī through Vajradehaka are dark blue, the mind wheel is dark blue. Since [the eight] from Aṅkura through Virūpākṣa are red, the speech wheel is red. And as [the eight] from Mahābala through Vajrasattva are white, the body wheel is white. They have two or four arms, as is claimed by the masters.
>
> *ebhir aṣṭabhiḥ khaṇḍakapālādibhir vajradehāntaiḥ kṛṣṇaiś cittacakraṁ kṛṣṇam / aṅkurikādibhir virūpākṣāntai raktai raktaṁ vākcakram / mahābalādibhir vajrasattvāntaiḥ śvetaiḥ śvetaṁ kāyacakram / eteṣāṁ dvibhujatvaṁ caturbhujatvaṁ vā ācāryamatena.* (F 141b.1–3, G 121.4–6; cf. Pandey 2002, 577, 578)

[12] Jayabhadra comments: "**Adept in all rites** means that all rites, such as pacifying, enriching, and so forth, will come to be in conformity with the appropriate ritual action by the mantrin endowed with the triple wheel" (D 56b.7–57a.2: *cakrasthā tu draṣṭavyā sarvakāryeṣu sādhakaṁ śāntipuṣṭyādisarvakārya[ṁ] yathā yathā karmānurūpataḥ tricakrānvite[na] mantriṇā bhavitavyam iti bhāvaḥ*).

[13] CS mss. A and C here read *yajeḍ ḍākinījālasamvaram*, which I have translated here. This is supported by Sumatikīrti's translation (SL 140b: *mkha' 'gro dra ba bde mchog mchod*). Ms. B, however, here reads *japeḍ*, "repeat," which is in turn supported by Mardo's translation (PM 244a: *mkha' 'gro dra ba'i bde mchog brjod*). I believe that the textual evidence is stronger for the former reading, which also seems to make more contextual sense. Pandey, however, follows Mardo in reading *japeḍ* (2002, 578). While Bhavabhaṭṭa does not cite this word, his commentary supports the idea that it is worship rather than mantra repetition that is called for here: "**By means of what was previously taught** means by means of the worship in the form of the outer, secret, and mind-made [types of worship]. That which is to be worshipped is the **binding of the ḍākinīs' network**." (2002, 578: *bāhyaguhyamanomaya-tatsvarūpābhiḥ pūjābhir ityarthaḥ / pūjyam āha ḍākinījālasamvaram iti*)

49. The Procedure of Transforming the Victim Who Is Born Seven Times

Now above all I will speak on the ritual action regarding the sacrificial victim in accordance with the rite, through mere knowledge of which there is rapid engagement with power. The mantrin should form a sacrificial victim made out of rice flour, in accordance with the procedure. There is the variegated hog[1] along with the donkey, man, tortoise, camel, jackal, and horse, and so forth; these truly are known to be the sacrificial victims. From these[2] I will explain the ritual action, in a manner which will accord with their defining characteristics.[3]

There are those with one and two births, and also three, four, and five. There are also those with six and seven births; have no doubt that these are the sacrificial victims.[4] He is one who always has a pleasant scent in his mouth,[5] gazes without blinking, is truthful, regards [all] with kindness, and

---

[1] Bhavabhaṭṭa explains that "the **variegated hog** is a type of wild animal with various coloration" (Pandey 2002, 580: *viśvavarāho nānāvarṇo mṛgaviśeṣaḥ*).

[2] Bhavabhaṭṭa here glosses "from these" as "from those born seven times as a man" (Pandey 2002, 580: *ebhyaḥ saptamanuṣyajanmabhyaḥ*).

[3] Vīravajra gives the following account of the rite to which he believes this text alludes:

> First, one prepares a tantric feast by the method of achieving the seven-birthed one. One should make an image of the **sacrificial victim** with **rice flour** equal in measure to the seven-birthed one. Making images of the seven, i.e., **man, tortoise, horse, camel, donkey, jackal, and hog,** fill their interiors with blood. As sacrificial offerings they should be offered as oblations and eaten. Having thus performed the *gaṇacakra*, the ḍākinīs are delighted, and one will know [the victim's] lineage of births from the first to the seventh, have no doubt. (PD 444b–445a)

Evidently this rite enables the adept to recognize the one born seven times as a man.

[4] Vīravajra explains that the following seven signs correspond to those who have been born a man from one to seven times, respectively. See PD 445a. Presumably the one born seven times a man would have all seven characteristics, as the text below suggests.

[5] This is a translation of the Tibetan, *kha yi dri zhim* (PM 244b, SL 140b: *kha'i dri zhim*; PD 445b: *kha dri zhim pa*). The CS mss. here read "very loud voice" (*susvanī vāṇī*), which while plausible is not attested elsewhere.

delights in the true teaching. He knows his own life, and always has a pleasant scent. He who is endowed with these characteristics is one born into the state of the seven-birthed.

Through merely having eaten this, or having smelled or touched it, one will become one who has a divine form. He who forms it into a drop will become accomplished and will assume his desired form. The wise one takes up the concretion in his heart.[6] Repeating the essence mantra, he forms it into a drop. If one desires to assume the form of whatever sentient being, have no doubt that one will transform into that form by means of the drop. If the wise one takes up tree sap together with concretion and forms it into a drop on his forehead, there is no doubt that he will assume the form of that.[7] Should one bind it to one's hand and head along with the body hair of the sacrificial victim, [or] should one bind it to one's hand and head together with the "five limbs"[8] mixed with body hair, one will assume its form, have no doubt.

One who has yoga conditioning and [mantra] repetition[9] and who is possessed of human capability should avert the path which achieves attachment to injury and affliction.[10] He can assume good forms, bad forms, or

---

[6] As CS ms. A misses a folio here, the Sanskrit text following this line through the middle of ch. 50 is lost, although it is partially recoverable via Bhavabhaṭṭa's and Jayabhadra's commentaries. The translation which follows is based on these as well as on the Tibetan translations. Any significant variants among these sources will be noted below.

[7] That is, he will transform himself into a tree. Vīravajra writes: "If one mixes the sap of whatever sort of tree with concretion and forms it into a drop on one's forehead, one will assume the form of that tree" (PD 445a).

[8] Kambala explains that the "five limbs" (*pañcāṅga*) are the "hair, nails, teeth, skin, and body hair" (SN 77a). The problem with this list, however, is that it is somewhat redundant, as the text states that these should be mixed with body hair. Bhavabhaṭṭa seems to interpret it in terms of the five ambrosias in the case of a living being, or the five parts of a plant should one seek to transform oneself into plant form. He writes: "Regarding the **five limbs** of him, one who desires the form of a sacrificial victim or of a tree [should acquire] the **five limbs**, i.e., the feces, and so forth, of him, or the leaf, flower, and so forth, [of that tree]" (Pandey 2002, 581–582: *tatpañcāṅgeti yasya paśor vṛkṣasya rūpam icchati tasya vairocanādīni pañcāṅgāni patrapuṣpādīni*).

[9] That is, one who has repeated the mantra many times.

[10] Bhavabhaṭṭa interprets this line as a warning not to remain in animal form, as follows: "As for the intention here, why should one not remain in the form of a sacrificial victim, and so forth? [It is because of] the **injury**, and so forth, which refers to the animal realm." (Pandey

divine forms, such as that of the elephant, horse, donkey, tortoise, camel, hog, jackal,[11] crow, owl, vulture, curlew, hawk, or crane.[12] Have no doubt here that the yogin who is a great hero will give rise to his desired form. Aside from this there is no greater power in the triple world.[13]

2002, 582: *prayojanam ihāpi paśvādirūpenaiva kuto na sthīyata ityāha kaṣṭetyādi tiryaggatir ityarthaḥ*)

[11] The Tibetan translations here read "fox" (*wa*). As was the case in ch. 46 above, the Tibetans used the term *wa* to translate the Sanskrit *jambukā*, "jackal."

[12] Sumatikīrti's text here reads *sa ra sa* (SL 141a), which I assume is a transliteration of *sārasa*, a crane. Mardo here reads *sa ra la* (PM 244b).

[13] The term which I translate as "power" (*grub pa*) occurs in Mardo's translation (PM 244b) but is omitted in Sumatikīrti's (SL 141b). It is attested in Bhavabhaṭṭa's commentary, who glosses it as "the power of the seven-birthed one" (Pandey 2002, 582: *saptajanmanaḥ siddhiṁ*). Vīravajra explains more fully as follows: "**Aside from this power** attained just by obtaining the flesh of one born seven times, without dependence on meditative concentration, **there is nothing greater in the triple world**, i.e., the underworld, the surface of the earth, and the heavens" (PD 445b).

50. The Procedure of the Domination Fire Sacrifice and the Teaching of the Stages in Relation to the Seats, and so forth

Next I will explain the ritual procedure of the fire sacrifice which accomplishes dominion, through mere knowledge of which[1] there is rapid engagement with power.[2] Should one mix beef with liquor and immolate it with one's left hand, even the Buddha will be subjugated.[3] What need is there to mention petty humans? The triple world will be subjugated [through a fire sacrifice] with saliva, tooth picks,[4] and thus also that which delights one's body,[5] and liquor, along with [the victim's] name. [The victim] will be summoned immediately with uterine blood, moistened food which has

---

[1] I translate here Sumatikīrti's *gang zhig shes pa tsam gyis ni* (SL 141b), which is also attested in Vīravajra's commentary: "**through mere knowledge of which**, i.e., of the rite of fire sacrifice, having attained the [auspicious sign]" (PD 445b: *gang gis mtshan ma thob nas sbyin sreg gi cho ga gang zhig shes pa tsam gyis*). Mardo, on the other hand, reads here "through the correct procedure of which" (PM 244b: *yang dag cho go gang gis ni*).

[2] This translates the text preserved by Bhavabhaṭṭa, *āśu siddhiḥ pravartate* (Pandey 2002, 583). The Tibetan translations read "power is rapidly attained" (PM 244b, SL 141b: *myur du dngos grub thob 'gyur bshad*).

[3] Vīravajra comments here:

> **Beef**, the flesh of cattle, illustrates the five meats. **Liquor** points particularly to beer—these are the substances to be immolated. **The left hand** refers to the gesture of the placement of the five heroes. Then, having generated the desired fire in the bow-shaped maṇḍala of domination, one immolates them within it along with the five ambrosias—the substances peculiar to the five heroes—enjoyable substances, requisite substances, and durable things. For the sake of that one arranges the solitary hero and the maṇḍala wheel in one's heart, into which they dissolve as light. Performing one hundred and eight immolations over seven days, **even** Indra, and so forth, **will be subjugated**. (PD 445b)

Presumably the gesture (*mudrā*) he mentions involves the visualization of the five deities as one's fingers, as is called for in CS ch. 31. See also the *Hastapūjāvidhi*, ed. in Meisezahl 1985.

[4] That is, *dantakāṣṭha* (D 57a.7), which are the small slivers of wood used as toothpicks.

[5] One would presume that this implies objects of sensuous enjoyment, as in the case of the previous comment by Vīravajra.

been eaten,[6] along with human hair.[7] Should the wise one employ that which is regurgitated from his own body[8] along with his own hair and Nimba wood,[9] [the victim] will be cleaved in an instant. Should the well equipoised one immolate mustard oil with crows' wings and [the victim's] name in a *datura* fire,[10] he will be immediately expelled or killed.

If the mantrin always repeats [the mantra],[11] while awake, asleep, or arising, eating, or engaging in sexual intercourse, there will be no fixed limit [to his lifespan].[12] Should one offer one hundred oblations with jackal flesh,[13]

---

[6] Bu-ston explains that this refers to regurgitated food (NS 268b).

[7] Both translations as well as Vīravajra's commentary read "human hair" (PM 245a: *mi yi skra*; SL 141b, PD 446a: *mi'i skra*). Bhavabhaṭṭa, however, reads here "dog hair" (Pandey 2002, 583: *śvakeśaḥ*). He further explains: "Seeing the victim coming positioned in the wind maṇḍala which arises from the syllable *yaṁ*, one should perform the fire sacrifice with the blood of a menstruating woman, and so forth" (2002, 583–584: *yaṁkārajavāyumaṇḍalasthasādhyam āgacchantaṁ paśyan rajasvalāraktādibhir homaṁ kuryād iti saṁkṣepaḥ*).

[8] This is the reading of the Tibetan translation. Again, Bhavabhaṭṭa reads *śvakāya*, which clearly is not a corruption as he glosses it as *śunaḥ kāyaḥ* (Pandey 2002, 584).

[9] That is, of the tree *Azadirachta indica*.

[10] That is, a fire made of dried material of the *datura* or thorn-apple plant.

[11] This word, *mantra*, is added in Jayabhadra's commentary (D 57b.1). Bhavabhaṭṭa explains that it is the two laughter mantras described in ch. 39 that are to be repeated (Pandey 2002, 584). Bhavabhaṭṭa also reads here *mahākālo japen mantrī*, "The Mahākāla mantrin should repeat." The Tibetan translations, however, do not support the *mahākālo* reading, attesting here only "always" (PM 245a, SL 142b: *rtag tu*). Pandey emends Bhavabhaṭṭa's text to *sadā kale* (2002, 584), presumably to accord with the Tibetan.

[12] This translates the reading preserved in Jayabhadra's commentary, *velā niyamā na vidyate* (D 57b.1–2). It is supported by an alternate reading quoted by Bhavabhaṭṭa, namely *samyag-velā na vidyate* (Pandey 2002, 584). Bhavabhaṭṭa also cites the term *māram*, supporting the readings preserved in the Tibetan translations, "there will be no Death for him" (SL 142a: *de la bdud ni yod ma yin*; PM 245a: *de la bgegs ni yod ma yin*). *Māra*, death personified (SL 142a: *bdud*), is also the major source of obstacles for serious meditators according to Buddhist mythology (hence Mardo's translation *bgegs*, PM 245a). Bhavabhaṭṭa comments here: "**Death** implies the [four] Māras, Skandha [Māra], and so forth. 'Death' is the mind, since, as it is said, 'it is the mind that is great death'." (2002, 584: *māram iti skandhādayo mārāḥ santyasyeti māraṁ cittaṁ / cittam eva mahāmāram iti vacanāt*)

[13] Sumatikīrti's text has the correct *lce sbyang* here (SL 142a), while Mardo, as before, reads "fox" (PM 245a: *wa*).

after three months the poverty of one's clan will be destroyed.[14] Should the adept offer great flesh together with liquor[15] up to one hundred and eight times over three watches [of the night],[16] all of the ground over which he ranges for six months will be subdued. Have no doubt that the satisfied ḍākinī will give him a kingdom.

Should one visualize all deities, and make oblations over two watches,[17] then one will attain flight with one's very own body. Should one make oblations, internally and externally, with jackal meat and liquor,[18] then engagement with the powers will quickly be at hand. One who has repeated the mantra[19] at night will overthrow countries.[20] Doing thus every day, one will become a king. There is nothing whatsoever in the triple world more excellent than this. The great yogin dies as he wishes, and plays, assuming various forms.

If one immolates a hundred thousand [times] with wood-apple,[21] palāśa,[22] and udumbara [wood],[23] one will quickly become a lord of great

[14] This translates the Tibetan *rigs kyi dbul ba 'jig par 'gyur* (PM 245a, SL 142a). Jayabhadra preserves the following: "then all poverty is destroyed" (D 57b.3: *tadā sarvadāridrya[ṁ] vinaśyatīti darśitaṁ*).

[15] That is, *myos byed* (presumably translating *madya* as is the case in Bhavabhaṭṭa's comment below), or perhaps *madana*.

[16] That is, the *prahara*, which is equal to approximately three hours.

[17] That is, *praharadvayam*, roughly six hours. Bhavabhaṭṭa specifies that the oblations are made "with all beef and intoxicants" (Pandey 2002, 584: *sarvagomāṁsamadyasaṁyuktaṁ*).

[18] That is, *gomāyumāṁsamadyena* (D 57b.5; PM 245a: *go mā yu dang sha chang gis*). Bhavabhaṭṭa preserves what appears to be a misreading, *gomāyumadyamāṁsena* (Pandey 2002, 584). He specifies that *gomāyumāṁsa* is "rotten meat of the jackal" (Pandey 2002, 584: *śṛgālasya śīrṇaṁ māṁsam*).

[19] To this Jayabhadra adds "making sacrificial cakes" (D 57a.6: *balikriyājapamantraṁ kṛto ratrau*).

[20] The plural is from Bhavabhaṭṭa's text, which reads *rāṣṭrakāni nipātayet* (Pandey 2002, 585). Mardo's text is ambiguous, reading only *yul 'khor* (PM 245a), while Sumatikīrti's is decidedly singular (SL 142a: *yul 'khor gcig*). Mardo reads the verb "summon," *'gugs par byed*, which makes no sense, but Sumatikīrti's *'jig par byed* does correspond to the Sanskrit.

[21] Bilva, the *Aegle marmelos* or wood-apple tree.

[22] Mardo and Vīravajra here read *pa la sha* (PM 245a, PD 446b), presumably a transliteration of the Sanskrit *palāśa*, indicating the tree *Butea frondosa*. Sumatikīrti reads "beef" (SL 142a: *ba lang sha*), which is plausible but makes less sense here, where apparently three species of trees are being listed.

[23] That is, the cluster fig, *Ficus glomerata*. Here the texts in the CS mss. resume, after a one folio lacuna (cf. p. 368 n. 6).

wealth. Mixing beef with liquor, it should be immolated by one who desires to be king. Encountering the lady of yogins,[24] who is deprived of a name?[25] [All desired things] are easily obtained by means of the jackal immolation. Should one immolate jackal [flesh], one will quickly become equal to a benefactor.[26] Even he who lacks purity in the practice of the observances will attain power through this instruction.[27]

[For] abundant life,[28] binding the mouth with wax gourd,[29] mung bean,[30] gram,[31] hemp,[32] beeswax,[33] Indian mustard,[34] and leaves of a

---

[24] Both the CS mss. and Bhavabhaṭṭa here read *yogīśvarīṁ*, "lady of yogins." Pandey emends this to *yogeśvarīṁ*, "lady of yoga" (Pandey 2002, 585), presumably on the basis of the Tibetan translations (PM 245a, SL 142b: *rnal 'byor dbang phyug*), despite the fact that this translation is ambiguous, and could serve as a translation of either Sanskrit appellation.

[25] This translates the Sanskrit which occurs in both the CS mss. and Bhavabhaṭṭa's commentary, *ko hi nāmadaridratā* (F 144b.2; A, B, C: *-daridratāḥ*). Note that Pandey erroneously reads here *draridratā* (2000, 585). The Tibetan translations differ, with "by what could one be impoverished" (PM 245a, SL 142b: *dbul po nyid du ga la 'gyur*).

[26] That is, a "wealth giver" (*dhanada*), a wealthy and generous person.

[27] Here I translate the text which is preserved in Jayabhadra's commentary, *ādiṣṭāt siddhim āpnuyāt* (D 60b.6), which appears to be closest to both Tibetan translations (PM 245b: *bstan pa'i dngos grub thob par 'gyur*; SL 142b: *gnang pas dngos grub thob par 'gyur*). The CS mss. read "will attain the power of command" (*adhiṣṭhānasiddhim āpnuyāt*). Bhavabhaṭṭa reads *āviṣṭāṁ* (Pandey 2002, 585), which does not make sense here.

[28] The term *adhikāyu[ḥ]* is at the front of a long list of edible plants. It is generally interpreted as referring to "abundant life," which presumably results from the procedure described here. Vīravajra begins his text here with the following: "If one desires to augment one's abundance of life…" (PD 476b). Jayabhadra claims that "**abundant life** means one becomes Amitāyus" (MP 78b; ms. D is corrupt here, reading: *abhikāyur…[a]mitāyu… bha[va]ti*, D 61a.1). Bhavabhaṭṭa glosses *abhikāyu* as *dūrvā* (Pandey 2002, 585), a grass species (*Panicum dactylon*), but I find this less likely as it is not attested elsewhere, nor is it edible, unlike the other items on the list.

[29] *Kuṣmāṇḍa* (*Beninkasa cerifera*). Jayabhadra explains that it is the seeds of this plant that are employed (D 61a.2: *kuṣmāṇḍabījaṁ*).

[30] *Mudga* (*Phaseolus mungo*).

[31] *Māṣa* (*Phaseolus radiatus*).

household tamāla tree,[35] one will become a yogin who does what he pleases and stays anywhere whatsoever.

Next, above all, I will explain the yoginīs'[36] stages, seats, and so forth.[37] Śrī Heruka has the body of bodies; his nature being the mobility and immobility of all bodies. The seats (*pīṭha*) are in relation to the Joyous stage (*pramuditā*);[38] the subsidiary seats (*upapīṭha*) are the Immaculate [stage] (*vimalā*). The fields (*kṣetra*) are known to be the Illuminating [stage] (*prabhākarī*); the Effulgent [stage] (*arciṣmatī*) correlates to the subsidiary fields (*upakṣetra*). The *chandoha*[39] is the Facing [stage] (*abhimukhī*); the

---

[32] *Śaṇa* (*Cannabis sativa*). Jayabhadra's commentary here reads *śala* (D 61a.2), which is undoubtedly a corruption of *śaṇa*. The Tibetan translation here read *tsa na ka* (PM 245b, SL 142b), presumably a transcription of *caṇaka*, "chick pea." On this basis, Pandey reads *caṇakam* (2002, 585).

[33] The CS mss. read *madhucchardi*, which is not particularly meaningful as a compound. *Madhu* means honey or a fermented beverage, and *chardi* "vomiting, expulsion, emetic," which could possibly be read as *chardikā*, the butterfly pea (*Clitoria ternatea*), the seeds and roots of which are used as a purgative. The *madhucchardi* reading is supported by Jayabhadra (D 61a.2), and also by Bhavabhaṭṭa, who glosses it as *madhūtsiṣṭa* (Pandey 2002, 585), which is presumably a corruption of *madhūcchiṣṭa*, "beeswax." This interpretation is supported by the Tibetan translation, *sbrang rtsi tshigs ma*, found in Bhavabhaṭṭa's (Pandey 2002, 866) and Jayabhadra's (MP 68b) commentaries, and *sbrang rtsi'i rtsigs ma*, found in Sumatikīrti's translation (SL 142b); Mardo's *sbrang rtsi gtsigs ma* (PM 245b) is likely a corruption of this. Another viable option occurs in Jayabhadra's Sanskrit commentary, in which we find *madhuśigru* (D 61a.2), "Indian horseradish" (*Moringa pterygosperma*), a shrub native to the sub-Himalayan region with edible roots, leaves, and flowers, which are also used medicinally. Jayabhadra's reading is certainly plausible, for it accords with the list of edible plants in which it is embedded. However, the *madhūcchiṣṭa* ("beeswax") reading is attested in more sources, and also makes sense as a substance to be used in "binding the mouth."

[34] *Rājikā* (*Brassia juncea* var. *ramosa*).

[35] *Xanthochymus pictorius*, a tree with black bark and white blossoms.

[36] Bhavabhaṭṭa correctly glosses the incorrectly declined *yoginī* as *yoginīnāṁ* (Pandey 2002, 586), which I translate here.

[37] This section of the text correlates the ten classes of pilgrimage place to the ten bodhisattva stages. See Table Three in section 3.1 of the Introduction above for the complete correlation here of pilgrimage places to the stages.

[38] The CS mss. read *muditā*, which is a common variant of *pramuditā*, the name of the first bodhisattva stage. See Dayal 1932, 284.

[39] *Chandoha* is not a Sanskrit term, and was usually transliterated by the Tibetans. It is of unclear derivation, perhaps deriving from an Apabhraṁśa dialect. I am tempted to translate

upachandoha is the Very-difficult-to-conquer [stage] (*sudurjayā*).[40] The Far-reaching [stage] (*dūraṅgamā*) is the meeting-place (*melāpaka*), and the subsidiary meeting-place (*upamelāpaka*) is of the Immovable [stage] (*acalā*). The charnel ground (*śmaśāna*) is the Accomplished [stage] (*sādhumatī*), and moreover the Cloud of Truth (*dharmameghā*) is the subsidiary charnel ground (*upaśmaśāna*).

This teaching of Śrī Heruka[41] concerns the inner stages.[42] With respect to the ten perfections and stages, there is the barbaric language [of the] yoginīs.[43] The hero's body, by nature mobile and immobile, is in heaven, the underworld, and in the mortal worlds. The teaching regarding Pullīramalaya, and so forth, is that they are positioned both outside and inside. The great yoga (*mahāyoga*) of Śrī Heruka is the mighty lord of all desires. With hands and feet everywhere, and eyes, faces, and heads everywhere, he is renowned everywhere in the world, and he abides turning toward all. It is through him that power will be attained, with a mind endowed with meditative states. The secret reality was stated for the sake of the welfare of the adepts.

---

it as "tryst" in the sense of "an appointed place of meeting," influenced by the possibility that it is connected with the Sanskrit terms *chanda*, "pleasing, alluring," and *chandas*, "desire, longing."

[40] The Tantra here reverses the typical order of *sudurjayā* and *abhimukhī*, which are usually the fifth and sixth stages, respectively.

[41] CS ms. A here clearly reads *śrīherukamatiś cāyaṁ*, which I translate here. Mss. B and C, however, read *śrīherukam abhiścāyaṁ*, which is clearly corrupt. Nevertheless, Pandey follows this reading, emending it slightly to *śrīherukam abhiścāryaṁ* (2002, 586). Bhavabhaṭṭa gives the alternate but comprehensible reading of *śrīherukam avadhārya*, "what is to be ascertained [concerning] Śrī Heruka," which he glosses as *niścitya*, "having ascertained." Mardo's translation reads "Śrī Heruka's text and practice" (PM 245b: *śrī he ru ka gzhung spyod pa'i*), which may have been based on text such as *śrīherukamaticaryā*. Sumatikīrti, however, reads "practicing in the land of Śrī Heruka" or "practicing with Śrī Heruka as one's object" (SL 142b: *śrī her ru ka'i yul du spyod*). Given this divergence, I am content to follow the oldest Sanskrit manuscript.

[42] Or, more literally, "the stages in relation to the self," *adhyātmabhūmayaḥ*. Note, however, that below *adhyātma* is juxtaposed to *bāhya*, "outer," suggesting that the simpler translation "inner" is particularly appropriate here.

[43] As above, here again *yoginī* is incorrectly declined, and should be read again as *yoginīnāṁ*.

51. Creation Stage Esoteric Instruction[1]

Now I will expound the esoteric instruction[2] very hard to attain—that which was spoken symbolically by the heroes, and hidden by me in the Tantra—[relating to the] garb[3] and the five insignia, and so forth,[4] of his body, the consort's body,[5] the stake, and the net.[6] Uttering the vowels and

---

[1] As this is the last chapter of the text, the Sanskrit mss. and the Tibetan translations do not provide a name for the chapter. Bhavabhaṭṭa, however, styles it the "Summary of Meditation, and so forth" (Pandey 2002, 588: *bhāvanāpiṇḍārthādi-paṭalam*). Vīravajra calls it "The Chapter on Creation Stage Esoteric Instruction" (PD 447b: *bskyed rim pa'i bsgom pa'i man ngag gi le'u*), which we might tentatively reconstruct as *utpattikramabhāvānāmnāya-paṭala*. I give the latter as the provisional title of the chapter, simply because it is more descriptive.

[2] Concerning the translation of *āmnāya* as "esoteric instruction," see Kapstein 1996, 275.

[3] According to Bhavabhaṭṭa, this consists of the tiger and elephant hides, the "garb" in which Heruka is clad in his iconic representations (Pandey 2002, 588: *nivasanaṁ vyāghracarma gajacarma ca*).

[4] Here *pañcamudrā* does not have its usual meaning but refers rather to the insignia of a Kāpālika yogin. Bhavabhaṭṭa explains that in this context they are the necklace (*kaṇṭhikā*), bracelet (*cūḍa*), armlet (*keyūra*), earring (*kuṇḍala*), and the sacred thread (*brahmasūtra*) (Pandey 2002, 588).

[5] This translation of *prajñāṅga* is based on Kambala's commentary, in which the term is glossed as indicating the *khaṭvāṅga* and also the consort's embrace (see SN 78a); *prajñā* is a euphemism of the consort, and the *khaṭvāṅga* can be a symbol for her. A quite different alternative is provided by Durjayacandra, who gives the less likely explanation that the term *prajñāṅga* refers to the "four vajras," evidently those of the *Guhyasamāja* creation stage, for he follows his explanation with what appears to be a somewhat garbled quotation from the *Uttaratantra* (*Guhyasamāja* ch. 18): */ dang po stong nyid byang chub sems // gnyis pa sa bon bsdus pa'o // gsum pa gzugs brnyan rdzogs pa ste // bzhi pa yi ge dgod pa'o /* (RG 314a). The Tibetan canonical citation for this passage is: */ dang po stong nyid byang chub ste // gnyis pa sa bon bsdu ba yin // gsum pa gzugs ni rdzogs pa ste // bzhi pa yi ge dgod pa'o /* (Tōh. 443, DK rgyud 'bum vol. ca, 154a); the Sanskrit reads: *prathamaṁ śūnyatābodhiṁ dvitīyaṁ bījasaṁhṛtam / tṛtīyaṁ bimbaniṣpattiś caturthaṁ nyāsam akṣaram /* (Matsunaga 1978, 123, v. 138); and this can be translated as: "The first is awakening to voidness, the second the accumulation of seed, the third the perfection of the image, and the fourth is syllable placement." While I have not encountered elsewhere a reference to the four vajra system in the context of the Cakrasamvara traditions, for more information regarding it in the context of the *Guhyasamāja*, see Wayman 1977, 155 ff.

consonants, the first being devoid of cause, and so forth, there are the sounds of manifestation, and so forth.[7] Insofar as there is the employment of condensation, and being satisfied with ambrosia, there is cessation, hand-worship, and consecration. Being guarded by the great armor, and worshipping with all mantras, these fourteen realities are concisely stated.[8]

---

[6] These latter two terms relate to the preliminary preparations in maṇḍala construction or preparation—i.e., staking the ground, constructing the vajra wall and the net of arrows, and so forth—as commentators such as Kambala point out. See SN 78a.

[7] This is a translation of the Tibetan *'jug pa sgra la sogs pa*, attested in both translations and in Vīravajra's commentary (PM 245b–246a, SL 143a, PD 448a), which is presumably a translation of *pravṛttinādādīni*, the meaning of which is explained in my translation of Vīravajra's text below. The CS mss. and Bhavabhaṭṭa (Pandey 2002, 588), however, read *pravṛttinādamādīni*, which may represent an erroneous addition of an *-m* termination to add an extra syllable.

[8] Vīravajra provides the following excellent commentary on the first four verses of this chapter, highlighting the "fourteen realities" of the creation stage:

> Having thus explained the method of attaining power, as for the statement of the chapter on the instruction on creation stage visualizations, there is the statement **Now I will expound**, and so forth. **The esoteric instruction very hard to attain** is the fourteen realities of the creation stage. They are **very hard to attain** in the sense that they integrate the stages of meditation of the sūtras which are the definitive meaning spoken by the Blessed Lord, which is not connected with the disputations of men. **Spoken symbolically by the heroes** means that the signs of all buddhas and bodhisattvas were **hidden in the Tantra** in human language by the Blessed Lord.
>
> The following will be an extensive explanation of what was taught succinctly [in the Tantra]. Regarding [his] **garb and the five insignia, and so forth,** the garb is his upper and lower coverings, the elephant and tiger skins, respectively. The **five insignia** excludes the ash [of the six Kāpālika insignia], and **and so forth** indicates the bearing of the six implements and the vajra and bell. This indicates the first reality. Regarding the second reality, the **consort's body** indicates either the *karmamudrā* for lay bodhisattvas, or the *dharma-* or *samayamudrā* for those on the path of liberation. The third reality begins with the production of the sign of the vajra, and concludes with the staking. Having expelled the obstacles, one produces the **net**, i.e., the arrow and vajra canopy, and the net of fiery light. Then the **stakes** are driven. As for the fourth reality, **uttering the vowels and consonants**, the lunar and solar maṇḍalas are visualized in the heart. In their midst is the syllable *hūṁ*, from which is uttered the eight line mantra, along with the mantras of worship, the heroes, and the heroines....
>
> Regarding the fifth reality, **the first being devoid of cause, and so forth,** indicates that *he* is placed in the forehead, *ru* in the throat, and *ka* in the heart. As it is said, "*he* is devoid of causality, *ru* is structure transcended, and *ka* is non-locality"

The excellent man who practices and whose nature is purified of all sins attains the Tathāgata stage.[9] In life after life he is born into the Tathāgata clan and becomes a righteous king. He who is deficient with regard to all of the [good] characteristics and has however many previous sins [will become] the lord of all desires on earth if he meditates constantly on this. Just as if a pot filled with grease is placed in the midst of a fire, the butter in the pot oozes, melts, and in time disappears,[10] likewise, sin is destroyed by

---

(HV 1.7.27; Snellgrove 1959, 2:24–25) one should meditate on the meaning of Heruka in terms of the three doors of liberation, taking these three syllables as the foremost. After that one visualizes the four elements and Mt. Sumeru, and one then inserts one's own consciousness into the abode of the syllable *hūṁ* in the midst of the united solar and lunar [disks] on top of the lotus inside of the palace. Regarding [the sixth reality], **the sounds of manifestation, and so forth**, the **sounds** are the syllables *hūṁ* and *vaṁ*. **And so forth** indicates the vajra, bell, and light rays which project and recollect, turning into the Causal Heruka divine couple. As it is said: "The moon is the mirror-like [wisdom], the sun the wisdom of equality. The syllables and implements are the [wisdom of] discrimination, and the projection and recollection of the light rays is the [wisdom of] accomplishment. The perfected body is the wisdom of reality." (See HV 1.8.6–7; Snellgrove 1959, 2:26–27) Regarding [the seventh reality,] **the employment of condensation**, the buddhas of the ten directions are gathered together and brought into the presence of the Causal Heruka divine couple. Having given rise to the womb-born wheel, the Causal Heruka divine couple melts and condenses into a drop. For this to happen one melts into the drop stimulated by the song of the goddesses of the five wheels. The syllable *he* which has the song is the eighth reality; it is said to be **satisfied with ambrosia**. These goddesses, in order to be free of the method of the melting of Causal Heruka, defeat Mṛtyupati Māra. Resultant Heruka delights the goddesses, hence they are satisfied with ambrosia.

The ninth reality, **cessation**, is the entry of the gnosis hero (*jñānasattva*). The tenth reality is the **hand-worship**, or the donning of the armors of the six heroes and heroines. The eleventh reality is **consecration**, namely, the water, secret, and wisdom-gnosis consecrations. The twelfth reality, **being guarded by the great armor**, is the visualization of the purified body and mind wheels. The thirteenth reality, **mantras**, is the repetition of the mantras of the principle deity and his retinue. The fourteenth reality, **worshipping**, is the offering of worship with the five ambrosias as well as praise and offering cakes. (PD 447b–448b)

[9] Bhavabhaṭṭa comments that "one attains the Tathāgata's stage of gnosis that is characterized by the destruction of all outflows" (Pandey 2002, 589–590: *tāthāgatīṁ ca labhate bhūmim iti sarvāsravakṣayarūpāṁ tāthāgatīṁ jñānabhūmiṁ labhate*).

[10] This translates the text preserved in the CS mss., *dravantaṁ dravate sarpiḥ kālaṁ naśyati bhāṇḍayoḥ*. I take *bhāṇḍayoḥ* to be an idiosyncratic use of the dual case. The Tibetan translations, in place of the indeclinable *kālaṁ*, read "taint" (PM 246a, SL 143b: *dri ma*), which

means of the name "Śrī Heruka,"[11] through meditation, mere reflection, or through reading, recitation, or writing.[12]

One attains the pleasure of heaven or of a universal monarch. At the yogins' time of death,[13] the heroes and yoginīs, Śrī Heruka, and so forth, [appear],[14] their hands occupied with various flowers, having various banners and flags, with the sound of various instruments, and with the offering of various songs. One is conducted from the thought of "death" to the aerial state. Thus the deity, the great heroes, and the yoginīs are difficult to attain on earth. Whoever knows Śrī Heruka's great Tantra yet is not devoted to it will always and forever have poverty and the agony of dissatisfaction.

---

makes less sense, as there is no obvious connection between a pot's taint and the melting of butter.

[11] Bhavabhaṭṭa comments here:

> **Likewise, sin is destroyed** refers to sentient beings who are immersed in the ocean of cyclic existence. Visualize that the totality [of] sinful karma is cast into a pot which is in the form of Śrī Heruka, in the fire of the gnosis of emptiness. Through the destruction of karma that is due to the engagement with the aggregates, and so forth, and characterized by attachment to objects, and so forth, the aggregates, and so forth, become faultless. Now, as for having a fault due to attachment to emptiness, such that one is bereft of purpose, it thus is said: "[Beings] are liberated by means of existence, Vajragarbha of Great Compassion—they are bound by means of the bond of existence and liberated through knowledge of that" (HT 1.10–11; Snellgrove 1959, 2:2–3).
>
> *tathā pāpaṁ vinaśyatīti pātayati saṁsārsāgare sattvān abhiniviṣṭān iti pāpaṁ sāmānyaṁ karma śūnyatājñānavahnau śrīherukākṛtibhāṇḍe ca bhāvyamāne skandhāder niveśitasya grāhyādyabhiniveśalakṣitasya karmaṇaś ca kṣayāt skandhādikaṁ nirdoṣī bhavati / atha ca śūnyatābhiniveśāt tad eva sadoṣaṁ yathāvad arthakriyāvirahāt / tathā cāha—bhāvenaiva vimucyante vajragarbha mahākṛpa / badhyante bhāvena mucyante tatparijñayā / iti /* (Pandey 2002, 590–591; note that the HT reads *bhāvabandhena* rather than *bhāvena*; I have translated the former reading.)

[12] This translates the Tibetan, *bsam gtan sems pa tsam gyis sam // klog cing kha ton bris pa yis /* (PM 246a). The CS mss. read *dhyāne cintitamātraṁ vā pāṭhaṁ svādhyāyalekhanāt*, which is inconsistently declined.

[13] This translates *cyutikāle tu yogināṁ*, which occurs thus in the parallel passage at YS 17.12 (Pandey 1998, 150). The other mss. give close variants of this (A, C: *yogīnāṁ*; B: *yoginaṁ*; Bhavabhaṭṭa [Pandey 2002, 591]: *yogīnā*), and it also accords with the Tibetan translations (PM 246a, SL 143b: *rnal rbyor pa rnams 'pho ba'i tshe*).

[14] The text here, *śrīherukādivīrayoginī*, is singular, although as Bhavabhaṭṭa indicates it should be read as plural (Pandey 2002, 591).

He has a necklace, bracelet, armlet, earrings, and a sacred thread, a throat ornament, a skull rosary, and a sash, with the sound of bells. On a stalk on the summit of the mountain are a universal lotus and the vowels and consonants. [There] he treads upon Gaurī's Lord,[15] his body embraced by the Adamantine Bell.[16] Contemplate the supreme state, the great king Śrī Heruka, endowed with half of twenty-four[17] and with hosts of heroes and yoginīs. In the middle is the one who has yoga, together with the assembly of all heroes and yoginīs.[18] All of them are delighted and have a nondual nature, and they bring about emanation and recollection.[19]

---

[15] This text, *gauryāḥ patiṁ*, refers to the Hindu deities who are under Śrī Heruka's feet, namely Bhairava and Kālarātri. Mardo here gives a literal translation of Gaurī, *dkar mo* (PM 246a). Sumatikīrti and Vīravajra read Umā here, which is an alternate name of Śiva's wife (SL 143b: *dbu ma'i*; PD 449a: *u ma'i*). The correct Sanskrit is given at YS 17.23 (Pandey 1998, 154); the CS mss. and Bhavabhaṭṭa (Pandey 2002, 592) read *gauryā*, which Bhavabhaṭṭa identifies as the third (instrumental) case, but this is clearly incorrect.

[16] This is a translation of the Tibetan, *rdo rje dril bus lus la 'khyud* (PM 246a, SL 143b–144a). The Sanskrit in the CS mss. reads *vajraghaṇṭāṅgaliṅgitam*, which might be emended to *vajraghaṇṭāṅgāliṅgitam* on the basis of the Tibetan. This refers to Śrī Heruka's consort, Vajravārāhī.

[17] This refers to Heruka's twelve arms, according to Vīravajra (PD 449a).

[18] This translates the CS mss.' text, *sarvavīrasya yoginyaḥ saparṣan madhye yogavān*. Note that, as is often the case, *yoginyaḥ* is given in place of *yoginīnāṁ*. This corresponds with Mardo's translation (PM 246a–b: *dpa' bo kun dang rnal 'byor ma'i // 'khor bcas dbus su sbyor ldan pa*), and is close to Vīravajra's (PD 449a: *rnal 'byor kun dang rnal 'byor ma'i // 'khor lo dbus su sbyor ldan pa*) and to Sumatikīrti's (SL 144a: *dpa' bo kun dang rnal 'byor ma'i // 'khor bcas dbus su reg ldan pa*). Bhavabhaṭṭa attests this text, "in the midst" (*madhye*), but also gives a variant here, *manthyā*, which yields the variant text: "He has union with her who is to be rubbed, together with the assembly of all heroes and yoginīs." He also indicates that "she who is to be rubbed" is Vajravārāhī (F 149a.5–6). This is a plausible variant, but one which I have only found in this text.

[19] Vīravajra, quoting this text, comments: "If one wonders what the manifestation body is like, **all of them**—i.e., the principal **nondual** deity couple **together with the assembly**—for the sake of sentient beings, **bring about emanation**, and, having finished this, **recollection**" (PD 449a). "Emanation" and "recollection" refer to the creation stage visualization concerning the emanation of light from the visualized maṇḍala for the purpose of benefiting beings, followed by the recollection of these light rays. "Emanation" here is a translation of *sṛṣṭi* (Tib. *'byin pa*).

The various faithful beings are taught the various methods of practice,[20] and they are instructed through diverse means and with various systems and disciplines.[21] Were one to have faith due to instruction in the profound teaching,[22] it should not be repudiated; the inconceivable reality should be contemplated. With regard to this I have no sense object, nor do I know reality.[23] Yet the great spirits, the completely awakened ones (*saṁbuddhāḥ*) and their offspring,[24] know it. Moreover, the production of the buddhas exists in non-production. The inconceivable, all-pervasive[25] reality lacks loss and gain. Contemplating thus, all of the worldly ones

---

[20] This translates the reading of the CS mss., *caryānānāvidhoditāḥ*. Bhavabhaṭṭa gives an alternate reading here, *nānācaryābhir vibodhitāḥ* (Pandey 2002, 593).

[21] Bhavabhaṭṭa describes the pedagogical background to the final portion of the chapter as follows: "The heroes and yoginīs listen to the teaching for the sake of others. The Blessed Lord was asked to teach by Vajravārāhī, for the sake of the disciples of Śrī Heruka." (Pandey 2002, 593: *vīrā yoginyaś ca parārthārthaṁ dharmaṁ śṛṇvanti / śrīherukavineyānām arthāya bhagavān api vajravārāhyādhyeṣitas*)

[22] Bhavabhaṭṭa describes this as "the instruction on the method of the nonduality of wisdom and art which is the profound teaching" (Pandey 2002, 593: *gambhīradharmasya prajñopāyādvayarūpasya nirdeśo*).

[23] Bhavabhaṭṭa explains here:

> **With regard to this**, i.e., with regard to the elements and the aggregates, **I have no sense object**, i.e., the form of an object, and so forth. Why is this? As it says, **nor do I know reality**—i.e., suchness which is emptiness—by means of the very nature of reality, since there is a contradiction in action with respect to oneself. Thus it is said: "The mind truly does not know the mind." The knowledge which discriminates objects, and so forth, is mind-only, which is emptiness. Thus it is said: "Apart from consciousness there is nothing whatsoever designated as emptiness, on account of which it is held that there is the exception of discrimination."
>
> *nātra dharmeṣu skandheṣu mama viṣayo grāhyādirūpo 'sti / kena kāraṇenety āha yenetyādi / dharmatātathatāśūnyatānāṁ na jānāmi dharmatārūpatvena svātmani kriyāvirodhāt / tathā cāha—na hi cittaṁ cittaṁ jānāti iti / grāhyādiviviktajñānaṁ cittamātraṁ śūnyatā / tad uktam—vijñānāc chūnyatānāma kācid anyā na vidyate / vyatiriktā vyatirekitvaṁ vivekasya yato matam iti.* (Pandey 2002, 594)

[24] That is, *sutāḥ*, which is the nominative plural for both the masculine and feminine forms of the word. According to Bhavabhaṭṭa, this refers to the bodhisattvas (Pandey 2002, 594).

[25] The CS mss. attest here the corrupt reading *sarvacintyā*. Bhavabhaṭṭa, however, reads here *sarvadā* and *acintyā*. He comments: "It is **all-pervasive** because it is always established through its mode of natural, continuous connection" (Pandey 2002, 594: *sarvadeti prakṛtipravāhaprabandharūpeṇa sadāvasthāpayitvāt*).

should not be faulted.[26] Their inconceivable way is the inconceivable play of the buddhas,[27] such that they delight in each and every disposition which manifests in sentient beings, in accordance with the divisions of the Sūtras, and of the Action (*kriyā*), Practice (*caryā*), Yoga, and Secret (*guhya*) [Tantras].[28]

This[29] concludes the fifty-first chapter of the Great King of Yoginī Tantras called the *Śrī-Cakrasamvara*, [30] the primordially established appendix (*uttaratantraṁ*) which is unsurpassed in omniscience achieved through the recitation of the Great Hero Śrī Heruka. It is the king of all

---

[26] Bhavabhaṭṭa explains: "**Contemplating thus,** and taking the awakened and non-awakened to be equal, **all of the worldly ones should not be faulted**" (Pandey 2002, 594: *evaṁ tulayitvā buddhābuddhau samīkṛtya na nindyāḥ sarvalaukikāḥ*).

[27] The word *nāṭaka* means "play" in the sense of a drama. Bhavabhaṭṭa explains this half-verse as follows: "How is **their**—the worldly ones'—established **way inconceivable**? [Because] is it is **the inconceivable play of the buddhas,** i.e., the 'play' in which the buddhas assume various forms." (Pandey 2002, 595: *teṣāṁ laukikānām api gativyavasthitir acintyā kuta ity āha—acintyaṁ buddhanāṭakam iti buddhā eva nānārūpā vyavasthitā iti nāṭakam*)

[28] These two lines, *sūtraṁ kriyābhicaryāṇāṁ yogaguhyaṁ tu bhedataḥ*, are generally understood by the commentators to refer to Buddhist doxography. Usually it is read as referring to the four categories of tantra, with *guhya* interpreted as referring to the Unexcelled Yoga Tantras. This interpretation is somewhat problematic, not accounting for the prefix *abhi-* that inconveniently lies between *kriyā* and *caryā*. There is nothing corresponding to it in the Tibetan translations. Bhavabhaṭṭa, somewhat implausibly, reads it as an abbreviation of *abhidharma*, and correlates the terms to schools of Buddhist thought, culminating in the Yogācāra, with *sūtra* refering to the *sūtrāntāḥ* (Sautrāntika), *kriyā* to the *vibhāṣā* (Vaibhāṣika), *abhidharma* to the *madhyamā* (Madhyamaka), and *yogaguhyaṁ* (the "secret of yoga") to the Yogācāra. Vīravajra's commentary quotes a rather different version of the first line, *ji srid kriya sogs sbyod nas* (PD 449b), evidently reading *kriyādi*. The Tibetan translations differ from the Sanskrit at another point, reading *rnal 'byor gsang mtha'i dbye ba nyid* (PM 246b, SL 144a), which is evidently based on a reading of *yogaguhyāntabhedataḥ*. Sachen reads into these lines an unprecedented six categories, dividing *yogaguhyāntabhedataḥ* and connecting *guhya* to the Unexcelled Yoga Tantras, **anta* to the "Unexcelled Yoginī Tantras," and *bhedataḥ* to "the even further unexcelled yoginī Cakrasamvaras" (*ma'i yang ma bla na med pa'i 'khor lo bde mchog rnams*), perhaps allowing his enthusiasm to carry him to the limits of commentarial plausability (PG 380.2).

[29] This concluding text occurs in the CS mss., Bhavabhaṭṭa's commentary, and the Tibetan translations.

[30] The CS mss. and Bhavabhaṭṭa read *śrīcakrasamvara-nāma* here, which is attested by Sumatikīrti (SL 144b: *dpal 'khor lo sdom pa zhes bya ba'i*). Mardo, however, reads *dpal he ru ka'i nges par brjod pa zhes bya ba*, attesting *śrīherukābhidhāna-nāma*.

teachings,[31] the appendix of the appendix (*uttarottaraṁ*),[32] included within the *Discourse of Śrī Heruka*, the one hundred thousand [stanza] great king of tantras.[33]

---

31 Bhavabhaṭṭa here reads *sarvaśāstrāṇāṁ* (Pandey 2002, 596), a reading supported by the Tibetan translations (PM 246b, SL 144b: *bstan bcos thams cad*). The CS mss., however, read *sarvamantrāṇāṁ*, "of all mantras."

32 I follow Bhavabhaṭṭa in translating this in terms of tantric Buddhist scriptural categories. He comments, succinctly, that "the word **and** shows that it is an **appendix of an appendix** that summarizes the import of other tantras" (Pandey 2002, 596: *cakārāt tantrāntarārtha-samuccāyakam uttarottaraṁ vyākhyātam*).

33 This translates *śrīherukābhidhāne mahātantrarājalakṣāntaḥpāti cottarottaraṁ rājā sarva-śāstrāṇāṁ*, following Bhavabhaṭṭa's commentary: "**included within**...**the end of the one hundred thousand** shows that it occurs within the *Khasama [Tantra]* which has the nature of a 100,000 [stanza text]. This means that it derives from that." (Pandey 2002, 596: *lakṣātmakaṁ khasamaṁ tanmadhyāntaḥ pāto nirgamanaṁ so 'syāstīti lakṣāntaḥpāti*)

Glossaries

English-Sanskrit-Tibetan Glossary

English	Sanskrit	Tibetan
accomplished, achieved	siddha	grub pa
accomplishment, achievement	siddhi	dngos grub
action	kriyā	bya ba
adept	sādhaka	sgrub pa po
aerial state	khecarīpada	mkha' spyod gnas mkha' la 'gro ba'i gnas
affliction	kleśa	nyon mongs
ambrosia	amṛta	bdud rtsi
appendix	uttaratantra	rgyud phyi ma
armor	kavaca	go cha
art	upāya	thabs
asceticism	tapas	dka' thub
astral spirit	graha	gdon
auspicious	śubha	dge ba
background [verse]	nidāna	gleng gzhi
barbarian	mleccha	kla klo
beast	paśu	phyugs
being	sattva	sems dpa'
beneficiary	sādhya	bsgrub bya
benefit, benefiting	anugraha	phen 'dogs
binding	samvara	sdom pa
birth place	yoni	skye gnas
Blessed Lady	bhagavatī	bcom ldan 'das ma
Blessed Lord	bhagavān	bcom ldan 'das
bliss	sukha	bde ba
blood	rakta, rudhira	khrag

body	aṅga	lus
	kāya	sku, lus
	gātra, deha, mūrti, vigraha, śarīra	lus
body wheel	kāyacakra	sku kyi 'khor lo
cake	saṁkulikā	snum 'khur
celestial musician	gandharva	dri za
central channel	avadhūti	rtsa dbu ma
characteristic	lakṣaṇa	mtshan nyid
charnel ground	śmaśāna	dur khrod
chastity	brahmacarya	tshangs spyod
clan	kula	rigs
clanswoman	kulikā	rigs ldan
commitment	samaya	dam tshig
communal enjoyment body	sambhogakāya	longs spyod rdzogs pa'i sku
concentration	samādhi	ting nge 'dzin
conception, conceptualization	vikalpa	rnam par rtog pa
concretion	rocanā	gi wang
conduct	caryā	spyod pa
consecration	abhiṣeka	dbang bskur ba
consort	mudrā, vidyā, prajñā	phyag rgya, rig pa, shes rab
counter-gesture	pratimudrā	phyag rgya'i lan
creation stage	utpattikrama	bskyed rim
cyclic existence	saṁsāra	'khor ba
dead person	preta	yi dags
death	mṛtyu	'chi ba
Death	māra	bdud
demon	rākṣasa	srin po
demoness	rākṣasī	srin mo
destroying	nigraha	tshar gcod
devil	māra	bdud

divinatory image	prasena	pra se na
disciple	śrāvaka	nyan thos
disposition	śīla	mos pa
dissatisfaction	duḥkha	sdug bsngal
distinguishing mark	lakṣaṇa	mtshan nyid
emanation	nirmāṇa	sprul pa
enveloping	sampuṭa	kha sbyar ba
esoteric instruction	āmnāya	man ngag
essence	hṛdaya	snying po
experiential scope	gocara	spyod yul
experiential unity	ekarasa	ro gcig
explanatory tantra	vyākhyātantra	bshad rgyud
Father Tantra		pha rgyud
fee	dakṣiṇā	yon
fervent	kruddha	khros pa
field	kṣetra	zhing
fierce one	krodha	khro bo
fire sacrifice	homa	sbyin sreg
vase	kalaśa	bum pa
flight	khecaratvaṁ	nam mkhar rgyu
floating	khecara	mkha' spyod, mkha' la rgyu ba
flying	khecara	mkha' spyod, mkha' la rgyu ba
	khecarī	mkha' la spyod
fury fire	caṇḍālī	gtum mo
gesture	mudrā	phyag rgya
ghost	preta	yi dags
goblin	pīśāca	sha za
gnosis	jñāna	ye shes
gnosis hero	jñānasattva	ye shes sems dpa'
great consort	mahāmudrā	phyag rgya chen po
great serpent	mahoraga	lto 'phye chen po

habitual propensity	vāsanā	bag chags
happiness	sukha	bde ba
heretic	tīrthika	mu stegs
hero	vīra	dpa' bo
	sattva	sems dpa'
Heruka	heruka	he ru ka, khrag 'thung ba
heteropraxy	vāmācāra	g-yon pa'i kun spyod
inauspicious	aśubha	mi dge ba
insight	vipaśyanā	lhag mthong
insignia	mudrā	phyag rgya
intercourse	sampuṭa	kha sbyar ba
joy	ānanda	dga' ba
joy of cessation	viramānanda	dga' bral
khatvanga staff	khaṭvāṅga	kha ṭvāṁ ga
knowledge	jñāna	she pa
lady	yoṣit	btsun mo
left channel	lalanā	rtsa rkyang ma
life-force	prāṇa	srog
limb	aṅga	yan lag
magical diagram	yantra	'khrul 'khor
manifestation body	nirmāṇakāya	sprul pa'i sku
means of achievement	sādhana	sgrub byed
means of achieving	sādhaka	sgrub byed
meditation, meditative state	dhyāna	bsam gtan
meeting-place	melāpaka	'dus pa
menstruating	puṣpavatī	me tog dang ldan pa
messenger	dūtī	pho nya mo
mind wheel	cittacakra	thugs kyi 'khor lo
Mother Tantra		ma rgyud
natural	sahaja	lhan cig skyes pa
natural joy	sahajānanda	lhan cig skyes pa'i dga' ba

nature	ātman	bdag nyid
	prakṛti	rang bzhin
net, network	jāla	dra ba
non-conceptual	nirvikalpa	rnam par mi rtog pa
non-conceptuality	nirvikalpatvam	mi rtog pa nyid
nondual	advaya	gnyis med
observance	vrata	brtul zhugs
obstacle demon	vināyaka	log 'dren
		rnam par log 'dren
omen	utpāta	ltas ngan
oral instruction	upadeśa	man ngag
origin of things	dharmodaya	chos 'byung ba
penis	liṅga	ling ga
perfected one	siddha	grub pa
perfecting stage	niṣpannakrama	rdzogs rim
power	siddhi	dngos grub
	śaktika	nus pa
practice	caryā	spyod pa
procedure	vidhi	cho ga
quiescence	śamathā	zhi gnas
quintessence	upahṛdaya	nye snying
race	yoni	skye gnas
reality	tattva	de nyid
	dharmatā	chos nyid
red	rakta	dmar po
reality body	dharmakāya	chos kyi sku
right channel	rasanā	rtsa ro ma
rite	vidhi	cho ga
ritual action	karma	las
	kriyā	bya ba
Root Tantra	mūlatantra	rtsa rgyud
sacred knowledge	vidyā	rig pa

sacrificial cake	bali	gtor ma
sacrificial victim	paśu	phyugs
sea monster	makara	chu srin
seal	mudrā	phyag rgya
seat	pīṭha	gnas
secret	guhya, rahasya	gsang ba
seed syllable	bīja	sa bon
semen	śukra	khu ba
seminal essence	bodhicitta	byang chub sems
seminal fluid	retas	rdzas
sentient being	sattva	sems dpa'
serpent deity	nāga	klu
serpent	uraga	lto 'phye
	sarpa	sbrul
solitary buddhas	pratyekabuddha	rang rgyal ba
speech wheel	vākcakra	gsung gi 'khor lo
spell	vidyā	rig pa
sphere of reality	dharmadhātu	chos kyi dbyings
spirit of awakening	bodhicitta	byang chub sems
spiritual discipline	sādhana	sgrub byed
strategy	upāya	thabs
subsidiary charnel ground	upaśmaśāna	nye ba'i dur khrod
subsidiary field	upakṣetra	nye ba'i zhing
subsidiary meeting-place	upamelāpaka	nye bar 'dus pa
subsidiary seat	upapīṭha	nye gnas
suffering	duḥkha	sdug bsngal
supreme bliss	samvara	bde mchog
supreme joy	paramānanda	mchog dga'
tantric feast	gaṇacakra	tshogs kyi 'khor lo
titan	asura, dānava	lha min
triple wheel	tricakra	'khor lo gsum
triple world	triloka, trailokya	'jig rten gsum

Unexcelled Yoga	*anuttarayoga	rnal 'byor bla med
unification	samāyoga	mnyam 'byor
union	yoga	rnal 'byor
	saṁyoga	yang dag 'byor
	samvara	sdom pa
universal monarch	cakravartin	'khor los sgyur ba
untimely death	apamṛtyu	dus min 'chi
uterine blood	rakta, rajas	khrag
vassal lord	sāmanta	rgyal phran
vermilion	rakta	dmar
victim	sādhya	bsgrub bya
victor	jina	rgyal ba
vow	samvara	sdom pa
vulva	yoni	skye gnas
	dharmodaya	chos 'byung ba
	bhaga	bha ga
war machine	yantra	'khrul 'khor
wisdom	prajñā	shes rab
yogic posture	yantra	'khrul 'khor
zombie	vetāla	ro langs

Sanskrit-Tibetan-English Glossary

aṅga	lus	body
	yan lag	limb
advaya	gnyis med	nondual
anugraha	phen 'dogs	benefit, benefiting
apamṛtyu	dus min 'chi	untimely death
abhiṣeka	dbang bskur ba	consecration
amṛta	bdud rtsi	ambrosia
avadhūti	rtsa dbu ma	central channel
aśubha	mi dge ba	inauspicious
asura	lha min	titan
ātman	bdag nyid	self, nature, oneself
ānanda	dga' ba	joy
āmnāya	man ngag	esoteric instruction
uttaratantra	rgyud phyi ma	appendix
utpattikrama	skyed rim	creation stage
utpāta	ltas ngan	omen
upakṣetra	nye ba'i zhing	subsidiary field
upadeśa	man ngag	oral instruction
upapīṭha	nye gnas	subsidiary seat
upamelāpaka	nye bar 'dus pa	subsidiary meeting-place
upaśmaśāna	nye ba'i dur khrod	subsidiary charnel ground
upahṛdaya	nye snying	quintessence
upāya	thabs	art, strategy
uraga	lto 'phye	serpent
ekarasa	ro gcig	experiential unity
karma	las	ritual action
kalaśa	bum pa	vase
kavaca	go cha	armor
kāya	sku, lus	body
kāyacakra	sku kyi 'khor lo	body wheel

kula	rigs	clan
kulikā	rigs ldan	clanswoman
kriyā	bya ba	action, ritual action
kruddha	khros pa	fervent
krodha	khro bo	fierce one
kleśa	nyon mongs	affliction
kṣetra	zhing	field
khaṭvāṅga	kha ṭvāṁ ga	khatvanga staff
khecara	mkha' spyod, mkha' l rgyu ba	flying, floating
khecaratvaṁ	nam mkhar rgyu	flight
khecarī	mkha' la spyod	flying
khecarīpada	mkha' spyod gnas, mkha' la 'gro ba'i gnas	aerial state
gaṇacakra	tshogs kyi 'khor lo	tantric feast
gandharva	dri za	celestial musician
gātra	lus	body
guhya	gsang ba	secret
gocara	spyod yul	experiential scope
graha	gdon	astral spirit
cakravartin	'khor los sgyur ba	universal monarch
cakrasamvara	'khor lo sdom pa	
caṇḍālī	gtum mo	fury fire
caryā	spyod pa	conduct, practice
cittacakra	thugs kyi 'khor lo	mind wheel
jāla	dra ba	net, network
jina	rgyal ba	victor
jñāna	ye shes	gnosis
	shes pa	knowledge
jñānasattva	ye shes sems dpa'	gnosis hero
tattva	de nyid	reality
tapas	dka' thub	asceticism
tricakra	'khor lo gsum	triple wheel

triloka, trailokya	'jig rten gsum	triple world
ḍākinī	mkha' 'gro ma, phra men ma	
dakṣiṇā	yon	fee
dānava	lha min	titan
duḥkha	sdug bsngal	dissatisfaction, suffering
dūtī	pho nya mo	messenger
deha	lus	body
dharmakāya	chos kyi sku	reality body
dharmatā	chos nyid	reality
dharmadhātu	chos kyi dbyings	sphere of reality
dharmodaya	chos 'byung ba	origin of things, vulva
dhyāna	bsam gtan	meditation, meditative state
nāga	klu	serpent deity
nigraha	tshar gcod	destroying
nidāna	gleng gzhi	background [verse]
nirmāṇa	sprul pa	emanation
nirmāṇakāya	sprul pa'i sku	manifestation body
nirvikalpa	rnam par mi rtog pa	non-conceptual
nirvikalpatvam	mi rtog pa nyid	non-conceptuality
niṣpannakrama	rdzogs rim	perfecting stage
paramānanda	mchog dga'	supreme joy
paśu	phyugs	beast, sacrificial victim
pīṭha	gnas	seat
pīśāca	sha za	goblin
puṣpavatī	me tog dang ldan pa	menstruating
prakṛti	rang bzhin	nature
prajñā	shes rab	wisdom, consort
pratimudrā	phyag rgya'i lan	counter-gesture
prasena	pra se na	divinatory image
prāṇa	srog	life-force
preta	yi dags	ghost, dead person

bali	gtor ma	sacrificial cake
bīja	sa bon	seed syllable
bodhicitta	byang chub sems	spirit of awakening, seminal essence
brahmacarya	tshangs spyod	chastity
bhaga	bha ga	vulva
bhagavatī	bcom ldan 'das ma	Blessed Lady
bhagavān	bcom ldan 'das	Blessed Lord
makara	chu srin	sea monster
mahāmudrā	phyag rgya chen po	great consort
mahoraga	lto 'phye chen po	great serpent
māra	bdud	devil, Death
mudrā	phyag rgya	gesture, consort, seal, insignia
mūrti	lus	body
mūlatantra	rtsa rgyud	Root Tantra
mṛtyu	'chi ba	death
melāpaka	'dus pa	meeting-place
mleccha	kla klo	barbarian
yantra	'khrul 'khor	magical diagram, yogic posture, war machine
yoga	rnal 'byor	union
yogin	rnal 'byor pa	
yoginī	rnal 'byor ma	
yoni	skye gnas	vulva, birth place, race
yoṣit	btsun mo	lady
rakta	dmar, dmar po, khrag	red, vermilion, blood, uterine blood
rajas	khrag	uterine blood
rasanā	rtsa ro ma	right channel
rahasya	gsang ba	secret
rākṣasa	srin po	demon
rākṣasī	srin mo	demoness

rudhira	khrag	blood
retas	seminal fluid	rdzas
rocanā	gi wang	concretion
lakṣaṇa	mtshan nyid	characteristic, distinguishing mark
lalanā	rtsa rkyang ma	left channel
liṅga	ling ga	penis
vākcakra	gsung gi 'khor lo	speech wheel
vāmācāra	g-yon pa'i kun spyod	heteropraxy
vāsanā	bag chags	habitual propensity
vikalpa	rnam par rtog pa	conception, conceptualization
vigraha	lus	body
vidyā	rig pa	consort, spell, sacred knowledge
vidhi	cho ga	procedure, rite
vināyaka	log 'dren, rnam par log 'dren	obstacle demon
vipaśyanā	lhag mthong	insight
viramānanda	dga' bral	joy of cessation
vīra	dpa' bo	hero
vetāla	ro langs	zombie
vyākhyātantra	bshad rgyud	explanatory tantra
vrata	brtul zhugs	observance
śaktika	nus pa	power
śamathā	zhi gnas	quiescence
śarīra	lus	body
śīla	mos pa	disposition
śukra	khu ba	semen
śubha	dge ba	auspicious
śmaśāna	dur khrod	charnel ground
śrāvaka	nyan thos	disciple
sattva	sems dpa'	(sentient) being, hero
samaya	dam tshig	commitment

samādhi	ting nge 'dzin	concentration
samāyoga	mnyam 'byor	unification
saṁkalpa	rnam par rtog pa	conception, conceptualization
saṁkulikā	snum 'khur	cake
sampuṭa	kha sbyar ba	enveloping, intercourse
saṁyoga	yang dag 'byor	union
samvara	sdom pa	binding, sanctuary, vow, union
	bde mchog	supreme bliss
saṁsāra	'khor ba	cyclic existence
sarpa	sbrul	serpent
sahaja	lhan cig skyes pa	natural
sahajānanda	lhan cig skyes pa'i dga' ba	natural joy
sādhaka	sgrub pa po	adept
	sgrub byed	means of achieving
sādhana	sgrub byed	means of achievement, spiritual discipline
sādhya	bsgrub bya	victim, beneficiary
sāmanta	rgyal phran	vassal lord
siddha	grub pa	accomplished, achieved, perfected one
siddhi	dngos grub	power, accomplishment, achievement
sukha	bde ba	bliss, happiness
hṛdaya	snying po	essence
heruka	he ru ka, khrag 'thung ba	Heruka
homa	sbyin sreg	fire sacrifice

Tibetan-Sanskrit-English Glossary

Tibetan	Sanskrit	English
kla klo	mleccha	barbarian
klu	nāga	serpent deity
dka' thub	tapas	asceticism
sku	kāya	body
skye gnas	yoni	vulva, birth place, race
skyed rim	utpattikrama	creation stage
kha ṭvāṁ ga	khaṭvāṅga	khatvanga staff
kha sbyar ba	sampuṭa	enveloping, intercourse
khu ba	śukra	semen
khrag	rakta	blood, uterine blood
	rajas	uterine blood
	rudhira	blood
khro bo	krodha	fierce one
khros pa	kruddha	fervent
mkha' 'gro ma	ḍākinī	
mkha' spyod	khecara	flying, floating
mkha' spyod gnas, mkha' la 'gro ba'i gnas	khecarīpada	aerial state
mkha' la rgyu ba	khecara	flying, floating
'khor ba	saṁsāra	cyclic existence
'khor lo sdom pa	cakrasamvara	"binding of the wheels"
'khor lo gsum	tricakra	triple wheel
'khor los sgyur ba	cakravartin	universal monarch
'khrul 'khor	yantra	magical diagram, yogic posture, war machine
gi wang	rocanā	concretion
go cha	kavaca	armor
grub pa	siddha	accomplished, achieved, perfected one
gleng gzhi	nidāna	background [verse]

dga' ba	ānanda	joy
dga' bral	viramānanda	joy of cessation
dge ba	śubha	auspicious
rgyal phran	sāmanta	vassal lord
rgyal ba	jina	victor
rgyud phyi ma	uttaratantra	appendix
sgrub pa po	sādhaka	adept
sgrub byed	sādhaka	means of achieving
	sādhana	means of achievement
bsgrub bya	sādhya	victim, beneficiary
dngos grub	siddhi	accomplishment, achievement, power
bcom ldan 'das	bhagavān	Blessed Lord
bcom ldan 'das ma	bhagavatī	Blessed Lady
chu srin	makara	sea monster
cho ga	vidhi	procedure, rite
chos kyi dbyings	dharmadhātu	sphere of reality
chos kyi sku	dharmakāya	reality body
chos nyid	dharmatā	reality
chos 'byung ba	dharmodaya	origin of things, vulva
mchog dga'	paramānanda	supreme joy
'chi ba	mṛtyu	death
'jig rten gsum	triloka, trailokya	triple world
nyan thos	śrāvaka	disciple
nye snying	upahṛdaya	quintessence
nye gnas	upapīṭha	subsidiary seat
nye ba'i dur khrod	upaśmaśāna	subsidiary charnel ground
nye ba'i zhing	upakṣetra	subsidiary field
nye bar 'dus pa	upamelāpaka	subsidiary meeting-place
nyon mongs	kleśa	affliction
gnyis med	advaya	nondual
mnyaṃ 'byor	samāyoga	unification

snying po	hṛdaya	essence
ting nge 'dzin	samādhi	concentration
gtum mo	caṇḍālī	fury fire
gtor ma	bali	sacrificial cake
ltas ngan	utpāta	omen
lto 'phye	uraga	serpent
lto 'phye chen po	mahoraga	great serpent
brtul zhugs	vrata	observance
thabs	upāya	art, strategy
thugs kyi 'khor lo	cittacakra	mind wheel
dam tshig	samaya	commitment
dur khrod	śmaśāna	charnel ground
dus min 'chi	apamṛtyu	untimely death
de nyid	tattva	reality
dra ba	jāla	net, network
dri za	gandharva	celestial musician
gdon	graha	astral spirit
bdag nyid	ātman	self, nature, oneself
bdud	māra	devil, Death
bdud rtsi	amṛta	ambrosia
bde mchog	samvara	supreme bliss
bde ba	sukha	bliss, happiness
'dus pa	melāpaka	meeting-place
sdug bsngal	duḥkha	dissatisfaction, suffering
sdom pa	samvara	binding, sanctuary, vow, union
nam mkhar rgyu	khecaratvaṁ	flight
nus pa	śaktika	power
gnas	pīṭha	seat
rnam par rtog pa	vikalpa, saṁkalpa	conception, conceptualization
rnam par mi rtog pa	nirvikalpa	non-conceptual
rnam par log 'dren	vināyaka	obstacle demon

rnal 'byor	yoga	union
rnal 'byor pa	yogin	
rnal 'byor bla med	*anuttarayoga	Unexcelled Yoga
rnal 'byor ma	yoginī	
snum 'khur	saṁkulikā	cake
pra se na	prasena	divinatory image
dpa' bo	vīra	hero
spyod pa	caryā	conduct
spyod yul	gocara	experiential scope
sprul pa	nirmāṇa	emanation
sprul pa'i sku	nirmāṇakāya	manifestation body
pha rgyud		Father Tantra
phen 'dogs	anugraha	benefit, benefiting
pho nya mo	dūtī	messenger
phyag rgya	mudrā	gesture, consort, seal, insignia
phyag rgya chen po	mahāmudrā	great consort
phyag rgya'i lan	pratimudrā	counter-gesture
phyugs	paśu	beast, sacrificial victim
phra men ma	ḍākinī	
bag chags	vāsanā	habitual propensity
bum pa	kalaśa	vase
byang chub sems	bodhicitta	spirit of awakening, seminal essence
dbang bskur ba	abhiṣeka	consecration
sbyin sreg	homa	fire sacrifice
sbrul	sarpa	serpent
bha ga	bhaga	vulva
ma rgyud		Mother Tantra
man ngag	upadeśa	oral instruction
	āmnāya	esoteric instruction
mi dge ba	aśubha	inauspicious
mi rtog pa nyid	nirvikalpatvam	non-conceptuality

mu stegs	tīrthika	heretic
me tog dang ldan pa	puṣpavatī	menstruating
mos pa	śīla	disposition
dmar	rakta	vermilion
dmar po	rakta	red
btsun mo	yoṣit	lady
rtsa rkyang ma	lalanā	left channel
rtsa rgyud	mūlatantra	Root Tantra
rtsa dbu ma	avadhūti	central channel
rtsa ro ma	rasanā	right channel
tshangs spyod	brahmacarya	chastity
tshar gcod	nigraha	destroying
tshogs kyi 'khor lo	gaṇacakra	tantric feast
mtshan nyid	lakṣaṇa	characteristic, distinguishing mark
rdzas	retas	seminal fluid
rdzogs rim	niṣpannakrama	perfecting stage
zhi gnas	śamathā	quiescence
zhing	kṣetra	field
yan lag	aṅga	limb
yang dag 'byor	saṁyoga	union
yi dags	preta	ghost, dead person
ye shes	jñāna	gnosis
ye shes sems dpa'	jñānasattva	gnosis hero
yon	dakṣiṇā	fee
rang bzhin	prakṛti	nature
rig pa	vidyā	consort, spell, sacred knowledge
rigs	kula	clan
rigs ldan	kulikā	clanswoman
ro gcig	ekarasa	experiential unity
ro langs	vetāla	zombie
las	karma	ritual action

ling ga	liṅga	penis
lus	aṅga, kāya, gātra, deha, mūrti, vigraha, śarīra	body
log 'dren	vināyaka	obstacle demon
sha za	pīśāca	goblin
shes pa	jñāna	knowledge
shes rab	prajñā	wisdom, consort
bshad rgyud	vyākhyātantra	explanatory tantra
sa bon	bīja	seed syllable
sems dpa'	sattva	(sentient) being, hero
srin po	rākṣasa	demon
srin mo	rākṣasī	demoness
srog	prāṇa	life-force
gsang ba	guhya, rahasya	secret
gsung gi 'khor lo	vākcakra	speech wheel
bsam gtan	dhyāna	meditation, meditative state
lha min	asura, dānava	titan
lhag mthong	vipaśyanā	insight
lhan cig skyes pa	sahaja	natural
lhan cig skyes pa'i dga' ba	sahajānanda	natural joy

Conspectus Siglorum

In the notes both to this translation and also the introduction that precedes it I have employed a number of *sigla* for the sake of brevity. The *sigla* that consist of single letters represent Sanskrit manuscripts that I have consulted in preparing my edition and translation of the root text. The *sigla* that consist of two letters represent Sanskrit and Tibetan texts that I have consulted. Regarding the latter, I first list the Tibetan CS translations that I have consulted, followed by a list of the commentaries. I provide the full bibliographic information for the latter in the bibliography following the translation. I cite a published edition by means of the editor's name and date of publication.

Sanskrit Manuscripts

A *Śrīherukābhidhāna*. Oriental Institute in Vadodara (ms. #13290). A palm-leaf manuscript written in Bhujimol variety of Nevārī script. No date, but likely dates to the twelfth or thirteenth century. It consisted of thirty-eight folia, eleven of which are lost (fols. 15, 18–22, 28–31, and 36).

B *Śrīherukābhidhāna*. Oriental Institute in Vadodara (ms. #13285). A Nepali paper manuscript written in Devanāgarī script. It contains 26 folia, and follows the pagination of ms. A. It is dated N. S. 1050, 1930 CE.

C *Śrīherukābhidhāna*. Kesar Library in Kathmandu (ms. #410). A Nepali paper manuscript in Devanāgarī script. It contains 25 folia, and follows the pagination of ms. A. It has no date, but it appears to have been written by the same hand as ms. B, and it is most certainly a twentieth-century copy.

D Jayabhadra. *Cakrasamvarapañjikā*. Institute for Advanced Studies of World Religions (Carmel, NY) microfiche no. MBB-II-75. Nepali paper, Devanāgarī script. Dated N. S. 1031, 1911 CE. A complete commentary on the root text.

E Jayabhadra. *Cakrasamvarapañjikā*. Institute for Advanced Studies of World Religions (Carmel, NY) microfiche no. MBB-I-122. Consists of 37 folia on Nepali paper, Nevārī script. No date. An older but incomplete version of Jayabhadra's commentary; ends in the middle of commenting on ch. 35 of the root text.

F Bhavabhaṭṭa. *Cakrasamvaravivṛtti*. Institute for Advanced Studies of World Religions (Carmel, NY) microfiche no. MBB-I-33. Consists of 153 folia on palm-leaves in the Bhujimol variety of Nevārī script. No date. A complete commentary on the root text.

G Bhavabhaṭṭa. *Cakrasamvaravivṛtti*. Institute for Advanced Studies of World Religions (Carmel, NY) microfiche no. MBB-I-70. Consists of 139 folia on Nepali paper, Nevārī script. No date. A complete commentary on the root text.

H *Abhidhānottara Tantra*. Institute for Advanced Studies of World Religions (Carmel, NY) microfiche no. MBB-I-100. Incomplete; consisted of a total of 194 folia, 6 of which are missing. Written on palm leaves in Bhujimol script by the scribe Paramānanda. Dated N. S. 258, 1138 CE.

I *Abhidhānottara Tantra*. Institute for Advanced Studies of World Religions (Carmel, NY) microfiche no. MBB-I-26. Consists of 92 folia on Nepali paper in Nevārī script. Dated N. S. 863, 1743 CE.[1]

J *Abhidhānottara Tantra*. A late ms. of 160 folia in Devanāgarī on Nepali paper, reproduced in Lokesh Chandra, ed. *Abhidhānottara-Tantra: A Sanskrit Manuscript from Nepal*. Śata-piṭaka series vol. 263. New Delhi: Sharada Rani, 1981.[2]

---

[1] The date of this manuscript is unclear, and may be incorrect. See Kalff 1979, 261 n. 2. However, the Nevārī script employed would not be out of place in the eighteenth century.

[2] The colophon of this ms. contains the date *samvat* 761. Usually, Nepali ms. use the Nepalese Samvat, but this would date the text to 1641 CE, which seems too early for a Devanāgarī text in Nepal. The colophon does not specify which *samvat* is indicated here, and also contains an additional anomaly, which is the presence of two *daṇḍa* between *samvat* and the date. Perhaps the date should read 1761, which, if counting from the beginning of the Vikram, era, would yield a date of 1819 CE, a more appropriate date for this ms.

Tibetan CS Translations

PM *Tantrarāja-śrīlaghusamvara-nāma. rgyud kyi rgyal po dpal bde mchog nyung ngu zhes bya ba.* Trans. by Padmākara and Rin-chen bZang-po, rev. by Prajñākīrti and Marpa Chos-kyi dbang-phyug. Tōh. 368, sDe-dge Kangyur rgyud 'bum vol. ka, 213b–246b; facsimile edition of the 18th century redaction of Situ Chos-kyi 'byung-gnas, Delhi, 1978.

SL *Laghusamvara-tantrarāja, bde mchog nyung ngu rgyud kyi rgyal po.* Trans. by Padmākara and Rin-chen bZang-po, rev. by Sumatikīrti and Locāna bLo-gros-grags. Phug-brag manuscript bka' 'gyur, Library of Tibetan Works and Archives (Dharamsala, H.P.); Institute for Advanced Studies of World Religions (Carmel, NY) microfiche no. Lmpj 016,901; vol. nga, 145a–191a.

Other Texts[3]

AN Vilāsavajra's *Ārya-Nāmasaṁgītiṭīkā-mantrārthāvalokinī-nāma*

AU *Abhidhānottaratantra*

AV Atīśa Dīpaṁkaraśrījñāna's *Abhisamayavibhaṅga*

BA Lūipa's *Śrībhagavad-abhisamaya*

CP Bhavabhaṭṭa's *Śrī Cakrasamvarapañjikā*

CS *Cakrasamvara Tantra*

DM *Ḍākārṇava-mahāyoginītantrarāja*

DS Bu-ston's *bde mchog nyung ngu rgyud kyi spyi rnam don gsal*

HA *Herukābhyudaya*

HV *Hevajra Mahātantrarājā*

---

3 Here I give only the full names of the texts; for the full references see the bibliography below.

IC Indrabhūti's *Śrīcakrasamvaratantrarāja-samvarasamuccaya-nāma-vṛtti*

JS The *Samayoga*, i.e., *Sarvabuddhasamayogaḍākinījālasamvara-nāma-uttaratantra*

KS Tsong Khapa's *bde mchog bsdus pa'i rgyud kyi rgya cher bshad pa sbas pa'i don kun gsal ba*

MP Jayabhadra's *Śrīcakrasamvara-mūlatantra-pañjikā*

NS Bu-ston's *bde mchog rtsa rgyud kyi rnam bshad gsang ba'i de kho na nyid gsal bar byed pa*

PD Vīravajra's *Padārthaprakāśikā-nāma-śrīsamvaramūlatantraṭīkā*

PG Sachen Kun-dga' snying-po's *dpal 'khor lo bde mchog gi rtsa ba'i rgyud kyi ṭīka mu tig phreng ba*

RG Durjayacandra's *Ratnagaṇa-nāma-pañjika*

SC Śūraṅgavajra's *Mūlatantrahṛdaya-saṁgrahābhidhānottaratantra-mūla-mūla-vṛtti*

SM Bhavyakīrti's *Śrīcakrasamvarapañjikā-śūramanojñā*

SN Kambala's *Sādhananidāna-śrīcakrasamvara-nāma-pañjikā*

SP *Sampuṭa-nāma-mahātantra*

SS Devagupta's *Śrīcakrasamvara-sarvasādhanaṁ-sanna-nāma-ṭīkā*

ST Vīravajra's *Samantaguṇaśālina-nāma-ṭīkā*

SU *Mahāsamvarodaya-tantrarāja*

TV *Śāśvatavajra (rtag-pa'i rdo-rje)'s *Śrītattvaviśada-nāma-śrīsamvaravṛtti*

UN Tathāgatarakṣita's *Ubhayanibandha*

VD *Vajraḍāka-nāma-mahātantrarāja*

YS *Yoginīsaṁcāra*

Bibliography

This bibliography is divided into the following sections: Indian Texts (in Sanskrit or Tibetan translation), Indigenous Tibetan Texts, Chinese Texts from the Taishō Canon, Other Chinese Texts, and Modern Sources. The Indian Texts are listed in the order of the Sanskrit alphabet, under the name of the author when there is authorial attribution, and under the title when not. When I refer to the text by a shortened form of its name, that is listed first, followed by the full form of the name. Indigenous Tibetan texts are listed under the author's name in Tibetan alphabetical order. The texts from the Taishō Canon are listed in the order of their enumeration. Modern sources are listed in order of the Roman alphabet. Editions and translations of Sanskrit and Tibetan texts are listed in this section under the name of the primary editor and/or translator.

Indian Texts (in Sanskrit or Tibetan translation)

Editions Consulted

DK, DT: sDe-dge *bka'-'gyur* and *bstan-'gyur*, facsimile edition of the 18th century redaction of Situ Chos-kyi 'byung-gnas, Delhi, 1978. Numbers from Tōhoku (Tōh.) catalogue (Tokyo, 1934).

QK, QT: *bka'-'gyur* and *bstan-'gyur* of the Beijing edition of the Kangyur and Tengyur prepared in 1737 under the Qianlong emperor, from the modern reprint. Numbers from Otani catalogue (PTT) (Kyoto, 1961).

Atīśa Dīpaṁkaraśrījñāna. *Abhisamayavibhaṅga* (AV). Tōh. 1490, DT rgyud 'grel vol zha 186a–202b.

———. *Bodhipathapradīpa*. Tōh. 3947, DT dbu ma vol. khi 238a–241a.

———. *Bodhimārgadīpapañjikā*. Tōh. 3948, DT dbu ma vol. khi 241a–293a.

Abhayākaragupta. *Niṣpannayogāvalī*. Sanskrit edited in Bhattacharyya 1949.

———. *Śrīsampuṭatantrarājaṭīkāmnāyamañjarī-nāma*. Tōh. 1198, DT rgyud 'grel vol. cha, 1b–316a.

Abhidhānottaratantra (AU). Tōh. 369, DK rgyud 'bum vol. ka, 247a–370a. Selected chapters of Sanskrit text edited and translated in Kalff 1979.

Asaṅga. *Mahāyāna-sūtrālakāra*. Sanskrit edited in Bagchi 1970.

Ānandagarbha. *Guhyasamājamahātantrarājaṭīkā*. Tōh. 1917, DT rgyud 'grel vol. bi, 1b–81a.

Indranāla. *Sarvabuddhasamayogaḍākinījālasamvaratantrārthodaraṭīkā*. Tōh. 1659, DT rgyud 'grel vol. ra, 245a–389a.

Indrabhūti. *Jñānasiddhi*. Tōh. 2219. Sanskrit and Tibetan edited in Samdhong and Dwivedi 1987, 89–154, 145–244.

———. *Śrīcakrasamvara-tantrarāja-samvarasamuccaya-nāma-vṛtti* (IC). Tōh. 1413, DT rgyud 'grel vol. tsa, 1a–119b.

Kambala. *Sādhananidāna-śrīcakrasamvara-nāma-pañjikā* (SN). Tōh. 1401, DT rgyud 'grel vol. ba, 1b–78a; PTT 2161, QT vol. 51, 189.5–201.1.

*Candrakumāra. (*zla-ba gzhon-nu*). *Herukābhyudaya-mahāyoginītantrarāja-katipayākṣarapañjikā*. Tōh. 1421, DT rgyud 'grel vol. wa, 101b–120a.

Cakrasamvara Tantra (CS), also known as the *Śrīherukābhidhāna* and *Tantrarāja-śrīlaghusamvara-nāma*. Tōh. 368, DK rgyud 'bum vol. ka, 213b–246b. Sanskrit and Tibetan edited in Pandey 2002.

Jayabhadra. *Śrīcakrasamvara-mūlatantra-pañjikā* (MP). Tōh. 1406, DT rgyud 'grel vol. ma, 41a–69a.

Ḍākārṇava-mahāyoginītantrarāja (DM). Tōh. 372, DK rgyud-'bum, vol. kha, 137a–264b.

Tattvasaṁgraha. *Sarvatathāgatatattvasaṁgraha-nāma-mahāyāna-sūtra*. Tōh. 479, DK rgyud 'bum vol. nya, 1b–142a. Sanskrit edited in Yamada 1981.

Tripiṭakamāla. *Nayatrayapradīpa*. Tōh. 3707, DT rgyud 'grel vol. tsu, 6b–26b.

Tathāgatarakṣita. *Ubhayanibandha* (UN). Tōh. 1409. DT rgyud 'grel vol. ma, 207a–253a.

———. *Yoginīsaṁcāranibandha.* Tōh. 1422, DT rgyud 'grel vol. wa, 120a–139a.

Dārika. *Śrīsamvarasādhana-tattvasaṁgraha-nāma.* Tōh. 1429, DT rgyud 'grel vol.wa, 197b–203b.

Durjayacandra. *Ratnagaṇa-nāma-pañjika* (RG). Tōh. 1404, DT rgyud 'grel vol. ba, 246b–315a.

Devakulamahāmati, *Ḍākinīvajrajāla-tantrarāja-tattvapauṣṭikapañjika-nāma.* Tōh. 1196, DT rgyud 'grel vol. ca, 54a–94b.

Devagupta. *Śrīcakrasamvara-sarvasādhanaṁ-sanna-nāma-ṭīkā* (SS). Tōh. 1407, DT vol. ma, 69a–156b; PTT 2123, QT vol. 49, 33.5–73.1.

Dharmakīrti. *Pramāṇavārttikakārikā* (Tōh. 4210), *Pramāṇavārttikavṛtti* (Tōh. 4216). Chapter one edited in Gnoli 1960.

Padmavajra. *Śrīḍākārṇavamahāyoginī-tantrarāja-vāhikaṭīkā.* Tōh. 1419, DT rgyud 'grel vol. dza, 1b–318a.

Bhavabhaṭṭa. *Śrīcakrasamvarapañjikā* (CP). Tōh. 1403, DT rgyud 'grel vol. ba, 141a–246b; PTT 2119. Sanskrit and Tibetan edited in Pandey 2002.

Bhavyakīrti. *Śrīcakrasamvarapañjikā-śūramanojñā-nāma* (SM). Tōh. 1405, DT rgyud 'grel vol. ma, 1–41a.

Buddhaguhya. *Ārya-subāhuparipṛcchā-nāma-tantrapiṇḍārthavṛtti.* Tōh. 2617. DT *rgyud-'grel* vol. thu, 38a–54b.

Mañjuśrīmūlatantra. Tōh. 543, DK rgyud 'bum vol. na, 88a–334a. Sanskrit edited in Vaidya 1964.

Mahāsamvarodaya-tantrarāja (SU). Tōh. 373, DK rgyud 'bum vol. kha, 265a–311a. Sanskrit and Tibetan partially edited in Tsuda 1974.

Māyājāla-mahātantrarāja. Tōh. 466, DK rgyud 'bum vol. ja, 94b–134a.

Yoginīsaṁcāra (YS). Tōh. 375, DK rgyud 'bum vol. ga, 34a–44b. Sanskrit and Tibetan edited in Pandey 1998.

Lakṣmīṁkarā. *Advayasiddhi.* Sanskrit and Tibetan edited in Samdhong and Dwivedi 1987.

Laṅkāvatārasūtra. Tōh. 107. DK mdo sde vol. ca, 56a–191b. Sanskrit edited in Vaidya 1963.

Lūipa. *Śrībhagavad-abhisamaya* (BA). Tōh. 1427, DT rgyud 'grel vol. wa, 186b–193a.

Vajraḍāka-nāma-mahātantrarāja (VD). Tōh. 370, DK rgyud-'bum vol. kha, 1b–125a.

Vajrapañjara. Āryaḍākinīvajrapañjara-mahātantrarājakalpa. Tōh. 419, DK rgyud 'bum vol. nga, 30a–65b.

Vilāsavajra. *Ārya-nāmasaṁgītiṭīkā-mantrārthāvalokinī-nāma* (AN). Tōh. 2533, DT rgyud 'grel vol. khu, 27b–115b.

Vīravajra. *Padārthaprakāśikā-nāma-śrīsamvaramūlatantraṭīkā* (PD). Tōh. 1412, DT rgyud 'grel vol. ma, 353b–450a. PTT 2128, QT vol. 49, 162.2–204.5.

———. *Samantaguṇaśālina-nāma-ṭīkā* (ST). Tōh. 1408, DT rgyud 'grel vol. ma, 156b–207a; PTT 2124, QT vol. 49, 73.1–95.4.

*Śāśvatavajra (rtag-pa'i rdo-rje). *Śrītattvaviśada-nāma-śrīsamvaravṛtti* (TV). Tōh. 1410, DT rgyud 'grel vol. ma, 253a–352a.

Śūraṅgavajra. *Mūlatantrahṛdayasaṁgrahābhidhānottaratantramūlamūlavṛtti* (SC). Tōh. 1414, DT rgyud 'grel vol. tsa, 120a–232a.

Sampuṭa-nāma-mahātantra (SP). Tōh. 381, DK rgyud 'bum vol. ga, 73b–158b. Sanskrit and Tibetan of first *kalpa* 1 edited in Skorupski 1996.

Samayoga. Sarvabuddhasamayogaḍākinījālasamvara-nāma-uttaratantra (JS). Tōh. 366, DK vol. ka, 151b–193a.

Sarvatathāgatakāyavākcittarahasya-guhyasamāja-nāma-mahākalparāja. Tōh. 442, 443. DK rgyud 'bum vol. ca, 90a–157b. Sanskrit edited in Matsunaga 1978.

Subāhuparipṛcchā-tantra. Tōh. 805. DK rgyud 'bum vol. wa, 118a–140b.

Surativajra. *Sarvabuddhasamayogaḍākinījālasamvaraṭīkā-samayogālaṁkāra*. Tōh. 1660, DT vol. ra, 389a–439a.

Herukābhyudaya (HA). Tōh. 374, DK rgyud 'bum vol. ga, 1b–33b.

Hevajra Mahātantrarājā (HV). Tōh. 417, 418, DK rgyud 'bum vol. nga, 1b–30a. Sanskrit and Tibetan edited and translated in Snellgrove 1959 (2 vols.).

Indigenous Tibetan Texts

Grags-pa rGyal-mtshan. *dpal he ru ka'i byung tshul.* In *The Complete Works of the Great Masters of the Sa Skya Sect of the Tibetan Buddhism. Vol. 3. The Complete Works of Grags Pa Rgyal Mtshan.* bSod nams rgya mtsho, compiler. Tokyo: The Toyo Bunko, 1968, 298.4–300.2.

'Jam-mgon A-myes-zhab Ngag-dbang Kun-dga'-bsod-nams. *grub thob brgyas cu rtsa bzhi'i rnam thar.* Reproduced from sDe-dge dGon-chen blocks. Dehra Dun: Sakya College, 1985.

Bu-ston Rin-chen-grub. *rgyud sde spyi'i rnam par gzhag pa rgyud sde rin po che'i mdzes rgyan zhes bya ba.* In *The Collected Works of Bu-ston.* Lokesh Chandra, ed. New Delhi: International Academy of Indian Culture, 1966, vol. ba, 1–610.

———. *bde mchog nyung ngu rgyud kyi spyi rnam don gsal* (DS). In *The Collected Works of Bu-ston.* Lokesh Chandra, ed. New Delhi: International Academy of Indian Culture, 1966. vol. cha, 1–118.

———. *bde mchog rtsa rgyud kyi rnam bshad gsang ba'i de kho na nyid gsal bar byed pa* (NS). In *The Collected Works of Bu-ston.* Lokesh Chandra, ed. New Delhi: International Academy of Indian Culture, 1966. vol. cha, 141–718.

Tsong Khapa bLo-bzang grags-pa. *bde mchog bsdus pa'i rgyud kyi rgya cher bshad pa sbas pa'i don kun gsal ba* (KS). bKra-shis Lhun-po edition, reprint. Delhi: Ngawang Gelek Demo, 1980, vol. nya, 1–502.

Sachen Kun-dga' snying-po. *dpal 'khor lo bde mchog gi rtsa ba'i rgyud kyi ṭīka mu tig phreng ba* (PG). In *The Complete Works of the Great Masters of the Sa Skya Sect of the Tibetan Buddhism. Vol. 1. The Complete Works of Kun dga' snying po.* bSod nams rgya mtsho, compiler. Tokyo: The Toyo Bunko, 1968, 288.3–380.3.

Chinese Texts from the Taishō Canon

Taishō Shinshū Daizōkyō (T), edited by Takakusu Junjirō and Watanabe Kaikyoku (Tokyo, 1924–1935)

T. 671. 入楞伽經 (*Laṅkāvatāra Sūtra*), trans. by Bodhiruci, 16.514c–586b.

T. 893a. 蘇悉地羯囉經 (*Susiddhikara Sūtra*), trans. by Śubhakarasiṁha, 18.603a–893a.

T. 895. 蘇婆呼童子請問經 (*Subāhuparipṛcchā Sūtra*), trans. by Śubhakarasiṁha, 18.719a–746b.

T. 1796. Śubhakarasiṁha and Yi-xing (一行). 大毘盧遮那成佛經疏。39.579a–789c.

T. 2066. Yi-jing (義淨), 大唐西域求法高僧傳。51.1a–12b.

Other Chinese Texts

勝樂略續. 1997。寶法稱 and 仁欽曲扎, 譯者。香港：佛教慈慧服務中心，台北：盤逸有限公司。

bod rgya tshig mdzod chen mo. 藏漢大辭典。張怡蓀，主編。n.p.: *mi rigs dpe skrun khang*, n.d., 3 vols.

Modern Sources

Abé, Ryūichi. 1999. *The Weaving of Mantra: Kukai and the Construction of Esoteric Buddhist Discourse*. New York: Columbia University Press.

Analayo. 2004. *Sattipatthana: The Direct Path to Realization*. Birmingham, UK: Windhorse Publications.

Apte, Vaman Shivram. 1965. *The Practical Sanskrit-English Dictionary*. Delhi: Motilal Banarsidass.

Bagchi, Prabodh Chandra. 1939. *Studies in the Tantra. Part I*. Calcutta: University of Calcutta.

Bagchi, S., ed. 1970. *Mahāyāna-Sūtrālakāra of Asaṅga*. Buddhist Sanskrit Texts no. 13. Darbhanga: The Mithila Institute.

Bangdel, Dina. 1999. "Manifesting the Maṇḍala: A Study of the Core Iconographic Program of Newar Buddhist Monasteries in Nepal." Ph.D. diss., Ohio State University. 3 vols.

Barron, Richard, trans. 2003. *The Autobiography of Jamgön Kongtrul: A Gem of Many Colors*. Ithaca, NY: Snow Lion Publications.

Beal, Samuel, trans. 1911. *The Life of Hiuen-Tsiang by the Shaman Hwui Li, with an Introduction Containing an Account of the Works of I-Tsing*. Reprint, New Delhi: Munishiram Manoharlal Publishers, 1973.

Beckwith, Christopher I. 1984. "A Hitherto Unnoticed Yüan-Period Collection Attributed to 'Phagspa." In Ligeti 1984, 1.9–16.

Bendall, Cecil. 1992. *Catalogue of the Buddhist Sanskrit Manuscripts in the University Library, Cambridge*. Verzeichnis der Orientalischen Handschriften in Deutschland, supplementband 33. Stuttgart: Franz Steiner Verlag.

Beyer, Stephan. 1973. *The Cult of Tārā: Magic and Ritual in Tibet*. Los Angeles: University of California Press.

Bhattacharya, Bholanath. 1977. "Some Aspects of the Esoteric Cults of Consort Worship in Bengal: A Field Survey Report." *Folklore* (Calcutta) 18.10 (October): 310–324, 18.11 (November): 359–365, 18.12 (December): 385–397.

Bhattacharyya, Benoytosh, ed. 1949. *Niṣpannayogāvalī of Mahāpaṇḍita Abhayākaragupta*. Gaekwad's Oriental Series vol. 109. Baroda: Oriental Institute.

Bharati, Agehananda. 1993. *Tantric Traditions*. 2nd rev. ed. Delhi: Hindustan Publishing.

Bisschop, Peter and Arlo Griffiths. 2003. "The Pāśupata Observance (Atharvavedapariśiṣṭa 40)." *Indo-Iranian Journal* 46.4: 315–348.

Boucher, Daniel. 1991. "The *Pratītyasamutpādagātha* and Its Role in the Medieval Cult of the Relics." *Journal of the International Association of Buddhist Studies* 14.1: 1–27.

Broido, Michael M. 1982. "Does Tibetan Hermeneutics Throw Any Light on *Sandhābhāṣa*." *Journal of the Tibet Society* 2: 5–39.

———.1983a. "*bShad Thabs*: Some Tibetan Methods of Explaining the Tantras." In Steinkellner and Tauscher 1983, 2.15–45.

———. 1983b. "A Note on dGos-'Brel." *Journal of the Tibet Society* 3: 5–19.

———. 1988. "Killing, Lying, Stealing, and Adultery: A Problem of Interpretation in the Tantras." In Lopez 1988, 71–118.

Brough, John. 1954. "The Language of Buddhist Sanskrit Texts." *Bulletin of the School of Oriental and African Studies* 16.2: 351–75.

Bühnemann, Gudrun. 1999. "Buddhist Deities and Mantras in the Hindu Tantras: I The *Tantrasārasaṁgraha* and the *Īśānaśivagurudeva-paddhati*." *Indo-Iranian Journal* 42: 303–334.

———. 2000. "Buddhist Deities and Mantras in the Hindu Tantras: II The *Śrīvidyārṇavatantra* and the *Tantrasāra*." *Indo-Iranian Journal* 43: 27–48.

———, ed. 2003. *Maṇḍalas and Yantras in the Hindu Traditions*. Leiden: Brill.

Buffetrille, Katia. 1999. "The Blue Lake of Amdo and Its Island: Legends and a Pilgrimage Guide." In Huber 1999b, 105–124.

Cabezón, José Ignacio. 1992. "Mother Wisdom, Father Love: Gender-Based Imagery in Mahāyāna Buddhist Thought." In *Buddhism, Sexuality and Gender*, edited by José Ignacio Cabezón, 181–99. Albany: State University of New York Press.

Caldwell, Sarah. 1999. *Oh Terrifying Mother: Sexuality, Violence and Worship of the Goddess Kāḷi*. New York: Oxford University Press.

Campbell, June. 1996. *Traveller in Space: In Search of Female Identity in Tibetan Buddhism*. New York: George Braziller.

Cantwell, Cathy. 1997. "To Meditate upon Consciousness as *Vajra*: Ritual 'Killing and Liberation' in the rNying-ma-pa Tradition." In Steinkellner and Tauscher 1983, 1.107–118.

Chandra, Lokesh. 1984. "Vaipulya Sūtras and the Tantras." In Ligeti 1984, 2.99–115.

Chattopadhyaya, Alaka. 1967. *Atīśa and Tibet: Life and Works of Dīpaṁkara Śrījñāna in Relation to the History and Religion of Tibet, with Tibetan Sources Translated under Professor Lama Chimpa.* Reprint, Delhi: Motilal Banarsidass, 1981.

Chaudhuri, Nagendra Narayan, ed. 1935. *Studies in the Apabhraṁśa Texts of the Ḍākārṇava.* Calcutta: Metropolitan Printing & Publishing House Ltd.

Chimpa, Lama and Alaka Chattopadhyaya, trans. 1970. *Tāranātha's History of Buddhism in India.* Simla: Institute of Advanced Studies. Reprint, Delhi: Motilal Banarsidass, 1990.

Chou Yi-Liang. 1945. "Tantrism in China." *Harvard Journal of Asiatic Studies* 8, 241–342.

Cicuzza, Claudio. 2001. *The Laghutantraṭīkā by Vajrapāṇi: A Critical Edition of the Sanskrit Text.* Serie Orientale Roma 86. Roma: Istituto Italiano per l'Africa e l'Oriente.

Coburn, Thomas B. 1984. *Devī-Māhātmya: The Crystallization of the Goddess Tradition.* Delhi: Motilal Banarsidass.

———. 1991. *Encountering the Goddess: A Translation of the Devī-Māhātmya and a Study of Its Interpretation.* Albany: State University of New York Press.

Cozort, Daniel. 1986. *Highest Yoga Tantra: An Introduction to the Esoteric Buddhism of Tibet.* Ithaca, New York: Snow Lion Publications.

Cuevas, Bryan J. 2003. *The Hidden History of the Tibetan Book of the Dead.* New York: Oxford University Press.

Davidson, Ronald M. 1981. "The *Litany of the Names of Mañjuśrī*: Text and Translation of the *Mañjuśrīnāmasaṁgīti*." In *Tantric and Taoist Studies in Honour of R.A. Stein,* edited by Michel Strickmann. Mélanges chinois et bouddhiques, vol. 1. Brussels: Institut belge des hautes études chinoises, 1–69.

———. 1991. "Reflections on the Maheśvara Subjugation Myth: Indic Materials, Sa-skya-pa Apologetics, and the Birth of Heruka." *Journal of the International Association of Buddhist Studies* 14.2: 197–235.

———. 1999. "Masquerading as *Pramāṇa*: Esoteric Buddhism and Epistemological Nomenclature." In Katsura 1999, 25–35.

———. 2002a. "Reframing *Sahaja*: Genre, Representation, Ritual and Lineage." *Journal of Indian Philosophy* 30: 45–83.

———. 2002b. *Indian Esoteric Buddhism: A Social History of the Tantric Movement*. New York: Columbia University Press.

Davis, Wade. 1988. *Passage of Darkness: The Ethnobiology of the Haitian Zombie*. Chapel Hill, NC: University of North Carolina Press.

Dawa-Samdup, Kazi, ed. 1919. *Śrī-Cakraśaṁvara-Tantra: A Buddhist Tantra*. Arthur Avalon's Tantrik Texts vol. VII, Calcutta: Thacker, Spink & Co. Reprint, New Delhi: Aditya Prakashan, 1987.

Dayal, Har. 1932. *The Bodhisattva Doctrine in Buddhist Sanskrit Literature*. London: Routledge & Kegan Paul. Reprint, Delhi: Motilal Banarsidass, 1970.

Decleer, Hubert. 1998. Review of *The Vajrabhairava Tantras*, by Bulcsu Siklos. *Indo-Iranian Journal* 41: 290–301.

Donaldson, Thomas E. 1986. "Erotic Rituals on Orissan Temples." *East and West* 36.1–3: 137–182.

Doniger, Wendy. 1999. *Splitting the Difference: Gender and Myth in Ancient Greece and India*. Chicago: University of Chicago Press.

Doniger, Wendy and Sudhir Kakar. 2002. *Kamasutra*. New York: Oxford University Press.

Dowman, Keith. 1985. *Masters of Mahamudra: Songs and Histories of the Eighty-four Buddhist Siddhas*. Albany: State University of New York Press.

Dundes, Alan. 1991. "The Ritual Murder or Blood Libel Legend: A Study of Anti-Semitic Victimization Through Projective Inversion." In *The Blood Libel Legend*, edited by Alan Dundes, 336–76. Madison: University of Wisconsin Press.

Eastman, Kenneth W. 1981. "The Eighteen Tantras of the Vajraśekhara/Māyājāla." Seminar paper presented at the 26th International Conference of Orientalists in Tōkyo, May 8, 1981. A summary of this paper is published in *Transactions of the International Conference of Orientalists in Japan* 24 (1981): 95–96.

Edgerton, Franklin. 1953. *Buddhist Hybrid Sanskrit Grammar and Dictionary.* New Haven: Yale University Press. Reprint, New Delhi: Motilal Banarsidass, 1970, 2 vols.

Elder, George Robert. 1978. "The Saṁpuṭa Tantra: Edition and Translation, Chapters I–IV." Ph.D. diss., Columbia University.

English, Elizabeth. 2002. *Vajrayoginī: Her Visualizations, Rituals, and Forms.* Boston: Wisdom Publications.

Falk, Nancy Auer. 1989. "The Case of the Vanishing Nuns: The Fruits of Ambivalence in Ancient Indian Buddhism." *Unspoken Worlds: Women's Religious Lives,* edited by Nancy Auer Falk and Rita M. Gross, 155–65. Belmont, CA: Wadsworth Publishing Company.

Faure, Bernard. 2003. *The Power of Denial: Buddhism, Purity, and Gender.* Princeton: Princeton University Press.

Ferrari, Alfonsa. 1958. *mK'yen brtse's Guide to the Holy Place of Central Tibet.* Completed and edited by Luciano Petech and Hugh Richardson. *Serie Orientale Roma* vol. 16. Roma: Istituto Italiano per il Medio ed Estremo Oriente.

Gellner, David. 1992. *Monk, Householder, and Tantric Priest: Newar Buddhism and Its Hierarchy of Ritual.* Cambridge: Cambridge University Press.

George, Christopher S. 1974. *The Caṇḍamahāroṣaṇa Tantra.* American Oriental Series vol. 56. New Haven: American Oriental Society.

Germano, David. 1994. "Architecture and Absence in the Secret Tantric History of the Great Perfection (*rdzogs chen*)." *Journal of the International Association of Buddhist Studies* 17.2: 203–335.

Gethin, Rupert. 1997. "Cosmology and Meditation: From the Aggañña-Sutta to the Mahāyāna." *History of Religions* 36.3: 183–217.

Gibson, Todd. 1997. “Inner Asian Contributions to the Vajrayāna.” *Indo-Iranian Journal* 40: 37–57.

Giebel, Rolf W. 1995. “The *Chin-kang-ting ching yü-ch'ieh shih-pa-hui chih-kuei*: An Annotated Translation.” *Journal of Naritasan Institute for Buddhist Studies*. 18: 107–201.

———. 2001. *Two Esoteric Sutras*. Berkeley: The Numata Center for Buddhist Translation and Research.

Goehring, James E. 2000. “Libertine or Liberated: Women in the So-called Libertine Gnostic Communities.” *Images of the Feminine in Gnosticism*, edited by Karen L. King, 329–344. Harrisburg: Trinity Press International.

Gombrich, Richard F. 1996. *How Buddhism Began: The Conditioned Genesis of the Early Teachings*. Reprint, New Delhi: Munshiram Manoharlal, 1997.

Gonda, Jan. 1972. “Mudrā.” *Studies in the History of Religions* 12.21–31.

Goudriaan, Teun. 1978. *Māyā Divine and Human*. Delhi: Motilal Banarsidass.

Gnoli, Raniero, ed. 1960. *The Pramāṇavārttikam of Dharmakīrti: The First Chapter with the Autocommentary*. Serie Orientale Roma vol. 23. Roma: Istituto Italiana per il Medio ed Estremo Oriente.

Granoff, Phyllis. 1979. “Maheśvara/Mahākāla: A Unique Buddhist Image from Kaśmīr.” *Artibus Asiae* 41: 64–82.

———. 2000. “Other People's Rituals: Ritual Eclecticism in Early Medieval Indian Religions.” *Journal of Indian Philosophy* 28.4: 399–424.

Gray, David B. 2001. “On Supreme Bliss: A Study of the History and Interpretation of the Cakrasamvara Tantra.” Ph.D. diss., Columbia University.

———. 2003. “The Chakrasamvara Tantra: The Text and Its Tradition.” In *The Circle of Bliss*, edited by John C. Huntington and Dina Bangdel, 51–54. Chicago: Art Media Resources, Ltd.

———. 2005a. “Eating the Heart of the Brahmin: Representations of Alterity and the Formation of Identity in Tantric Buddhist Discourse.” *History of Religions* 45.1: 45–69.

———. 2005b. "Disclosing the Empty Secret: Textuality and Embodiment in the *Cakrasamvara Tantra.*" *Numen* 52.4: 417–444.

———. 2006. "Mandala of the Self: Embodiment, Practice, and Identity Construction in the Cakrasamvara Tradition." *Journal of Religious History* 30.3: 294–310.

———. 2012. *The Cakrasamvara Tantra (The Discourse of Śrī Heruka): Editions of the Sanskrit and Tibetan Texts.* New York: American Institute of Buddhist Studies.

———. 2017. *Illumination of the Hidden Meaning: Maṇḍala, Mantra, and the Cult of the Yoginīs (Chapters 1–24).* By Tsong Khapa Losang Drakpa. New York: American Institute of Buddhist Studies.

———. 2019. *Illumination of the Hidden Meaning: Yogic Vows, Conduct, and Ritual Praxis (Chapters 25–51).* By Tsong Khapa Losang Drakpa. New York and Boston: American Institute of Buddhist Studies and Wisdom Publications.

Gross, Rita M. 1993. *Buddhism After Patriarchy: A Feminist History, Analysis, and Reconstruction of Buddhism.* Albany: State University of New York Press.

———. 1998. *Soaring and Settling. Buddhist Perspectives on Contemporary Social and Religious Issues.* New York: Continuum.

van Gulik, R. H. 1953. *Siddham: An Essay on the History of Sanskrit Studies in China and Japan.* Leiden: E. J. Brill. Reprint, Delhi: Jayyed Press, 1980.

Gutschow, Kim. 2004. *Being a Buddhist Nun: The Struggle for Enlightenment in the Himalayas.* Cambridge, MA: Harvard University Press.

Gyalzur, Losang Paldhen and Antony H. N. Verwey. 1983. "Spells on the Life-Wood: An Introduction to the Tibetan Buddhist Ceremony of Consecration." In *Selected Studies on Ritual in the Indian Religions: Essays to D. J. Hoens,* edited by Ria Kloppenborg, 169–202. Studies in the History of Religions, vol. 45. Leiden: E. J. Brill.

Gyurme Dorje and Matthew Kapstein, ed. 1991. *The rNying ma School of Tibetan Buddhism.* vol. 2. Boston: Wisdom Publications.

Harding, Sarah, trans. 1996. *Creation and Completion: Essential Points of Tantric Meditation.* Boston: Wisdom Publications.

Harle, J. C. 1971. "Remarks on *ālīḍha.*" In *Mahayanist Art After A.D. 900*, edited by William Watson, 10–16. London: University of London.

Hebdige, Dick. 1979. *Subculture: The Meaning of Style.* London: Methuen & Co.

Heller, Amy. 2001. "On the Development of the Iconography of Acala and Vighnāntaka in Tibet." In *Embodying Wisdom: Art, Text and Interpretation in the History of Esoteric Buddhism*, edited by Rob Linrothe and Henrik H. Sørensen, 209–228. Copenhagen: The Seminar for Buddhist Studies.

Herrmann-Pfandt, Adelheid. 1992. *Ḍākinīs: Zur Stellung und Symbolik des Weiblichen im Tantrischen Buddhismus.* Indica et Tibetica band 20. Bonn: Indica et Tibetica Verlag.

———. 1996. "The Good Woman's Shadow: Some Aspects of the Dark Nature of Ḍākinīs and Śākinīs in Hinduism." In *Wild Goddesses of India and Nepal: Proceedings of an International Symposium, Berne and Zurich, November 1994*, edited by Axel Michaels et al. Vol. 2, 39–70. New York: Peter Lang.

———. 1997. "Yab Yum Iconography and the Role of Women in Tibetan Tantric Buddhism." *Tibet Journal* 22.1: 12–34.

Hodge, Stephen. 1994. "Considerations on the Dating and Geographic Origins of the *Mahāvairocanābhisaṁbodhi-sūtra.*" In *The Buddhist Forum volume III Seminar Papers 1991–1993*, edited by Tadeusz Skorupski and Ulrich Pagel, 57–83. London: School of Oriental and African Studies, University of London.

———, trans. 2003. *The Mahā-Vairocana-Abhisaṁbodhi Tantra with Buddhaguhya's Commentary.* London: RoutledgeCurzon.

Hoey, W. 1907. "The Five Rivers of the Buddhists." *Journal of the Royal Asiatic Society of Great Britain and Ireland*: 41–46.

Huber, Toni. 1990. "Where Exactly are Cāritra, Devikoṭa and Himavat? A Sacred Geography Controversy and the Development of Tantric Buddhist Pilgrimage Sites in Tibet." *Kailash* 16.3–4: 121–164.

———. 1999a. *The Cult of Pure Crystal Mountain: Popular Pilgrimage and Visionary Landscape in Southeast Tibet.* New York: Oxford University Press.

———, ed. 1999b. *Sacred Spaces and Powerful Places in Tibetan Culture.* Dharamsala: Library of Tibetan Works and Archives.

Huntington, John C. and Dina Bangdel. 2003. *The Circle of Bliss.* Chicago: Art Media Resources, Ltd.

Inden, Ronald. 1981. "Hierarchies of Kings in Medieval India." *Contributions to Indian Sociology* 15.1–2, 99–125.

Iyanaga, Nobumi. 1985. "Récits de la soumission de Maheśvara par Trailokyavijaya–d'après les sources chinoises et japonaises." In *Tantric and Taoist Studies in Honour of R.A. Stein,* edited by Michel Strickmann, 633–745. Mélanges chinois et bouddhiques vol. 12. Brussels: Institut belge des hautes études chinoises.

Jamison, Stephanie W. 1996. *Sacrificed Wife/Sacrificer's Wife: Women, Ritual and Hospitality in Ancient India.* New York: Oxford University Press.

Jan, Yün-hua. 1966. "Buddhist Relations Between India and Sung China." *History of Religions* 6.1, 24–42.

Kalff, Martin M. 1978. "Ḍākinīs in the Cakrasaṁvara Tradition." In *Tibetan Studies,* edited by Martin Brauen and Per Kvaerne, 149–163. Zürich: Völkerkundemuseum der Universität Zürich.

———. 1979. "Selected Chapters from the Abhidhānottara-Tantra: The Union of Female and Male Deities." Ph.D. diss., Columbia University. 2 vols.

Kaneko, Eiichi. 1982. *Ko-Tantora zenshū kaidai mokuroku.* Tokyo: Kukusho Kankōkai.

Kangle, R. P. 1986. *The Kauṭilīya Arthaśāstra.* reprint ed. Delhi: Motilal Banarsidass, 3 vols.

Kapstein, Matthew. 1980. "The Shangs-pa bka'-brgyud: An Unknown Tradition of Tibetan Buddhism." In *Tibetan Studies in Honour of Hugh Richardson: Proceedings of the International Seminar of Tibetan Studies, Oxford 1979*, edited by Michael Aris and Aung San Suu Kyi, 138–144. Warminster, U.K.: Aris & Phillips Ltd.

———. 1988. "Mi-pham's Theory of Interpretation." In Donald S. Lopez, ed. *Buddhist Hermeneutics*. Honolulu: University of Hawaii Press, 149–174.

———. 1992. "The Illusion of Spiritual Progress: Remarks on Indo-Tibetan Buddhist Soteriology." In *Paths to Liberation: The Mārga and Its Transformations in Buddhist Thought*, edited by Robert E. Buswell, Jr. and Robert M. Gimello, 193–224. Honolulu: University of Hawaii Press.

———. 1996. "*gDams ngag*: Tibetan Technologies of the Self." In *Tibetan Literature: Studies in Genre*, edited by José Ignacio Cabezón and Roger R. Jackson, 275–289. Ithaca, NY: Snow Lion.

———. 2001. *Reason's Traces: Identity and Interpretation in Indian & Tibetan Buddhist Thought*. Boston: Wisdom Publications.

Kara, Georg and Peter Zieme. 1976. *Fragmente tantrischer Werke in uigurischer Übersetzung*. Berliner Turfantexte 7. Berlin: Akademie-Verlag.

Karmay, Samten G. 1980a. "The Ordinance of Lha Bla-ma Ye-shes-'od." In *Tibetan Studies in Honour of Hugh Richardson: Proceedings of the International Seminar of Tibetan Studies, Oxford 1979*, edited by Michael Aris and Aung San Suu Kyi, 150–162. Warminster, U. K.: Aris & Phillips.

———. 1980b. "An Open Letter by the Pho-brang Zhi-ba-'od." *The Tibet Journal*, 5: 2–28.

Katsura Shoryu, ed. 1999. *Dharmakīrti's Thought and Its Impact on Indian and Tibetan Philosophy*. Wien: Verlag der Österreichischen Akademie der Wissenschaften.

Kelsang Gyatso, Geshe. 1997. *Essence of Vajrayana: The Highest Yoga Tantra Practice of Heruka Body Mandala*. London: Tharpa Publications.

Kimura, Toshihiko. 1999. "A New Chronology of Dharmakīrti." In Katsura 1999, 209–214.

King, Winston L. 1992. *Theravāda Meditation: The Buddhist Transformation of Yoga.* Delhi: Motilal Banarsidass.

Kloetzli, Randy. 1983. *Buddhist Cosmology from Single World System to Pure Land: Science and Theology in the Images of Motion and Light.* Delhi: Motilal Banarsidass.

Kohn, Richard J. 2001. *Lord of the Dance: The Mani Rimdu Festival in Tibet and Nepal.* Albany: State University of New York Press.

Krapivina, Raisa N. 1991. "Materials on the History of the Saskya School: The History of the Life of the Great Saskya Teacher." *Central Asian Journal* 35.1–2: 62–66.

Kripal, Jeffrey J. 1995. *Kālī's Child: The Mystical and the Erotic in the Life and Teachings of Ramakrishna.* Chicago: University of Chicago Press.

Kuijp, Leonard W.J. van der. 1992. "Notes Apropos of the Transmission of the Sarvadurgatipariśodhanatantra in Tibet." *Studien zur Indologie und Iranistik* 16: 109–25.

Kuwayama, Shoshin. 1991. "L'inscription du Gaṇeśa de Gardez et la chronologie des Turki-Ṣāhi." *Journal Asiatique* 279: 267–287.

Kvaerne, Per. 1975. "On the Concept of Sahaja in Indian Buddhist Tantric Literature." *Temenos* 11: 88–135.

———. 1977. *An Anthology of Buddhist Tantric Songs: A Study in the Caryāgīti.* Det Norske Videnskaps-Akademi, II Hist.-Filos. Klasse Skrifter Ny Serie No. 14. Oslo: Universitetsforlaget.

Lienhard, Siegfried, with Thakur Lal Manandhar. 1988. *Nepalese Manuscripts, Part 1, Nevārī and Sanskrit, Staatsbibliothek Preussischer Kulturbesitz.* Verzeichnis der Orientalischen Handschriften in Deutschland, band 33,1. Stuttgart: Franz Steiner Verlag.

Ligeti, Louis, ed. 1984. *Tibetan and Buddhist Studies Commemorating the 200th Anniversary of the Birth of Alexander Csoma de Korös.* 2 vols. Reprint, New Delhi: Munshiram Manoharlal Publishers.

Lessing, Ferdinand D. and Alex Wayman, trans. 1978. *Introduction to the Buddhist Tantric Systems*. Delhi, Motilal Banarsidass.

Lopez, Donald S., ed. 1988. *Buddhist Hermeneutics*. The Kuroda Institute Studies in East Asian Buddhism No. 6. Honolulu: University of Hawaii Press.

———. 1995. "Authority and Orality in the Mahāyāna." *Numen* 42: 21–47.

Lorenzen, David N. 1972. *The Kāpālikas and the Kālāmukhas: Two Lost Śaivite Sects*. 2nd rev. ed. Delhi: Motilal Banarsidass, 1991.

———. 1989. "New Data on the Kāpālikas." In *Criminal Gods and Demon Devotees: Essays on the Guardians of Popular Hinduism*, edited by Alf Hiltebeital, 231–238. Albany: State University of New York Press.

Macdonald, A. W. 1990. "Hindu-isation, Buddha-isation, then Lama-isation, or: What Happened at La-phyi?" In *Indo-Tibetan Studies: Papers in Honour and Appreciation of Professor David L. Snellgrove's Contribution to Indo-Tibetan Studies*, edited by Tadeusz Skorupski, 199–208. Tring, U.K.: The Institute of Buddhist Studies.

Macdonell, A. A. 1898. *Vedic Mythology*. Reprint, Delhi: Motilal Banarsidass, 1974.

Makransky, John. 1997. *Buddhahood Embodied: Sources of Controversy in India and Tibet*. Albany: State University of New York Press.

Marriott, McKim. 1976. "Hindu Transactions: Diversity Without Dualism." In *Transaction and Meaning: Directions in the Anthropology of Exchange and Symbolic Behavior*, edited by Bruce Kapferer, 109–142. Philadelphia: Institute for the Study of Human Issues.

Matsunaga, Yukei. 1977. "A History of Tantric Buddhism in India with Reference to Chinese Translations." In *Buddhist Thought and Asian Civilization: Essays in Honor of Herbert V. Guenther*, edited by Leslie S. Kawamura and Keith Scott, 167–81. Emeryville, CA: Dharma Publishing.

———, ed. 1978. *The Guhyasamāja Tantra*. Osaka: Toho Shuppan.

———. 1980. *Mikkyō kyōten Seiritsu-shi Ron* (密 教 經 典 成 立 史 論). Kyōto: Hōzōkan.

McEvilley, Thomas. 1981. "An Archaeology of Yoga." *Res: Anthropology and Aesthetics* 1: 44–77.

———. 2002. "The Spinal Serpent." In *The Roots of Tantra*, edited by Katherine Anne Harper and Robert L. Brown, 93–113. Albany: State University of New York Press.

McMahan, David. 1998. "Orality, Writing, and Authority in South Asian Buddhism: Visionary Literature and the Struggle for Legitimacy in the Mahāyāna." *History of Religions* 37.3: 249–74.

———. 2002. *Empty Vision: Metaphor and Visionary Imagery in Mahāyāna Buddhism*. London: RoutledgeCurzon.

Meisezahl, R. O. 1985. *Hastapūjāvidhi-Texte: Der Handritus im anuttara-yogischen Kult des Götterpaares Cakrasambara und Vajravārāhī*. Beiträga zur Zentralasienforschung, band 6. Sankt Augustin: VGH-Wissenschaftsverlag.

Mimaki, Katsumi and Tōru Tomabechi, eds. 1994. *Pañcakrama: Sanskrit and Tibetan Texts Critically Edited with Verse Index and Facsimile Edition of the Sanskrit Manuscripts*. Bibliotheca Codicum Asiaticorum vol. 8. Tokyo: The Centre for East Asian Cultural Studies for Unesco, Toyo Bunko.

Monier-Williams, Sir Monier. 2002. *A Sanskrit-English Dictionary*. Originally published 1899. Corrected edition, Delhi: Motilal Banarsidass.

Mudiyanse, Nandasena. 1967. *Mahayana Monuments in Ceylon*. Columbo: M. D. Gunasena & Co. Ltd.

Mullin, Glenn H., trans. 1996. *Tsong Khapa's Six Yogas of Naropa*. Ithaca, NY: Snow Lion Publications.

Naudou, Jean. 1980. *Buddhists of Kaśmīr*. Delhi: Agam Kala Prakashan.

Negi, J. S. 1993–2002. *Tibetan-Sanskrit Dictionary*. Sarnath: Central Institute of Higher Tibetan Studies, vols. 1–9.

Newman, John. 1990. "Vajrayāna Deities in an Illustrated Indian Manuscript of the *Aṣṭasāhasrikā-prajñāpāramitā*." *Journal of the International Association of Buddhist Studies* 13.2: 117–32.

———. 1998. "The Epoch of the Kālacakra Tantra." *Indo-Iranian Journal* 41.4: 319–49.

Ñāṇamoli, Bhikkhu, trans. 1976. *The Path of Purification*. Berkeley: Shambhala Press, 2 vols.

Obeyesekere, Gananath. 2002. *Imagining Karma: Ethical Transformation in Amerindian, Buddhist, and Greek Rebirth*. Berkeley: University of California Press.

O'Flaherty, Wendy Doniger. 1971. "The Origin of Heresy in Hindu Mythology." *History of Religions* 10.4: 271–333.

———. 1976. *The Origins of Evil in Hindu Mythology*. Los Angeles: University of California Press.

———. 1980. *Women, Androgynes, and Other Mythical Beasts*. Chicago: University of Chicago Press.

———. 1983. "Image of the Heretic in the Gupta *Purāṇas*." In *Essays on Gupta Culture*, edited by Bardwell L. Smith, 107–127. Delhi: Motilal Banarsidass.

———. 1985. *Tales of Sex and Violence: Folklore, Sacrifice, and Danger in the Jaiminiya Brahmana*. Chicago: University of Chicago Press.

Olivelle, Patrick. 1998. *The Early Upanishads: Annotated Text and Translation*. New York: Oxford University Press.

Orofino, Giacomella. 1994a. "Divination with Mirrors: Observations on a Simile Found in the Kālacakra Literature." In *Tibetan Studies: Proceedings of the 6th Seminar of the International Association of Tibetan Studies. Fagernes 1992*, edited by Per Kvarene, 2: 612–29. Oslo: Institute for Comparative Research in Human Culture.

———. 1994b. *Sekoddeśa: A Critical Edition of the Tibetan Translations*. Serie Orientale Roma vol. 72. Roma: Istituto Italiano per il Medio ed Estremo Oriente.

Pandey, Janardan Shastri, ed. 1998. *Yoginīsaṁcāratantram with Nibandha of Tathāgatarakṣita and Upadeśānusāriṇīvyākhyā of Alakakaśala*. Rare Buddhist Texts Series no. 21. Sarnath: Central Institute of Higher Tibetan Studies.

———. 2002. *Śrīherukābhidhānam Cakrasamvaratantram with the Vivṛti Commentary of Bhavabhaṭṭa*. Rare Buddhist Texts Series no. 26. Sarnath: Central Institute of Higher Tibetan Studies, 2 vols.

Parpola, Asko. 1988. "The Coming of the Aryans to India and the Cultural and Ethnic Identity of the Dāsas." *Studia Orientalia* 64: 194–302.

———. 1992. "Metamorphoses of Mahiṣa Asura and Prajāpati." In *Ritual, State and History in South Asia. Essays in Honour of J. C. Heesterman*, edited by A. W. van den Hoek, D. H. A. Kolff and M. S. Oort, 275–308. Leiden: E.J. Brill.

Paul, Diana Y. 1979. *Women and Buddhism: Images of the Feminine in the Mahāyāna Tradition*. Los Angeles: University of California Press.

Payne, Richard Karl. 1991. *The Tantric Ritual of Japan, Feeding the Gods: The Shingon Fire Ritual*. New Delhi: Aditya Prakashan.

Rājavaṁśī, Śaṁkaramāna. 1959. *Prācīna Lipi Varṇamālā*. Kathmandu: Sarakāra.

Ray, Reginald. 1989. "Accomplished Women in Tantric Buddhism of Medieval India and Tibet." In *Unspoken Worlds: Women's Religious Lives*, edited by Nancy Auer Falk and Rita M. Gross, 191–200. Belmont, CA: Wadsworth Publishing Company.

Reinders, Eric. 1997. "Ritual Topography: Embodiment and Vertical Space in Buddhist Monastic Practice." *History of Religions* 36.3: 244–264.

Rhys-Davids, T. W. and J. E. Carpenter, eds. 1975, 1982, 1976. *The Dīgha Nikāya, Vol. II*. London: Pali Text Society. 3 vols.

Rhys-Davids, T. W. and William Stede, eds. 1949. *Pali-English Dictionary*. London: Pali Text Society.

Rigzin, Tsepak. 1986. *Tibetan-English Dictionary of Buddhist Terminology*. Dharamsala: Library of Tibetan Works and Archives.

Roerich, George N. 1949. trans. *The Blue Annals* by gZhon-nu dPal. 2nd ed., Delhi: Motilal Banarsidass, 1976.

Ruegg, David Seyfort. 1966. *The Life of Bu ston Rin po che with the Tibetan Text of the Bu ston rNam thar. Serie Orientale Roma* vol. 34. Roma: Istituto Italiano per il Medio ed Estremo Oriente.

———. 1976. "The Meaning of the Term *Gotra* and the Textual History of the *Ratnagotravibhāga*." *Bulletin of the School of Oriental and African Studies* 34.2: 341–63.

———. 1984. "Problems in the Transmission of Vajrayāna Buddhism in the Western Himalaya about the Year 1000." In *Studies of Mysticism in Honor of the 1150th Anniversary of Kobo Daishi's Nirvāṇam, Acta Indologica* (Indo koten kenkyū), 4.369–81. Narita: Naritasan Shinshōji.

———. 1989a. "Allusiveness and Obliqueness in Buddhist Texts: *Saṁdhā, Saṁdhi, Saṁdhyā* and *Abhisaṁdhi*." In *Dialectes dans les litteratures indo-aryennes: actes du colloque international*, edited by C. Caillat, 295–328. Paris: Institut de civilisation indienne.

———. 1989b. *Buddha-nature, Mind and the Problem of Gradualism in a Comparative Perspective: On the Transmission and Reception of Buddhism in India and Tibet.* London: School of Oriental and African Studies, University of London.

Śākya, Hemarāja. 1974. *Nepāla Lipi Prakāśa.* Kathmandu: Nepāla Rājakīya Prajñā-pratiṣṭhāna.

Samdhong Rinpoche and Vrajvallabh Dwivedi, eds. 1987. *Guhyādi-Aṣṭasiddhi-Saṅgraha.* Rare Buddhist Text Series 1. Sarnath, Varanasi: Central Institute of Higher Tibetan Studies.

Sanderson, Alexis. 1985. "Purity and Power among the Brahmans of Kashmir." In *The Category of the Person: Anthropology, Philosophy, History*, edited by Michael Carrithers et al., 190–216. Cambridge: Cambridge University Press.

———. 1988. "Śaivism and the Tantric Traditions." In *The World's Religions*, edited by Stewart Sutherland et al., 660–704. Boston: G. K. Hall & Co.

———. 1994. "Vajrayāna: Origin and Function." In *Buddhism into the Year 2000: International Conference Proceedings*, no editor, 87–102. Los Angeles: Dhammakaya Foundation.

———. 2001. "History through Textual Criticism in the Study of Śaivism, the Pañcarātra and the Buddhist Yoginītantras." In *Les Source et le temps,* edited by François Grimal, 1–47. Pondicherry: École française d'Extrême Orient.

Saunders, E. Dale. 1960. *Mudrā: A Study of Symbolic Gestures in Japanese Buddhist Sculpture.* Princeton: Princeton University Press.

Scharfe, Hartmut. 1993. *Investigations in Kauṭalya's Manual of Political Science.* Wiesbaden: Harrasowitz Verlag.

Sferra, Francesco. 1999. "The Concept of Purification in Some Texts of Late Indian Buddhism." *Journal of Indian Philosophy* 27.1–2: 83–103.

Shaw, Miranda. 1994. *Passionate Enlightenment: Women in Tantric Buddhism.* Princeton: Princeton University Press.

Sherburne, Richard. 2000. *The Complete Works of Atīśa.* Delhi: Aditya Prakashan.

Siklos, Bulcsu. 1996. *The Vajrabhairava Tantras.* Tring, U.K.: The Institute of Buddhist Studies.

Simmer-Brown, Judith. 2001. *Dakini's Warm Breath: The Feminine Principle in Tibetan Buddhism.* Boston: Shambhala Publications.

Simpson, J.A. and E.S.C. Weiner, eds. 1989. *The Oxford English Dictionary.* 2nd ed. Oxford: Clarendon Press, 20 vols.

Singh, Bireshwar Prasad. 1968. "A Tibetan Account of Abhayākaragupta." *Journal of the Bihar Research Society* 54: 179–198.

Sircar, D.C. 1971. *Studies in the Geography of Ancient and Medieval India.* 2nd rev. ed. Delhi, Motilal Banarsidass.

———. 1973. *The Śākta Pīṭhas.* Second revised edition. Delhi: Motilal Banarsidass.

Skorupski, Tadeusz. 1996. "The *Saṁpuṭa-Tantra*: Sanskrit and Tibetan Versions of Chapter One." In *The Buddhist Forum volume IV Seminar Papers 1994–1996*, edited by Tadeusz Skorupski, 191–244. London: School of Oriental and African Studies, University of London.

Smith, Brian K. 1994. *Classifying the Universe: The Ancient Indian Varṇa System and the Origins of Caste*. New York: Oxford University Press.

Smith, Jonathan Z. 1982. *Imagining Religion: From Babylon to Jonestown*. Chicago: University of Chicago Press.

Snellgrove, David L. 1959. *The Hevajra Tantra: A Critical Study*. London: Oxford University Press, 2 vols.

———. 1987. *Indo-Tibetan Buddhism*. London: Serindia Publications.

———. 1988. "Categories of Buddhist Tantras." In *Orientalia Iosephi Tucci Memoriae Dicata*, edited by G. Gnoli and L. Lanciotti. *Serie Orientale Roma* 56.3: 1353–1384.

Soothill, William Edward and Lewis Hodous. 1937. *A Dictionary of Chinese Buddhist Terms with Sanskrit and English Equivalents and a Sanskrit-Pali Index*. Reprint, Delhi: Motilal Banarsidass, 1994.

Sperling, Elliot. 1994. "Rtsa-mi Lo-tsā-ba Sangs-rgyas grags and the Tangut Background to Early Mongol-Tibetan Relations." In *Tibetan Studies: Proceedings of the 6th Seminar of the International Association of Tibetan Studies, Fagernes 1992*, edited by Per Kvarene, 2: 801–24. Oslo: Institute for Comparative Research in Human Culture.

Staal, Frits, ed. 1983. *Agni: The Vedic Ritual of the Fire Altar*. Berkeley, CA: Asian Humanities Press, 2 vols.

Steinkellner, Ernst and Helmut Tauscher, ed. 1983. *Contributions on Tibetan and Buddhist Religion and Philosophy. Proceedings of the Csoma de Körös Symposium Held at Velm-Vienna, Austria, 13–19 September 1981*. 2 vols. Wein: Arbeitskreis für Tibetische und Buddhistische Studien, Universität Wien.

Stewart, Tony K. and Carl W. Ernst. 2003. "Syncretism." *South Asian Folklore: An Encyclopedia*, edited by Margaret Mills et al., 586–588. London: Routledge.

Strickmann, Michel. 1983. "Homa in East Asia." In Staal 1983, 2.418–455.

Stutchbury, Elisabeth. 1999. "Perceptions of Landscape in Karzha: 'Sacred' Geography and the Tibetan System of 'Geomancy'." In Huber 1999b, 154–186.

Sutherland, Gail Hinich. 1991. *The Disguises of the Demon: The Development of the Yakṣa in Hinduism and Buddhism*. Albany: State University of New York Press.

Sutton, Florin G. 1991. *Existence and Enlightenment in the Laṅkāvatāra-sūtra*. Albany: State University of New York Press.

Suzuki, Daisetz Teitaro, trans. 1932. *The Lankavatara Sutra: A Mahayana Text*. Reprint, Delhi: Motilal Banarsidass, 1999.

Tambiah, Stanley J. 1985. *Culture, Thought and Social Action: An Anthropological Perspective*. Cambridge: Harvard University Press.

Tanaka Tyōzaburō. 1976. *Tanaka's Cyclopedia of Edible Plants of the World*. Tokyo: Keigaku Pub. Co.

Tatz, Mark. 1988. "Maitrī-pa and Atiśa." In *Tibetan Studies: Proceedings of the 4th Seminar of the International Association for Tibetan Studies. Schloss Hohenkammer–Munich 1985*, edited by Helga Uebach and Jampa L. Panglung, 473–81. Studia Tibetica, Quellen und Studien zur tibetischen Lexikographie, band 2. München: Kommission für Zentralasiatische Studien Bayerische Akademie Der Wissenschaften.

Templeman, David. 1981. "Taranatha the Historian." *Tibet Journal* 6.2: 41–46.

———. 1983. *The Seven Instruction Lineages*. Dharamsala: Library of Tibetan Works and Archives.

———. 1999. "Internal and External Geography in Spiritual Biography." In Huber 1999b, 187–197.

Thurman, Robert A. F. 1976. *The Holy Teaching of Vimalakīrti, A Mahāyāna Scripture*. University Park: Pennsylvania State University Press.

———. 1988. "Vajra Hermeneutics." In Lopez 1988, 119–148.

Torricelli, Fabrizio and Sangye T. Naga, trans. 1995. *The Life of the Mahāsiddha Tilopa by Mar-pa Chos-kyi bLo-gros*. Dharamsala: Library of Tibetan Works and Archives.

Trungpa, Chögyam, director, Nālandā Translation Committee. 1982. *The Life of Marpa the Translator*. Reprinted, Boston: Shambhala Publications, 1995.

Tsuda, Shinichi. 1974. *The Saṁvarodaya-Tantra: Selected Chapters.* Tokyo: The Hokuseido Press.

———. 1978. "A Critical Tantrism." *Memoirs of the Research Department of the Toyo Bunko* 36: 167–231.

———. 1982. "*Vajrayoṣidbhageṣu vijahāra* Historical Survey from the Beginnings to the Culmination of Tantric Buddhism." In *Indological and Buddhist Studies: Volume in Honour of Professor J.W. de Jong on his Sixtieth Birthday.* ed. L.A. Hercus et al., 595–616. Canberra: Faculty of Asian Studies.

———. 1990. "The cult of śmaśāna, the realities of Tantra." In *The Sanskrit Tradition and Tantrism,* edited by Teun Goudriaan, 96–108. Panels of the VIIth World Sanskrit Conference. Kern Institute, Leiden: August 23–29, 1987, vol. 1. Leiden: E. J. Brill.

———. 1999. "The Original Formation and Performance of the "Secret Assembly" (*guhyasamāja*), an Integration of the *Guhyasamāja-Tantra* into the History of Tantric Buddhism in India." *Journal of the International College for Advanced Buddhist Studies* 2: 103–146.

Tucci, Guiseppe. 1956. *Minor Buddhist Texts, Part I.* Serie Orientale Roma 9. Roma: Istituto Italiano per il Medio ed Estremo Oriente.

———. 1988. *Rin-chen-bzaṅ-po and the Renaissance of Buddhism in Tibet Around the Millenium.* trans. by Nancy Kipp Smith and Thomas J. Pritzker, ed. by Lokesh Chandra. New Delhi: Aditya Prakashan. Originally published as *Indo-Tibetica II.* Rome: Reale Academia d'Italia, 1932.

———. 1989. *The Temples of Western Tibet and their Artistic Symbolism.* Lokesh Chandra, ed., Uma Marina Vesci, trans. New Delhi: Aditya Prakashan. English trans. of *Indo-Tibetica III.2.* Rome: Reale Accademia d'Italia, 1935.

Türstig, Hans-Georg. 1985. "The Indian Sorcery Called Abhicāra," *Wiener Zeitschrift für die Kunde Südasiens und Archive für Indische Philosophie* 29: 69–117.

Urban, Hugh. 2001a. *The Economics of Ecstacy: Tantra, Secrecy, and Power in Colonial Bengal.* New York: Oxford University Press.

———. 2001b. "The Path of Power: Impurity, Kingship, and Sacrifice in Assamese Tantra." *Journal of the American Academy of Religion* 69.4: 777–816.

Vaidya, P. L., ed. 1963. *Saddharmalaṅkāvatārasūtram.* Buddhist Sanskrit Texts no. 3. Darbhanga: The Mithila Institute.

Vaidya, P. L., ed. 1964. *Mahāyāna-sūtra-saṁgraha part II.* Buddhist Sanskrit Texts no. 18. Darbhanga: The Mithila Institute.

Verardi, Giovanni. 1994. *Homa and Other Fire Rituals in Gandhāra.* Napoli: Istituto Universitario Orientale.

Wallace, Vesna A. 1995. "The Inner Kālacakratantra: A Buddhist Tantric View of the Individual." Ph.D. diss., University of California, Berkeley.

———. 2001. *The Inner Kālacakratantra.* New York: Oxford University Press.

Wallis, Glenn. 2002. *Mediating the Power of the Buddhas: Ritual in the Mañjuśrīmūlakalpa.* Albany: State University of New York Press.

Walshe, Maurice, trans. 1995. *The Long Discourses of the Buddha: A Translation of the Dīgha Nikāya.* Boston: Wisdom Publications.

Wayman, Alex. 1973. *The Buddhist Tantras: Light on Indo-Tibetan Esotericism.* New York: Samuel Weiser.

———. 1977. *The Yoga of the Guhyasamājatantra: The Arcane Lore of Forty Verses.* Delhi: Motilal Banarsidass.

Weber, Max. 1968. *On Charisma and Institution Building: Selected Papers.* S. N. Eisenstadt, ed. Chicago: University of Chicago Press.

Wedemeyer, Christian. 2001. "Tropes, Typologies, and Turnarounds: A Brief Genealogy of the Historiography of Tantric Buddhism." *History of Religions* 40.3: 223–259.

White, David Gordon. 1996. *The Alchemical Body: Siddha Traditions in Medieval India.* Chicago: University of Chicago Press.

———. 1998. "Transformations in the Art of Love: Kāmakalā Practices in Hindu Tantric and Kaula Traditions." *History of Religions* 38.2: 172–98.

———. 2003. *Kiss of the Yoginī: "Tantric Sex" in South Asian Contexts.* Chicago: University of Chicago Press.

Whitney, W. D. 1962. *Artharva-Veda-Saṁhitā, Part I.* The Harvard Oriental Series vol. 7. Indian repr. ed. Delhi: Motilal Banarsidass.

Willemen, C. 1983. *The Chinese Hevajratantra: The Scriptural Text of the Ritual of the Great King of the Teaching, the Adamantine One with Great Compassion and Knowledge of the Void.* Orientalia Gandensia vol. 8. Leuven, Belgium: Uitgeverij Peeters.

Wilson, Liz. 1996a. *Charming Cadavers: Horrific Figurations of the Feminine in Indian Buddhist Hagiographic Literature.* Chicago: University of Chicago Press.

———. 1996b. Review of *Passionate Enlightenment: Women in Tantric Buddhism,* by Miranda Shaw. *History of Religions* 36.1: 60–4.

Wujastyk, Dominik. 2003. *The Roots of Ayurveda.* rev. ed. New York: Penguin Books.

Wylie, Turrell V. 1978. "Reincarnation: A Political Innovation in Tibetan Buddhism." In *Proceedings of the Csoma de Koros Memorial Symposium Held at Mátrafüred, Hungary, 24–30 September 1976,* edited by Louis Ligeti, 579–86. Budapest: Akadémiai Kiadó.

———. 1982. "Dating the Death of Nāropa." In *Indological and Buddhist Studies: Volume in Honour of Professor J. W. de Jong on His Sixtieth Birthday,* edited by L. A. Hercus et al., 687–92. Canberra: Faculty of Asian Studies.

Yamada, Isshi, ed. 1981. *Sarva-tathāgata-tattva-saṅgraha: A Critical Edition Based on a Sanskrit Manuscript and Chinese and Tibetan Translations.* Śata-piṭaka Series, Indo-Asian Literatures vol. 262. Delhi: Jayyed Press.

Yarnall, Thomas F. 2003. "The Emptiness that Is Form: Developing the Body of Buddhahood in Indo-Tibetan Buddhist Tantra." Ph.D. diss., Columbia University.

Yelle, Robert A. 2003. *Explaining Mantras: Ritual, Rhetoric and the Dream of a Natural Language in Hindu Tantra.* New York: Routledge.

Index

A

Abhayākaragupta, 44, 45, 69, 70, 71
Abhidhānottara, 9, 16, 17, 18, 19, 20, 140, 141, 142, 143, 208
Abhisamayavibhaṅga, 128
Advayasiddhi, 95
Akṣobhya, 50, 171, 296
Amitābha, 49, 172, 295, 365
Amoghasiddhi, 50, 295
Amoghavajra, 12, 13
appendix (*uttaratantra*), 19, 20, 27, 30, 31, 279, 382
Arthaśāstra, 38
Atīśa, 17, 83, 124–29, 131, 143

Ā

Ākāśagarbha, 155, 298, 365
Ānandagarbha, 82, 83

B

Bhāvaviveka, 79, 80, 89
Bhairava, 7, 10, 43, 44, 50, 51, 52, 304, 380
 of the twenty-four heroes, 365
Bhavabhaṭṭa, 10, 19, 21–25, 32–35, 37, 54, 91, 100, 101, 113, 114, 122, 139, 142, 146, 147, 152, 160, 356, 370
Bhavabhadra. *See* Bhavabhaṭṭa
Bhavyakīrti, 22, 30, 32, 53, 92, 93
Bhūtaḍāmara Tantra, 90
bLo-gros-grags, 144
bodhipakṣikadharma, 163
bodhisattva stages, 27, 28, 47, 66, 67, 374
Brahmā, 26, 41, 43, 45
brahmacarya, 123
Buddhaghoṣa, 61, 72
Buddhaguhya, 72, 73, 88
Buddhajñānapāda, 12, 13, 76
Bu-ston, 16, 17, 19, 24, 25, 44, 52, 81, 82, 145
Byang-chub-'od, 83

C

Cakrasamvara
 Chinese translation, 3
 definition of, 4
Cakrasamvara Tantra
 ḍākinīs in, 77
 Śaiva influence upon, 9
Cakrasamvara tradition
 Hevajra and *Guhyasamāja* influence upon, 71
Cakrasamvarapañjikā, 139
Cakrasamvaravivṛtti, 139
cakravartin. *See* universal monarch
Cāmuṇḍā, 89
caṇḍāla, 77, 98, 103, 200, 212, 229, 258, 291, 335, 351
caṇḍālī. *See* fury fire
Caṇḍamahāroṣaṇa, 9, 29, 97, 114
Candrakumāra, 22, 31

caru oblation, 201, 266, 272, 274, 279, 283, 286, 299
Catuḥpīṭha Tantra, 220
Caturdevīparipṛcchā, 75
Caturyoginīsampuṭa, 16, 17
celibacy, 7, 76, 125, 126, 128, 129, 280, 339
channels, 4, 69, 74, 113, 121, 149, 155, 162, 163, 172, 198, 199, 220, 253, 270, 309, 312, 319, 326, 337, 339
charnel ground, 7, 40, 42, 50, 51, 55, 67, 87, 89, 90, 97, 136, 1, 164, 199, 200, 212, 223, 237, 257, 302, 314, 324, 330, 351, 352, 354, 355, 375
chastity, 123, 124, 268, 339
Cicuzza, Claudio, 25, 36, 139, 159
communal enjoyment body, 46, 54, 56, 203
concretion, 84, 206, 207, 210, 211, 354, 355, 356, 368
consecration, 56, 95, 103, 111, 116, 120, 125, 135, 159, 274, 275, 276, 284, 363, 377, 378
  ceremony of, 15, 55, 92, 114, 117, 129, 132, 171, 179, 217, 335
  fourth, 49, 163
  of objects, 50, 137, 210, 224, 301, 338
  secret, 76, 108–14, 125, 127, 160, 162, 171–75, 216
  set of four, 111
  vase, 111, 162, 171
  wisdom-gnosis, 76, 111, 116, 125, 127, 128, 150, 162, 171, 172, 216, 305
consort. *See* mudrā; vidyā; wisdom as consort (*prajñā*); women as consorts
creation stage, 26, 55, 71, 72, 73, 110, 121, 132, 157, 216, 300, 303, 317, 376, 377, 380
Cumbikā, 233, 299, 334

D

Dāsa Śambara. *See* Śamvara/Śambara deity
Davidson, Ronald, 7, 8, 12–14, 33, 39, 40, 43, 44, 45, 46, 65, 71, 76, 78, 79, 82, 87, 88, 96, 97, 100, 102, 126, 128
Devagupta, 23
Devakulamahāmati, 6
Devarakṣita, 3
Devī-Māhātmya, 38
Dharma blo-gros, 22
Dharmakīrti, 3, 78, 79, 81, 85
Dharmapāla
  King, 12, 13
  translator, 24
Dīpaṁkarabhadra, 12
Doniger, Wendy, 105, 114, 119, 284
Durjayacandra, 17, 22, 24, 25, 115
dūtī. *See* messenger
Dvikramatattvabhāvana-mukhāgama, 76

Ḍ

Ḍākārṇava, 16, 17, 18, 20, 31, 74
Ḍākinī Tantras, 78, 79, 83, 85
ḍākinīs
  as buddhas, 86
  as carnivores, 323
  as companions, 323
  as delighted by *gaṇacakra*, 367
  as enlightened, 155
  as heretics, 84
  as human, 90, 119, 129
  as messengers, 289
  as non-human, 41, 84, 92
  as servants, 209
  as terrifying, 325
  bali, 359
  characteristics of, 250
  clans of, 236
  early references to, 77
  etymology of, 85
  in the *Sarvabuddhasamayoga*, 85, 86
  in the Yoginī Tantras, 77
  negative depiction of, 176
  nonduality of, 317
  pervasiveness of, 329
  pleasing of, 328
  summoning of, 212
  the seven, 233
  twenty-four, 169, 178, 179, 290, 336
  worship of, 362

E

English, Elizabeth, 4, 55, 61, 99
explanatory tantra, 4, 5, 15–20, 31, 32, 74, 75, 135, 262

F

Faure, Bernard, 95, 98, 101
fire sacrifice, 15, 68, 80, 99, 121, 136, 219, 282, 287, 297, 301, 302, 308, 309, 317, 327, 328, 347, 348, 351, 356, 361, 370, 371
five sacrifices, 309
four joys, 23, 24, 52, 95, 110, 119, 129, 155, 222, 337
fury fire, 172, 199, 220, 253

G

gaṇacakra, 52, 109, 110, 111, 130, 160, 201, 268, 283, 301, 362, 367
Gaurī, 42, 44, 380
Germano, David, 73
gnosis (*jñāna*), 70, 155, 156, 158, 162, 172, 173, 199, 201, 202, 203, 204, 222, 251, 257, 275, 283, 329, 335, 339, 357, 378, 379
gnosis hero, 26, 172, 378
Grags-pa rGyal-mtshan, 44, 52, 53, 82, 126
Granoff, Phyllis, 10, 79, 85, 123
Guhyagarbha, 6
Guhyakośa, 279
Guhyasamāja, 5, 12, 13, 27, 29, 71, 74, 82, 83, 87, 108, 109, 110, 171, 177, 207, 279, 283, 295, 297, 307, 376

H

Hayagrīva, 187, 295, 298, 365
heroes
  as world pervading, 56, 366

twenty-four, 56, 179, 265, 290, 312, 336, 365, 366
Heruka
as a buddha, xii–xiii, 10, 27, 28, 49, 52, 54
as omnipresent, 61, 68, 157, 177, 374
deity couple, 9, 42, 45, 46, 51, 55, 128, 156, 168, 172, 173, 277, 298, 304, 378, 380
etymology of, 40
origin of, 7, 35–54, 54, 304
union with, xiii, 27, 36, 54, 132, 155, 202, 325
Herukābhyudaya, 3, 16, 17, 22, 31, 261, 262
heteropraxy, 8, 98, 229, 267, 286, 322, 336
Hevajra, 5, 6, 17, 23, 29, 50, 71, 120, 379
Hodge, Stephen, 21, 72, 73, 115
homa. *See* fire sacrifice.

I
Indra, 37, 39, 40, 41, 166, 178, 197, 289, 328, 370
Indrabhūti, 14, 23, 44, 45, 46, 52, 53, 54, 162, 171, 199, 222, 223, 224, 226, 257, 258, 261, 262, 268
Indranāla, 40, 41
Iyanaga, Nobumi, 43, 77

J
jackal, 234, 300, 301, 359, 367, 369, 371, 372, 373
'Jam-mgon A-myes-zhab Ngag-dbang Kun-dga'-bsod-nams, 126, 130
'Jam-mgon Kong-sprul, 91, 129
Jayabhadra, 9, 10, 11, 12, 15, 21–26, 85, 92, 107, 111–15, 123, 124, 139, 142, 143, 146–50
Jñānasiddhi, 14

K
Kākāsyā, 55, 170, 179, 218, 267, 295, 334
Kālacakra, 25, 125, 127, 345
Kālarātri, xiii, 44, 45, 50, 380
Kambala, 23–26, 108, 118, 119, 120, 146
Kāṇha, 22
Kāpālika, xvii, 7, 8, 45, 65, 81, 85, 87, 91, 92, 165, 168, 330, 376, 377
Kapstein, Matthew, xviii, 6, 71, 79, 89, 97, 376
Kāśyapa Buddha, 40
Khaṇḍarohā, 211, 224, 234, 237, 287, 308, 310, 311, 314, 315, 317, 335
khaṇḍarohā goddesses, 364
khecarī, 108, 344
khecarīpada, 326
Kṛṣṇācārya, 68

L
Lakṣmīṁkarā, 95, 103
Lāmā
origin of term, 233
lāmās, 334, 364
clans of, 239–42

Laṅkāvatāra Sūtra, 41, 77, 78, 98, 106, 107
Lha bLa-ma Ye-shes-'od, 83, 131
Locanā, 295, 299
Lūipa, 17, 35, 65, 68, 124

M

Magadha, 50
Mahābala, 324, 365
Mahābhairava, 9, 52, 167, 168, 169, 334, 365
  Tantra, 279
Mahādeva, 26, 41, 42, 43, 47, 48, 49, 52
Mahākālā ḍākinīs, 334, 335
Mahākāla, 7, 9, 10, 84, 85, 89, 334, 371
Mahākālī, 9, 10, 339
Mahāsatipaṭṭhāna Sutta, 61, 62, 63
Mahāvairocana-abhisambodhi, 15, 21, 68, 72, 84, 115
Mahāvajradhara, 32, 41, 43, 46, 49, *See also* Vajradhara
Maheśvara, 48, 85, 168, 332
Mahiṣa Samvara, 38
Maitrīpa, 18, 126
Mal-gyo blo-gros-grags, 144, 145
Mal-gyo Lotsāwa, 25
Māmakī, 295, 299
maṇḍala, 72, 156, 364
  body maṇḍala, 18, 36, 56, 61, 65, 68, 74, 99, 135, 165, 329, 336, 339
  Cakrasamvara, 4, 36, 42, 44, 51, 54–76, 55, 155, 158, 310
  construction of, 55, 133, 135, 162–64, 165–67, 170, 171, 307, 377
  empowering vision of, 180
  revelation of, 111, 174
  ritual use of, 287, 301
  worship of, 111, 171
Mañjuśrīmūlakalpa, 86
Mañjuśrī-nāmasaṁgīti, 14, 30
Mañjuvajra, 296
mantra
  armor, 132, 133, 135, 187, 194, 195, 214, 218, 230, 276, 278
  eightfold, 325
  envelopment of, 314
  essence, 174, 186, 193, 194, 195, 204, 207, 209, 210, 218, 219, 220, 318, 344, 360, 364, 368
  etymology of, 159
  interconnection of, 312, 320
  quintessence, 174, 186, 193, 194, 195, 207, 209–13, 218, 220, 343–49, 360
  root, 181, 192, 196, 263, 287, 290, 324, 344
  seven syllable, 348, 350
  trailokyavijaya, 38, 132, 295–96
  śumbha-niśumbha, 292
mantra body, 326
Māra, 41, 43, 207, 295, 314, 371, 378
Mardo (Marpa Chos-kyi dbang-phyug), 137, 143, 144, 146
Marpa Lho-brag-pa (Lo-tsā-wa), 18, 144

Māyājāla, 13, 33, 295
messenger, 90, 92, 113, 158, 222, 265, 269, 270, 271, 272, 273, 283, 284, 286, 290, 305, 310, 311, 312, 350, 355, 356
  characteristics of, 289
mudrā, 86, 283
  as consort, 121, 128, 149, 150, 275, 306, 317, 338, 343, *See also dharmamudrā*, etc., below
  as gesture, 41, 48, 90, 132, 149, 229, 232, 239, 242
  as insignia, 129, 165, 278, 304
  as seal, 26, 127, 149, 196, 200, 201, 259, 318, 354
  as soma drinking, 283
  as yogic seal, 120, 123, 340
  dharmamudrā, 27, 127, 161, 171, 172, 173, 377
  identification with types of *pūjā*, 161
  insignia, 52, 109
  jñānamudrā, 127, 128
  karmamudrā, 27, 127, 128, 150, 161, 171, 173, 250, 343, 357, 377
  mahāmudrā, 6, 27, 120, 150, 161, 168, 171, 172, 251, 275, 283, 306, 325, 327
  meanings of, 149, 150
  samayamudrā, 27, 127, 161, 171, 172, 173, 377
mūlatantra. *See* Root Tantra

N

nāḍī. *See* channels
Nāgabodhi, 14
Nālandā, 19, 79, 81, 115, 126
Nāropa, 18, 23, 97, 115, 144, 145
Navaślokī, 24
Nayatrayapradīpa, 124
Nikāya-saṅgraha, 3, 11
nirvāṇa, 30, 48, 76, 282
niṣpannakrama. *See* perfecting stage
Niṣpannayogāvalī, 45

O

obstacle demons, 41, 49
obstacles, 41, 94, 171, 238, 371, 377
Oḍḍiyāna, 23, 67, 332

P

Padmākaravarman, 11, 143
Padmanartaka, 298
Padmanarteśvara, 187, 236, 298, 365
Padmavajra, 171, 262
Pañcakrama, 71, 75
Pāṇḍarā, 295, 299
perfecting stage, 20, 26, 27, 69–76, 118, 217, 220, 251, 275, 326, 336, 365
perfections, xi, 5, 70, 95, *See also* wisdom
  six, 163, 172, 299
  ten, 68, 375
'Phags-pa, 3
pilgrimage, 64, 66, 68, 70
  places of, 9, 18, 50, 51, 55, 65–71, 178, 326, 330–36, 374
Piṇḍārtha, 72

Piṇḍīkramasādhana, 71
pīṭha, xi, 50, 67, 69, 92, 118, 158, 162, 173, 222, 266, 331, 332, 335, 374
prajñā. *See* wisdom
Prajñākīrti, 144
Prajñāpāramitā, 30
Pramāṇavārttika, 78
prasenā, 345
Pratyutpanna-buddha-saṁmukhāvasthita-samādhi Sūtra, 215

R

Ratneśa, 295
reality body, 32, 46, 54, 56, 106, 157, 202, 203, 297
Rin-chen bZang-po, 11, 22, 83, 124, 143, 144
Rin-chen-grags, 22, 24
Root Tantra, 15, 16, 18–21, 28–35, 55, 71, 118, 135
Rudra, xiii, 9, 10, 42, 43, 53, 228, *See also* Vajrarudra
Rūpavajrā, 216

S

Sachen Kun-dga' sNying-po, 22, 25, 101, 118, 145
sacrificial victim, 92, 206, 258, 260, 300, 301, 323, 355, 356, 367, 368
Samayoga. *See Sarvabuddha-samayoga*
Sampuṭa, 16, 17, 26, 27, 148, 295
Samvara. *See also Sarvabuddha-samayoga*, *See also* Śamvara/Śambara deity
  as binding/vow, 35–37, 155, 193, 251
  as communities of yoginīs, 222
  as sanctuary, 222
  as union/supreme bliss, 36–37, 251
  definitions of, 4, 35–37
Samvarodaya, 16, 17, 20, 36, 74, 230
Sanderson, Alexis, 7, 8, 45, 54, 65, 78, 79, 91, 92, 102, 297, 330
Saraha, 35, 129, 130, 131
Sarvabuddhasamayoga, 3, 6, 12, 13, 29, 32, 36, 37, 38, 40, 77, 83, 85, 109, 176, 279
Sarvatathāgata-tattvasaṁgraha, 9, 29, 38, 43, 47, 176, 279, 295
Sarvatathāgata-tattvasaṁgraha Sūtra, 12, 85
Sa-skya school, 3, 22, 145
seat (*pīṭha*). *See pīṭha*
semen, 88, 91, 104–10, 117, 118, 121–24, 149, 150, 159, 160, 161, 214, 235, 266, 268, 321, *See also* seminal essence; sexual fluids
seminal essence, 108, 110, 113, 121–24, 149, 155, 157, 158, 161, 163, 196, 198, 215, 220, 251, 253, 268, 283, 285, 286, 288, 317, 318, 326, 337, 338, 339, 340, *See also* semen; sexual fluids

sexual fluids, 76, 104–14, 117–24, 127, 149, 151, 174, 286, *See also* semen; seminal essence; uterine blood
sexual intercourse, 78, 105, 114, 115, 118, 119, 254, 255, 262, 280, 371
sexual practices, 5, 7, 39, 52, 76, 84, 86, 103–31, 149, 150, 163, 171, 197, 270, 280, 284, 317, 318
sexual union, 6, 78, 117, 119, 121, 123, 124, 129, 261, 280, 288, 318, 336
sexuality, 74, 76, 79
  female, 99, 104–6, *See also* women
Shaw, Miranda, 93–101, 114
siddhi
  meanings of, 150
Snellgrove, David, xiv, 5, 22, 29, 38, 43, 50, 53, 65, 70, 95, 109, 111, 120, 148, 150, 173, 378, 379
soma, 109, 110, 112, 151, 160, 174, 198, 199, 223, 279, 283, 285
Strickmann, Michel, 68, 81, 105
Subāhuparipṛcchā Tantra, 39, 40, 87, 88, 89, 91, 106
Subāhuparipṛcchā-nāma-tantrapiṇḍārthavṛtti, 88
sukhāvatī, 326
Sumatikīrti, 25, 137, 144, 147, 348
Surativajra, 40, 41, 42, 110, 111
Susiddhikara, 89

Ś

Śaiva, xvii, 7–10, 20, 21, 22, 40, 43, 51, 53, 54, 65, 68, 79, 85, 89, 91, 167, 168, 228, 275, 297, 330–34
Śakra, 354
Śākyamuni Buddha, 28, 29, 30
Śamvara/Śambara deity, 35, 37, 38, 221
Śāśvatavajra, 24
Śiva, xii, xiii, 26, 39, 43, 54, 156, 167, 234, 304, 380
Śrī Paramādya, 12, 13, 26, 279, 295
Śrī Vajravārāhī Sādhana. See Vajravārāhī: *sādhana*
Śrīdhara, 22
Śubhakarasiṁha, 40, 68, 81, 84, 85, 89

T

Tārā, 296, 299
Tāranātha, 11, 12, 23, 24, 82
tantric feast. *See gaṇacakra.*
Tarkajvāla, 89
Tathāgatarakṣita, 22
Tilopa, 23
Trailokyavijaya, 49, *See also* mantra, trailokyavijaya
transgressive practice, xvii, 7–8, 78–84, 89, 98, 106, 126, 129, 130, 131, 206, 207, 284, *See also* heteropraxy
trikāya. See triple body
Tripiṭakamāla, 124
triple body, 46, 54, 202, 204, 353
tripurāntaka, 39, 53, 54

Tsong Khapa, 17, 19, 25, 75, 113, 136, 143, 145, 351
Tsuda, Shinichi, 7, 16, 19, 20, 74, 75, 89

U

Umā, 48, 51, 380
Umāpatideva, 99
universal monarch, 280, 295, 328, 355, 379
Urban, Hugh, 7, 151
uterine blood, 91, 104–14, 117, 118, 121, 160, 163, 198, 235, 266, 285, 337, 338, 339, 358, 370, 391, 396, 399, *See also* sexual fluids
utpattikrama. *See* creation stage
uttaratantra. *See* appendix (*uttaratantra*)

V

Vairocana, 29, 47, 49, 72, 84, 85, 172, 187, 217, 229, 295, 298, 365
Vajrāmṛta Tantra, 6
Vajraḍāka, 16, 17, 18, 20, 32, 75
Vajrabhairava, 10, 38
  Tantra, 12, 177, 295
Vajradhara, 26, 35, 40, 42, 46, 47, 54, 157, 171, 272, 295, *See also* Mahāvajradhara
Vajragarbha, 49, 379
Vajrahūṁkāra, 49, 365
Vajrajvālānalārka, 49
Vajrapāṇi
  author, 25, 139, 159
  bodhisattva, 32, 35, 43, 47–49, 85, 340
Vajrapañjara Tantra, 5, 6
Vajrarudra, 211, 275, *See also* Rudra
Vajrasattva, 29, 31, 32, 36, 50, 95, 109, 111, 146, 155, 156, 172, 187, 190, 191, 229, 295, 298, 303, 365, 366
Vajraśekhara, 12, 26
Vajravārāhī, 9, 10, 23, 32–35, 44, 45, 55, 99, 108, 112, 128, 135, 156, 157, 162, 166, 168, 169, 195, 229, 235, 237, 242, 277, 281, 298, 299, 304, 324, 333, 336, 339, 360, 364, 380, 381
  sādhana, 4, 55, 99
Vajravārāhī-abhibhava Tantrarāja, 9
Vajrayoginī, 46, 51, 69, 99
vāmācāra. *See* heteropraxy
Vārāhī-abhisambodhi, 16
vetāla. *See* zombie (*vetāla*).
vidyā
  as consort, 6, 118, 150, 162, 199, 231, 275
  as mantra spell, 73, 185, 192, 231, 272, 295, 320, 325
  meanings of, 150
Vikramaśīla, xvii, 10, 12, 13, 21–23, 32, 96, 126
Vilāsavajra, 13–14, 23
Vimalakīrti Sūtra, 98
Vimalaprabhā, 69, 125, 127
Vināyaka, 238, *See also* obstacle demons
Vīracandra Buddha, 40

Vīravajra, 24, 25, 26, 28, 31, 113, 120–23, 127, 146, 149, 150
Virūpa, 126
Viṣṇu, xii, 26, 39, 41, 42, 49, 53, 83, 156
Visuddhimagga, 61, 72
vyākhyātantra. *See* explanatory tantra

W

Weber, Max, 98, 116
White, David, 105, 106, 109, 114, 118, 120, 122
wisdom, xi, 27, 46, 48, 51, 128, 203, 215, 251, 275, 288, 327, 346, *See also* consecration; *Prajñāpāramitā*.
  and art, 27, 42, 81, 159, 163, 215, 251, 326, 336
  as consort (*prajñā*), 95, 376
  as goddess, 27, 95, 98, 108, 163
  perfection of, 5, 95, 128
  set of five, 108, 378
  sword of, 198, 276
women, 6, 109, 163, 199, 206, 230, 231, 240, 251, 262, 265, 320, 334, 335, 356, 357
  as consorts, 115, 124, 150, 198, 230, 333, *See also* consort
  portrayals, roles, status of, 70, 76, 77–103, 105, 106, 115, 285, 333, 335
Woodruff, Sir John, 4

X

Xuan-zang, 81

Y

yakṣiṇī
  as dangerous females, 105
  as sexual vampires, 105
  in the *Mañjuśrīmūlakalpa*, 86–90, 92
  in the *Subāhuparipṛcchā*, 87
  sādhana of, 87, 129
yantra, 308
  as magical diagram, 136, 212, 314, 315, 329, 346, 347
  as war machine, 348, 357
  yogic posture, 119, 120, 123, 149, 172, 222, 253, 318, 336
Yi-jing, 19, 79
Yi-xing, 68, 81, 84, 85
Yoga Tantras, 5, 6, 111, 150, 207, 266, 306
Yoginī Tantras, 3–11, 23, 28, 35, 77, 81, 89, 93, 97, 99, 122
yoginīs
  as ḍākinīs, 77
  as discipliners, 51
  as girls, 333
  as human, 69, 90, 101
  as non-human, 92
  as pleasing assistants, 226
  as servants, 214
  bands of, 266
  classes of, 227
  four essence yoginīs, 55, 161, 175, 179, 214, 217, 224, 262, 310, 334, 336, 366
  worship of, 282

yoginī-sādhana, 90
Yoginīsaṁcāra, 8, 16, 18, 62, 63, 217, 317

Z

Zhi-ba-'od, 83
zombie (*vetāla*), 87, 89, 300, 303, 324
sādhana of, 300, 303